The Influence of Technology on Social Network Analysis and Mining

Lecture Notes in Social Networks (LNSN)

For further volumes:
www.springer.com/series/8768

Tansel Özyer
Jon Rokne
Gerhard Wagner
Arno H.P. Reuser
Editors

The Influence of Technology on Social Network Analysis and Mining

Springer

Editors
Tansel Özyer
Department of Computer Engineering
TOBB University
Sogutozu Ankara
Turkey

Gerhard Wagner
IPSC
European Commission Joint Research Centre
Ispra
Italy

Jon Rokne
Department of Computer Science
University of Calgary
Calgary
Canada

Arno H.P. Reuser
Leiden
Netherlands

SpringerWienNewYork is a part of Springer Science+Business Media
springer.at

Typesetting: SPi, Pondicherry, India

Printed on acid-free and chlorine-free bleached paper
SPIN: 86130600

With 216 Figures

Library of Congress Control Number: 2013933244

ISBN 978-3-7091-1345-5 e-ISBN 978-3-7091-1346-2
DOI 10.1007/978-3-7091-1346-2
SpringerWienNewYork

Preface

This edited book contains extended versions of selected papers from ASONAM 2010 which was held at the University of Odense, Denmark, August 9–11, 2010. From the many excellent papers submitted to the conference, 28 were chosen for this volume. The volume explores a number of aspects of social networks, both global and local, and it also shows how social networks analysis and mining may aid web searches, product acceptances and personalized recommendations just to mention a few areas where social networks analysis can improve results in other mostly web-related areas. The application of graph theoretical aspects to social networks analysis is a recurrent theme in many of the chapters, and terminology from graph theory has influenced that of social networks to a large extent.

The theme of the book relates to the influence of technology on social networks and mining. This influence is not new. Technology is the enabling tool for all social networks except for the most trivial. Indeed without technology the only possible social networks would be extremely local and the cohesion of the network would simply have been by oral communication. Wider social networks only became a possibility with the advent of some sort of pictorial representation, for example, the technology of carving on stone. This meant that a message of some form could be read by others when the individual creating the representation was no longer present. Abstractions in the form of pictographs representing ideas and concepts and alphabets improved the technology. The advent of the movable print further sped up the technology. The printing press technology enabled a significant increase in speed for social network communication. These technologies were still limited in what could be disseminated both in time and space, however.

The advent of the electronic means of disseminating ideas and communications together with the development of the Internet opened up the possibility of transmitting ideas and to make connections with an essentially unlimited number of actors (people) with no geographical limitation at very low cost. This technological advance enabled the growth of social networks to sizes that could not be realized with previous technologies. The papers in this volume describe a number of aspects of this new ability to form such networks and they provide new tools and techniques for analyzing these networks effectively.

The first chapter is: *EgoClustering: Overlapping Community Detection via Merged Friendship-Groups* by Bradley S. Rees and Keith B. Gallagher. In this chapter, the authors identify communities through the identification of friendship groups where a friendship-group is a localized community as seen from an individual's perspective that allows him/her to belong to multiple communities. The basic tools of the chapter are those of graph theory. An algorithm has been developed that finds overlapping communities and identifies key members that bind communities together. The algorithm is applied to some standard social networks datasets. Detailed results from the Caveman and Zachary data sets are provided.

The chapter *Evolution of Online Forum Communities* by Mikolaj Morzy is a perfect example of a chapter discussing a theme relating the theme of the volume since the concept of an "online forum" did not exist prior to the current advances in technology. While one can trace the forum idea back to posters on bulletin boards and discussion in the printed literature, the current online forums are highly dependent on the speed and ease of transmission made possible by the Internet. The chapter discusses the evolution of these forums and their social implications. There are large number of forums and that are established that expand, contract, develop, and wither depending on the interest they generate. The paper introduces a micro-community-based model for measuring the evolution of Internet forums. It shows how the simple concept of a micro-community can be used to quantitatively assess the openness and durability of an Internet forum. The authors apply the model to a number of actual forums to experimentally verify the correctness and robustness of the model.

In *Integrating Online Social Network Analysis in Personalized Web Search* by Omair Shafiq, Tamer N. Jarada, Panagiotis Karampelas, Reda Alhajj, and Jon G. Rokne, the authors discuss how a web search experience can be improved through the mining of trusted information sources. From the content of the sources preferences are extracted that reorders the ranking of the results of a search engine. Search results for the same query raised by different users may differ in priority for individual users. For example a search for "The best pizza house" will clearly have a geographical component since the best pizza house in Miami is of no interest to someone searching for the best pizza in New York. It is also assumed that a query posed by a user correlates strongly with information in their social networks. To find the personal interest and social context, the paper therefore considers (1) the activities of users in their social network and (2) relevant information from a user's social networks, based on proposed trust and relevance matrices. The proposed solution has been implemented and tested.

The latent class models (LCMs) used in social science are applied in the context of social networks in *How Latent Class Models Matter to Social Network Analysis and Mining: Exploring the Emergence of Community* by Jaime R. S. Fonseca and Romana Xerez. The chapter discusses the advantages of reducing complex data to a limited number of typologies from a theoretical and empirical perspective. A relatively small dataset was obtained from surveying a community while using the notion of homophile to establish the survey criteria. The methodology is applied in the context of a three-latent class social network and the findings are in terms of (1) network structure, (2) trust and reciprocity, (3) resources, (4) community engagement, (5) the Internet, and (6) years of residence.

In *Extending Social Network Analysis with Discourse Analysis: Combining Relational with Interpretive Data* by Christine Moser, Peter Groenewegen, and Marleen Huysman the authors investigate social networks that are related to specific interest groups such as Dutch Cake Bakers (DCB). These communities may be quite large (DCB had about 10,000 members at the time of writing the chapter) and they are characterized by a high level of activity; a strong, active, and small core; and an extensive peripheral group. They were able to gather very detailed and massive relational data from their example online communities from which they explored the connections within the communities. The authors then performed a discourse analysis on the content of the gathered messages and by this characterized the interactions in terms of we-them, compliments and empathy, competition and advice, and criticism, thus enabling a deeper understanding of the communities.

Viewing relational databases through their information content for social networks is the topic of the chapter *DB2SNA: An All-in-one Tool for Extraction and Aggregation of Underlying Social Networks from Relational Databases* by Rania Soussi, Etienne Cuvelier, Marie-Aude Aufaure, Amine Louati, and Yves Lechevallier. The authors propose a heterogeneous object graph extraction approach from a relational database which they use to extract a social network. This step is followed by an aggregation step in order to improve the visualization and analysis of the extracted social network. This is followed by an aggregation step using the k-SNAP algorithm which produces a summarized graph in order that the resulting social network graphs can be more easily understood.

The next chapter, *An Adaptive Framework for Discovery and Mining of User Profiles from SocialWeb-Based Interest Communities* by Nima Dokoohaki and Mihhail Matskin, introduces an adaptive framework for semi- to fully automatic discovery, acquisition, and mining of topic style interest profiles from openly accessible social web communities. Their techniques use machine learning tools including clustering and classifying for their algorithms. Three schemes are defined as follows: (1) depth-based, allowing for discovering and crawling of topics on a certain taxonomy tree-depth at each time; (2) n-split, allowing iterative discovery and crawling of all topics while at each iteration gathered data is split for n-times; and finally (3) greedy, which allows for discovery and crawling the network for all topics and processing the cached data. They apply the developed techniques to the social networking site LiveJournal.

The chapter *Enhancing Child Safety in MMOs* by Lyta Penna, Andrew Clark, and George Mohay considers the general issue of how the Internet can be made safe for children, specifically when Massively Multiplayer Online (MMO) games and environments are involved. A particular issue with respect to children and MMOs is the potential for luring a child into an off-line encounter which would in many cases present a hazard to a child. Typical message threads are analyzed for contextual content that might lead to such harmful encounters. The techniques developed to detect potentially unfavorable situations are applied to World of Warcraft as a case study. The chapter extends previous work by the authors.

Virtual communities are studied in *Towards Leader-Based Recommendations* by Ilham Esslimani, Armelle Brun, and Anne Boyer with the aim of discovering community leaders. These leaders influence the opinion and decision making of the rest of the community. Discovering these leaders is important, for example, in the area of marketing, where detecting opinion leaders allows the prediction of future decision making (about products and services), the anticipation of risks (due, e.g., to negative opinions of leaders) and the follow-up of the corporate image (e-reputation) of companies. Their algorithm considers the high connectivity and the potentiality of propagating accurate appreciations so as to detect reliable leaders through these networks. Furthermore, studying leadership is also relevant in other application areas, such as social network analysis and recommender systems.

Name and author disambiguation is an important topic for today's electronic article databases. For example, J. Smith, Jim Smith, J. Peter Smith may be (a) one author using different variations of his name Jim Smith, (b) two authors with variations in the use of their names, or (c) three authors. The chapter *Learning from the Past: An Analysis of Person Name Corrections in the DBLP Collection and Social Network Properties of Affected Entities* by Florian Reitz and Oliver Hoffmann tackles this problem for the DBLP bibliographic database of computer science and related topics. Given the name of an author, the intent is that the DLBP database will provide a list of papers by that author. Although there are a large number of algorithmic approaches to solve this problem, little is known on the properties of inconsistencies in the information in the databases such as variations of names of one individual. The present paper applies a historical and social network approach to the problem. Their algorithms are able to calculate the probability that a name will need correction in the future.

Factors Enabling Information Propagation in a Social Network Site by Matteo Magnani, Danilo Montesi, and Luca Rossi discusses the phenomenon that information propagates efficiently over social networks and that it is much more efficient than traditional media. Many general formal models of network propagation that might be applied to social network information dissemination have been developed in different research fields. This paper presents the result of an empirical study on a Large Social Database (LSD) aimed at measuring specific socio-technical factors enabling information spreading over social network sites.

In the chapter *Detecting Emergent Behavior in a Social Network of Agents* by Mohammad Moshirpour, Shimaa M. El-Sherif, Behrouz H. Far, and Reda Alhajj, the entities of the social networks are agents, that is, computer programs that exchange information with other computer programs and perform specific functions. In this chapter, there are agents handling queries, learning and managing concepts, annotating documents, finding peers, and resolving ties. The agents may work together to achieve certain goals, and certain behavior patterns may develop over time (emergent behavior). The chapter presents a case study of using a social network of a multiagent system for semantic search.

In *Detecting Communities in Massive Networks Efficiently with Flexible Resolution* by Qi Ye, Bin Wu, and Bai Wang the authors are concerned with data analysis on real-world networks. They consider an iterative heuristic approach to extract the community structure in such networks. The approach is based on local multi-resolution modularity optimization and the time complexity is close to linear and the space complexity is linear. The resulting algorithm is very efficient, and it may enhance the ability to explore massive networks in real time.

The topic of the next chapter *Extraction of Spatio-temporal Data for Social Networks* by Judith Gelernter, Dong Cao, and Kathleen M. Carley is using social networks for the identification of locations and their association with people. This is then used to obtain a better understanding of group changes over time. The authors have therefore developed an algorithm to automatically accomplish the person-to-place mapping. It involves the identification of location and uses syntactic proximity of words in the text to link the location to a person's name. The contributions of this chapter include techniques to mine for location from text and social network edges as well as the use of the mined data to make spatiotemporal maps and to perform social network analysis.

The chapter *Clustering Social Networks Using Distance-Preserving Subgraphs* by Ronald Nussbaum, Abdol-Hossein Esfahanian, and Pang-Ning Tan considers cluster analysis in a social networks setting. The problem of not being able to define what a cluster is causes problems for cluster analysis in general; however, for the data sets representing social networks, there are some criteria that aid the clustering process. The authors use the tools of graph theory and the notion of distance preservation in subgraphs for the clustering process. A heuristic algorithm has been developed that finds distance-preserving subgraphs which are then merged to the best of the abilities of the algorithm. They apply the algorithm to explore the effect of alternative graph invariants on the process of community finding. Two datasets are explored: CiteSeer and Cora.

The chapter *Informative Value of Individual and Relational Data Compared Through Business-Oriented Community Detection* by Vincent Labatut and Jean-Michel Balasque deals with the issue of extracting data from an enterprise database. The chapter uses a small Turkish university as the background test case and develops algorithms dealing with aspects of the data gathered from students at the university. The authors perform group detection on single data items as well as pairs gathered from the student population and estimate groups separately using individual and relational data to obtain sets of clusters and communities. They then measure the overlap between clusters and communities, which turns out to be relatively weak. They also define a predictive model which allows them to identify the most discriminant attributes for the communities, and to reveal the presence of a tenuous link between the relational and individual data.

Considering the data from blogs in a social network context is the topic of *Cross-Domain Analysis of the Blogosphere for Trend Prediction* by Patrick Siehndel, Fabian Abel, Ernesto Diaz-Aviles, Nicola Henze, and Daniel Krause. The authors note first the importance of blogs for communicating information on the web. Blogging over advanced communications devices such as smartphones and other handheld devices has enabled blogging anywhere at any time. Because of this facility, the blogged information is up to date and a valuable source for data, especially for companies. Relevant date, extracted from blogs, can be used to adjust marketing campaigns and advertisement. The authors have selected the music and movie domains as examples where there is a significant blogging activity and they used these domains to investigate how chatter from the blogosphere can be used to predict the success of products. In particular, they identify typical patterns of blogging behavior around the release of a product by analyzing the terms of posting relevant to the product, point out methods for extracting features from the blogosphere, and show that we can exploit these features to predict the monetary success of movies and music with high accuracy.

Betweenness computation its the topic of *Efficient Extraction of High-Betweenness Vertices from Heterogeneous Networks* by Wen Haw Chong, Wei Shan Belinda Toh, and Loo Nin Teow. The efficient computation of betweenness in a network is computationally expensive, yet it is often the set of vertices with high betweenness that is of key interest in a graph. The authors have developed a novel algorithm that efficiently returns the set of vertices with the highest betweenness. The convergence criterion for the algorithm is based on the membership stability of the high-betweenness set. They also show experimentally that the algorithm tends to perform better on networks with heterogeneous betweenness distributions. The authors have applied the algorithm developed to the real-world cases of Protein, Enron, Ticker, AS, and DBLP data.

Engagingness and Responsiveness Behavior Models on the Enron E-mail Network and their Application to E-mail Reply Order Prediction deals with user interactions in e-mail systems. The authors note that user behaviors affect the way e-mails are sent and replied. They therefore investigate user engagingness and responsiveness as two interaction behaviors that give us useful insights into how users e-mail one another. They classify e-mail users in two categories: engaging users and responsive users. They propose four model types based on e-mail, e-mail thread, e-mail sequence, and social cognitively. These models are used to quantify the engagingness and responsiveness of users, and the behaviors can be used as features in the e-mail reply order prediction task which predicts the e-mail reply order given an e-mail pair. Experiments show that engagingness and responsiveness behavior features are more useful than other non-behavior features in building a classifier for the e-mail reply order prediction task. An Enron data set is used to test the models developed.

In the chapter *Comparing and Visualizing the Social Spreading of Products on a Large Social Network* by Pøal Roe SundsØy, Johannes Bjelland, Geoffrey Canright, Kenth Engø-Monsen, and Rich Ling, the authors investigate how products and services adoption is propagated. By combining mobile traffic data and product adoption history from one of the markets for the telecom provider Telenor the social network among adopters is derived. They study and compare the evolution of adoption networks over time for several products: the iPhone handset, the Doro handset, the iPad 3G, and video telephony. It is shown how the structure of the adoption network changes over time and how it can be used to study the social effects of product diffusion. Supporting this, they find that the adoption probability increases with the number of adopting friends for all the products in the study. It is postulated that the strongest spreading of adoption takes place in the dense core of the underlying network, and gives rise to a dominant LCC (largest connected component) in the adoption network, which they call the social network monster. This is supported by measuring the eigenvector centrality of the adopters. They postulate that the size of the monster is a good indicator for whether or not a product is going to "take off."

The next chapter is *Virus Propagation Modeling in Facebook* by W. Fan and K. H. Yeung, where the authors model virus propagation in social networks using Facebook as a model. It is argued that the virus propagation models used for e-mail, IM, and P2P are not suitable for social networks services (SNS). Facebook provides an experimental platform for application developers and it also provides an opportunity for studying the spreading of viruses. The authors find that a virus will spread faster in the Facebook network if Facebook users spend more time on it. The simulations in the chapter are generated with the Barabasi-Albert (BA) scale-free model. This model is compared with some sampled Facebook networks. The results show that applying BA model in simulations will overestimate the number of infected users a little while still reflecting the trend of virus spreading.

The chapter *A Local Structure-Based Method for Nodes Clustering. Application to a Large Mobile Phone Social Network* by Alina Stoica and Zbigniew Smoreda and Christophe Prieur presents a method for describing how a node of a given graph is connected to a network. They also propose a method for grouping nodes into clusters based on the structure of the network in which they are embedded using the tools of graph theory and data mining. These methods are applied to a mobile phone communications network. The paper concludes with a typology of mobile phone users based on social network cluster, communication intensity, and age.

In the chapter *Building Expert Recommenders from E-mail-Based Personal Social Networks* by Veronica Rivera-Pelayo, Simone Braun, Uwe V. Riss, Hans Friedrich Witschel, and Bo Hu, the authors investigate how to identify knowledgable individuals in organizations. In such organizations, it is generally necessary to collaborate with people in any organization, to establish interpersonal relationships, and to establish sources for knowledge about the organization and its activities. Contacting the right person is crucial for successfully accessing this knowledge. The authors use personal e-mail corpora as a source of information of a user since it contains rich information about all the people the user knows and their activities. Thus, an analysis of a person's e-mails allows automatically constructing a realistic image of the surroundings of that person. They develop ExpertSN, a personalized Expert Recommender tool based on e-mail Data Mining and Social Network Analysis. ExpertSN constructs a personal social network from the e-mail corpus of a person by computing profiles including topics represented by keywords and other attributes.

The most common way of visualizing networks is by depicting the networks as graphs. In *Pixel-Oriented Network Visualization: Static Visualization of Change in Social Networks* by Klaus Stein, René Wegener, and Christoph Schlieder, the networks are described in a matrix form using pixels. They claim that their approach is more suitable for social networks than graph drawing since graph drawing results in a very cluttered image even for moderately sized social networks. Their technique implements activity timelines that are folded to inner glyphs within each matrix cell. Users are ordered by similarity which allows to uncover interesting patterns. The visualization is exemplified using social networks based on corporate wikis.

The chapter *TweCoM: Topic and Context Mining from Twitter* by Luca Cagliero and Alessandro Fiori is concered with knowledge discovery from user-generated content from social networks and online communities. Many different approaches have been devoted to addressing this issue. This chapter proposes the TweCoM (Tweet Context Miner) framework which entails the mining of relevant recurrences from the content and the context in which Twitter messages (i.e., tweets) are posted. The framework combines two main efforts: (1) the automatic generation of taxonomies from both post content and contextual features and (2) the extraction of hidden correlations by means of generalized association rule mining. In particular, relationships holding in context data provided by Twitter are exploited to automatically construct aggregation hierarchies over contextual features, while a hierarchical clustering algorithm is exploited to build a taxonomy over most relevant tweet content keywords. To counteract the excessive level of detail of the extracted information, conceptual aggregations (i.e., generalizations) of concepts hidden in the analyzed data are exploited in the association rule mining process. The extraction of generalized association rules allows discovering high-level recurrences by evaluating the extracted taxonomies. Experiments performed on real Twitter posts show the effectiveness and the efficiency of the proposed technique.

In the chapter *Application of Social Network Metrics to a Trust-Aware Collaborative Model for Generating Personalized User Recommendations* by Iraklis Varlamis, Magdalini Eirinaki, and Malamati Louta, the authors discuss trustworthiness of recommendations in social networks which discuss product placement and promotion. The authors note that community-based reputation can aid in assessing the trustworthiness of individual network participants. In order to better understand the properties of links, and the dynamics of social networks, they distinguish between permanent and transient links and in the latter case, they consider the link freshness. Moreover, they distinguish between the propagation of trust in a local level and the effect of global influence and compare suggestions provided by locally trusted or globally influential users. The dataset extended Epinions is used as a testbed to evaluate the techniques developed.

Optimization Techniques for Multiple Centrality Computations by Christian von der Weth, Klemens Böhm, and Christian Hütter applies optimization techniques to identify important nodes in a social network. The authors note that many types of data have a graph structure and that, in this context, by identifying central nodes, users can derive important information about the data. In the social network context, it can be used to find influential users and in a reputation system it can identify trustworthy users. Since centrality computation is expensive, performance is crucial. Optimization techniques for single centrality computations exist, but little attention so far has gone into the computation of several centrality measures in combination. In this chapter, the authors investigate how to efficiently compute several centrality measures at a time. They propose two new optimization techniques and demonstrate their usefulness both theoretically as well as experimentally on synthetic and on real-world data sets.

Movie Rating Prediction with Matrix Factorization Algorithm by Ozan B. Fikir, Îlker O. Yaz, and Tansel Özyer discusses a movie rating recommendation system. Recommenation systems is one of the research areas studied intensively in the last decades and several solutions have been elicited for problems in different recommendation domains. Recommendations may differ by content, collaborative filtering, or both. In this chapter, the authors propose an approach which utilizes matrix value factorization for predicting rating i by user j with the sub matrix as k-most similar items specific to user i for all users who rate all items. Previously predicted values are used for subsequent predictions and they investigate the accuracy of neighborhood methods by applying the method to the prizing of Netflix. They have considered both items and users relationships on Netflix dataset for predicting ratings. Here, they have followed different ordering strategies for predicting a sequence of unknown movie ratings and conducted several experiments.

Finally, we would like to mention the hard work of the individuals who have made this valuable edited volume possible. We also thank the authors who submitted revised chapters and the reviewers who produced detailed constructive reports which improved the quality of the papers. Various people from Springer as well deserve much credit for their help and support in all the issues related to publishing this book. In particular, we would like to thank Stephen Soehnlen for his dedication, seriousness, and generous support in terms of time and effort. He answered our e-mails on time despite his busy schedule, even when he was traveling.

A number of organizations supported the project in various ways. We would like to mention the University of Odense, which hosted ASONAM 2010; the National Sciences and Reserch Council of Canada, which supported several of the editors financially through its granting program; the Joint Research Centre (JRC) of European Commission, which supported one of the editors from its Global Security and Crisis Management Unit.

Sogutozu Ankara, Turkey — Tansel Özyer
Calgary, AB, Canada — Jon Rokne
Ispra, Italy — Gerhard Wagner
Leiden, The Netherlands — Arno Reuser

Contents

Contributors

Fabian Abel Web Information Systems, Delft University of Technology, Delft, The Netherlands

Reda Alhajj Department of Computer Science, University of Calgary, Calgary, AB, Canada; Department of Information Technology, Hellenic American University, Manchester, NH, USA; Department of Computer Science, Global University, Beirut, Lebanon

Marie-Aude Aufaure Ecole Centrale Paris, MAS Laboratory, Business Intelligence Team, Chatenay-Malabry, France; INRIA Paris-Rocquencourt, Axis Team, Rocquencourt, France

Klemens Böhm Institute for Program Structures and Data Organization, Karlsruhe Institute of Technology (KIT), Karlsruhe, Germany

Jean-Michel Balasque Computer Science Department, Galatasaray University, Ortaköy/Istanbul, Turkey

Johannes Bjelland Corporate Development, Telenor ASA, Oslo, Norway

Anne Boyer KIWI Team-LORIA, Nancy University, Villers-Lès-Nancy, France

Simone Braun FZI Forschungszentrum Informatik, Haid-und-Neu-Str. 10–14, 76131 Karlsruhe, Germany braun@fzi.de

Armelle Brun KIWI Team-LORIA, Nancy University, Villers-Lès-Nancy, France

Luca Cagliero Politecnico di Torino, Corso Duca degli Abruzzi, Torino, Italy

Geoffrey Canright Corporate Development, Telenor ASA, Oslo, Norway

Dong Cao School of Computer Science, Carnegie-Mellon University, Pittsburgh, PA, USA

Kathleen M. Carley School of Computer Science, Carnegie-Mellon University, Pittsburgh, PA, USA

Wen Haw Chong DSO National Laboratories, Singapore, Singapore

Andrew Clark Information Security Institute, Queensland University of Technology, Brisbane, QLD, Australia

Etienne Cuvelier Ecole Centrale Paris, MAS Laboratory, Business Intelligence Team, Chatenay-Malabry, France

Ernesto Diaz-Aviles L3S Research Center, Leibniz University Hannover, Hannover, Germany

Nima Dokoohaki Software and Computer Systems (SCS), School of Information and Telecommunication Technology (ICT), Royal Institute of Technology (KTH), Stockholm, Sweden

Magdalini Eirinaki Computer Engineering Department, San Jose State University, San Jose, CA, USA

Shimaa M. El-Sherif Department of Electrical and Computer Engineering, University of Calgary, Calgary, AB, Canada

Kenth Engø-Monsen Corporate Development, Telenor ASA, Oslo, Norway

Abdol-Hossein Esfahanian Michigan State University, East Lansing, MI, USA

Ilham Esslimani KIWI Team-LORIA, Nancy University, Villers-Lès-Nancy, France

W. Fan Department of Electronic Engineering, City University of Hong Kong, Hong Kong, China

Behrouz H. Far Department of Electrical and Computer Engineering, University of Calgary, Calgary, AB, Canada

Ozan Bora Fikir Aydin Yazilim Elektronik Sanayi A.Ş., TOBB University, Ankara, Turkey

Alessandro Fiori Politecnico di Torino, Corso Duca degli Abruzzi, Torino, Italy

Jaime R. S. Fonseca Univ Tecn Lisboa, ISCSP, P-1349055 Lisbon, Portugal jaimefonseca@iscsp.utl.pt

Keith B. Gallagher Department of Computer Science, Florida Institute of Technology, Melbourne, FL, USA

Judith Gelernter School of Computer Science, Carnegie-Mellon University, Pittsburgh, PA, USA

Peter Groenewegen Faculty of Social Science, Department of Organization Science, VU University Amsterdam, Amsterdam, The Netherlands

Christian Hütter Institute for Program Structures and Data Organization, Karlsruhe Institute of Technology (KIT), Karlsruhe, Germany

Nicola Henze L3S Research Center, Leibniz University Hannover, Hannover, Germany

Oliver Hoffmann University of Trier, Trier, Germany; Schloss Dagstuhl – Leibniz-Zentrum für Informatik GmbH, Warden, Germany

Bo Hu Fujitsu Laboratories of Europe Limited, Hayes Park Central, Hayes End Road, Hayes, Middlesex, United Kingdom, UB4 8FE bo.hu@uk.fujitsu.com

Marleen Huysman Faculty of Economics and Business Administration, Department of Information Systems and Logistics, VU University Amsterdam, Amsterdam, The Netherlands

Tamer N. Jarada University of Calgary, Calgary, AB, Canada

Jing Jiang School of Information Systems, Singapore Management University, Singapore, Singapore

Panagiotis Karampelas Department of Information Technology, Hellenic American University, Manchester, NH, USA

Daniel Krause L3S Research Center, Leibniz University Hannover, Hannover, Germany

Vincent Labatut Computer Science Department, Galatasaray University, Ortaköy/Istanbul, Turkey

Yves Lechevallier INRIA Paris-Rocquencourt, Axis Team, Rocquencourt, France

Ee-Peng Lim School of Information Systems, Singapore Management University, Singapore, Singapore

Rich Ling IT-University, Copenhagen, Denmark

Amine Louati ENSI, RIADI-GDL Laboratory, Campus Universitaire de la Manouba, 2010, Manouba, Tunisia; INRIA Paris-Rocquencourt, Axis Team, Rocquencourt, France

Malamati Louta Department of Informatics and Telecommunications Engineering, University of Western Macedonia, Kozani, Greece

Matteo Magnani Department of Computer Science, University of Bologna, Bologna, Italy

Mihhail Matskin Computer and Information Science (IDI), Norwegian University of Science and Technology (NTNU), Trondheim, Norway

George Mohay Information Security Institute, Queensland University of Technology, Brisbane, QLD, Australia

Danilo Montesi Department of Computer Science, University of Bologna, Bologna, Italy

Mikolaj Morzy Institute of Computing Science, Poznan University of Technology, Poznan, Poland

Christine Moser Faculty of Social Science, Department of Organization Science, VU University Amsterdam, Amsterdam, The Netherlands

Mohammad Moshirpour Department of Electrical and Computer Engineering, University of Calgary, Calgary, AB, Canada,

Ronald Nussbaum Michigan State University, East Lansing, MI, USA

Byung-Won On Advanced Digital Sciences Center, Singapore, Singapore

Tansel Özyer TOBB University, Ankara, Turkey

Lyta Penna Information Security Institute, Queensland University of Technology, Brisbane, QLD, Australia

Christophe Prieur LIAFA, Paris-Diderot, Paris, France

Bradley S. Rees Department of Computer Science, Florida Institute of Technology, Melbourne, FL, USA

Florian Reitz University of Trier, Trier, Germany

Uwe V. Riss SAP AG, Dietmar-Hopp-Allee 16, 69190 Walldorf, Germany Uwe. Riss@sap.com

Verónica Rivera-Pelayo FZI Forschungszentrum Informatik, Haid-und-Neu-Str. 10–14, 76131, Karlsruhe, Germany rivera@fzi.de

Jon G. Rokne Department of Computer Science, University of Calgary, Calgary, AB, Canada

Luca Rossi Department of Communication Studies, University of Urbino Carlo Bo, Urbino, Italy

Christoph Schlieder Computing in the Cultural Sciences, University of Bamberg, Bamberg, Germany

Omair Shafiq Department of Computer Science, University of Calgary, Calgary, AB, Canada

Patrick Siehndel L3S Research Center, Leibniz University Hannover, Hannover, Germany

Zbigniew Smoreda Orange Labs, Issy les Moulineaux, France

Rania Soussi Ecole Centrale Paris, MAS Laboratory, Business Intelligence Team, Chatenay-Malabry, France

Klaus Stein Computing in the Cultural Sciences, University of Bamberg, Bamberg, Germany

Alina Stoica EDF R&D, Clamart, France

Pål Roe Sundsøy Corporate Development, Telenor ASA, Oslo, Norway

Pang-Ning Tan Michigan State University, East Lansing, MI, USA

Loo-Nin Teow DSO National Laboratories, Singapore, Singapore

Wei Shan Belinda Toh DSO National Laboratories, Singapore, Singapore

Iraklis Varlamis Department of Informatics and Telematics, Harokopio University of Athens, Athens, Greece

Bai Wang Beijing University of Posts and Telecommunications, Beijing, China

René Wegener Information Systems, Kassel University, Kassel, Germany

Christian von der Weth School of Computer Engineering, Nanyang Technological University (NTU), Singapore, Singapore

Hans Friedrich Witschel Fachhochschule Nordwestschweiz, Riggenbachstraße 16, 4600 Olten, Switzerland hansfriedrich.witschel@fhnw.ch

Bin Wu Beijing University of Posts and Telecommunications, Beijing, China

Romana Xerez Univ Tecn Lisboa, ISCSP, P-1349055 Lisbon, Portugal rxerez@iscsp.utl.pt

İlker O. Yaz TOBB University, Ankara, Turkey

Qi Ye Beijing University of Posts and Telecommunications, Beijing, China

K. H. Yeung Department of Electronic Engineering, City University of Hong Kong, Hong Kong, China

Chapter 1
EgoClustering: Overlapping Community Detection via Merged Friendship-Groups

Bradley S. Rees and Keith B. Gallagher

Abstract There has been considerable interest in identifying communities within large collections of social networking data. Existing algorithms will classify an actor (node) into a single group, ignoring the fact that in real-world situations people tend to belong concurrently to multiple (overlapping) groups. Our work focuses on the ability to find overlapping communities. We use egonets to form friendship-groups. A friendship-group is a localized community as seen from an individual's perspective that allows an actor to belong to multiple communities. Our algorithm finds overlapping communities and identifies key members that bind communities together. Additionally, we will highlight the parallel feature of the algorithm as a means of improving runtime performance, and the ability of the algorithm to run within a database and not be constrained by system memory.

1.1 Introduction

An escalation in the number of Community Detection algorithms [2,9,11–14,22,24, 26,34–36,38,40,45,46] has occurred in recent years. The focus of the algorithms shifted away from the classical clustering principles of grouping nodes based upon some type of shared attribute [20,36], to one where the relationships and interactions between individuals are emphasized. The shift has caused algorithms to view the data as a graph and focus on exploiting (detecting) the "small-world effect" [44] found in social networks – the phenomena that a small path length separates any two randomly selected nodes – and on detecting the clustering property of social networks in which the density of the edges is higher within the group than between the groups [2,13,14,22,24,26,34–36,38,40,45].

B.S. Rees (✉) · K.B. Gallagher
Department of Computer Science, Florida Institute of Technology, Melbourne, FL, USA
e-mail: brees2011@my.fit.edu; kgallagher@fit.edu

T. Özyer et al. (eds.), *The Influence of Technology on Social Network Analysis and Mining*, Lecture Notes in Social Networks 6, DOI 10.1007/978-3-7091-1346-2_1,

Moody and White [33] reasoned that communities are held together by the presence of multiple independent paths between members. Extrapolating from the goal of discovering clusters, where internal edge density is maximized, it follows that the identification of cliques [15, 26, 38] {k-cliques, k-clans, or k-cores, where k is the number of nodes comprising the group} would be a viable approach; the density is maximal within those structures. However, given that a five-clique, for example, contains a number of overlapping four-cliques, each of which is a community in its own right [15], presents the question of whether the algorithm is really revealing communities or just doing pattern matching.

Other approaches have focused on centrality [17] to identify key nodes or edges, and follow a hierarchical clustering approach to recursively extract clusters [13, 22, 26]. While centrality is a powerful and useful idea for identifying key (central) actors in a network, many of the centrality approaches require that the centrality measurement be recalculated after each graph edit, causing the algorithms to be highly inefficient [13, 35, 36].

In this paper, which is an expanded version of the one we presented at ASONAM 2010 [41], we present a radically different approach to group detection that finds communities based on the collective viewpoint of individuals. The notion postulated is that each node in the network knows, by way of its egonet [16, 18], who is in its *Friendship-Groups*. We use the term friendship-group to represent the small clusters, extracted from egonets, containing the central node and communal neighbors. Therefore, by calculating the aggregation of each individual's friendship-groups, we find overlapping communities, in a process we term *EgoClustering*. Additionally, the algorithm is designed to be highly parallelizable as a means of improving runtime, and able to operate within a database and therefore not constrained by system memory.

The contributions of this paper are:

1. A precise mathematical formulation of a Friendship-Group
2. A full fledged implementation of the EgoClustering algorithm
3. An algorithm producing communities with maximal size by allowing for overlap
4. A more intuitive approach to community detection
5. An algorithm that can be run on disk-based data
6. An Algorithm that can be easily parallelized.

1.1.1 Terminology

Social Network Analysis derives from the social sciences with its own taxonomy and argot, while graph theory derives from mathematics with a different taxonomy. In graph theory [6], the terms vertex and edge are used to describe a graph, while social networking [10, 43] uses node or actor and edge, link, or arc to describe a graph. For the purpose of this paper, the terms are used interchangeably, with a slight preference toward nodes and edges.

A graph is defined as $G = \{V, E\}$ where V is a set of vertices (nodes) and E is a set of edges, represented by unordered pairs of vertices, called the *start node* and *end node*. The edge set defines connections between pairs of vertices. An optional weighting can be assigned to the pair. If the pairs are ordered, the graph is directed. A *path* is an ordered sequence of edges in the graph where the end node of an edge is the start node of the next in the sequence. Any two nodes on a path are *connected*. The shortest path between to nodes is one with the least number of edges. If there is no path between two nodes, they are *disconnected*.

The neighbors of a vertex, v, is defined as the set of vertexes connected by way of an edge to vertex v, or $\mathrm{N}(v) = \{U\}$ where $v \in V$ and $\forall \mathrm{u} \in \mathrm{U} \; \exists \; \mathrm{edge(v, u)} \in \mathrm{E}$. The degree of a vertex, $\delta(v)$, is the number of edges incident to that vertex. In the case where the graph contains no loops (edges that have the same starting and ending vertex) the degree of a vertex is also equal to the number of neighbors, $\delta(v) = |\mathrm{N}(v)|$.

The density of a graph, or subgraph, is the measure of the number of edges in the graph, over the maximum number of possible edges. A value of 1 indicates that all possible edges are present, while a value of 0 indicates the absence of any edges. The most edges a node can have is $(n-1)$; the maximum number of edges possible in an undirected graph is $\frac{n(n-1)}{2}$. Density can then be defined as: $d(n) = \frac{2m}{n(n-1)}$, where n is the number of nodes and m is the number of edges. A sparse graph is one where the number of edges is close to the number of nodes, and a dense graph is one where the density measurement approaches, or is equal to, 1. There is no agreed upon threshold between a sparse graph and a dense graph.

Centrality [17] is a measure of how important, or central, a node is in relation to the whole graph. The *betweenness centrality* of a node, n, is number of paths that contain n in the *all-pairs-shortest-path* set of the graph G. Betweenness centrality can also be obtained for edges [36].

The term egonet [10, 16, 18] derives from egocentric network. An egonet is an induced subgraph consisting of a central node, (the *ego-node*), its neighbors, and all edges among the neighbors. The individual's viewpoint reduces the network under consideration to just those vertices adjacent to the central "ego" node and any edges between those nodes.

Given a graph G, the egonet on a node, n, is:
ego(n) = the subgraph H of G where

$$
\begin{aligned}
&V(H) = \{v, N(v)\} \\
&E(H) = \\
&\quad \forall (n_1, n_2) \in V(H) \text{ if} \\
&\quad \exists\, e(n_1,\ n_2) \in E(G) \text{ then} \\
&\quad \exists\, e(n_1, n_2) \in E(H)
\end{aligned}
$$

A dyad is two nodes joined by an edge. A triad is three nodes connected by a minimum of two edges and a maximum of three edges.

All graphs in this work are considered to be "sparse", unweighted, undirected, and containing no loops. For this work, we define sparse as being graphs with density less than 0.4.

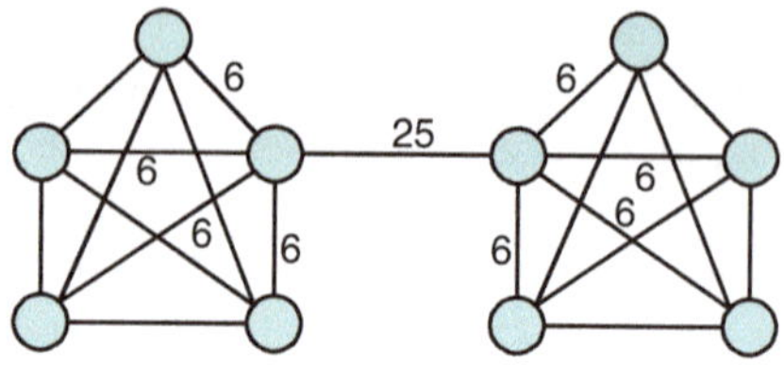

Fig. 1.1 Edge betweenness centrality scores

1.2 Related Work

One of the more prevalent algorithms comes from work by Girvin and Newman [22, 36] (GN). The GN algorithm follows a divisive hierarchical method, which iteratively removes edges with the highest edge-betweenness centrality score. This is based on the principle that *between community* edges have higher centrality than *within community* edges, as shown in Fig. 1.1.

The GN algorithm recognized that the centrality score must be recalculated after each edge removal. However, the recalculating of centrality causes the algorithm to have high computational demands, running in $O(n3)$ to $O(n4)$ time on sparse graphs. Newman addressed the performance factor in a subsequent paper [35] by developing an agglomerative method that reduced runtime to $O(n2)$.

Hierarchical clustering approaches, divisive or agglomerative, present some problems. As Newman points out [35] "...the GN community structure algorithm always produces some division of vertices into communities, regardless of whether the network has any natural such divisions." Moreover, the "fast-Newman" [35] algorithm suffers from an NP-complete subproblem [46].

The notion of using some form of centrality as the means for determining edge removal was extended by Hwang et al. [34], by the concept of Bridging Centrality. A bridge, in graph theory terms, is an edge whose removal will break the graph into two disconnected subgraphs. Hwang et al. defined Bridging Centrality as the ranked product of betweenness centrality and a bridging coefficient. Informally, the bridging coefficient is the probability of having common neighbors.

Agglomerative methods start with one node per cluster and iteratively joins clusters; divisive methods start with one cluster and iteratively divides. The iterations of both processes can be represented as a *dendrogram*. Selecting different stopping points in those processes will produce different numbers of communities [34, 36]. The challenge is that the decision of where to stop should to be done a priori. The following illustration, Fig. 1.2, shows a dendrogram with three possible cut points (A, B, and C), producing two, four, or six possible clusters, each of which does not necessarily equate to a community [40]. *Modularity* (a probabilistic method) and density have both been used as means of determining the stopping point [26, 36].

Modularity was first introduced by Newman and Girvan [36] as a means of determining when to stop processing within their divisive algorithm. Since then, modularity has become a widely studied community quality measure [7, 8, 37, 42] (non-exhaustive list). More recently, Brandes et. al. [5] published a critique of

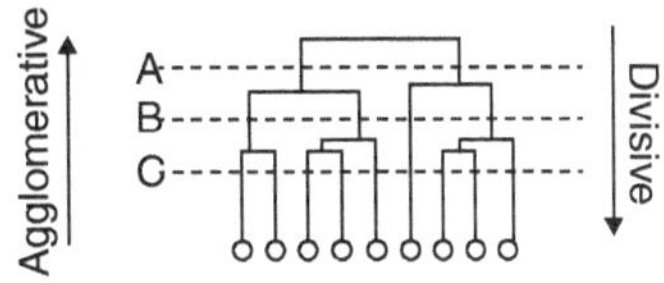

Fig. 1.2 Dendrogram with three possible cuts

modularity and illustrated how finding the optimal modularity value is an NP-complete problem. Modularity can be described as the notion that communities do not occur by random change. The Modularity, denoted Q, is the measure of a cluster against the same cluster in a null (or random) graph. A greater than random probability indicates a good cluster.

These approaches suffer the additional problem that nodes are forced to exist only in a single community. Real-world networks are not so nicely constrained, and contain realistic amounts of overlap between communities [9, 33, 38]. Each person (node) could have a community for family, friends, work, and interest, for example, and community detection algorithms must allow for, and detect, overlapping groups. Forcing a node into a single community and not allowing for overlap could prevent the detection of the true underlying community structures [9, 30, 38].

A number of solutions for finding overlapping communities have been developed [2, 9, 13, 14, 24, 38]. Gregory [24], for example, modified the GN algorithm to highlight overlapping communities by splitting nodes, thus permitting a node to be represented in the graph multiple times, and allowing each instance of the node to clustered into a different community. While the modification does find overlapping communities, it also degrades the algorithm's performance.

Local clustering has been explored in a number of algorithms [1, 8, 30]. This technique, which builds communities independently, does not remove nodes from the graph for subsequent iterations. Overlapping communities can be found using local clustering. Baumes et al. [2, 3] present a unique two-step approach to finding overlapping communities. The first part of the algorithm is called Rank Removal, or *RaRe*, which iteratively removes high ranked nodes, thus breaking the network into disconnected clusters. Baumes et al. discuss the use of PageRank and high degree nodes (degree-centrality) as a means of finding important nodes, however it would seem logical to expand that process to leverage any of the previously discussed community detection approaches. The second step is the truly unique portion of their algorithm, and involves adding nodes that were not part of the cluster and evaluating whether the clusters density increased. This step considers all neighboring nodes, rather than all nodes, as a means of improving performance. Additionally, it is this step that permits the assumption that nodes belong to multiple communities and therefore overlap.

The notion of local-based community construction was also used by Lancichinetti et al. [30] in what they termed as finding the "natural community" of a node. Lancichinetti's algorithm works by randomly selecting a node and iteratively adding neighboring nodes, checking for an increase in "fitness." Fitness is roughly similar to modularity [35] or Radicchi's definition of community [40], and is defined as the measure of edges within a community over the sum of edges within and leaving the community: $f_G = \frac{k_{in}^G}{(k_{in}^G + k_{out}^G)\alpha}$.

The factor, α, is used to control, or limit, community size. However, as Lancichinetti points out, the best results are obtained where $\alpha = 1$. The values of *kin* and *kout* are the degree of edges within the community and leaving the community respectively. Since each community is built independently, and based on the full graph, overlap between the communities can occur.

The notion of a clique (a subgraph with maximal density) being synonymous with a community is not new, and approaches for finding cliques originated as early as the late 1940s [15]. Palla et al. [38] extended the theory of cliques as communities by introducing the definition that a community, specifically a *k-clique-community*, is a union of all k-cliques that can be reached via adjacent k-cliques. The process works by rolling, or *percolating*, a k-clique over the network to find other k-cliques that share $k-1$ nodes. The percolating [11] is performed by moving the selection of one node within the k-clique to an unselected neighbor node that also form a k-clique. Since only one node is selected each time, the subsequent k-clique must share exactly $k-1$ nodes.

1.3 Our Approach

1.3.1 Defining Community

There is no formal, or conventional, definition of social community [12] beyond "a collection of individuals linked by a common interest" [32]. Rather than trying to define, or redefining community, we turn instead to work by Moody and White [33], who focused on defining four characteristics that bind a community together, referred to as "structural cohesion." One definition of interest from Moody and White is that community cohesion is tied to the number of independent paths between members. That definition is supported by the qualitative observations [40] that communities have greater internal edge density than external, inter-community, density. Consider the graph in Fig. 1.3a; it contains two obvious communities with a single edge between them. As the number of links between communities increases, the ability of clustering algorithms to find distinct communities degrades [22]. Increasing the number of edges between the two communities, Fig. 1.3a, b poses the question: Are there still two communities, have the two merged into one, or are there now three communities?

A second definition from Moody and White is that the removal of one member (node) should not cause the community to collapse. Therefore, for this version of the algorithm, a dyad is not a community; likewise a node of degree 1 cannot be part of a community. However, nodes of degree 1 could be easily subsumed into its neighbor – future version of the algorithm.

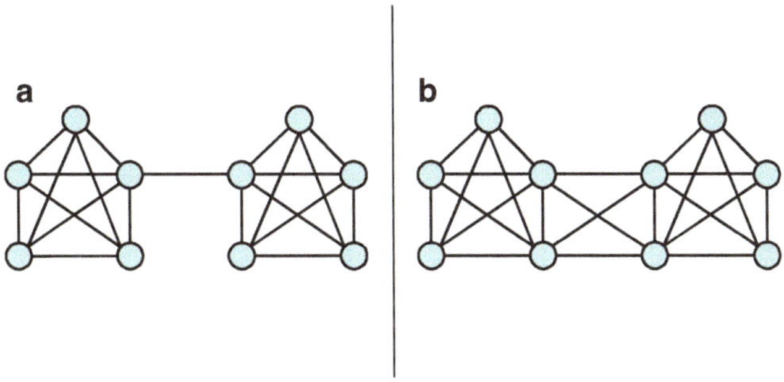

Fig. 1.3 Example of increased edges between communities

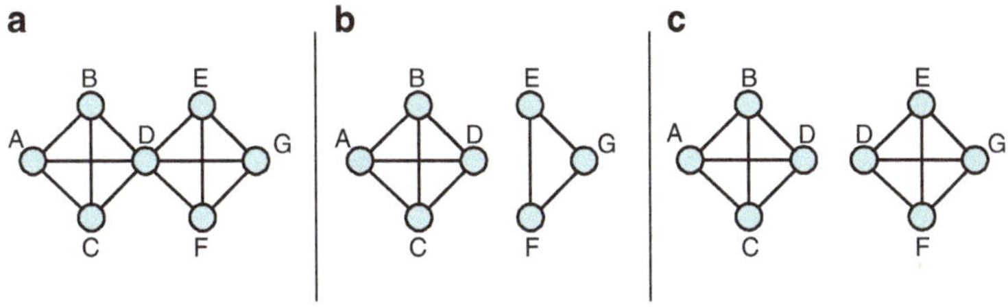

Fig. 1.4 Need to allow overlap

1.3.2 The Need to Allow Overlapping

A key feature [11] of most real-world communities from social networks is that they overlap [9, 13, 24, 30], allowing a single node to belong to multiple communities. The notion should be intuitive, and empirically evident [9, 19] that individuals can belong to multiple simultaneous groups, for example families, social circles, and work communities. Moreover, in hierarchical clustering, as several have pointed out [9, 30, 38, 39], the assignment of a node to a single community can cause the remaining communities to fall apart, thus preventing the detection, or discovery, of the true social structures. A simple proof to this statement can be seen in the following example.

We ran two popular community detection algorithms on the simple and very small graph – for illustration purposes – shown in Fig. 1.4a. In this case, the *FastModularity* algorithm of Clauset and Newman [7], and the modified GN [22] algorithm, called "A Fast Algorithm", from Radicchi et al. [40]. Each of the algorithms detected the same two communities shown in Fig. 1.4b.

If we examine the smaller community, {E, G, F}, Fig. 1.4b, independent of the other communities and under the premise that all nodes and edges not within that community are available for consideration in the community, we can then evaluate the effect of adding each neighbor node into the community. In this case the inclusion of node D within the smaller community increases the modularity score, and therefore uncovers the true community. Both local clustering and our

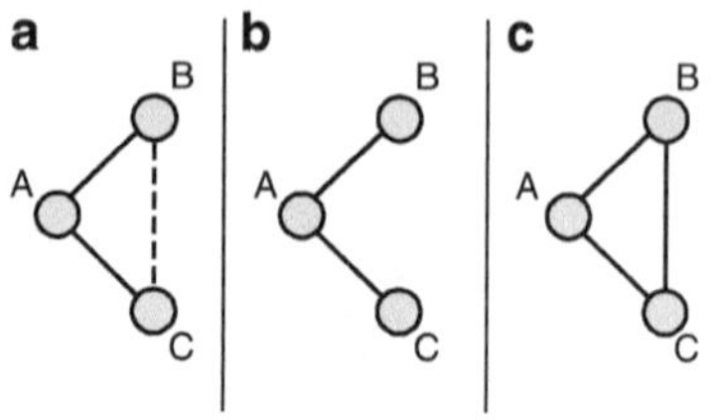

Fig. 1.5 Triangles and the Forbidden triad

EgoClustering algorithms produce the result of Fig. 1.4c, which we believe are the valid communities of the graph.

For the purpose of this study, we are interested in finding all communities within a social network, and not simply on partitioning nodes into clusters. Therefore we make the statement that detected communities can only be guaranteed to be maximal if overlap is allowed, and by not allowing overlap, erroneous results can be obtained; moreover all overlapping nodes must be found.

1.3.3 Triangles

When examining undirected, unweighted, and unlabeled graphs, a few assumptions need to be made: (1) That there is some form of *homophily* (common interest) that binds communities together; (2) that each edge represents the same level of relationship strength; and, (3) that there is an equal amount of reciprocity in each edge. With those assumptions in mind, we can look at triads and their relationship to communities.

Consider a triad comprised of the three nodes {A, B, C}, Fig. 1.5a. If there is a tie between A and B, and A and C, the probability that B and C are linked is so much greater than random that Granovetter [23, 27] deemed the absence of such a link as the "Forbidden" triad. The presence of a triad indicates that there is a strong tie [23] between the nodes and therefore some type of shared interest, which could be called a community.

For the purpose of this work, we are considering the absence of a link between node B and C, Fig. 1.5b, to be an indication that B and C are not similar and therefore, initially, not within the same community. Conversely, the presence of a tie between B and C, Fig. 1.5c, is an indication of a community.

1.3.4 Friendship-Groups

With the rudimentary definition of community, the need to allow overlap, and the value of triad defined, we can now define the basic building block of our algorithm, the *Friendship-Group*. Consider the graph shown in Fig. 1.6a, an egonet build around node A.

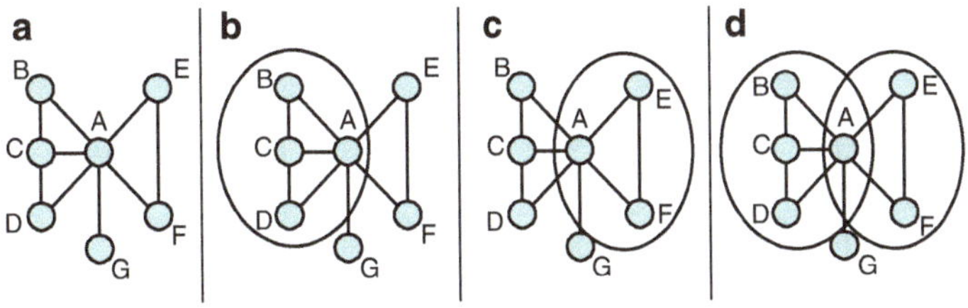

Fig. 1.6 Friendship-Groups

Node A has a strong connection to nodes B and C, since nodes B and C are connected. Additionally, node A has a strong connection to nodes C and D, which are also connected. Without additional information we can infer that node A, B, C, and D form a community, Fig. 1.6b. At the same time, node A has a strong connection to nodes E and F, due to the connection between E and F. Since nodes are allowed to belong to multiple communities, we conclude that nodes A, E, and F form a community as shown in Fig. 1.6c. The connection between node A and G fits the definition of a dyad, which we have previously defined as not constituting a community.

We define a Friendship-Group to be the local view of communities within an egonet from the perspective of the ego node. Or, an induced subgraph extracted from an egonet, adhering to the same constraints mentioned above for a community; multiple paths and no dyads or single nodes. We make the distinction between communities and friendship-group since the friendship-group is myopic view of the egonet, and one or more friendships-groups can be combined to form a community. The egonet in Fig. 1.6 contains two friendship-groups as shown in Fig. 1.6d.

1.3.5 Algorithm

The algorithm executes in two phases; the first phase is the detection of friendship-groups, the second phase comprises the aggregation of friendship-groups into communities.

In phase 1, the algorithm iterates through every vertex in the graph and derives the egonet for that vertex. From that derived egonet, friendship-groups are extracted. The process for finding friendship-groups from the egonet is performed by first removing the central, or ego, node, since it is known to exist in multiple friendship-groups. By removing the ego vertex, the graph breaks into multiple connected components, each of which can be easily found. The egocentric vertex is then added back to each found component to form the friendship-groups.

For example, given the following simple network, Fig. 1.7a, the egonet for vertex D would be just those vertices connected to D, or B, C, E, and F, as shown in Fig. 1.7b.

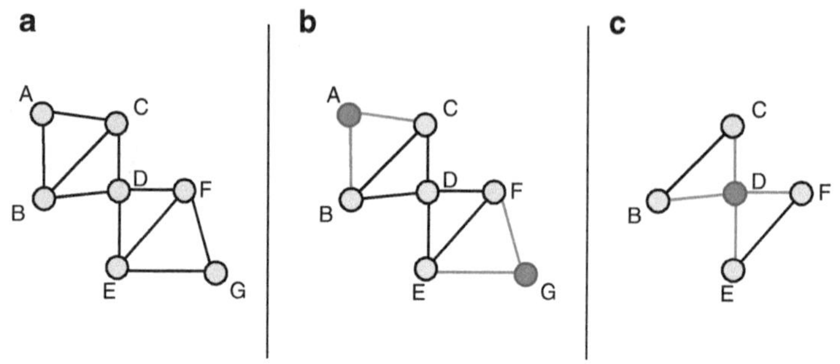

Fig. 1.7 Detecting Friendship-Groups

Pseudo code:

1. For each node $\forall n \in \{V\}$
   - Get egonet of n: H = ego(n)
   - Find Friendship-Groups:
     - Remove n from the egonet
     - Find the connected components of the remaining subgraph
     - Add n to each component
2. Merge and Reduce Sets
   - Remove proper subsets
   - Merge "close" matches
   - Repeat until no more merges can be performed

From the point-of-view of vertex D, nodes B and C are friends and E and F are friends. The removal of D, grayed out in Fig. 1.7c, creates two distinct components. That yields two friendship-groups, with the ego vertex added back in, of {B, C, D} and {D, E, F}. That process is repeated for every vertex in the network. The result of that first phase is a collection of friendship-groups, from an egocentric point-of-view.

The next step, phase 2, is to merge all the friendship-groups into communities. That process is done by first merging all exact matches, groups that are either complete or proper subsets of other groups. The final step is to merge groups that are "relatively close"; in this case, groups that match all but one item from the smaller group. Given two sets, Sl and Ss, where Sl is larger than, or equal to, Ss, then the sets are merged (union) if the size of the intersection is equal to one less than the size of the smaller set: $S_l \bigcap S_s| = |S_s| - 1$; i.e., the size of the set difference is 1. This step compensates for egonets not having a complete picture of the community, and allows communities of different sizes to be compared. Continuing the example from above, Fig. 1.7a, group {A, B, C}, obtained from egonet centered on node A, would merge with group {B, C, D}, from egonet centered on B and/or C, to form {A, B, C, D}. Notice that even though A and D are not directly connected, they are in the same community.

1.3.6 Performance

The runtime performance of the algorithm is greatly influenced by the density of the graph being analyzed. Consequently, we will compute performance for the boundary conditions, density $= 0$ and density $= 1$, and for the anticipated runtime when applied to sparse graphs, typical of social networks. For performance definition, we use n to represent the number of nodes, m to represent the number of edges, δ to represent the average degree of a node, and s to represent the number of friendship-groups sets identified. We will delay reducing any equation until after the base equation has been defined. Lastly, as with any algorithm, the method of implementation can affect performance. Here we assume that the graph is stored either as an adjacency matrix, or spared edge list.

The first phase of the algorithm comprises the identification of friendship-groups within derived egonets. The process of identifying the egonet can be done in constant time, since the base graph does not have to be modified. The process only needs to identify the neighbors of the selected node. If the data is stored in an edge matrix, then the neighbors are specified in the row corresponding to the ego-node. The complexity of iterating over each node is captured in the following description.

The process of finding the egonet friendship-groups, or disjoint connected components, can be done using the classic union-find algorithm, in $O(log(n))$ time. The process of finding the friendship groups requires that the approximately δ incident nodes of the egonode be compared against the δ incident nodes of each neighbor of the egonode, gives $O(\delta^2)$. Since the process of finding friendship-groups is done for each node in the network, the runtime for the first phase is $O(n\delta^2)$.

The second step is filtering and merging, which can be accomplished with a modified merge-sort algorithm. A traditional merge-sort runs in $O(slog(s))$, however the merging process in this case produces a new set (partial community) that needs to be reexamined and compared to the remaining set. That modification increases runtime to $O(s^2log(s))$.

Lower Boundary: When density equals 0 (i.e. there are no edges), all nodes are disconnected. Therefore, the average degree of a node is 0 and $\delta = 0$. That reduces the first phase to $O(n)$. As detected friendship-groups consist of only the ego-node, the number of sets is equal to the number of nodes, $s = n$. Additionally, since we know that each set is unique, no merges will occur and the algorithm will not need to reexamine any merged sets. This brings the runtime of the second phase down to $O(nlog(n))$. The total runtime is then $O(n^2log(n))$. Since we know that single node sets cannot merge during the second phase, we could programmatically have removed those sets and not done the all-pair comparison, further reducing runtime to: $O(n)$.

Upper Boundary: When density equals 1 (i.e. every possible edge exists), then the graph is one large clique. The average degree of every node is $\delta = (n - 1)$, which we reduce to just $\delta = n$. This causes the first phase to have a runtime of $O(n^3)$.

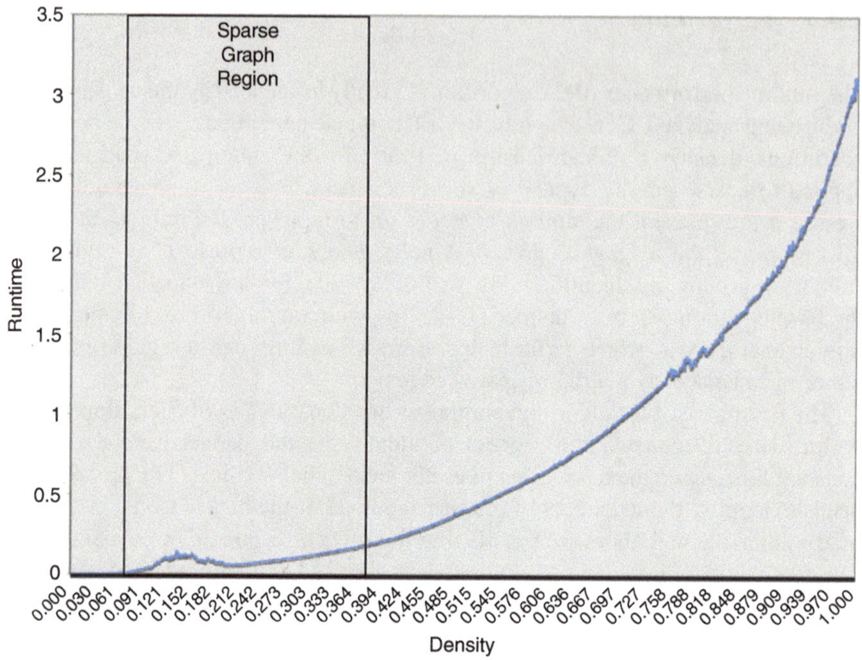

Fig. 1.8 Runtime

For the second phase, each node will have detected only a single friendship-group, $s = n$. However, all friendship-groups will be the same, hence the first pass will merge all sets down to a single set. This reduces the runtime of the second phase to $O(n)$. The total runtime is thus: $O(n + n^3)$.

Anticipated Runtime: For sparse graphs where the number of edges scales linearly with the number of nodes, Hwang et al. [26] points out that the average degree is approximately *logn*, which we will use for the anticipated engonet size of a sparse graph, $\delta = log(n)$. The first phase becomes: $O(nlog^2(n))$. For the second phase, we assume that the maximum number of sets per friendship-groups is the same as the average degree, or $s = log(n)$. Runtime for phase 2 then becomes: $O(n^2 log(n))$, and the total runtime is: $O(n(log^2(n)) + n^2 log(n))$.

The runtime performance of the algorithm can now be expressed as:

$$O(n) < O(n(log^2(n)) + n^2 log(n)) < O(n^3)$$

Figure 1.8 depicts the performance of running the algorithm over a graph with 100 nodes and increasing the density from 0 to 1. The inserted box represents the targets sparse area.

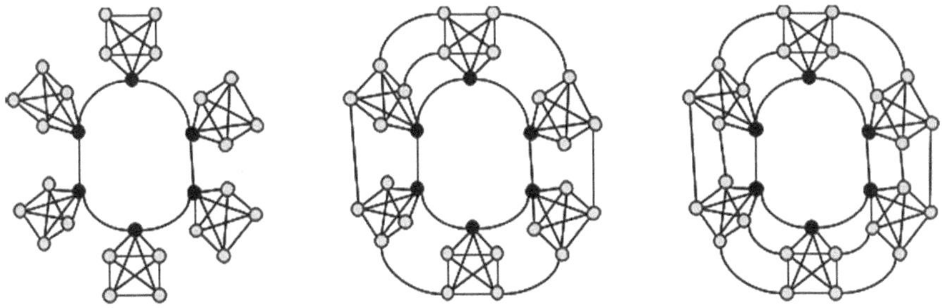

Fig. 1.9 Caveman graph

1.3.7 Improving Performance

The runtime performance shown above is not an improvement, and in some cases inferior, to existing algorithms. Conversely, our algorithm is designed to operate in a parallel fashion as a means of improving performance and scalability.

The initial phase of the algorithm is the identification of friendship groups by iterating over all nodes in the graph. Friendship groups are found for each node, independent of the other nodes, and therefore can be performed in a parallel fashion. The second phase is an all-pair comparison, where a selected set (friendship-group or community) is compared with all others to determine if the set warrants merging, deletion, or retention. As each comparison is acted independently from the previous examination, these processes can also be performed in parallel.

Disk-Resided Processing

One advantage of the algorithm is that it does not need to operate on the graph as a whole; this is true for sparse graphs that are the focus of this work. The algorithm can extract egonets from database resident adjacency matrixes and save detected friendship-groups as sets within a caches database table for the merge and reduce phase. This allows the algorithm to operate against very large graphs that would be too large to fit within available memory.

1.4 Application

1.4.1 Caveman

The algorithm was first applied against a Caveman graph, Fig. 1.9, a term coined by Watts and Strogatz [44] for a network containing a number of fully-connected clusters (cliques) or "caves." The number of connections between the caves is increased to determine at which point the algorithm stops identifying the core cave groups.

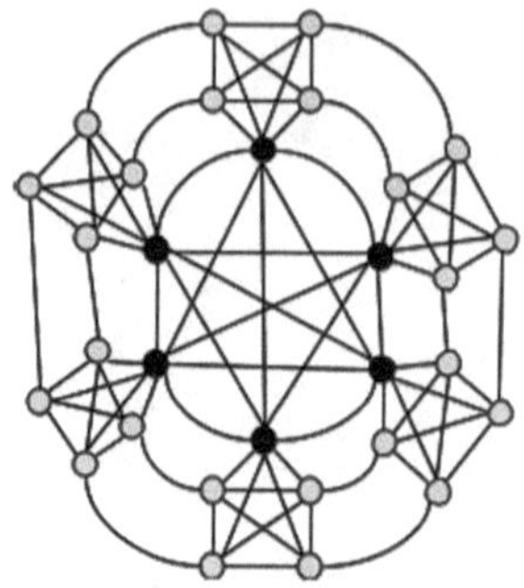

Fig. 1.10 Fully connected Caveman graph

In the case of the three examples shown in Fig. 1.9, the algorithm found the groups with no errors. Although this was a simple case and the links were not really added at random – additional links did not form any new triads and thus no additional groups were detected. When additional links were added linking all the center nodes, Fig. 1.10, the algorithm then detected the six original groups plus a new overlapping community formed by the center nodes. The introduction of a new community is an indication that linkages between communities cannot be added without regard for the implication of the newly formed relationships.

1.4.2 Zachary

The Zachary [47] Karate Club dataset is well studied, and widely utilized as a test bed for many community detection algorithms [13, 22, 24, 34–36, 45]. Zachary observed the social interactions of members of his karate club over a period of 2 years. By chance a dispute broke out between two members that caused the club to split into two smaller groups.

When our algorithm was applied to the Zachary dataset, four communities were found. The following graph, Fig. 1.11, illustrates the discovered networks as well as highlighting the two clubs formed after the split, group 1 is shown by the circles hexagons and group 2 shown by squares and triangles.

Cluster A: [1, 17, 7, 11, 6, 5]
Cluster B: [13, 33, 1, 4, 14, 3, 22, 20, 2, 9, 18, 8]
Cluster C: [25, 32, 26]
Cluster D: [29, 33, 1, 21, 3, 31, 9, 15, 34, 28, 24, 30, 16, 27, 32, 19, 23]
Not a member of a community: 10, 12

At first glance, it might appear that our algorithm was in error when it detected four communities in contrast with what the Zachary states as the final outcome. However, the focus of the Zachary paper was on group fission and not on communities, or overlapping communities, within the group. Additionally, the Zachary paper presented a method for creating edge weights based on an aggregation of the number

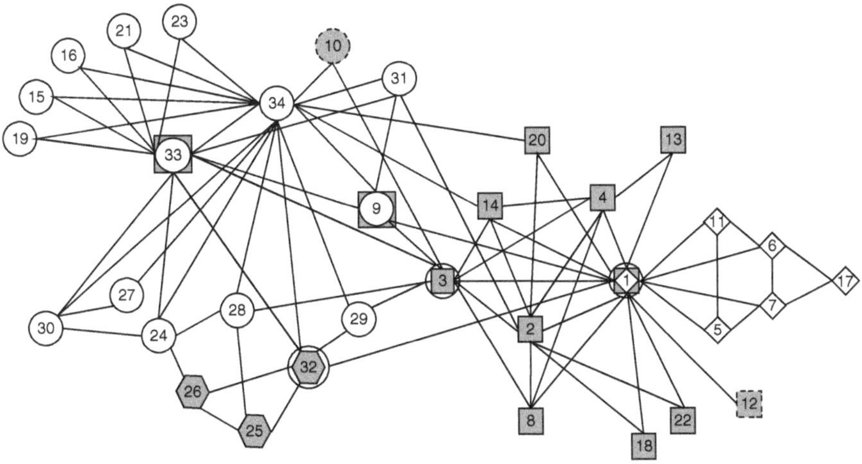

Fig. 1.11 The Zachary Karate club dataset

of different social interaction domains at individuals attended together. Each of these domains has the possibility of defining a community.

Hierarchical clustering allows for the algorithm to be stopped at various points, producing from 1 to n clusters. Since the anticipated results were two clusters, that is the stopping point of most benchmarks against the Zachary dataset. The GN [22] algorithm, for example, identifies the two communities within the dataset, when programmed to extract only two communities.

The FastModularity algorithm of Clauset and Newman [7], selects a stopping point by optimizing modularity. Their algorithm finds three communities, denoted as circles, squares, and triangles as shown in Fig. 1.12.

As we mentioned in Sect. 1.3.2, a community can only be guaranteed to be maximal – inclusion or removal of one additional node decreases quality of the community – if overlap is allowed. Since the FastModularity algorithm does not allow for overlap, it appears as if one community, denoted as squares, is a collection of left over nodes. The inclusion of node "1" within the square community would increase modularity and density.

As an additional comparison, Donetti and Muñoz [12] presented an overlapping algorithm based on modularity that stops processing when modularity is maximized. Their algorithm finds four clusters and one single node.

If the goal was to simply produce two clusters, then a few additional communities merging would have to occur. Looking at Community A, this community is virtually independent from the rest of the communities, with the overlap occurring solely due to node "1". When the split in the karate group happened, this group would follow node "1" and community A would merge in with community B. Looking at the dendrogram from the GN [22] and the Donetti [12] papers, the node comprising cluster A and B are merged in the final step. Community C is less independent than A, but only has an overlap with community D at node "32" and would merge in

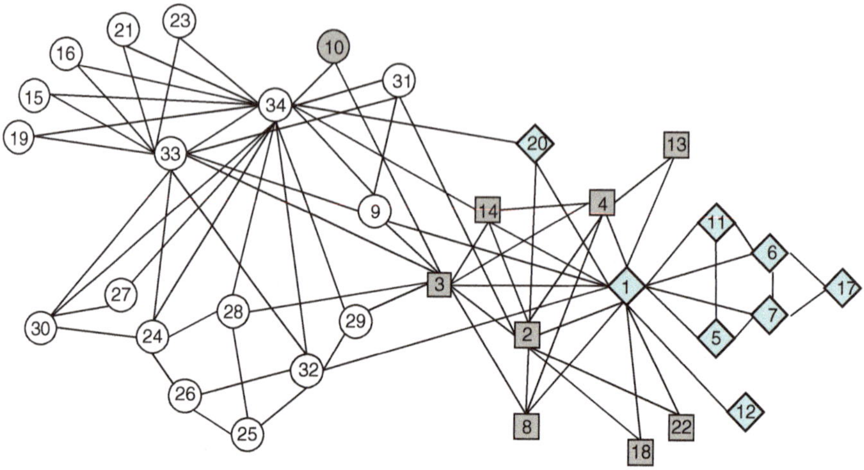

Fig. 1.12 Results using FastModularity

with that cluster. A merger of cluster A with cluster B and cluster C with cluster D would produce two communities, with the only error being the overlapping nodes that appear within both communities.

Yet the purpose of our algorithm was to find overlapping communities and not graph partitioning. In detecting communities, the algorithm also identifies those nodes that form the overlap and act as brokers, or social bridges, between communities. Of particular interest from the karate club are nodes 1, 3, 9, and 33. Those four nodes appear to be the glue that held the groups together. For example, breaking the edge between nodes 3 and 33 and nodes 9 and 1 causes our algorithm to remove the overlap between the two groups. From that we can deduce that any strife within the group affected those four nodes, has the potential to impact the entire karate club.

1.4.3 Other Datasets and Follow-on Work

A number of other datasets were processed by our algorithm and are shown in Table 1.1. However, as the sizes of the graphs being examined grew, so did the complexity of displaying and analyzing the results. The table shows some basic metrics – number of nodes (order), the number of edges (size), the average degree, and the density – on each dataset along with the number of detected communities and the number of nodes not assigned to any community, show in parentheses. Additionally, the number of communities detected from running the FastModularity from Clauset and Newman [7] and the CFinder algorithm of Palla et al. [38] are shown for comparison. For CFinder, the results for k = 3 were used. (Each author on his or her respected web sites generously provided source code for each algorithm).

Table 1.1 Additional datasets and number of communities detected

Dataset	Nodes	Edges	Avg. degree	Density	Communities detected # (single)	Runtime (s)	Fast modul-arity	CFinder
Dolphins[a]	62	159	5.13	0.084	6 (16)	0.117	4	4
Zachary[b]	34	78	4.6	0.14	4 (2)	0.45	3	3
Football[c]	115	613	10.66	0.0935	23 (0)	0.277	7	4
Jazz[d]	198	2,742	27.69	0.14	64 (6)	0.86	4	2
Email[e]	1,133	5,452	9.6	0.008	390 (293)	24.38	12	41
PGP[f]	10,680	24,316	4.55	0.26	793 (7,181)	654.74	698	734

Datasets from http://deim.urv.cat/~Eaarenas/data/welcome.htm
[a]See reference [31].
[b]See reference [47].
[c]See reference [22].
[d]See reference [21].
[e]See reference [25].
[f]See reference [4].

1.5 Follow-on Work

Since our algorithm presents a new definition of community, it was anticipated that there would be significant deviation in results between our algorithm and what others have achieved. Identifying the most efficient methods to measure and compare our results against other algorithms, beyond a simple Jaccard similarity score, is an area for future research. As our algorithm also identifies the nodes that form the overlap, an analysis of those nodes for their ability to act as brokers, and as structural holes, should be cultivated.

In processing the larger datasets, a growing number of nodes not belonging to any community were detected, raising two questions that we plan to further investigate: (1) Is our assumption that a single edge node does not belong to a community valid? (2) Can link weighting be used to further cast a node into one community or another?

Another technique for evaluating our algorithm is to compare it using the LFR [28, 29] benchmark from Lancichinetti, Fortunato, and Radicchi. The benchmark includes a data generator that produces a graph with a known number of communities, and a known internal structure of those communities. Furthermore, the generator does allow communities to overlap. The generator can produce a number of graphs with varying amount of interaction (i.e. links) between the communities. The benchmark measures an algorithm's ability to detect communities as the numbers of cross-community edges are increased. Excepting the algorithm to constantly detect the original communities as the number of cross-community edges increases we believe to be erroneous.

The main focus of this research has been on the community detection portion of the algorithm and not on the merging of the friendship groups. An investigation of that set merging is expected to aid in the reduction of overall runtime. Lastly, we would like to further study the parallel capabilities of the algorithm by exploring multi-threading options or rewriting the algorithm in OpenCL.

1.6 Conclusion

Detection of the underlying community structure is an important part of intuitive network analysis. Failure to consider and account for overlapping groups creates a situation where the true community structure can go undetected. In this paper, we have presented a new approach for detecting overlapping communities, based on the unique perspective of individual group members, which we called friendship-groups. This approach, we believe, defines a more insightful notion of community and creates a potential for future performance enhancements.

Acknowledgements The authors are grateful to Graham Cruickshank for his proofreading skill.

References

1. Bagrow, J.P.: Evaluating local community methods in networks. J. Stat. Mech. **2008**(05), P05001 (2008)
2. Baumes, J., Goldberg, M., Magdon-Ismail, M.: Efficient identification of overlapping communities. In: IEEE International Conference on Intelligence and Security Informatics (ISI), pp. 27–36. Springer, Berlin/Heidelberg (2005)
3. Baumes, J., Goldberg, M.K., Krishnamoorthy, M.S., Magdon-Ismail, M., Preston, N.: Finding communities by clustering a graph into overlapping subgraphs. In: Guimarães, N., Isaías, P. (eds), Proceedings of the IADIS International Conference on Applied Computing, Algarve, Portugal, 97–104. IADIS Press (2005)
4. Bogua, M., Pastor-Satorras, R., Diaz-Guilera, A., Arenas, A.: Models of social networks based on social distance attachment. Phys. Rev. E **70**, 056122 (2004)
5. Brandes, U., Delling, D., Gaertler, M., Gorke, R., Hoefer, M., Nikoloski, Z., Wagner, D.: On modularity clustering. IEEE Trans. Knowl. Data Eng. **20**(2), 172–188 (2008)
6. Chartrand, G.: Introductory Graph Theory. Dover, New York (1985) [1977]
7. Clauset, A., Newman, M.E.J., Moore, C.: Finding community structure in very large networks. Phys. Rev. E **70**, 066111+ (2004)
8. Clauset, A.: Finding local community structure in networks. Phys. Rev. E **72**, 026132 (2005)
9. Davis, G., Carley, K.: Clearing the fog: fuzzy, overlapping groups for social networks. Soc. Netw. **30**, 201–212 (2008)
10. de Nooy, W., Mrvar, A., Batagelj, V.: Exploratory Social Network Analysis with Pajek. Cambridge University Press, Cambridge (2005)
11. Der enyi, I., Palla, G., Vicsek, T.: Clique percolation in random networks. Phys. Rev. Lett. **94**, 160202+ (2005)
12. Donetti, L., Munoz, M.A.: Detecting network communities: a new systematic and efficient algorithm. J. Stat. Mech. **2004**(10), 10012 (2004)
13. Du, N., Wu, B., Pei, X., Wang, B., Xu, L.: Community detection in large-scale social networks. In: WebKDD/SNA-KDD '07: Proceedings of the 9th WebKDD and 1st SNA-KDD 2007 Workshop on Web Mining and Social Network Analysis, pp. 16–25. ACM, New York (2007)

14. Du, N., Wang, B., Wu, B.: Overlapping community structure detection in networks. In: CIKM '08: Proceeding of the 17th ACM Conference on Information and Knowledge Management, pp. 1371–1372. ACM, New York (2008)
15. Everett, M.G., Borgatti, S.P.: Analyzing clique overlap. Connections **21**(1), 49–61 (1998)
16. Everett, M., Borgatti, S.P.: Ego network betweenness. Soc. Netw. **27**, 31–38 (2005)
17. Freeman, L.C.: Centrality in social networks conceptual clarification. Soc. Netw. **1**(3), 215–239 (1979)
18. Freeman, L.C.: Centered graphs and the structure of ego networks. Math. Soc. Sci. **3**, 291–304 (1982)
19. Freeman, L.C.: The sociological concept of group; an empirical test of two models. Am. J. Sociol. **98**(1), 152–166 (1992)
20. Getoor, L., Diehl, C.P.: Link mining: a survey. SIGKDD Explor. Newsl. **7**(2), 3–12 (2005)
21. Gleiser, P.M., Danon, L.: Community structure in jazz. Adv. Complex Syst. (ACS) **6**(4), 565–573 (2003)
22. Girvan, M., Newman, M.E.: Community structure in social and biological networks. Proc. Nat. Acad. Sci. **99**, 7821–7826 (2002)
23. Granovetter, M.S.: The strength of weak ties. Am. J. Sociol. **78**(6), 1360–1380 (1973)
24. Gregory, S.: An algorithm to find overlapping community structure in networks. In: PKDD 2007: Proceedings of the 11th European Conference on Principles and Practice of Knowledge Discovery in Databases, pp. 91–102, Springer, Berlin/Heidelberg (2007)
25. Guimera, R., Danon, L., Diaz-Guilera, A., Giralt, F., Arenas, A.: Self-similar community structure in a network of human interactions. Phys. Rev. E **68**, 065103(R) (2003)
26. Hwang, W., Kim, T., Ramanathan, M., Zhang, A.: Bridging centrality: graph mining from element level to group level. In: KDD '08: Proceeding of the 14th ACM SIGKDD International Conference on Knowledge Discovery and Data Mining, pp. 336–344. ACM, New York (2008)
27. Kossinets, G., Watts, D.J.: Empirical analysis of an evolving social network. Science **311**, 88–90 (2006)
28. Lancichinetti, A., Fortunato, S.: Benchmarks for testing community detection algorithms on directed and weighted graphs with overlapping communities. Phys. Rev. E **80**, 016118 (2009)
29. Lancichinetti, A., Fortunato, S., Radicchi, F.: Benchmark graphs for testing community detection algorithms. Phys. Rev. E **78**, 046110 (2008)
30. Lancichinetti, A., Fortunato, S., Kertesz, J.: Detecting the overlapping and hierarchical community structure of complex networks. New J. Phys. **11**, 033015 (2009).
31. Lusseau, D., Schneider, K., Boisseau, O.J., Haase, P., Slooten, E., Dawson, S.M.: The bottlenose dolphin community of Doubtful Sound features a large proportion of long-lasting associations. Behav. Ecol. Sociobiol. **54**, 396–405 (2003)
32. Marriam-Webster online dictionary. http://www.merriam-webster.com
33. Moody, J., White, D.R.: Structural cohesion and embeddedness: a hierarchical concept of social groups. Am. Sociol. Rev. **68**(1), 103–127 (2003)
34. Newman, M.E.J.: Detecting community structure in networks. Eur. Phys. J. B **38**, 321–330 (2004)
35. Newman, M.E.J.: Fast algorithm for detecting community structure in networks. Phys. Rev. E **69**(6), 066133+ (2004)
36. Newman, M.E.J., Girvan, M.: Finding and evaluating community structure in networks. Phys Rev. E, **69**(12), 026113 (2003)
37. Noack, A., Rotta, R.: Multi-level algorithms for modularity clustering. In: SEA '09: Proceedings of the 8th International Symposium on Experimental Algorithms, pp. 257–268. Springer, Berlin/Heidelberg (2009)
38. Palla, G., Derenyi, I., Farkas, I., Vicsek, T.: Uncovering the overlapping community structure of complex networks in nature and society. Nature **435**, 814 (2005)
39. Pinney, J.W., Westhead, D.R.: Betweenness-based decomposition methods for social and biological networks. In: Barber, S., Baxter, P.D., Mardia, K.V., Walls, R.E. (eds.) Interdisciplinary Statistics and Bioinformatics, Leeds, England, 87–90. Leeds University Press (2006)

40. Radicchi, F., Castellano, C., Cecconi, F., Loreto, V., Parisi, D.: Defining and identifying communities in networks. Proc. Nat. Acad. Sci. U.S.A. **101**, 2658–2663 (2004)
41. Rees, B.S., Gallagher, K.B.: Overlapping community detection by collective friendship group inference. Int. Conf. Adv. Soc. Netw. Anal. Min. **0**, 375–379 (2010)
42. Wakita, K., Tsurumi, T.: Finding community structure in mega-scale social networks. In: WWW '07: Proceedings of the 16th International Conference on World Wide Web, pp. 1275–1276. ACM, New York (2007)
43. Wasserman, S., Faust, K.: Social Network Analysis: Methods and Applications. Cambridge University Press, Cambridge/New York (1994)
44. Watts, D.J., Strogatz, S.H.: Collective dynamics of 'small-world' networks. Nature **393**, 440–442 (1998)
45. Wu, F., Huberman, B.A.: Finding communities in linear time: a physics approach. Eur. Phys. J. B **38**, 331–338 (2004)
46. Xu, X., Yuruk, N., Feng, Z., Schweiger, T.A.J.: Scan: a structural clustering algorithm for networks. In: KDD '07: Proceedings of the 13th ACM SIGKDD International Conference on Knowledge Discovery and Data Mining, pp. 824–833. ACM, New York (2007)
47. Zachary, W.: An information flow model for conflict and fission in small groups. J. Anthropol. Res. **33**, 452–473 (1977)

Chapter 2
Optimization Techniques for Multiple Centrality Computations

Christian von der Weth, Klemens Böhm, and Christian Hütter

Abstract A broad range of data has a graph structure, such as the Web link structure, online social networks, or online communities whose members rate each other (reputation systems) or rate items (recommender systems). In these contexts, a common task is to identify important vertices in the graph, e.g., influential users in a social network or trustworthy users in a reputation system, by means of centrality measures. In such scenarios, several centrality computations take place at the same time, as we will explain. With centrality computation being expensive, performance is crucial. While optimization techniques for single centrality computations exist, little attention so far has gone into the computation of several centrality measures in combination. In this paper, we investigate how to efficiently compute several centrality measures at a time. We propose two new optimization techniques and demonstrate their usefulness both theoretically as well as experimentally on synthetic and on real-world data sets.

2.1 Introduction

Centrality measures [30] allow identifying important vertices in graphs. Such measures assign a numerical score to each vertex to quantify its importance among all nodes, based on the graph structure. On a large scale, Eigenvector-based measures have been successfully applied to the Web graph to rank search

C. von der Weth (✉)
Digital Enterprise Research Institute (DERI), National University of Ireland, Galway (NUIG), Galway, Ireland
e-mail: christian.vonderweth@deri.org

K. Böhm · C. Hütter
Institute for Program Structures and Data Organization, Karlsruhe Institute of Technology (KIT), Karlsruhe, Germany
e-mail: klemens.boehm@kit.edu; christian.huetter@kit.edu

T. Özyer et al. (eds.), *The Influence of Technology on Social Network Analysis and Mining*, Lecture Notes in Social Networks 6, DOI 10.1007/978-3-7091-1346-2_2,

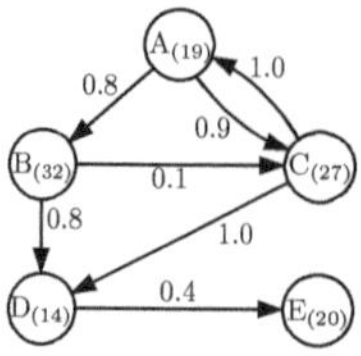

P_1	$\text{PageRank}_{\text{adult}}$
1:	D
2:	C
3:	A
4:	B
5:	E

P_2	PageRank	HITS
1:	E	D
2:	D	A
3:	C	C
4:	A	B
5:	B	E

Fig. 2.1 Example of a feedback graph

results, e.g., [16, 19]. Further applications include online social network analysis to identify individuals that are influential, e.g., [6, 13], and recommender systems to find similar items, e.g., [1, 35]. In this work, we use reputation systems [21] as our running example. With such systems, participants of social networks or members of online communities can issue *feedback*, i.e., rate previous interactions with others. Reputation systems differ in the way they process feedback to derive the reputation of participants. Various existing reputation systems [15, 22, 33] make use of centrality measures, the feedback forms a graph, the *feedback graph*. Vertices are the participants, edges represent the feedback items. However, existing reputation systems use fixed evaluation schemes to determine the reputation of participants, i.e., a centrality measure together with fixed parameter values is given. This is restrictive from a user perspective. We envision a more flexible system where participants can formulate *behavioral trust policies*. Such policies allow participants to specify how to compute the reputation of others. This includes the flexible application of various centralities measures on arbitrary subgraphs of the feedback graph; see the following example.

Examples 1. Figure 2.1 (left) shows a feedback graph. The nodes A–D represent the individuals. The label of each node is its age. Edges represent feedback between individuals. Edge weights represent the rating scores of the corresponding feedback items. Various trust policies are conceivable, e.g.:

P_1: "A participant is trustworthy if he belongs to the top 2 individuals according to PageRank based on the feedback from adult participants ($\text{PageRank}_{\text{adult}}$)."
P_2: "A participant is trustworthy if he belongs to the top 2 individuals according to both PageRank and HITS."

P_1 is true for members D and C, P_2 is true for member D; see Fig. 2.1 (right). This example illustrates that the evaluation of trust policies may require several centrality computations at the same time. □

When participants formulate policies themselves, we observe that several centrality computations take place at the same time, for the following reasons: (a) While centrality measures in general are accepted to determine the reputation of individuals, it is not obvious which one should be used in which situation [27]. An approach from data mining is to compute several measures at a time and to pay attention to the data objects whose values regarding one measure are distinctive. (b) In environments with a large number of individuals, the frequency of interactions is high; hence, the number of policies that need to be evaluated at the same time is large. (c) Literature has investigated attacks against centrality-based reputation systems and has proposed countermeasures [34]. A proposal that identifies vertices with different centrality indices for 'similar' centrality measures is particularly promising.

To illustrate that our concern is broad, we briefly leave aside our running example. In social network analysis (see Example 2), one might be interested in the centrality values of individuals according to different centrality measures (Q_1), in the centrality values of individuals with respect to different subgraphs of the network (Q_2), or in the temporal development of centrality values, e.g., by looking at snapshots of a social network (Q_3).

Examples 2. Consider the following analysis questions given the friendship network between members of a social networking platform like FACEBOOK:

Q_1: "Who is most influential according to both PAGERANK and HITS?"
Q_2: "What is the PAGERANK value of a female member with respect to the complete friendship network and with respect to the network consisting of female members only?"
Q_3: "The PAGERANK value of which member shows the most significant increase over the last month?"

□

From a performance perspective, centrality computation is expensive. While the optimization of a single centrality computation has been addressed, e.g., [14, 17], the computation of more than one measure at a time is challenging and remains to be investigated. This work focuses on *Eigenvector-based centrality measures* where the centrality score of a vertex depends on the centrality scores of the vertices it is adjacent to. PageRank [19] and HITS [16] serve as examples. Algorithms for these measures incorporate the power method [10], a numerical method to compute the largest Eigenvector of a matrix. This chapter makes the following contributions.

Classification of combined centrality computation. Centrality computations may 'overlap' in various ways, i.e., they share different commonalities which give way to a combined computation. For instance, one may want to compute two (different) measures on the same data set or to compute the same measure on data sets that are slightly different. We provide a classification of these variants of overlap and say how centrality computations can be combined in each case, at least in theory.

Techniques for combined centrality computation. We propose two new optimization approaches: (1) *Loop fusion techniques* exploit commonalities of centrality computations on the physical level, i.e., the data structures representing the graph data as well as the algorithms, allowing for the computation of several measures within one execution of the power method. (2) The power method starts with an initialization of the centrality values and adapts them in subsequent iterations. *Re-use of computation results* means that the result of a previous centrality computation serves as initialization. This results in fewer iterations.

Theoretical analysis. The improvements due to loop fusion depend on the internal representation of the graph data. Thus, we first present the graph representation we have used for our evaluation. Based on this we provide a theoretical analysis of the performance of loop fusion in the worst and in the best case as well as in average cases. One result is that the improvement depends on how different graph data overlaps. While the analysis is general in its nature, we present specific numbers for our graph representation, to compare them with our experimental results.

Evaluation. We have carried out extensive experiments both with synthetic and with real-world data to investigate the performance improvements of our optimization techniques. We conducted experiments for each 'overlap variant' according to our classification. Our main results are as follows: While re-use yields an improvement in specific situations only, loop fusion always yields an improvement. However, its extent in quantitative terms depends on various parameters and may be difficult to predict. For example, fusing centrality computations on the same data set yields a much higher speed-up than fusing centrality computations on different sets.

Chapter outline: Section 2.2 reviews related work. We discuss centrality computation in Sect. 2.3. Section 2.4 presents our optimizations and Sect. 2.5 our implementation. Section 2.6 presents the theoretical analysis regarding the effect of loop fusion. Section 2.7 features an evaluation. Section 2.8 concludes. This article is an extended version of [28]. It contains a comprehensive theoretical analysis of loop fusion and an extended evaluation section.

2.2 Related Work

Researchers have successfully applied centrality measures on graphs in various settings, see [9]. PageRank [19] and HITS [16] are popular measures for web-graph analysis. Variants of those algorithms have been proposed, e.g., personalization of the ranking [5, 12], stability of the algorithms [18], and distributed environments [20, 29]. Applications of centrality measures include social network analysis [6, 13] to identify influential participants, and recommender systems [1, 35] to find similar items. Several reputation systems rely on centrality measures, e.g., [15, 22, 33]. While these systems use fixed evaluation schemes for trust, [26] proposes behavioral trust policies based on centrality. von derWeth and Böhm [27] compares centrality measures for reputation systems. It shows that various measures yield good results, but only Eigenvector-based ones have good runtime performance as well. Other centrality-based reputation systems take into account social relations between participants [23, 24] and propose decentralized trust models for P2P systems [8, 32].

Loop fusion is a technique for compiler optimization [2, 3]. It exploits commonalities of loops (e.g., centrality computations) on the physical level. Optimization techniques for Eigenvector-based centrality computation deal with the power method itself. There are two main research thrusts, to modify the method to reduce the work per iteration [17], and to reduce the number of iterations [14]. However, these optimizations exploit a priori knowledge regarding the structure of the graph. In general – given dynamic data sets like feedback – this knowledge is not available. Other optimizations focus on parallelization, e.g., [7, 31]. While parallelization can bring down absolute runtimes, the total extent of resources required is not reduced. We are the first to address the combined computation of several centrality measures.

2.3 Centrality Computation

In the following, we first review the power method which serves as the basis of centrality computation. See [10] for the mathematical background. We then categorize how centrality computations may differ from each other.

2.3.1 *The Power Method*

Eigenvector-based centrality-index values are the largest Eigenvector of an $n \times n$ Matrix M representing the graph structure, and n is the number of vertices. To compute the centrality index values, numerical methods are typically used. One is the so-called power method (Algorithm 1). It consists of a loop which multiplies a vector with M in each iteration. According to theory [10], for an arbitrary non-zero start vector $\overrightarrow{v}_0$, $\overrightarrow{v}_t$ converges to the largest Eigenvector of M. The process stops when the norm of the difference of $\overrightarrow{v}_t$ and $\overrightarrow{v}_{t-1}$ is smaller than a user-specified threshold ϵ, i.e., $\overrightarrow{v}_t$ does not change significantly any more. Different centrality measures lead to different matrices M. Some measures have a argument list L; Function f in Line 5 reflects this. To give an example, the PageRank definition features the so-called damping factor d, i.e., $L =< d >$, and function f is defined as $\mathrm{f}(\overrightarrow{\mathrm{v}_t}, \mathrm{d}) = (1 - \mathrm{d}) \cdot \overrightarrow{\mathbf{1}} + \mathrm{d} \cdot \overrightarrow{\mathrm{v}_t}$, where $\overrightarrow{\mathbf{1}}$ is the vector with all elements equal to 1.

Thus, four parameters describe the execution of a power method for centrality measures: M, f, the measure-specific argument list L, and error threshold ϵ. – Our evaluation will cover PageRank, HITS and Positional Weakness (PW). The power iterations for these three measures are as follows:

$$\overrightarrow{v}^{(k+1)}_{\mathrm{PageRank}} = (1 - \mathrm{d})\overrightarrow{\mathbf{1}} + \mathrm{d} \cdot \mathbf{T}\overrightarrow{v}^{(k)}_{\mathrm{PageRank}}$$

$$\overrightarrow{v}^{(k+1)}_{\mathrm{Authority}} = \mathbf{A}^{\mathrm{T}}\overrightarrow{v}^{(k)}_{\mathrm{Hub}}, \quad \overrightarrow{v}^{(k+1)}_{\mathrm{Hub}} = \mathbf{A}\overrightarrow{v}^{(k)}_{\mathrm{Authority}}$$

$$\overrightarrow{v}^{(k+1)}_{\mathrm{PW}} = \frac{1}{|\mathrm{V}|}\mathbf{B}^{\mathrm{T}}(\overrightarrow{\mathbf{1}} + \overrightarrow{v}^{(k)}_{\mathrm{PW}})$$

$\mathbf{A} = (a_{ij})$ is the *adjacency matrix* of a graph $G(V, E)$ with $a_{ij} = w_{ij}$, where w_{ij} is the weight on an edge from v_i to v_j, 0 if there is no such edge. $\mathbf{A}^{\mathrm{T}}$ is the transposed adjacency matrix. $\mathbf{T} = (t_{ij})$ is the *transition matrix* of G with $t_{ij} = w_{ji} / \sum_{v_k \in Out(v_j)} w_{jk}$; $Out(v)$ denotes the set of vertices with an edge from v. $\mathbf{B}^{\mathrm{T}}$ is a variant of the transposed adjacency matrix $\mathbf{B} = (b_{ij})$ with $b_{ij} = w_{ij}/\max_{i,k}(w_{ik})$. For all definitions, $1 \leq i, j, k \leq n$, with $n = |V|$.

Algorithm 1 Basic algorithm of power method

```
t=0;
repeat
    t=t+1;
    v⃗_t = M · v⃗_(t−1);
    v⃗_t = f(v⃗_t, L);
    δ = ‖v⃗_t − v⃗_(t−1)‖;
until δ < ε
```

2.3.2 *Classes of Multiple Computations*

We see three main situations where the computation of several centrality measures within one power iteration or other, similar optimizations are likely to be useful, or other optimizations might be possible: (1) *several measures*, i.e., computation of several measures on the same data set, (2) *multiple data sets*, i.e., the computation of one measure with identical parameter settings on different data sets, and (3) *multiple parameter settings*, i.e., the computation of one measure with different parameter settings on the same data set. Combinations of these cases can of course happen. We now discuss each case separately.

Several measures. We observe that behavioral trust policies which require the evaluation of several centrality measures are natural (cf. Policy P_2 in Example 1), or that a system frequently has to evaluate several trust policies containing different centrality measures at the same time (cf. Sect. 2.1).

Multiple data sets. Different data sets induce different graph structures, like two behavioral trust policies referring to the same centrality measure, but using different feedback (see P_1 and P_2 in Example 1). Two directed, weighted graphs G(V, E) and G′(V′, E′) can differ in several ways. The sets of vertices V/V′ and the sets of edges E/E′ can either be equal, be distinct, intersect or have a subset relationship. Note that there are dependencies between relationships, e.g., two distinct set of vertices imply, in general, distinct sets of edges. Finally, the weights of the edges may differ for otherwise identical graphs. While V determines the size of Matrix M, E and the weights determine its elements.

Multiple parameter settings. Eigenvector-based centrality computation using the power method depends on parameters, and different parameter settings yield

Table 2.1 Classes of multiple centrality computations

Type of overlap	**M**	**f**	**L**	ϵ
Several measures	✓	✓	✓	
Multiple data sets	✓			
Multiple parameter settings (MPS_{CM})			✓	
Multiple parameter settings (MPS_{ϵ})				✓

different results. There are two kinds of parameters: (1) Inherent arguments determining the semantics of a centrality measure, e.g., the damping factor d of PageRank. This is the measure-specific argument list L mentioned before. MPS_{CM} denotes this class of parameters. (2) Parameters controlling the centrality computation. In particular, the parameter ϵ (MPS_{ϵ}) of the power method specifies the stop condition. It does not depend on the centrality measure.

To sum up, Table 2.1 shows how the cases differ with regard to the parameters for the execution of a power method. A checkmark indicates where the parameters have to be different in order to fall into the respective category.

2.4 Optimization of Combined Centrality Computations

We now present *Loop Fusion* and *Re-use of Results* which optimize the combined computation of Eigenvector-based centrality measures.

2.4.1 Loop Fusion

With the number n of nodes typically being large, the resulting $n \times n$ Matrix M is large as well and may not fit into main memory. Thus, each matrix multiplication requires costly access to secondary storage, e.g., the hard disk. When computing several Eigenvector-based centrality measures, we therefore propose applying loop-fusion techniques to reduce the number of accesses to secondary storage. Loop fusion is a concept from compiler optimization to replace several loops with one. It aims to improve the performance by exploiting commonalities of the individual loops. For instance, if k loops require the same data from secondary storage, the data is read once and is used for all k loops.

Fusing two loops requires them to have the same number of iterations [3]. In general, two power-method executions do not satisfy this requirement. Since the stop condition of an execution is evaluated at runtime, the number of iterations cannot be computed a priori. Thus, the execution with the highest iteration count would result in further (unnecessary) iterations for all other executions. [3] overcomes this limitation via *guarding iterations*, i.e., the insertion of conditional statements to ensure that no unnecessary work is done in iterations. In this way we extend the basic power-method algorithm for the parallel computation of two or more centrality measures; see Algorithm 2. We derive the additional conditions from the stop condition for each execution of the power method (Line 5). The algorithm stops if the stop conditions of all executions are fulfilled. Variable `finished` is `false` as long as at least one execution has not converged.

Algorithm 2 Extended power method with loop fusion

1: finished=**false**; t=0;
2: **while** (finished$\neq$**true**) **do**
3: finished=**true**; t=t+1;
4: **for all** single computations c **do**
5: **if** ($\delta^{(c)} > \epsilon^{(c)}$) **then**
6: finished=**false**;
7: $\vec{v}^{(c)}_{t} = M^{(c)} \cdot \vec{v}^{(c)}_{(t-1)}$;
8: $\vec{v}^{(c)}_{t} = f^{(c)}(\vec{v}^{(c)}_{t}, L^{(c)})$;
9: $\delta^{(c)} = \|\vec{v}^{(c)}_{t} - \vec{v}^{(c)}_{(t-1)}\|$;
10: **end if**
11: **end for**
12: **end while**

The extended algorithm requires more computation steps than the basic version, cf. Algorithm 1, due to the additional conditions and the modification of `finished`. Another reason is the extended data structures required to distinguish between the parameters of the different executions. Thus, if both algorithms execute one power iteration, we expect the extended algorithm to be slightly slower than the basic one. With different classes of overlap, other parameters may be different (cf. Table 2.1). We now discuss the challenges and improvements expected from loop fusion for each class.

Several measures. Different measures result in different matrices M. However, their processing is identical: In one iteration, any execution requires access to the entries at the same positions of the matrices. This congruence suggests having one integrated data structure, the so-called *multi matrix*. Each matrix entry consists of several values, one from each underlying matrix.

Examples 3. In the following, two $n \times n$ matrices ($n = 3$) are transformed into one multi matrix:

$$\begin{pmatrix} 0 & 5 & 1 \\ 0 & 0 & 2 \\ 8 & 1 & 0 \end{pmatrix} \begin{pmatrix} 0 & 0 & 2 \\ 1 & 0 & 3 \\ 4 & 1 & 0 \end{pmatrix} \Rightarrow \begin{pmatrix} 0 & 5|0 & 1|2 \\ 0|1 & 0 & 2|3 \\ 8|4 & 1|1 & 0 \end{pmatrix}$$

□

On the logical level, 'single' matrices and multi matrices do not show any difference, so the total number of entries does not change. Thus, regarding the entries, the number of accesses to secondary storage required is the same in both cases. On the physical level however, the data structure representing a matrix also contains meta-data, e.g., data describing the rows and the columns. Hence, the size of a multi matrix is less than the sum of the sizes of the single matrices. The effective improvement depends on the ratio between the size of the multi matrix and the overall size of all single matrices. This ratio in turn depends on the internal representation of the graph. See Sect. 2.7.

Multiple data sets. Different data sets result in different matrices for the power method. While the multi-matrix concept is applicable in general, it is less obvious how to construct the multi matrix. First, if two graphs have a different number of vertices, the corresponding matrices are of different size. In this case, the larger matrix determines the size of the multi matrix. Further, there typically is more than one matrix representing a graph; it depends on the assignment of the vertices to the rows/columns of the matrix.

Examples 4. The following two matrices are possible adjacency matrices for the same graph.

$$\begin{array}{c} \\ \mathbf{A} \\ \mathbf{B} \\ \mathbf{C} \\ \mathbf{D} \end{array} \begin{array}{c} \begin{array}{cccc} \mathbf{A} & \mathbf{B} & \mathbf{C} & \mathbf{D} \end{array} \\ \begin{pmatrix} 0 & 1 & 1 & 0 \\ 0 & 0 & 1 & 1 \\ 1 & 0 & 0 & 1 \\ 0 & 1 & 0 & 0 \end{pmatrix} \end{array} \qquad \begin{array}{c} \\ \mathbf{B} \\ \mathbf{C} \\ \mathbf{D} \\ \mathbf{A} \end{array} \begin{array}{c} \begin{array}{cccc} \mathbf{B} & \mathbf{C} & \mathbf{D} & \mathbf{A} \end{array} \\ \begin{pmatrix} 0 & 1 & 1 & 0 \\ 0 & 0 & 1 & 1 \\ 1 & 0 & 0 & 0 \\ 1 & 1 & 0 & 0 \end{pmatrix} \end{array}$$

□

Since there are many representations of a graph, there also are various multi matrices. The optimal multi matrix maximizes the ratio of its size and the added size of all corresponding single matrices. In other words, a multi matrix is optimal if the number of non-zero entries in the multi matrix is minimal. From an algorithmic perspective, the problem of computing the optimal multi matrix for a set of single matrices is related to the problem of finding an isomorphism between (sub-)graphs.

While the (sub-)graph isomorphism problem concerns the question whether a (sub-)graph isomorphism between graphs exists, finding an optimal multi matrix concerns to the task of finding the largest sub-graph isomorphism. Since the complexity of finding graph isomorphisms is still unknown – finding subgraph isomorphisms is NP-hard – and beyond the scope of this work. We therefore consider in our theoretical analysis and evaluation only the cases where the sets of vertices V_1 and V_2 in two graphs are either identical or form subset relationship. To be more precise, to construct a multi matrix, we map each vertex $v \in V_1 \cap V_2$ to itself. Note that his restriction does not guarantee an optimal multi matrix, since mapping a vertex to another one might result in a better overlap of two graphs. It allows, however, for comparable results when evaluating the effect of the remaining cases two graphs can differ (see Sect. 2.3.2).

Multiple parameter settings. If only the parameter settings of different centrality computations differ, all computations make use of the same Matrix M, i.e., the same accesses to matrix entries when executing the combined power method. The implementation is straightforward, and we expect the highest improvement, compared to the other classes.

2.4.2 Re-Use of Computation Results

With the power method, the actual choice of the start vector affects the number of iterations required. We expect a start vector that is similar to the result vector to require fewer iterations to converge. Here, we quantify the similarity of two vectors as the norm of their difference, cf. the stop condition in Algorithm 1. With one centrality computation, no a priori knowledge is available to identify a 'good' start vector. Thus, single centrality computations use 'naive' start vectors, e.g., vectors where all elements have the same value. With multiple centrality computations, the idea now is that the result vector of one computation can serve as the start vector of another one. The rationale is that both result vectors might be similar so that the second computation requires fewer iterations. 'Bad' start vectors in turn, i.e., very different from the result, yield a slower rate of convergence than naive ones. To assess a priori whether two results are similar, we have to look at the kinds of overlap. For each class of multiple centrality computation we now discuss the difficulties and expected improvement.

Similarity of measures. The potential of the re-use of results seems to be limited. For two measures to yield similar result vectors on the same graph, (a) they have to assign a similar relative importance to the vertices, and (b) the absolute values of the centrality indices must be from a similar range. Speaking casually, *two measures are similar if they give similar importance to the various characteristics of graphs.* For example, PageRank and Positional Weakness are relatively similar, since they take the in-links of a vertex into account. In general, the absolute values of the centrality indices vary significantly between measures. To overcome this limitation, we normalize the centrality indices. However, normalization requires knowing the range of the result vector. This is the case for PageRank, where the centrality indices of the vertices add up to the number of vertices n. The result vector of Positional Weakness in turn does not have this characteristic, to give an example. To summarize, re-use is only meaningful here if both measures are similar, and if at least the second measure allows for normalization.

Similarity of data sets. Two data sets can be different because the vertices, the edges or the weights are different. These kinds of differences may affect the centrality indices to different extents: For instance, multiplying each weight with the same factor has no effect on the resulting PageRank values. In contrast, one additional edge, from a vertex with a high centrality index to one with a low index, can alter the result significantly. Thus, a reliable prediction whether the re-use of results is beneficial would require an analysis of the underlying graphs. The overhead of such an analysis, even though it is only preliminary, is likely to be high; we therefore do not consider this variant here.

Similarity of parameter settings. In general, the same measure with different parameters yields different results. We expect that the more similar two parameter settings, the more similar are the results. However, the impact of the inherent parameters (MPS_{CM}) is hard to assess without experiments. For values of ϵ in turn (MPS_{ϵ}) we can estimate the improvement a priori. Consider two power-method executions p_1 and p_2 that only differ with regard to ϵ such that $\epsilon_1 > \epsilon_2$. Let i_1 be the number of iterations for p_1 and i_2 the one for p_2, with $i_1 \leq i_2$. If the result of p_1 is used as start vector of p_2, p_2 requires $i_2 - i_1$ iterations. Thus, experiments concerning the effect of various error thresholds are not necessary.

2.5 Implementation

Most of our optimizations for multiple centrality computation do not depend on the graph representation. This is particularly true for the re-use of results, since it aims for an optimization on a logical level. For loop fusion, the impact of the graph representation on performance depends on the type of overlap between the graphs (cf. Sect. 2.3). In case of multiple parameter settings (MPS_{CM} and MPS_{ϵ}), the combined centrality computation takes place on the same matrix for all single computations. Here the performance benefit is obvious, all single computations access the same matrix entries at the same time. However, for multiple measures or multiple datasets the graph representation matters, since it affects the ratio of the size of the resulting multi matrix and the corresponding single matrices. We now describe the graph representation we use for our theoretical analysis and evaluation.

Representation of graphs. There are various ways to store graphs, e.g., adjacency matrices/lists/tables, incidence matrices/lists/tables, and others, cf. [11]. The expected improvement depends on the sum of the sizes of the individual matrices divided by the size of the multi matrix. This ratio might differ with different graph representations. However, all representation techniques require meta-data, be it the rows/columns of a matrix or the links between list elements. A combined representation of several graphs saves storage space by using the same meta-data, and the more similar the graphs, the higher these savings.

In our evaluation we store all feedback data in a relational database, and represent graphs by means of an *incidence table* [4, 25]. An incidence table stores the information on the edges, i.e., each tuple stores the source (v_s), the target (v_t) and the weight (w) of an edge. Thus, an incidence table might not contain all vertices. This requires an additional *vertex table*.

Examples 5. The following figure (see Example 1) shows an example graph and its incidence table.

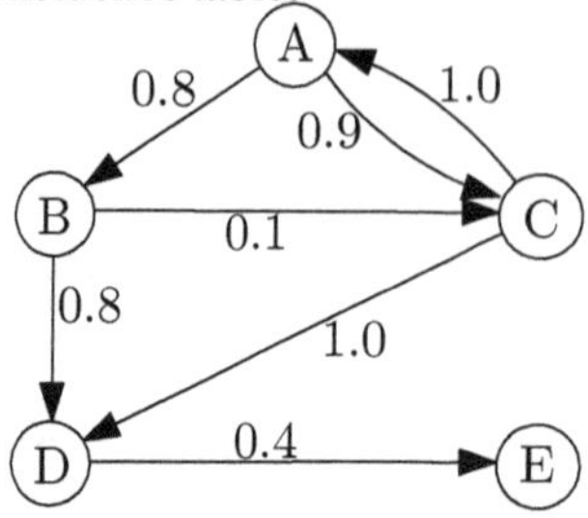

Incidence table

v_s	v_t	w
A	B	0.8
A	C	0.9
B	C	0.1
B	D	0.8
C	A	0.9
C	D	1.0
D	C	1.0
D	E	0.4

Vertex table

v
A
B
C
D
E

□

From the structure of an incidence table we can now derive the one of a multi incidence table. Since an incidence table represents the edges of a graph, storing the edges of several graphs in one table requires a Column w_i for each single graph. However, all combined graphs can share Columns v_s and v_t.

Examples 6. The following multi incidence table contains n graphs. The values of Column w_i represent the graph in Example 5.

Multi incidence table

v_s	v_t	w_1	...	w_i	...	w_n
A	B	0	...	0.8	...	0
A	C	0.5	...	0.9	...	0
A	D	0.9	...	0	...	0
B	C	0	...	0.1	...	0.8
B	D	0	...	0.8	...	0.3
...	...	...	...	...	...	...

Vertex table

v
A
B
C
D
E

Obviously, the vertex table remains unchanged. □

In the multi incidence table 'zero' values for Attribute w_i are possible if there is an edge between two vertices in one graph, but not in another one.

Computing centrality measures. With a relational database as back-end, we have implemented Algorithm 1 of the original power method and Algorithm 2 of our extended power method using PL/SQL. We also have experimented with Java stored procedures. The results are very similar, so we will omit them in our evaluation.

2.6 Theoretical Analysis

The expected benefits of the re-use of results depend on the convergence behavior of the power method. The number of required iterations, in turn, depends on the actual input, i.e. the graph data. Qualifying the convergence behavior of the power method w.r.t the input, and therefore a theoretical analysis of the benefits due to the re-use of results, is beyond the scope of this work. In contrast, loop fusion exploits the commonalities of two or more centrality computations on a physical level. The notion of the multi matrix as combined data structure (cf. Sect. 2.4.1) is particularly attractive in this context. The speed-up due to loop fusion depends on the ratio of the physical size of a multi matrix and the sum of the sizes of the data structures for each graph in isolation. The more compact the combined graph representation, the fewer accesses to secondary storage are necessary.

Depending on the graphs to be combined, however, loop fusion does not necessarily yield an improvement. In general, the more similar the graphs are, the more compact the combined representation. The question arises how to determine a-priori whether loop fusion should be applied or not. We now offer a respective analysis on graphs with varying degrees of similarity. While our examples and figures are limited to the incidence table, the analysis is general.

Examples 7. Below are fragments of a multi incidence table representing the sets of edges of n graphs and the corresponding incidence tables.

Multi incidence table

v_s	v_t	w_1	...	w_i	...	w_n
A	B	0	...	**0.8**	...	0
A	C	0.5	...	**0.9**	...	0
...	...	...	...	...	...	...

***n* single incidence tables**

v_s	v_t	w_1
A	C	0.9
B	C	0.1
...	...	...

...

v_s	v_t	w_i
A	C	0.9
B	C	0.1
...	...	...

...

v_s	v_t	w_n
B	C	0.8
B	D	0.3
...	...	...

All single incidence tables share the Columns v_s and v_t, representing the start and target vertex of an edge. Thus, the multi incidence table has fewer columns than all single incidence tables together. However, the number of tuples varies depending on the similarity of the graphs. If an edge is not present in all graphs, the corresponding tuple in the multi incidence table contains 'zero' values. This increases the physical size of the table. □

For any representation of a graph, we can distinguish between meta data and the actual data describing the graph. Meta data refers to the part of a graph representation that does not depend on the actual graph and can be shared among several graphs. Regarding incidence tables, for example, the meta data are the columns describing the source and the target vertices of edges. For an edge, s_m denotes the required physical size required to store the meta data, and s_w denotes the physical size required to store the weight. We assume that the values of s_m and

s_w are fixed for a certain graph representation. Further, let $\mathcal{E}$ denote the set of edges $\{E_1, E_2, \ldots, E_n\}$. Now we can express the ratio q of the size of a combined data structure and the n single data structures as follows:

$$q = \frac{|\bigcup_{i=1}^{n} E_i| \cdot (s_m + n \cdot s_w)}{\sum_{i=1}^{n} [|E_i| \cdot (s_m + s_w)]} = \frac{s_m + n \cdot s_w}{s_m + s_w} \cdot \frac{|\bigcup_{i=1}^{n} E_i|}{\sum_{i=1}^{n} |E_i|} \tag{2.1}$$

If $q < 1$, the multi incidence table is smaller than all corresponding single incidence tables. This makes a combined centrality computation using loop fusion on different data sets beneficial.

The factor $K(n) = \frac{s_m+n \cdot s_w}{s_m+s_w}$ in Eq. 2.1 describes the ratio of the required storage of an edge in a single and in a multi incidence table, with n being the number of combined data structures. For a given graph representation, i.e., fixed values for s_m and s_w, $K(n)$ only depends on the number of combined graphs, but not on the data, i.e., the appearance of the graph itself. Naturally, $K(1) = 1$, and $K(n)$ increases monotonously for larger n. Further, $K(n)$ decreases for an increasing ratio of $\frac{s_m}{s_w}$. This is intuitive, since the larger the storage required for the meta data, the more a combined representation can save.

Worst case and best case analysis. Factor $F(\mathcal{E}) = \frac{|\bigcup_{i=1}^{n} E_i|}{\sum_{i=1}^{n} |E_i|}$ in Eq. 2.1 depends on the actual graph data and reflects the similarities between a set of edges $\mathcal{E}$. Intuitively, the more similar the sets $E_i \in \mathcal{E}$ are, the smaller is $F(\mathcal{E})$. In the worst case, the sets of edges are completely disjunct. Note that this is a rather hypothetical case, since by re-labeling vertices, subsets of edges always can be mapped between all E_i, even in the absence of a (complete) graph isomorphism. In this case, each edge $e_i \in E_i$ results in a distinct edge in the combined data structure. This means that, in a multi incidence table, each tuple has only one weight column w_i with a non-zero entry. Thus, with no similarities between the sets of edges, $|\bigcup_{i=1}^{n} E_i| = \sum_{i=1}^{n} |E_i|$ holds. This yields a worst-case ratio of

$$q^{worst} = K(n) \cdot \frac{|\bigcup_{i=1}^{n} E_i|}{\sum_{i=1}^{n} |E_i|} = K(n) \cdot \frac{\sum_{i=1}^{n} |E_i|}{\sum_{i=1}^{n} |E_i|} = K(n) \tag{2.2}$$

In the best case, the sets of edges of all n graphs are identical, and therefore the n single incidence matrices are identical. As a result, no tuple in the corresponding multi incidence table has a 'zero' value for all weight columns w_i. Thus, $|\bigcup_{i=1}^{n} E_i| = |E|$, and $F(\mathcal{E}) = \frac{|E|}{|E| \sum_{i=1}^{n} 1} = \frac{1}{n}$ respectively. Now, in the bast case, q is as follows:

$$q^{best} = \frac{K(n)}{n} = \frac{s_m + n s_w}{n(s_m + s_w)} = \frac{s_w}{s_m + s_w} + \frac{s_m}{n(s_m + s_w)} \tag{2.3}$$

The latter addend in the previous formula decreases monotonously with n. Thus, for $n \to \infty$, $q^{best}_{n\to\infty} = \frac{s_w}{s_m+s_w}$. $q^{best}_{n\to\infty}$ defines the lower bound for ratio q, and it depends on the given graph representation. Again, higher values of ratio $\frac{s_m}{s_w}$ are more beneficial since the absolute value for the lower bound $q^{best}_{n\to\infty}$ decreases.

Analysis of expected improvements. Besides the worst case, i.e., completely distinct sets of edges, and the best case, i.e., identical sets of edges, arbitrary relationships between the sets $E_i \in \mathcal{E}$ are conceivable. In the following we consider three different commonalities of sets of edges: (1) *Different edge weights*, i.e., only the weights of the edges differ among all E_i. (2) *Subset relationships*, i.e., all sets E_i form subset relationships. (3) *Intersecting sets of edges*, i.e., the sets E_i do not have subset relationships but have non-empty intersections. In general, these three commonalities appear in combination. However, we now discuss the expected performance benefits in the three cases separately.

Different edge weights. The sets of edges $E_i \in \mathcal{E}$ differ only in their weights. Varying the weights has no impact on the overall size of a (multi) incidence table, since it does not alter the number of tuples within the table. Thus, the resulting multi incidence matrix is always optimal, i.e., storing no 'zero' values. As a result, in case of different edge weights, the expected improvement equals the best case q^{best}, making loop fusion always beneficial.

Subset relationships. In this case, one set of edges $E^{sup} \in \mathcal{E}$ is a superset of all other sets. Note that we do not make any further restrictions. Since E^{sup} contains all edges, it follows that $|\bigcup_{i=1}^{n} E_i| = |E^{sup}|$, i.e., E^{sup} determines the number of tuples in the multi incidence table. For the sum of the sizes of each single set E_i, the lower and upper limit are $|E^{sup}| \leq \sum_{i=1}^{n} |E_i| \leq n \cdot |E^{sup}|$. Now, let $t^{sup} = |E^{sup}| / \sum_{i=1}^{n} |E_i|$, $0 < t^{sup} \leq 1$, be the relative coverage of all subsets $E_i \in \mathcal{E} \setminus E^{sup}$ by superset E^{sup}. With that, the expected improvement for subset relationships is $q = \frac{1}{t^{sup}(n-1)+1} \cdot K(n)$. If we set $q \overset{!}{=} 1$ to evaluate the minimum threshold of similarity, given a subset relationship between all E_i to determine when loop fusion is beneficial we can solve $1 = \frac{1}{t^{sup}(n-1)+1} \cdot K(n)$ for t^{sup}, and denote the solution as t^{sup}_{min}:

$$t^{sup}_{min} = \frac{K(n)-1}{n-1} = \frac{\frac{s_m+ns_w}{s_m+s_w}-1}{n-1} = \frac{s_w(n-1)}{(s_m+2_w)(n-1)} = \frac{s_w}{s_m+s_w} \tag{2.4}$$

If the relative coverage $t^{sup} > t^{sup}_{min}$, loop fusion yields a performance improvement. It is worth noting that for subset relationships the threshold depends only on the graph representation but not on the number of combined data sets. Figure 2.2 illustrate this for various values of n. For this example we set $s_m = 2s_w$; this is the situation of the attributes v_s, v_t and w_i in our incidence tables have the same data type (cf. Example 7). With these values $K(n) = \frac{n+2}{3}$. Given $K(n)$ we can calculate the worst and best case, e.g. for $n = 2$, $q^{worst} = \frac{4}{3}$ and $q^{best} = \frac{2}{3}$. Further, we can calculate threshold $t^{sup} = \frac{1}{3}$. Naturally, all these values show up in Fig. 2.2.

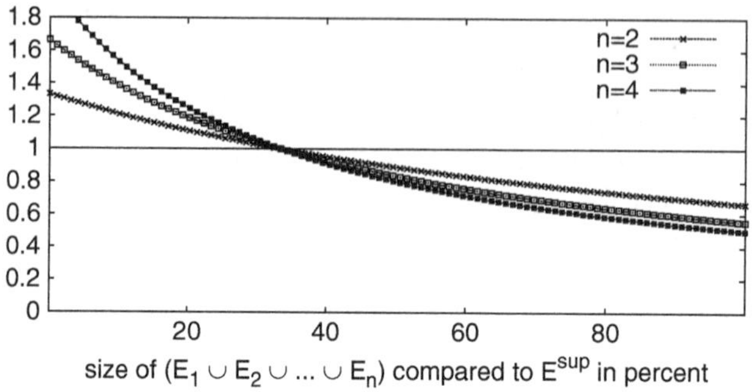

Fig. 2.2 Development of q for different subset relationships

Intersecting sets of edges. This case refers to sets of edges E_i that overlap to some degree, without explicitly forming a subset relationship. To ease the analysis, and to pronounce the distinction to the case subset relationships, we assume that all sets of edges are of an equal size l, i.e., $\forall E_i \in \mathscr{E} : |E_i| = l$. As a consequence, regarding Factor $F(\mathscr{E})$, $\sum_{i=1}^{n} |E_i| = n \cdot l$ is fixed. $|\bigcup_{i=1}^{n} E_i|$ depends on the size of the intersection, but is bounded by $l \leq |\bigcup_{i=1}^{n} E_i| \leq n \cdot l$. Compared to subset relationships, quantifying the relative overlap of intersecting sets of edges E_i is slightly more complex. Firstly, let $E_i^* = E_i \setminus \bigcup_{j=1, j \neq i}^{n} E_i$ be the subset of E_i that contains all edges which are only in E_i. We can then define the relative overlap $t^\wedge$ of all sets E_i as $t^\wedge = \frac{n \cdot l - \sum_{i=1}^{n} |E_i^*|}{n \cdot l}$, where $0 \leq t^\wedge \leq 1$. With this, the expected improvement for intersecting sets of edges is $q = \frac{t^\wedge (n-1)+1}{n} \cdot K(n)$. Setting $q \stackrel{!}{=} 1$ and solving equation $1 = \frac{t^\wedge (n-1)+1}{n} \cdot K(n)$ for $t^\wedge$, and denoting the solution as $t_{min}^\wedge$, yields

$$t_{min}^\wedge = \frac{\frac{n}{K(n)} - 1}{n-1} = \frac{\frac{n(s_m + s_w)}{s_m + s_w} - 1}{n-1} = \frac{s_m(n-1)}{(s_m + n s_w)(n-1)} = \frac{s_w}{s_m + n s_w} \tag{2.5}$$

Again, if $t^\wedge > t_{min}^\wedge$, the application of loop fusion is beneficial. Compared to t_{min}^{sup}, threshold $t_{min}^\wedge$ does not only depend on the graph representation but also on the number n of combined data sets. The more data sets one intends to combine the higher has to be their similarity (here: their intersection) between them to gain a speed-up due to loop fusion. Figure 2.3 shows the development of q for various values of n; again we set $s_m = 2s_w$ yielding $K(n) = \frac{n+2}{3}$. Since both q^{worst} and q^{best} to not depend on the actual data sets, their values are the same as for the subset relationships (cf. Fig. 2.2). However, threshold $t^\wedge$ is no longer constant but decreases for larger values of n. For example, for $n = 2$, $t^\wedge = \frac{1}{2}$.

Our analysis provides some interesting insight into the performance of loop fusion. Considering the parameters s_m and s_w for a given graph representation as fixed values emphasizes the effect of storing unnecessary 'zero' values. In real

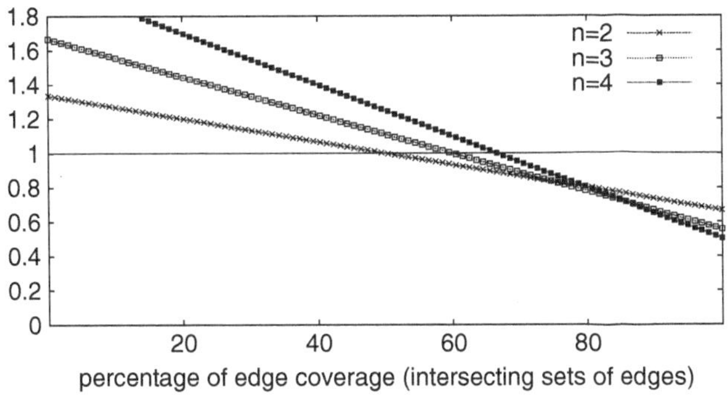

Fig. 2.3 Development of q for different intersection sizes

systems like relational databases, 'zero' values are stored more efficiently. This results in a better performance of loop fusion techniques.

2.7 Evaluation

We compare the isolated computation of centrality measures to the combined execution with loop fusion or re-use. The testbed for our experiments was a dual 2.2 GHz Opteron 64 bit platform, 2 GB main memory, SCSI Ultra 320 hard drive running Red Hat Enterprise Linux 3 and Oracle Database 10g Release 2. In contrast to the worst-case assumptions in our theoretical analysis, i.e., a fixed number of bytes required to store the edge in a (multi) incidence table, Oracle allocates storage according to the actual number of bytes required to store a data value. Thus, Oracle stores 'zero' values using a minimum number of bytes, compared to non-zero values. We therefore expect much better results in the worst-case (no or hardly any similarities between the combined graphs) compared to our theoretical analysis for loop fusion.

For the experiments we use both synthetic and real-world data. The real-world data is from two platforms: ADVOGATO (www.advogato.org) is a platform for a community of software developers. Participants can certify others on four different trust levels: *Observer* (0.0), *Apprentice* (0.6), *Journeyer* (0.8), *Master* (1.0). The data set[1] contains 7,383 participants and 51,797 trust relationships. EPINIONS (www.epinions.com) is a consumer-review site. A participant can add others to his "Web of Trust" whose reviews are likely to be of value. The data set[2] consists of 49,290 participants and 487,182 trust relationships. Regarding the synthetic data, we have generated it with a *feedback generator* that simulates cooperation among

[1] www.advogato.org/person/graph.dot

[2] www.trustlet.org/datasets/downloaded_epinions/

individuals [27]. This lets us study the influence of specific characteristics of the data set in a much more controlled way. We have conducted experiments in graphs of various sizes, up to 100,000 vertices. Our 'default' data set consists of three graphs, each with 1,000 vertices, but with different numbers of edges. They have the densities 0.05/0.15/0.25, where the density D of a directed graph G(V, E) is $D(G) = |E|/|V|^2$. The results for graphs with a low density are particularly relevant, since graphs derived from online scenarios tend to be sparse.

In this work we are interested in the speed-up of our optimization techniques. In addition, focusing on the absolute runtimes would be less helpful and might even be misleading. This is because (a) our datasets have different sizes and therefore give way to different absolute runtimes and (b) different datasets as well as modifications of the datasets throughout the evaluation – e.g., the removal of edges to generate subset relationships – result in different numbers of required iterations of the power method. To ease comparability of our results, if not stated otherwise, we normalize the runtimes so that the one of an isolated computation is 1. This also allows to limit ourselves to presenting only the results for the synthetic data. This is because the relative improvement due to our optimization techniques has always been the same for both the synthetic and the real-world data, as we will demonstrate.

2.7.1 Loop Fusion Techniques

To quantify the benefit of loop fusion, we compare the runtime to the total duration of the isolated executions.

Size of graphs. We first investigate whether the size of a graph influences the effectiveness of loop fusion in combination with a multi matrix. This experiment tells us how much attention we should put to the graph size in subsequent experiments. We perform two single PageRank computations and a combined computation, each on both synthetic and on real-world data. The graphs generated are of various sizes, from 10,000 to 100,000 vertices. For the real-world data, we start with the complete data set and gradually reduce the number of participants/vertices together with the adjacent edges. To fill the multi matrix, which contains two or more different graphs, we pretend that there are two graphs (even though there actually is only one), i.e., each matrix cell contains the same value twice. The advantage of using the same graph twice is that both an individual and a combined computation require the same number of iterations to converge. If the number of iterations was very different, the centrality computation with more iterations would dominate the combined one. This in turn would make seeing the effective improvement more complicated.

Figure 2.4a shows the runtimes of the power method for the synthetic data. (The results for the real-world data are very similar and are omitted here.) Naturally, the runtimes increase with the number of vertices. Figure 2.4b shows that there is no significant difference between the sizes regarding the relative improvement due to loop fusion. The other centrality measures yield the same behavior. The similarities

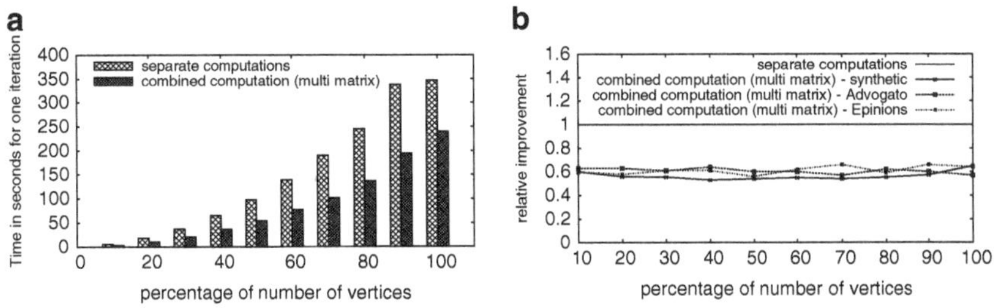

Fig. 2.4 Loop fusion: two PageRank computations in graphs of various sizes. (**a**) Absolute runtimes for the synthetic dataset. (**b**) Relative improvements for the synthetic dataset and the real-world datasets from ADVOGATO and EPINIONS

between the results for the various datasets appear in all of our experiments. We therefore only present the results for the synthetic data from now on.

Several measures. In our evaluation we explicitly consider three Eigenvector-based centrality measures, PageRank (PR), Positional Weakness (PW) and HITS. Table 2.2 shows the relative improvement using loop fusion. The values are normalized with 1. This corresponds to the runtime of the isolated computation of the two measures. Loop fusion yields an improvement, and the density of a graph has no significant impact. The differences between the combinations depend on the runtimes of the computations of the individual measures. In general, different measures on the same data set require a different number of iterations to converge. If these numbers differ significantly, the measure with the larger number dominates the runtime of the combined computation. The results are very similar for other data sets.

Multiple data sets. Two directed weighted graphs have different vertices, edges, or edge weights. We first consider the edges. Two sets E and E′ can either be equal, be distinct, intersect or have a subset relationship. We carry out two experiments: (1) We start with two identical graphs and successively modify the edges to make them intersect at various degrees (from equal to distinct). The number of edges stays the same in both sets. (2) For the subset relationship we again start with two identical graphs and then delete the edges of one graph one by one. Figure 2.5a shows the results for PageRank and intersecting set of edges, Fig. 2.5b for subset relationships between sets of edges. The results for Positional Weakness and HITS are similar. The more similar both sets of edges, the greater is the improvement. Compared to the results of our theoretical analysis, the most noticeable difference is the much better performance in the worst case (no similarities between graphs.) The reason for this is the efficient handling of 'zero' values; the 'zero' values in the multi incidence case affect the physical size only slightly. However, the improvement depending on the degree of similarity – for both subset relationships and intersecting sets of edges – is very similar in theory and in the experiments.

Table 2.2 Relative improvement using loop fusion for a combined computation of two different centrality measures

	PR + PW	PR + HITS	PW + HITS
$D = 0.05$	0.66	0.8	0.73
$D = 0.15$	0.58	0.81	0.76
$D = 0.25$	0.58	0.83	0.79

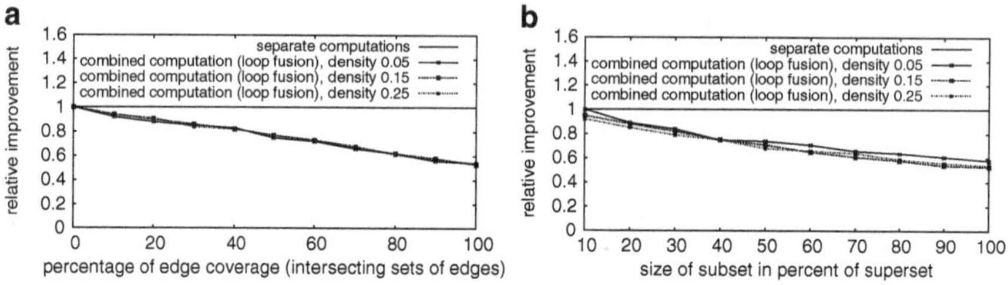

Fig. 2.5 Loop fusion: two PageRank computation on different sets of edges. (**a**) Intersecting sets. (**b**) Subset relationships

As mentioned, we consider only graphs whose sets of vertices are disjoint or have a subset relationship. To obtain sets of vertices with different degrees of overlap, we start with two identical graphs and remove vertices step by step. Figure 2.6 shows the result for PageRank. The other measures yield very similar results. Again, the improvement depends on the similarity of the sets of vertices. When the subset becomes smaller, the computation for the larger graphs dominates the combined computation more and more. Still, results for the worst case are better than expected, compared to theory. (Note that subset relationships between sets of vertices generally imply subset relationships between the corresponding sets of edges.) This has two reasons. Firstly, again, the negative effect of 'zero' values in the multi incidence table is much less pronounced in the implementation. Secondly, if the subset becomes very small, loop fusion does not have a noticeable impact any more. When a single computation completely dominates the combined one, the overhead of the extended power method starts to affect the runtime, decreasing the performance.

Finally, we investigate the impact of the weights of the edges. To do so, we run an experiment where we randomly modify the weights of a random subset of edges. On both the source and the modified graphs we compute the relative speedup with loop fusion, compared to sequences of isolated computations. In all runs – independently from the size of the subset or from the densities – loop fusion reduces the runtime by Factor 0.55–0.6. This is expected and in line with our theoretical findings: Modifying the edges does not change the size of the multi incidence table nor the number of its entries. So the costs of an iteration should not change.

Multiple parameter settings. We investigate both inherent parameters of centrality measures (MPS_{CM}) and the error threshold ϵ of the power method (MPS_ϵ) in one series of experiments. We use PageRank for two reasons. Firstly, only PageRank has an inherent parameter (damping factor d) and, secondly, the results concerning ϵ are very similar among all measures. See Fig. 2.7. The graph density has no

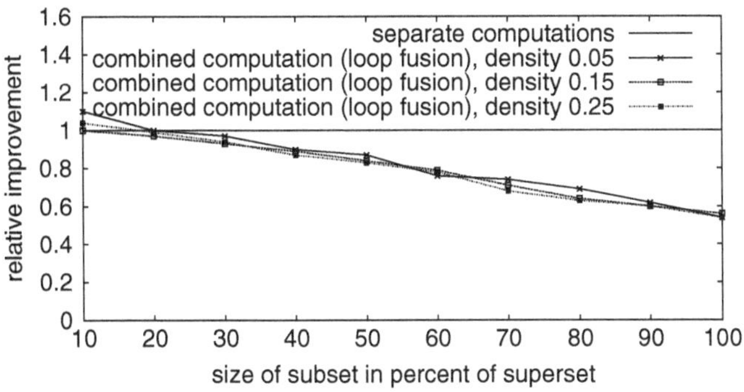

Fig. 2.6 Loop fusion: PageRank computation; different sets of vertices

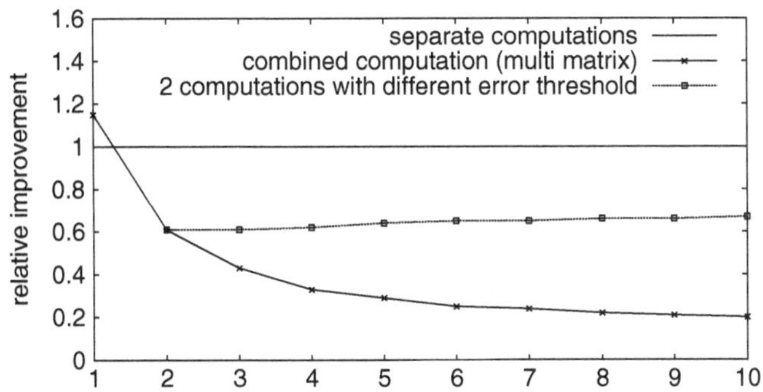

Fig. 2.7 Loop fusion: PageRank computations with different parameter settings

significant effect, and we omit the plots. The dashed line shows the improvement when executing various numbers of PageRank computations with different damping factors using loop fusion. As expected, a single computation using the extended power method is slightly slower, due to the additional computation steps in the extended algorithm. But the more centrality computations are done at the same time, the more loop fusion can reduce the runtime. The dotted line stands for two PageRank computations where we make the error threshold ϵ of the second computation smaller step by step. Starting with $\epsilon = 10^{-4}$ for both computations, we decrease ϵ for the second computation down to 10^{-10}. As expected, the improvement due to loop fusion becomes less. The computation with the decreasing threshold value requires more and more iterations and dominates the combined computation more and more.

The sum up, loop fusion is suited to improve the performance of the computation of several Eigenvector-based centrality measures. Due to the efficient handling of 'zero' values in particular, the improvement is significant even with different data sets. Only if the costs of one computation stand out by much, the overhead of the extended power-method algorithm can lead to slightly weaker results.

2.7.2 Re-Use of Results

In each experiment we consider two subsequent centrality computations, comparing the isolated computation to the combined one with re-use of results. The improvement is the number of iterations saved with the second computation. We normalize the number of iterations, such that the number of iterations for the second centrality-computation using an isolated computation is 1.

Several measures. In Section 2.4.2 we have argued that the re-use of results is promising only if two measures are similar, and the range of the scores of the second measure is known. Among the centrality measures considered, the latter condition is only true for PageRank. We carry out an experiment where we re-use the centrality computation result obtained with other measures (Positional Weakness, HITS) as start vector for the PageRank computation on the same data set. HITS provides two centrality indices, the authority index ($\text{HITS}_{\text{Authorities}}$) and the hub index ($\text{HITS}_{\text{Hubs}}$). PageRank, Positional Weakness and $\text{HITS}_{\text{Authorities}}$ are similar measures, they all consider the in-links of a vertex. For better comparability, we also re-use the result of $\text{HITS}_{\text{Hubs}}$ which considers the out-links of the vertices. As data sets, we use our three graphs with different densities. Table 2.3 shows the results. In all cases, the re-use of the result of PositionalWeakness and $\text{HITS}_{\text{Authorities}}$ for a PageRank computation yields no or only a small improvement, although these measures are similar. A rather unexpected result is that $\text{HITS}_{\text{Hubs}}$, which is not similar to PageRank, does not necessarily lead to additional iterations for the PageRank computation. Our explanation is that the rate of convergence of a power method is logarithmic, being high in the first iterations. In other words, the result of the first centrality computation must already be very close to the one of the second computation to see an improvement. At least, re-use of results does not increase the number of iterations among similar measures.

Multiple data sets. To evaluate the effect of re-use of results on the computation of one centrality measure on two different data sets, we proceed analogously to Sect. 2.7.1: For two graphs G(V, E) and G′(V′, E′) we consider (a) different degrees of the overlapping and different subset relationships of E and E′, (b) different subset relationships of V and V′, and (c) different weights of the edges. Again, we only show the results for PageRank.

For two overlapping sets of edges E and E′ we use the result of the PageRank computation on E as the start vector for the PageRank computation on E′. To study the case of a subset relationship of two sets of edges ($E' \subseteq E$), we compute PageRank on the subset using the result of the PageRank computation on the superset as the start vector. Figure 2.8a shows the results for overlapping sets of edges, Fig. 2.8b

Table 2.3 Relative improvement of the combined computation of different centrality measures using the re-use of results

	Positional Weakness	$HITS_{Authorities}$	$HITS_{Hubs}$
$D = 0.05$	1	1	1
$D = 0.15$	1	1	1.06
$D = 0.25$	0.92	0.92	1

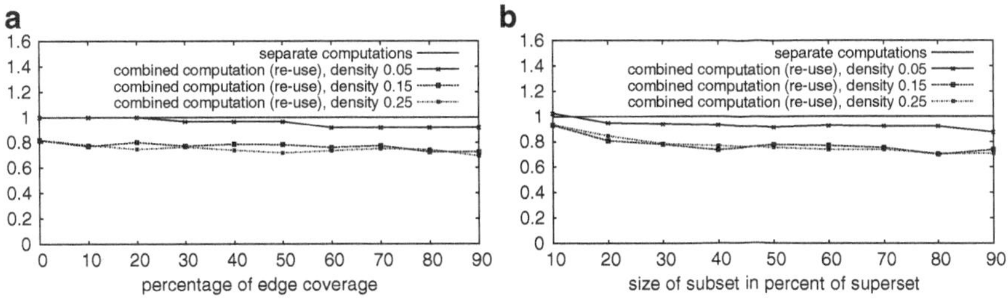

Fig. 2.8 Re-use of results: two PageRank computation on different sets of edges. (**a**) Intersecting sets. (**b**) Subset relationships

for a subset relationship between the sets of edges. The more similar the set of edges, the greater is the improvement. Another finding is that for sparse graphs the improvement is rather small, even if the sets of edges are very similar.

Analogously, we consider the subset relationship of two sets of vertices ($V' \subseteq V$). We first compute PageRank on V and use its result as the start vector for the second computation on V'. Note that, here, re-use requires the normalization of the start vector. Figure 2.9 shows the result. For dense graphs the improvement is about 0.8–0.85, independently from the size of the subset. For sparse graphs however, re-use can worsen the runtime of the second centrality computation, and for larger subsets the improvement is less than for dense graphs.

Regarding the third issue, we randomly change the edge weights. We first compute PageRank on the original graph and use the resulting vector for the PageRank computation on the modified graph. Figure 2.10 shows the result. Again, the two key findings are as follows: (1) The more similar the weights are, the greater the improvement, and (2) the sparser the graph, the less the improvement.

Multiple parameter settings. Since we can assess the improvement with re-use for two centrality computations that differ only with regard to ϵ (MPS_{ϵ}) a priori, we focus on the inherent parameters of centrality measures (MPS_{CM}). Among the measures considered here, only PageRank features such a parameter, damping factor d. To quantify its effect, we conduct several runs where we perform two computations with different damping factors, using the result of the first computation as start vector for the second one. Figure 2.11 shows the result for a single run. Here, $d = 0.85$ for the first computation and $d \in [0.75 \dots 0.95]$ for

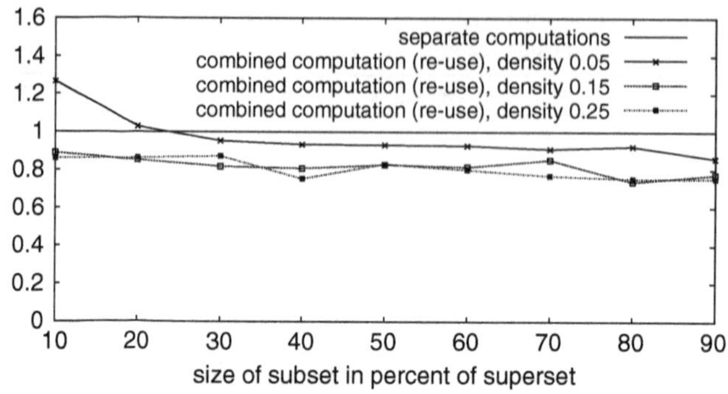

Fig. 2.9 Re-use of results: Two PageRank computation on two graphs with different sets of vertices (subset relationship)

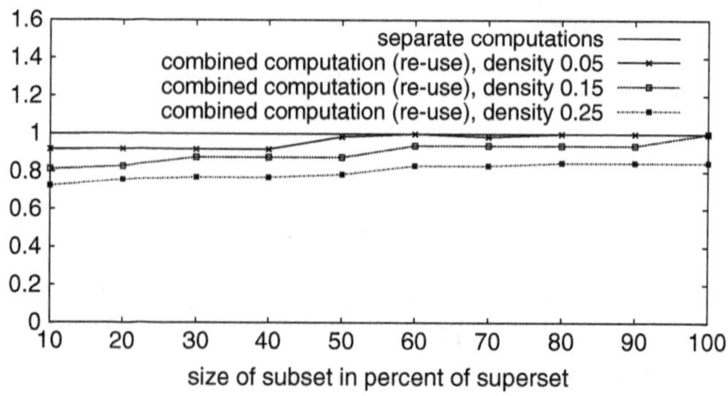

Fig. 2.10 Re-use of results: Two PageRank computations on two graphs with different edge weights

the second computation. The results for other runs with various combinations of d are very similar.

There only is a significant improvement if the damping factor in both computations is very close. For larger differences between the damping factors of two PageRank computations, the improvement for the second computation vanishes. However, re-use never requires more iterations than using a generic start vector.

To sum up, re-use only achieves a significant speedup if the results of two centrality computations are very similar. The evaluation shows that this is typically not true for several measures (SM). For the other classes MDS and MPS the improvement depends on the density of the graph. For sparse graphs in particular – note that the graphs of online scenarios tend to be sparse – re-use often cannot reduce the number of iterations of subsequent centrality computations, but increases it in some cases.

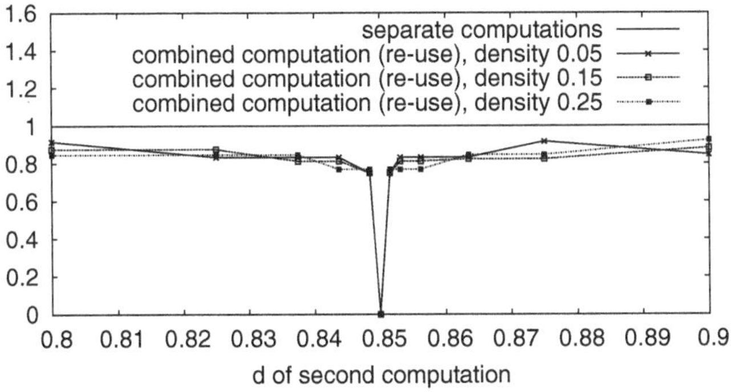

Fig. 2.11 Re-use of results: Two PageRank computations with various damping factors *d*

2.8 Conclusions

An accepted way to identify of trustworthy participants in online communities relies on Eigenvector-based centrality measures. However, centrality computation is expensive. While existing work has focused on the optimization of one centrality computation, little attention has gone into the computation of several centrality measures in combination. We have proposed and evaluated two optimization schemes, namely loop fusion and re-use of computation results. Re-use yields an improvement in distinct cases only. Loop fusion improves the performance in almost all situations, except when the cost of one computation is much higher than the costs of the other computations. Additionally, re-use is bound to the power method and therefore to Eigenvector-based centrality measures. The improvements due to loop fusion, result from the compact representation of the multi matrix. Thus, one can apply loop fusion to various graph algorithms at least in principle. Evaluating the actual benefit however requires further investigation.

References

1. Abbassi, Z., Mirrokni, V.S.: A recommender system based on local random walks and spectral methods. In: Proceedings of the 9th WebKDD and 1st SNA-KDD 2007 Workshop on Web Mining and Social Network Analysis, WebKDD/SNA-KDD '07. ACM, New York (2007)
2. Bacon, D.F., Graham, S.L., Sharp, O.J.: Compiler transformations for high-performance computing. ACM Comput. Surv. **26** (1994)
3. Blainey, B., Barton, C., Amaral, J.: Removing impediments to loop fusion through code transformations. In: Languages and Compilers for Parallel Computing, Springer, Berlin/Heidelberg (2002)
4. Bowen, B., Kocura, P.: Implementing conceptual graphs in a RDBMS. In: Proceedings on Conceptual Graphs for Knowledge Representation. Springer, London (1993)

5. Cho, J., Schonfeld, U.: RankMass crawler: a crawler with high personalized PageRank coverage guarantee. In: Proceedings of the 33rd International Conference on Very Large Data Bases, VLDB '07. VLDB Endowment (2007)
6. Cummings, J.N.: NetVis module: Dynamic visualization of social networks. Available online at http://www.netvis.org (2001–2012)
7. Dean, J., Ghemawat, S.: MapReduce: simplified data processing on large clusters. Commun. ACM **51**(1), 107–113 (2008)
8. Delaviz, R., Andrade, N., Pouwelse, J.: Improving accuracy and coverage in an internet-deployed reputation mechanism. In: Peer-to-Peer Computing. IEEE, New York (2010)
9. Getoor, L., Diehl, C.P.: Link mining: a survey. SIGKDD Explor. Newsl. **7**, 3–12 (2005)
10. Golub, G.H., van Loan, C.F.: Matrix Computations (Johns Hopkins Studies in Mathematical Sciences), 3rd edn. Johns Hopkins University Press, Baltimore (1996)
11. Gross, J., Yellen, J.: Graph Theory and its Applications. CRC, Boca Raton (1999)
12. Gyöngyi, Z., Garcia-Molina, H., Pedersen, J.: Combating web spam with TrustRank. In: Proceedings of the 13th International Conference on Very Large Data Bases, VLDB '04. VLDB Endowment (2004)
13. Hütter, C., Hartmann, B.O., Böhm, K., Heistermann, T., Kohlmeyer, K.S., Reckling, R., Reiche, M., Parra, D.S.: SONAR: towards user-centric social network analysis and visualization. In: Proceedings of the 2010 IEEE/WIC/ACM International Conference on Web Intelligence and Intelligent Agent Technology, WI-IAT '10. IEEE Computer Society, New York (2010)
14. Kamvar, S., Haveliwala, T., Manning, C., Golub, G.: Extrapolation methods for accelerating PageRank computations. In: Proceedings of the 12th International Conference on World Wide Web, WWW '03. ACM, New York (2003)
15. Kamvar, S.D., et al.: The eigen trust algorithm for reputation management in P2P networks. In: Proceedings of the 12th International Conference on World Wide Web, WWW '03. ACM, New York (2003)
16. Kleinberg, J.M.: Authoritative sources in a hyperlinked environment. J. ACM **46**, 604–632 (1999)
17. Lee, C.P., Golub, G.H., Zenios, S.A.: A fast two-stage algorithm for computing PageRank and its extensions. Tech. rep., Stanford University (2004)
18. Ng, A.Y., Zheng, A.X., Jordan, M.I.: Link analysis, eigenvectors and stability. In: Proceedings of the 17th International Joint Conference on Artificial Intelligence. Morgan Kaufmann, San Francisco (2001)
19. Page, L., Brin, S., Motwani, R., Winograd, T.: The PageRank citation ranking: bringing order to the web. Tech. rep., Stanford (1998)
20. Parreira, J.X., et al.: Efficient and decentralized PageRank approximation in a P2P web search network. In: Proceedings of the 32nd International Conference on Very Large Data Bases, VLDB '06. VLDB Endowment (2006)
21. Resnick, P., Kuwabara, K., Zeckhauser, R., Friedman, E.: Reputation systems: facilitating trust in internet interactions. Commun. ACM **43**, 45–48 (2000). ACM
22. Richardson, M., Agrawal, R., Domingos, P.: Trust management for the semantic web. In: Proceedings of the International Semantic Web Conference, ISWC'03. Springer, Berlin/Heidelberg (2003)
23. Sabater, J., Sierra, C.: Reputation and social network analysis in multi-agent systems. In: Proceedings of the 1st International Joint Conference on Autonomous Agent and Multi-Agent Systems, AAMAS '02. ACM, New York (2002)
24. Sierra, C., Debenham, J.: Information-based reputation. In: 1st International Conference on Reputation Theory and Technology, ICORE '09. New York (2009)
25. Stephens, S., Rung, J. Lopez, X.: Graph data representation in oracle database 10*g*: case studies in life sciences. IEEE Data Eng. Bull. **27**, 61–66 (2004)
26. von der Weth, C., Böhm, K.: A unifying framework for behavior-based trust models. In: Proceedings of the International Conference on Cooperative Information Systems, CoopIS '06. Springer, Berlin/Heidelberg (2006)

27. von der Weth, C., Böhm, K.: Towards an objective assessment of centrality measures in reputation systems. In: Proceedings of the 9th IEEE International Conference on E-Commerce Technology and The 4th IEEE International Conference on Enterprise Computing, E-Commerce and E-Services, CEC/EEE '07. IEEE Computer Society, New York (2007)
28. von der Weth, C., Böhm, K., Hütter, C.: Optimizing multiple centrality computations for reputation systems. In: Proceedings of the International Conference on Advances in Social Networks Analysis and Mining, ASONAM '10. IEEE Computer Society, New York (2010)
29. Wang, Y., DeWitt, D.: Computing PageRank in a distributed internet search system. In: Proceedings of the 30th International Conference on Very Large Data Bases, VLDB '04. VLDB Endowment (2004)
30. Wassermann, S., Faust, K.: Social Network Analysis: Methods and Applications. Cambridge University Press, Cambridge/New York (1994)
31. Wicks, J., Greenwald, A.: More efficient parallel computation of PageRank. In: Proceedings of the 30th International Conference on Research and Development in Information Retrieval, SIGIR '07. ACM, New York (2007)
32. Xiong, L., Liu, L.: PeerTrust: supporting reputation-based trust for peer-to-peer electronic communities. IEEE Trans. Knowl. Data Eng. **16**(7), 843–857 (2004)
33. Yamamoto, A., Asahara, D., Itao, T., Tanaka, S., Suda, T.: Distributed PageRank: a distributed reputation model for open peer-to-peer networks. In: Proceedings of the 2004 Symposium on Applications and the Internet-Workshops, SAINT-W '04. IEEE Computer Society (2004)
34. Zhang, H., Goel, A., Govindan, R., Mason, K., Roy, B.V.: Improving eigenvector-based reputation systems against collusions. In: Workshop on Algorithms and Models for the Web Graph. Springer, New York (2004)
35. Zhang, L., Zhang, K., Li, C.: A topical PageRank based algorithm for recommender systems. In: Proceedings of the 31st International Conference on Research and Development in Information Retrieval, SIGIR '08. ACM, New York (2008)

Chapter 3
Application of Social Network Metrics to a Trust-Aware Collaborative Model for Generating Personalized User Recommendations

Iraklis Varlamis, Magdalini Eirinaki, and Malamati Louta

Abstract Social network analysis has emerged as a key technique in modern sociology, but has recently gained a lot of interest in Web mining research, because of the advent and the increasing popularity of social media, such as blogs, social networks, micro-blogging, customer review sites etc. Such media often serve as platforms for information dissemination and product placement or promotion. One way to improve the quality of recommendations provided to the members of social networks is to use trustworthy resources. In this environment, community-based reputation can help estimating the trustworthiness of individual users. Consequently, influence and trust are becoming essential qualities among user interactions. In this work, we perform an extensive study of various metrics related to the aforementioned elements, and of their effect in the process of information propagation in social networks. In order to better understand the properties of links and the dynamics of social networks, we distinguish between permanent and transient links and in the latter case, we consider the link freshness. Moreover, we distinguish between the propagation of trust in a local level and the effect of global influence and compare suggestions provided by locally trusted or globally influential users.

I. Varlamis (✉)
Department of Informatics and Telematics, Harokopio University of Athens, Athens, Greece
e-mail: varlamis@hua.gr

M. Eirinaki
Computer Engineering Department, San Jose State University, San Jose, CA, USA
e-mail: magdalini.eirinaki@sjsu.edu

M. Louta
Department of Informatics and Telecommunications Engineering, University of Western Macedonia, Kozani, Greece
e-mail: louta@uowm.gr

T. Özyer et al. (eds.), *The Influence of Technology on Social Network Analysis and Mining*, Lecture Notes in Social Networks 6, DOI 10.1007/978-3-7091-1346-2_3,

3.1 Introduction

Social network analysis has been a major area of research for sociologists for many years, but recently has attracted the interest of the Web mining research community. The advent of participatory Web (Web 2.0) and the enormous increase in the use of social networking websites, customer review sites, blogs etc. has turned Web users from information consumers to information producers, thus creating for Web researchers a huge repository of user-provided content. Such content presents features, which are unique to the Web, in terms of shared authorship, multitude of user-provided tags, inherent connectivity between users and the content they provide, and high update rate. All these characteristics provide a platform that can be exploited in order to mine interesting information about the dynamics of users' interactions.

One common type of analysis is the detection of communities of users with similar interests, and within such communities the identification of the most "influential users". We may define influential users as individuals with many connections within the community, but in general other definitions are possible depending on the type of the community and the social network that interconnects the community members. Influential users act as authorities or hubs within their community and thus play a key role in spreading information. This has obvious implications on "word of mouth" and viral marketing, as indicated in recent studies [5, 16], which in turn makes influential users important for the promotion and endorsement of new products or ideas.

On a slightly different note, another common type of analysis is that of content ranking, in other words finding "influential content", whether this is a product review, a blog or a tweet. Such ranking is becoming increasingly important since online social media expand, in terms of content and users, on a very rapid pace, making navigation cumbersome and time-consuming. This process helps in that the top-ranked items (reviews, blogs, comments, tweets, etc.) can be used as recommendations to the users. Most of existing work in this area generates overall rankings [1,21,27], and only recently there have been some efforts in personalizing the rankings [32,35].

Finally, the notion of trust prediction and propagation, used primarily to find trustful (or distrustful) nodes in P2P networks [15] has been adopted in the context of virtual communities [24, 28, 36, 37]. It has been shown empirically [9, 13] that in a specific context, it can be assumed that trust may propagate (with appropriate discounting) through the relationship network [13, 28]. Trust has also been shown to be highly correlated to profile similarity and the model is used for recommending items [10, 11, 25, 26].

In this work, we bridge these research directions. Our objective is to generate personalized *user recommendations* based on the analysis of implicit or explicit link information between users and user provided content. Depending on the nature of each specific social network, the link information may express trust to the user or simply interest to the content being pointed by the link. Since hyperlinks do not explicitly carry semantic information, our graph analysis model can either discover trustful, influential or interesting nodes depending on the social network.

This paper extends our previous work [32, 33], employing the notion of trust among users as expressed with links, to generate personalized user rankings and recommendations. In this work we incorporate the notion of influence in the ranking algorithm along with the freshness of the trust connections between users and perform an extensive study by integrating several link analysis algorithms in the ranking process in order to get insights of how different influence metrics, such as the degree, closeness, betweenness and centrality or the hub, authority or PageRank scores of a node affect the overall ranking.

The remaining of this paper is organized as follows; in the following section, we present an overview of related research in ranking, influence and trust in social networks. In Sect. 3.3 we present the background of our work, concerning user recommendations based on collaborative knowledge from locally trusted or globally influential users. In Sect. 3.4, we introduce our model, which combines recommendations from trusted (or neighboring) users with those of "influential" users. Section 3.5 presents the results of the evaluation we performed on a social network which comprises users, links of trust between them and product reviews and ratings. Finally, Sect. 3.6 summarizes our findings and presents our next steps in this work.

3.2 Related Work

Studying and analyzing Web 2.0 media, such as social networks, blogs, forums, wikis etc. has gained momentum, resulting in an increase of research in the related fields. Among the several facets of these social media, *trust*, *influence*, and *ranking* are receiving a lot of attention.

The notion of trust propagation within a network was first introduced in the context of P2P networks. The most well-known algorithm in this context is EigenTrust [15]. This reputation management algorithm, is based on the fact that trust is transitive, in that, if a node i trusts another node j, then it also trusts the nodes trusted by j. The algorithm first allows each node to perform a local ranking of the neighboring nodes. These local rankings are then accumulated to give a global "trustfulness" rank to each node in the network. The more "trustworthy" a node is, the more weight their rating of other nodes has.

This idea of trust transitivity, prediction, and propagation, has lately been adopted in the context of virtual communities [13, 24, 28, 36, 37]. Golbeck [11] defines the trust rating between two users (called source and sink) as the weighted average of the source's neighbors' ratings of the sink. It has been shown empirically [9, 13] that, in a specific context, it can be assumed that trust may propagate (with appropriate discounting) through the relationship network [13, 28]. Massa and Avesani assume that the users state how much they consider trustworthy each other user and his/her ratings and exploit trust propagation over the network in order to infer more trust relationships [26]. A detailed survey of the use of trust in recommender systems is presented in [10].

In our work we introduce the notion of trust in a social network, assuming that trust between a pair of users is already known, either explicitly or implicitly. Our model builds on the idea of integrating local trust and global influence, as suggested in [15]. More specifically, in our model the propagation of trust within a social network is complemented by the more general notion of "influence" within the network and as a result personalized user recommendations are formed considering people that the user trusts and people that have big influence on the whole social network.

Influence in social networks, a topic extensively studied in the pre-WWW era [34], has again emerged as a research topic. One common approach is to model the identification of influencers as a combinatorial optimization problem: given a fixed number of nodes that can be initially activated or infected, find the set of nodes with maximum influence over the entire network – the one that generates the largest cascade of adoptions [5]. Several works build on this Information Cascade (IC) notion proposing various machine learning algorithms [6, 16, 18, 19, 30]. Even though such approaches have been shown to improve over traditional social network analysis metrics, they are solely based on the link structure of social networks, and do not take into consideration other important parameters, such as activity, rate of updates, and trust among users. In the same vein, researchers have investigated the identification of likely influential users through a combination of link analysis techniques [31, 35], as well as user activity-related parameters in order to identify influential users in blogs [2,3] and social networks [17]. As shown from the analysis above, most of the work in identification of influencers within a social network (real or online) is based on extensions of well known link analysis algorithms and as such, exploit the structural characteristics of the network. In this work we follow a similar approach and incorporate such metrics in our ranking method.

Ranking on the Web is primarily based on the analysis of the Web graph as it is formulated by hyperlinks. In the case of blogs, several ranking algorithms have been suggested that exploit explicit (EigenRumor algorithm [27]) and/or implicit (BlogRank [1,21]) hyperlinks between blogs. All these algorithms formulate a graph of blogs, based on hyperlinks and then apply PageRank or a variation of it in order to provide an overall ranking of blogs. However, all these algorithms provide a static measure of blog importance that does not reflect the temporal aspects accompanying the evolution of the blogosphere.

In our previous work [32] we introduced a collaborative rating mechanism, which exploits the explicit connections between users and other implicit connections and provides each user with personalized rankings of other users in the network. The rating mechanism employs direct and indirect information from a user's neighborhood. In [23] we presented a global rating model for the blogosphere. The model distinguishes between explicit links between blogs (the links in the blogroll) and implicit links (links between individual posts). The model also captures the time dimension of links. Using links' freshness, we manage to punish blogs that artificially receive a large number of links in a small period of time and are ignored thereafter, we reward blogs that are constantly being referenced by other blogs and successfully distinguish between normal and spam blogs.

To the best of our knowledge, this is the first extensive study of the effect of both overall "influence", as expressed by the analysis of the whole social graph, as well as by personalized aspects of "influence" such as trust, in ranking and recommending other users or content. This paper is an extended version of the paper presented in [33], including more detailed overview of the various algorithms employed, an updated ranking algorithm that incorporates the notion of "freshness" of connections, and a more extensive experimental evaluation.

3.3 Preliminaries

Social network analysis is the study of social entities (*actors*) and their interactions and relationships. The interaction and relationships are represented as a graph, where each node represents an actor (user), and the edge between two nodes represents their relationship. Several link analysis algorithms have been proposed, that are applied on such graphs in order to identify and analyze the role, position, and influence of each user.

In our work, we employ social network analysis metrics such as centrality and rank prestige, in order to identify the "influential" actors in a social network, in terms of their position in the graph and their connections/interactions with other users [4, 7, 8, 34]. *Centrality* identifies as important actors (i.e. users) those that are linked (i.e. involved) extensively with other actors. *Prestige* is a more refined measure since it differentiates between in-links and out-links, focusing on in-links. In other words, the importance of an actor depends on the opinion of other actors, expressed by their ties to her. More specifically, we are interested in *rank prestige*,that also takes into account the prominence of individual actors that participate in this "voting" process. Rank prestige has been the basis upon which both HITS [20] and PageRank [29] were built.

In addition to these global metrics, influence in a local scale is important for all actors. In this context, actors collaborate with the actors they trust and are influenced by their opinions. Moreover, trust and influence are reinforced for certain actors in the circle of trust and decrease for others. In order to model the dynamics of trust and influence in the "neighborhood" of a user, we employ our *collaborative local* scoring mechanism. In what follows, we provide a brief overview of the aforementioned metrics [22, 32].

3.3.1 Social Network Analysis Metrics

Centrality. The three centrality metrics, namely degree, closeness, and betweenness centrality, identify "key" users of the graph, in terms of information dissemination. Let n denote the size of the graph (i.e. the number of actors/users).

Degree Centrality $Gd(i)$ takes into consideration the node degree $d(i)$ of a user i. The higher the node degree, the more central the user is:

$$Gd(i) = \frac{d(i)}{n-1} \tag{3.1}$$

Closeness Centrality $Gc(i)$ of a user i signifies how easily this user interacts with all other users j $(j \in [1 \ldots n])$. Let $d(i, j)$ denote the distance of user i from user j, equal to the number of links in a shortest path. Then, according to closeness centrality, the shorter the distance of the user to all other actors, the more central the user is:

$$Gc(i) = \frac{n-1}{\sum_{j=1}^{n} d(i, j)} \tag{3.2}$$

Finally, *Betweenness Centrality* $Gb(i)$ signifies the importance of user i with regards to the flow of information in the social network. If the user is between two non-adjucent users j and k then i has control over their interactions. If i is on the paths of many such interactions (i.e. *between* many users), then this is an important user, having a great amount of *influence* on what happens in the network. Let sp_{jk} be the number of shortest paths between j and k, and $sp_{jk}(i)$, $(j \neq i$ and $k \neq i)$ be the number of shortest paths that pass i. Betweenness centrality of a user i is defined as follows:

$$Gb(i) = \sum_{j<k} \frac{sp_{jk}(i)}{sp_{jk}} \tag{3.3}$$

Hubs and Authorities. Both terms were introduced as part of the well-known algorithm HITS [20]. A *hub* is a node with many out-links and an *authority* is a node with many in-links. The key idea of HITS is that hubs and authorities have a mutual reinforcement relationship, since a good hub points to many good authorities, and a good authority is pointed to by many good hubs. Transferring the algorithm to the social network paradigm, the authority score $Ga(i)$ of user i is the sum of all hub scores $Gh(j)$ of users j that have a (directed) relationship with i (this directed relationship can be, for example, a declaration of trust in a social network or a comment on a blog post). The hub score $Gh(i)$ of user i is defined similarly. Let E be the set of directed edges (i.e. links) in the graph, then the authority $Ga(i)$ and hub $Gh(i)$ scores are iteratively calculated as follows:

$$Ga(i) = \sum_{(j,i) \in E} Gh(j) \tag{3.4}$$

$$Gh(i) = \sum_{(i,j) \in E} Ga(j) \tag{3.5}$$

PageRank. PageRank [29] also identifies "authorities" in a graph. The intuition is that the more actors "endorse" or vote for an actor i (i.e. add a link pointing to i), the more important i is. What is more, prominence of the endorsers is crucial, since the vote of important actors is more valuable. Transferring this notion to the social network paradigm, a user i is considered to be influential if (a) many other users endorse i (for example by "trusting" i, adding i's blog in their blogroll, or becoming i's followers), and (b) these users are in turn influential. The PageRank score $Gp(i)$ of user i is iteratively computed as follows:

$$Gp(i) = (1 - d) + d \sum_{(j,i) \in E} \frac{Gp(j)}{O_j} \tag{3.6}$$

where O_j denotes the number of out-links of node j and d is the so-called damping factor.

3.3.2 Collaborative Rating in Social Networks

In [32, 33] we presented a personalized recommendation model, which capitalizes on a collaborative rating mechanism that exploits the structure of the social network. The model represents the social network as a directed graph $G = (V, E)$, where users are the nodes V and the implicit or explicit links between users are the edges E of the graph. Explicit links between two users in a social network denote a permanent recommendation and trust, while on the other hand, implicit links represent a temporary interest and thus, a more transient reference to the user being pointed. In any case, it has been assumed that the intention of a user i when adding a link towards user j is to provide a positive recommendation for j to other users in the network.

The model suggests a quantification of user's i opinion with respect to user j, called local score (*LS*), which is updated in time, so as to follow the dynamic nature of the social networks and capture the "freshness" of information available.

$$LS_t(i, j) = w_{BR} \cdot BR_t(i, j) + w_{EP} \cdot EP_t(i, j) \tag{3.7}$$

In Eq. (3.7), the local score for a user j as expressed by another user i, at a certain time period t, is the weighted combination of two factors: (a) $BR_t(i, j)$, which corresponds to what i explicitly denotes about j, and (b) $EP_t(i, j)$, which corresponds to what i implicitly believes about j. The first factor constitutes of the number of explicit/permanent links, which, for example, in the case of blogs, can be those in the blogroll list of a user, in the case of social networking applications can be the "friend" links or in the case of consumer networks can be the links to the "members of trust". The second factor considers implicit links and can be, for example, the number of links from blog i to blog j (e.g. if user X, the owner of blog i, adds a link to a post in blog j, owned by user Y, this implicitly means that X likes Y). The definition of weights depends on the type of social network we examine and the relative significance we give to explicit and implicit expressions of trust or interest. Local score estimation takes place at consecutive, equally distributed, time intervals.

Due to the dynamic nature of social networks, users may add new links (i.e. new recommendations) to the same targets, thus, reinforcing their initial recommendations or withdraw some old links, weakening their former positions. In order to capture the links' "freshness", we proposed an extension, named *local accumulative score* (*LAS*), which aggregates the local scores $LS_t(i, j)$ of previous time periods t in order to find the score in the current period c, attributing higher significance to recent time periods.

$$LAS_c(i, j) = \sum_{\substack{t=c-m+1 \\ t>0}}^{c} w_t \cdot LS_t(i, j) \tag{3.8}$$

Weights are given by the following equation:

$$w_t = \frac{f(t)}{\sum\limits_{\substack{l=c-m+1 \\ l>0}}^{c} f(l)} \tag{3.9}$$

where $f(t) = \begin{Bmatrix} m - c + t, c \geq m \\ t, c < m \end{Bmatrix}$ and $\sum\limits_{\substack{t=c-m+1 \\ t>0}}^{c} w_t = 1$.

For the calculation of the local accumulative score at time period c, only the m most recent local scores formed are considered. Parameter m stands for the "system memory",[1] which in essence determines the number of periods back in time that we consider for aggregating the local scores. A small value for the parameter m means that the memory of the system is small, whereas large value considers a large memory for the system. Depending on the type of the social network considered, the definition of the value of the parameter m may yield interesting results. Equation (3.9) in essence models the fact that more recent local scores should weigh more in the overall *LAS* evaluation.

We subsequently extend the local accumulative scores produced in a first step, introducing the concept of *collaborative local score (CLS)*. $CLS_c(i, j)$ score aggregates at time period c the direct accumulative scores $LAS_c(i, j)$, assigned by user i to any user j, with the indirect accumulative scores $LAS_c(k, j)$ attributed to user j by all users k belonging in the WS_i set, a subset of the set V, formed by users that user i trusts (hereafter referred to as the "witnesses"). WS_i set comprises the users that are explicitly connected to user i (as determined by user's i explicit links – depth = 1), while adoption of the transitivity property of trust leads to its more general form including the users that are explicitly connected to user's i trusted

[1] We assume that the system does not process the complete history of user ratings and friendship links from the very beginning of the community, but only the most recent interactions. Thus we use the term "system memory" to refer to the size (in time units) of this history log.

users (depth = 2), the users that are explicitly connected to the trusted users of user's i trusted users (depth = 3), etc.

$$CLS_c(i, j) = w_i \cdot LAS_c(i, j) + \sum_{k \in WS_i} w_k \cdot LAS_c(k, j) \tag{3.10}$$

As may be observed, the collaborative local score is a weighted combination of the user's i direct opinion and the recommendations collected from a number of user's i witnesses with respect to user j. In general, weight w_k is a measure of the trustworthiness of witness k in the eyes of user i, depends on the transitivity horizon considered and may be a function of the LAS attributed to each user in the respective trust chain formed. Considering transitivity horizon equal to n, the weight w_k along a specific trust chain may be given by the following equation:

$$w_k = \frac{w_{u(d=1)} \cdot w_{u(d=2)} \cdot \ldots \cdot w_{u(d=n)}}{n} \tag{3.11}$$

where $w_{u(d=x)}$ denotes the weight of user u in the position/depth x of the trust chain and $w_{u(d=x)} = \frac{LAS(u(d=x-1),u(d=x))}{\sum LAS(u(d=x-1),u(d=x))}$. At this point it should be noted that we have assumed that user i is connected to witness user k only through the specific trust chain. This assumption may be readily relaxed. Besides the multiplicative function considered in Eq. (3.11), other functions could be defined as well.

3.4 Influence Model

Our objective is to generate personalized recommendations to the members of social networks. These recommendations may refer to users, blogs/blog posts, comments, tweets, content reviews, etc. In order for such recommendations to be personalized, a ranking algorithm is needed.

In this work, we propose a model that enhances our previous approach on social networks, by involving both the circle of trust of a user, as well as the overall influential users of a social network in the ranking process. Our objective is to compare and evaluate the importance of different types of users in a social network. Such users might belong to the immediate network of trust of the user, the extended network of trust of the user, or the overall conception of trust among all users in the network. Please note that the same model can be applied to any social medium, for example blogs (where "trust" is expressed by adding a blog in one's blogroll), tweets (where "trust" is shown by following a tweeter), or consumer networks (where "trust" is shown explicitly by endorsement or reviews).

To this direction, we extend the collaborative model of Eq. (3.10) to include a *Global Influence* model GI. This global influence model results to a global ranking of all users in the social network, based on their position in the social graph and their connections to all other users. In essence, the global influence $GI(i)$ of user

i is an indication of the importance of this user in the whole social graph and is a linear combination of the six models presented in Sect. 3.3.1:

$$\begin{aligned} GI(i) = w_d \cdot Gd(i) + w_c \cdot Gc(i) + \\ w_b \cdot Gb(i) + w_h \cdot Gh(i) + \\ w_a \cdot Ga(i) + w_p \cdot Gp(i) \end{aligned} \tag{3.12}$$

Note that using the aforementioned formula, we may give more importance to one (or more) global influence metric(s) and diminish others.

Our proposed model computes the influence score $INF^i_c(j)$ as a function of the ratings/trust provided for any user j by (a) user i, (b) the network of trust of user i, and (c) the globally influential users:

$$\begin{aligned} INF_c(i,j) = f(LAS_c(i,j), \sum_{k \in WS_i} w_k \cdot LAS_c(k,j), \\ \sum_{(m,j) \in E} GI(m) \cdot LAS_c(m,j)) \end{aligned} \tag{3.13}$$

This function could be, for instance, a weighted sum of the three factors of Eq. (3.13):

$$\begin{aligned} INF_c(i,j) = w_{local} \cdot LAS_c(i,j) + \\ w_{collab} \cdot \sum_{k \in WS_i} w_k \cdot LAS_c(k,j) + \\ w_{global} \cdot \sum_{(m,j) \in E} GI(m) \cdot LAS_c(m,j) \end{aligned} \tag{3.14}$$

Equation (3.14) assumes that the weights are normalized. The weighted sum approach has been used in a related context (identification of influential bloggers) with great success [2]. Alternatively we can produce different rankings using each local and global metric and then merge the rankings in a single ranked list [12], or use an ensemble ranking [14].

The combined model for social networks has a dual meaning: a member of the social network decides upon her own beliefs and upon suggestions of people she trusts and is influenced by the central/powerfull members of the network. The three different weights in Eq. (3.14) represent the balance between the three different types of influence: w_{local} for the user's own beliefs, w_{collab} for the user's extended network beliefs and w_{global} for influential users' beliefs. Moreover, each component weighs differently each participant, with each user k in the network of trust of user i receiving a different weight $w(k)$, and each globally influential user m receiving a weight proportional to her importance in the graph ($GI(m)$). We should point out that the aforementioned model can be easily adjusted to cater for newcomers to a social network. Newcomers don't have a "circle of trust" yet so the local metrics cannot be applied. In that case the ranking can be made on the basis of the global influence of each user, and be personalized/adjusted when the user starts making more connections in the network.

The final outcome of our model is a personalized set of influence scores for all other users in a social network. These influence scores can be used to rank the users, and this ranking can be subsequently used to generate recommendations to the current user i. For example, in the blogosphere, the model recommends the personalized top-k list of influential blogs, taking into consideration the user's personal network of trust and overall influence of blogs. In a micro-blogging site such as Twitter, the model will generate a personalized set of trusted and influential "followees", whereas in a social network, the model will generate a personalized set of trusted and influential users.

In the case of decentralized networks (e.g. p2p networks, ad-hoc social networks etc.), finding the global influence is difficult or even infeasible, so the local alternative is the only solution. On the other hand, in a web-based social networking application (e.g. Twitter), trust scores and item ratings are all stored in a central node thus permitting the application of both local and global approaches. In the following section we evaluate the local and global approaches and their combinations in a centralized social networking application.

3.5 Experimental Evaluation

The aim of our study is to compare the performance of local and global models of influence in providing recommendations to the users of social networks and combine them in a single model. For the evaluation of the different models, we employed a dataset which refers to a network of buyers. The *extended Epinions dataset*, which was provided by Epinions and is available through the Trustlet wikipage[2] contains information about product reviews written by the members of the Epinions community. It contains approximately 132,000 users who issued 841,372 statements. More specifically, each user provides ratings for users (1 and -1 for trusted and distrusted users respectively) and ratings for the reviews written by other users (ranging from 1 to 6). Finally, the dataset contains information about the author and subject of each review, thus, giving us evidence on the interests of each author.

We model our social graph as follows: The users are the nodes, and the user ratings are the permanent links of the network, used to define the circle-of-trust of each user. The article ratings are considered as the transient expressions of trust or influence. During the preprocessing phase, we kept the 717,667 positive trust ratings and removed self-references, i.e., statements about users trusting themselves.

We divided the dataset in three distinct subsets: (a) one that includes users with a narrow circle-of-trust (set A: users having between 5 and 10 outlinks), (b) one

[2]http://www.trustlet.org/wiki

that includes users with a medium-sized circle-of-trust (set B: users having 15–25 outlinks) and (c) one that includes users with an extended circle-of-trust (set C: users having more than 30 outlinks). Sets A and C are of equal size (set A contains 5,425 and set C contains 5,405 users) but significantly differ in the connectivity of their nodes. The size of set B is 2,349.

As mentioned in the introduction, depending on the nature of each social network, the proposed model can be appropriately adapted to provide users with personalized recommendations that correspond to trustful or influential users. In the context of the *Epinions* network, user-to-user links express the trust between users, and user-to-item links imply the interest of a user to a specific item, formulating a network of trust among users. A recommendation for a user U_i of this network will be a set of users U that U_i can trust. Since *Epinions* is a buyers' network, recommending user U_j to user U_i based on the analysis of the graph means that U_i can trust U_j's opinion and product reviews. As a result, we expect a big overlap in the lists of items bought (or reviewed) by U_i and U_j. Thus, in order to evaluate our approach, we examine whether the users recommended to U_i (users in U) have matching interests with U_i.

The similarity between two users U_i and U_j is defined as the number of items rated by U_i that have been also rated by U_j. This measure is similar to the bibliographic measure of *coupling* which is based on the number of common references between two users. We compute the average similarity between U_i and the top-k recommended users of each ranking and compare it to the baseline T, which is the average similarity between U_i and the users U_t to whom U_i is connected via an explicit trust link ($(U_i, U_t) \in E$).

The first experiment, examines the effect of the memory size to the performance of the accumulative local model. In the subsequent experiments, we first evaluate each model (namely, the local, the collaborative local, and each one of the global influence models) individually (setting the respective weight in Eq. (3.12) to 1 and the remaining weights to 0). Based on the results of this experiment, which show that the collaborative local model outperforms the local one, we combine the collaborative local model with each of the global influence models (setting equal weights for w_{collab} and w_{global} and $w_{local} = 0$ in Eq. (3.14)). Finally, based on our findings, we combine those global influence models that performed better in the second step with the collaborative local models. The detailed weight values for this experiment are explained in Sect. 3.5.5. We performed each set of experiments for all sets of users.

3.5.1 The Effect of Memory in the Accumulative Local Model

In the first experiment, we examine how the memory size affects the performance of the accumulative local model. For this reason, we vary the memory size m between 0 and 15 months, which means that we do not take into account links that have been issued before the last m months in the dataset. For a memory size m and a link issued in period t ($t \in [c - m + 1, c]$) the freshness-related weight w_t for the

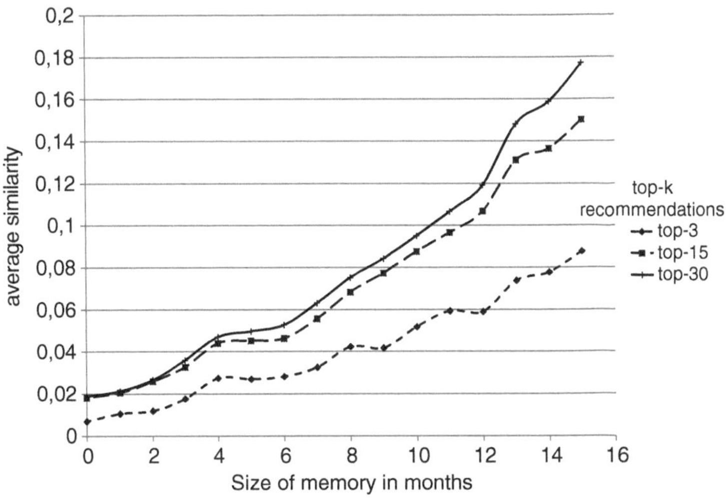

Fig. 3.1 The effect of links' freshness and memory size in the performance of the local accumulative score (*LAS*)

current period c is given by Eq. (3.9). We employ the users in set B and generate for each user U a ranked list of recommended users, using the local accumulative (L) formation. The average similarity is measured for all users in set-C compared against the top-k users in the recommendation list after removing the current friends of each user. Experimental results on sets A and C have been omitted, since these two sets contain users either with too few trusted users (set A), which results in very few fresh links or with too many trusted users (set C), which results in huge lists of links.

In Fig. 3.1, we present the performance curves for the top-3, top-15 and top-30 users. All intermediate curves (top-5, top-10 etc.) have been omitted, to improve readability of the chart. However, they all fall between the top-3 and top-30 curves depicted in Fig. 3.1. All curves show that an increase in memory size results in an increase to the average similarity. An interpretation of the results is that the use of a user's rating history can improve the performance of the accumulative local metric. The role of link weighting, according to Eq. (3.9), is crucial, since it prioritizes the fresh links and punishes obsolete ones. For example, recommendations from a friend that has been added a year ago, and whose rating has never been updated again (e.g. with a "like" link), will receive lower values than recommendations from a friend that has been added recently. In this way, we manage to provide recommendations that reflect the recent activity of each user.

In all the following experiments, we decide to use the complete recommendation history for articles and authors. Although it is more expensive, it can significantly boost the system performance as will be demonstrated in the following paragraphs. For example, keeping only the links to authors and articles that have been created in the last 15 months (m = 15) results in ignoring more than 50 % of the link information of the dataset, since more than half of the article links are older than 15 months. As a consequence, the performance of the local accumulative formation measured using average similarity (as depicted in Fig. 3.1) ranges between 0.02 and 0.18, whereas in all the experiments that follow it is constantly above 0.20.

3.5.2 Evaluation of the Individual Models

In the second experiment, we generate for each user U (member of sets A, B and C respectively) a ranked list of recommended users, using the local accumulative (L) and the collaborative local (CL) formation. We also generate the overall (global) rankings of all users using each centrality metric (*Gd* using degree centrality, *Gc* using closeness centrality, *Gb* using betweenness centrality, *Gh* using hub score, *Ga* using authority score and *Gp* using PageRank score). We then select the top-k users from each list. These are the recommended users.

The following Figs. 3.2–3.13 show the similarity between a user and the users in the top-k positions of the recommendations' list. As explained previously, similarity is measured in terms of commonalities, i.e. of items that have been rated by both the user and a user in his/her top-k list. When the top-k list contains users with similar interests, the similarity is expected to increase for higher k values, because the number of items that have been rated by both the user and a user in the list is expected to increase. When the top-k list contains users with completely dissimilar interests, the similarity will remain stable. The y-axis in all the following figures is labeled "average similarity", because it averages the similarity values of all users in the examined set.

A reference ranking is not available so we cannot measure the correlation with our rankings (using Spearman's ρ or Kendall's τ). Golden standards (lists of correct and incorrect recommendations per user) are not available too, so we cannot measure performance using IR metrics in our top-k lists. The use of blind user testing is not feasible in this scale, so we decided to comparatively evaluate our approaches. A standard baseline for comparison could be to recommend to each user k randomly selected users from the epinion dataset. However, this *random* baseline results in very low average similarity values, and is not helpful for comparison. The users who already are in the friend list of a user constitute a more antagonistic baseline for our methods, which is identified as T in Figs. 3.2–3.7 and 3.11–3.13. When a method outperforms T in a certain k value, it means that the top-k users in the corresponding recommendation list have more similarities with the target user, than his/her own friends.

Figure 3.2 presents the average similarity values for the top-k matches ($k =$ 3, 5, 7, 10, 15, 20, 25, 30) for set A, which comprises users with few trusted nodes. Figure 3.3 refers to members of set B, who have between 15 and 25 direct neighbors, whereas Fig. 3.4 shows users of set C, who have many trusted nodes in their circle.

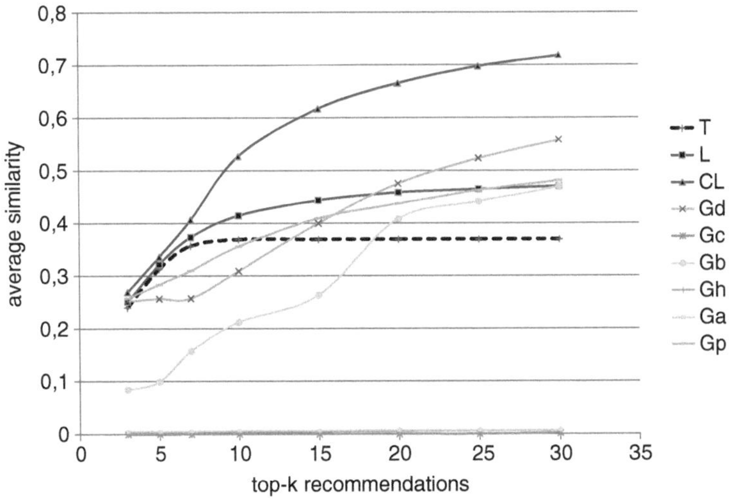

Fig. 3.2 Comparison of the local, collaborative and individual global rating models for users with few trusted nodes (set A)

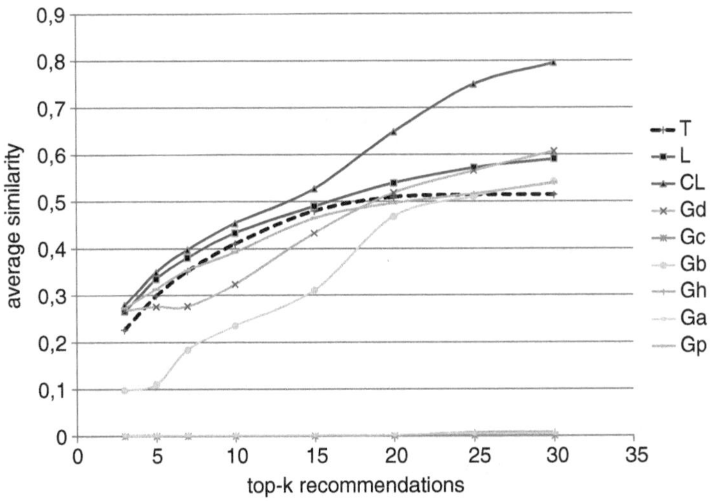

Fig. 3.3 Comparison of the local, collaborative and individual global rating models for users with many trusted nodes (set B)

From the results presented in Figs. 3.2–3.4 we observe that the collaborative local model (*CL*) significantly improves the performance of the baseline (*T*), especially for users with a small circle of trust (set A). This implies that it is useful for a recommendation model to check for suggestions beyond the direct neighbors of a node, in the extended neighborhood of users (in terms of links of trust).

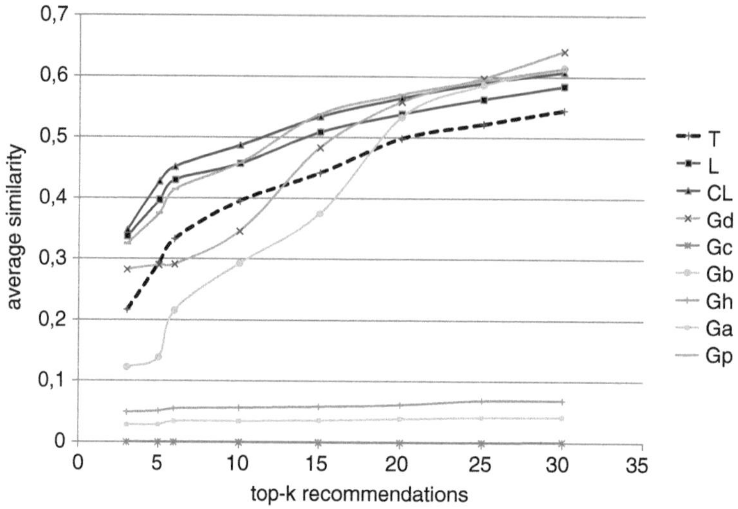

Fig. 3.4 Comparison of the local, collaborative and individual global rating models for users with too many trusted nodes (set C)

On the contrary, the performance of the global rating models is comparable or even worse than the baseline. In several cases (i.e. when hub, authority or centrality are employed) the performance reaches zero. This means that there are no similarities between the user's likes and those of the top ranked users in the whole network.

On the other hand, for users with more neighbors (sets B and C), certain global models (i.e. degree, betweenness and PageRank) perform better than local models when the top-k recommendations are examined. An explanation of this is that users in set B and even more in set C have many direct or indirect neighbors so these users are probably connected to some of the highly connected users of the graph, who also have a high global rating. This is an indication that global rating models in general and "influential" or "central" users can be valuable resources for a recommendation engine, mainly in the absence of local sources of recommendation. Such models can be used to address the "cold-start" problem, in which a user is new and hasn't yet formed a network of trust. The results also indicate that the three aforementioned global rating models perform better than the remaining global models.

This behavior of the global rating models was anticipated, since, even the top-*k* users are influential, they do not affect the whole network (especially when a network comprises of thousands of users, as in the *Epinions* case). Thus a recommendation engine might not benefit by looking at such metrics alone, without taking into consideration the direct network of each user. However, some models are able to discover powerful "influentials" and can be combined with collaborative local models. All other global models confuse rather than assist the recommendation engine.

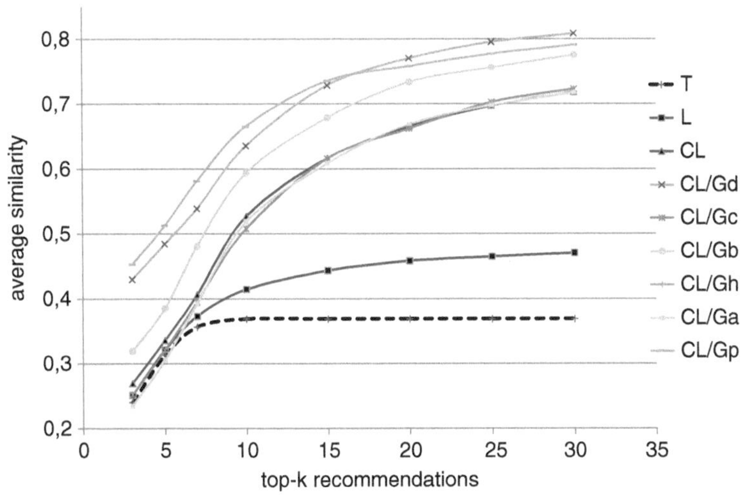

Fig. 3.5 Comparison of the combination of individual global rating models with the collaborative local model for users with few trusted nodes (set A)

The comparison of results for sets A, B and C shows a higher baseline for set C, where users have many trusted users and thus a lot of recommendations to choose from. The local and collaborative local models manage to further improve performance. The results for users in set B are similar, with the baseline ranging from 0.22 to 0.51 and the collaborative local ranging from 0.28 to 0.79 for k=3 and k=30 respectively.

Based on the aforementioned results, it is expected that the quality of recommendations is better when they are based on local sources than on globally "influential" nodes. The boost is bigger for smaller values of k, which means that the local models are able to distill the long lists of trusted users and find the most influential users in each circle of trust.

3.5.3 Combination of Collaborative Local and Global Models

Based on the results of our first set of experiments, we decide to combine the collaborative local model with each of the global models. Although the outcome of the experiments showed that only some of the models perform well, we experiment with all combinations of collaborative local with each global model. We assign equal weights to the collaborative local and each of the global scores and evaluate the respective top-k lists. The comparative results are depicted in Figs. 3.5–3.7. They present the average similarity values for all users in each set (Fig. 3.5 for set A, Fig. 3.6 for set B and Fig. 3.7 for set C), comparing each user with the top-k recommended users ($k = 3, 5, 7, 10, 15, 20, 25, 30$) when ranked using the

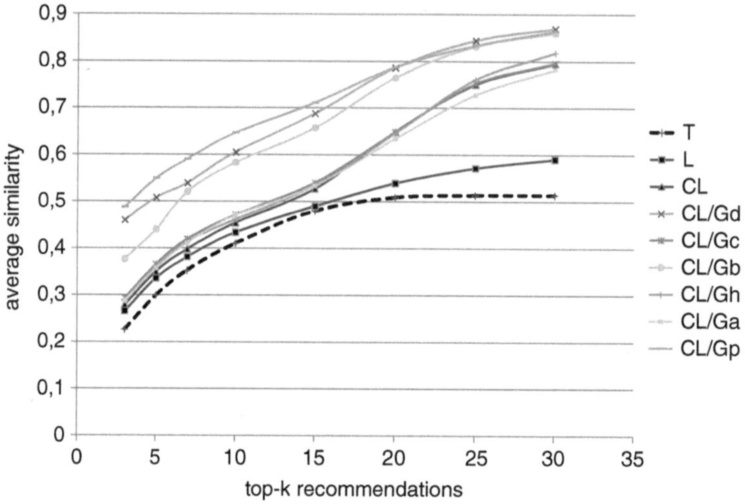

Fig. 3.6 Comparison of the combination of individual global rating models with the collaborative local model for users with many trusted nodes (set B)

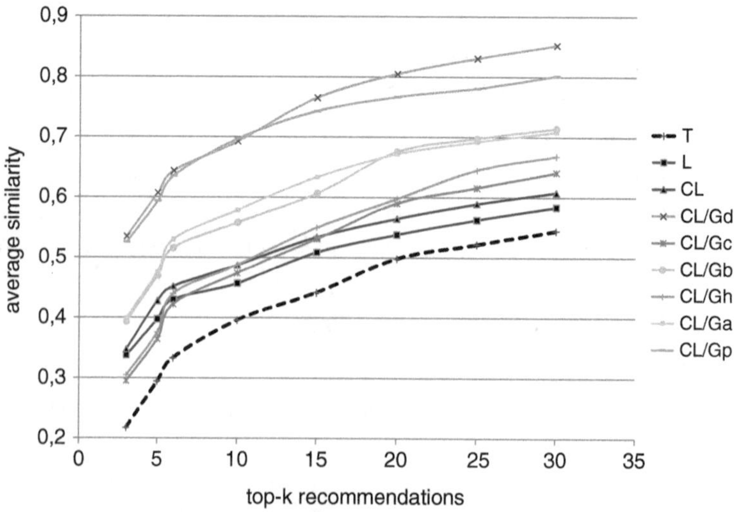

Fig. 3.7 Comparison of the combination of individual global rating models with the collaborative local model for users with too many trusted nodes (set C)

collaborative local model (*CLS* of Eq. 3.10) with $w_{CLS}= 0.5$ and each one of the global influence measures (*Gd*, *Gc*, *Gb*, *Gh*, *Ga*, *Gp* in Eq. 3.12) with $w_x= 0.5$ (where $w_x \in \{w_d, w_c, w_b, w_h, w_a, w_p\}$). For example the value for CL/Gd and $k = 3$ represents the average similarity between a user i and the top-3 users with the highest weighted combination of degree centrality rating and collaborative local rating using w_d=0.5 and w_{CLS}= 0.5.

Results in Figs. 3.5–3.7 show that highly ranked users (i.e. influential users) may provide additional recommendations which are useful to all authors. Several metrics, such as hub, authority and closeness provide little improvement compared to the collaborative local model. However, degree (CL/Gd), PageRank (CL/Gp) and betweenness (CL/Gb) have further improved the recommendations of the collaborative local model for all the different k values. The average improvement for all the values of k is in average 0.12, 0.13 and 0.06 for (CL/Gd), (CL/Gp) and (CL/Gb) respectively. This strengthens our initial belief that global rating models can address the "cold-start" problem, especially when the recommendations coming from globally influential users are combined with those coming from the few people that a user trusts. The results are in accordance to those of the first set of experiments, where PageRank, betweenness and degree centrality outperformed all other global rating models.

More specifically, when we compare the results for the three sets (A, B and C) for the two sets of experiments, we notice that:

- The local methods (local and collaborative local) demonstrate slightly improved results for set C in comparison to set A (average improvement is 0.037)
- The combined methods further increase this improvement (average improvement for PageRank and degree is 0.05)
- The improvement is smaller for users in set B (users with 15–25 links) when compared to users of set A (average improvement is 0.035 and 0.018 for the local and combined methods respectively).

3.5.4 *Effect of Individual Global Influence Models to the Collaborative Local Model*

In an attempt to further improve our results, we combine the local with multiple global models using weighted combinations. However, in order to better understand the influence of each global metric to the collaborative local decisions, we first perform an extended evaluation of the combinations of collaborative local and a single global metric. We decide to evaluate only PageRank, Degree and Betweeness, which are the ones with the stronger influence as shown in Figs. 3.5–3.7. We provide results only for set B, which contains users with 15–25 outlinks (trusted friends).

In the previous set of experiments, we combined each individual global influence score with the collaborative local score using equal weights. For example, the combination of the collaborative local metric with PageRank corresponds to $w_{collab} = 0.5$ and $w_{global} = 0.5$ in Eq. (3.14) and $w_p = 1, w_d = w_c = w_b = w_h = w_a = 0$ in Eq. (3.12). In this step, we employ only a percentage of the global influence score (provided by PageRank, Degree or Betweenness) ranging from 10 to 100 %. For example, the combination of the collaborative local metric with a

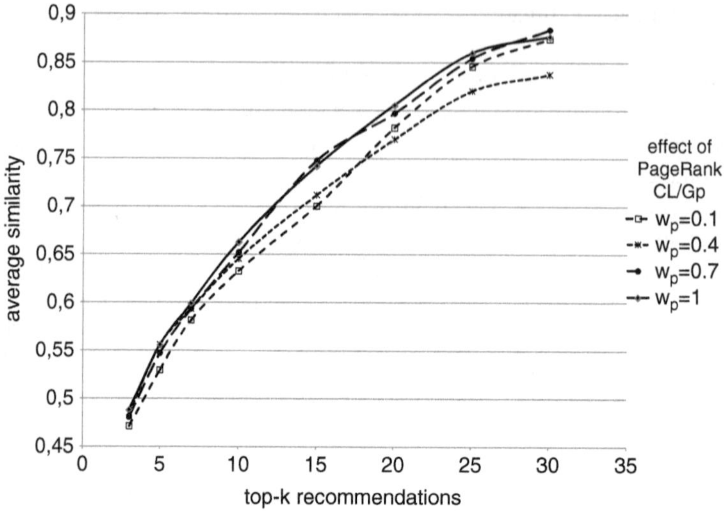

Fig. 3.8 The effect of PageRank-based global influence on the collaborative model (set B)

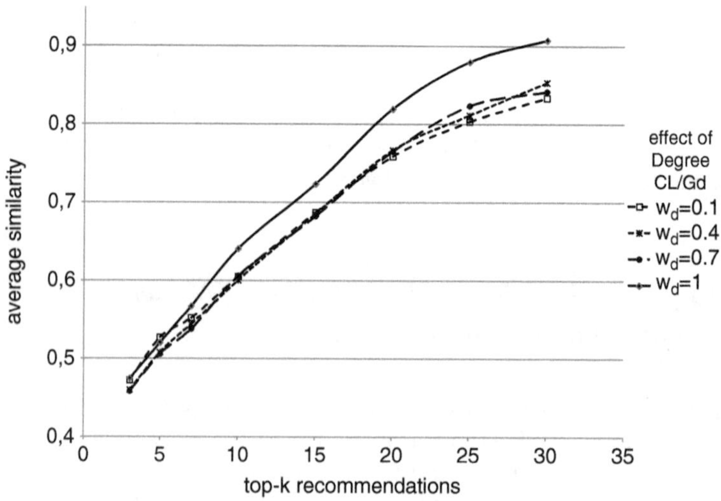

Fig. 3.9 The effect of Degree-based global influence on the collaborative model (set B)

10% of PageRank corresponds to $w_{collab} = 0.5$ and $w_{global} = 0.5$ in Eq. (3.14) and $w_p = 0.1, w_d = w_c = w_b = w_h = w_a = 0$ in Eq. (3.12). The results are depicted in Figs. 3.8 (PageRank), 3.9 (Degree) and 3.10 (Betweenness). For readability reasons, we only show the results for combinations of the global and collaborative local scores with $w_i \in \{0.1, 0.4, 0.7, 1\}$.

The results show that PageRank contributes more to the overall performance when its percentage is high (close to 100%). Similarly, Degree reaches its top

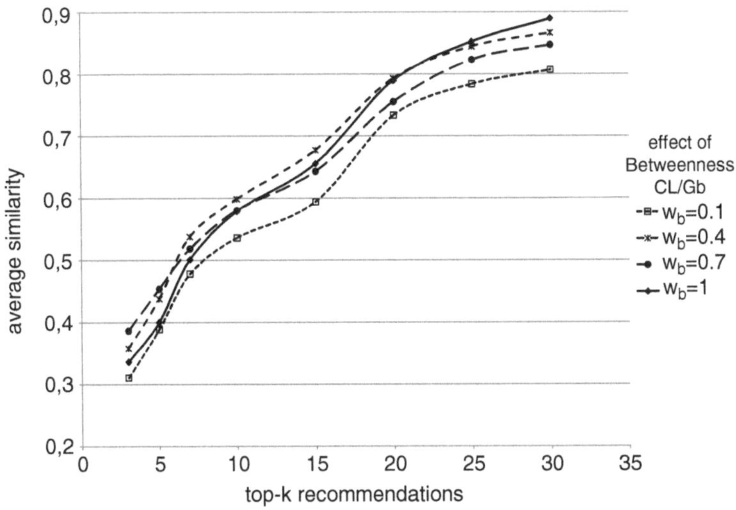

Fig. 3.10 The effect of Betweenness-based global influence on the collaborative model (set B)

performance when its percentage is 100 %, whereas Betweenness performs better for lower percentage values (e.g. 40 %). These are indications that in a combined global influence metric, the weights of the individual global metrics must vary in order to achieve maximum performance. Based on the results of this section, in the following step, we test different combinations of the three (or two) aforementioned global metrics with the collaborative local model using different ratios for each metric.

3.5.5 Combination of Multiple Collaborative Local and Global Models

In the previous steps, we evaluated each individual global rating model combined with the collaborative local model. The degree, PageRank and betweenness showed the highest performance improvement, so we combine these metrics using Eq. (3.12) and produce a single combined global rating for each user. We further combine this rating with the collaborative local rating (using w_{CLS}=0.5 and w_{global} =0.5) and produce the final rating for each user.

In Figs. 3.11–3.13 we present the results of the baseline T versus the local L, collaborative local CL and six combinations of the collaborative local rating with a combined global rating for user sets A, B and C respectively. We evaluate the following combinations of global metrics: ($CL/GdGbGp$) with emphasis on the PageRank metric ($w_d = 0.2$, $w_b = 0.2$, $w_p = 0.6$), ($CL/GdGbGp(2)$) using

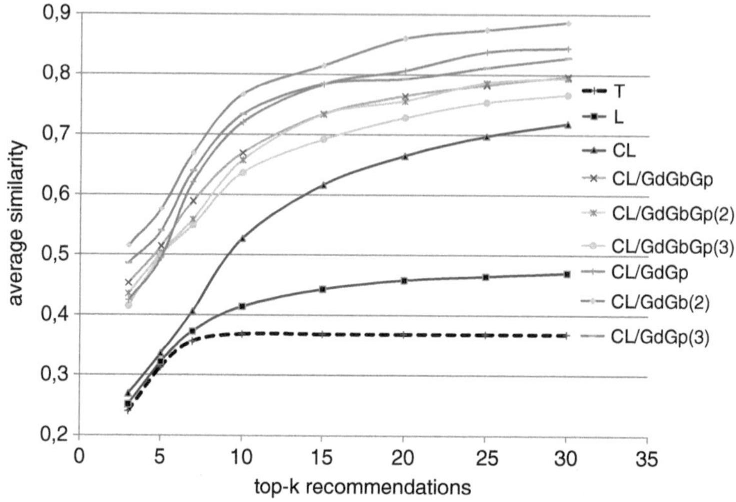

Fig. 3.11 Collaborative local plus combo of global models (set A)

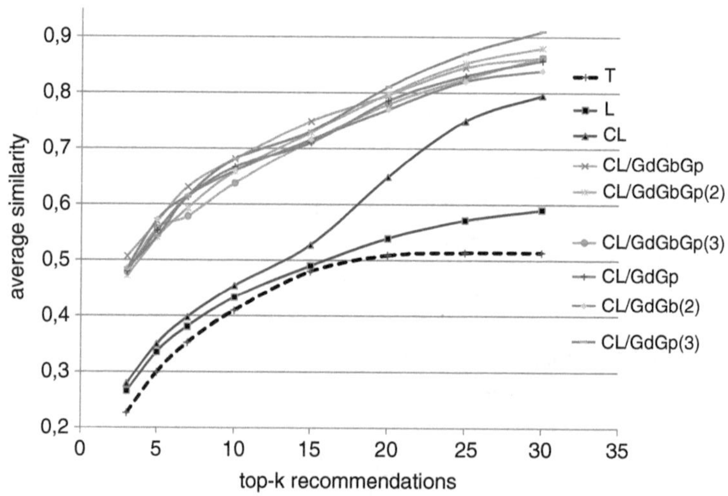

Fig. 3.12 Collaborative local plus combo of global models (set B)

equal weights ($w_d = 1/3$, $w_b = 1/3$, $w_p = 1/3$), $CL/GdGbGp(3)$ with ($w_d = 0.2$, $w_b = 0.4$, $w_p = 0.4$), $(GL/GdGp)$ with ($w_d = 0.5$, $w_p = 0.5$), $CL/GdGp(2)$ with ($w_d = 1/3$, $w_p = 2/3$) and $CL/GdGp(3)$ with ($w_d = 2/3$, $w_p = 1/3$).

The results show that most of the combinations improve the results of the baseline and the collaborative local model with the combinations of PageRank and degree to outperform all other combinations. However only the combinations of

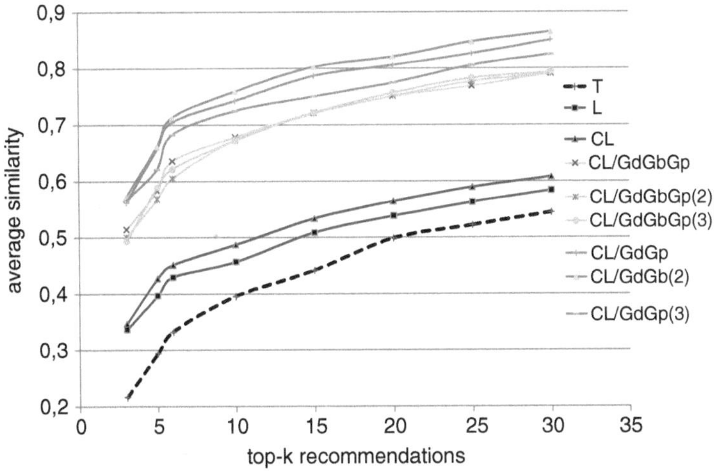

Fig. 3.13 Collaborative local plus combo of global models (set C)

the combined PageRank and Degree metrics (i.e. the best global metrics in the previous experiments) manage to further improve the results of the combinations of collaborative local and a single global measure.

Our overall observation based on this experimental evaluation is that the combination of centrality and prestige metrics cannot outperform local metrics in providing recommendations for a specific user. However they can improve the performance of a recommendation engine when combined with collaborative local metrics. Finally, our findings in the performance of combinations of global metrics is that, depending on the nature of the social network and the weights' setup, it is possible to further improve the recommendation engine performance.

3.6 Conclusions and Future Work

In this work we studied the contribution of various measures in identifying trustworthy or influential actors in a social network in order to recommend them to a specific user. The actors can be users, blogs, or tweets. The measures take into consideration the opinion/trust of the actor for other actors, the opinion/trust of the actor's network of trust, and the overall ranking of all actors, as computed by their position and interconnections in a graph.

Global metrics can be easily manipulated with the creation of fake users and fake links (e.g. Google bombing). On the other hand, local trust metrics are more resistant to attacks, since users get recommendations only from users of trust and ignore the artificially created spam users and their links. A disadvantage of local trust metrics is that they do not apply to the new members of a social network, who have not formed a network of trust yet. The use of global metrics can be beneficial for those users, since it recommends users with raised global influence. Of course, the risk of recommending spam users to the new members of the network exists, but is quickly balanced, as soon as the user starts to add friends. The combination of local and global methods can help us tackle the shortcomings of each separate approach and improve the recommendations' quality.

Our model extends our previous work that generated personalized recommendations based on the network of trust, by incorporating global measures of influence and the notion of time "freshness" of the various user connections. We experimentally compared and evaluated various models, along with several combinations of them. The results showed that global measures are not very useful by themselves in providing recommendations to users, however, when combined with the collaborative local measures, they have a positive impact in the final recommendation set. In the future, we plan to extend our model and study the negative influence as expressed with negative values for trust. Finally, although the aforementioned model is meant to be used offline, it is on our plans to study the complexity of the different measures, a topic of great practical importance in case this model would be adjusted to run for large datasets and/or generate real-time recommendations.

References

1. Adar, E., Zhang, L., Adamic, L.A., Lukose, R.M.: Implicit structure and the dynamics of blogspace. In: Workshop on the Weblogging Ecosystem at the 13th International World Wide Web Conference, New York (2004)
2. Agarwal, N., Liu, H., Tang, L., Yu, P.S.: Identifying the influential bloggers in a community. In: WSDM '08: Proceedings of the International Conference on Web Search and Web Data Mining, pp. 207–218. ACM, New York (2008)
3. Akritidis, L., Katsaros, D., Bozanis, P.: Identifying influential bloggers: time does matter. In: Proceedings of the 2009 IEEE/WIC/ACM International Joint Conference on Web Intelligence and Intelligent Agent Technology, WI-IAT '09, vol. 1, pp. 76–83. IEEE Computer Society, Washington (2009)
4. Bonanich, P.: Power and centrality: a family of measures. Am. J. Sociol. **5**(92), 1170–1182 (1987)
5. Domingos, P., Richardson, M.: Mining the network value of customers. In: KDD '01: Proceedings of the Seventh ACM SIGKDD International Conference on Knowledge Discovery and Data Mining, pp. 57–66. ACM, New York (2001)
6. Estévez, P.A., Vera, P.A., Saito, K.: Selecting the most influential nodes in social networks. In: The International Joint Conference on Neural Networks, IJCNN. IEEE, Piscataway (2007)
7. Freeman, L.: A set of measures of centrality based on betweenness. Sociometry **40**(1), 35–41 (1977)
8. Freeman, L.: Centrality in social networks: Conceptual clarification. Soc. Netw. **3**(1), 215–239 (1979)
9. Golbeck, J.: Generating predictive movie recommendations from trust in social networks. In: Stølen, K., Winsborough, W.H., Martinelli, F., Massacci, F. (eds.) Proceedings of the 4th International Conference on Trust Management (iTrust). Lecture Notes in Computer Science, pp. 93–104. Springer, Berlin (2006)
10. Golbeck, J.: Trust on the world wide web: a survey. Found. Trend Web Sci. **1**, 131–197 (2006)

11. Golbeck, J.: Trust and nuanced profile similarity in online social networks. ACM Trans. Web **3**, 12:1–12:33 (2009)
12. Guha, S., Koudas, N., Marathe, A., Srivastava, D.: Merging the results of approximate match operations. In: Proceedings of the Thirtieth International Conference on Very Large Data Bases, VLDB '04, Toronto, vol. 30, pp. 636–647. VLDB Endowment, Morgan Kaufmann Publishers, St. Louis (2004)
13. Guha, R., Kumar, R., Raghavan, P., Tomkins, A.: Propagation of trust and distrust. In: Proceedings of the 13th International Conference on World Wide Web, WWW '04, pp. 403–412. ACM, New York (2004)
14. Hoi, S.C.H., Jin, R.: Semi-supervised ensemble ranking. In: Proceedings of the 23rd National Conference on Artificial Intelligence, vol. 2, pp. 634–639. AAAI Press, Menlo Park (2008)
15. Kamvar, S.D., Schlosser, M.T., Garcia-Molina, H.: The eigentrust algorithm for reputation management in p2p networks. In: Proceedings of the 12th International Conference on World Wide Web, WWW '03, pp. 640–651. ACM, New York (2003)
16. Kempe, D., Kleinberg, J., Tardos, E.: Maximizing the spread of influence through a social network. In: Proceedings of the Ninth ACM SIGKDD International Conference on Knowledge Discovery and Data Mining, KDD '03, pp. 137–146. ACM, New York (2003)
17. Kim, E.S., Han, S.S.: An analytical way to find influencers on social networks and validate their effects in disseminating social games. In: Proceedings of the 2009 International Conference on Advances in Social Network Analysis and Mining, pp. 41–46. IEEE Computer Society, Washington, DC (2009)
18. Kimura, M., Saito, K., Nakano, R.: Extracting influential nodes for information diffusion on a social network. In: Proceedings of the 22nd National Conference on Artificial Intelligence, Vol. 2, pp. 1371–1376. AAAI Press, Menlo Park (2007)
19. Kimura, M., Yamakawa, K., Saito, K., Motoda, H.: Community analysis of influential nodes for information diffusion on a social network. In: The International Joint Conference on Neural Networks, IJCNN. IEEE, Piscataway (2008)
20. Kleinberg, J.: Authoritative sources in a hyperlinked environment. J. ACM **46**(5), 604–632 (1999)
21. Kritikopoulos, A., Sideri, M., Varlamis, I.: Blogrank: ranking blogs based on connectivity and similarity features. In: Proceedings of the 2nd International Workshop on Advanced Architectures and Algorithms for Internet Delivery and Applications AAA-IDEA'06. ACM, New York (2006)
22. Liu, B.: Web Data Mining. Exploring Hyperlinks, Contents, and Usage Data. Springer, Berlin (2007)
23. Louta, M., Varlamis, I.: Blog rating as an iterative collaborative process. In: Wallace, M., et al. (eds.) Semantics in Adaptive and Personalized Services. Springer Series on Studies in Computational Intelligence SCI 279, pp. 187–203. Springer, Berlin/Heidelberg (2010)
24. Massa, P., Avesani, P.: Controversial users demand local trust metrics: an experimental study on epinions.com community. In: Proceedings of the 20th National Conference on Artificial Intelligence (AAAI-05). AAAI, Menlo Park (2005)
25. Massa, P., Avesani, P.: Trust metrics on controversial users: balancing between tyranny of the majority and echo chambers. Int J. Semant. Web Inf. Syst. **3**, 39–64 (2007)
26. Massa, P., Avesani, P.: Trust metrics in recommender systems. In: Golbeck, J. (ed.) Computing with Social Trust, Chap. 10. Springer, London (2009)
27. Nakajima, S., Tatemura, J., Hino, Y., Hara, Y., Tanaka, K.: Discovering important bloggers based on analyzing blog threads. In: 2nd Annual Workshop on the Blogging Ecosystem: Aggregation, Analysis and Dynamics, Chiba, Japan, May 10–14, (2005)
28. O'Donovan, J.: Capturing trust in social web applications. In: Golbeck, J. (ed.) Computing with Social Trust, Chap. 9. Springer, London (2009)
29. Page, L., Brin, S., Motwani, R., Winograd, T.: The pagerank citation ranking: bringing order to the web. Technical report. Stanford InfoLab (1998). http://ilpubs.stanford.edu:8090/422/1/1999-66.pdf

30. Richardson, M., Domingos, P.: Mining knowledge-sharing sites for viral marketing. In: Proceedings of the 8th ACM SIGKDD International Conference on Knowledge Discovery and Data Mining, KDD '02, pp. 61–70. ACM, New York (2002)
31. Song, X., Chi, Y., Hino, K., Tseng, B.: Identifying opinion leaders in the blogosphere. In: Proceedings of the 16th ACM conference on Conference on Information and Knowledge Management, CIKM '07, pp. 971–974. ACM, New York (2007)
32. Varlamis, I., Louta, M.: Towards a personalized blog site recommendation system: a collaborative rating approach. The International IEEE Workshop on Semantic Media Adaptation and Personalization, SMAP, San Sebastián, Spain, December 14–15, (2009)
33. Varlamis, I., Eirinaki, M., Louta, M.: A study on social network metrics and their application in trust networks. In: Proceedings of the 2010 International Conference on Advances in Social Networks Analysis and Mining, ASONAM '10, pp. 168–175. IEEE Computer Society, Washington, DC (2010)
34. Wasserman, S., Faust, K.: Social Network Analysis. Cambridge University Press, Cambridge/New York (1994)
35. Weng, J., Lim, E.P., Jiang, J., He, Q.: Twitterrank: finding topic-sensitive influential twitterers. In: Proceedings of the third ACM international conference on Web search and data mining, WSDM '10, pp. 261–270. ACM, New York (2010)
36. Ziegler, C.N.: On propagating interpersonal trust in social networks. In: Golbeck, J. (ed.) Computing with Social Trust, Chap. 6. Springer, London (2009)
37. Ziegler, C.N., Lausen, G.: Spreading activation models for trust propagation. In: Proceedings of the 2004 IEEE International Conference on e-Technology, e-Commerce and e-Service (EEE'04), pp. 83–97. IEEE Computer Society, Washington, DC (2004)

Chapter 4
TweCoM: Topic and Context Mining from Twitter

Luca Cagliero and Alessandro Fiori

Abstract Social networks and online communities are taking a primary role in enabling communication and content sharing (e.g., posts, documents, photos, videos) among Web users. Knowledge discovery from user-generated content is becoming an increasingly appealing research context. Many different approaches have been devoted to addressing this issue.

This chapter proposes the TweCoM (Tweet Context Miner) framework which entails the mining of relevant recurrences from the content and the context in which Twitter messages (i.e., tweets) are posted. The framework combines two main efforts: (i) the automatic generation of taxonomies from both post content and contextual features, and (ii) the extraction of hidden correlations by means of generalized association rule mining. Since generalized association rule mining is commonly driven by user-provided taxonomies, discovered recurrences are often unsatisfactory. To overcome this issue, two different taxonomy inference procedures have been applied, depending on the kind of information. In particular, relationships holding in context data provided by Twitter are exploited to automatically construct aggregation hierarchies over contextual features, while a hierarchical clustering algorithm is exploited to build a taxonomy over most relevant tweet content keywords. To counteract the excessive level of detail of the extracted information, conceptual aggregations (i.e., generalizations) of concepts hidden in the analyzed data are exploited in the association rule mining process. The extraction of generalized association rules allows discovering high level recurrences by evaluating the extracted taxonomies. Experiments performed on real Twitter

L. Cagliero (✉)
Politecnico di Torino, Corso Duca degli Abruzzi, 24 10129 Torino, Italy
e-mail: luca.cagliero@polito.it

A. Fiori
IRC@C: Institute for Cancer Research at Candiolo, Str. Prov. 142 Km. 3.95 10060 - Candiolo (TO) - Italy
e-mail: alessandro.fiori@ircc.it

T. Özyer et al. (eds.), *The Influence of Technology on Social Network Analysis and Mining*, Lecture Notes in Social Networks 6, DOI 10.1007/978-3-7091-1346-2_4,

posts show the effectiveness and the efficiency of the proposed framework in analyzing tweet content and related context as well as highlighting relevant trends in tweet propagation.

4.1 Introduction

Social networks are becoming one of the most commonly used resources to communicate news or share documents, photos, and videos with a large community. Social networks sites, such as Facebook or Twitter, are accessed by millions of people every day. The huge amount of data generated by social network users represents a powerful source of knowledge to support the investigation of different aspects of online social communities. Recently, many different research efforts have been devoted to exploiting user-generated content (UGC) to define user profiles and behaviors, mine opinions about products, and define models to represent the shared knowledge. Different applications are based on these studies. For instance, online communities have been exploited in recommender systems to either suggest new products to their customers (e.g., books, CDs, movies) or enhance the quality of the offered services [13, 21, 31, 38]. The study and the extraction of knowledge stored in the user-generated content is a very interesting and challenging research topic. A large variety of media data (e.g., documents, photos, videos, tags, news) is suitable for effectively supporting semantics-based knowledge representations (e.g., taxonomies, ontologies) and building models to classify new media content. For instance, ontology extraction from the infoboxes of Wikipedia has been thoroughly investigated (e.g., [17]).

The aim of this chapter is to present the TweCoM (Tweet Context Miner) framework that addresses the discovery, by means of generalized association rule mining, of information hidden in short messages posted on Twitter, which is one of the most famous social networks. Generalized association rule mining has been introduced in [33] in the context of market basket analysis. It aggregates concepts at higher levels of abstraction by exploiting a taxonomy (i.e., is-a hierarchy) built over data items. To efficiently accomplish this task, we follow a support-driven approach, first proposed in [5], to pattern generalization, i.e., we generalize a pattern only if it is infrequent with respect to the minimum support threshold. The framework focuses on discovering knowledge of interest from Twitter messages by also considering the impact of knowledge propagation. To achieve this goal, it retrieves and categorizes tweets by following the sequence of responses/citations to an initial set of tweets of highest interest (i.e., the toptweets). Unlike traditional approaches to generalized rule mining, which commonly rely on user-provided taxonomies, the TweCoM framework automatically builds different taxonomies according to the type of analyzed data feature. Depending on the kind of information, two different approaches have been proposed. A hierarchical clustering algorithm is exploited to build a tree-based hierarchy over most relevant tweet content keywords, while a set of aggregation functions defined on the structure of the tweet contextual knowledge is employed to aggregate temporal and spatial concepts into higher level ones.

Finally, the framework allows effectively querying the extracted association rules according to either the schema or the content of the mined patterns. An example of application context in which the TweCoM framework may effectively support domain expert analysis is the investigation of most relevant trends in tweet content propagation. The proposed approach may be employed to effectively discover and select strong high level recurrences hidden in tweet contents. The user may get more benefits from the generalized associations mined from topical and contextual features (i.e., space, time and keywords) by analyzing their variations, in terms of their quality indexes, in the sequence of responses/citations. Moreover, the rule selection step, supported by the TweCoM rule query engine, prevents experts from looking into a huge amount of uninteresting rules. Examples of use cases for the presented framework are reported in Sect. 4.4.

This chapter is organized as follows. Section 4.2 overviews most relevant related works concerning data mining from online communities, taxonomy inference, and generalized association rule mining. Section 4.3 presents the architecture of the proposed framework and describes its main blocks. Section 4.4 assesses the effectiveness of the TweCoM framework in extracting hidden information from Twitter posts, while Sect. 4.5 draws conclusions and presents future developments of this work.

4.2 Previous Works

In last years, online communities have shown a steadfast growth. Community users continuously produce a huge amount of heterogeneous data. The user-generated content (UGC) has taken a significant role in the Internet culture by allowing the establishment of novel forms of social behavior. Thus, many research efforts have been devoted to studying the characteristics and the propagation of the UGC. This section reviews previous works concerning the application of data mining techniques to online communities. Moreover, it overviews most relevant literature concerning both generalized rule mining algorithms and taxonomy inference techniques with the aim at providing a strong foundation on the data mining approaches employed in the proposed framework.

4.2.1 Data Mining from Online Communities

Online communities provide a powerful resource suitable for discovering relevant social knowledge by means of data mining algorithms and tools tailored to most common user interests. In the last years, many different research efforts have been devoted to (i) developing new recommender systems to enhance the quality of product suggestions to the customers, (ii) improving the understanding of online resources by means of the categorization of UGC, and (iii) building query engines that take advantage of emerging semantics in social networks. For example, recommender systems are focused on identifying the objects (e.g., products, news) that highlight the highest correlation with the user behavior and preferences. Different approaches have been proposed according to the features employed to characterize the users and the items to be suggested. In [38] a news recommendation system that takes into account the opinion of readers is discussed. For each news discussion thread that has been posted on a social bookmarking site a topic profile is built. An extension of the previous approach exploited a graph-based representation to model the content similarity between comments and logic relationships among them [21]. In [27], authors proposed to combine RSS news and UGC coming from microblogs to recommend news. They mined Twitter message content to identify emerging topics and breaking events. Moreover, RSS stories have been ranked based on a weighted scoring that considers the Lucene tf-idf score of each article term. Finally, the information provided by tweets is exploited to adjust the rank of RSS news feeds in order to promote topical articles.

Recommendation systems can be also exploited to enhance the quality of tags by analyzing the interest of a single user and/or the trend of social communities. For example, in [6] a classification system identified the documents and the associated tags that are more likely to be of user interest. Differently, in [31] the authors exploited a hierarchical clustering algorithm to identify the correlations among groups of tags in order to reduce tag redundancy and ambiguity. To improve the quality of suggested tags for photo annotation, [32] proposed a method based on two steps. Given a photo with user-defined tags, for each tag an ordered list of candidate tags is first provided based on co-occurrence measure. Next, the lists of candidate tags are aggregated to generate a ranked list of recommended tags. An interesting overview of most popular algorithms for both computing similarity between users in online communities and recommending items in common between users is presented in [13].

The user-generated content has been extensively analyzed to improve the understanding of online resources (e.g., web pages, photos, videos). For example, the discovery of most relevant social interests and the categorization of web objects have been both addressed in [20] by exploiting tags assigned by users. Differently, TwitterMonitor [23] performs trend detection in Twitter streams. It first identified and clustered, by means of a co-occurence measure, the "bursty" keywords (i.e., keywords that appear in tweets at unusually high rate). Secondly, it employed context knowledge extraction to compose a more accurate description of the identified trend. In [39], an optimization framework to assign the correct category to web resources has been proposed. They focused on representing, by means of a graph-based model, the relationships between Web objects and social tags provided by del.icio.us and propagating the category information of training samples from one domain to another.

Other kinds of applications are targeted to advanced analysis of UGC retrieved from online communities. As pointed out by Heymann et al. [14], query engines can take advantage of folksonomies and ontologies extracted from social networks sites. For example, [7] proposed a framework to improve query results according to the user interest. The social relationships between users and the correlations among tags associated with media resources are represented by a unified graph model. Finally, the information provided by posts on social network sites has been exploited to improve the quality of online news searches. In [1] Twitter messages are exploited to retrieve keywords that are highly correlated with the user query. In particular, the authors analyzed the geographical content of Twitter message to determine which messages are more relevant according to the user query and retrieve a set of semantically related keywords. To further improve search queries on long document sequences (e.g., UGC) produced over a large time period, [19] addressed the problem of burstiness detection. They exploited the well-founded discrepancy theory [3] to describe the deviation of a situation from the normal behavior and, thus, perform an efficient document indexing and ranking process.

Despite several works (e.g., [1, 23, 27]) already addressed data mining from the Twitter UGC, to best of our knowledge the TweCoM framework is the first attempt to address generalized association rule mining from both tweet content and contextual features, driven by not user-provided taxonomies.

4.2.2 Taxonomy Inference

Semantics-based models support analysts in understanding the meaning of the resources within a knowledge domain. Among them, taxonomies provide a hierarchical organization of concepts, topics, and keywords among which is-a relationships hold. Despite the construction of conceptual taxonomies is becoming an increasingly appealing target in several research fields (e.g., information retrieval, data mining), the creation of taxonomies still heavily relies on human intervention. Indeed, a significant research effort has been devoted to either building or automatically inferring taxonomies from data.

Several works addressed taxonomy construction by exploiting well-known data mining techniques. Most of them proposed to exploit hierarchical clustering algorithms to provide a well-founded structuring of concepts of interest. Hierarchical clustering produces a set of nested clusters organized as a tree, called dendrogram, over data. It has been largely employed to address taxonomy generation, especially in document analysis [9, 10, 12, 16].

Other approaches have been proposed in the context of textual data analysis. For example, [25] proposed to exploit neural networks to produce a compound similarity measure of words, while in [37] documents keywords were hierarchically organized by considering the term co-occurrence frequency as an indicator of the semantic closeness between terms. Differently, other approaches are tailored to semantics-based knowledge representations. Hovy and Lin [15] adopted a lexical thesaurus (e.g., WordNet) to generalize concepts and identifies topics within a text document, while [30] exploited association rule mining with the two-fold aim at (i) analyzing and structuring folksonomies, and (ii) supporting ontology learning.

The focus of TweCoM framework differs from the aforementioned ones. We focus on automatically generating taxonomies over data items to drive the generalized rule mining process over UGC and related publication context. To this aim, we employ, similarly to [9, 10, 12, 16], a hierarchical clustering algorithm to discover hierarchical relationships among most relevant tweet content keywords, while a set of aggregation functions, defined on the structure of the tweet context, are exploited to aggregate temporal and spatial concepts.

4.2.3 Generalized Association Rule Mining

Association rule mining is a widely used exploratory technique to discover valuable correlations among data. It has been introduced in [2] in the context of market basket analysis. To focus on patterns that are relatively strong, e.g., which occur frequently and hold in most cases, several quality indexes, such as support and confidence [2], have been introduced. The mining task is typically performed by following a two-step process: (i) frequent itemset mining, driven by a minimum support threshold, and (ii) rule generation from the previously mined frequent itemsets, driven by a minimum confidence threshold. However, in some cases, this approach is not effective in discovering relevant data recurrences due to the excessive level of detailed of the analyzed data.

Generalized rules [33] have been introduced to provide a high level abstraction of the mined knowledge. By evaluating a taxonomy (i.e., is-a hierarchy), data items are aggregated based on different granularity concepts. Each generalized itemset, which is a high level representation of a set of "lower level" itemsets, provides a higher level view of patterns hidden in the analyzed data. The first generalized association rule mining algorithm [33] generates itemsets by considering, for each item, all its parents in a taxonomy. Hence, candidate frequent itemsets are generated by exhaustively evaluating the taxonomy. To reduce the mining complexity, several approaches have been proposed. For instance, [34] proposed to integrate into the mining process user-provided constraints in the form of boolean expressions over the presence and the absence of items into the mined set. Differently, in [35], subset-superset and parent-child relationships in the lattice of generalized patterns are exploited to constrain the mining process.

Many approaches based either on the Apriori [2] and FP-growth [11] mining algorithms were devoted to improving the efficiency of generalized association rules extraction (e.g., [24, 29, 33]). In [8] the authors addressed the elimination of redundant uninteresting knowledge by both generating closed itemsets [26] and exploiting schema dependencies [18] to drive the mining process. Differently, a support-driven approach to generalized itemset mining has been presented in [5]. To avoid exhaustive taxonomy evaluation followed by a post-pruning step, the generalization of an itemset is performed only if its support is below the minimum support threshold.

Most of the above mentioned approaches exploited analyst-provided taxonomies to drive the generalization process. This may lead to inconsistencies or errors due to (i) high data sparsity, (ii) limited analyst experience, or (iii) limited time spent in context learning and data processing. To address this issue, we exploited a hierarchical clustering algorithm to discover hierarchical relationships among keywords, while a set of aggregation functions to aggregate temporal and spatial concepts.

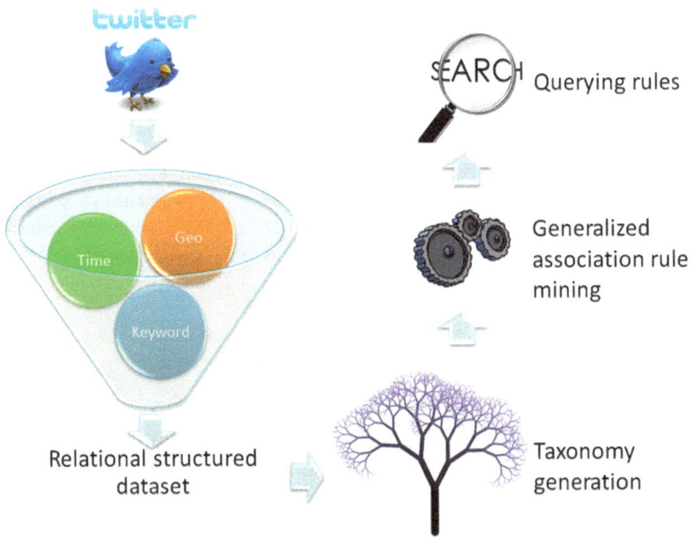

Fig. 4.1 The TweCoM framework architecture

4.3 The TweCoM Framework

The TweCoM (Tweet Context Miner) framework is a data mining environment that effectively addresses data mining and knowledge discovery from Twitter user-generated content and related context. The main architectural blocks of the TweCoM framework are shown in Fig. 4.1. A brief description of each block follows.

Representation of user-generated content. The most relevant Twitter posts (i.e., tweets) are retrieved by means of an ad-hoc crawler. Each tweet is represented as a record (i.e., set of items) which describes both content features (e.g., the most relevant keywords) and contextual features (e.g., the geographical location).

Taxonomy generation. This block addresses the automatic generation of taxonomies over content and contextual data items. Depending on the kind of information, different approaches are exploited for the taxonomy generation. Taxonomies provide a high level abstraction of the mined knowledge which allows representing tweet features at different levels of abstraction.

Generalized association rule mining. Generalized association rule mining discovers relevant high level recurrences hidden in the tweet collection. The generalization process is driven by the previously generated taxonomies. The extraction of generalized association rules is performed by means of a two-step process: (i) frequent generalized itemset extraction and (ii) rule generation from the extracted frequent itemsets.

```
2 - UserA: {results: [{profile_image_url:..., created_at: Sun, 10 Oct 2010
12:43:31 +0000, from_user:.., metadata: {result_type:recent}, to_user_id: X,
text: This is a text message, id: Y, from_user_id: X, to_user: UserB,
geo:{coordinates:+X -Y id: Z, place: New York City, place_type: city
Country: NY-United States of America}, iso_language_code: en, source..

2 - UserB: {results: [{profile_image_url:..., created_at: Wed, 20 Oct 2010
13:30:12 +0000, from_user:.., metadata:{result_type: recent}, to_user_id: X,
text: This is another message, id: X, from_user_id: X, to_user: User2,
geo:{coordinates: +X -Y id: Z, place: Los Angeles, place_type: city
Country: California-United States of America}, iso_language_code:en, source..
```

Fig. 4.2 A simplified example of tweets in the JSON data format

Querying rules. The extracted rules are queried, based on either their content or their schema, to more efficiently retrieve the information of interest. The resulting rules are ranked according to their confidence and support values to better support in-depth analysis.

A more detailed description of each block and its functionalities is presented in the following sections.

4.3.1 Representation of User-Generated Content

Twitter (http://twitter.com) is one of the most popular microblogging and social networking service. The Web service is mainly based on the messages, named tweets, posted by users. Tweets are posts, of at most 140 characters, that are publicly visible by default. The user-generated content (i.e., tweets) can be accessed by means of Search Application Programming Interfaces (APIs) provided by the social network site. Data returned by Twitter APIs is stored in the JSON format (Java Script Object Notation), which is an XML-based standard for client-server data exchange. A simplified example of two tweets tailored to the JSON format is reported in Fig. 4.2.

As shown in Fig. 4.2, tweets are characterized by a short text message enriched with several context pieces of information (e.g., source location coordinates, city, date, hour). Some contextual features are peculiar characteristics of the context in which tweets are posted by users (e.g., the source location coordinates), while others are just high level aggregations of the previous ones (e.g., the city). Consider the text message and low level contextual features first. Couples (*attribute*, *value*), where *attribute* is the text message or the description of the context feature (e.g., the date) and *value* is the collected information (e.g., "This is a text message", $2010-10-10$), are denoted as items in the following. In the case of continuous attributes, the value range is discretized into intervals and the intervals are mapped to consecutive positive integers. A relational (structured) dataset D is a set of records,

TWEETS
((**Tweet ID, 1**), (Propagation level,2), (Username, UserA), (Place, New York City), (Date, 2010-10-10), (Time, 12:43:31 +000), (Text, key_{1a} key_{1b}))
((**Tweet ID, 2**), (Propagation level,2), (Username, UserB), (Place, Los Angeles), (Date, 2010-10-20), (Time, 13:30:12 +000), (Text, key_{2a} key_{2b}))

Fig. 4.3 A simplified structured dataset generated from two tweets

where each record r is a set of items (e.g., $(Date, 2010 - 10 - 10)$) such that each attribute appears at most once in r.

Since data retrieved by Twitter is not compliant with a relational structured dataset, a preprocessing phase is needed. During the joining process, data are tailored to a common relational data format by means of a data cleaning process. Data cleaning also discards useless and redundant information and correctly manages missing values.

For each tweet, the following information are extracted:

- Geographical information
- Tweet publication date and timestamp
- Response/citation level of propagation
- Tweet keywords

While the first two tweet features can be directly extracted from the JSON data format, the tweet propagation level and keywords are usually not defined. Therefore, we record the tweet response/citation propagation level during data crawling and process the collection to select the of most representative words within each tweet content. Tweet contents are represented by means of the bag-of-word (BOW) representation in which stopwords, numbers, and website URLs are removed to avoid noisy information and on which the Porter stemming algorithm [28] is applied. The BOW representation is associated with the statistical measure of the term frequency-inverse document frequency (tf-idf) that evaluates the relevance of a word in the whole collection. The representative tweet keywords are thus defined as the top-k words with highest tf-idf values.

After preprocessing, the collected information can be modeled as a structured dataset, where records represent Twitter messages (i.e., tweets) by means of (i) their most representative tweet keywords, and (ii) their related contextual features. This representation will be exploited to effectively address generalized association rule mining from tweet collections. An example of structured context dataset record obtained by including the content of a portion of two Twitter messages, presented in Fig. 4.2, is reported in Fig. 4.3. The primary key (Tweet ID attribute) is in boldface.

4.3.1.1 Tweet Crawler

Twitter APIs are general-purpose libraries that allow the efficient retrieval of tweets from the Web. However, a procedure to extract a collection of tweets and their corresponding relationships (e.g. citations or responses) is not provided yet. Thus, we

Algorithm 3 Tweet crawler

Input: k /*number of top tweets*/, *keys* /*set of keywords*/, d /*search maximum depth*/
Output: T /*collection of tweets*/
1: $T = \emptyset, i = 0$
2: // initialization of the source set
3: **if** *keys* $= \emptyset$ **then**
4:     $S =$ set of top-k toptweets
5: **else**
6:     $S =$ set of top-k tweets retrieved by means of keyword search using *keys*
7: **end if**
8: **repeat**
9:     $C = \emptyset$ // candidate set initialization
10:     **for all** s in S **do**
11:         $C = C \cup \{c_i$ tweets directly linked to $s | c \notin \{S \cup T\}\}$
12:     **end for**
13:     $T = T \cup S$ // update of tweet collection
14:     $S = C$ // update of source set
15:     $i = i + 1$
16: **until** $i \neq d$
17: $T = T \cup S$ // it includes the tweets in S in the final collection set T
18: **return** T

introduced a tweet crawler to effectively query Twitter web service and retrieve a collection of linked tweets. To this aim, we define the following two sets of tweets: (i) the source S and (ii) the collection T sets. Different parameters are provided to the crawler: (i) the number of top-k tweets that will be retrieved during the first step of the procedure, and (ii) an optional set of keywords *keys*. If the *keys* set is empty the source set is initialized with the tweets belonging to the toptweet category, else with the top-k results retrieved by means of a keyword search (lines 3–7). For each tweet belonging to the source set S, all the tweets that are directly linked to the original post (i.e., answers and/or citations) and are not just visited by the procedure are inserted in a candidate set C (lines 10–12). Then, the original posts in the source set S are moved into the collection set T (line 13), while the candidate set becomes the new source set (line 14). This step is recursively repeated for each tweet belonging to the source set until a termination condition is satisfied. When the stop condition is reached, all the tweets belonging to the source set are moved into the collection set. Different termination conditions can be employed. To investigate tweet propagation, we defined a maximum depth level d of responses/citations as crawler stop condition (see line 16). Since Twitter system enforces some upper bound constraints for tweet download by means of APIs, we adopt an approach, similar to TPC congestion control, to efficiently query the Twitter API.

4.3.2 Taxonomy Generation

A taxonomy is a hierarchical knowledge representation that defines is-a relationships between concepts and their instances (i.e., the items). Taxonomies are used to classify objects, define semantic relationships between concepts and provide additional information on data. Most of the previously proposed generalized rule mining approaches (e.g., [11, 33]) commonly rely on user-provided taxonomies. Moreover, these taxonomies are usually general-purpose, thus they may not reflect the real meaning of the information stored in the data collection. The automatic extraction of taxonomies from data items in a relational dataset is definitely a challenging task. Since Twitter APIs provide contextual knowledge as "flat" attributes (i.e., relationships among data objects are not provided yet), we introduce this block to automatically generate a taxonomy over a selection of tweet record attributes.

Since, the generated taxonomies will be used to drive the generalization process during the rule mining phase, we formalize the concept of generalized item. Generated taxonomies are hierarchies of aggregations built over data items. Data items are leaf nodes, while generalized items, which represent higher level aggregations of lower level items, are not-leaf nodes. Given a taxonomy T_i, a generalized item $(t_i, expression_i)$ assigns the value $expression_i$ to attribute t_i. $expression_i$ is an aggregation value over values in Ω_i. $leaves(expression_i) \subseteq \Omega_i$ is the set of leaf nodes descendants of $expression_i$ in T_i. A root node aggregates all lower level nodes. Generated taxonomies will be used to drive the generalization process during the rule mining phase. The support of a generalized item $(t_i, expression_i)$ in a dataset D is the (observed) frequency of $leaves(expression_i)$ in D. For instance, $(date, October\ 2010)$ is a generalized item and its support is 100 % as depicted in Fig. 4.3. In the following, we thoroughly describe the extraction approaches exploited to infer taxonomies over tweet features.

4.3.2.1 Context Taxonomy Generation

Taxonomies over contextual features (e.g., spatial and temporal information) can be derived by means of aggregation functions based on a hierarchical model. The hierarchical model represents the relationships between different levels of aggregation. Similarly to what usually done in data warehousing, these pieces of information are extracted by means of Extraction, Transformation and Load (ETL) processes, named here aggregation functions, defined by the user. For example, in the relational tweet representation, aggregations functions may define either associations among different context attributes (e.g., *City* $\Rightarrow$ *State*) or aggregations over a singular context attributes (e.g., *Date* $\Rightarrow$ *Semester*) which could be derived by simply parsing the corresponding attribute domain values.

Given a set of aggregation functions among UGC features, the taxonomy generation block allows automatically building a taxonomy. It associates with each item the corresponding set of generalizations organized in a hierarchical fashion. For instance, consider a temporal context feature included in the UGC (e.g., *Month*) that represents high level knowledge abstraction of another context feature (e.g., *Date*). A conceptual hierarchy of aggregations may be devised by mapping the two attribute domains by means of the corresponding aggregation function

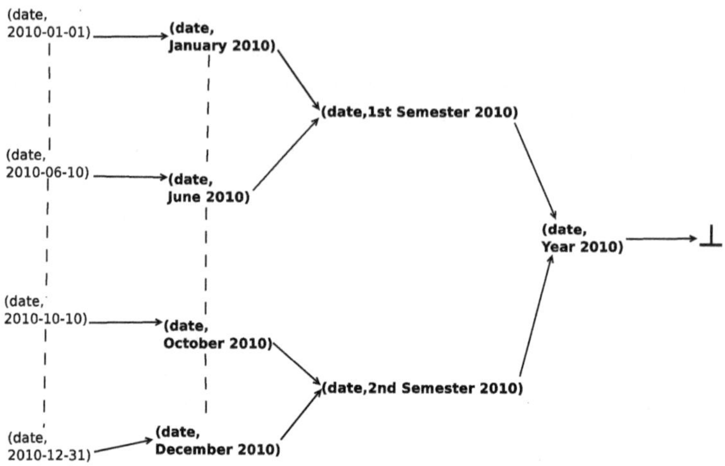

Fig. 4.4 A portion of an aggregation tree over the date attribute

Table 4.1 Aggregation functions used for the taxonomy generation over the temporal and the spatial context features

Data feature	Aggregation function
Temporal	*Date* ⇒ *WeekDay*
	Date ⇒ *Month*
	Month ⇒ *Year*
	Time ⇒ *Hour*
	Hour ⇒ *TimeSlot*
Spatial	*GPSCoordinates* ⇒ *Id*
	Id ⇒ *Place*
	Place ⇒ *Region*
	Region ⇒ *State*

(e.g., *Date* ⇒ *Month*). Consider again the *Date* attribute and its high level aggregation *Semester*. Although the corresponding higher level attribute does not exist yet, the corresponding mapping may be simply derived by parsing the lower level *Date* domain values (e.g., $2010 - 10 - 10$) and generating upper level concepts (e.g., *2nd Semester* 2010) according to the corresponding aggregation function (i.e., *Date* ⇒ *Semester*). An example of taxonomy built over the *date* attribute is reported in Fig. 4.4.

In Table 4.1 the aggregation functions exploited for the automatic generation of the taxonomy over temporal and spatial data features are resumed. However, the framework allows the usage of different aggregation functions as well.

4.3.2.2 Keyword Taxonomy Generation

In literature several hierarchical organizations of concepts have been proposed in textual data analysis (e.g., [4, 17]). We focus on combining both content and context high level data features by generating a taxonomy over tweet content keywords as well. The generation of a taxonomy directly from the user-generated content (UGC) collection may provide additional knowledge about the content and the relationships between words/concepts that are of major interest for the social community. In the following, we address this issue by adopting a clustering-based approach.

As discussed in Sect. 4.3.1, a tweet content collection can be represented by means of a tf-idf matrix. For each tweet content, we apply both the Porter stemming algorithm [28], which reduces words belonging to the collection to their base or root form, and a filter on stopwords, numbers, and webpage URLs, to remove redundant and noisy information.

Next, the tweet content collection can be represented in a matricial form TC in which each row represents a stemmed word (i.e., a term) of the collection while each column corresponds to the content of a tweet. Each element of the matrix TC is denoted as the tf-idf (Term Frequency – Inverse Document Frequency) value for a term. It is computed as follows:

$$tc_{ij} = \frac{n_{ij}}{\sum_{k \in \{q \,:\, t_q \in tw_j\}} n_{kj}} \cdot \log \frac{|TW|}{|\{tw \in TW \,:\, t_i \in tw\}|} \tag{4.1}$$

where n_{ij} is the number of occurrences of i-th term t_i in the j-th tweet content tw_j, TW is the collection of tweet contents, $\sum_{k \in \{q \,:\, t_q \in tw_j\}} n_{kj}$ is the sum of the number of occurrences of all terms in the j-th tweet content tw_j, and $\log \frac{|TW|}{|\{tw \in TW \,:\, t_i \in tw\}|}$ represents the inverse document frequency of the i-th term t_i (i.e., the logarithm of the ratio between the tweet collection cardinality and the number of tweets whose content includes term t_i).

Since a taxonomy is a hierarchical structure, we apply a hierarchical clustering to the tf-idf matricial representation of the tweet content collection. The hierarchical clustering approaches build a tree-based structure, called dendrogram, that represents how the tweet contents are grouped together at different levels of aggregation. Despite the algorithm may support different approaches and similarity measures to build the dendrogram structure, we exploited a centroid linkage approach using the cosine similarity measure. The cosine similarity measure is one the mostly used measures to compute similarity between documents in the BOW representation. The similarity between two tweet contents/clusters, represented by means of their corresponding tf-idf vectors A and B, is computed as the dot product between the two vectors normalized by the product of their magnitude. The employed clustering approach assigns a vector to each cluster which represents the cluster itself. It is computed as the average between all the tweets belonging to the cluster. Thus, the centroid provides the set of the most representative (i.e., highest tf-idf values) keywords of the tweet group.

Our approach exploits the dendrogram structure and the centroid representation to automatically generate a taxonomy over the tweet text content. The method cuts the hierarchical clustering scheme at different levels l according to the analyst request. For each cluster C_l at level l, the representative keywords of the tweets are the top-t terms with the highest tf-idf values. Since a cluster at level $l + 1$ is

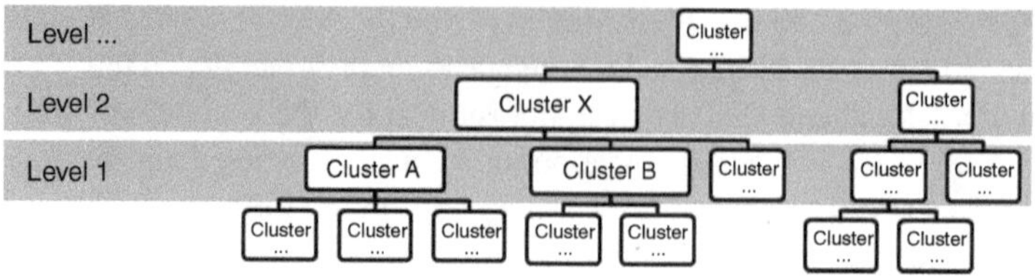

Fig. 4.5 An example of dendrogram cut for keyword taxonomy generation

composed of two or more clusters belonging to the level l, we exploit keyword aggregation functions, formally defined in Definition 1, to construct a taxonomy over tweet content keywords.

Definition 1 (Keyword aggregation function). Let t_l and t_{l+1} be the sets of keywords representing two clusters C_l and C_{l+1} obtained by two different cuts of dendrogram (i.e., two different levels). If C_l is a subset of C_{l+1} (i.e., $C_i \subseteq C_j$), the aggregation function between two keywords $key_l \in t_l$ and $key_{l+1} \in t_{l+1}$ is: $key_l \Rightarrow key_{l+1}$.

In the following an example of the taxonomy generation process over the tweet content keywords is reported. Consider the dendrogram shown in Fig. 4.5. Suppose that the analyst decides to cut the dendrogram between levels 1 and 2. At level 1, clusters A and B are characterized by the keywords "Obama" and "Bush" respectively. At level 2 the two clusters are merged in cluster X that is represented by keyword "President", i.e., the term with highest tf-idf value among all tweet contents belonging to X. Thus, the taxonomy generation process, according to the Definition 1, exploits the following keyword aggregation functions: $Obama \Rightarrow President$ and $Bush \Rightarrow President$.

4.3.3 Generalized Association Rule Mining

Correlations hidden in a dataset D may be effectively represented by means of association rules [2]. An association rule is an implication $X \Rightarrow Y$, where X and Y are itemsets, i.e., sets of items. By following the approach first proposed in [33], this block focuses on extending the problem of association rule mining to the discovery of high level correlations. The generalization process is performed by evaluating a taxonomy. To introduce generalized rule mining, we preliminarily defined the concept of generalized itemset as a set of items and/or generalized items in which each attribute may occur at most once. For instance, according to the aggregation relationships reported in Table 4.1, $\{(Place, New\ York), (date, October\ 2010)\}$ is a generalized itemset of length 2 (i.e., a generalized 2-itemset).

A generalized itemset matches a given record $r \in D$ if all its (possibly generalized) items $x \in X$ are either (i) included in r, or (ii) ancestors of items $i \in r$ (i.e., $\exists\ i \in leaves(x) |\ i \in r$). The support of a generalized itemset X is given by the number of records $r \in D$ matching X divided by the cardinality of D.

For instance, consider the example dataset reported in Fig. 4.3. The generalized itemset $\{(Place, New\ York), (date, October\ 2010)\}$ has support 50 % as it cover half of the dataset records.

By exploiting the notion of generalized itemset, we extend the notion of association rule to generalized association rule in the relational data format as an implication $A \Rightarrow B$, where A and B are disjoint generalized itemsets, i.e., generalized itemsets having no attributes in common.

Definition 2 (Generalized Association Rule). Let A and B be two generalized itemsets such that $attr(A) \cap attr(B) = \emptyset$, where $attr(X)$ is the set of attributes belonging to itemset X. A generalized association rule is represented in the form $A \Rightarrow B$, where A and B are the body and the head of the rule respectively.

A and B are respectively denoted as antecedent and consequent of the generalized rule $A \Rightarrow B$. Generalized association rule extraction is driven by rule support and confidence quality indexes. The support is defined as the prior probability of A and B (i.e., its observed frequency) in the source dataset. The confidence of a rule $A \Rightarrow B$ is the conditional probability of the generalized itemset B given the generalized itemset A and it represents the strength of the implication. For example, the generalized association rule $\{(Keyword, Sport) \rightarrow (Location, U.S)\}$ ($s = 10\%$, $c = 88\%$) states that sport tweets are frequently posted in the U.S. It occurs in 10 % of the context dataset records and it holds in 88 % of the cases.

The generalized rule mining block takes as input the generated taxonomies, the structured dataset of tweets, and, possibly, some mining constraints (e.g., minimum support and confidence thresholds). It discovers all the generalized association rules that satisfy the enforced constraints.

The mining task follows the usual two-step approach [33]: (i) extraction of the frequent generalized itemsets, and (ii) generation of the corresponding generalized rules. Since the first step is considered the most computationally intensive step [2], plenty of algorithms (e.g., Cumulate [33], GenIO [5], ML_T2LA-C [11]) have been proposed to efficiently perform this task. To perform the generalized itemset extraction task, we select the GenIO algorithm [5], a recently proposed support-driven approach, while the generalized rule generation is performed by exploiting our implementation of the Apriori rule mining algorithm [33]. However, generalized association rule mining may be successfully addressed by means of different mining algorithms as well. A brief outline of the adopted algorithms is presented in the following sections.

4.3.3.1 The GenIO Algorithm

GenIO is a generalized itemset mining algorithm that focuses on discovering only a smart subset of all the possible frequent generalized itemsets. The adopted constraint on the generalized mining process is strictly related to the concept of generalized itemset descendance. A (generalized) itemset X is a descendant of a generalized itemset Y if (i) X and Y have the same length and (ii) for each item $y \in Y$ exists at least one item $x \in X$ that is a descendant of y.

GENIO discovers all frequent itemsets and all generalized itemsets having at least an infrequent descendant. The generalization process, driven by a given taxonomy, is support-driven, i.e., it generalizes an itemset only if it is infrequent with respect to the minimum support threshold. It is based on Apriori [2], which is a level-wise algorithm. Apriori generates, at each iteration, all frequent itemsets of a given length. At arbitrary iteration k, two steps are performed: (i) candidate generation, the most computationally and memory intensive step, in which all possible k-itemsets are generated from $(k-1)$-itemsets, (ii) candidate pruning, which is based on the property that all subsets of frequent itemsets must also be frequent, to discard candidate itemsets which cannot be frequent. Finally, actual candidate support is counted by reading the dataset.

GENIO approach follows the same level-wise pattern. However, it (i) manages rare itemsets by lazily evaluating the given taxonomy Γ, and (ii) exploits the characteristics of the structured datasets to effectively prune candidates. The taxonomy evaluation is performed by applying on each item $(t_j, value_j)$ in a (infrequent) itemset c the corresponding aggregation tree AT_j. All the itemsets obtained by replacing one or more items in c with their generalized versions are generalized itemsets of c. Hence, the taxonomy evaluation on itemset c potentially generates a set of generalized itemsets. The generalization process of c is triggered if and only if c is infrequent with respect to the minimum support threshold. During the candidate generation step, GENIO exploits the uniqueness of attributes in a given record of a structured dataset to further prune candidate itemsets and reduce the computational and memory cost. A more detailed description of this method is provided by Baralis et al. [5].

4.3.3.2 The RuleGen Algorithm

The *RuleGen* algorithm generates the generalized rules given the complete set of frequent generalized itemsets. Thus, it performs the second step of the Apriori algorithm [2]. The Apriori rule generation step finds all rules that satisfy a minimum confidence constraint. Since confidence of rules generated from the same itemset has the anti-monotone property, candidate rules of length k are generated by merging two $(k-1)$-length rules that share the same prefix in the rule consequent [2]. Rule mining is typically constrained by a minimum confidence threshold to reduce the amount of generated rules. However, many different rule quality indexes may be easily integrated as well (e.g., lift [36]).

4.3.4 Querying Rules

The block entails the selection and ranking of most valuable rules for better supporting in-depth analysis. Rule selection is constrained by either (i) the rule schema (i.e., the attributes that have to appear in the rule body or head), or (i) some specific rule items of interest. An example of schema constraint may be: $(Keyword, *) \rightarrow (Place, *)$. It selects all 2-length rules that include, respectively, an item characterized by attribute *Keyword* in the rule body and attribute *Place* in the rule head. For instance, the generalized rule $(Keyword, Sport) \rightarrow (Place, U.S.))$ satisfies the above schema constraint. Differently, an example of item constraint is: $\{*\} \rightarrow \{(Place, U.S.)$. It selects all rules that contain item $(Place, U.S)$ as rule consequent. Rule $(Keyword, Sport) \rightarrow (Place, U.S.))$ also satisfies the proposed item constraint.

Results of rule querying are sorted according to confidence and support quality indexes to better support in-depth analysis. Although confidence and support are the most popular rule quality indexes [2], the TweCoM framework allows to easily integrate different quality indexes as well (e.g., lift [36]).

4.4 Experimental Results

We evaluated the efficiency and the effectiveness of the proposed approach by addressing the following issues: (i) the efficiency of the tweet crawler (see Sect. 4.4.1), (ii) the effectiveness of the adopted taxonomy inference procedure (see Sect. 4.4.2), and (ii) the propagation analysis of tweet answers and/or citations by means of generalized rule mining (see Sect. 4.4.3).

4.4.1 Data Retrieval

The TweCoM framework exploits a crawler to effectively retrieve tweets from the Web. We exploited the retrieval procedure, described in Sect. 4.3.1.1, to follow the sequence of responses/citations to the top-k results of a keyword search until a maximum search depth is reached. We performed a campaign of keyword searches starting from a set of commonly used American terms and famous names (e.g., *Soccer*, *Obama*, *Society*). Searches are performed with the aim of discovering most significant trends in UGC generation and propagation. Searches are contextualized into Examples of use-cases for the proposed TweCoM framework that concern the collected tweets are deeply discussed in Sect. 4.4.3. We investigated the impact of the following parameters on both the number of extracted tweets and the time spent in tweet retrieval: (i) the number of top results of the keyword search k, and (ii) the maximum search depth d. In Table 4.2 we reported the number of tweets retrieved for the most relevant keyword searches and the corresponding time elapsed in tweet crawling by setting the maximum search depth $D = 4$ and by varying the number of retrieved top results from 4 to 20. Both the elapsed time and the cardinality of the tweet set scale roughly linearly with the number of top results as long as the cardinality of different chains of answers/citations related to different top results are similar.

Table 4.2 Tweet set cardinality and elapsed time in tweet crawling by varying the number of retrieved top results. $d = 4$

	$k = 4$		$k = 10$		$k = 15$		$k = 20$	
Keyword	Tweets	Time (s)	Tweets	Time (s)	Tweets	Time (s)	Tweets	Time (s)
Obama	19,242	15.2	25,342	20.0	27,291	24.2	34,321	28.4
Clinton	16,543	13.3	18,765	15.3	21,454	18.2	24,652	22.9
Society	14,532	12.7	16,119	14.1	19,665	16.8	23,552	20.0
Health	11,683	10.7	12,753	12.1	14,664	15.7	18,421	18.1
War	9,332	8.6	11,356	10.2	13,568	12.7	16,742	15.9
Sport	12,687	12.3	14,331	15.1	17,876	17.1	19,864	19.5
Soccer	18,238	15.1	19,594	17.0	21,303	18.9	23,643	20.0
Los Angeles galaxy	12,687	11.3	14,223	13.2	17,352	15.8	18,992	18.0
Stadium	9,623	9.8	11,200	11.1	12,782	12.9	14,782	14.8

Table 4.3 Tweet set cardinality and elapsed time in tweet crawling by varying the number of top results. $k = 10$

	$d = 3$		$d = 4$		$d = 5$		$d = 6$	
Keyword	Num. Tweets	Time (s)	Num. Tweets	Time (s)	Num. Tweets	Time (s)	Num. Tweets	Time (s)
Obama	21,112	16.1	25,342	20.0	29,345	28.6	65,345	47.7
Clinton	16,543	13.3	18,765	15.3	25,876	25.1	56,323	42.2
Society	14,112	11.2	16,119	14.1	23,453	23.1	49,075	36.0
Health	10,301	10.9	12,753	12.1	26,360	25.9	68,102	45.1
War	9,993	7.2	11,356	10.2	19,342	18.4	34,795	39.1
Sport	11,633	11.5	14,331	15.1	22,098	26.2	50,061	40.0
Soccer	15,114	15.1	19,594	17.0	28,026	27.0	52,037	44.5
Los Angeles galaxy	12,996	11.4	14,223	13.2	21,753	19.1	42,664	39.0
Stadium	9,453	9.1	11,200	11.1	18,553	17.9	44,118	39.3

In Table 4.3 we reported the number of tweets retrieved for the most relevant keyword searches and the corresponding time elapsed in tweet crawling by setting the number of top results $k = 10$ and by varying the maximum search depth from 3 to 6. Both the elapsed time and the cardinality of the gathered tweet set scale more than linearly with the maximum depth search because of the combinatorial growth of the number of considered answers/citations. We denoted the setting $k = 10$ and $d = 4$ as standard configuration in the rest of the experimental section.

4.4.2 Taxonomy Inference

Depending on the kind of processed information, the taxonomy generation procedure exploits either (i) semantic relationships among tweet contextual features, or (ii) hierarchical clustering over Twitter textual message content. We analyzed tweets retrieved by means of the tweet crawler by setting its standard configuration

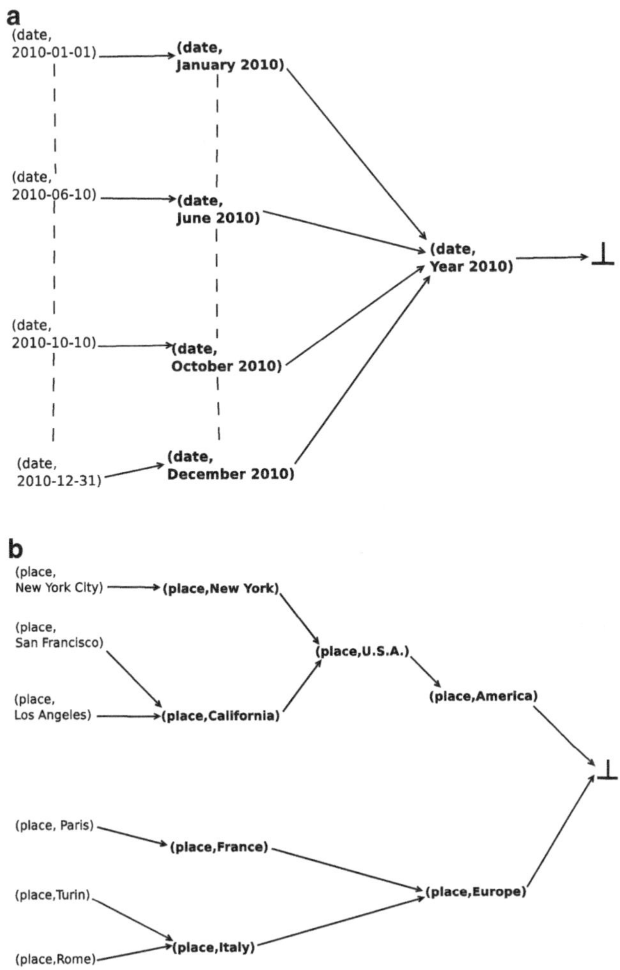

Fig. 4.6 A portion of the aggregation tree built over the date and place attributes. (**a**) Date attribute. (**b**) Place attribute

(see Sect. 4.4.1). By exploiting the aggregation relationships reported in Table 4.1 over geographical and temporal tweet contextual features, we build up a set of aggregation hierarchies. A portion of the inferred taxonomy is reported in Fig. 4.6.

The hierarchical clustering has been exploited to generate a taxonomy over tweet content keywords. For each cluster the keyword characterized by the highest tf-idf value is selected as representative (i.e., $t = 1$). To capture soccer teams, we introduced their names in the BOW representation. A portion of the resulting taxonomy built over tweet content keywords is reported in Fig. 4.7. The devised aggregations are deemed relevant by domain experts. Thus, they are employed in the generalized rule mining process. The selected aggregation relationships between

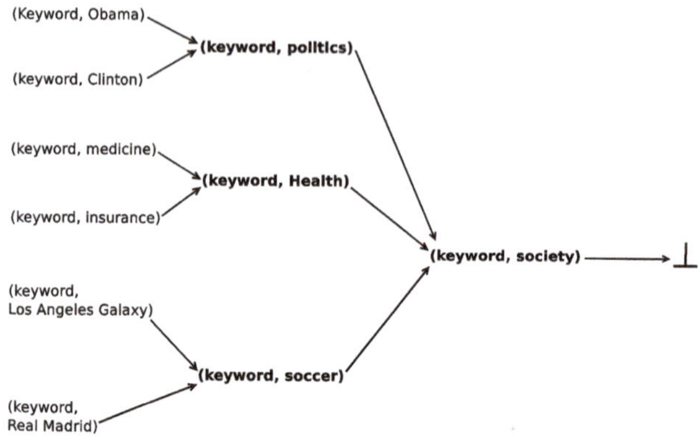

Fig. 4.7 A portion of the aggregation tree built over the tweet content keywords

Fig. 4.8 Tf-idf distribution in the Obama tweet collection

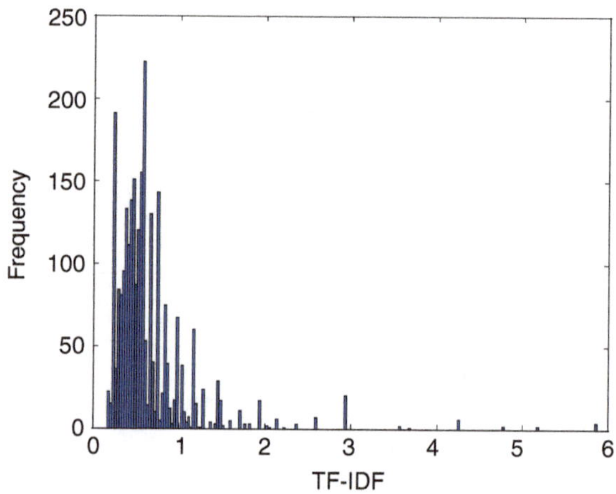

tweet contextual features (e.g., between *Los Angeles*, *California*, and *U.S.A.*) and content keywords (e.g., between *Soccer* and *Los Angeles Galaxy*) will be exploited in Sect. 4.4.3 to effectively characterize tweet propagation.

We also analyzed the distribution of the tf-idf weight among tweet contents. In particular, in Fig. 4.8 we reported the tf-idf distribution of tweet collection concerning Obama. Since tweets are characterized by a few number of words due to the post length limitation imposed by Twitter (i.e., at most 140 characters), the inverse document frequency impact becomes dominant. In fact, term frequencies are usually close to one and their distributions follow a power law. The inverse document frequency allows normalizing this distribution by assigning a score to the most relevant words in the tweet collection.

We compared the performance of the hierarchical clustering algorithm employed in our approach with the ones of the traditional k-means algorithm [22]. The cosine distance was used as similarity measure for both algorithms. We measured the

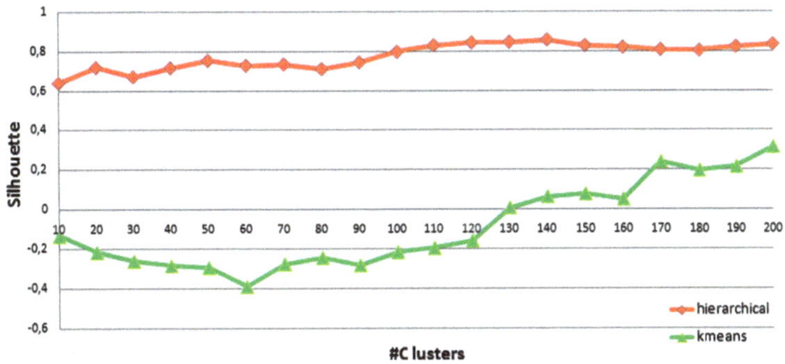

Fig. 4.9 Silhouette coefficient trend in a tweet collection

overall average silhouette achieved by the previously described tweet collections. In the reported experiments, we cut the dendrogram at the levels at which the overall average silhouette is still higher than 0.8. In Fig. 4.9, the variation of the silhouette coefficient values yielded by the two algorithms in terms of the number of generated clusters is reported for one tweet representative collection. Similar results were obtained for the others. The hierarchical algorithm outperformed k-means for any number of generated clusters. Moreover, the silhouette for the hierarchical algorithm was averagely equal 0.77, while for the k-means was −0.08. Thus, the hierarchical approach could more efficiently identify well-formed clusters with respect to the k-means approach.

4.4.3 Propagation Analysis of Tweet Content

In this section, we investigated the effectiveness of the TweCoM framework in discovering valuable correlations from Twitter user-generated content. To address this issue, we separately analyzed three different examples of use-cases for TweCoM.

Use-Case 1: Spatial Propagation Analysis of Tweet Content

This application scenario drives the analyst to retrieve and select the most relevant rules involving spatial information. To achieve this goal, the analyst performed the following steps: (i) post retrieval and categorization based on their propagation level (in the chain of answers/citations), (ii) generalized rule mining from each generated tweet set, and (iii) rule querying based on user-specified constraints involving spatial information (e.g., $(Keyword, *) \rightarrow (Location, *)$). The generalized rule mining process is performed by exploiting both (i) the tweets retrieved by the tweet crawler with the standard configuration, and (ii) the taxonomy reported in Sect. 4.4.2. During the generalized rule mining, the analyst enforced a minimum support threshold equal to 0.5% and a minimum confidence threshold equal to 50%. The analyst sorted rules according to, respectively, their confidence and support values to select the strongest and most recurrent patterns. The selection task is first performed by enforcing the schema constraint $(Keyword, *) \rightarrow (Location, *)$ over the set of mined patterns. From the set of tweets characterized by propagation level 1 (i.e., direct answers/citations of the top-k tweets), the following rules have been extracted:

Propagation Level = 1

(i) (*Keyword, Los Angeles Galaxy*) → (*Location, Los Angeles*) ($sup = 1.0\%$, $conf = 87\%$)
(ii) (*Keyword, Los Angeles Galaxy*) → (*Location, San Francisco*) ($sup = 0.7\%$, $conf = 74\%$)

They state that the American soccer team name *Los Angeles Galaxy* frequently occurs in the content of tweets posted from Los Angeles and San Francisco. The analysis of the next propagation level (2) highlighted the following generalized rule:

Propagation Level = 2

(iii) (*Keyword, Soccer*) → (*Location, Los Angeles*) ($sup = 1.5\%$, $conf = 87\%$)

The above rule is a generalization of the former ones. It states that a significant part of tweets whose content includes keyword *Soccer* have been posted from Los Angeles, where one of the most famous American soccer teams (i.e., the Los Angeles Galaxy) plays. At this level, patterns that involve singular teams became infrequent and, thus, they have not been extracted. However, due to the support-driven generalization process exploited by GenIO [5], their generalization is triggered over the taxonomy (see Fig. 4.7). Indeed, singular soccer team names are generalized in their upper level aggregation *Soccer*. Among the all possible generalizations, one of them (i.e., rule (iii)) becomes frequent with respect to the minimum support threshold. The discovered knowledge prompted the analyst to deepen the investigation into some selected keywords (e.g., *Soccer*). Spatial propagation of tweets whose content includes keyword *Soccer* has been investigated by enforcing the following item and schema constraint $(Keyword, Soccer) \rightarrow (Location, *)$ on the set of mined rules. Most of the answer/citation authors were located nearby at submission time, as shown by the following rules extracted from tweets characterized, respectively, by propagation level 3 and 4.

Propagation Level = 3

(iv) (*Keyword, Soccer*) → (*Location, California*) ($sup = 0.9\%$, $conf = 71\%$)

Propagation Level = 4

(v) (*Keyword, Soccer*) → (*Location, California*) ($sup = 0.6\%$, $conf = 76\%$)

Twitter users that were interested in citing these kind of tweets are mainly located close to the city in which their favorite soccer team plays.

Use-Case 2: Temporal Propagation Analysis of Tweet Content

This application scenario drives the analyst to retrieve and select most relevant rules involving temporal recurrences in tweet content posting. The TweCoM framework steps of usage are similar to the ones adopted in the previous use-case. A temporal propagation analysis of tweets whose content includes keyword *Obama* has been performed by enforcing the constraint $(Keyword, Obama) \rightarrow \{(Date, *), (Time, *)\}$ on the set of mined rules. The selected rules, among which the two reported below have been selected, highlight a typical propagation trend.

Propagation Level = 1

(vi) $(Keyword, Obama) \rightarrow \{(Date, November\ 2010), (Time, from\ 5\ p.m.\ to\ 8 p.m.\}$ $(sup = 0.9\%, conf = 83\%)$

Propagation Level = 3

(vii) $(Keyword, Obama) \rightarrow \{(Date, November\ 2010), (Time,\ p.m.)\}$ $(sup = 0.7\%, conf = 62\%)$

When a significant amount of toptweets about *Obama* are posted in limited time period, i.e., when a newsworthy political event happens, the answers/citations up to propagation level 3 are posted within the following 4–8 h. This information may be deemed relevant for bandwidth shaping and service monitoring.

Use-Case 3: Conbined Spatial and Temporal Propagation Analysis of the Tweet Content

The last usage scenario introduces the analysis of the temporal propagation of tweet content, in conjunction with the spatial dimension. By following the same approach presented in the previous use-cases, the analyst enforces the constraint $\{(Keyword, Soccer), (Location, *)\} \rightarrow \{(Date, *), (Time, *)\}$ on the set of mined rules. He discovered, amongst others, the following rules:
Propagation Level = 2

(viii) $\{(Keyword, Soccer), (Location, Los\ Angeles)\} \rightarrow \{(Date, November\ 2010), (Time, from\ 7\ p.m.\ to\ 8\ p.m.)\}$ $(sup = 0.6\%, conf = 72\%)$

Propagation Level = 3

(ix) $\{(Keyword, Soccer), (Location, California)\} \rightarrow \{(Date, October\ 2010), (Time, p.m.)\}$ $(sup = 0.9\%, conf = 85\%)$

The above rules highlight temporal daily recurrences holding in a specific month (November 2010). Discovered rules are supported by the fact that Los Angels Galaxy team won 5 games out of 7 from October to November 2010.

To consider also spatial and temporal propagation in tandem of tweets whose content includes keyword *Obama* the analyst enforced the constraint $\{(Keyword, Obama), (Location, *) \rightarrow \{(Date, *), (Time, *)\}$ on the set of mined rules.

Propagation Level = 1

(vi) $\{(Keyword, Obama), (Location, Paris)\} \rightarrow \{(Date, November\ 2010), (Time, p.m.)\}$ $(sup = 0.6\%, conf = 62\%)$

The above rule may suggest that a number of European newsworthy events have engaged president Obama in November 2010. This information may be worth mentioning, for instance, for news recommendation.

4.5 Conclusions and Future Works

This chapter addresses the discovery of relevant high level correlations hidden in both Twitter message contents and the context in which they have been posted. It presents the TweCoM framework that entails generalized association rule mining from tweet collections. The generalization process is driven by an automatically generated taxonomy. To track knowledge propagation, the mining process is triggered over tweet sets characterized by a common level of propagation in the sequence of responses/citations to a initial set of tweets of major interest (i.e., the toptweets). The rule querying and ranking step allows selecting relevant sets of strong patterns from Twitter messages able to effectively support analysts in analyzing the temporal evolution, the geographical distribution, and the dealing with specific topics of interest of incoming tweets.

Future works will address: (i) the usage of more efficient disk-based structures to compactly store and retrieve user-generated content, (ii) the application of more efficient clustering algorithms to address taxonomy inference, (iii) integration of clustering quality indexes to identify the best clustering results employed for keyword taxonomy generation, and (iv) the enforcement of analyst-provided constraints into the generalized association rule mining process.

References

1. Abrol, S., Khan, L.: Twinner: understanding news queries with geo-content using twitter. In: Proceedings of the 6th Workshop on Geographic Information Retrieval, pp. 1–8. ACM, New York (2008)

2. Agrawal, R., Imieliński, T., Swami, A.: Mining association rules between sets of items in large databases. In: ACM SIGMOD Record, vol. 22, pp. 207–216. ACM, New York (1993)
3. Agarwal, D., Phillips, J., Venkatasubramanian, S.: The hunting of the bump: on maximizing statistical discrepancy. In: Proceedings of the Seventeenth Annual ACM-SIAM Symposium on Discrete Algorithm, pp. 1137–1146. ACM, New York (2006)
4. Auer, S., Bizer, C., Kobilarov, G., Lehmann, J., Cyganiak, R., Ives, Z.: Dbpedia: A Nucleus for a Web of Open Data. The Semantic Web, pp. 722–735. Springer, Heidelberg (2007)
5. Baralis, E., Cagliero, L., Cerquitelli, T., D'Elia, V., Garza, P.: Support driven opportunistic aggregation for generalized itemset extraction. In: IEEE Conference of Intelligent Systems, pp. 102–107. IEEE, Washington, DC (2010)
6. Basile, P., Gendarmi, D., Lanubile, F., Semeraro, G.: Recommending Smart Tags in a Social Bookmarking System, pp. 22–29. IEEE, Washington, DC (2007)
7. Bender, M., Crecelius, T., Kacimi, M., Michel, S., Neumann, T., Parreira, J., Schenkel, R., Weikum, G.: Exploiting social relations for query expansion and result ranking. In: IEEE 24th International Conference on Data Engineering Workshop, pp. 501–506. ACM, New York (2008)
8. Bogorny, V., Valiati, J., da Silva Camargo, S., Engel, P., Alvares, L.: Towards Elimination of Redundant and Well Known Patterns in Spatial Association Rule Mining, pp. 343–360. Springer, Berlin/Heidelberg (2008)
9. Clifton, C., Cooley, R., Rennie, J.: TopCat: data Mining for Topic Identification in a Text Corpus, pp. 949–964. IEEE, Washington, DC (2004)
10. Gates, S., Teiken, W., Cheng, K.: Taxonomies by the numbers: building high-Performance taxonomies. In: Proceedings of the 14th ACM International Conference on Information and Knowledge Management, pp. 568–577. ACM, New York (2005)
11. Han, J., Fu, Y.: Mining multiple-level association rules in large databases. IEEE Trans. Knowl. Data Eng. **11**(5), 798–805 (2002)
12. Hatzivassiloglou, V., Gravano, L., Maganti, A.: An investigation of linguistic features and clustering algorithms for topical document clustering. In: Proceedings of the 23rd Annual International ACM SIGIR Conference on Research and Development in Information Retrieval, pp. 224–231. ACM, New York (2000)
13. Herlocker, J., Konstan, J., Terveen, L., Riedl, J.: Evaluating collaborative filtering recommender systems. ACM Trans. Inf. Syst. **22**(1), 5–53 (2004)
14. Heymann, P., Ramage, D., Garcia-Molina, H.: Social tag prediction. In: Proceedings of the 31st Annual International ACM SIGIR Conference on Research and Development in Information Retrieval, pp. 531–538. ACM, New York (2008)
15. Hovy, E., Lin, C.: Automated text summarization in SUMMARIST. In: Advances in Automatic Text Summarization, vol. 94. MIT, Cambridge (1999)
16. Ienco, D., Meo, R.: Towards the Automatic Construction of Conceptual Taxonomies, pp. 327–336. Springer, London (2008)
17. Kasneci, G., Ramanath, M., Suchanek, F., Weikum, G.: The YAGO-NAGA approach to knowledge discovery. ACM SIGMOD Rec. **37**(4), 41–47 (2009)
18. Kivinen, J., Mannila, H.: Approximate inference of functional dependencies from relations. Theor. Comput. Sci. **149**(1), 129–149 (1995)
19. Lappas, T., Arai, B., Platakis, M., Kotsakos, D., Gunopulos, D.: On burstiness-aware search for document sequences. In: Proceedings of the 15th ACM SIGKDD International Conference on Knowledge Discovery and Data Mining, pp. 477–486. ACM, New York (2009)
20. Li, X., Guo, L., Zhao, Y.: Tag-based social interest discovery. In: Proceeding of the 17th International Conference on World Wide Web, pp. 675–684. ACM, New York (2008)
21. Li, Q., Wang, J., Chen, Y., Lin, Z.: User comments for news recommendation in forum-based social media. Inf. Sci. **180**, 4929–4939 (2010)
22. MacQueen, J.B.: Some methods for classification and analysis of multivariate observations. In: Proceedings of 5-th Berkeley Symposium on Mathematical Statistics and Probability, pp. 281–297. University of California Press, Berkeley (1967)

23. Mathioudakis, M., Koudas, N.: TwitterMonitor: trend detection over the twitter stream. In: Proceedings of the 2010 International Conference on Management of data, pp. 1155–1158. ACM, New York (2010)
24. Mennis, J., Liu, J.: Mining association rules in spatio-temporal data: an analysis of urban socioeconomic and land cover change. Trans. GIS **9**(1), 5–17 (2005)
25. Neshati, M., Hassanabadi, L.: Taxonomy construction using compound similarity measure. In: Proceedings of the OTM Confederated International Conference on On the Move to Meaningful Internet Systems, pp. 915–932. Springer, Berlin/Heidelberg (2007)
26. Pasquier, N., Bastide, Y., Taouil, R., Lakhal, L.: Discovering frequent closed itemsets for association rules. In: Database Theory, pp. 398–416, Springer, Berlin (1999)
27. Phelan, O., McCarthy, K., Smyth, B.: Using twitter to recommend real-time topical news. In: Proceedings of the Third ACM Conference on Recommender Systems, pp. 385–388. ACM, New York (2009)
28. Porter, M.F.: An algorithm for suffix stripping. In: Readings in Information Retrieval pp. 313–316. Morgan Kaufmann, San Francisco (1997)
29. Pramudiono, I., Kitsuregawa, M.: Fp-tax: tree structure based generalized association rule mining. In: Proceedings of the 9th ACM SIGMOD Workshop on Research Issues in Data Mining and Knowledge Discovery, p. 63. ACM, New York (2004)
30. Schmitz, C., Hotho, A., Jaschke, R., Stumme, G.: Mining association rules in folksonomies. In: Data Science and Classification, pp. 261–270. Springer, Berlin (2006)
31. Shepitsen, A., Gemmell, J., Mobasher, B., Burke, R.: Personalized recommendation in social tagging systems using hierarchical clustering. In: Proceedings of the 2008 ACM Conference on Recommender Systems, pp. 259–266. ACM, New York (2008)
32. Sigurbjornsson, B., Van Zwol, R.: Flickr tag recommendation based on collective knowledge. In: Proceedings of the 17th International Conference on World Wide Web, pp. 327–336. ACM, New York (2008)
33. Srikant, R., Agrawal, R.: Mining generalized association rules. In: International Conference on Very Large Data Bases, pp. 407–419. Morgan Kaufmann, San Fransisco (1995)
34. Srikant, R., Vu, Q., Agrawal, R.: Mining association rules with item constraints. In: Conference on Knowledge Discovery and Data Mining, vol. 97, pp. 67–73. AAAI, Menlo Park (1997)
35. Sriphaew, K., Theeramunkong, T.: A new method for finding generalized frequent itemsets in generalized association rule mining. In: Seventh International Symposium on Computers and Communications, pp. 1040–1045. IEEE, Washington, DC (2002)
36. Tan, P., Kumar, V., Srivastava, J.: Selecting the right interestingness measure for association patterns. In: Proceedings of the Eighth ACM SIGKDD International Conference on Knowledge Discovery and Data Mining, p. 41. ACM, New York (2002)
37. Woon, W., Madnick, S.: Asymmetric information distances for automated taxonomy construction. Knowl. Inf. Syst. **21**(1), 91–111 (2009)
38. Xue, Y., Zhang, C., Zhou, C., Lin, X., Li, Q.: An effective news recommendation in social media based on users' preference. In: International Workshop on Education Technology and Training, vol. 1, pp. 627–631. IEEE, Washington, DC (2009)
39. Yin, Z., Li, R., Mei, Q., Han, J.: Exploring social tagging graph for web object classification. In: Proceedings of the 15th ACM SIGKDD International Conference on Knowledge Discovery and Data Mining, pp. 957–966. ACM, New York (2009)

Chapter 5
Pixel-Oriented Network Visualization: Static Visualization of Change in Social Networks

Klaus Stein, René Wegener, and Christoph Schlieder

Abstract Most common network visualizations rely on graph drawing. While without doubt useful, graphs suffer from limitations like cluttering and important patterns may not be realized especially when networks change over time. We propose a novel approach for the visualization of user interactions in social networks: a pixel-oriented visualization of a graphical network matrix where activity timelines are folded to inner glyphs within each matrix cell. Users are ordered by similarity which allows to uncover interesting patterns. The visualization is exemplified using social networks based on corporate wikis.

5.1 Introduction

One important aspect of social network analysis consists in finding interaction patterns between social actors by appropriate visualization paradigms.[1] Social network visualizations offer great help in getting deeper insights in structure and relations. Most commonly graphs are used to represent social networks giving an overview especially over smaller networks, but normally do not cover network dynamics. Too little attention has been paid to networks changing over time: new users come in, old ones leave, new links between users get established, interaction between certain users declines, etc.

[1]This chapter is based on a conference paper at ASONAM 2010.

K. Stein (✉) · C. Schlieder
Computing in the Cultural Sciences, University of Bamberg, Bamberg, Germany
e-mail: klaus.stein@uni-bamberg.de; christoph.schlieder@uni-bamberg.de

R. Wegener
Information Systems, Kassel University, Kassel, Germany
e-mail: wegener@uni-kassel.de

T. Özyer et al. (eds.), *The Influence of Technology on Social Network Analysis and Mining*, Lecture Notes in Social Networks 6, DOI 10.1007/978-3-7091-1346-2_5,

Techniques like animated graphs give some insights into network dynamics but also inherit several shortcomings: graphs tend to clutter when larger networks are being displayed, and animation requires digital media as well as more cognitive resources compared to static visualizations. A static visualization technique able to display dynamics even in large social networks is needed.

The visualization problem addressed in this chapter first arised when we analyzed user collaboration in organizational wikis where we missed a good visualization for temporal dynamics which could be used in the context of visual data mining. The social networks studied are extended coauthor networks extracted from organizational wikis using the interlocking measure.[2] The idea of interlocking is simple: if an user *B* edits a page previously edited by another user *A*, a directed link from *B* to *A* is established. An user *C* editing the same page afterwards establishes links to *A and B* and so on. Each link is associated with a time stamp, so the network holds the interaction record of users in time.

The analysis of interlocking networks can be applied to many different data sets from SVN or GIT repositories over email corpuses to newsgroups, discussion boards, CMS. Interlocking gives a directed network, as each user action is considered as an "answer" to actions of other users before. The visualizations presented in this chapter are nevertheless also useful on undirected graphs, as long as time stamps of interaction are available.

This chapter describes the following contributions to the state of the art: (1) We introduce a new kind of social network visualization based on the pixel-oriented visualization paradigm and extend it for the presentation of networks evolving in time in a way that supports visual data mining; (2) We compare different glyph layout patterns and their application to the problem domain; (3) We provide measures for arranging (sorting) nodes; and (4) We show that temporal patterns indicating cooccurrence and similar behavior are perceptually salient in our visualization even on larger networks.

The chapter is organized as follows. We discuss common visualization approaches for social networks and time series in Sect. 5.2. Section 5.3 introduces our pixel-oriented network visualization approach and describes the adequate choices of glyph layouts and node arrangement. Section 5.4 presents a case study that illustrates how to apply our approach to real-world network data. We conclude in Sect. 5.5 with a discussion of the results and an outlook on future work.

5.2 Related Work

Visual data mining techniques take advantage of the efficient perceptual grouping processes of the human visual system (see e.g. [7, 26]). Even in large data sets, perceptual saliency draws the observer's attentions to patterns. Visualization is most

[2] See [32] for a detailed discussion of this measure.

useful to generate hypothesis about regularities in a data set. On the other hand visualization does not provide a proof. For instance nodes positioned close together by a layout algorithm suggest some correlation which vanishes by using another layout.

Shneiderman [29] gives an overviews on visualization of large datasets, a detailed description can be found in [33].

5.2.1 Social Network Graphs

Much research has been conducted in the field of social network visualization (for an overview see [8, 20]). For a discussion of the explanatory power of network visualization see [6]. The most common way to present a social network is the network graph. The nodes are arranged by one of various graph layout algorithms which continue to be improved in their computational properties as well as their usability (see e.g. [11]). Most software packages for network analysis include graph drawing functionality. Furthermore, a variety of specialized graph drawing packages are available.[3]

Alternatively networks can be presented by adjacency matrices that represent the network by some kind of numbers for actors and relations. Ghoniem et al. [13] compare node-link diagrams and matrices. While probably less appealing to the user, matrix visualizations avoid common problems like cluttering. The authors conclude that node-link representations are best suited for smaller graphs while a higher number of nodes and higher degree of density are better visualized as matrix representations. Shneiderman and Aris [30] state that network graphs can be understood best if they contain between 10–50 nodes and 20–100 links. A higher number of nodes and links makes it more difficult to follow the links, count or identify nodes etc.

One way to avoid cluttering is to group related nodes. For example Shi et al. [28] and Balzer and Deussen [3] use hierarchical clustering, Peng and SiKun [25] propose a subgroup analysis layout algorithm based on attributes and Chen et al. [9] create subgraphs for subgroups. Leung and Carmichel [22] also group nodes and arrange them in a rectangular grid using horizontal edges to show relations between different actors.

Henry et al. [15] take a different approach. They combine node-link layouts and matrix representations in order to give an easy to understand overview of a

[3]For example UCINET (http://www.analytictech.com/ucinet/), JUNG (http://jung.sourceforge.net/), Graphviz (http://www.graphviz.org/), GUESS (http://graphexploration.cond.org/), Pajek (http://pajek.imfm.si/), Visone (http://visone.info/), and others. See also http://www.google.com/Top/Science/Math/Combinatorics/Software/Graph_Drawing/, http://www.graphdrawing.org/ and the INSNA software list (http://www.insna.org/software/).

network while also revealing details that couldn't be recognized in a pure node-link visualization (see also [27]).

5.2.2 Change in Time

For visualizing time-oriented data a variety of methods is available, for an overview see [1]. Broadly speaking, the methods for visualizing time oriented data in social networks fall into two classes: sequences of snapshots and (interactive) animations. Moody [24] considers a third class: network summary statistics plotted as a line graph over time. Since the network topology cannot be recovered from this visualization, we will not consider it.

Two major problems arise with using a temporal sequence of snapshots as visualization: (1) The temporal resolution, i.e., the number of elements of the sequence, is severely restricted, (2) The optimization of the layout algorithm conflicts with changes. We illustrate the problems of visualizations using sequences of snapshots with a network from our own data.

The network presented in Fig. 5.1 shows students working on a larger project across three terms using a wiki as documentation platform. So in each term a bunch of new students join, others leave. The visualization uses a spring embedding layout algorithm that optimizes the length of the edges between the nodes (see [16]) in order to achieve a grouping of highly interconnected sets of nodes. Figure 5.1b–d show snapshots of the network at different times that illustrate the temporal change. While for each subgraph both spatial dimensions are used to lay out the graph on the big scale, the x-axis represents time from left (past) to right (future). The spatial extension of each "data point" (network graph) restricts the temporal resolution to few (three) time points.

We could not layout each of the graphs with spring embedding but had to keep each node at a fixed position to be able to compare the graphs. So while the change shows up very well in Fig. 5.1b–d the grouping in the single graphs is not optimal.

Moody states that the "poor job" of representing change in the network is a problem "fundamental to the media" and suggests to use animations. Network animation software is available either stand alone (e.g. SoNIA,[4] see [4]) or as part of dedicated network analysis software (e.g. SONIVIS[5]) as most of the network visualization libraries support dynamic node and edge change. By interpolating between the graphs that represent the different intervals of the network, nodes are moved to smoothly re-layout the graph responding to changing edges. One drawback here is that this representation cannot be published in print, some kind

[4]http://www.stanford.edu/group/sonia/

[5]http://sonivis.org

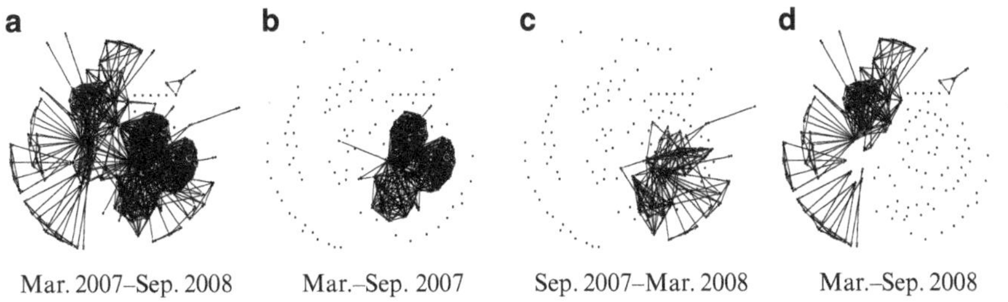

Fig. 5.1 Network evolution in time (*students wiki*). (**a**) Full timespan. (**b**) First term. (**c**) Second term. (**d**) Third term

of digital medium is needed.[6] More important, animations are nice and striking in presentations but less useful for analysis as they do not give an overview at a glance. Animations inherit the issues of change blindness which means that some changes (maybe just because the glimpse of an eye) will not be realized by the user [7].

The static graphical presentation of data allows to externalize concepts as everything is available on paper. The visual system provides the data analyst with scanning routines that permit a very efficient processing of externalized data. Presenting all the information on one single figure instead of using an animation takes advantage of this ability. In fact, switching our attention from one area of a single figure to another will usually not only be much faster than finding the right interval of an animation with the help of a slide bar [34], it will also allow to for deeper inspection. Human's visual working memory only stores a handful of objects at a time [34] and watching animations forces us to *remember* what we have seen while a static representation keeps everything accessible in parallel.

5.3 Pixel-Oriented Visualization of Network Data

The idea of pixel-oriented visualization was introduced by Keim et al. [18] and further developed in [17, 19] and other publications. Although the original publications do not provide a concise definition, the basic idea of the visualization methods is simple to describe. Each pixel of the screen is used to visualize one data point, representing its value by its color. This allows to visualize great amounts of data while avoiding overlapping and cluttering. Pixel-oriented visualization has been applied by Guo et al. [14] for the visualization of very large scale network matrices (BOSAM,[7]) but to the best of our knowledge it has not been tried on temporal and weighted networks.

---

[6]For an animated representation of the network shown in Fig. 5.1 see http://www.kinf.wiai.uni-bamberg.de/mwstat/examples/wiki_1_weekly_network.swf.

[7]Bitmap of sorted adjacency matrix.

In this section we show, how to adapt the idea of pixel-oriented visualization for a static representation of social network data in time.

5.3.1 Collaboration in Time

Figure 5.2a shows typical time series data in graph representation: the x-axis represents time as the independent variable, while the dependent variable (interaction activity) is displayed on the y-axis. Different colors (levels of gray) are used to distinguish the different users. Figure 5.2c gives exactly the same data in pixel-oriented representation. The x-axis again represents time, the y-axis now is used to separate the users line by line. Color (grayscale) represents interaction intensity.

The advantage of the graph-based representation consists in a visually salient rendering of extreme values (intensity spikes around June 07, August 08 and April 09) but makes it hard to distinguish the different users (Fig. 5.2a) as their graphs overlap.

In the pixel-oriented representation the activity of different users is clearly visible as there is no overlapping. The user timelines are easy to compare (we see in Fig. 5.2c which users where active in August 08 and which in April 09), but we do not get the absolute intensity values, only the relative intensity distribution is visible.

Figure 5.2b, d present the same data in higher resolution, i.e. day by day instead of month by month following the idea that "to map each data value to a colored pixel [...] allow[s] us to visualize the largest amount of data which is possible on current displays" [17]. The pixel-oriented visualization delivers additional implications: As you can see high collaboration values in 1 month are usually generated by the high collaboration rates of only a few days and not by continuing collaboration during this month.

Figure 5.2d uses the calendar metaphor which means to arrange the timeline in a weekly zigzag:

user	1	8	15	22	29	36		*Monday*
	2	9	16	23	30	37		*Tuesday*
	3	10	17	24	31	38	...	*Wednesday*
	4	11	18	25	32	39		*Thursday*
	5	12	19	26	33	40		*Friday*
	6	13	20	27	34	41		*Saturday*
	7	14	21	28	35			*Sunday*

Although the single dots are too fine to be able to tell which day exactly it represents we nevertheless get the interesting patterns. We not only get an impression which users collaborate a lot at which time during the year (as every pixel column represents a week), we additionally see[8] that only users U6 and U1 are working on Sunday while no one works on Saturday.

[8] At least I hope this is visible in the printout.

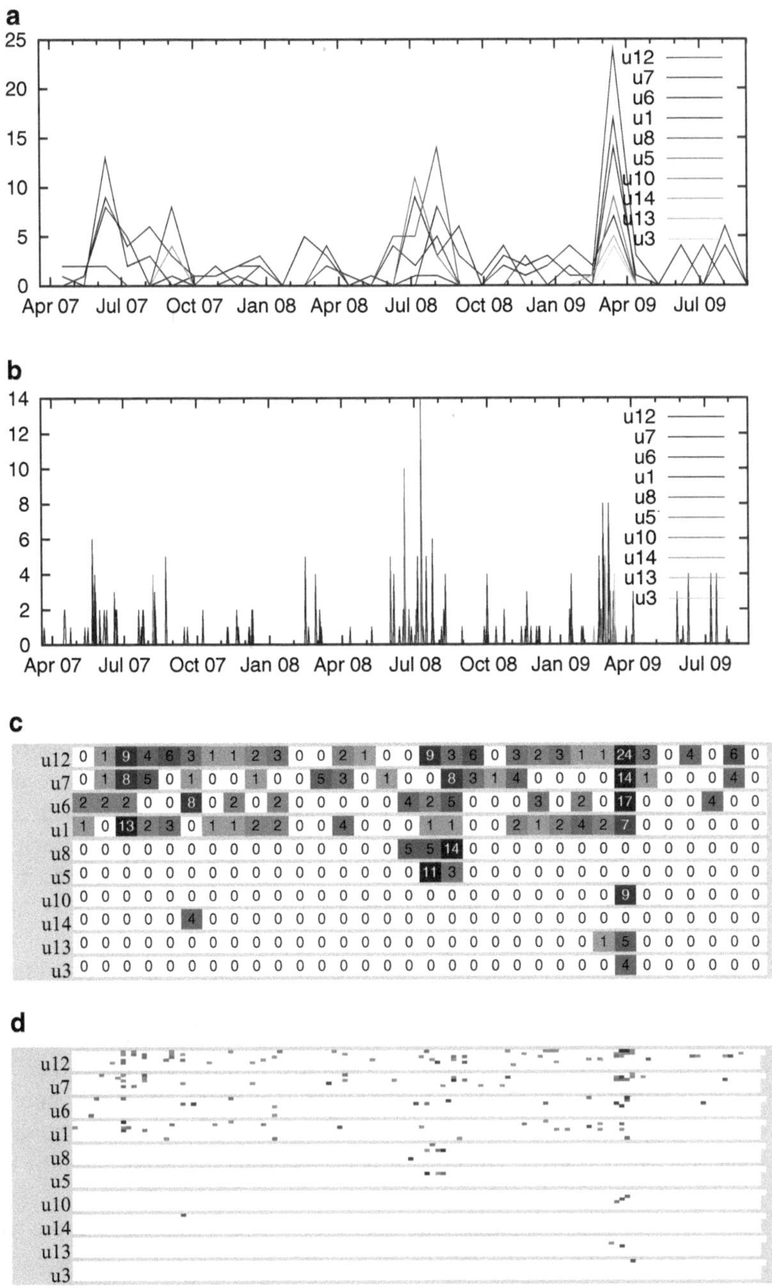

Fig. 5.2 Collaboration activity per user (*workgroup wiki*). All figures show the same timespan from April 2007 to September 2009 (x-axis), only the resolution is different. (**a**) Monthly. (**b**) Daily. (**c**) Monthly. (**d**) Daily

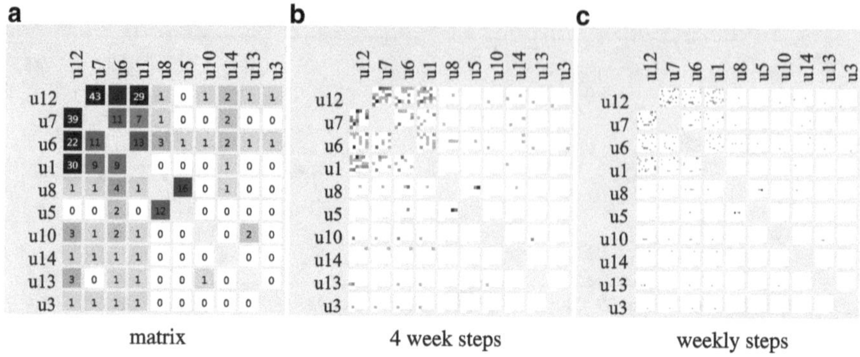

Fig. 5.3 *Workgroup wiki* network matrix. (**a**) Shows the adjacency matrix of the network. Each matrix element is colored according to its value. In (**b**) and (**c**) each glyph shows the folded timeline row by row. The nodes are sorted by their (weighted) degree

5.3.2 *The Pixel Matrix*

We adapt the idea of pixel-oriented visualization applying it to social network graphs. We present the network as an adjacency matrix with each row and each column corresponding to one node and the matrix elements giving the weight of the edge between the corresponding nodes, as shown in Fig. 5.3a.

Following the pixel-oriented visualization paradigm to present each value by one colored pixel we can inject the whole timeline of user interaction in one matrix element by folding it. Figure 5.3b gives the network matrix with each matrix element showing one glyph which holds the timeline folded row by row, each pixel representing the user-user-interaction within 4 weeks. This is somehow the inverse representation to Fig. 5.1 where time is given on the outer x-axis while now time is folded at the inside, i.e. within each glyph.

The scale is changed from monthly to 4 weeks to get timespans of equal length. While monthly data is easier to present and describe it has the disadvantage that each month covers a different *number* of days and a different number of certain weekdays: June 2010 has four Fridays, July has five. This is important when work is organized weekly, e.g. the workgroup has a weekly meeting on Friday generating extra social interaction. On a monthly raster this generates 20 % more activity for July while everything is even. The other way around if there is some monthly event the 4-weeks raster would show irritating data.

We see users U12, U7, U6 and U1 interacting a lot with each other over the whole timespan. Users U8 and U5 come in after around 1 year for 3 months, working closely together with small interaction with others (U8 has few connections to the most prominent four users while U5 only meets U6). And users U10, U13 and U3 join the network even later, interacting mainly with the prominent four and not with each other.

This small example gives first insight on the potential of pixel-oriented network visualization (PONV). We do not know exactly at which time users U8 and U5 came in and we do not get a detailed analysis on the interaction between users U12 to U1, but we see gray dots sprinkled over the whole glyph telling us that there was interaction between these users all the time. And we see that U10, U13 and U3 came in at the same time even though their timelines are not layed out side by side. Our visual perception is perfect in detecting that these gray dots are on the same position within their glyph. While we are not able to read absolute data from the graph (neither exact times nor exact intensity values of collaboration) we get a good overview over the temporal behavior of each user as well as temporal cooccurrence of certain events.

And this is exactly what visual data mining is meant for: an exploratory analysis of the data to detect regularities. In a next step, all evidence in the data set is evaluated that supports the hypothetical regularity or conflicts with it. For instance, it could be checked at what time U5 did his first edit operation, at what time U8 her last edit operation and so on. In other words, the cues from visual examination are backed up with hard data.

An additional remark about U14. As we see in the U14 *row* he comes in rather early, interacts once and is gone, but in the U14 *column* there are several interactions visible even at later times. This is a result of the network creation method we used. Interlocking response graphs are directed and an edge from user B to user A is set at the time B edits a page A edited before. And in the network matrix as presented in Fig. 5.3 the row gives the tail node (R) and the column gives the head node (C), so the edge points from R to C. So what we see here is that U14 edited a page users U12 to U1 edited before, and months later users U12 to U8 "responded" by editing this page. And we can also see some closer interaction between U6 and U14 as the (U6,U14)-glyph shows us U6 must have edited this page shortly before U14.

5.3.3 *Inner Glyphs*

Our visual perception is good in pattern recognition and edge detection. Looking at Fig. 5.3b we detect some interesting vertical bars at (U6,U12), (U6,U1) and (U7,U12). Unfortunately these findings are arbitrary. The timeline is packed into the glyph row by row (see Fig. 5.4a) and each glyph has 6×6 pixel. This means that two pixel aligned vertically contain data that is 24 weeks apart. Looking at the same data with glyphs of width 7 would reveal other arbitrary vertical bars. On the other hand we may miss timespans of high activity which start at the end of one column and end at the beginning of the next one. The latter problem can be reduced by laying out the rows in a snake-like way (see Fig. 5.4b) as here continuous timespans are not ripped apart.

Things are different in the example before (Fig. 5.2d).[9] Each column represents 1 week with Monday in the top and Sunday in the bottom row which allowed us to

[9]Where the timeline was presented column by column.

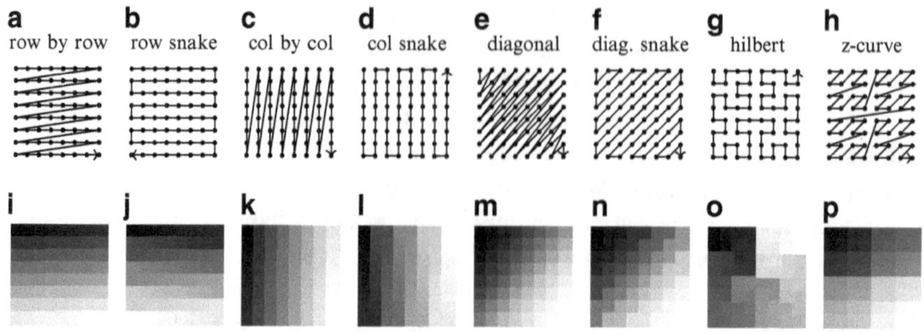

Fig. 5.4 Layout patterns for inner glyphs. (a) to (h) give the layout path while (i) to (p) show example glyphs for a color gradient from black to white in the corresponding layout. (See also [17, 19])

see who is working on weekends, and obviously a snake pattern (Fig. 5.4d) would disturb.

While Fig. 5.3b kind of allows to distinguish single pixels and – with some effort – even to see which row a pixel belongs to we are lost in Fig. 5.3c with a weekly resolution. There are darker and lighter regions and you can hardly see how many rows are involved, in other words: you see darker and lighter region patterns which may be incidental as our vision groups events which are layed out next to each other in successive rows while in fact being numbers of weeks apart.

Space-filling curves like the well-known Hilbert curve (Fig. 5.4g) are one answer to this problem as these curves lay out one-dimensional data in two-dimensional space in a locality-preserving way, i.e. data points being close together in the one-dimensional representation are kept close in the two-dimensional layout. Unfortunately it also brings data points close which were *very* far away from each other as visible in Fig. 5.4o.

A second disadvantage of this layout is that the main data order is non-linear. While the layouts Fig. 5.4a–f show a main linear direction (top→down, left→right, topleft→downright)[10] the main timeline for the Hilbert curve is U-shaped which is kind of irritating not only for the uninformed reader.

The recursive z-curve Fig. 5.4h roughly maintains an overall topleft→downright direction with partly more locality than the pure diagonal layouts Fig. 5.4e, f but on the other hand shows leaps.

We found the row and column layouts least irritating to the uninformed as well as expert user, they are easy to explain and the more complicated layouts are not capable of solving all the issues described above. And finally its up to the decision of the user which layout he or she prefers.

If the data timeline is known to be structured by periods relevant to the problem domain, e.g. quarters or terms, the pixel-oriented visualization can easily adapt to

[10]Which could be flipped e.g. for Arabic readers who may prefer right→left.

that fact. For example, to present 10 years of data month by month use a row by row or column by column layout with 12×10, and you may be able to see some pattern for Christmas time, for 1 year (52 weeks) day by day use 14×26 or 21×18 and so on. If no such rhythm applies choose quadratic glyphs with any layout you may like but keep in mind how to interpret it and which patterns may show up spuriously.

5.3.4 Arranging the Glyphs

Displaying the timelines of the users row by row as in Fig. 5.2c, d raises the question about the best order to arrange them. A similar issue arises with the matrix representation (Fig. 5.3).

In many cases additional background knowledge is available about the members of the social network. They belong to some part of the organization, work together in a certain project, have a certain role (manager, clerk, intern etc.). Grouping users by one of this aspects can help to identify certain patterns (are members of the same projects working together within certain timespans? Are there different patterns showing up for different roles?).

A second criterion for grouping is some node feature. For the examples up to now we used the (weighted) degree of each node, that is we sorted by a network parameter. This is reasonable as such parameters provide well-defined sorting criteria, but it is also kind of arbitrary as one would need to argue why not to base sorting on content-based criteria such as activity, timespan, or grouped nodes highly connected in the network.

The pixel-oriented network visualization supports the identification of *patterns* in the timelines. The layout algorithm can support the pattern recognition process by choosing arrangements placing similar objects side by side. Figure 5.5 shows the same user collaboration timelines as Fig. 5.2 with users grouped by similarity of their timelines. The most outstanding change is that U10, U13 and U3, the three users only working in April 2009, are grouped together and not longer disturbed by U14. We give a larger and more substantial example in Sect. 5.4 (Figs. 5.9 and 5.10).

The rest of this section focusses on ordering by these similar patterns. First an approach for computing distances (dissimilarities) on user timelines is given. Based on these distances the timelines are then ordered by multidimensional scaling (MDS). And finally we describe additional considerations for matrix ordering.

5.3.4.1 Comparing Timelines

Each user timeline gives a high dimensional vector, where each data point (user activity at a certain time) is mapped to one vector component. So each timeline is represented as a point in a high dimensional space. This allows to compute the distance (i.e. the discrepancy) between each pair of timelines and to group users

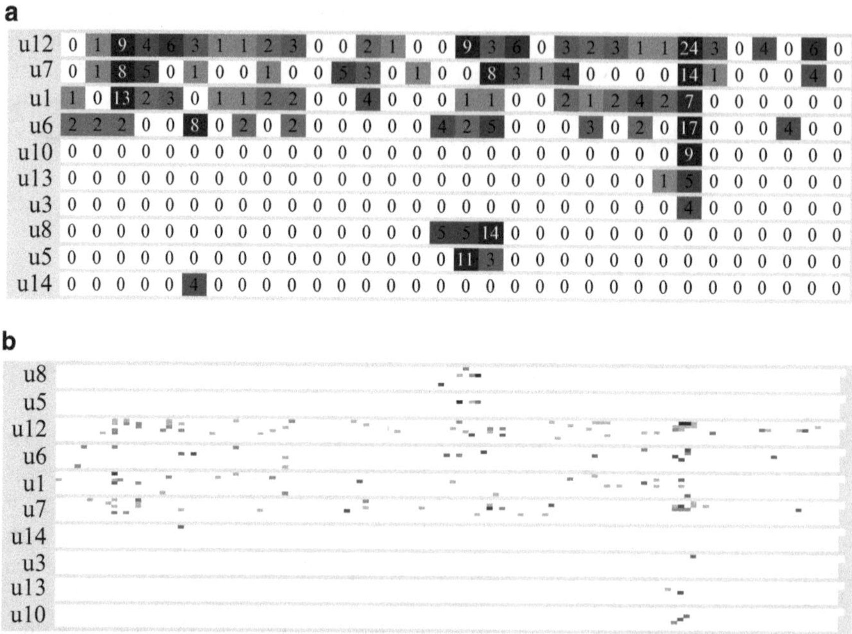

Fig. 5.5 Collaboration activity per user (*workgroup wiki*), users arranged by similarity of timelines (**a**) Monthly (**b**) Daily

with close timelines and put them side by side. We will not discuss the large number of algorithms for high dimensional clustering[11] but concentrate on the specifics of the network data.

Consider the following timelines (■ = 5, ▣ = 1, □ = 0):

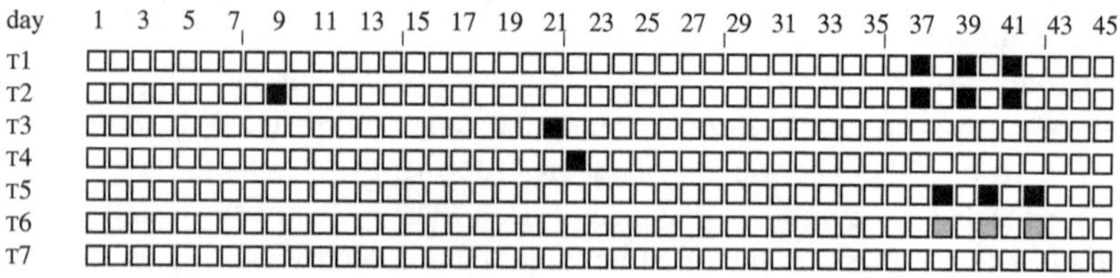

Each timeline is a vector presenting a point in 45-dimensional space. Simply computing the distance between these points using some metric works for T1 and T2. They are close compared to the others as they only differ in their 9. component, so with euclidean distance we get: $d(\text{T1}, \text{T2}) = 5$, compared to $d(\text{T1}, \text{T3}) = 10$, $d(\text{T2}, \text{T3}) = 11.18$, $d(\text{T1}, \text{T4}) = 10$ and so on.

[11]For example CLIQUE [2]. For an overview on cluster analysis see Everitt et al. [12].

But $d(\text{T}1, \text{T}5) = 12.25$, so T1 is closer to T4 than to T5. Mathematically, this is obvious as dimensions are independent to each other and T4 and T5 differ in six coordinates by $|5 - 0| = 5$, but it may not be what we want. Users T1, T4 and T5 were active in the 6 week so it may be reasonable to count their timelines as similar, even if they did not show active on the same days.

One way to solve this would be to use a coarser raster for computing the distances, we can use weekly timelines for ordering and daily timelines for presentation. So T1 and T5 show activity intensity of 15 in week 6 and no activity in other weeks giving a complete match. But it would not work for users T3 and T4, as we are unlucky with the weekly border: T3 shows activity in week 3 while T4 is active in week 4.

Therefore, we propose another solution. The basic idea consists in not computing the distances on the timelines as given above but instead to smoothen (blur) them. For each component a_i of the timeline vector the neighbors $a_{i-k}, a_{i-k+1}, \ldots, a_{i-1}$ and $a_{i+1}, a_{i+2}, \ldots, a_{i+k}$ are modified by the value of a_i, e.g. by addition of $\frac{1}{2}a_i$. For example with $k = 1$ by computing: $a_i' = \frac{1}{2}a_{i-1} + a_i + \frac{1}{2}a_{i+1}$ we get the ordering timeline for all timepoints[12] i.

This gives modified timelines (■ = 5, ■ = 2.5, ■ = 1, □ = 0):

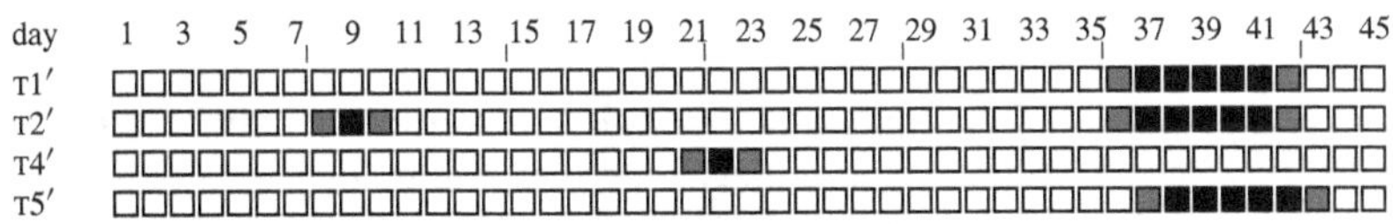

$d(\text{T}1', \text{T}2') = 6.12$, $d(\text{T}1', \text{T}4') = 13.23$, $d(\text{T}1', \text{T}5') = 5$, $d(\text{T}2', \text{T}5') = 7.9$. So T1′ and T5′ are closer than T1′ and T4′, as requested. So in general smoothing works. How to do the smoothing exactly, e.g. how to choose the size of the neighborhood k, depends on the specific problem domain. For the daily timelines of the *workgroup wiki* (Fig. 5.5b) we used $k = 7$ which means that activities of two users are overlapping as long as they are not more than 1 week apart which is feasible for users collaborating in a wiki over several years.

5.3.4.2 Distance Measures

In the examples given the distances are computed using the euclidean distance metric. Comparing the timelines for T5, T6 and T7 gives the euclidean distances $d(\text{T}5, \text{T}6) = 6.93$ and $d(\text{T}6, \text{T}7) = 1.73$, so T6 is much closer to T7 than to T5. This holds for all minkowski (p-norm) metrices, e.g. manhattan metric gives $d(\text{T}5, \text{T}6) = 12$ and $d(\text{T}6, \text{T}7) = 3$ and maximum metric gives $d(\text{T}5, \text{T}6) = 4$ and $d(\text{T}6, \text{T}7) = 1$.

[12] For indices outside the time range (e.g. a_{-1}) the value 0 is substituted.

Whether this is the desired result depends on the scenario. Are two users which are active at the same time similar even if the activity of one is very high and of the other is very low or is low activity more similar to no activity?

The former can be achieved in several ways. Adding some δ to each value greater than 0 increases the relative gap between 0 (no activity) and other values. Alternatively transforming the activity values by $a_i' = \sqrt[m]{a_i}$ reduces the importance of high values, for very large m it is similar to setting all non-zero values to 1. Now a distance measure can be applied to the modified timelines. For example, with $m = 5$ and the euclidean metric we get $d(\text{T5}, \text{T6}) = 0.66$ and $d(\text{T6}, \text{T7}) = 1.73$ as expected.

Other measures like the Pearson correlation (known as r) or the cosine coefficient[13] (which computes the cosine of the angle between two vectors) can be used to compare timelines by their relative intensity pattern. As they compute the similarity s of two vectors with 1 indicating maximum similarity, and not the distance, we define $d(\text{TA}, \text{TB}) = 1 - s(\text{TA}, \text{TB})$ to get a distance measure as required for MDS. Two timeline vectors with $\text{TA} = \lambda \cdot \text{TB}, (\lambda > 0)$ are considered similar by these measures, so we get $d(\text{T5}, \text{T6}) = 0$. With cosine similarity we get $d(\text{T1}', \text{T2}') = 0.11$, $d(\text{T1}', \text{T4}') = 1$ (the maximum distance possible) and $d(\text{T1}', \text{T5}') = 0.09$, i.e. sensible values.

Unfortunately both measures do not allow to compare with the zero vector (which has no direction). While this is not a problem for ordering collaboration activities as in Fig. 5.5 where users with empty timelines could simply be put at the end, it will give problems for ordering matrices (Sect. 5.3.4.4) as here a lot of glyphs with empty timelines are normal (see e.g. Fig. 5.6). Therefore comparison with the zero vector has to be handled as special case. Two empty timelines have distance 0. As absolute intensity is ignored by cosine, it seems natural to take the limes for $\lambda \to 0$ and set the distance of any to the zero vector to 0. As this does not give the desired effect a possible solution is to use a fixed maximum distance of 2 (which is larger than all other distances).

5.3.4.3 From Timeline Distances to User Arrangement

Applying distance measures as described for all pairs of timelines gives a distance matrix. Now timelines with low distances can be clustered together. Using multidimensional scaling[14] down to one dimension assigns a one dimensional position to each timeline. Please note that this even works if the distance matrix does not fulfil all properties of a metric space (e.g. triangle inequality).

Sorting the users according to these positions of their corresponding timelines arranges similar ones next to each other as visible in Fig. 5.5. While the sorting

[13]Which are in fact very similar, see e.g. [23].

[14]Multidimensional scaling (MDS, [21]) in several variants [10].

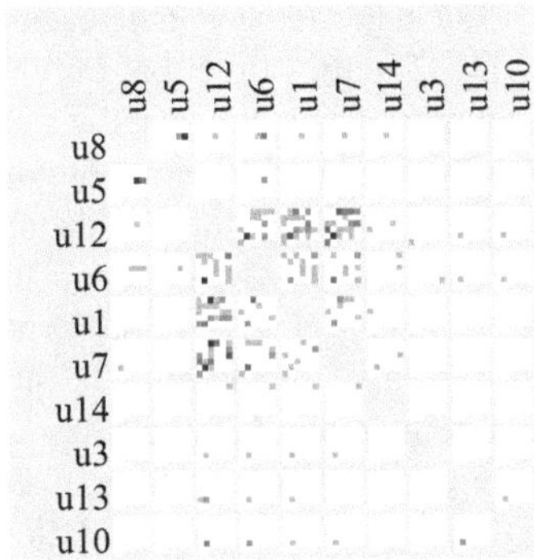

Fig. 5.6 *Workgroup wiki* network matrix ordered by collaboration activity

is done on the smoothened timelines which, as noted above, may have coarser resolution than the original timelines, the original ones are used in visualization.

Choosing good projections for MDS is known as a difficult problem [5], especially to only one dimension. We tested a lot of distance measures and parameters (more than described above) on social network data of several wikis (examples are given in Sect. 5.4) and found the ordering of the nodes to be very sensitive even to small changes of the distance matrix while the grouping of users with very similar timelines stays rather robust. This means small parameter changes give different layouts, but within these similar users (e.g. U5 and U8 in Fig. 5.5) are grouped together. So it is important to choose the right distance measure for the general decision whether to focus on absolute intensity or on relative cooccurrence of activity, as this defines which timelines should be grouped together, and adjusting the parameters can improve the visual appearance.

5.3.4.4 Arranging Matrix Rows and Columns

For the network matrix further parameters have to be considered for sorting the nodes. While grouping by external knowledge or some node feature stays the same arranging by similarity gets more complex as now each node does not longer correspond to exactly one timeline but (for n nodes) is connected to $2(n-1)$ timelines (the corresponding row and column).

We cannot simply arrange these $n(n-1)$ timelines by similarity as this would destroy the matrix structure. We can only rearrange whole columns and rows so that rows/columns containing similar timelines are placed next to each other. While it is possible to have a different order for rows and columns we would not recommend this, as it is unintuitive for a network matrix.

An easy and often sufficient approach is to use the node arrangement computed on their collaboration activity timelines for the matrix (Figs. 5.5b and 5.6). Our *workgroup wiki* example will not gain any further improvements by more sophisticated measures.

For other (larger) networks things are different as we will see later (Figs. 5.9–5.11). The user timelines only show the unspecific activity pattern of the users. So two users being active at the same time are grouped together even if their activity is totally unrelated. To compute the similarity of two user rows in the network matrix we therefore compute the distances of their glyphs column by column, e.g. for the users U3 and U13 in Fig. 5.6 (third and second bottommost row) we compare the glyph distances $d(\text{U3/U8}, \text{U13/U8})$, $d(\text{U3/U5}, \text{U13/U5}), \ldots, d(\text{U3/U10}, \text{U13/U10})$. The distance of the rows U3 and U13 is the sum of the distances of their glyphs. Please note that for comparison of the single glyph timelines everything described in Sect. 5.3.4.1 (smoothing, distance measures etc.) can be used.

Pairs involving diagonal elements (in the example i.e. $d(\text{U3/U3}, \text{U13/U3})$ and $d(\text{U3+/U13}, \text{U13/U13})$) cannot be computed and are either skipped or the diagonal glyph is virtually set to a timeline with each point set to the maximum of all values in the matrix. The latter measure supports users working closely together to be considered more similar, e.g. $d(\text{U1/U12}, \text{U12/U12}) < d(\text{U10/U12}, \text{U12/U12})$. Both options work and we found the effect of the latter negligible on large networks.

5.3.5 *Interactive Visual Data Mining*

The visualization paradigm described in this section has been implemented as part of a network analysis package. Figure 5.7 gives a screenshot of PONVA, our interactive pixel-oriented network visualization application, which allows us to experiment with different layout algorithms and settings on various networks.[15]

Zooming into the full plot as well as "zooming" the glyphs by changing the resolution (Fig. 5.3b, c) allows to switch between overview and detailed inspection. Selecting the active timespan within one glyph or one column or row and highlighting the corresponding pixels in the other glyphs helps comparing user activity in time. Same holds for selecting one user or a pair of users and highlighting the corresponding row(s), column(s) (and intersections). And clicking on a pixel reveals detailed data from the point in time it represents to its numeric value.

Selecting one of the different glyph layout mechanisms, color scales and some γ-correction appropriate to the network to be analyzed is done interactively. And finally rows and columns can be sorted according to various similarity measures, which are not discussed within this chapter due to limited space.

Additionally an interactive application allows to use the distance information available from MDS. Figure 5.8 shows a two-dimensional configuration of the timelines (folded to row-by-row glyphs) scaled to two dimensions. This places the users/glyphs according to the similarity relations of their timelines, so similar glyphs are visually clustered together. This representation is not too useful on a printed

[15]POVNA [35] is written in Java. Not all features described are included in the current stable release.

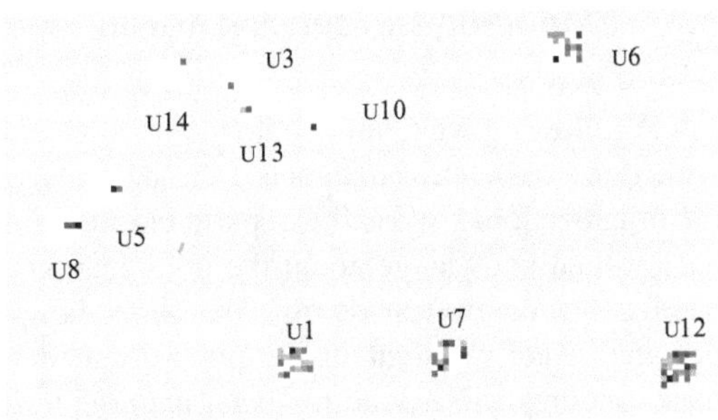

Fig. 5.7 Two-dimensional MDS representation of the *workgroup wiki* timelines

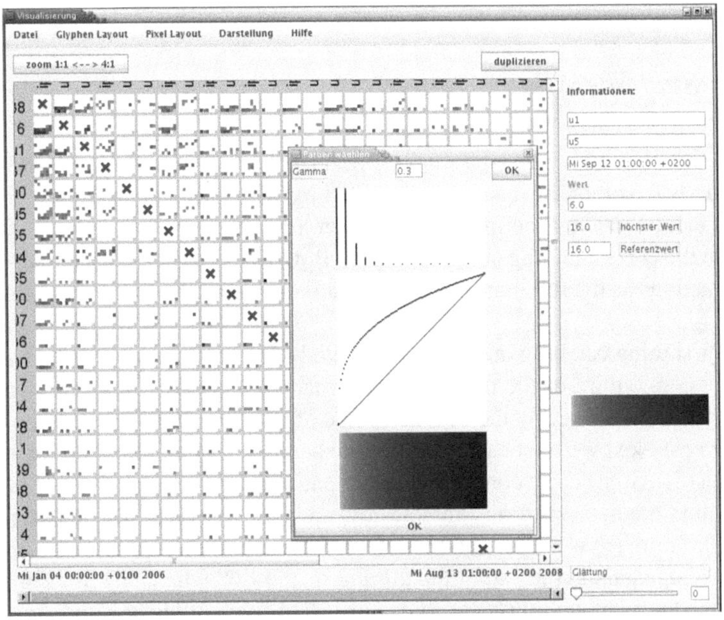

Fig. 5.8 Graphical user interface of PONVA. The main window shows a pixel-oriented visualization of the network matrix while the dialog in front allows to change γ-correction. To the right detailed information about one selected pixel is displayed

paper as it takes a larger amount of space which conflicts with the paradigm of pixel-oriented visualization that requires to use every pixel on the screen to represent one data point. The visualizations also suffers from cluttering as there are problems with overlapping glyphs and the annotation of the user names. However it is useful for interactive exploration where one can scroll and zoom in and annotations are dynamically displayed on mouseover or mouseclick.

5.4 Exploring Larger Networks

In the following we demonstrate the practical value of pixel-oriented visualization with three real world data sets. The datasets were collected during our research on organizational wikis.[16] A particularity of the data set is the fact that rich background knowledge about the organization context of the social networks has been collected independently. We show how user interaction patterns in time become visually salient in the pixel-oriented visualization and demonstrate that these findings correspond to social patterns in the organization. Additionally whe show how different node ordering methods improve the visualization.

5.4.1 Students Wiki

In Sect. 5.2.1 we introduced the *students wiki* (Fig. 5.1). Figure 5.9 shows the pixel-oriented visualization of this network sorted by (weighted) node degree: Fig. 5.9b gives the interaction timeline for each user (day by day grouped weekly) and Fig. 5.9a the corresponding network matrix. Both plots only give users with at least 50 interactions as the full matrix with 142 users would not be readable on this paper size.[17]

The first thing catching our eye in Fig. 5.9b is this dotted horizontal bar showing up at about one third of the timeline (users marked with •). This is the start of the second term and obviously the new and some of the older students did a lot of work in this week. Next we see heavy traffic at the beginning of the timeline for a 2 week timespan (□). Some users continue to participate, others leave, but most of the active users within the first two terms do not show up in the third one, and the users active in the third term (○) were not present before. Exceptions are only users U8 and U105 who show up again at the end of the third term and U68 who came in the middle of the second term but without being very active. The users of the first and second term overlap but there is low connection to the third term, and this confirms what we see in Fig. 5.1b–d.

While all this is visible in Fig. 5.9b, it gets more obvious in Fig. 5.10b where the user timelines are arranged by similarity as described in Sect. 5.3.4.3. The students active in the first, second and third term are now grouped together with the ones active during a whole year (first and second term) nicely placed in between.

The network matrix in Fig. 5.9a presents a nearly regular pattern of similar glyphs interrupted by rows and columns with rather empty glyphs and some few darker ones. By looking closer we can distinguish users with different glyph patterns. The

[16] In-depth case studies of the wikis used here including other types of (not pixel-oriented) visualizations are provided by Stein and Blaschke [31].

[17] This is less a problem in interactive usage where we can scroll.

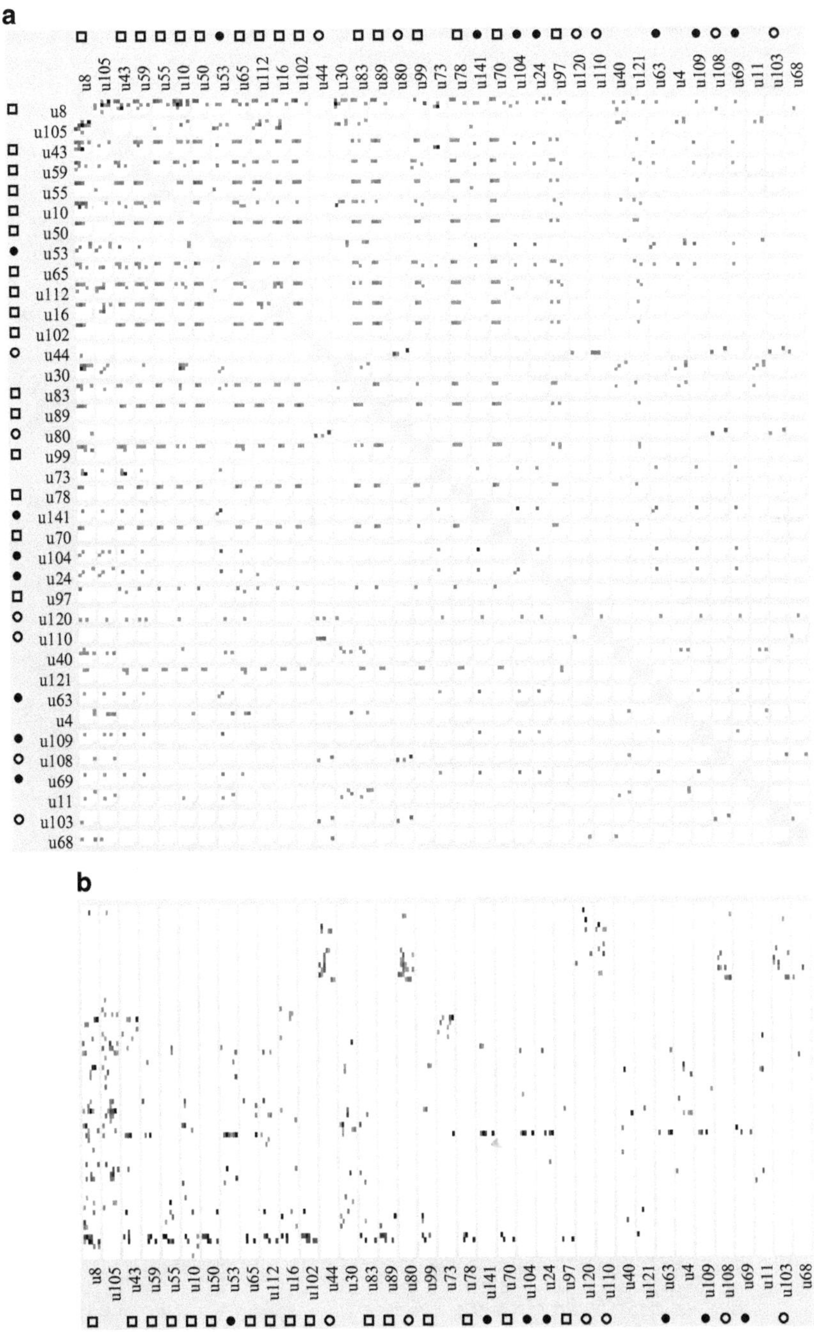

Fig. 5.9 *students wiki* (users with at least 50 links). (**a**) Network matrix. (**b**) Collaboration intensity. Time goes from *bottom* to *top*

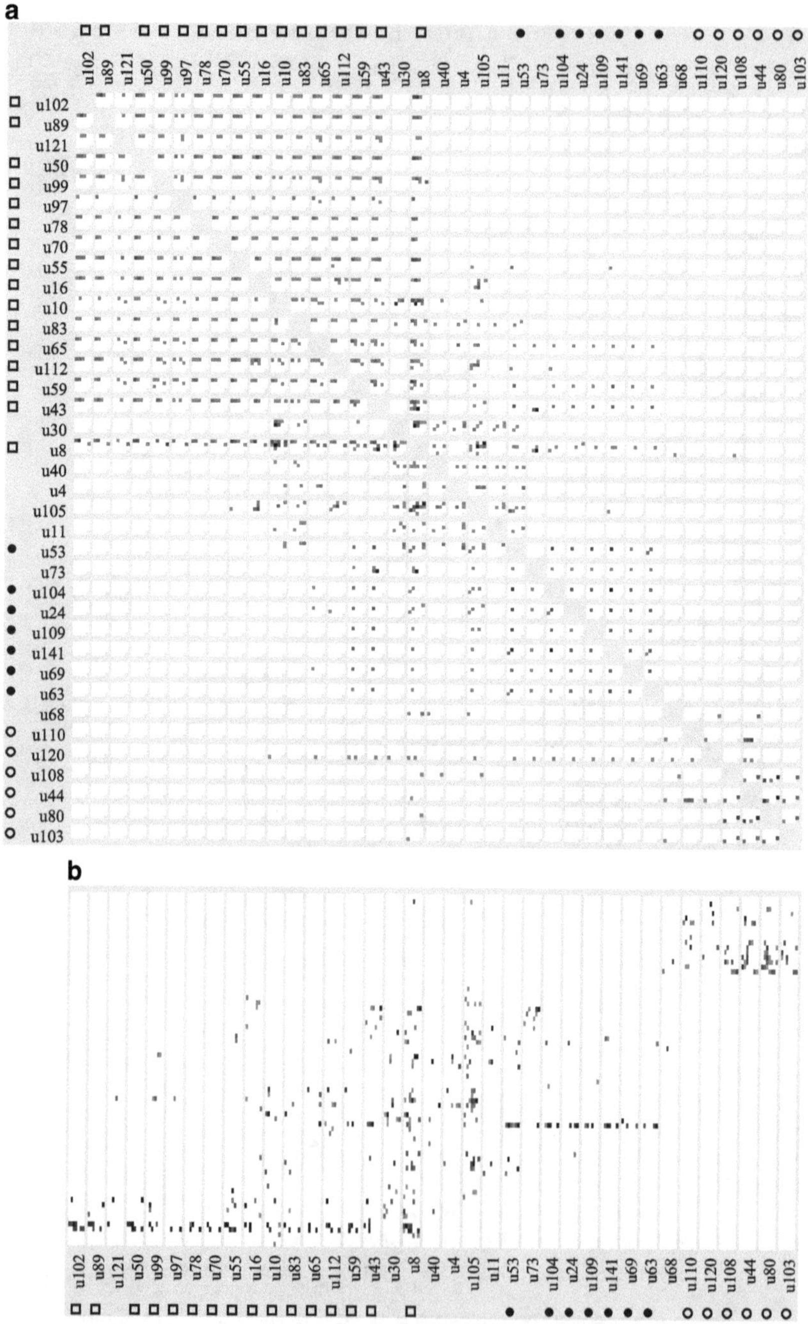

Fig. 5.10 *Students wiki* (users with at least 50 links), grouped by collaboration intensity timeline similarity. (**a**) Network matrix. (**b**) Collaboration intensity. Time goes from *bottom* to *top*

changed arrangement of rows and columns in Fig. 5.10a makes things easier by revealing patterns which give further insights: while there is collaboration between the students of the first and second term visible in the matrix the third term is nearly fully disconnected. Most of the students present in the first term collaborate with most of their fellows, for the wiki this means they all worked on the same wiki pages, they did not split up in subgroups working on different pages. Only user U120 stands out. While joining the wiki in the third term contrary to his fellows, he connects to most of the users of the first and second term, i.e. works on the pages they edited before.

In Fig. 5.11 not the collaboration intensity of the student timelines but the similarity of the glyph rows in the matrix is used to arrange the students. The difference to Fig. 5.10 is not as big as between Figs. 5.9 and 5.10 but noticeable. The three groups of students are clearly visible in the matrix, as well as the connection between the first and second group (users U83 to U43, i.e. the first six rows/columns in the matrix, plus some connection for rows/columns U112 to U16).

The exact configuration of rows and columns is highly dependent from the parameters chosen (smooth factor, distance metric, etc.) as if the distances between rows are small even small changes give different MDS to the one-dimensional space. Nevertheless the general patterns visible in the figure are rather stable.

So Figs. 5.9–5.11 are a good example for the perceptual salience of regular temporal collaboration patterns on one hand and the improvements possible by sophisticated grouping of the nodes. They not only show cooccurrence of activity of single users but also which users and groups of users are connected at which time.

5.4.2 Facilitation Wiki

Figure 5.12 introduces a new network. It shows the internal wiki of an organization that lends support for information and communication technologies to small and medium enterprises. The wiki features mostly research articles, project reports, and later publications thereof. The wiki is maintained as a dedicated project, and employees are enforced to generate a certain amount of input per anno.

The first thing catching the eye when inspecting the collaboration intensity timelines Fig. 5.12a is that users U35 (•) and U48 (∘) stand out.[18] U35 was the project manager of the wiki project and obviously did a lot of work until she left the company after three quarters of the timeline, where U48 had to take over this position. Both users were connected to almost everybody else as we can see in the first two rows of the network matrix (Fig. 5.12b). Only a connection from U35 to U33 is missing and as we can see in the user timelines U33 joined the wiki after U35 left.

[18] We may also see that they never edited the wiki on weekends.

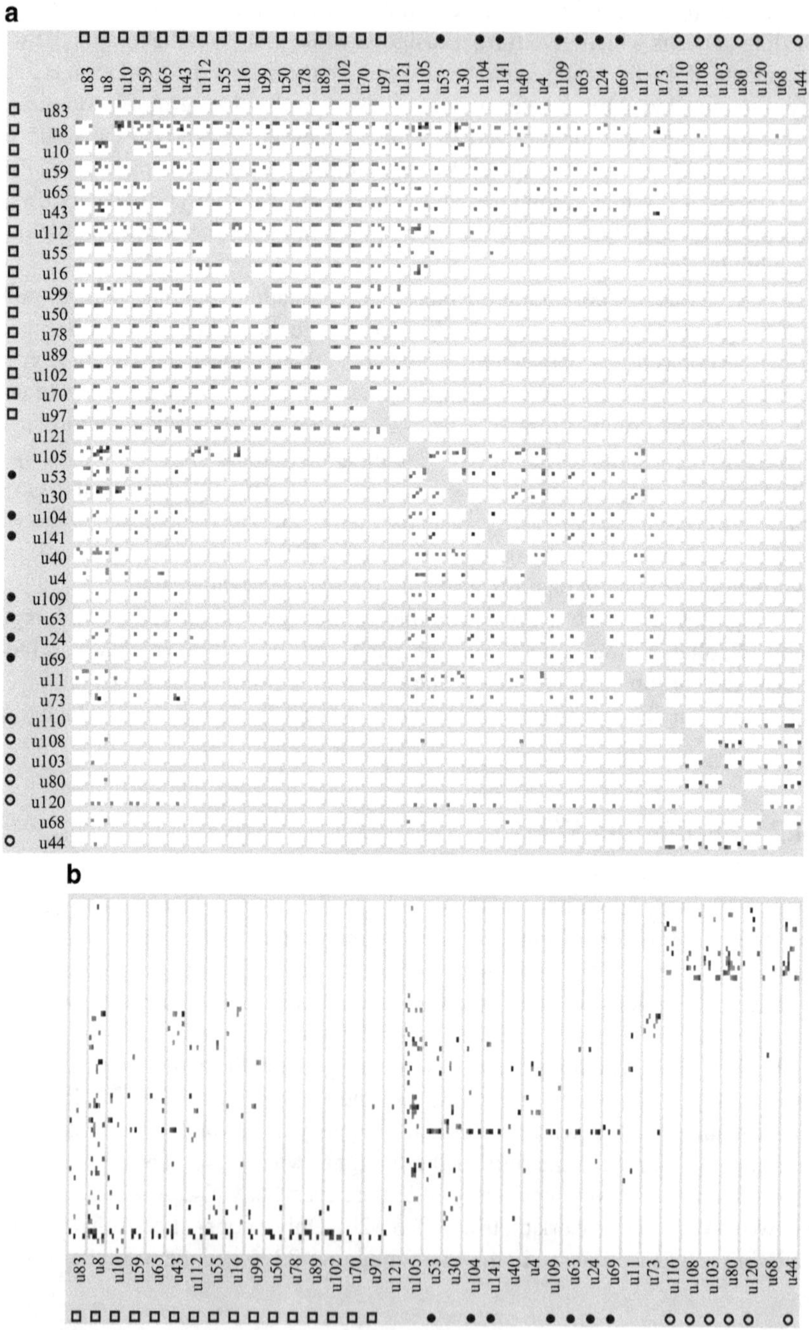

Fig. 5.11 *Students wiki* (users with at least 50 links), grouped by glyph row similarity. (**a**) Network matrix. (**b**) Collaboration intensity. Time goes from *bottom* to *top*

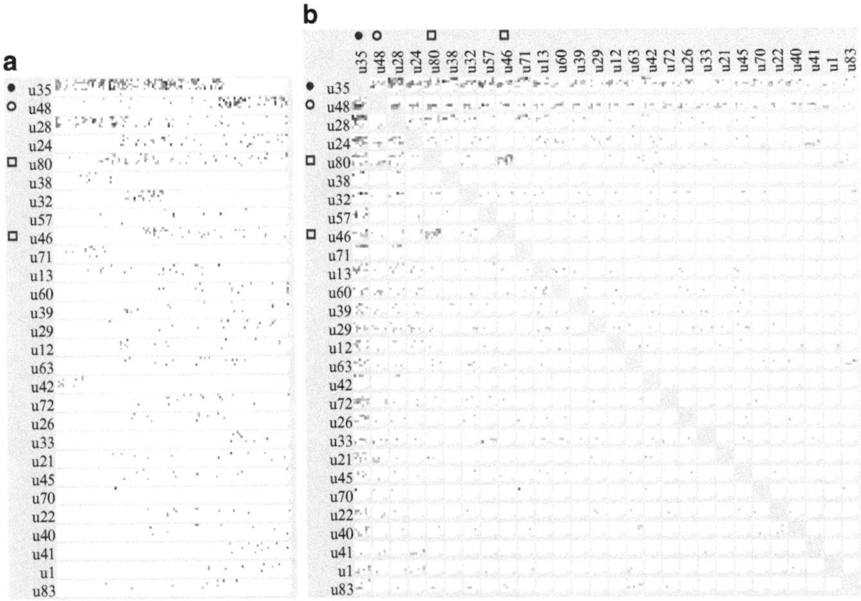

Fig. 5.12 *Facilitation wiki* (users with at least 50 links). (**a**) Collaboration intensity. (**b**) Network matrix

We could backup our findings by interviews where we learned that U35 (and later U48) was asked by all others to assist them with the wiki. However, the wiki was never really accepted by the users, and almost nobody started to use the wiki as a collaboration tool, so she had to work as a "gardener", formating the articles others had written. And the missing collaboration is visible in the network matrix, most of the glyphs are empty or very sparsely filled, only the pair U80 and U46 □ stands out, here direct collaboration shows up.

Contrary to the last example no uniform patterns are visible, but temporal cooccurrence as well as temporal connection draw attention when present in the fuzzy gray-spotted area of glyphs as our visual perception smoothens single dots to larger areas.

5.4.3 *Startup Wiki*

Our last example (Fig. 5.13) shows the *startup wiki* . It is the company wiki of an European market leader for one-stop solutions and services in mobile or proximity marketing. It was installed during the founding of the company and since then keeps its role as primary collaboration and main content management system for

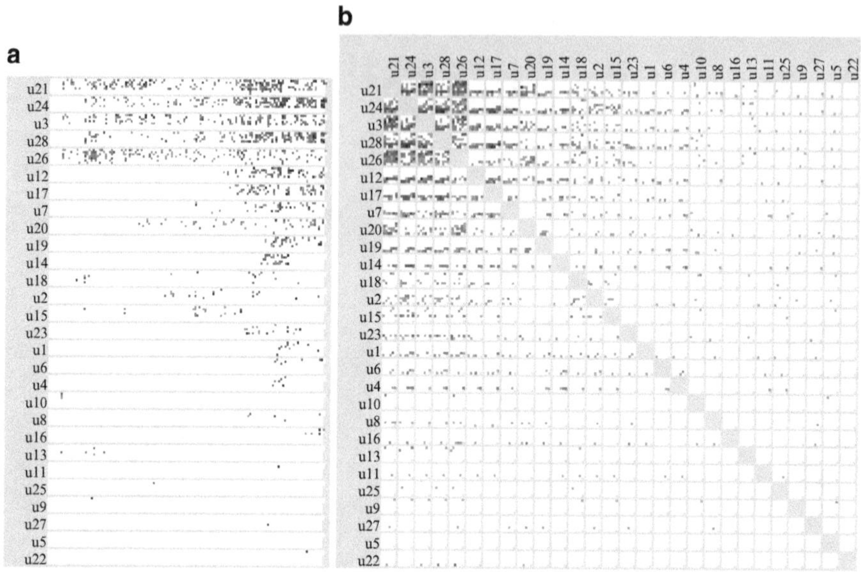

Fig. 5.13 *Startup wiki* network matrix. (**a**) Collaboration intensity. (**b**) Network matrix

the engineers. Growing from 3 to 26 users the primary users never stopped to use the wiki and new employees joining get connected to the others. Wiki growth at its best, and nicely visible in the user interlocking network matrix.

We see users with high activity as well as ones showing up only once which is not surprising as e.g. accounting uses other specialized software and other groups only need to read wiki contents without editing.

Contrary to the *facilitation wiki* users connect to each other, we do not have this one "gardener" getting all the connections but collaboration between the active users. Not everyone is using the wiki intensely but those who do are connected to each other.

5.5 Conclusions and Outlook

In this chapter we introduced pixel-oriented network visualization (PONV), a new visualization for weighted social networks changing in time. Our approach focuses on using static visualization of dynamic network data as a method of data exploration by the means of visual data mining which works best on medium-size networks where the whole matrix fits on the screen or paper at once.

We discussed different patterns for pixel as well as the glyph arrangement. Furthermore, we presented different pixel layouts from simple ones like plain rows to more complex space-filling curves. It turns out that the arrangement of the glyphs should be adapted according to the actual task and can be lead by external knowledge, some node feature or similarity. We therefore introduced different distance measures.

The interpretation of PONV is not immediately obvious but easily learned by the interested expert. Using several interlocking coauthor networks extracted from organizational wikis we could show how pixel-oriented network visualization reveals perceptual salient patterns for temporal cooccurrence of user collaboration as well as user-user-connection. In our examples we tended to stick to the simple row by row approach for the arrangement of the pixels which we found to be least irritating. In addition a glyph arrangement according to similarity lead to the visually most appealing results.

PONV allows to detect similar collaboration patterns across users and to reveal the collaboration between a pair of users across time. It is nevertheless meant as complementary visualization besides network graphs and others and not as a substitution, as interactions between groups of more than two users only show up indirectly, it focuses on temporal patterns, not on the detection of network clusters. This also means that PONV is less useful on rather sparse networks with low traffic where no visual patterns emerge.

Topics for future work are the development of more sophisticated glyph layouts as well as combining pixel-oriented visualization with other layout algorithms like using the glyphs as nodes in a graph representation integrating both visualization techniques. Finally the understandability and usefulness of PONV shall be examined and at best improved by user studies.

The analysis and graphics in this chapter are produced using the pixvis/PONV module of our own Wiki Explorator library.[19] It is available for download under an open source licence.[20]

Acknowledgements Part of this work was supported by the Volkswagenstiftung through Grant No. II/82 509.

We thank the reviewers for their helpful comments.

References

1. Aigner, W., Miksch, S., Müller, W., Schumann, H., Tominski, C.: Visualizing time-oriented data, a systematic view. Comput. Graph. **31**(3), 401–409 (2007)
2. Ankerst, M., Berchtold, S., Keim, D.A.: Similarity clustering of dimensions for an enhanced visualization of multidimensional data. In: INFOVIS '98: Proceedings of the 1998 IEEE Symposium on Information Visualization. IEEE Computer Society, Washington, DC (1998)
3. Balzer, M., Deussen, O.: Level-of-detail visualization of clustered graph layouts. In: APVIS'07, pp. 133–140. IEEE, Piscataway (2007)

[19] Wiki Explorator is written in Ruby using R, Gnuplot, Graphviz and other open source software.

[20] http://wiki-explorator.rubyforge.org. We also provide an online wiki analysis service based on this library at http://www.kinf.wiai.uni-bamberg.de/mwstat.

4. Bender-deMoll, S., McFarland, D.A.: The art and science of dynamic network visualization. J. Soc. Struct. **7**(2), 1–46 (2006). http://www.cmu.edu/joss/content/articles/volume7/deMollMcFarland
5. Beyer, K., Goldstein, J., Ramakrishnan, R., Shaft, U.: When is "nearest neighbor" meaningful? In: Database Theory—ICDT'99, pp. 217–235. Springer, Berlin/New York (1999)
6. Brandes, U., Kenis, P., Raab, J.: Explanation through network visualization. Methodology **2**(1), 16–23 (2006)
7. Chen, C.: Information Visualization: Beyond the Horizon, 2nd edn. Springer, London (2006)
8. Chen, I.X., Yang, C.Z.: Visualization of social networks. In: Furht, B. (ed.) Handbook of Social Network Technologies and Applications, pp. 585–610. Springer, New York (2010)
9. Chen, W., Ji, M., Tang, X., Zhang, B., Shi, B.: Visualization tools for exploring social networks and travel behavior. In: 2010 International Conference on Environmental Science and Information Application Technology (ESIAT), vol. 3, pp. 239–243. IEEE, Piscataway (2010)
10. Cox, M.A.A., Cox, T.F.: Multidimensional scaling. In: Chen, C.h., Härdle, W., Unwin, A. (eds.) Handbook of Data Visualization. Springer Handbooks Computational Statistics, pp. 315–347. Springer, Berlin/Heidelberg (2008). doi:http://dx.doi.org/10.1007/978-3-540-33037-0_14
11. Eppstein, D., Gansner, E.R. (eds.): Graph Drawing: 17th International Symposium, GD 2009. LNCS, vol. 5849. Springer, Berlin/New York (2010)
12. Everitt, B.S., Landau, S., Leese, M.: Cluster Analysis, 4th edn. Wiley, Chichester (2009)
13. Ghoniem, M., Fekete, J.D., Castagliola, P.: A comparison of the readability of graphs using node-link and matrix-based representations. In: INFOVIS '04: Proceedings of the IEEE Symposium on Information Visualization, pp. 17–24. IEEE, Washington, DC (2004). doi:http://dx.doi.org/10.1109/INFOVIS.2004.1
14. Guo, Y., Chen, C., Zhou, S.: Fingerprint for network topologies. In: Zhou, J. (ed.) Complex Sciences, pp. 1666–1677. Springer, Berlin/Heidelberg (2009)
15. Henry, N., Fekete, J.D., McGuffin, M.J.: Nodetrix: a hybrid visualization of social networks. IEEE Trans. Vis. Comput. Graph. **13**(6), 1302–1309 (2007). doi:http://dx.doi.org/10.1109/TVCG.2007.70582
16. Kamada, T., Kawai, S.: An algorithm for drawing general undirected graphs. Inf. Process. Lett. **31**(1), 7–15 (1989)
17. Keim, D.A.: Designing pixel-oriented visualization techniques: theory and applications. IEEE Trans. Vis. Comput. Graph. **6**(1), 59–78 (2000). doi:http://dx.doi.org/10.1109/2945.841121
18. Keim, D.A., Keim, D.A., Kriegel, H.P., Kriegel, H.P.: Visdb: database exploration using multidimensional visualization. IEEE Comput. Graph. Appl. **14**, 40–49 (1994)
19. Keim, D.A., Ankerst, M., Kriegel, H.P.: Recursive pattern: a technique for visualizing very large amounts of data. In: VIS '95: Proceedings of the 6th Conference on Visualization '95. IEEE Computer Society, Washington, DC (1995)
20. Krempel, L.: Network visualization. In: Scott, J., Carrington, P.J. (eds.) Sage Handbook of Social Network Analysis. SAGE, London/Thousand Oaks (2009)
21. Kruskal, J.B., Wish, M.: Multidimensional Scaling. Sage University Paper Series on Quantitative Application in the Social Sciences. Sage, Beverly Hills/London (1978)
22. Leung, C., Carmichael, C.: Exploring social networks: a frequent pattern visualization approach. In: IEEE International Conference on Social Computing/IEEE International Conference on Privacy, Security, Risk and Trust, pp. 419–424. IEEE, Los Alamitos (2010)
23. Leydesdorff, L.: On the normalization and visualization of author co-citation data: Salton's cosine versus the jaccard index. J. Am. Soc. Inf. Sci. Technol. **59**(1), 77–85 (2008)
24. Moody, J., McFarland, D., Bender-deMoll, S.: Dynamic network visualization. Am. J. Sociol. **110**(4), 1206–1241 (2005). doi:10.1086/421509
25. Peng, W., SiKun, L.: Social network visualization via domain ontology. In: International Conference on Information Engineering and Computer Science, pp. 1–4. IEEE, Piscataway (2009)
26. Reeve, L., Han, H., Chen, C.: Information visualization and the semeantic web. In: Geroimenko, V., Chen, C. (eds.) Visualizing the Semantic Web: XML-Based Internet and Information Visualization. Springer, London (2006)

27. Riche, N.H., Fekete, J.D.: Novel visualizations and interactions for social networks exploration. In: Furht, B. (ed.) Handbook of Social Network Technologies and Applications, pp. 611–636. Springer, New York (2010). doi:http://dx.doi.org/10.1007/978-1-4419-7142-5_28
28. Shi, L., Cao, N., Liu, S., Qian, W., Tan, L., Wang, G., Sun, J., Lin, C.: HiMap: adaptive visualization of large-scale online social networks. In: Visualization Symposium, PacificVis '09. IEEE, Piscataway (2009)
29. Shneiderman, B.: Extreme visualization: squeezing a billion records into a million pixels. In: Proceedings of the 2008 ACM SIGMOD International Conference on Management of Data, pp. 3–12. ACM, New York (2008)
30. Shneiderman, B., Aris, A.: Network visualization by semantic substrates. IEEE Trans. Vis. Comput. Graph. **12**(5), 733–740 (2006). doi:http://dx.doi.org/10.1109/TVCG.2006.166
31. Stein, K., Blaschke, S.: Corporate wikis: comparative analysis of structures and dynamics. In: Hinkelmann, K., Wache, H. (eds.) Proceedings of the 5th Conference on Professional Knowledge Management. Lecture Notes in Informatics, pp. 77–86. Gesellschaft für Informatik, Bonn (2009)
32. Stein, K., Blaschke, S.: Interlocking communication, measuring collaborative intensity in social networks. In: Social Networks Analysis and Mining: Foundations and Applications. Springer, New York (2010)
33. Unwin, A., Theus, M., Hofmann, H.: Graphics of Large Datasets: Visualizing a Million. Springer, New York (2006)
34. Ware, C.: Visual Queries: The Foundation of Visual Thinking. Springer, Berlin/Heidelberg (2005)
35. Wegener, R.: Kollaborationsprozesse in Wikis: Entwurf und Umsetzung eines Analysewerkzeugs. Master's thesis, University of Bamberg (2009)

Chapter 6
Building Expert Recommenders from Email-Based Personal Social Networks

Verónica Rivera-Pelayo, Simone Braun, Uwe V. Riss, Hans Friedrich Witschel, and Bo Hu

Abstract In modern organisations there is the necessity to collaborate with people and establish interpersonal relationships. Contacting the right person is crucial for the success of the performed daily tasks. Personal email corpora contain rich information about all the people the user knows and their activities. Thus, an analysis of a person's emails allows automatically constructing a realistic image of the surroundings of that person. This chapter aims to develop ExpertSN, a personalised Expert Recommender tool based on email Data Mining and Social Network Analysis. ExpertSN constructs a personal social network from the email corpus of a person by computing profiles—including topics represented by keywords and other attributes such as recency of communication—for each contact found in the emails and by extracting relationships between people based on measures such as co-occurrence in *To* and *CC* fields of the emails or reciprocity of communication. Having constructed such a personal social network, we then consider its application for people search in a given work context. Through an analysis of several use cases, we have derived requirements for a query language that allows exploiting the personal social network for people search, taking into account a variety of

V. Rivera-Pelayo (✉) · S. Braun
FZI Forschungszentrum Informatik, Haid-und-Neu-Str. 10–14, 76131, Karlsruhe, Germany
e-mail: rivera@fzi.de; braun@fzi.de

U.V. Riss
SAP AG, Dietmar-Hopp-Allee 16, 69190 Walldorf, Germany
e-mail: Uwe.Riss@sap.com

H.F. Witschel
Fachhochschule Nordwestschweiz, Riggenbachstraße 16, 4600 Olten, Switzerland
e-mail: hansfriedrich.witschel@fhnw.ch

B. Hu
Fujitsu Laboratories of Europe Limited, Hayes Park Central, Hayes End Road, Hayes, Middlesex, United Kingdom, UB4 8FE
e-mail: bo.hu@uk.fujitsu.com

T. Özyer et al. (eds.), *The Influence of Technology on Social Network Analysis and Mining*, Lecture Notes in Social Networks 6, DOI 10.1007/978-3-7091-1346-2_6,

information needs that go well beyond classical expert search scenarios known from the literature. We further discuss the application of the people search interface in a personal task management environment for effectively retrieving collaborators for a work task. Finally, we report on a user study undertaken to evaluate the personal social network in ExpertSN that shows very promising results.

6.1 Introduction

Currently we witness a significant increase in the uptake of social network technologies that have almost become an omnipresent phenomenon. The impact of such networks on organisations has become a vividly discussed topic. While initially extra-organisational social networks such as Facebook[1] or LinkedIn[2] were used for organisational purposes [41], we now observe a certain trend of implementing purposely designed intra-organisational social networks such as IBM's Beehive [13]. The motivation behind the introduction of social network applications into large organisations was to foster new ways of communication and collaboration between the employees and motivate them to share work-related personal experiences. The importance of social network support has been further increased by the growing agility requirements of organisations and their workforce, which continuously raise the need for IT support in collaboration and expert identification [15, 34].

In the enterprise environment, a widely accepted use of social networks is the "expert search" that is finding the right person with the right expertise. In such a field, there is, however, a particular challenge resulting from the fact that collaboration always takes place in a restricted social context and not in a global network [6]. As a consequence the willingness to collaborate often depends on the personal proximity to the respective expert. Beside the use of extra- and intra-organisational social networks, which bring about various privacy issues [1, 20], recently the use of so-called egocentric social networks (ESNs) has entered the discussion. They serve similar purposes as global public networks but are tailored to and controlled by the individual users [17]. To this end they take the personal communication (e.g. emails, blogs, etc.) of the users into account to help them find a potential expert. On this basis ESNs allow exploring the relations to and between other people within and outside the user's organisation. Among other communication channels, email as the most extended and accepted way of communication in and between organisations provides a rich reservoir of data, of which the full potential has not been exploited yet. Emails are being used for various purposes that go far beyond their original aim of mere communication [49]. Since especially in large organisations people can only sporadically be reached at their desks, emails are used for all kinds of purposes such as requesting answers to questions, discussing

[1] http://www.facebook.com/

[2] http://www.linkedin.com/

problems, summoning up meetings, managing projects, aligning work tasks and so on. Each email establishes connections of varying intensity depending on the nature of the recipients, e.g. who was directly addressed or who was included via a distribution list. The connections may also be regulated by other characteristics of emails, e.g. time interval, subject, etc. All this information is, however, hidden in the massive body of personal emails and thus not accessible to the users. The situation is aggravated due to a lack of suitable visualisers that assist us to harness the vast amount of information.

In this chapter, we present an approach that has been developed at SAP Research and consists in the design, implementation and evaluation of an expert search tool, called ExpertSN, based on a Personal Social Network (PSN). ExpertSN extracts and analyses the hidden treasure in the personal email corpus to build up the PSN that is focused on the owner of the email corpus. Hence, individual users have full control over the resultant PSN without jeopardising data privacy and safety. The analysis of this corpus provides information about all contacts that appear in the email and is used as a data pool for the expert recommender. The aim of this recommender is to identify potential collaborators for specific tasks. Identifying the experts is normally not the end of process, it is also important to select the most appropriate one judged by other criteria [31]. This is facilitated by additional information about the particular foci of expertise that the respective expert is bringing along and their general availability.

A particular characteristic of the current approach is that the entire data management and persistence is based on semantic technologies. This approach opens up opportunities to exploit the analysis results for a semantically integrated Personal Information and Task Management framework that we have started to develop [19, 38, 39]. Here the aim is to provide a seamless infrastructure that allows users to get desktop-wide access to personal information resources as well as to the corresponding metadata and offer analytic tools to exploit the resulting semantic network so as to enrich the PSN.

In order to simplify the interaction with the ExpertSN system, we developed a Social Network Query Language (SNQL) for expressing the users' search requirements in the PSN. This query language helps exploit the email data pool and thus supports users to find suitable collaborators for their daily tasks.

In summary, the design and development of ExpertSN was directed towards the following objectives:

- Analysis of actual work situations that require expert search;
- Data extraction from the user's email corpus;
- Development of use cases and requirements for such extraction;
- Construction of a social network graph of persons from the email corpus;
- Keyword extraction methodology that automatically annotates persons with keywords found in emails;
- Definition of a relationship between two persons based on email corpus;
- Recommendations based on both keywords and network proximities.

Before we explain the ExpertSN approach in more detail, we would like first give an overview of the current state of the art in email based network development and expert search in Sect. 6.2. In Sect. 6.3 we derive the requirements of an expert search system as they appear in the context of social networks. In Sect. 6.4 we describe the chosen approach, turning to technical aspects of architecture and implementation. In Sect. 6.5 we detail the experience of using the system and the lessons learned. We conclude the chapter in Sect. 6.6 where we briefly summarise the results and envision the prospective further research and development of the ExpertSN system.

6.2 State of the Art

In this section we review the related work of using email corpora as knowledge source. This is followed by a survey of existing approaches to social network analysis (SNA) and expert recommendation systems.

6.2.1 Email Corpora as Knowledge Source

Email systems provide a rich source of information and the analysis of email communication [16, 35, 36] has been a quite popular research topic in social and computer science for many years [17, 28, 45, 47]. An email is not only a simple text message but also yields information on interactions and user behaviour [42] and knowledge transfer among people within a specific context.

Clustering and classification techniques are used to analyse the email content that might be trained with manual user input [33, 43]. Carvalho and Cohen [8] showed methods for automatically identifying the different parts in a plain-text email message, e.g. of significant importance are signature blocks and reply lines. Aalst and Nikolov [45] aimed to discover the interaction patterns and processes in the email corpora of a company's employees to support business process management. They created an organisation wide sociogram from such information. Culotta et al. [11] extracted one's social network from his or her email inbox and enriched the network with expertise and contact information for each person obtained from the Web.

Balog and de Rijke [2] found out that (1) the fielded structure of email messages can be effectively exploited to find pieces of evidence of expertise, which can then be successfully combined in a language modelling framework, and (2) email signatures are a reliable source of personal contact information. Campbell et al. [7] compared two algorithms for determining expertise from email: a content-based approach that mines email text and a graph-based ranking algorithm adapting HITS (Hyperlink-Induced Topic Search [27]). Their results suggest that HITS makes more specific or targeted predictions than the simple algorithm. However better algorithms are needed to capture more knowledge.

Several studies have been carried out in order to analyse personal relationships via email messages. The study by Whittaker et al. [48] has shown that frequency, reciprocity, recency, longevity and affiliation of email interaction are strong predictors of the importance of email contacts. Similarly, the study by Ogata et al. [36] reveals that the social relationship is strong if email between two persons is exchanged frequently, recently and reciprocally. Van Reijsen et al. [46] propose to extract email based social networks (who–knows–who) from email header data as well as knowledge (who–knows–what) from email bodies. They have developed tools, ESNE (email social network extractor) and EKE (email knowledge extractor) and discuss an integration of both.

Carvalho and Cohen [9] and Pal and Mccallum [37] approached the problem of recipient prediction; i.e. identifying and suggesting potentially intended recipients when composing the email. The prediction is based on the written content. This problem is closely related to the expert finding approach, since it involves identifying people within an organisation or social network who are working on similar projects, dealing with similar issues or who have relevant skills.

6.2.2 *Social Network Analysis*

There is a wide range on SNA tools that support examining social networks and performing common SNA routines like *UCINET*[3] or *Pajek*[4] or *Vizster*[5] for visualisation. *InFlow 3.1*[6] maps and measures knowledge exchange, information flow, emergent communities, networks of alliances and other networks within and between organisations and communities. The *Email Mining Toolkit* [42] and *EmailNet* [44] analyse email usage patterns at the individual and group level and compute behaviour profiles or models of user email accounts.

Farnham et al. [16] used public corporate mailing lists to automatically approximate corporate social networks. They have shown that co-occurrence in mailing lists provided a good predictor of who works with whom. With their *Point to Point* tool, they let users explore these networks and decide whom they want to contact. Based on this, the authors had also found that the network visualisation had a meaningful impact on users' ratings with respect to the similarities between others and themselves—people appeared less similar with the presence of the visualisation. Rowe et al. [40] introduce an algorithm for extracting a special kind of social relationships, namely hierarchical ones, from email communication.

Flink by Mika [32] is a system for extracting, aggregating and visualising online social networks, specifically of researchers together with their interests and research

[3]http://www.analytictech.com/ucinet

[4]http://pajek.imfm.si/doku.php

[5]http://hci.stanford.edu/jheer/projects/vizster

[6]http://www.orgnet.com/inflow3.html

topics. It employs semantic technologies for reasoning with personal information extracted from different electronic information sources including web pages, emails, publications and FOAF profiles. FOAF[7] is intended to create a Web of machine-readable pages describing people, the links between them and the things they like. SIOC[8] (Semantically-Interlinked Online Communities) is an ontology for semantically representing Social Web data in order to integrate the information from online communities. Similarly, RELATIONSHIP[9] is a vocabulary for describing relationships among people with a specific nomenclature of terms like "ancestor of", "colleague of" or "employer of".

As mentioned before, the analysis of egocentric social networks has become a more active area of research due to the consideration of privacy. Fisher [17] makes a first attempt to view social networks from an individual's perspective and to understand how people manage group communication. He uses data from email or newsgroups [17, 18] to construct egocentric social networks, other approaches focus on mobile call networks [50]. In [22], the authors make an attempt to compare public global social networks with egocentric ones derived from email.

6.2.3 Expert Systems for People Recommendation

A key issue of expert recommender systems is the determination of expert profiles, which Balog and de Rijke [3] described as the record of topical profile (types and fields of skills) plus social profile (collaboration network). Determining a user's expertise is usually based on and often limited to topic extraction from documents. Becerra-Fernandez [4] provided a review on expertise locator systems from a knowledge and human resource management perspective. Balog and de Rijke [3] presented a formalisation in order to automatically determine an expert profile of a person from a heterogeneous corpus of an organisation. Hofmann and Balog [24] explored in a pilot study how contextual factors identified by expertise seeking models can be integrated with topic-centric retrieval performance. Based on the vision of the social semantic desktop [21] that includes the extraction of metadata about people and the extraction of content from the desktop files, Demartini and Niederée [12] presented a new system for finding experts in the user's desktop content.

Recently expert recommendation systems have attracted strong interests in major enterprises. For instance, the social networking web application *SmallBlue* by IBM Research [15, 29] aims to locate knowledgeable colleagues, communities, and knowledge networks in companies based on analysing a user's outgoing email and instant messages. Different components provide functionalities such as expertise search, profile information, social search showing the social distance and combining

[7] http://www.foaf-project.org/

[8] http://sioc-project.org

[9] http://vocab.org/relationship/.html

it with social bookmarking and web search, as well as displaying the social network of top experts associated with a topic.

In conclusion, email corpora provide a rich source of information. The extraction of knowledge from these email corpora is a new trend in the field of expert recommender systems, in contrast with the conventional methods for searching experts based on documents. Meanwhile, most of the approaches that offer expert recommendation are only based on content information, neglecting the importance of relationships among people. The approach of combining the content and metadata extraction from emails with the characterisation of the relationships between the people based on network analysis is one of the innovative aspects that differentiates our approach from apparently similar ones. In other words: previous research has concentrated on either email-based expert search or analysis of email-based social networks, but there is few work that brings both together. Our main motivation for doing so is the possibility to cover a broader variety of information needs in expert search—i.e. to be able to search for facets, introducing e.g. a distinction between finding (results known largely in advance) and searching (completely open results)—and thus to go beyond the simplistic notion of "expertise" that is so widely used in the existing expert search literature. The systematisation and formalisation of the varying information needs via the Social Network Query Language (SNQL) is another distinctive feature of our research.

6.3 Information Needs in Expert Search

The task of finding collaborators in an organisational environment—which we refer to as "people retrieval" hereinafter—can involve more aspects than a person's expertise. Therefore, a prerequisite of designing an expert recommendation system is to gain an understanding of different information needs that support different use cases of people retrieval.

Categorisation of information needs is extensively studied in Information Retrieval research, namely in the area of web search, where tasks like homepage finding or on-line service location were identified in addition to the traditional topic relevance searches. Taxonomies of search tasks have been brought forward e.g. based on the number of results that a searcher expects (see the TREC web track [23]). Similar to web search, information needs in people retrieval can also be generally classified into two groups: *finding* and *searching* based on both the goals of the user and the expected results. In *people finding*, the result set is known in advance. In other words, the user is looking for a particular person or a group of persons whose existence is already known. He/She is seeking to enrich the known information, e.g. contact details and sometimes name(s). The search criteria in the people finding use case are very clear and sometimes well-defined for the user. In *people search*, the situation is different: the user is looking for people with specific characteristics. He/She does not know if such people exist or, in case they do exist, how many candidates there are. The search criteria in the people searching use case are rather vague. Typically, retrieved experts will match the criteria to different extents and thus ranking become necessary.

The rest of this section provides a detailed analysis of information needs in the context of people finding and people search, which are compilations of situations that the authors have experienced in their daily work activities. The first of these use cases is centred around a researcher, Philipp, who—having worked in a research project for some years—now joins a new project that started 2 years ago. Philipp needs to catch up with the work that has been done and, even more importantly, get acquainted with the people who are working on the same project and who can help him with his new tasks. We will use the task of writing a project report as an example. The second use case is that of a project manager, Jan, who has taken up a new position as software release manager where he needs to communicate with a large number of people, including developers, testers and customers. Jan needs to release the new software EasyWay and wishes to set up a meeting with all key persons involved in the production. Fortunately, he had been involved since the early stages of the EasyWay project.

6.3.1 People Finding

There are several situations that can lead to looking for a person or a group of persons of whose existence is known. Based on our two use cases, we have extracted the following categories:

Substitute (single person). This case occurs when one of the collaborators in the past is no longer available, e.g. due to a job change. In this case, it is desirable to find a replacement of that person. In the example of our first use case, imagine that Philipp, who needs to work on a software prototype that is part of his new project, finds the name of a programmer in the source code of the prototype. Let us assume that this person has left the project and the company. Philipp then has to search for the substitute.

Representative (single person). Sometimes one faces the need to contact a person in another department or organisation in order to acquire answers to a specific question. In such a situation, one needs to find the right representative in the target group. Imagine, for example, that Philipp would like to access a versioning system as a repository for important project documents. He knows which partner organisation is hosting the system and also knows that there is a dedicated contact person, but is lacking name and contact details of that person.

Group members (group of persons). Frequently, one needs to contact all members of a certain group, e.g. to set up a meeting or distribute an announcement. In the case where no mailing lists already exist for the given group, finding all members of a group becomes challenging. In the example of our second use case, we can imagine that Jan is trying to set up a meeting with all members of the EasyWay project.

6.3.2 People Search

As mentioned above, people search has more uncertainty in the result set than people finding. In addition, it often involves less clear criteria, e.g. the personal relationships among people. We have discovered the following categories of criteria that characterise information needs:

Expertise. This is the conventional expert search where people with a particular expertise are to be identified. However, it is possible to further sub-categorise this kind of information need with respect to the kind of knowledge that one wishes to obtain from the expert—by distinguishing between procedural and factual knowledge:

Procedural expertise: Often, one needs to find a person that has (successfully) performed a certain task in order to draw from their experience—in the form of advice or resources that have applied or produced. For instance, Philipp might need to write a report describing the outcomes of the accomplished work in the project. He suspects that someone has done this task before and thus he can use as a guide the templates and examples that were used by other before. In order to find such information, he needs to look for a person who has actually performed this task in the past.

Factual expertise: This corresponds to the topical relevance in document retrieval where a document conveys the information about a certain topic. It occurs in cases where one is searching for persons interested and knowledgeable in a certain topic in order to collaborate with them or engage in discussions. Here, the primary focus is not necessarily on sharing concrete experience, but rather on common interests and factual knowledge that can lead to a fruitful collaboration. For instance, we can imagine that Jan would like to contact people from another department—which he has not previously worked with—in order to discuss a potential future collaboration aiming at extending EasyWay with new functionalities. The system should recommend collaborators from the department who are working on or interested in topics that are relevant to EasyWay.

Closeness. Sometimes a person (*P*) that one usually works with or whom one knows to be knowledgeable about something is unavailable or too busy to respond. In such cases, the user may be interested in contacting a person who is close enough to *P*. We can further distinguish two types of closeness:

Close collaboration: This refers to persons who work closely together with *P*—it could be that they are in the same department and project or share an office. In our example, let us imagine that Philipp is looking for people who know a certain software; he knows that John is among the few people who do and is the most knowledgeable one about the software. Unfortunately, John is on vacation. Philipp would like the system to propose from those who collaborate closely with John, with the hope that there is another expert among these. Moreover, Philipp would prefer those who know John personally because he has a good relationship with John and believes that in this way he is more likely to get good answers.

Close expertise: Here, we are looking at cases where the user knows potentially rather little about *P*, except the fact that John is a knowledgeable person on a certain topic. The user would like to find other people with similar expertise. That is, there is no strict need for the retrieved person to know *P*, apart from using *P*'s profile as an exemplary case. In our example, consider Jan looking for someone in the Change Management Department who could help him with a particular problem. He knows that Michael has the necessary expertise, but is unavailable. Therefore he needs to find other people in Change Management who have a matching profile with Michael's.

Availability. The (regular) availability of a person may be an important criterion for fruitful collaboration: someone can be a very renowned expert in a field; but if he/she never has time, there is no hope for good collaboration. For instance, assume Philipp needs the expertise of an analyst for his report. He finds out that the head analyst of the project is not responsive. He would like to find another analyst, e.g. using *close collaboration* as a criterion with an additional constraint on availability.

It is typical for people retrieval that two or more of the criteria mentioned above are combined. For instance, it is often possible to restrict the search for a person with a certain expertise to a specific group of persons (Group members) or it may be desirable to combine expertise with availability.

6.3.3 General Ranking Criteria

In addition to analysing and categorising the information needs mentioned above, we propose the following general considerations about how the results of people retrieval should be ranked—taking into account the *personal relationship* between the user and the contacts that are retrieved:

Affluence of communication. Depending on the situation, a high or low affluence can be desirable. In many situations, a user would prefer well-known persons to be ranked close to the top of the list because it is easier to get in contact and collaborate with these. On the other hand, a searcher might be more interested in *novelty*, i.e. retrieving contacts of whom he or she would otherwise not have thought. Hence, it is important for a retrieval system to be able to retrieve persons with whom he/she has never communicated before.

Time. The date of last and first activity or communication between a retrieved contact and the user may be an important ranking criterion. It is often desirable to rank experts at a higher position if they have been in contact with the user recently and/or for a long period of time.

Table 6.1 Constructs of the SNQL

Constructs	Explanation	Information need/ranking criterion
SUBSTITUTE *person*	Find the substitute for *person*	Substitute
REPRESENTATIVE *q*	Given a set of results for SNQL query *q*, find a representative person	Representative
Keywords	Set of keywords associated to a contact describing his/her expertise	Factual Expertise
NOT *person*	Allows the exclusion of a person from the result set	
REG AVAILABILITY	Find a contact with availability to establish a continuous collaboration	Availability
REL *person*	Find a contact with a relationship with *person*	(Close) collaboration
CLOSE *person*	Find a contact close to *person*	Close collaboration
UNAVAILABLE *person*	Indicates that *person* is unavailable, the user needs a contact with similar characteristics	Close expertise
COMPARE *keywords*	Search for contacts close to the current collaborator in a field described by *keywords*	Close expertise
RECENT *date*	Retrieve contacts with evidence of activity more recent than *date*	Time factor
RECENT	Rank by recency of communication	Time factor
ORDER *criteria*	Order candidates following the *criteria*	Affluence of communication

6.3.4 A Social Network Query Language

The means to express both the "atomic" information needs described above and combinations thereof is provided by a Social Network Query Language (SNQL).

In the field of web search, considerable effort has been invested into automatically classifying queries according to search task categories (e.g. homepage finding versus topical relevance, see e.g. the TREC-2004 web track [10] with its query classification task), in order to apply different ranking algorithms based on the outcome of classification. Since we are not sure whether an automatic query classification (differentiating people finding and people search) is possible for people retrieval and since this is beyond the scope of this work, we will present SNQL for the *explicit* formulation of all information needs that we have identified.

```
query = keywords, { ";", [ "NOT", blank ], person },
        [ ";REG AVAILABILITY" ], [ options ]
        | "REPRESENTATIVE", blank, query;
options = closeness | unavailable | compare | substitute
        | compound;
keywords = words, { ",", words };
closeness = ";", "CLOSE", blank, person;
unavailable = ";", "UNAVAILABLE";
compare = ";", "COMPARE", blank, words;
substitute = ";", "SUBSTITUTE", blank, person;
compound = [ recency ], { relationship } , [ order ];
recency = ";", "RECENT", [ blank, date];
relationship = ";", "REL", blank, person;
order = ";", "ORDER", blank, [ "weight" | "reciprocity"
        | "co-occurrence" ];
person = "name=", words | "email=", address;
words = word, { blank, word };
date = day, month, year;
blank=" ";
```

Fig. 6.1 SNQL in EBNF

The SNQL intends to offer a suitable mean to specify in which conditions and contexts a user is seeking collaborators to do a specific task.

Table 6.1 summarises the atomic constructs from which SNQL queries can be composed. In addition to the explanation in the second column, the table also lists the types of information needs (see Sect. 6.3) that are satisfied by each constructs. The SNQL is formalised using the Extended Backus-Naur Form (EBNF) in Fig. 6.1. For simplicity, we do not further detail the syntax of the non-terminals word, address, day, month, and year, for which we assume standard definitions.

In the next section, we will describe ExpertSN and show how an egocentric social network, gained from an analysis of a person's emails, can be exploited for satisfying many of the discussed information needs and thus how that social network can help implementing SNQL.

6.4 ExpertSN—a Personalised Expert Recommender

ExpertSN system is an Expert Recommender based on email mining and social network analysis including the construction of an egocentric Personal Social Network. The general architecture of ExpertSN is based on two main modules, as shown in Fig. 6.2. The first module involves the construction of the egocentric Social Network from the email corpora and consequently has the email corpora as input and the PSN as output. The second module constitutes the Expert Recommender, taking as input the PSN and generating a personalised expert recommendation.

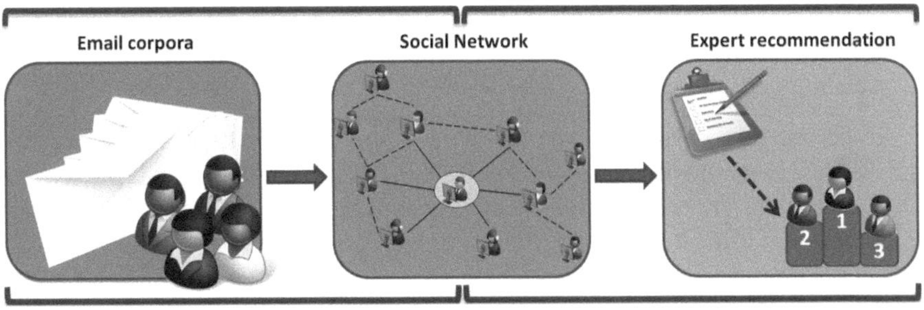

Fig. 6.2 The two ExpertSN modules. The first module involves the construction of the Personal Social Network from the email corpora and the second module constitutes the Expert Recommender based on this PSN

6.4.1 ExpertSN Architecture

Technically, ExpertSN is composed of:

- A presentation layer, through which users interact with the system, comprising the visualisation of the PSN and the console terminal that allows the communication with the Expert Recommender (e.g. entering SNQL queries).
- A logic layer consisting of modules that implement the steps in Fig. 6.2, i.e. crawl the raw data, create the PSN and allow to access the PSN data for use in the presentation layer. Crawling of emails is performed by the *Outlookcrawler* of the *Aperture* Framework,[10] which interacts with Microsoft Outlook (the main email management tool being used at SAP Research) to extract all email content and metadata into RDF.[11] Another important part of the logic layer consists of the extraction of keywords from the body of an email and the co-occurrence analysis of contacts from its header, handled by the *TE* [5] and *TinyCC*[12] modules, respectively (see below for details). Finally, the *Render* module in the logic layer helps to visualise the PSN through its interaction with *Protégé*[13] and the *Expert Recommender* module performs all the necessary tasks to generate a personal recommendation from the PSN based on the user's request/query.
- A data layer that contains the persistent data of the ExpertSN system, namely the email corpora, the RDF repository storing the email corpora, and the RDF repository storing the Social Network. We used the Sesame triple store[14] in

[10]http://aperture.sourceforge.net/

[11]http://www.w3.org/TR/PR-rdf-syntax/

[12]http://wortschatz.uni-leipzig.de/~cbiemann/software/TinyCC2.html

[13]http://protege.stanford.edu

[14]http://www.openrdf.org/

conjunction with the *RDFReactor*[15] and *Jena*[16] libraries for the actual storage and retrieval of the RDF data—thus, all issues such as optimisation of queries, scalability etc. are handled by these components.

To describe the design of ExpertSN we will use one running example. Suppose that Jan is a user who has installed ExpertSN in his system. In the next two sections we will explain the construction of the Personal Social Network and the Expert Recommender using the context of Jan.

6.4.2 Construction of the Personal Social Network

The construction of the PSN provides the basis that can be fed into the Expert Recommender to discover answers to user's queries.

The first step towards constructing the PSN consists of crawling the email corpus, technically implemented by Outlookcrawler from the Aperture Framework. Outlookcroawler connects to the MS Outlook instance. In the ExpertSN system, we leverage mainly two types of information provided by the Outlookcrawler, i.e. the emails and contacts.

The raw RDF file output by Outlookcrawler may contain invalid XML characters and can also have multiple string representations for the same email address. In order to guarantee the right performance of the next stages, this raw file must be cleaned.

The nodes of the resultant PSN are persons, including the user (owner of the email corpus, i.e. Jan) and the contacts, whereas the edges are undirected representing the relationships between pairs of persons. The relationships are classified into two categories according to the nodes that define the edge: if the user is one of the nodes defining the edge, the relationship is classified as *first* (first level); if both nodes are contacts from the network, it is denoted as *second* (second level).

The attributes that define each of the PSN nodes and edges were derived from the formalisation of the requirements. The formalisation allowed us to know which information is necessary in the PSN to enable the Expert Recommender. The attributes of each contact, first relationship, and second relationship were defined as follows: where $\mathscr{C}$ denotes the Contact nodes and $\mathscr{R}$ the relationship—note that we do not differentiate first and second level relationships when defining the attributes.

$\mathscr{C}$. Frequency: the total number of messages exchanged between the contact and the user, divided by the longevity of their relationship.

$\mathscr{C}$. Availability: the probability of keeping a constant contact, based on the frequency of communication of the most recent days.

[15] http://semanticweb.org/wiki/RDFReactor

[16] http://jena.sourceforge.net/

$\mathscr{C}$. Longevity: the number of days since the first communication of the contact with the user.
$\mathscr{C}$. Recency: the number of days since the last communication of the contact with the user.
$\mathscr{C}$. Keywords: the list of words from the email bodies related to each contact, represented as pairs (t,w) where t is the term and w its significance.

$\mathscr{R}$. Reciprocity: the measurement of the act of returning/responding emails (only for *first* relationships).
$\mathscr{R}$. Co-occurrence: the joint appearance as receivers in emails.
$\mathscr{R}$. Weight: strength of the relationship based on the attributes of the adjacent contacts and the previous two attributes.

The cleaned RDF graph that represents the email corpus will be queried using SPARQL[17] to extract the following information: the sent date, the sender, the receivers in *To* and *CC* fields, the message subject and the message body. This information is analysed to construct the PSN as follows.

A link is created between the body of the email and each contact that appears on it in order to perform the subsequent extraction of keywords. Regarding the relationships between the contacts of the email, we can distinguish between the emails that the user has sent and the emails that he/she has received (including the list emails). In case the email is sent by the user, the first and second relationships are added to the PSN between: (1) the user and the receivers of the email (first relationship) and (2) all the receivers in To and CC (second relationship). In case the email is received by the user, the relationships are added to the PSN between: (1) the user and the sender (first relationship) (2) the user and the other receivers, i.e. co-receivers (first relationship) (3) the sender and all the receivers in To and CC (second relationship) (4) all the receivers in To and CC, excluding the user (second relationship).

The Source Code 6.1 shows two SPARQL query examples used to obtain all this information. The first query would obtain the body content and the second query would obtain all the recipients in *To* field of an email identified by 'mailID'.

```
PREFIX rdf: <http://www.w3.org/1999/02/22-rdf-syntax-ns#>
PREFIX nmo: <http://www.semanticdesktop.org/ontologies/2007/03/22/nmo#>
PREFIX nco: <http://www.semanticdesktop.org/ontologies/2007/03/22/nco#>

SELECT ?body
WHERE {?email rdf:type nmo:Email.
FILTER regex(str(?email), 'mailID', 'i' ).
?email nmo:plainTextMessageContent ?body. }

SELECT ?name ?mID
WHERE {?email rdf: type nmo:Email.
FILTER regex(str(?email), 'mailID', 'i' ).
?email nmo:to ?to.
?to nco:fullname ?name.
?to nco:hasEmailAddress ?mail.
?mail nco:emailAddress ?mID.}
```

Source Code 6.1 SPARQL query examples

[17]http://www.w3.org/TR/rdf-sparql-query/

Besides, all the receivers (in both *To* and *CC* fields) of each email are added to a file to serve as input for the TinyCC module. TinyCC 1.5 is used to calculate the frequency of joint occurrence between two co-receivers (sentence-based co-occurrence) and the co-occurrence significance, i.e. the log-likelihood ratio of joint occurrence. The computation of this significance is based on a null hypothesis that states that the occurrence of two items A and B (e.g. two email receivers) is probabilistically independent, i.e. $p(AB) = p(A)p(B)$; the likelihood ratio [14] indicates how much the data deviates from the null hypothesis.

The body of each email undergoes a special process to identify forwarded or replied emails, which appear as simple strings without any RDF identification of its components (e.g. sender, receiver or date). This requires a string identification process to find the potential headers of embedded emails. Implementation is done in two languages: German and English. The analysis of these headers allows finding information about contacts who have not exchanged (send, received or co-receive) emails with the user but appear in forwarded or response emails of him/her.

For each contact, we extract keywords from the body of emails that are related to it. The keyword extraction is performed using TE, which extracts terminologically relevant terms and phrases from short documents based on a large background corpus. This extraction is again based on a statistical test using a likelihood ratio [14]. Here, however, the null hypothesis is that the probability of a term occurring in the emails of a person is the same as that of occurrence in the large background corpus. That means that the weights associated to extracted terms indicate how strongly a term's relative frequency in the emails deviates from its relative frequency in the background corpus.

Figure 6.3 shows the morphology of the Personal Social Network through an example of the PSN that we would obtain from the email corpus of Jan. We use solid lines for the first relationships, i.e. relationships between Jan and the people who appear in emails exchanged with him. For the second relationships, dashed lines are used to link contacts that appear together in the emails exchanged with Jan or contacts who appear in forwarded/replied emails found in the body of Jan's emails. These last contacts do not have a relationship with Jan because they have not directly exchanged emails with him (e.g. that would be the case of the contact A, who would appear in a thread that B has emailed to Jan).

After the analysis of the emails and construction of the network, the calculation of all the measures that characterise a PSN is performed. For each contact, the following values are calculated:

Availability (Θ) is derived from the summation of frequencies of emails sent each day. Recent days are more important and thus the weight of each day is modified by an exponential factor:

$$\Theta = \sum_i f_i \times w_i, \qquad \text{with } w_i = \mathrm{e}^{-\left(\frac{x_i}{\alpha}\right)^2}, \tag{6.1}$$

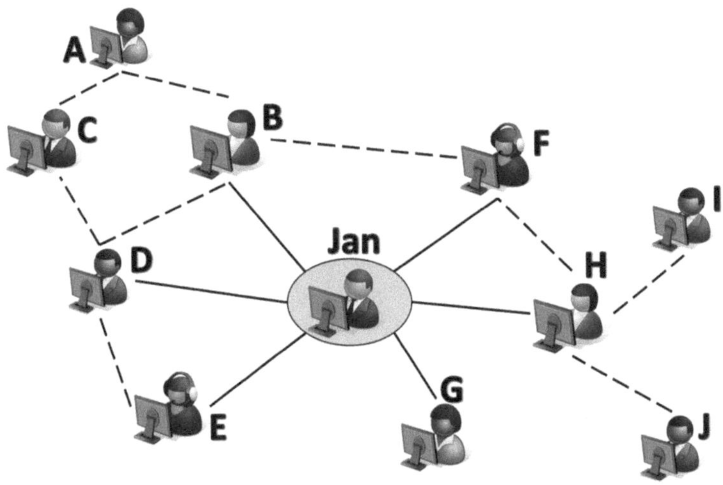

Fig. 6.3 Morphology of the PSN obtained from the email corpus of Jan. The illustration shows the first relationships (*solid line*) and the second relationships (*dashed line*) of the social network

where f_i is the total number of emails on the ith day, x_i the number of passed days since the ith day, and α the relevance period. Currently, α is set to 4 weeks.

Longevity (Δ_{lg}) is the total number of days since the first message exchanged between the contact and the user (cf. [48]).

Recency (Δ_{rec}) is the total number of days since the last message exchanged between the contact and the user (cf. [48]).

Frequency (Φ_{freq}) is the total number n_{exch} of messages exchanged between the contact and the user divided by the duration of their relationship (cf. [48]):

$$\Phi_{freq} = \frac{n_{exch}}{\Delta_{lg} - \Delta_{rec}} \,. \tag{6.2}$$

The *relationship* is weighted in the following way:

Reciprocity (ϕ_{recip}) results from the comparison between sent and received messages with respect to a contact (for first relationships, cf. [48]):

$$\phi_{recip} = 1 - \left| \frac{n_{sentBy} - n_{sentTo}}{n_{exch}} \right| \,, \tag{6.3}$$

where n_{sentBy} is the number of emails sent by the user and n_{sentTo} the number of emails sent to the user.

First Relationship Weight: ($W_{firstRel}$) General strength of the relationship based on the other specific measures and weighted according to their importance and influence on a relationship:

$$W_{\text{firstRel}} = w_{\text{high}}(\phi_{\text{freq}} + \phi_{\text{to}} + \phi_{\text{recip}}) + w_{\text{low}}\left(e^{-w_{\text{rec}}\times\Delta_{\text{rec}}} \times e^{-\left(\frac{w_{\text{rel}}}{\Delta_{\text{lg}}-\Delta_{\text{rec}}}\right)} + \phi_{\text{cc}} + \phi_{\text{ct}}\right), \tag{6.4}$$

where $w_{\text{high}} = 1$ weights the most important contributing factors, $w_{\text{low}} = 0.5$ weights the less important factors, $w_{\text{rec}} = w_{\text{rel}} = 1$ scale the recency and the inverse difference of longevity and recency, ϕ_{freq} is the normalised frequency, ϕ_{to} is the number of emails received from the user in *To* field divided by the total number of received emails, ϕ_{cc} is the number of emails received from the user in *CC* field divided by the total number of received emails, and ϕ_{ct} is the *c*entrality of the related person defined as the number of this person's relations by the total number of persons in the network (excluding the user). $\Delta_{\text{lg}} - \Delta_{\text{rec}}$ defines the duration of the relationship with the user. ϕ_{freq}, ϕ_{to} and ϕ_{recip} are considered the most important measures when evaluating a relationship whereas Δ_{lg}, Δ_{rec}, ϕ_{cc} and ϕ_{ct} indicate in a lower level a relationship and therefore have a lower weight. The number of emails sent with contacts in the *To* field have a higher weight than those appearing in the *CC* field, due to the consideration that the relation is stronger in the first case than in the latter. All the parameters of the Eq. 6.4 have been chosen and experimented empirically to have the desired behaviour, i.e. obtain a normalised value that rewards when the contacts exchange more emails, the exchange is reciprocal and they have a long recent relationship, and penalizes otherwise.

Second Relationship Weight: ($W_{\text{secondRel}}$) General strength of the relationship based on the other specific measures, weighted according to their importance and influence on a relationship:

$$W_{\text{secondRel}} = w_{\text{exch}} \times \phi_{\text{exch}} + w_{\text{ct}} \times \phi_{\text{ct}} + w_{\text{co}} \times \phi_{\text{co}}, \tag{6.5}$$

where $w_{\text{exch}} = 1$, $w_{\text{co}} = 0.7$ and $w_{\text{ct}} = 0.5$ are weights for the individual factors, while ϕ_{co} is the co-occurrence divided by the highest co-occurrence in the network. The *co-occurrence* is determined according to [5] by the TinyCC module. The used weight factors reflect the importance of the individual contributions and were determined empirically.

After computing the value, both first and second relationship weights are normalised in the network, divided by the highest value among all the first and second relationships respectively.

The structure of the PSN is stored in an RDF repository. *RDFReactor* allows the creation and management of new instances, following the ontology that defines the domain of the PSN.

The visualisation of the resultant PSN is too complicated for an RDF visualisation tool due to the amount of information that the network contains. A new representation of the PSN, therefore, was needed to allow the user visualise his PSN using *Protégé*. As a result, the ontology of the network was simplified to show the key point of the network: the relationships between the people. Still, in order to make the visualisation more manageable, the user can decide what relationships should be included in the user interface.

6.4.3 Expert Recommender Based on the PSN

Once the PSN is constructed, the Expert Recommender can use it as input to make its personalised recommendations. The Social Network Query Language (SNQL) was designed and implemented to give the user a mean for expressing his search request. For each SNQL construct, we translate it according to the PSN structure and its attributes. The formalisation of the requirements allowed us to perceive which constructs of the SNQL could be implemented from the email data pool. As a result, *substitute* and *representative* were not practical and thus were not implemented. In the following, we present the translation of SNQL constructs in terms of metrics of the PSN.

<Keywords> Sum of significance values of the matching keywords in each person adjusted by the BM25 score of the person.
NOT <name|email> list of candidates—Person(name|email).
REG AVAILABILITY attribute availability higher than the arithmetic mean of the availabilities of the candidates.
REL <name|email > weight of relationship with Person(name|email).
CLOSE <name|email> weight of relationship and coincidence in keywords and co-occurrence, all the attributes related to Person(name|email).
UNAVAILABLE <name|email> maximise co-occurrence of the contacts with Person(name|email) and NOT Person(name|email).
COMPARE <keyword> compare significance values of the keyword(s) between the current collaborator and the candidates.
RECENT minimise (Today.date—Person.recency).
RECENT <date> Person.recency >date.
ORDER <criteria> order final list of candidates according to criteria. Possible values for criteria: weight, reciprocity or co-occurrence.

BM25 [25] is a ranking function used by search engines to rank matching documents according to their relevance to a given search query that is specified by keywords. The ranking is done based on the query terms appearing in each document. For ExpertSN, a document is tantamount to all sent and received emails of a person together in the persons *profile*.

Given a search query Q, containing keywords $q_1,\ldots,q_n$, the BM25 score of a person P is shown in the Eq. 6.6.

$$\text{Score}(P, Q) = \sum_{i=1}^{n} \text{IDF}(q_i) \times \frac{f(q_i, P) \times (k_1 + 1)}{f(q_i, P) + k_1 \times \left(1 - b + b \times \frac{|l_{\text{profile}}|}{L_{\text{avg}}}\right)}, \quad (6.6)$$

where $f(q_i, P)$ is q_i's term frequency in the profile of person P, $|l_{\text{profile}}|$ is the length of the profile of P (number of words), L_{avg} is the average profile length in the persons collection from which persons are drawn (i.e. the social network), $k_1 = 2.0$ and $b = 0.75$. IDF(q_i) is the IDF (Inverse Document Frequency) weight of the query term q_i and is computed as follows:

$$\text{IDF}(q_i) = \epsilon + log\frac{N - n_{q_i} + 0.5}{n_{q_i} + 0.5}\ , \tag{6.7}$$

where N is the total number of persons in the network, $n(q_i)$ is the number of persons containing q_i as related keyword, ϵ is a floor constant to avoid negative values without ignoring common terms at all.

A query can be composed of more than one SNQL construct. Different constructs have different behaviour when the results are interpreted.

Generally, we classify SNQL constructs into the following groups:

1. Group A: the return values must be calculated and then the retrieval function is applied. The constructs in this group are: keywords, relationship, closeness, recency, unavailable and compare.
2. Group B: the return values present a restriction, directly filtering out some candidates from the recommendation set. The constructs of this group are: not, forced recency and regular availability.
3. Group C: the action of the return value is made at the end, when the candidate collaborators are already chosen. The construct order is part of this group.

The retrieval function applied to the measures of group A is the Arithmetic Mean as given in the Eq. 6.8:

$$A = \frac{1}{n}\sum_{i=1}^{n} x_i\ , \tag{6.8}$$

where n is the total number of return values specified in the query; $x_1, x_2, \ldots, x_n$ would be the return value of the interpretation of each construct of the query.

We chose the Arithmetic Mean because it weights all the constructs of the query equally. Besides, experimentation to compare the Arithmetic Mean and Harmonic Mean was carried out and it was concluded, that the first function gives the desired behaviour (there is no necessity to avoid the influence of outliers).

In order to get a concrete idea of the construction and results of a query, we present below a query that Jan would do. Suppose that Jan is looking for someone in the Change Management Department who has worked with Mary, who is currently on holidays, and who has a regular availability to work with him. Jan would introduce the following query:

```
Task Description: change management department
Search query: REL name=Mary Sandens; REG AVAILABILITY
```

Jan would receive a list of recommended candidates, ordered in increasing order of punctuation:

```
Hope, Peter hope@sap.com 0.0
Winter,Martin winter@sap.com 0.031849
Schmidt,Maxwell schmidt@sap.de 0.854
```

6.4.3.1 Functionalities of the Expert Recommender

Generally speaking, the final ExpertSN system supports two types of high level queries posted to the PSN:

1. "Who can be a collaborator for a certain task?"—the user posts a query to the system and receives a list of candidates to collaborate with him/her. Moreover, the system creates a network that is a part of the PSN, containing the recommended candidates and their relationships.
2. "What are the connections between person X and Y?"—the user can specify which relationship he/she wants to see between himself/herself and a contact or among contacts. The system shows the measures that qualify the relationship.

6.5 Discussion of the Results

The evaluation of the ExpertSN system includes firstly feedback of end users regarding the usability of the people search interface in a personal task management environment. We then report on a user study that evaluates the quality of the Personal Social Network extracted by ExpertSN.

6.5.1 Analytical Evaluation of the Search Interface

In order to study the usability of the people search interface, an analytical evaluation of ExpertSN was carried out, which uses a variation of the Activity-Oriented Evaluation Method (AOEM). This practical and analytical evaluation method utilises activity theory and was developed by Jurisch [26].

The main objective of ExpertSN's analytical evaluation was to assess users' experience about the interaction with the system and the user acceptance of the system. According to the description from Jurisch, AOEM intends to be a semi-structured method, which is flexible enough to adapt to the situation under investigation according to specific goals and context.

For the user acceptance evaluation of ExpertSN, the main objective was to understand what the user is expecting from the system and how the users interact with ExpertSN when searching for personal collaboration in their daily tasks. This allows evaluating the overall design principle of ExpertSN. The outcome of the acceptance evaluation is to answer whether the ExpertSN tool supports the users in selecting persons to collaborate with them in their daily tasks.

Due to practical reasons (imposed by the parent company), the testing of the tool within the system of each user was not possible. It was substituted by a qualitative description of the tool itself and the use of the SNQL. This description was materialised in a detailed presentation of the interface, functionalities and examples of ExpertSN in the framework of collaborators search. We introduced the tool to the subjects of the evaluation and showed the available functionalities and features. We designed a questionnaire based on the defined main goals and assessed it by the decomposition of the Activity System done in the previous steps. We additionally evaluated contradictions found during the design of the ExpertSN system with the questionnaire. Most of the items in the questionnaire were open-ended in order to permit the respondents to elaborate their opinions.

We performed the analytic evaluation with 11 participants, who were knowledge workers from three different companies. The results of the questionnaire confirmed most of the contradictions previously identified and addressed in the questionnaire. Regarding the necessity of computer-based recommenders, a majority of the answers were positive, pointing out the functionalities as an additional help, as a mean of saving time and having extra/new information about people. Three of the participants gave negative response in term of "unnecessary" or "had doubts about their performance". All the participants could identify expected benefits of using a personalised Expert Recommender and the possibility of adapting ExpertSN to a task management tool, especially because of usability, low turnaround time and faster performance of their tasks. Overall, the users had a positive opinion about the system and specified benefits like "easy access to potential collaborators", "semantical crawling of email corpora", "access to information they currently do not have" or "taking into account new measures e.g. availability or co-occurrence".

Referring to the features of ExpertSN, there was unanimity that the visualisation of the PSN would help the users choose a potential collaborator, if the visualisation can be easily configured according to certain attributes, measures or queries. The feature of consulting a relationship in the Social Network created diversity of opinions: some did not know what to answer while others found it useful and suitable to have a perception. However, one participant stated that he could not imagine that PSN based on a personal email corpus can provide the real quality of relationships.

Among the ExpertSN Recommender design features, the ones that sparked more controversy were *regular availability* and *relationship*. For some participants, it was clearly evident that the activity in email communication can be used to approximate the availability because in many organisations emails play an important role in communication and sent and received emails were informative enough to show the availability of a person. On the other hand, other users suggested that it depends on the context and calendars should be used for this purpose. Additionally, most of the participants thought that *compare* could be useful in situations like comparing skills in a concrete field, looking for specific competencies or impossibility to collaborate with the current collaborators.

Table 6.2 Quantitative results of the analytical evaluation

Question	Negative (%)	Neutral (%)	Positive (%)
Benefits/limitations of ExpertSN	22	0	78
Perception of the feature relationship in the PSN	55	27	18
Visualization would help to choose a collaborator	0	18	82
Integration with outlook	27	18	55
Explicit exclusion of collaborators with the SNQL	9	18	73
Regular availability as a criteria to choose a collaborator	36	0	64
Email as an approximation of regular availability	27	27	45
Email as an approximation of a personal relationship	9	64	27
Reciprocity as a factor to characterize a relationship	9	9	82
Recency as a factor to characterize a relationship	0	73	27

The search criteria *relationship* created some doubts among the participants due to the limitation of having only email communication to approximate a real life aspect. Eight of the eleven participants affirmed being more likely to contact someone with a high *reciprocity*, because this contact is more reliable suggesting that it is more certain to obtain an answer and it indicates a higher participation level of the contact. Finally, the importance of contacting *recent* people depends on the situation, as asserted by the majority (8 out of 11).

In general, discovering information in the email corpus of the same user triggered discussion in most of the evaluations. Some participants even affirmed it in their answers. Two participants emphasised the *reciprocity* and the *co-occurrence* as promising measures to evaluate relationships between people, although one of them pointed out the problems that administrative emails can deviate the results in the case of co-occurrence.

Table 6.2 summarises the results of the questionnaire. It shows the percentage of negative, neutral and positive answers given to the questions that were not completely open.

6.5.2 *Quality of the Personal Social Network*

The evaluation of the ExpertSN PSN (and its characterising measures) involves obtaining feedback from the end users regarding the accuracy of the extracted social network graph. For this purpose, ExpertSN was executed with the email corpus of the main author. The obtained PSN was examined against a manually crafted social network. The email corpus contained 581 mails in a 160 day window and the resulting PSN was formed with 145 contacts.

In the manually crafted version, the owner of the email corpus divided her contacts into three classes according to their role in her work life. Class A contains the professionals and tutors that advised/supervised her during her time in SAP

Research. Class C contains all the students and colleagues that shared their time with her. Class B was formed according to the importance and closeness of friendship with a subgroup of the students and colleagues. Afterwards, the author indicated the membership of each the class. This classification was validated by those who understood the surrounding of the author very well.

In order to allow a comparison between the constructed PSN and the classes defined by the user, there should be an equivalent categorisation of the contacts in the network. This is done as follows: (1) the contacts were sorted in a decreasing order according to their edge strengths; and (2) a filtering rule was applied grouping the contacts in three categories:

```
if(strength >= 67%)                 Class A
if(strength < 67% and >=33%)        Class B
if(strength < 33%)                  Class C
```

The manually crafted social network was compared against the categorised results obtained from the system. First of all, the size of the classes followed the same pattern as the classes obtained from the system. In both categorisations, Class A contained a reduced number of contacts (three to four persons); Class B had slightly more contacts than Class A; and finally Class C was the class which contains more members.

Regarding the class membership, the first disagreement was the non-overlapping part between the contacts that the user mentioned and the contacts that are really part of the ExpertSN PSN. This was specially evident in Class C, where the user only mentioned 11 contacts, whereas the ExpertSN PSN had 124 contacts. This supports one of the motivations for this research work: enriching and revealing the existence of new collaborators and increasing the user's awareness with respect to these contacts.

Secondly, we made the following observations when analysing the exact members in each class: Class A in the PSN contains all the three members given by the user. Interestingly, the PSN Class A contains one extra member, who was placed by the user in Class B for being a student who has a close relationship with the user. The majority of contacts specified by the user as members of Class B were already contained in the corresponding PSN Class. There is one exception, who is a member of Class B according to the user, but was classified into Class C according to the PSN. This could be explained by the fact that this contact, besides being part of the most trusted students, only started working with the user on the same project 2 months ago and thus has a lower level of activity in her email communication. Finally, the people identified by the user as members of Class C were included in the corresponding Class produced based on ExpertSN PSN. It, however, must be noticed (as stated before) that the entire set of email contacts were relatively small and Class C was served as the final catchment of all the contacts not classified to Class A and B by the ExpertSN system. After the analysis of class C, we noticed that there were new contacts whose existence the user ignored. These contacts mainly came from long threads and forwarded/replied emails which were embedded in emails of the user.

6.6 Conclusion and Future Work

With the deepening of globalisation and virtualisation, it becomes increasingly important to establish the right teams of specialities for consultation, coordination, and collaboration. Social network, as the signature of Enterprise 2.0 [30], was leveraged to assist the discovery and management of the expertise landscape in enterprises. In this paper, we focused on the enterprise social network solely based on one's work email. We developed the ExpertSN system which parses a given email corpus and constructs the user-centred egocentric social network covering all the contacts that the user may benefit from. The resultant social network then serves as the basis for identifying and discovering experts when special needs arise. The preliminary evaluation results of ExpertSN are promising: automatically generated social network largely agreed with inputs manually crafted by human users.

Building social network solely with work email is based on both practical and theoretical considerations. On the one hand, work email is normally available under organisational regulations and has less restrictive privacy and safety concerns than private email. This ensures that a further large scale evaluation can be performed. On the other hand, work email is tightly bound with one's daily work activity. A personal network constructed therefrom can fully align with one's work duties and thus facilitate a well-focused and well-targeted expert recommendation mechanism.

There are several points that need further investigation. The crux of our immediate future work lies in the evaluation of ExpertSN in a larger scale. Feedbacks from users can then serve to optimise the proposed mining and recommendation algorithms and to improve system usability. Modern enterprises generally have multiple internal information systems in parallel with the email system. The information contained in these systems can enhance and refine ExpertSN personal networks as well as validate the accuracy of such networks. We, therefore, will investigate what information sources are particularly useful for ExpertSN and how they can be effectively incorporated. Finally, though expert recommendation is the most evident application of ExpertSN personal networks, there are other potential use cases that can exploit the results of ExpertSN. For instance, work-based personal network can be the basis of sophisticated SNA methods to derive patterns in employee behaviours and organisational structures.

Acknowledgements This work is supported by the European Union IST fund through the EU FP7 MATURE Integrating Project (Grant No. 216356).

References

1. Acquisti, A., Gross, R.: Imagined communities: awareness, information sharing, and privacy on the facebook. In: Proceedings of 6th Workshop on Privacy Enhancing Technologies, Cambridge (2006)

2. Balog, K., de Rijke, M.: Finding experts and their details in e-mail corpora. In: 15th International World Wide Web Conference (WWW2006), Edinburgh (2006)
3. Balog, K., De Rijke, M.: Determining expert profiles (with an application to expert finding). In: IJCAI'07: Proceedings of the 20th International Joint Conference on Artifical Intelligence, Hyderabad, India, pp. 2657–2662. Morgan Kaufmann, San Francisco (2007)
4. Becerra-Fernandez, I.: Searching for experts on the web: a review of contemporary expertise locator systems. ACM Trans. Int. Technol. **6**(4), 333–355 (2006)
5. Biemann, C., Quasthoff, U., Heyer, G., Holz, F.: Asv toolbox – a modular collection of language exploration tools. In: Proceedings of the 6th Language Resources and Evaluation Conference (LREC) 2008, Marrakech (2008)
6. Brown, J.S., Duguid, P., Duguid, P.: The Social Life of Information. Harvard Business School Press, Boston (2000)
7. Campbell, C.S., Maglio, P.P., Cozzi, A., Dom, B.: Expertise identification using email communications. In: CIKM '03: Proceedings of the Twelfth International Conference on Information and Knowledge Management, New Orleans, pp. 528–531. ACM (2003)
8. Carvalho, V.R., Cohen, W.W.: Learning to extract signature and reply lines from email. In: CEAS-2004 (Conference on Email and Anti-Spam), Mountain View (2004)
9. Carvalho, V.R., Cohen, W.W.: Recommending recipients in the enron email corpus. Technical Report, Carnegie Mellon University (2007)
10. Craswell, N., Hawking, D.: Overview of the TREC-2004 web track. In: Proceedings of TREC-2004, Gaithersburg (2004)
11. Culotta, A., Bekkerman, R., Mccallum, A.: Extracting social networks and contact information from email and the web. In: CEAS-1, Mountain View (2004)
12. Demartini, G., Niederée, C.: Finding experts on the semantic desktop. In: Personal Identification and Collaborations: Knowledge Mediation and Extraction (PICKME 2008) Workshop at ISWC 2008, Karlsruhe (2008)
13. DiMicco, J., Millen, D.R., Geyer, W., Dugan, C., Brownholtz, B., Muller, M.: Motivations for social networking at work. In: CSCW '08: Proceedings of the 2008 ACM Conference on Computer Supported Cooperative Work, San Diego, pp. 711–720. ACM, New York (2008)
14. Dunning, T.: Accurate methods for the statistics of surprise and coincidence. Comput. Linguist. **19**, 61–74 (1993)
15. Ehrlich, K., Lin, C.Y., Griffiths-Fisher, V.: Searching for experts in the enterprise: combining text and social network analysis. In: GROUP '07: Proceedings of the 2007 International ACM Conference on Supporting Group Work, Sanibel Island, pp. 117–126. ACM, New York (2007)
16. Farnham, S., Portnoy, W., Turski, A.: Using email mailing lists to approximate and explore corporate social networks. In: Proceedings of the CSCW'04 Workshop on Social Networks, Chicago (2004)
17. Fisher, D.: Using egocentric networks to understand communication. IEEE Int. Comput. **9**(5), 20–28 (2005)
18. Fisher, D., Smith, M., Welser, H.T.: You are who you talk to: detecting roles in usenet newsgroups. Hawaii Int. Conf. Syst. Sci. **3**, 59 (2006)
19. Grebner, O., Riss, U.V.: The social semantic desktop in an enterprise environment – integrating personal and organizational knowledge for an enterprise research department. In: 9th European Conference on Knowledge Management, Southampton, pp. 233–240 (2008)
20. Gross, R., Acquisti, A.: Information revelation and privacy in online social networks. In: Proceedings of the 2005 ACM Workshop on Privacy in the Electronic Society, WPES '05, Alexandria, pp. 71–80. ACM, New York (2005)
21. Groza, T., Handschuh, S., Moeller, K., Grimnes, G., Sauermann, L., Minack, E., Mesnage, C., Jazayeri, M., Reif, G., Gudjonsdottir, R.: The nepomuk project – on the way to the social semantic desktop. In: Proceedings of the Third International Conference on Semantic Technologies (I-SEMANTICS 2007), Graz (2007)
22. Guy, I., Jacovi, M., Meshulam, N., Ronen, I., Shahar, E.: Public vs. private: comparing public social network information with email. In: Proceedings of the 2008 ACM Conference on Computer Supported Cooperative Work, CSCW '08, San Diego, pp. 393–402 (2008)

23. Hawking, D.: Overview of the TREC-9 web track. In: Proceedings of TREC-9, Gaithersburg (2000)
24. Hofmann, K., Balog, K., Bogers, T., de Rijke, M.: Integrating contextual factors into topic-centric retrieval models for finding similar experts. In: SIGIR 2008 Workshop on Future Challenges in Expertise Retrieval (fCHER), Singapore, pp. 29–36 (2008)
25. Jones, K.S., Walker, S., Robertson, S.E.: A probabilistic model of information retrieval: development and comparative experiments. Inf. Process. Manag. **36**, 779–840 (2000)
26. Jurisch, M.: User acceptance of a complex knowledge management tool. Master's thesis, University of Konstanz, Faculty of Law, Economics and Politics, Department of Politics and Management (2009)
27. Kleinberg, J.M.: Authoritative sources in a hyperlinked environment. J. ACM **46**(5), 604–632 (1999)
28. Krebs, V.: Social capital: the key to success for the 21st century organization. IHRIM J. **XII**(5), 38–42 (2008). Orgnet.com
29. Lin, C.Y., Cao, N., Liu, S.X., Papadimitriou, S., Sun, J., Yan, X.: SmallBlue: social network analysis for expertise search and collective intelligence. In: ICDE '09: Proceedings of the 2009 IEEE International Conference on Data Engineering, Shanghai, pp. 1483–1486 (2009)
30. McAfee, A.P.: Enterprise 2.0: The dawn of emergent collaboration. MIT Sloan Manag. Rev. **47**(3), 21–28 (2006)
31. McDonald, D.W., Ackerman, M.S.: Just talk to me: a field study of expertise location. In: Proceedings of the 1998 ACM Conference on Computer Supported Cooperative Work, CSCW '98, Seattle, pp. 315–324. ACM, New York (1998)
32. Mika, P.: Flink: semantic web technology for the extraction and analysis of social networks. J. Web Semant. **3**, 211–223 (2005)
33. Mock, K.: An experimental framework for email categorization and management. In: SIGIR '01: Proceedings of the 24th Annual International ACM SIGIR Conference on Research and Development in Information Retrieval, New Orleans, pp. 392–393. ACM, New York (2001)
34. Nardi, B.A., Whittaker, S., Schwarz, H.: It's not what you know it's who you know **5**(5), First Monday (2000)
35. Nardi, B.A., Whittaker, S., Isaacs, E., Creech, M., Johnson, J., Hainsworth, J.: ContactMap: integrating communication and information through visualizing personal social networks. Commun. ACM **45**, 89–95 (2001)
36. Ogata, H., Yano, Y., Furugori, N., Jin, Q.: Computer supported social networking for augmenting cooperation. Comput. Support. Coop. Work **10**(2), 189–209 (2001)
37. Pal, C., Mccallum, A.: Cc prediction with graphical models. In: CEAS 2006 – The Third Conference on Email and Anti-Spam, Mountain View (2006)
38. Riss, U.V., Jurisch, M., Kaufman, V.: E-mail in semantic task management. IEEE Conference on Commerce and Enterprise Computing (CEC '09), Vienna, pp. 468–475 (2009)
39. Riss, U.V., Grebner, O., Taylor, P., Du, Y.: Knowledge work support by semantic task management. Comput. Ind. **61**(8), 798–805 (2010)
40. Rowe, R., Creamer, G., Hershkop, S., Stolfo, S.J.: Automated social hierarchy detection through email network analysis. In: Proceedings of the 9th WebKDD and 1st SNA-KDD 2007 Workshop on Web Mining and Social Network Analysis, San Jose, pp. 109–117 (2007)
41. Skeels, M.M., Grudin, J.: When social networks cross boundaries: a case study of workplace use of Facebook and LinkedIn. In: GROUP '09: Proceedings of the ACM 2009 International Conference on Supporting Group Work, Sanibel Island, pp. 95–104. ACM, New York (2009)
42. Stolfo, S.J., Hershkop, S., Wang, K., Nimeskern, O., Hu, C.W.: Behavior profiling of email. In: ISI, Tucson, pp. 74–90 (2003)
43. Udoh, E.: Mining e-mail content for a small enterprise. In: Innovations and Advanced Techniques in Computer and Information Sciences and Engineering, pp. 179–182. Springer, Dordrecht (2007)
44. van Alstyne, M., Zhang, J.: EmailNet: a system for automatically mining social networks from organizational email communications. In: North American Association for Computational Social and Organizational Science (NAACSOS), Pittsburgh (2003)

45. van der Aalst, W.M., Nikolov, A.: EMailAnalyzer: an e-mail mining plug-in for the ProM framework. BPM Center Report BPM-07-16, BPMCenter.org (2007)
46. van Reijsen, J., Helms, R., Jackson, T., Vleugel, A., Tedmori, S.: Mining e-mail to leverage knowledge networks in organizations. In: Proceedings of the 10th European Conference on Knowledge Management, Vicenza (2009)
47. Wasserman, S., Faust, K.: Social Network Analysis: Methods and Applications. Cambridge University Press, New York (1994)
48. Whittaker, S., Jones, Q., Terveen, L.: Contact management: identifying contacts to support long-term communication. In: CSCW '02: Proceedings of the 2002 ACM Conference on Computer Supported Cooperative Work, New Orleans, pp. 216–225. ACM, New York (2002)
49. Whittaker, S., Bellotti, V., Gwizdka, J.: Email in personal information management. Commun. ACM **49**(1), 68–73 (2006)
50. Ye, Q., Wu, B., Hu, D., Wang, B.: Exploring temporal egocentric networks in mobile call graphs. In: 6th International Conference on Fuzzy Systems and Knowledge Discovery (FSKD '09), Tianjin, pp. 413–417 (2009)

Chapter 7
A Local Structure-Based Method for Nodes Clustering: Application to a Large Mobile Phone Social Network

Alina Stoica, Zbigniew Smoreda, and Christophe Prieur

Abstract In this paper we present a method for describing how a node of a given graph is connected to the network. We also propose a method for grouping nodes into clusters based on the structure of the network in which they are embedded, so on the description provided by the first method. We apply these methods to a mobile phone communications network. When confronting the obtained clusters of individuals to their age and to their intensity of communication, the results are quite promising: the two measures are correlated to the social network cluster. We finish by providing a typology of the mobile phone users based on social network cluster, communication intensity and age.

7.1 Introduction

In this paper, we want to describe how each individual of a given social network is connected to the network and to cluster nodes that are connected in a similar way to the network. One can see this distribution of nodes into clusters as an identification of network "roles". Without pretending to have solved the problem of identification of roles, we present a method to distribute nodes into clusters based on the local structure of the network.

A. Stoica (✉)
EDF R&D, 1 av. du Gen. de Gaulle Clamart, Clamart, France
e-mail: alina.stoica@edf.fr

Z. Smoreda
Orange Labs, 38-40 rue du Gen. Leclerc, Issy les Moulineaux, France
e-mail: zbigniew.smoreda@orange-ftgroup.com

C. Prieur
LIAFA, Paris-Diderot, 75 rue du Chevaleret, 75013 Paris, France
e-mail: prieur@liafa.jussieu.fr

T. Özyer et al. (eds.), *The Influence of Technology on Social Network Analysis and Mining*, Lecture Notes in Social Networks 6, DOI 10.1007/978-3-7091-1346-2_7,

We apply the method to a large mobile phone network. The obtained results are quite promising, in particular when the clusters are confronted to other characteristics of the individuals. Indeed the probability that an individual belongs to a certain cluster depends on his or her age; even more, using these probabilities we are able to group together different ages, thus discovering four groups containing consecutive ages, corresponding to four life stages. The probability that a person belongs to a certain cluster also depends on his or her mobile phone communication intensity; moreover the intensity of communication allows us to predict with rather high accuracy the cluster membership of a person.

We begin by recalling some work related to the subject. Next we present the method for describing how a node of a given graph is embedded in the network. We then propose a method for clustering nodes based on the structure of the network surrounding them. Next we present the results of the application of the methods to the mobile phone communications network: the obtained clusters of individuals, the correlations with the age and the intensity of communication and a typology of mobile phone users based on social network cluster, communication intensity and age.

7.2 Related Work

Social roles. The notion of role refers to the position of an actor in society and it is based on the relationships that the actor in question has with other actors. Actors playing a particular social role are connected in the same way to the network. Generally, the nodes in a network can be grouped into equivalence classes based on the roles they play, so nodes having the same role have to be equivalent or similar to each other by some metric. Probably the best known equivalence relations for this purpose are the structural, the automorphic and the regular equivalence.

Structural equivalence [11]. Two nodes are considered equivalent if and only if they have exactly the same neighbors in the graph, so they are linked to exactly the same set of nodes with (in the case of directed graphs) the arrows pointing in the same directions. Thus, two structurally equivalent actors can exchange their positions without changing the network.

However, it is not frequent to find two persons with identical relations. There are examples of actors who play the same role without being connected to exactly the same people, but rather have similar relations with people who have themselves a same role. The two following relations express this idea.

Automorphic equivalence. Two nodes are considered equivalent if one is the automorphic image of the other one. Formally, two vertices u and v of a graph G are *automorphically equivalent* if there is an automorphism φ of G such that $\varphi(u) = v$.[1]

[1] The notion of automorphism is presented in Sect. 7.3.

Regular equivalence [3, 18]. Two nodes are considered equivalent if they are connected to equivalent nodes. Imagine that nodes having the same role are given the same color (and nodes with distinct roles are given distinct colors). If two nodes are equivalent, the colors found in the neighborhood of one node are also found (possibly in different numbers) in the neighborhood of the other node. Also, the definition can be understood in the following way: every equivalence class is represented by a single node in an "image graph" (also called "blockmodel" or "role model"). The nodes of the image graph are connected (disconnected) if the nodes in the corresponding classes are connected (disconnected) in the original graph.

A lot of research has been devoted to blockmodeling. Some authors focused on efficient algorithms for blockmodeling [2], others on its mathematical foundations [1, 5, 18], others proposed problem relaxations [15] or generalizations for different types of relations [5]. The method we propose here is different from the research on blockmodels. Although the goal is the same, to cluster nodes that share some network characteristics, our method can be applied to nodes that belong to the same graph as well as to nodes belonging to different graphs (as for example nodes in personal networks obtained by interviews). The blockmodeling, on the other hand, searches for roles in a same graph. Also, our method can be easily applied to (very) large networks, taking a few dozens of minutes to compute clusters of nodes in a graph containing millions of nodes.

The method we propose here is somehow related to the equivalence of roles introduced by Burt [4] who published in English the work of Hummell and Sodeur [8]. In this paper the authors characterized each node of a given network by the number of occurrences of the node in triads. One looks for the presence/absence of links between the given node and every other two nodes of the network. As the graph where the triads are computed is directed, one counts the presence of the node in 36 types of triads. Then the Euclidian distance is used in order to find similar nodes. In a way, the method we propose here follows this idea. However, we look for patterns of a higher order than the triads. Also, one major difference is that, when characterizing a node, we look only at its neighbors and the connections between them, while Hummell and Sodeur look at its relation with every pair of nodes in the network. Their characterization is therefore more detailed, but way too complex for large networks. Looking at $\binom{n-1}{2}$ nodes in order to characterize one node of a network with n nodes is impossible when n is high, so this method cannot be applied to large social networks. Another difference is that our method is designed for undirected networks, but it can be easily modified to take into consideration directed graphs.

Mobile phone social networks. We apply the method proposed here to a large network built from mobile phone communications. Different properties have been already identified in such networks [12, 13]. Onnela et al. [13] show with no surprise that the distributions of degree and of the duration of calls are power-laws. They also give a definition for the strength of ties depending on the duration of calls and they analyze the connection between the strength and the connectivity or the community structure.

Using mobile phone communication data, Lambiotte et al. [10] were able to test the sociological hypothesis that the existence of a call between two persons depends on the geographical distance between them. They thus show that the probability of a mobile phone call is inversely proportional to the square of the geographical distance between the two persons. Several researchers analyzed the temporal dynamics of mobile phone networks e.g. the temporal stability of links [7, 14]. In [7], Hidalgo and Rodriguez-Sickert define the persistence of a link over a set of time periods as the number of periods where the link is activated (i.e. there are reciprocal calls between the two persons during that period). They find that persistent links are more common with people with low degree and high clustering.

However, the properties of mobile phone social networks computed in these studies are global, characterizing the network as a whole. Here, our aim is to characterize the local structure of the graph. We thus propose methods to describe the way each node is embedded into the network and to find similarly connected nodes. We then apply the methods to a large mobile phone network.

7.3 Preliminaries

7.3.1 Basic Graph Notions

Let $G = (V, E)$ be a graph; V is the set of its vertices, $E \subseteq V \times V$ is the set of its edges. The graph G is *undirected* if for all $(u, v) \in E$ also $(v, u) \in E$ i.e. edges are unordered pairs of nodes. G is *connected* if there exists a finite path between every two vertices and it is *simple* if it has no multiple edges (i.e. for all $u, v \in V$ there is at most one edge connecting u to v) and no self-loops ($(v, v) \notin E$, for all $v \in V$). All the graphs we consider here are simple and undirected.

Given a vertex $v \in V$, a vertex $u \in V$ is a *neighbor* of v if and only if $(u, v) \in E$. The set of neighbors of v represents its *neighborhood* denoted by $N(v) = \{u \in V, (u, v) \in E\}$ and the cardinal of this set represents its *degree*. Two graphs $G = (V, E)$ and $H = (V', E')$ are *isomorphic* if and only if there exists a bijective function $\varphi : V \to V'$ such that, for any two vertices u and v in V, $(u, v) \in E$ if and only if $(\varphi(u), \varphi(v)) \in E'$. If G and H represent the same graph, the function φ is called *automorphism* of the graph G. The subgraph *induced* by a set of vertices $V' \subseteq V$ in G is the graph $H = (V', E')$ with $E' = \{((u, v) \in E \mid u, v \in V')\}$.

7.3.2 Data Mining Notions

ANOVA test. This test measures the correlation between a continuous variable and a categorization. It tells if the mean of the continuous variable is the same for the different categories. If this is true then the two variables are independent.

For instance, one can use the ANOVA test in order to see if the salary (the continuous variable) is independent from the gender (the categories, male and female). However, this test says only if the means are different or not, but it does not say for which categories the means are significantly different and for which they are not. A test that can provide such information is called a multiple comparison test. Such tests are the Bonferroni [6] and the Scheffé tests [16].

We also present briefly two widely-used methods for clustering objects.

K-means clustering. Given a set of objects, the *k-means* algorithm groups them into a given number k of clusters using the distance between the objects. If each object is characterized by a feature vector with n elements, one usually uses the Euclidian distance between the feature vectors as distance between objects. The Euclidian distance is defined as

$$d(u,v) = \sqrt{(u_1 - v_1)^2 + (u_2 - v_2)^2 + \cdots + (u_n - v_n)^2} = \sqrt{\sum_{i=1}^{n}(u_i - v_i)^2}$$

where u and v are two objects characterized by two feature vectors with n elements $(u_1, \ldots u_n)$ and $(v_1, \ldots v_n)$ respectively.

Given a cluster K containing n_K objects characterized by feature vectors of n elements, the center (or centroid) C_K of the cluster is a vector representing the average of all the objects in the cluster i.e. for each variable i from 1 to n, the i-th value of the vector is the arithmetic mean of the i-th values of the feature vectors of the objects in the cluster: $C_K(i) = \frac{1}{n_K} \sum_{v \in K} v_i$ where v is an object in the cluster and v_i is the i-th value of its feature vector.

Kohonen self organizing maps. Given a set of p individuals (or objects) characterized by feature vectors with n variables, the aim of the *Kohonen self-organizing map*[9] is to cluster the individuals and also to build a bi-dimensional map with n layers (a layer for each variable describing the individuals) where the individuals are placed depending on their topological proximity. The map's smallest entity is a cell, and each individual is placed in only one cell (the individual has the same position and therefore cell on all the layers); there are $\sqrt{|p|}$ cells. The method has three steps. The first one is the learning. The feature vectors of the cells are randomly initialized. Then a subset of the population to model is randomly selected; for each individual in this selection the SOM finds the ("winner") cell whose feature vector is the most similar (i.e. is the closest by a given distance). The feature vector of the winner cell is updated to take into account the feature values of the individual. The feature vector of the neighbor cells are then modified to reduce the vectors gradient with the new values of the cells' feature vector. The second step of the algorithm is the processing of the global population to model: each individual is placed in the cell with the closest feature vector. Finally the last step is the clustering of the cells with, for instance, a k-means algorithm, based on the similarity of their feature vectors.

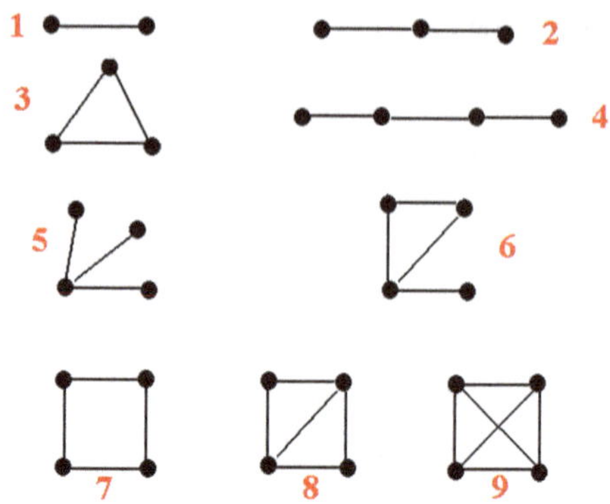

Fig. 7.1 The nine patterns with at most four vertices and at least one edge

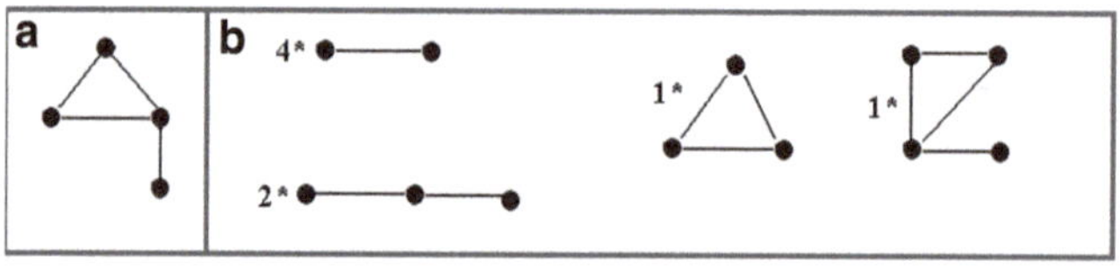

Fig. 7.2 A graph (*a*) and its patterns (*b*)

7.4 Local Structure-Based Node Characterization

Suppose that we are given a network that represents a set of individuals and some connections between them. We want to study how each one of the individuals is connected to the network. For that, we analyze the connections between each node and its neighbors and between these neighbors. More precisely, we characterize the egocentred network of each one of the nodes in the network. By egocentred network of a given node we mean the network formed by its neighbors and the links between them.

Formally, let $G = (V, E)$ be a simple undirected graph such that V corresponds to the set of individuals and E to the set of connections between them: two vertices u and v are connected by an edge (u, v) if there is a connection between the two individuals u and v. We call *egocentred network* of the node $v \in V$ the graph $Eg(v)$ induced by the neighbors of v in G i.e. the graph whose vertices are the neighbors of v and whose edges are the edges between these neighbors in G.

We call *patterns* the nine non-isomorphic undirected connected graphs with at most four vertices and at least one edge (Fig. 7.1). We say that a pattern P appears in a graph $G = (V, E)$ if there exists a set of vertices $V_P \subseteq V$ such that the subgraph induced by V_P in G is isomorphic to P. Listing all the occurrences of the pattern P in the graph G means finding all the sets of vertices V_P according to the previous definition. As an example, Fig. 7.2 represents a graph (a) and the patterns it contains and their number of occurrences (b).

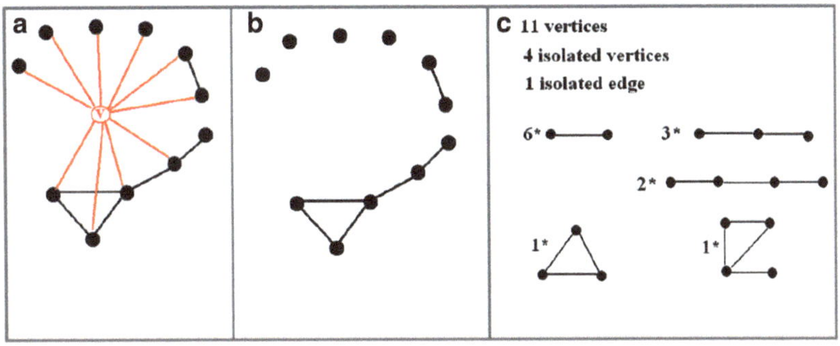

Fig. 7.3 A vertex v and its neighbors (*a*), the egocentred network $Eg(v)$ of v (*b*) and the patterns of $Eg(v)$ (*c*)

Now, to characterize a node v of a graph G we proceed as it follows (method ***characterize(v)***; this is part of the method *local_structure* that we introduced in [17]):

Step 1. Extract the egocentred network $Eg(v)$ of v i.e. the subgraph induced by the neighbors of v in G;
Step 2. List the patterns of $Eg(v)$;

Let us explain the two steps of the method with an example. In Fig. 7.3a, the black circles correspond to the neighbors of v. The egocentred network $Eg(v)$ of v is represented in Fig. 7.3b and the patterns of $Eg(v)$ in Fig. 7.3c.[2] We chose not to include v in its egocentred network because we know that it is connected to all the vertices in this graph, its presence doesn't bring any information. After performing the two steps of the method one has a rich description of the way v is connected to the graph G. For a more detailed description of the local structure of G around v one can list the patterns of a higher order (with five vertices or more); the patterns with four vertices are however a good compromise between the variety of forms and their number, providing, in many cases, a detailed enough picture.

We call *pattern-frequency vector* of v the vector containing the number of occurrences of the different patterns in its egocentred network (along with the number of isolated vertices and edges in its network):

Definition 1. Given a vertex v of a graph $G = (V, E)$, we call pattern-frequency vector of v the vector

$$f(v) = (f_{iv}(v), f_{ie}(v), f_{\sqcup}(v), f_{\llcorner\!\lrcorner}(v), f_{\triangle}(v), f_{\sqsubset}(v), f_{\angle}(v), f_{\boxslash}(v), f_{\square}(v), f_{\boxslash}(v), f_{\boxtimes}(v))$$

[2]We have also counted the number of isolated vertices and edges in $Eg(v)$.

where:

- $f_{iv}(v)$ is the number of isolated vertices in the egocentred network $Eg(v)$,
- $f_{ie}(v)$ is the number of isolated edges

and the subsequent components are the numbers of occurrences of the patterns as induced subgraphs in the egocentred network $Eg(v)$ of v:

- $f_{\_}(v)$, pattern 1, edges,
- $f_{\llcorner}(v)$, pattern 2, paths with two vertices,
- $f_{\triangle}(v)$, pattern 3, triangles,
- $f_{\sqsubset}(v)$, pattern 4, paths with three vertices,
- $f_{\angle}(v)$, pattern 5, stars,
- $f_{\boxslash}(v)$, pattern 6,
- $f_{\square}(v)$, pattern 7, chordless squares,
- $f_{\boxslash}(v)$, pattern 8, squares with one chord,
- $f_{\boxtimes}(v)$, pattern 9, four-cliques.

For instance, for the vertex in Fig. 7.3a, its pattern-frequency vector is

$$f(v) = (4, 1, 6, 3, 1, 2, 0, 1, 0, 0, 0).$$

Note that this method provides a description of how a given vertex is connected to the network; it can be applied to the set of all the vertices of the graph or only to some of them. As it is local, one doesn't need to have all the vertices and edges in the graph, but only the neighbors of each studied vertex and the edges between them.

7.5 Pattern Frequency Clustering of Nodes

In this section we want to group together nodes that are connected in a similar way to the network. We use the previously defined pattern-frequency vectors in order to describe how the different nodes are connected to the network. Now we have to define what "connected in similar ways" represents.

One possibility is to define an equivalence relation on nodes using the pattern-frequency vectors. For instance:

Definition 2. Two vertices of the graph G are said to be equivalent if and only if they have identical pattern-frequency vectors. We call this pattern equivalence.

Note that this equivalence is less strict than the structural and the automorphic equivalences. Indeed, vertices that have exactly the same neighbors in the network (so are structurally equivalent) have identical egocentred network, so identical feature vectors, and therefore are pattern equivalent. Also, vertices that are automorphically equivalent have isomorphic egocentred networks, so identical feature vectors and are thus pattern equivalent. For the two definitions, the opposite is not always true, so one can say that the pattern equivalence is included in the structural and automorphic equivalences. This means that the pattern equivalence is less strict than these two relations. However, it is still not enough flexible for real-world networks where nodes having exactly the same patterns in exactly the same amounts are rare (at least for values of the degree higher than, let's say, 10). Thus, the equivalence classes obtained when applying the definition to large graphs are much too numerous. Here we want to group the nodes of a given large network into a small number of classes (i.e. smaller than a given constant, for instance 20). Each class should contain similar nodes in terms of network structure. It is the local structure of the network surrounding the node that should matter when attributing a node to a class, and not its degree or the fact of being connected to other nodes in the class. The interest of computing such classes is that they are very easy to use. Thus, one can measure correlations with other properties of the nodes or make predictions (e.g. predict a property when knowing the class and vice-versa).

Instead of grouping together nodes that have identical pattern-frequency vectors (as in the pattern equivalence), we cluster nodes that have similar vectors. For that, we use a classical clustering method, the k-means algorithm. The advantage of performing a clustering to define vertex equivalence is its flexibility: one can distribute the vertices into a small number of clusters (if this is his or her goal) or a large number of clusters (where vertices in the same cluster are very similar to each other).

Before performing the clustering, we filter out vertices that have identical pattern-frequency vectors. These vertices are not distinguishable by using only the patterns; their egocentred networks contain exactly the same patterns in exactly the same number. By default, they belong to the same cluster. The elimination of multiple copies of the same pattern-frequency vector insures a smaller complexity of computation and also allows us to perform a finer clustering. Of course, after having clustered the remaining vertices (we call them the reduced population), we put the filtered out vertices into the clusters where the vertices with identical vectors have been already placed.

Definition 3. Given a graph G, we call reduced population of G a maximal set of vertices of G that have distinct pattern-frequency vectors. Given a positive integer d, we denote by $Pop_d(G)$ the set of vertices in the reduced population of G that have degree d (in G).

7.5.1 The Issue of the Degree

There is an important factor that must be taken into consideration prior to the clustering: the degree of vertices. It is difficult to compare the number of occurrences of patterns in egocentred networks of vertices with different degrees because these values are biased by the degree. For vertices with high degrees, the number of

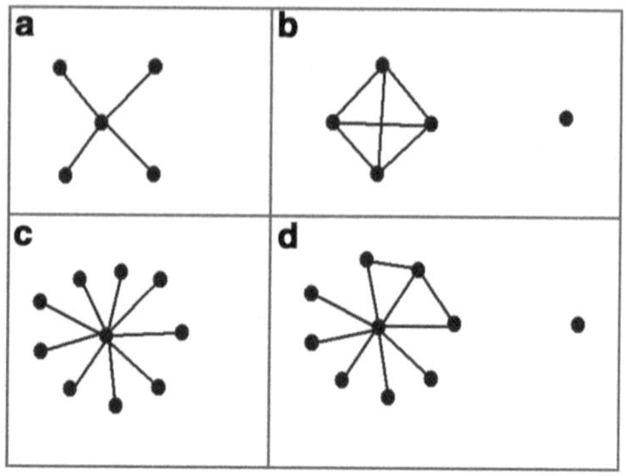

Fig. 7.4 An example of four egocentred networks with five vertices (*a* and *b*) and ten vertices (*c* and *d*) respectively (ego has been removed)

occurrences can have high values, too. Actually, for a vertex (ego) with degree d, a pattern with k vertices can occur at most $\binom{d}{k}$ times in its egocentred network. So, while the minimal value of the number of occurrences of a pattern is always 0, the maximal value depends on the degree of ego. Therefore, the exact values of the number of occurrences of patterns can be misleading. Look, for instance, at the four egocentred networks in Fig. 7.4 (ego has been removed). Their pattern-frequency vectors are presented in Table 7.1 where one can see that the values of many variables are higher for C and D than for A and B. Even more, the networks C and D look more similar to each other than A and B, so the vectors of C and D should be closer to each other than those of A and B. However, the Euclidian distance between the pattern-frequency vectors is 74 for A and B and 1,726 for C and D.

In order to avoid the problem of the degree, we choose to perform a clustering for each degree. Thus, the distance between the vertices C and D in the previous example will be compared to the distances between other pairs of vertices of degree 10 and not to all the input vertices. If we manage to group together the vertices of each degree in a same number of clusters and to match together the clusters obtained for the different degrees, then we have that each cluster contains vertices of all the degrees. This is exactly our goal here: we want a vertex to belong to a given cluster because it has a certain type of connection to the network and not because it has a certain degree. Thus, if a vertex gets another degree during time, we can see if the type of structure in which it is connected also changes by checking if its cluster changes. It is not the difference of degree that we want to capture but the difference of structure. If we don't have exactly the same clusters for all the degrees, we cannot do this. And this is exactly what might happen if we perform a single clustering for all the degrees (and not for each degree separately): there might be clusters with no vertices of some degrees (because, for instance, there are fewer vertices of that degree).

Table 7.1 The pattern-frequency vectors of the egocentred networks in Fig. 7.4

net.	f_{deg}	f_{iv}	f_{ev}	$f_{\text{—}}$	$f_{\text{∟}}$	$f_{\triangle}$	$f_{\text{⊏}}$	$f_{\text{∠}}$	$f_{\text{◸}}$	$f_{\square}$	$f_{\text{◪}}$	$f_{\boxtimes}$
A	5	0	0	4	6	0	0	4	0	0	0	0
B	5	1	0	6	0	4	0	0	0	0	0	1
C	10	0	0	9	36	0	0	84	0	0	0	0
D	10	1	0	10	26	2	0	45	10	0	1	0

7.5.2 Pattern-Frequency Clustering of Nodes

We proceed as it follows:

1. For each degree, we perform several k-means clusterings on the vertices with that degree in the reduced population, using different numbers of clusters; we compute the best number of clusters;
2. We keep as final number of clusters the number indicated as best for most degrees; let this number be n_c;
3. For each degree, we divide the vertices with that degree into n_c clusters;
4. We finally match the clusters found for the different degrees.

Let us explain the different steps.

STEP 1. Given that we base our clustering on occurrences of patterns with four vertices and less, we cluster only vertices with degree at least 4. For each degree, we use the k-means algorithm on modified versions of the pattern-frequency vectors of the nodes. As k-means starts by randomly picking the first centers, we perform 50 clusterings for each degree and each number of clusters and choose the clustering with the lowest intra-cluster variance. The best number of clusters is computed by comparing the average silhouette values obtained for the different numbers of clusters.

Let us explain why and how we modify the pattern-frequency vectors. The k-means algorithm uses a given distance between elements in order to compute the clusters; this distance is usually the Euclidian distance between the feature vectors of the elements. We need to modify the pattern-frequency vectors before computing the Euclidian distance on them. There are several reasons for that.

(a) Modifying the ranges of values. Even if we focus on each degree at a time, the numbers of occurrences of the different patterns are not placed in the same ranges of values. For instance, the maximal number of occurrences of the ∠–pattern is generally a lot higher than the maximal number of the $\boxtimes$–pattern. We need to place the ranges of values of all the variables participating to the Euclidian distance between the same extreme values. This can be done for instance by centering and scaling the variables or by giving them new values, obtained from a computation of slices. It is the second solution that we adopt here.

Generally, given a group of n elements that have values $a_1, a_2 \ldots a_n$ for a given attribute (or variable) a, one can compute k bins (or slices) such that there is a fairly equivalent number of elements whose values are placed in each bin. For that, one needs to compute $k + 1$ ascendant values (called limits) such that the first limit is the minimal value of a_i for $i \in \{1, 2, \dots n\}$, the last limit is the maximal value of a_i and there is a fairy equivalent number of elements (i.e. $\frac{n}{k}$) whose values are placed between two consecutive limits. Now, one can use instead of the values $a_1, a_2 \dots a_n$ the corresponding slices: instead of the value a_i one uses the value x if a_i belongs to the x–th bin. Note that the computation of only two bins ($k = 2$) is equivalent to the computation of the median value of the attribute a. In this case, one can use, instead of the real value a_i of the attribute, a value that is either 1 or 2 depending on a_i : if a_i is inferior to the median value, then one uses 1, otherwise 2.

This is the technique that we apply here. Instead of using the real values of the pattern-frequency vectors, we compute and use slices of values. There are several advantages in doing this. First, we eliminate the problem of comparing very different values for different patterns: now we have, for all the patterns, the same possible values. Second, the new values are established using the ranges of values, as found in the network. Thus, the number of occurrences of a given pattern in a given egocentred network can be very small comparing to the maximal possible value and, in the same time, very high comparing to its value in the other egocentred networks. We want to emphasize the fact that this value is high in *our* network, which the slices do. Third, the extreme values (often difficult to handle) are simply put in the marginal slices and are no longer seen as extreme.

For each degree d and each one of the 11 components of the pattern-frequency vector, we choose five bins such that an equivalent number of nodes in Pop_d (the reduced population with degree d) have values in each one of the bins.

(b) Using the absent patterns. By using the pattern-frequency vectors we take into consideration the presence of different structures in the egocentred networks. Besides this, it can be useful to take into consideration also the absence of different structures. Thus, two nodes are similar if they have many common patterns in their egocentred networks, but also if patterns that are not present in one are not present in the other one either. To take this information into consideration, we add to the pattern-frequency vector of each node the pattern-frequency vector of the complement graph of its egocentred network. The complement graph of a graph $G = (V, E)$ is a graph $G' = (V', E')$ where the vertices are the same as in G (i.e. $V' = V$) and the edges are all the possible edges between vertices in V that are not present in E (i.e. $E' = \{(u, v), u, v \in V \text{ and } (u, v) \notin E\}$).We thus have, for each vertex v, a vector containing the number of occurrences of patterns in the egocentred network $Eg(v)$, followed by the number of occurrences of patterns in the complement graph $Eg'(v)$ of the egocentred network. Next we replace the real values in this new vector by the corresponding slices as previously explained; we thus obtain the *extended pattern-frequency vector.*

Definition 4. Given a vertex v of a graph G, we call extended pattern-frequency vector of v the vector with 22 components containing first the slice values of the pattern-frequency vector of v and then the slice values of the pattern-frequency vector of the complement graph $Eg'(v)$ of the egocentred network $Eg(v)$ of v.

It is on the extended pattern-frequency vectors that we compute the Euclidian distance and we perform the k-means clustering.

STEP 3. Suppose n_c was found as best number of clusters for most degrees, so we need to divide the nodes with each degree in the reduced population into n_c clusters. We perform again 50 k-means clusterings with $k = n_c$ for each degree and we keep the clustering with the lowest intra-cluster variance.

STEP 4. We have now n_c clusters for each degree greater than 3. We need to match the clusters obtained for the different degrees so that, every node, no matter its degree, belongs to one of the n_c clusters. In order to do the matching, we compute the center (or centroid) of each cluster for each degree. Recall that the center of a cluster is the average of all the points in the cluster i.e. a vector where each component is the arithmetic mean of the values of that component for all the elements in the cluster.

We match clusters for consecutive degrees by using the centers: for each degree $d > 4$, we compute the centers of the clusters obtained for d (let C_i be the center of the ith cluster, with i from 1 to n_c) and for $d - 1$ (let C'_i be the center of the ith cluster, with i from 1 to n_c) and the Euclidean distances between these centers. For each one of the clusters obtained for degree d we have to choose exactly one cluster from those obtained for degree $d - 1$, and each one of these clusters must be chosen exactly once. This corresponds to a permutation of n_c elements: each cluster with index 1 to n_c obtained for degree d is given a new index, also from 1 to n_c, corresponding to the cluster for degree $d - 1$ with which it is matched. We choose the permutation σ that minimizes the sum of distances between centers of matched clusters: $\sum_{i=1,\ldots,n_c} dist(C_i, C'_{\sigma(i)})$. For that, let us observe that if there is a valid permutation σ such that, for all i from 1 to n_c, $dist(C_i, C'_{\sigma(i)})$ is the minimum distance between C_i and any C'_j, with j from 1 to n_c, then σ is the permutation that minimizes the sum of distances. This case may occur for many pairs of consecutive degrees, so in this case no other computation is needed. After having computed the permutation σ that minimizes the sum of distances, one has a bijective matching of clusters for the given pair of consecutive degrees. By doing this for each pair, we obtain a matching of all the clusters.

Each vertex in the reduced population thus belongs to one of the n_c clusters. We now distribute into clusters the vertices that we have previously filtered out by putting them in the clusters of the vertices with the same pattern-frequency vector.

7.6 Mobile Phone Communications Network

We apply the previously presented methods to a large mobile phone communication network. We first present the dataset and some statistics on duration and frequency of communication depending on the age of the person. Then we describe how each node is connected to the network using the method that we have introduced in Sect. 7.4. Next, we group the individuals in the social network into clusters using the method presented in Sect. 7.5. Finally, we compare the obtained clusters to the age and communication intensity of the people in the social network.

7.6.1 Data Description

The analyzed dataset contains the CDRs (call detail records) of the mobile phone communications of the customers of a mobile phone operator (we call it O) in a European country during the month of October 2006. O has approximately 30 % share market in the country. The dataset contains several details of each mobile phone communication in the O network: the identifiers of the two persons in communication, their mobile phone operators (for the communication to be recorded, at least one of the two persons must be a O customer), the type of communication (this can be call or short message SMS), the time when the communication began and its duration (in the case of a phone call). The phone numbers have been hashed and each person has been given a unique identifier that does not allow finding the identity of the person. The dataset contains over one billion records involving ten millions users. As we do not have the mobile phone communications between the persons not belonging to O, we keep in our analysis only the communications where the two persons are both O customers. We thus analyze 3.3 million users that have exchanged more than 170 million phone calls and SMS during the followed month. For these customers the database contains also their age. We compared the age distribution of the mobile phone customers in our dataset to the census distribution in the population of the analyzed country. The differences between the two are very small, so there is no systematic bias in our data as regarding this characteristic (except for people over 55 who are underrepresented among mobile phone users). The following analysis has been done on customers aged 18–55 thus the older age groups under-representation in the mobile phone dataset does not affect our results.

First, we computed some statistics of mobile phone usage by age. The age seems an interesting variable here as different generations of people began to use the mobile phone at different ages. As the mobile phone diffusion started in the mid-1990s, there is only the nowadays youngest part of population who entered in their "communication age" directly with a cell phone at hand. We thus expected a different usage of the mobile phone between age groups. Figure 7.5 shows the average number of out-going calls and SMS by age during the studied month. We observe no important difference in the number of calls by age. The main distinction concerns SMS usage: younger users send more SMS than older ones. In the age group 18–25 this tendency is really impressive: the SMS is used four times more frequently than a conversational exchange. This means that to recognize a younger customer in the dataset, one can look at the number of SMS sent. Figure 7.6 shows the average of the total duration of calls by age. We observe that people from 22 to 34 have in average the greatest total durations (these are out-going calls, so the age is that of the caller); for older people, the total duration of calls decreases with the age.

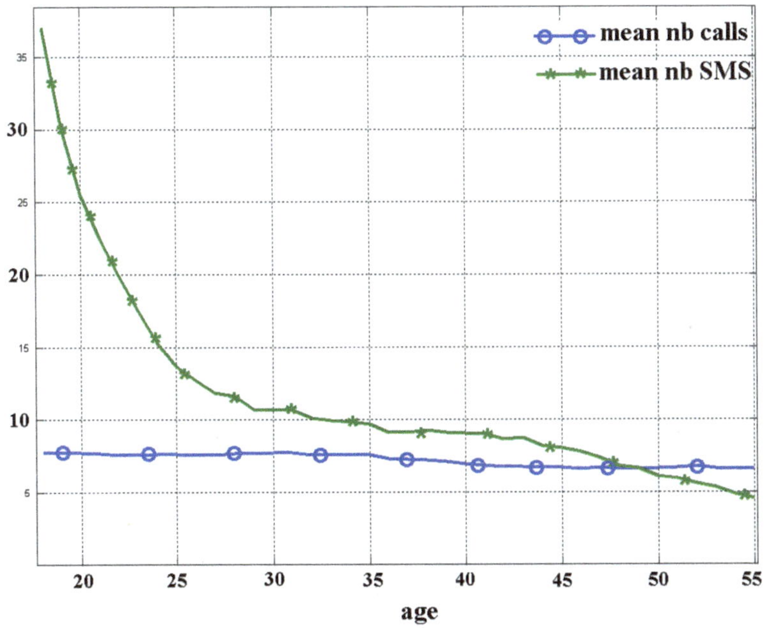

Fig. 7.5 Average number of calls and SMS as a function of phone user's age

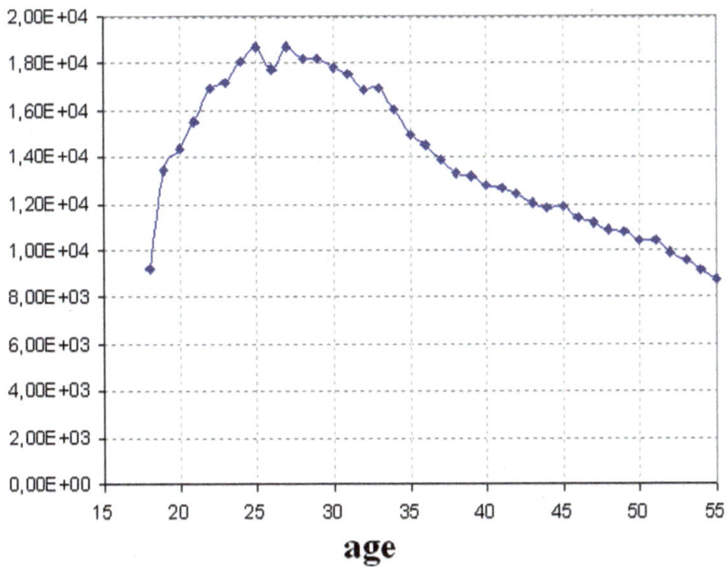

Fig. 7.6 Average total duration of calls (in seconds) as a function of phone user's age

While these measures represent a first analysis of the mobile phone communication data, our purpose is to study the social network modeling this data. The remaining part of this paper deals with the clustering of individuals using the social network structures and with the correlation between clusters and intensity of communication or age.

7.7 Personal Network Clusters

We model the mobile phone communications set by a simple undirected graph G. In this graph the vertices are the customers; we connect such two vertices by an undirected link if there had been at least one communication in each direction between the two persons during the followed period. This way we do not take into consideration the one-way contacts (calls or messages), single events in most of the cases suggesting that the two individuals do not know each other personally. We keep only the vertices with degree greater than 0, thus obtaining a graph G with 2.7×10^6 vertices and 6.4×10^6 edges.

In this graph, we apply the method *characterize* introduced in Sect. 7.4 in order to analyze how each one of the $2.7M$ vertices is connected to the network. Next, we apply the method introduced in Sect. 7.5 in order to group the nodes into clusters based on their network insertion.

The best number of clusters is found to be 6. Figure 7.7 represents the distribution into clusters of the egocentred networks of vertices with degrees 4 (up) and 5 (bottom). In our graph, all the possible egocentred networks for these degrees are present; these are all the possible undirected graphs with four and five vertices respectively. For each network, we have marked the cluster to which it belongs.

We observe that cluster 1 contains dense networks, while cluster 6 contains very sparse networks. Networks in cluster 2 seem to have a high number of stars, while those in cluster 5 have both isolated vertices and a rather dense group. For clusters 3 and 4 we can say that networks in cluster 3 are denser than those in cluster 4. These observations have been made by simply analyzing the clusters obtained for degrees 4 and 5. When looking at the centers of the clusters obtained for the different degrees, we observe that, for all degree:

- The center of cluster 1 has the maximal value for the number of edges and for the number of triangles i.e. vertices in cluster 1 have the highest average of $f_{\_}$ and of $f_{\triangle}$;
- The opposite situation happens for cluster 6: the center of this cluster has the minimal value for the number of edges and for the number of triangles i.e. vertices in cluster 6 have the lowest average of $f_{\_}$ and of $f_{\triangle}$;
- From the remaining clusters, the center of cluster 5 has the maximal value for the number of isolated vertices multiplied by the number of edges i.e. vertices in cluster 5 have the highest average of $f_{iv} \times f_{\_}$;

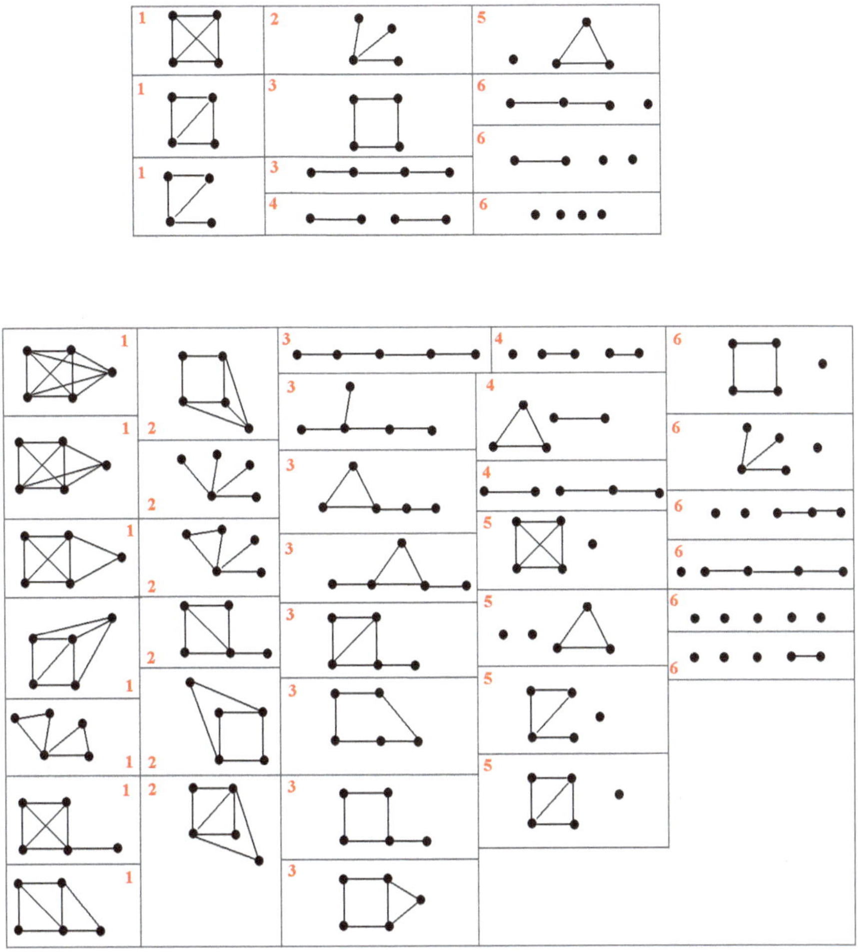

Fig. 7.7 All the possible egocentred networks of vertices with degrees 4 (*up*) and 5 (*bottom*) and their clusters

- The center of cluster 2 has the maximal value for the number of stars i.e. vertices in cluster 2 have the highest average of $f_{\angle}$;
- From the remaining two clusters, the center of cluster 3 has a higher value for the number of edges than the center of cluster 4 i.e. vertices in cluster 3 have a higher average of $f_{\_}$ than vertices in cluster 4.

This sustains our previously made observations for degrees 4 and 5: cluster 1 contains the densest networks, while cluster 6 contains the sparsest ones. Networks in cluster 2 have many stars, while those in cluster 5 have both isolated vertices and a dense group. Finally, networks in cluster 3 are denser than those in cluster 4.

Fig. 7.8 The distribution of the reduced population into the six clusters

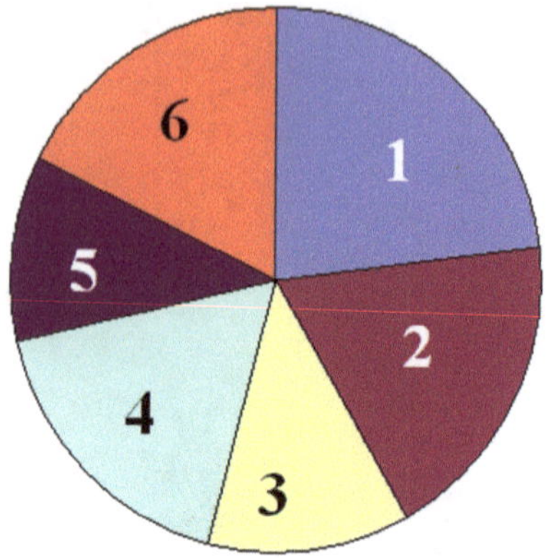

Table 7.2 The distribution of the reduced and total population into the six clusters

Cluster	% of the reduced population	% of the total population
1	23.16	4.15
2	18.6	2.91
3	12.24	2.54
4	17.05	26.93
5	11.12	5.04
6	17.83	58.43

Remember that before computing the clusters we have eliminated the multiple copies of pattern-frequency vectors. It is in this reduced population that we have computed the six clusters. The different resulting clusters contain fairly similar percentages of the reduced population (see Fig. 7.8 and Table 7.2).

However, when reintroducing the filtered out vertices, the population is not equally divided into clusters any more. This is caused by the low local density of the graph: most vertices have very sparse egocentred networks, so the different patterns occur in their networks in a small number. Thus the majority of the eliminated vertices belongs to cluster 6. After the introduction of the previously filtered out vertices, the new repartition into clusters becomes very unbalanced (Table 7.2).

In the following sections we confront the identified clusters to other characteristics of the mobile phone customers.

7.7.1 Clusters Versus Age

For the mobile phone customers who have provided their birth year when subscribing to the studied operator, we want to see if there is a connection between the age of a person and his or her cluster. Remember that in Sect. 7.6 we have presented some statistics on mobile phone use. There are some differences in call frequency and duration between ages, but the main distinction concerns SMS usage,

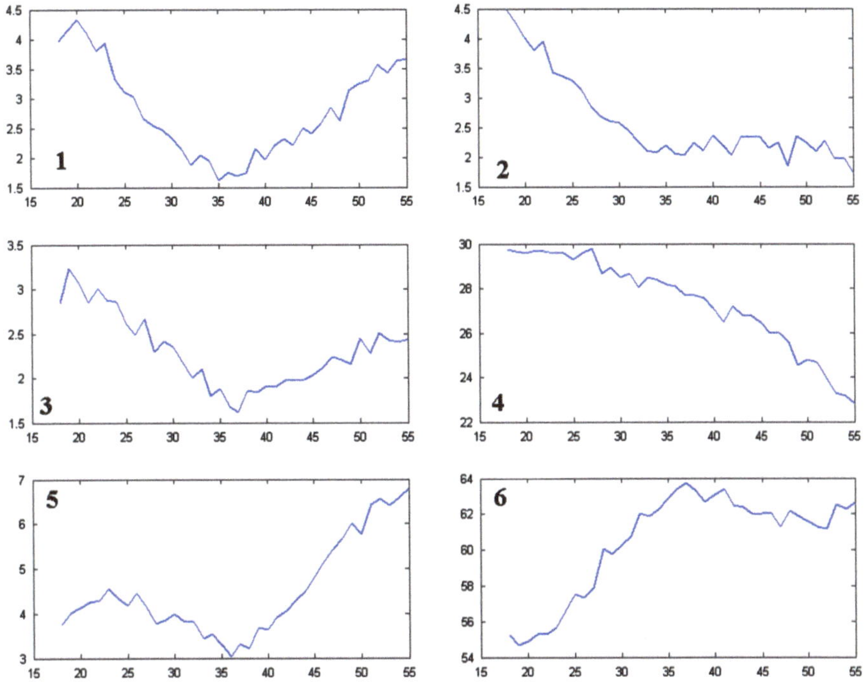

Fig. 7.9 For each cluster (each image), the probability of belonging to that cluster by age (on x-axis)

the younger users sending a lot more SMS than the older ones. Here we want to see if these differences in mobile phone uses are visible in the structure of the network surrounding each person.

We compute, for each cluster k from 1 to 6 and for each age a from 18 to 55,[3] the probability that a person of age a who has at least four contacts belongs to cluster k :

$$P(a,k) = \frac{\text{nb. persons of age } a \text{ and cluster } k}{\text{nb. persons of age } a \text{ and degree} > 3}$$

The plot of these probabilities is presented in Fig. 7.9. We observe that middle age people (30–45) have the lowest probability of belonging to cluster 1, so generally they are not involved in dense structures. This can be seen also in the plot for cluster 6 (the cluster containing the sparsest networks), where there is a peak for 35–40. Younger people belong generally to clusters 2, 3 and 4 and rarely to cluster 6 (in any case, a lot less frequently than older people). The oldest people are generally

[3] 18 is the minimal age to have a mobile phone subscription, while for persons of more than 55 years old, 70 % of them have degree smaller than 4.

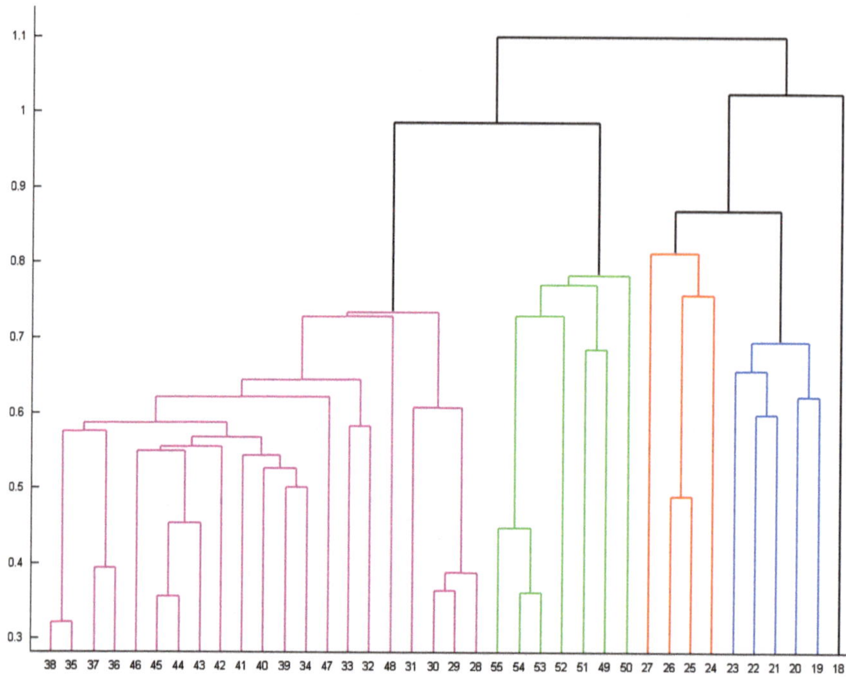

Fig. 7.10 Hierarchical clustering of ages on probabilities of belonging to the six clusters

placed in cluster 5: there is an increasing probability of having a densely connected group and some isolated contacts when going from 40 years old to 55.

Let us now group together the ages that have similar probabilities for the six clusters. We perform a hierarchical clustering on the ages using the cluster probabilities previously computed, after having centered and scaled the probabilities so that they have the same mean and standard deviation for each profile. The result of this analysis is shown in Fig. 7.10. We observe that there are four principal, homogeneous age groups similar to life stages categories: 19–23 (who can be associated with "students"), 24–27 (young people starting their active life), 28–48 (the age of living in couple, often with children), and 49–55 (people at an advanced stage of the professional life, whose children are adult or living apart). Note that this classification is based exclusively on structural characteristics of the local communication network where the degree was neutralized.

To sum up, there are some differences in the mobile phone usage and in the network structure depending on the age that allow recovering homogeneous age groups from mobile phone data. The personal network structure changes with age and the communication practices follow this transformation. Our analysis shows that the particular ways of interconnection to a personal network are in fact markers of age-related sociability of the mobile phone user.

7.7.2 *Clusters Versus Intensity of Communication*

7.7.2.1 Basic Statistics

We compute for each person (ego) the total number of calls he or she had during the followed period (both in-coming and out-going calls), the total duration of the calls and the total number of SMS (similarly, in-coming and out-going SMS). Also, we compute the average number of calls, total duration and number of SMS he or she had with each one of the contacts. We limit the contacts to the persons who initiated at least one communication (call or SMS) with ego and who also received at least one call or SMS from ego; these persons correspond to ego's neighbors in our graph. Besides the average values, we also compute the standard deviation for the number of calls, the duration and the number of SMS per contact. We thus have for each ego a vector with nine variables characterizing ego's communications. We use these vectors to measure the relation between communication intensity and the previously obtained clusters.

We begin by testing, for each one of the nine variables, the independence of the variable and the clusters by performing an ANOVA test: we test the hypothesis that the mean value of the variable is the same for the different clusters. As the distributions for the nine components are heavily right-skewed, we use the log values instead of the real ones. The ANOVA test rejects the hypothesis of equal means for each one of the components with $p = 0$. However, the ANOVA test specifies only that the means are different (i.e. they are not all equal) but does not say for which pairs of clusters these means are significantly different and for which they are not. In order to find this information, we perform a Bonferroni multi-comparison test for each one of the nine variables. We thus have:

- For the total number of calls, all the means are significantly different, except for the clusters 1 and 2; the order of the mean values of the total number of calls for the six clusters is, from low to high: 6, 4, 5, 3, 2, 1;
- Similarly, for the total duration of calls and the total number of SMS, all the means are significantly different, except for the clusters 1 and 2; in this case the order is 6, 5, 4, 3, 1, 2;
- Very similar results are obtained for the other variables; the ascending order of the values is always 6, 4, 5, 3, 2, 1, maybe with an interchange of 4 and 5 and of 1 and 2; the average duration of calls per contact is the only variable for which there isn't a significant difference between the mean values for the six clusters.

So, for each one of the nine components, cluster 6 has the lowest mean, followed by clusters 5 and 4 (or 4 and 5), cluster 3 and finally 2 and 1 (or 1 and 2). However, using the mean values is not satisfying as the different variables have a right-skewed distribution. Therefore, for each variable, we compute ten slices as we did in Sect. 7.5: we divide its spectrum of values into ten slices or bins such that a fairly equal number of values belong to each one of the bins. Then, we compute the probability that an individual belonging to a given cluster has values in a certain bin:

$$P(\text{variable, cluster, bin}) = \frac{\#\text{individuals} \in \text{cluster s.t. value(variable)} \in \text{bin}}{\#\text{individuals} \in \text{cluster.}}$$

We plot these probabilities for the first three variables in Fig. 7.11: the number of calls in (a), the total duration of calls in (b) and the number of SMS in (c). Each bar corresponds to a bin, going from the bin with the lowest values (left side) to the bin with the highest ones (right side). For each cluster, the height of each bin represents the previously computed probability i.e. the probability that an individual in that cluster has values in that bin; the sum of heights of bins of one cluster is thus equal to 1. For the three variables, individuals in clusters 1, 2 and 3 have a greater probability to have values in the highest bins than in the lowest ones, while for cluster 6 the opposite situation happens. Cluster 4 has values especially in the intermediate bins, while cluster 5 has values both in high and low bins, but fewer in the intermediate ones.

7.7.2.2 Predicting the Cluster from the Communications

Given these differences in quantity of communications for the different clusters, we want to see if we can guess in which cluster an individual is placed given his or her communications. For that, we use a decision tree to unveil the relation between communication intensity and cluster and thus to predict the cluster of each individual. The explanatory variables are the nine characterizing the communications of an individual: the number of calls, the total duration of calls, the number of SMS, the average number of calls, duration and number of SMS per contact, and the standard deviation of the number of calls, duration and number of SMS per contact. Based on the learning population, the tree learns the associations between intensity of communication and cluster; then it predicts the cluster of the individuals in the test population. If the predicted cluster is the same with the real cluster of the person, then the prediction is correct; otherwise the prediction is false. To measure the accuracy of the tree, one counts the correct predictions as compared to the size of the test population: the higher this number, the better the prediction. This number is then compared to the random prediction, where one attributes individuals into clusters randomly, with an equal probability.

Remember that the number of individuals in the six clusters is very uneven, with cluster 6 over-represented. If the decision tree learns and tests its rules of association on populations with such uneven distribution of clusters, it will associate everybody with cluster 6: no matter the communication characteristics of the different persons, if everybody is put in cluster 6, the tree gives the correct class to all the individuals in cluster 6 and the wrong cluster to all the others. As the individuals in cluster 6 are much more numerous then the others, the tree has a high rate of success. We want to avoid this situation and impose to the tree to search for associations between communications and clusters. Therefore, we give it a learning population where there is an equal number of individuals belonging to each cluster; the individuals are randomly chosen from the individuals in each cluster. We do the same thing

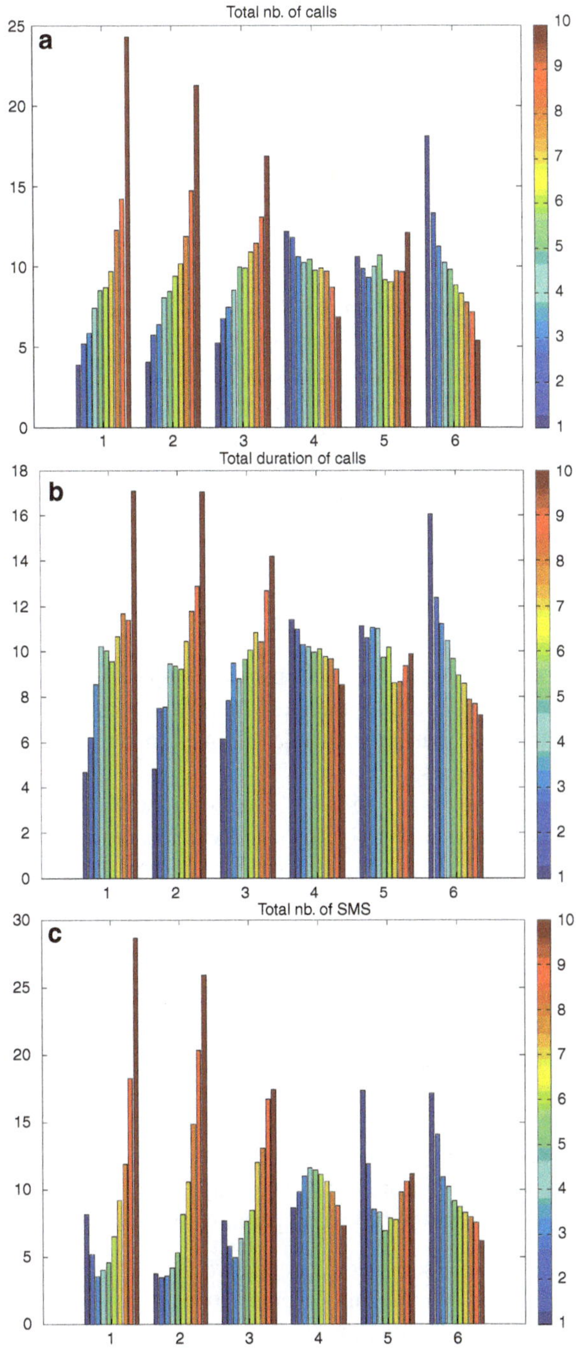

Fig. 7.11 For each cluster (Ox-axis), the probability that the communications of an individual in that cluster are in a given slice of values of the number of calls (*a*), total duration of calls (*b*) and number of SMS (*c*). In each image, the ten slices for each cluster are grouped together, with the lowest values in the *left side*

Table 7.3 The proportion of correct predictions in the six clusters

Cluster	Rate of success (%)
1	31.2
2	22.6
3	24.3
4	40.4
5	51.8
6	37.1

for the test population. As we want to predict six clusters, the rate of success of the random prediction is $\frac{100}{6} = 16.66\,\%$. Our decision tree has a rate of success of $34.6\,\%$, so more than twice the random one. The rate of correct predictions in the different clusters is presented in Table 7.3.

This result shows that there is a correlation between the intensity of communication and the cluster to which an individual belongs. Even more, we are able to predict the cluster with a rather high accuracy (as compared to the random prediction) given a set of variables characterizing the communications of each person.

7.7.3 A Typology of Customers

In the previous two sections we compared the social network clusters first to customers' age and then to their communication intensity, observing that the probability that an individual belongs to a given cluster is not independent from these measures.

Here we want to take into consideration, in the same time, all the three dimensions characterizing the individuals: the age, the communication intensity and the social network cluster. We want to see how these characteristics are distributed in the population and also to create a typology of customers based on these three dimensions. We would thus obtain groups of individuals such that the persons in a same group have similar communication practices and about the same age and cluster.

We use the Kohonen self organizing map. Remember that this clustering method produces a map with several layers, one for each variable characterizing the individuals. This shows how the different variables are distributed in the population. Also, the algorithm produces cells grouping individuals with close characteristics. In a second step, the algorithm computes a clustering of the individuals. The obtained clustering will represent our typology.

We choose the following parameters to characterize the individuals:

- Thier age (socio-demographic variable);
- Cluster membership (social network variable, from 1 to 6, as obtained in the previous sections); as it takes only six values, this variable can be seen as a class or a label of each individual;
- Communication intensity: number of calls, total duration of calls and number of SMS; (three communication variables).

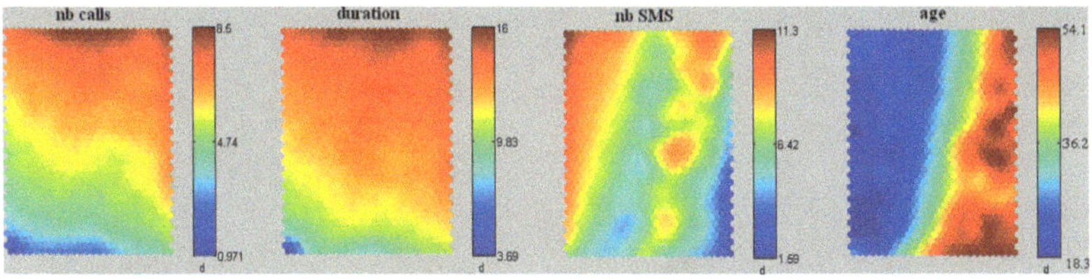

Fig. 7.12 SOM results: the individuals are grouped into cells depending on their communication intensity and age

Each individual is thus characterized by a vector with five elements. For the communication variables, we use a log transformation instead of the values themselves as these variables are heavily right-skewed. Also, recall that the distribution of individuals into clusters is very uneven, with cluster 6 being overrepresented. As we want to measure the influence of the variable "cluster", too, we randomly choose a same number of individuals in each cluster.

The set of individuals is then processed by the Kohonen self organizing map. This algorithm does not take labels into consideration when building the map, so it builds the map using only the other variables.

The processing of the set of individuals by the Self Organizing Map (SOM) provides Fig. 7.12. We observe that, unsurprisingly, the number of calls and the total duration are highly correlated, with increasing values on the south-north axis: the individuals with the lowest number of calls and total duration are placed in the south part of the map, while those with the highest values are placed in the north part. The number of SMS, however, is not correlated to the two previous ones, its values increasing from east to west. This variable seems to be correlated to the age: the highest values of the number of SMS are in the west part, where the youngest people are placed, while the lowest values are placed in the east part, where the oldest persons are placed. All these observations sustain our previous ones, presented in Sect. 7.6: there is no influence of the age on the call frequency and duration, but there is a high influence on the number of SMS.

Let us now analyze the distribution of the variable "cluster" in the different cells. Figure 7.13 shows this distribution, cluster by cluster. Each image in the figure corresponds to a cluster: the dark cells contain mostly individuals of the given cluster, while the white cells contain mostly individuals of other clusters. Recall that the different clusters are not taken into consideration when building the map; the cells are colored depending on the clusters of the people present in the cell, after all the computations. We observe that clusters 1, 2 and 3 are present especially in the north-west side of the map, while clusters 4, 5 and 6 are placed especially in the south-east side. Most of the cells labeled cluster 1 contain individuals with very high number of SMS or very high number of calls and total duration. Cluster 2 is generally associated with cells containing individuals with a high number of SMS or a high number of calls and total duration. Clusters 3 and 4 are generally present in cells where the individuals have a medium number of calls, total duration and

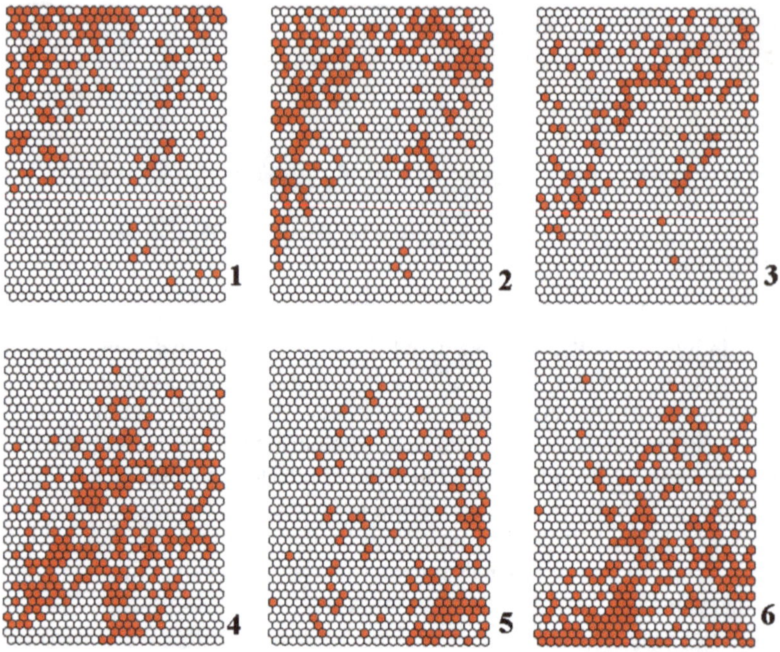

Fig. 7.13 For each cluster (each image), the cells where the cluster is in the majority (the *dark cells*)

number of SMS. Cluster 6 is especially placed in the south-east part of the area, where there are individuals with low number of calls, total duration and number of SMS. There seems to be no clear relation between the label of the cell and the average age of the persons in the cell, except for cluster 5 which is present especially in the cells containing the oldest people.

We now cluster the cells using the k-means algorithm. We thus obtain nine profiles, as showed in Fig. 7.14. We present the different characteristics of the people with each profile in Table 7.4. This result represents a typology of individuals based on their age, communication intensity and social network cluster.

7.8 Conclusions

In this paper we presented a method for clustering nodes, thus relating to the problem of identification of roles in a network. In this problem often encountered in social network analysis, one wants to group together the nodes of the network that are connected in similar ways to the network. There are however several questions that make this problem difficult to solve: What is a good characterization of the way a node is connected to the network? What does "similar connections" mean?

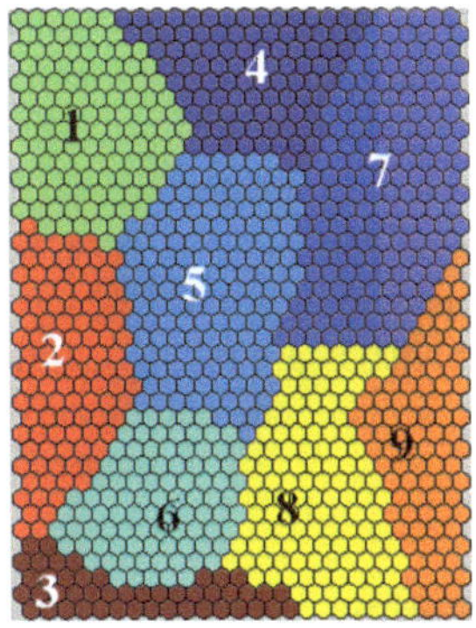

Fig. 7.14 The nine profiles produced by the Kohonen SOM

Table 7.4 The different characteristics of the individuals in the nine profiles produced by the SOM

Profile	Age	Nb. calls and duration	nb. SMS	Most represented cluster(s)
1	Youngest	High	Very high	1(45 %), 2(41 %)
2	Youngest	Medium	High	2(38 %), 3(20 %)
3	Young-middle	Very low	Low	6(70 %)
4	Young-middle	Very high	Medium	1(31 %), 2(31 %)
5	Young-middle	Medium-high	Low	4(39 %), 6(24 %)
6	Young-middle	Low	Low	4(45 %), 6(43 %)
7	Oldest	High	High	2(29 %), 1(19 %)
8	Oldest	Low	Low	4(34 %), 6(29 %)
9	Oldest	Low	Very low	5(42 %), 6(35 %)

Can the solution be applied to large graphs? How can one check the relevance of the different groups of nodes? In which conditions can one say that there is no better way of grouping the nodes?

We have made several choices in order to answer the different questions. First, we have characterized the way a node is connected to the network by counting the patterns present in its egocentred network; we have stored the number of occurrences of the different patterns in a pattern-frequency vector characterizing the node. Second, we have considered that nodes connected in a similar way to the network have close pattern-frequency vectors; here "close" is defined with respect to a set of transformations made on the pattern-frequency vectors. We have thus proposed a method for nodes clustering that groups together vertices that are embedded in similar egocentred networks. The clustering is done efficiently, so the method can be applied to large graphs. As said before, we have made several choices in order to answer the different questions. The proposed method gives promising results when applied to our real-world graph. As always, in this kind of methods, the solution validation is a delicate problem, but the results we have obtained for our large social network sustain the relevance of our method.

We have applied the proposed method to a mobile phone graph. This graph models 1-month mobile phone communications between the three million individuals.

The clusters produced by the method can be seen as a segmentation of the set of customers based on their social network insertions. We have compared the different clusters to the other information we had on the individuals (age and communication intensity), showing that the different parameters characterizing the individuals are not independent. Thus, the probability that a node belongs to a given cluster is not independent from the age and the mobile phone use of the person represented by the node. These results confirm the soundness of our method, even though, as always, many concurrent clusterings for various purposes may as well be relevant.

References

1. Batagelj, V.: Notes on blockmodeling. Soc. Netw. **19**, 143–155 (1997)
2. Batagelj, V., Ferligoj, A., Doreian, P.: Direct and indirect methods for structural equivalence. Soc. Netw. **14**, 63–90 (1992)
3. Borgatti, S.P., Everett, M.G.: The class of all regular equivalences: algebraic structure and computation. Soc. Netw. **11**(1), 65–88 (1989)
4. Burt, R.S.: Detecting role equivalence. Soc. Netw. **12**, 83–97 (1990)
5. Doreian, P., Batagelj, V., Ferligoj, A.: Generalized Blockmodeling. Cambridge University Press, Cambridge, England (2005)
6. Dunnett, C.W.: A multiple comparisons procedure for comparing several treatments with a control. J. Am. Stat. Assoc. **50**, 1096–1121 (1955)
7. Hidalgo, C.A., Rodriguez-Sickert, C.: The dynamics of a mobile phone network. Phys. A Stat. Mech. Appl. **387**(12), 3017–3024 (2008)
8. Hummell, H., Sodeur, W.: Strukturbeschreibung von positionen in sozialen beziehungsnetzen. In: Pappi, F.U. (ed.) Methoden der Netzwerkanalayse. Oldenbourg, Munich (1987)
9. Kohonen, T.: The self-organizing map. Proc. IEEE **78**(9), 1464–1480 (1990)
10. Lambiotte, R., Blondel, V.D., de Kerchove, C., Huens, E., Prieur, C., Smoreda, Z., Van Dooren, P.: Geographical dispersal of mobile communication networks. Phys. A **387**(21), 5317–5325 (2008)
11. Lorrain, F., White, H.: Structural equivalence of individuals in social networks. J. Math. Sociol. **1**, 49–80 (1971)
12. Onnela, J.P., Saramäki, J., Hyvönen, J., Szabó, G., de Menezes, A.M., Kaski, K., Barabási, A.L., Kertész, J.: Analysis of a large-scale weighted network of one-to-one human communication. New J. Phys. **9**(6), 179+ (2007)
13. Onnela, J.P., Saramäki, J., Hyvönen, J., Szabó, G., Lazer, D., Kaski, K., Kertész, J., Barabási, A.L.: Structure and tie strengths in mobile communication networks. Proc. Natl. Acad. Sci. **104**(18), 7332–7336 (2007)
14. Palla, G., Barabasi, A.-L., Vicsek, T.: Quantifying social group evolution. Nature **446**(7136), 664–667 (2007)
15. Reichardt, J., White, D.R.: Role models for complex networks. EPJ Manuscr. **60**, 217–224 (2007)
16. Scheffé, H.: The Analysis of Variance. Wiley, New York (1959)
17. Stoica, A., Couronné, T., Beuscart, J.S.: To be a star is not only metaphoric: from popularity to social linkage. In: Proceedings of the 4th International AAAI Conference on Weblogs and Social Media (ICWSM). AAAI, Washington, DC (2010)
18. White, D., Reitz, K.: Graph and semigroup homomorphisms on netwoks and relations. Soc. Netw. **5**, 193–234 (1983)

Chapter 8
Virus Propagation Modeling in Facebook

Wei Fan and Kai-Hau Yeung

Abstract In recent years, online social network services have become part of people's life. One of the consequences these services bring about is the security problem. In this paper, we propose a virus model based on the application platform of Facebook. We also model virus propagation through emails and compare the behaviors of virus spreading in Facebook and email network. It is found that while Facebook provides a platform for application developers, it also provides the same chance for virus spreading. Virus will spread faster in Facebook network if users of Facebook spend more time on it. Moreover, users' network generated with BA scale-free model is compared with some sampled networks of Facebook in this paper. The results show that applying BA model in simulations will overestimate the number of infected users a little, but still reflect the trend of virus spreading.

8.1 Introduction

Computer viruses can spread through the Internet in many ways, such as email, instant messengers (IM), and P2P file sharing. Currently, online social network service (SNS) becomes popular. This kind of service provides a platform for people to have fun. People can share interesting things in their life with their friends on these websites, and they can also take part in some activities or join groups online. But these characteristics give hackers opportunity to attack these users. The virus spreading in SNS network is similar to that in an email network or an instant messenger network. All of them can spread virus by sending or sharing files which contain malicious codes. If a user of these networks gets infected, the infected

W. Fan (✉) · K.-H. Yeung
Department of Electronic Engineering, City University of Hong Kong, Hong Kong, China
e-mail: fanwei.fw@gmail.com; eeayeung@cityu.edu.hk

T. Özyer et al. (eds.), *The Influence of Technology on Social Network Analysis and Mining*, Lecture Notes in Social Networks 6, DOI 10.1007/978-3-7091-1346-2_8,

account will automatically send the same email or file to the users in his/her contact list, which helps virus spread quickly.

There have been some models to simulate the virus propagation in those networks. C. Zou et al. describe their email virus propagation model in [19–21]. They assume that email virus spreads though network by containing virus in email attachments. This model accounts for users' email checking time intervals and the probability of users to open these attachments. And they found that as users' email checking time becomes more variable, the virus spreads faster. In this model, the probability that a certain user gets infected is a constant. In [9, 10] T. Komninos et al. propose a worm propagation model for email, IM and P2P networks. They consider that as time grows, users' behaviors should be different. So the probability that a user opens a malicious attachment is not a fixed value, but will decrease as time goes, which is different from Zou's model. And the model of virus propagation in P2P network in [17] assumes that the probability of a user to download an infected file is a function of the ratio of infected files to total files. And this ratio can be affected by users' downloading and executing behaviors.

Although virus propagation models have been proposed for email, IM and P2P networks, these models are not suitable for SNS networks. Besides sending messages while using email services, users of SNS networks can upload files to the Internet. To ensure that users can share their life in time, the activities that a user takes will appear in his/her friends' news feed, so all the friends can read the news when they are online. Moreover, different from email or IM networks, some people use SNS for entertainment, and spend many hours on that every day. These features are helpful for virus propagation. As the behavior of SNS users can be more complex than that in other networks, it is necessary to construct new models for virus propagation in SNS networks. Recently, there are reports that some SNS websites, such as Facebook and MySpace, were attacked by hackers [8, 18]. Among these SNS providers, Facebook attracts the largest population. Also, there is an application platform in Facebook. Everyone can build their applications with this platform, which can be easily utilized by hackers. So in this paper Facebook is the focused network in our study.

In this paper, two models of virus propagation in Facebook are proposed. The first is based on the Facebook application platform. In this model, it is assumed that hackers may utilize this platform to post applications along with viruses. Users may install these malicious applications in turn. After being infected, these users will send invitations to their friends. As will be reported later, installations of malicious application spread through network faster than other normal applications with the same initial conditions. In the second model, virus spreads through sending messages to friends. It is a traditional way, just like sending email with malicious attachments. More generally, hackers can post pictures or links that contain Trojans or worms. For simplicity, we assume that these methods are similar and we will describe them as sending messages. As will be reported later from our simulation results, it is found that if some people take SNS networks as entertainment tools and spend more time on them, virus will spread faster.

8.2 Facebook User Network Topology

We present the users of Facebook as a network with N_{user} nodes in this paper. Users are nodes in the network and each node is assigned a number $i, i = 1, 2, \ldots N_{user}$. An edge between two nodes i and j means these two users are friends. In Facebook, user i becomes a friend of user j with their names in each other's friends list, so this network is undirected. We also define that the node degree is the number of friends a user has. Some results have shown that email networks have a scale-free topology [5, 14]. And recently, researchers have studied the structure of some online social networks topology, such as MySpace, orkut, cyworld, and so on [2, 11, 13]. They found that these networks all have power-law degree distributions. Their degree distribution can be described as $P(k) \sim k^{-\gamma}$, here the probability that a node connects to k other nodes is $P(k)$, and the power-law exponent $\gamma > 0$. Most nodes of these networks have small degrees but a few nodes have many connections. This structure has been demonstrated to be vulnerable and the well connected nodes are crucial in epidemic spreading [4, 12, 15, 16].

In our simulations, we assume that the nodes' degrees of Facebook users' network exhibit the power-law distribution, as it is also one of the online social networks. Firstly, we will construct the users' network with Barábasi-Albert (BA) scale-free network model [3] to study both virus propagation models. The algorithm of BA model is as follows: (1) Starts with m_0 connected nodes, and $m_0 > 1$. (2) At each time step, add a new node to this network, and this node is connected to m existing nodes ($1 \leq m \leq m_0$). The probability that a new node connects to node i is $\prod(k_i) = k_i/(\sum_j k_j)$. In BA model, $\gamma = 3$. Edges are added with a preferential attachment, so the nodes with greater degrees will get more connections.

In this paper, the actual Facebook network will be sampled to verify that whether BA model can fit Facebook well. Firstly we take a user from Facebook randomly. This user is the source node and then snowball method is used to gain users. After enough nodes are obtained, connections among these nodes are kept, but the edges pointing to the nodes outside the sampled network will be removed. This method is repeated and several sampled networks are obtained. We will apply two of these sampled networks in simulations. The sampled networks and BA networks will be compared in this paper.

8.3 A Model Based on Facebook Application Platform

One of the Facebook's successes is its application platform. By using this platform, companies and individuals can develop their applications. Users of Facebook can add these applications to their accounts. And if they like the applications which they installed, they can send invitations to their friends and invite them to join. Because there will be more fun if more friends are using the same applications. Most applications are also designed to remind users to invite their friends. More

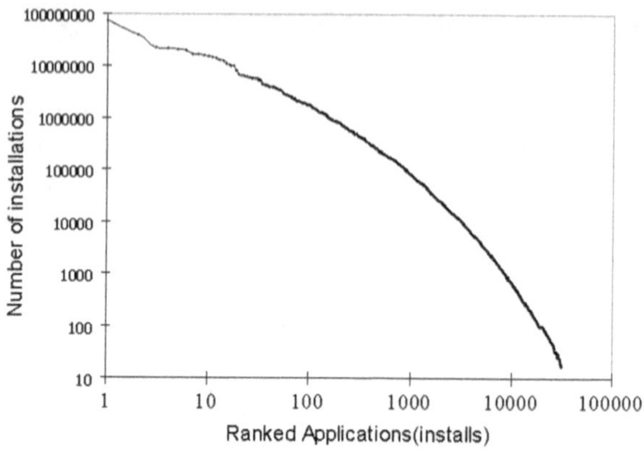

Fig. 8.1 The distribution of number of installations of each application

than 95 % of users have used at least one application, and on average, every day there are 140 new applications added [6]. However, it has been reported that some new applications become available along with virus [8]. If a user installs this kind of application, his/her account is infected and fake messages are forwarded to all his/her friends automatically to persuade them to install the same application. This will increase the probability that a user installs it. Considering the great number of daily installations, damage of this kind of applications may be severe. So it is necessary to construct a virus propagation model based on these applications. It has been shown that the installation of applications has a preferential characteristic in [7]. That means an application with greater number of installations can attract more new users. This is because this application has more chances to be seen by people, and people are more willing to install such a popular application. Moreover, a user who has installed more applications has a higher probability to install new applications. The distribution of number of installations per application is shown in Fig. 8.1. The data is obtained from Adonomics [1].

Gjoka developed a model to simulate the users' number of installations of Facebook applications [7]. With the input of the list of applications, number of installations per application and number of users, this model can generate a graph which shows the power-law distribution of number of installations per user. This model is helpful for us to model the existing number of installations for each user, but it cannot reflect the behavior when a user encounters an application invitation. In this paper we proposed a Facebook virus propagation model based on the application platform. This model not only follows the spreading law of normal applications, but also contains the characteristics of virus spreading.

Our Facebook user network has N_{user} nodes, and each node is assigned a number $i, i = 1, 2, \ldots N_{user}$. We assume that the total number of available applications is N_{app}, and each one is denoted by $k, k = 1, 2, \ldots N_{app}$. Each application has a number of installations to show how many users have installed it. Since there are new installations every day, the number of installations per application is not a fixed value. So the number of installations of application k at time step t is $Install_k(t)$,

$k = 1, 2, \ldots N_{app}$. From the data of Adonomics we can get the knowledge of initial number of installations per application before the virus begins attacking. We assume that the virus starts spreading at $t = t_0$. We will study our model in a network which is much smaller than the real Facebook network, so we will not use the original data of installations. We scale down the size of the network, total number of applications, and the number of installations per user/application. We can create a list of applications and assign a $Install_k(t_0)$ for each application k. The distribution of $Install_k(t_0)$ is similar to the curve in Fig. 8.1. Next we will model the behaviors of applications as described below.

1. Construct the initial number of installations for users

   With the list of existing applications and $Install_k(t_0), k, k = 1, 2, \ldots N_{app}$, we can construct the initial number of installations per user using the model defined in [7]. In the beginning, $Install_k(t_0)$ is ready for each application, but all the users in our network have not installed any application. We need to distribute each installation to users. At each step, each installation of $Install_k(t_0)$ over all the N_{app} applications is assigned to one of the users with a probability. The probability of one installation to be installed by user i is

$$P_{user}(i,t) = \frac{Apps_i(t)^{\rho} + init_{user}}{\sum_{j=1}^{N_{user}} (Apps_j(t)^{\rho} + init_{user})}. \tag{8.1}$$

   In [7] it is found that the number of installations per user has power-law distribution. That means a user who installs more applications has more chances to be selected to install other applications in our simulations. So we use preferential selection in this equation. Here $Apps_i(t)$ is the number of applications that user i has installed at time step t. The parameter ρ reflects the effect of preferential installation. $init_{user}$ is used to show the initial probability $P_{user}(i,t)$ for a user i who does not install any application at that time step. That is, if $Apps_i(t) = 0$, the initial probability for user i is $init_{user}/(\sum_{j=1}^{N_{user}}(Apps_j(t)^{\rho} + init_{user}))$. This probability would make sure that, even a user has no installation can also have the opportunity to be chosen in our simulations. This step is repeated until all $Install_k(t_0)$ installations of all N_{app} applications are exhausted. When the initialization is completed, the simulation steps described in Part 2 will be run.
2. Virus propagation

   The propagation of virus follows the steps described below:

   (a) Select the users who are infected in the beginning:

   The virus spreading starts from I_0 infected users at time step t_0. We randomly select the I_0 initial infected users from the network. Then the total number of applications N_{app} is added by 1. We label the malicious application by M. And we have $I(t_0) = I_0$, here $I(t)$ is the number of infected users in the network at t-th time step. The initial infected user(s) will send invitation messages to their friends.

(b) Maintain the distribution of installations:

The statistics of Facebook shows that there are many new installations every day, but the curve showed in Fig. 8.1 does not change significantly. The distributions of installation of applications are similar from time to time. So we should maintain the preferential characteristic of installations of applications. As we mentioned before, from Adonomics we can know how many installations are taken every day. We assume that in our simulations the number of new installations per day is m. The value of m is also scaled down due to the small size of our network. In this step, we select one application from the application list, the probability of application k being selected is

$$P_{app}(k,t) = \frac{Install_k(t) + init_{app}}{\sum_{j=1}^{N_{app}} (Install_j(t) + init_{app})}. \tag{8.2}$$

Here $init_{app}$ defines the initial probability $P_{app}(k,t)$ for an application without any installation, which has the same function as $init_{user}$. Figure 8.1 in this chapter shows that the number of installations per application also has power-law distribution. Therefore, this equation in our model uses preferential selection, as well. It means that an application with more installations has higher probability to be selected to be installed by users. Then a user i is selected from the network with the probability $P_{user}(i,t)$. If this selected user i has installed this application k before, we will pick another user. We select application and assign it to a user for m times in this step. So we have m new installations at this step b. And if the malicious application is selected in this step, we will change the value of $I(t)$, and the infected users would send invitations to his/her friends.

(c) Dealing with the invitations:

Every user who has received c invitation(s) at this time step will install the malicious application with the probability

$$P_{virus} = \frac{\sigma}{(1 - \frac{Install_M(t)}{N_{user}} \times \frac{Apps_i(t)}{N_{app}})^c}. \tag{8.3}$$

In this equation, the numerator $\sigma = 0.05$, which is the real data we obtain from an application. And we use the denominator to reflect the number of installations' influence on the probability of invitations acceptance. The reason is similar to that of equations (1) and (2): the increments of installations of application/user can raise the possibility that a user accepts invitations. If the user i accepts the invitations, we will change the value of $I(t)$. In our model, a user receives more invitation messages means that he/she has higher risk to be infected.

(d) Time step t is added by 1 and we repeat step b and c for the next time step.

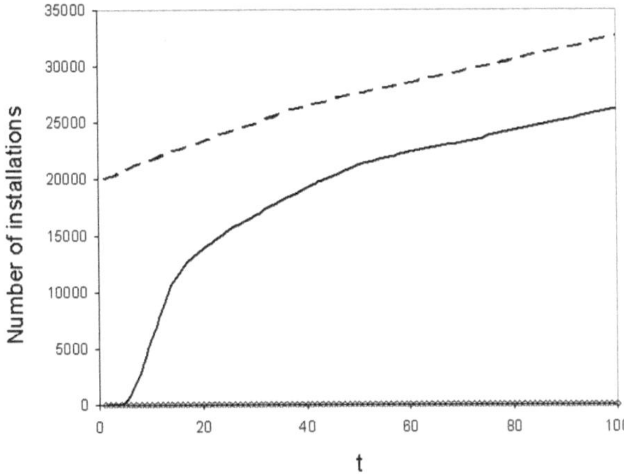

Fig. 8.2 The behavior of three applications over time. In this simulation, $N_{user} = 50,000$, $N_{app} = 100$ before the virus spreads, and $I_0 = 10$

8.3.1 Comparison of Malicious Application and the Top One

In this simulation, we record $I(t)$ at every time step t to show the virus spreading process in the network and the size of infected users in the end. In Fig. 8.2 we plot the behavior of malicious application, as the solid line shows. The dash line shows the behavior of the application which attracts the most users in the beginning. In this figure, the number of installations of the malicious application increases rapidly, and comes close to that of the top application. That is because the step c helps the virus to spread. But when the number of infected users reaches a certain value, its growth mainly comes from step b. So we can see from the figure that the growth rate is as the same as that of the top application after $t = 50$. And we also record the behavior of the application which has the same number of installations at $t = t_0 = 1$, as the diamond spots show. The line composed by these spots is nearly parallel and close to the x-axis. That is because its installations do not increase much. This implies that the number of installations of the application which has the same condition in the beginning does not change significantly.

8.3.2 Comparison of BA Networks with Different User's Average Degree

Users' decisions can be affected by their friends' behaviors. A user with higher degree may be infected easier, since he/she would receive more invitations. In BA scale-free network we can change the users' average degree, which is the average number of friends. Figure 8.3 plots the installations of malicious application in two different networks with average degree $< k >= 6$ and $< k >= 14$. This figure shows that a network with greater $< k >$ has more infected users, and the virus can spread faster in it.

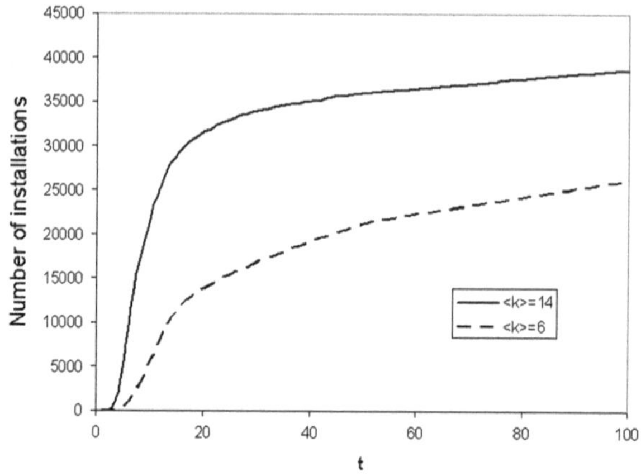

Fig. 8.3 The behavior of malicious application in networks with different average degrees

8.3.3 *Comparison of Sampled Facebook Networks and BA Networks*

In order to know whether BA model fits the Facebook network well, we take part of the users of Facebook and simulate our model in these sampled networks. Figure 8.4 shows the virus spreading in two sampled networks. These two networks have small power-law exponents that $\gamma \approx 1.5$, which is much smaller than BA network ($\gamma = 3$). Their average degrees are almost the same ($< k >= 34.2$ and $< k >= 35$), and the numbers of users of these two networks are 18,802 and 18,249, respectively. Their curves in this figure are close. We also draw the virus spreading processes in corresponding BA networks, which own the same average degrees and numbers of users. Although the clustering coefficients of the sampled networks are much larger ($c \approx 0.42$ while this value is about 0.009 in BA networks), the virus spread faster in BA networks. The reason is their small power-law exponents. The sampled networks are more heterogeneous than the BA networks, so more users have low degrees, which would slow down the speed of virus spreading.

In our model, infected users send invitations to their friends. This affects the behavior of users significantly, as we see from the results. Users who are friends in Facebook may be also friends in real life, so they will easily trust the invitations they received. So the virus can spread rapidly even there are only a few users installing it in the beginning. By comparing virus propagation in BA networks and that in sampled networks, it is found that the spreading in BA networks shows the general trend of the real situation. However, it is necessary to find a better network model if more accurate simulation results are required. This is because the number of infected users is overestimated on condition that BA model is used.

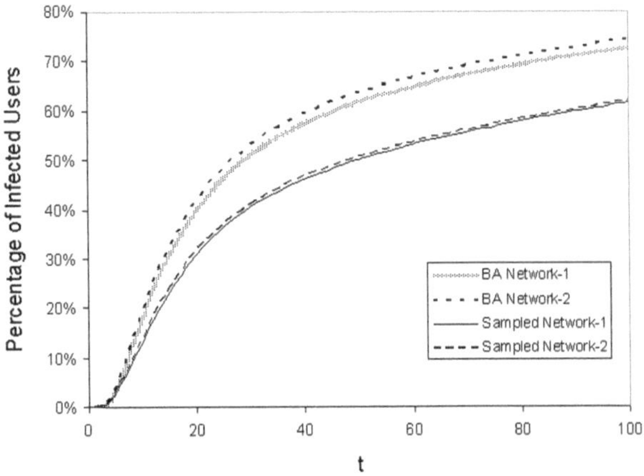

Fig. 8.4 The behavior of malicious application in BA network and sampled networks

8.4 A Model Based on Sending Messages

Our proposed second model is similar to an email virus propagation model. Email virus spreads by sending mails which contain attachments to users. If users open these email attachments, they will become infected. However, users can not add attachments to messages on Facebook, so hackers try to lead users to some third-party websites. These websites will inform users that their flash players are out of date, so users may download the new version of flash player, which is actually the virus, and install it [8]. The virus spreading process can be described like that: users log in Facebook from time to time. When a user is online and receives a message with a link to malicious website, he/she may delete this message without clicking this link, or click it and then become infected. If a user receives this message when he/she is offline, this user will process this message next time he/she logs in. And if a user is infected, the virus will send the same messages to all the friends of this user.

We can see that this spreading process seems to be the same as the email virus described in [19]. Both of them depend on users' interactions. And users check their accounts with dynamic time intervals. However, they have differences. In normal cases, while using email application,[1] people only check that if there is new mail and then log out. They may check email many times in a day, but will not stay on the web page and "play" their mailbox. On the contrary, people spend more time on Facebook and play online games. Every day more than 23 billion minutes are spent on Facebook which has 500 million active users [6]. That means on average each user spends more than 40 min on Facebook per day. If users get new messages when they are online, they can check mailbox immediately. For the ones who are online for hours every day, virus can spread faster. As a result, besides the time between two

[1] In this paper we only consider the case of Web mails.

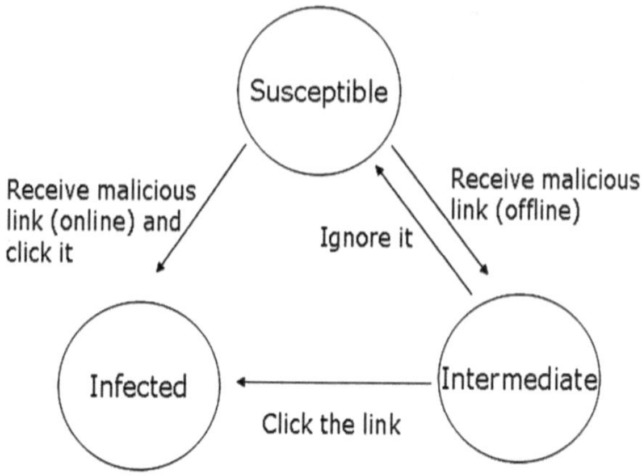

Fig. 8.5 Three kinds of status of a user: susceptible, intermediate, and infected

log-in attempts of a user and the probability that a user clicks the direct malicious URL, we need the online time as another factor that affects virus propagation. And we assume that the probability that a user click the URL may not be a constant value, which may decreases if some users realize there is virus spreading in the network.

We still present our model in BA scale-free networks and sampled Facebook networks with N_{user} nodes. Users of Facebook are described as $i, i = 1, 2, \ldots N_{user}$. In our model nodes have three kinds of status–susceptible, intermediate, and infected, as Fig. 8.5 shows. In the beginning, all nodes are susceptible. If a node gets a message with malicious link in inbox but it is offline, this node becomes intermediate. An intermediate node can return back to the status of susceptible if it ignores this message. But it will become infected if the user clicks this link with a clicking probability. Infected nodes cannot return other status. The three users' interaction factors are as follows:

- Facebook log-in time $T_{login}(i)$ for node i $(i = 1, 2, \ldots N_{user})$, follows exponential distribution. It is the time intervals between user i's two log-ins. Its mean $E[T_{login}(i)]$ is independent Gaussian random variable that $E[T_{login}] \sim N(\mu_{Tl}, \sigma_{Tl}^2)$. In our simulation $E[T_{login}] \sim N(40, 400)$.
- Facebook online time $T_{online}(i)$ for node i $(i = 1, 2, \ldots N_{user})$, it is independent Gaussian random variable that $T_{online} \sim N(\mu_{To}, \sigma_{To}^2)$. It is reasonable that $T_{online}(i) < T_{login}(i)$. In our simulation we have $T_{online} \sim N(1, 100)$, and we assume that in the original email virus model $T_{online}(i) \equiv 1, i = 1, 2, \ldots N_{user}$.
- The probability that user i clicks a malicious link $P_{click}(i, t)$ is also independent Gaussian random variable. It is assumed that $P_{click}(t) \sim N(\mu_p(t), \sigma_p^2)$, in which $\mu_p(t)$ will decrease as time goes on, because more users would be aware of this scam if the number of infected users increases. We have $\mu_p(t) = \mu_0(1 - N_{infect}(t)/N_{user})$, here μ_0 is a constant and $N_{infect}(t)$ is the number of infected user at time step t. In our simulation $\mu_0 = 0.5, \sigma_p^2 = 0.09$.

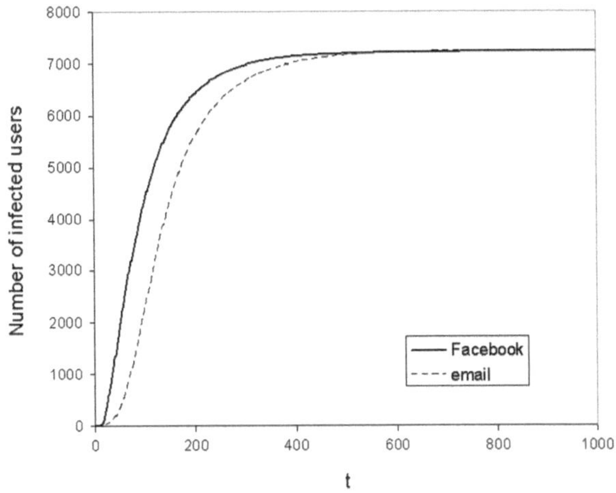

Fig. 8.6 The behavior of number of infected user. In this simulation, $N_{user} = 10,000$, $N_{infect}(t_0) = 10$, and $\mu_p(t) \equiv \mu_0$. The data is averages over 20 simulations

Virus propagation follows the steps below:

1. The propagation begins at $t_0 = 1$. We randomly select $N_{infect}(t_0)$ users who have malicious mails in their mailboxes in the beginning. These mails contain malicious links. If a user clicks the link, he/she will be infected and send the same mails to his/her friends.
2. At every time step, we check all the users who log in Facebook or are online at this step. If a user i has malicious mails in the mailbox, he/she would click the links with $P_{click}(i,t)$, or ignore these mails with probability $1 - P_{click}(i,t)$. After a user i logs out, we will generate new $T_{login}(i)$ and $T_{online}(i)$ for this user's next log-in. All our simulations are under the non-reinfection case, that is, infected users will not send the virus to their friends if they click the malicious link again.
3. Repeat step 2 for the next time step t.

8.4.1 Comparison of Facebook Networks and Email Networks

In this simulation, we present the Facebook network with BA network, and record the number of infected users $N_{infect}(t)$ at each time step. Figure 8.6 plots the $N_{infect}(t)$ in Facebook network with a constant $\mu_p(t) \equiv \mu_0$ and $T_{online}(i) > 1$, as the solid line shows. The dash line is the number of infected users in the original email network, which does not consider the users' online time. By comparing these two lines, we find that the virus will spread faster as some users spend lots of time on Facebook.

But users may be aware of this virus if more and more users are infected. So the probability that they click the links would decrease, and the number of infected users

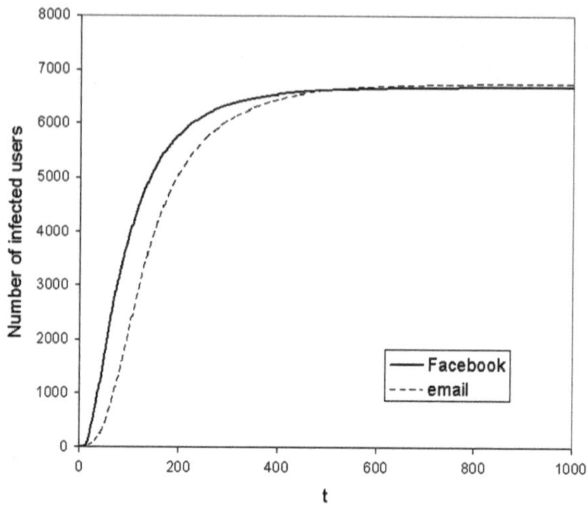

Fig. 8.7 The behavior of number of infected user. In this simulation, $N_{user} = 10,000$, $N_{infect}(t_0) = 10$, and $\mu_p(t) = \mu_0(1 - N_{infect}(t)/N_{user})$. The data is averages over 20 simulations

will be different. We plot it in Fig. 8.7, in which the $\mu_p(t)$ changes over time. We find that the sizes of infected users are smaller in both Facebook and email networks than those in Fig. 8.6. In Fig. 8.7, the solid line still rises faster than the dash line.

Our results indicate that under the same conditions, virus spreads faster in Facebook network than that in the original email network. But if we assume that the probability of a user to click the malicious link is not constant, the size of infected users will be smaller.

8.4.2 Comparison of BA Networks with Different User Average Degree

We also compare the virus' behavior in BA networks with different average degrees. Figure 8.8 plots the virus propagation process in two BA networks with $< k >= 6$ and $< k >= 14$. We also get the same conclusion that a network with greater $< k >$ has more infected users.

8.4.3 Comparison of Sampled Facebook Networks and BA Networks

The virus spreading in sampled Facebook networks and BA networks are compared, as well. As the characteristics of the two sampled networks that we mentioned in the first model are similar, we only plot the curve of one sampled network in Fig. 8.9. The corresponding BA network owns the same number of nodes and average degree.

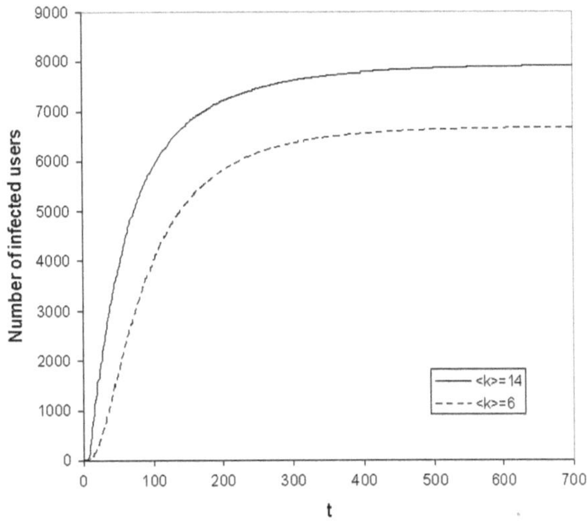

Fig. 8.8 The virus behavior in networks with different average degrees. In this simulation $N_{user} = 10,000$, $N_{infect}(t_0) = 10$, and $\mu_p(t) = \mu_0(1 - N_{infect}(t)/N_{user})$. The data is averages over 20 simulations

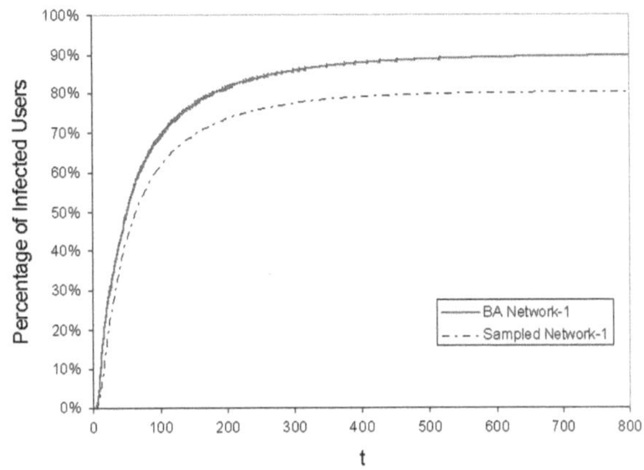

Fig. 8.9 The behavior of virus in BA network and sampled Facebook network

The same conclusion as that of the first model is obtained: virus still makes more users infected in BA network due to the high power-law exponent. But the difference is little.

8.5 Conclusion

In this paper, two models for virus propagation in Facebook network were proposed. In the first model based on Facebook's application platform, if the malicious application is installed by more users, it will become more popular and attract more installations. The results of the simulations showed that, although the malicious application attracts only a few users in the beginning, it can still spread rapidly. That is because users may trust their friends of Facebook and install it. While in the second model, which is similar to the email virus propagation model, the probability that a user is infected becomes smaller as more and more users get infected. We have found that the virus spread faster in Facebook than in the original email network, if we assume that people use Facebook for entertainment and spend more time on it. And it is demonstrated that the virus will spread faster in a network with higher average degree.

In the investigation of both models, we crawled part of the actual Facebook network and simulate our models in the sampled networks. It is found that virus spreads faster and makes more users infected in BA networks, which are more homogeneous than the sampled Facebook networks. This is because users' decisions may be affected by their friends' behaviors. So users with few friends of the sampled networks may slow down the spreading. Our results showed that, from the viewpoint of virus spreading, BA model is a good model and fit the Facebook network approximately. But if we would like to study Facebook from other point of view, we should look for other complex network models which can generate networks of similar power-law exponents and clustering coefficients to those of Facebook.

Acknowledgements This work was supported by Hong Kong Government General Research Fund (grant No. CityU-123608).

References

1. Adonomics: http://www.adonomics.com. Retrieved 10 June 2009
2. Ahn, Y., Han, S., Kwak, H., Moon, S., Jeong, H.: Analysis of topological characteristics of huge online social networking services. In: WWW '07: Proceedings of the 16th International Conference on World Wide Web, Banff (2007)
3. Barabási, A.-L., Albert, R.: Emergence of scaling in random networks. Science **286**, 509–512 (1999)
4. Dezsö, Z., Barabási, A.-L.: Halting viruses in scale-free networks. Phys. Rev. E **65**, 055103(R) (2002)
5. Ebel, H., Mielsch, L.-I., Bornholdt, S.: Scale-free topology of e-mail networks. Phys. Rev. E **66**, 035103 (R) (2002)
6. Facebook: http://www.facebook.com/press/info.php?statistics. Retrieved 20 July 2010
7. Gjoka, M., Sirivianos, M., Markopoulou, A., Yang, X.W.: Poking facebook: characterization of OSN applications. In: ACM SIGCOMM Workshop on Social Networks (WOSN'08), Seattle, Aug 2008
8. Kaspersky Lab: Kaspersky lab detects new worms attacking mySpace and facebook. Message posted to: http://www.kaspersky.com/news?id=207575670 (2008)
9. Komninos, T., Spirakis, P., Stamatiou, Y.C., Vavitsas, G.: A worm propagation model based on scale free network structures and people's email acquaintance profiles. Int. J. Comput. Sci. Netw. Secur. **7**, 2 (2007)
10. Komninos, T., Stamatiou, Y.C., Vavitsas, G.: A worm propagation model based on people's email acquaintance profiles. In: WINE 2006, Patras (2006)

11. Kumar, R., Novak, J., Tomkins, A.: Structure and evolution of online social networks. In: KDD '06: Proceedings of the 12th ACM SIGKDD International Conference on Knowledge Discovery and Data Mining, Philadelphia (2006)
12. May, R.M., Lloyd, A.L.: Infection dynamics on scale-free networks. Phys. Rev. E **64**, 066112 (2001)
13. Mislove, A., Marcon, M., Gummadi, K.P., Druschel, P., Bhattacharjee, S.: Measurement and analysis of online social networks. In: IMC '07: Proceedings of the 7th ACM SIGCOMM Conference on Internet Measurement, San Diego (2007)
14. Newman, M.E.J., Forrest, S., Balthrop, J.: Email networks and the spread of computer viruses. Phys. Rev. E **66**, 035101 (2002)
15. Pastor-Satorras, R., Vespignani, A.: Epidemic spreading in scale-free networks. Phys. Rev. Lett. **86**(14), 3200–3203 (2001)
16. Pastor-Satorras, R., Vespignani, A.: Epidemic dynamics and endemic states in complex networks. Phys. Rev. E **63**, 066117 (2001)
17. Thommes, R.W., Coates, M.J.: Modeling virus propagation in peer to peer networks. In: Information, Communications and Signal Processing, 2005 Fifth International Conference, Bangkok, pp. 981–985 (2005)
18. Ward, M.: Facebook users suffer viral surge. Message posted to http://news.bbc.co.uk/2/hi/technology/7918839.stm (2009)
19. Zou, C.C., Towsley, D., Gong, W.: Email virus propagation modeling and analysis. Technical Report TR-03-CSE-04, Umass ECE Department (2003)
20. Zou, C.C., Towsley, D., Gong, W.: Email worm modeling and defense. In: 13th International Conference on Computer Communications and Networks (ICCCN'04), Chicago, pp. 409–414 (2004)
21. Zou, C.C., Towsley, D., Gong, W.: Modeling and simulation study of the propagation and defense of internet e-mail worms. IEEE Trans. Dependable Secur. Comput. **4**(2), 105–118 (2007)

Chapter 9
Comparing and Visualizing the Social Spreading of Products on a Large Social Network

Pål Roe Sundsøy, Johannes Bjelland, Geoffrey Canright, Kenth Engø-Monsen, and Rich Ling

Abstract By combining mobile traffic data and product adoption history from one of the markets of the telecom provider Telenor, we define and measure an adoption network—roughly, the social network among adopters. We study and compare the evolution of this adoption network over time for several products—the iPhone handset, the Doro handset, the iPad 3G and videotelephony. We show how the structure of the adoption network changes over time, and how it can be used to study the social effects of product diffusion. Specifically, we show that the evolution of the Largest Connected Component (LCC) and the size distribution of the other components vary strongly with different products. We also introduce simple tests for quantifying the social spreading effect by comparing actual product diffusion on the network to random based spreading models. As videotelephony is adopted pairwise, we suggest two types of tests: transactional- and node based adoption test. These tests indicate strong social network dependencies in adoption for all products except the Doro handset. People who talk together, are also likely to adopt together. Supporting this, we also find that adoption probability increases with the number of adopting friends for all the products in this study. We believe that the strongest spreading of adoption takes place in the dense core of the underlying network, and gives rise to a dominant LCC in the adoption network, which we call "the social network monster". This is supported by measuring the eigenvector centrality of the adopters. We believe that the size of the monster is a good indicator for whether or not a product is going to "take off".

P.R. Sundsøy (✉) · J. Bjelland · G. Canright · K. Engø-Monsen
Corporate Development, Telenor ASA, Oslo, Norway
e-mail: pal-roe.sundsoy@telenor.com

R. Ling
IT-University, Copenhagen, Denmark
e-mail: rili@itu.dk

T. Özyer et al. (eds.), *The Influence of Technology on Social Network Analysis and Mining*, Lecture Notes in Social Networks 6, DOI 10.1007/978-3-7091-1346-2_9,

9.1 Introduction

This paper is an extended version of [28], where new methodology is developed and applied to existing datasets. A new longitudinal dataset is also added. The new methodology quantifies the social spreading effects for transactional products, and is applied on the video telephony data. In addition we enrich the paper by adding spreading studies of the recent iPad 3G tablet.

The current study is motivated by the question of how people adopt new products and services, and what role the underlying social network structure plays in this process. The effect of the social network on product adoption and diffusion has been well documented in early market research, see e.g. [29] for an overview of this research. Most of the early studies have suffered from limited network data availability, since social networks have traditionally been difficult to measure. Several theoretical network models have been developed. Some are less realistic due to the evolutionary nature and power law degree distributions [5, 14]. Analyses of more realistic models can be found in [6, 18, 31].

In recent years massive social network data have been made available to researchers through electronic phone logs [9, 15, 23, 26] and online social network services [2, 21]. These studies have confirmed that "the network matters" when customers decide to churn [4, 9] and when purchase decisions are made [8, 15]. Most of the existing research on product diffusion on networks has been focused on a single product, with a static snapshot of the social network. For an overview of analyses of large networks, the reader is referred to [1, 10, 11, 18, 24, 27, 30]. A few papers study the evolution of real-world networks [12, 19, 20, 22, 25]. In this paper we will present an empirical study of how the social network among adopters of telecom-products develops over time. In addition we will show how the product diffusion depends on the underlying social network.

We know that, for many products, a person's adoption probability increases with the number of that person's friends or contacts that have adopted the same product [9, 15]. This can be interpreted as inter-personal or social influence, and can be measured empirically. These measurements do not typically say anything about the large-scale structure of the social network. In telecommunications it is possible to obtain detailed anonymized mobile traffic data for a large connected network of users. One can then use this telephony network as a proxy for the underlying social network. Studies show that a telephony network is a very good proxy for the real social network [13]. Furthermore, by combining telephone network data over time with the adoption history for a product of interest, it is possible to observe how different products spread over the social network.

Using anonymized datasets from one of Telenor's markets, we will show how two different handsets have spread over the social network. The cases being used in this study are the highly buzzed iPhone, and the less fancy, but user-friendly, Doro type handset, which is more common among elderly people.

Both handsets are tracked from their early introduction and followed for a period of 2 years. We also present the tracking of a *transactional* product, mobile video telephony, a potentially useful product which allows users to talk to each other, while simultaneously viewing one another (or one another's surroundings)—given certain technological preconditions.

At the end we will show how a computer tablet, specifically iPad 3G, is spreading over the network. We include this as a preview on ongoing research due to the recent introduction in the market.

We start by introducing the *adoption network*, a construction which is readily visualized and which gives insight into the spreading of a product or service. Our figures will include many visualizations, which, we believe, are useful in understanding the product diffusion process on the underlying social network.

9.2 The Adoption Network

We will in this section define what we mean by the adoption network, followed by an empirical example.

9.2.1 *Definition of Adoption Network*

We define an adoption network as follows. Given a measured telephony network, the node set of the adoption network is the set of subscribers that have adopted a given product, and the links are the communication links belonging to this subset.

Mathematically, an adoption network is thus a subgraph of the whole mobile communication network $C = (c_{ij})$, where C represents (most generally) a weighted, directed, and possibly disconnected graph.

The mobile communication matrix C places a link between each pair of communicating subscribers, so that each nonzero element c_{ij} represents communication. The communication can be based for example on a weighted sum of SMS and voice duration (in which case we call these weighted links *W-links*), or other transactional data like video telephony traffic. All the results in this paper depend only on whether the communication link exists or not, without consideration to weight or direction. We consider traffic between Telenor subscribers in one market, which implies that the matrix will be $n \times n$ large, where n is the size of the customer base (several million subscribers).

The adoption network is then simply the subgraph of C formed by including only the adopting nodes and their common links. As we will see, for a *transactional* product (video telephony), there are two distinct useful choices for the communication links to be used in defining the adoption graph: (i) the standard (voice + SMS) links, or (ii) the links representing the use of the transactional service.

9.2.2 *Introducing the "Social Network Monster" by Example*

Figure 9.1 shows the empirical iPhone adoption network from Q4 2007 (This was measured before the iPhone had been introduced into the Telenor net; hence these

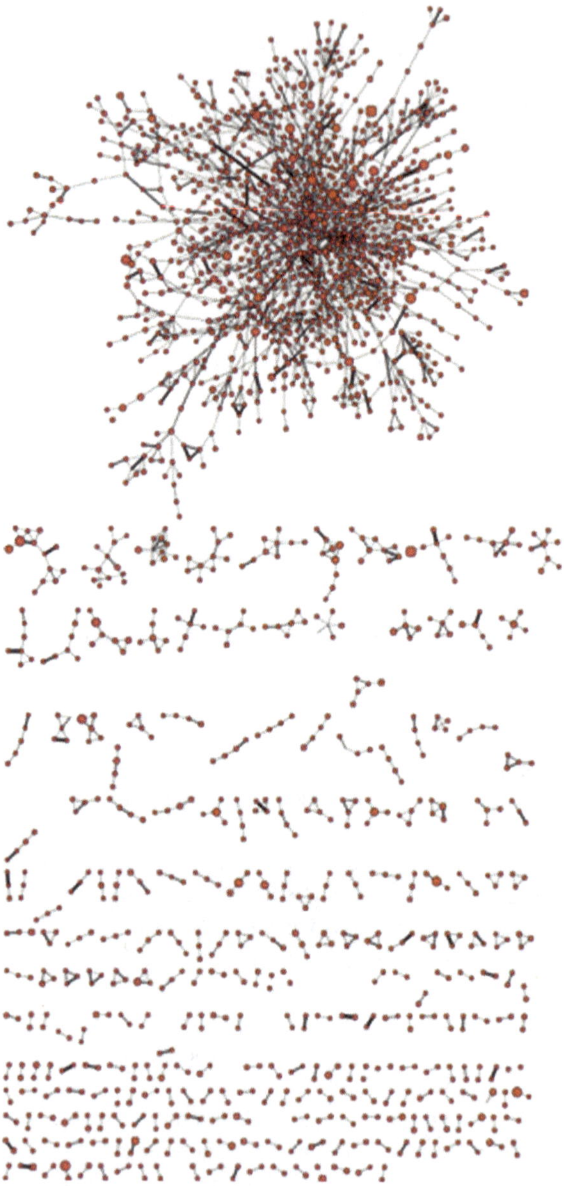

Fig. 9.1 iPhone Q4 2007 adoption network. One node represents one subscriber. Node size represents downloaded internet volume. Link width represents a weighted sum of SMS + voice. Isolates-adopters who are not connected to other adopters-are not shown in the picture

users have presumably bought their iPhones in the US and "cracked" them for use on the Telenor net). The data show that 42 % of the iPhone users communicated with at least one other iPhone-user, which speaks to the social nature of technology consumption, while 58 % did not have any iPhone contacts. We call the latter *isolates*. We do not include isolates in any of our visualizations of adoption networks, but do include them in all results counting number of users. We also study the connected components of the adoption network, where the connected components are subgraphs in which any two nodes are connected to each other by paths. Using this convention, we find for example that the largest connected component (LCC) in the adoption network of Fig. 9.1 includes 24.7 % of the total number of adopters (while representing over half of the nodes visible in Fig. 9.1). When the LCC in the adoption network is much bigger than all other connected components, and also represents a large fraction of all adopters, we will call the LCC a "social network monster". We note that this is not a precise definition; but we find that such monsters are typically found in adoption networks, and hence believe that the concept is useful.

9.3 Time Evolution of Adoption Networks

By studying the time evolution of an adoption network, we can get some insight into how the product which defines the adoption network is diffusing over the underlying social network. In particular we will often focus on the time evolution of the LCC of the adoption network—which may or may not form a social network monster. We recall from Fig. 9.1 that the other components are often rather small compared to the LCC. Hence we argue that studying the evolution of the LCC itself gives useful insight into the strength of the network spreading mechanisms in operation. It also gives insight into the broader context of adoption. As described in [20], two friends adopting together does not necessarily imply social influence—there might also be external factors that control the adoption. In this paper we will not try to separate the 'influence-effects' from external effects such as network homophily. Instead, when we observe a tendency that people who talk together also adopt together, we will use the term 'social spreading'—without making any implicit claim as to the underlying mechanism.

9.3.1 The iPhone Case

The iPhone 2G was officially released in the US in late Q2 2007 followed by 3G in early Q3 2008 and 3GS late Q2 2009. It was released on the Telenor net in 2009. Despite the existence of various models, we have chosen to look at the iPhone as one distinct product, since (as we will see) the older models are naturally substituted in our network. Figure 9.2 shows the development of the iPhone monster in one particular market. We observe how the 2G phone is gradually substituted by 3G (red to green), followed by 3GS in Q3 2009 (yellow nodes). The 2G model falls from 100 to 10 % with respect to all the iPhone subscribers in the adoption network. In Q1 2009 we observe the same amount of 2G as 3G models.

We show only the LCC in Fig. 9.2 because the other components are visually very much like those seen in Fig. 9.1; the main change over time is that the non-LCC components increase greatly in number, but not in size. That is, essentially all

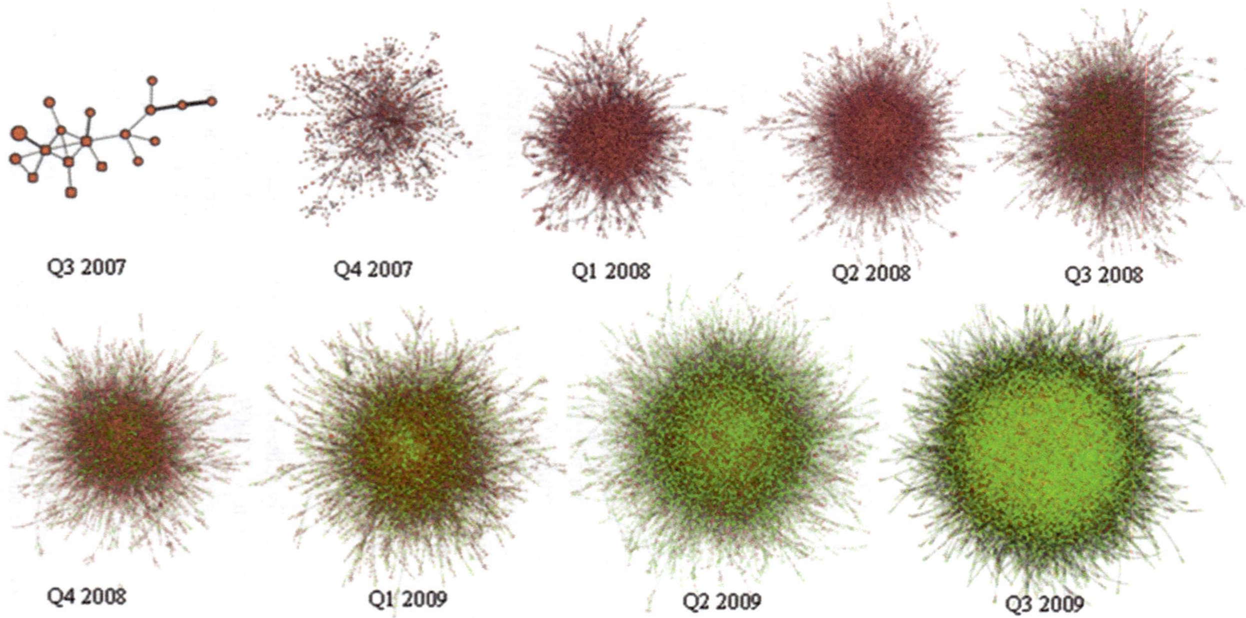

Fig. 9.2 Time evolution of the iPhone adoption network. One node represents one subscriber. Node color: represents iPhone model: *red* = 2G, *green* = iPhone 3G, *yellow* = 3GS. Node size, link width, and node shape (attributes which are visible in Q3 2007) represent, respectively, internet volume, weighted sum of SMS and voice traffic, and subscription type. *Round* node shape represents business users, while *square* represents consumers

significant growth in component size occurs (in the iPhone case) in the LCC. We regard this growth as a sign that the iPhone is spreading strongly ("taking off") over the social network. It is worth noting that there is a significant marketing "buzz" and external social pressure associated with the iPhone that is perhaps unique. We will offer in later Sections other kinds of measurements which support this conclusion.

9.3.2 The DORO Case

The next example is the Doro. As with the iPhone, there are several different models that are considered collectively. It is a handset which is easy to use, and mainly targeted towards elderly people [17]. Since Doro has a relatively low number of non-isolated users in all quarters studied, we present in Fig. 9.3 visualizations of the whole adoption network (minus isolates) over the entire time period, from introduction (in Q4 2007) to Q3 2009. Figure 9.3 shows that most Doro users that are not isolates appear in pairs in the adoption network. The social network monster never appears—the contrast with the iPhone case is striking. We believe that the kind of adoption network evolution seen in Fig. 9.3 is indicative of a product where "buzz" effects—social influence in the spreading of adoption—are weak or absent, whereas what we see in Fig. 9.2 indicates strong buzz effects. It is possible to argue that the adoption of the Doro is more of an individual choice, or perhaps even the choice of the user's children who wish to be in contact with their elderly parents. We note finally that the tiny "monster" (LCC) seen in Q3 2009 of Fig. 9.3 consists entirely of enterprise subscribers. Hence we speculate that these users are not the elderly of the target segment, but rather users with some other interest in the product.

9.3.3 Mobile Video Telephony Case

Compared to iPhone and Doro, video telephony has no value for an isolated user; thus users will always appear in pairs. A similar (pairs-only) constraint may be seen in [3], where the connections are based on romantic relations. In the video telephony case we actually have two distinct link sets which may be used to define an adoption network: W-links (voice + SMS), and video links. Thus for mobile video telephony we create and study two distinct adoption networks:

- The video-link set gives rise to the video adoption network (VAN)
- The W-linkset (voice + SMS) gives rise to the W-Video adoption network (WVAN).

We find that these two networks for video telephony have quite different behavior. We consider first the WVAN. This network connects users who (i) have a communication link (voice and/or SMS) and (ii) both use video telephony—not necessarily with each other. For the WVAN we find consistently a large social monster, much like the one seen in Fig. 9.2 that starts to form. However, differently

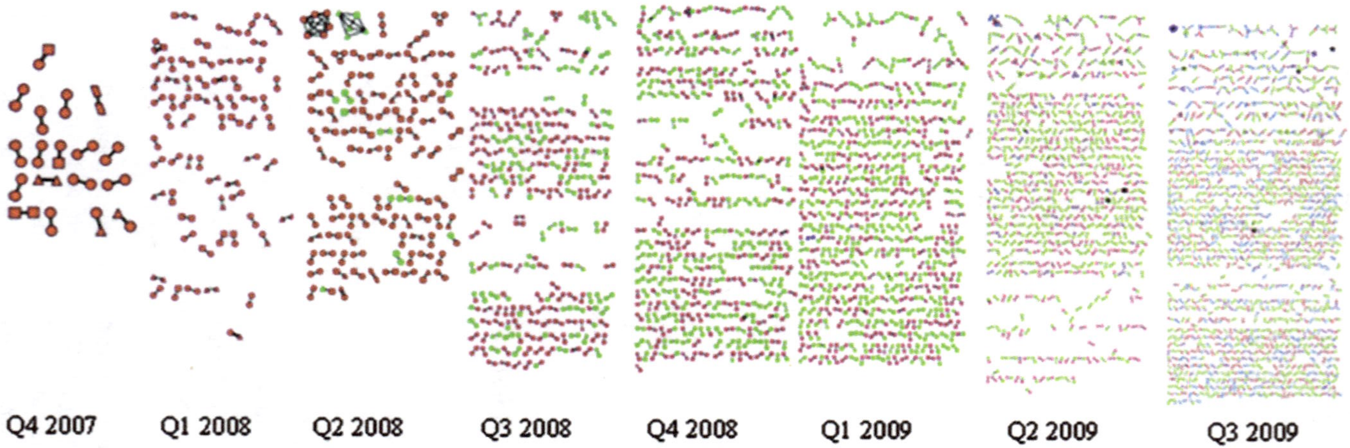

Fig. 9.3 Time evolution of Doro adoption network. One node represent one subscriber. Node color represents Doro Model: *red* = HandleEasy 326,328, *green* = HandleEasy 330, *blue* = PhoneEasy 410, *Purple* = Other Doro models. Node shape represents age of user: A *circle* means that user is older than 70 year. Link width represents weighted sum of SMS and Voice traffic

from Fig. 9.2, the monster in the WVAN actually diminishes in size over time—both in absolute number of users, and in the percentage of users in the LCC. Figure 9.4 illustrates this by showing two WVAN video-monsters which are 2 years apart.

We gain even more insight by looking at the time evolution of the VAN. Figure 9.5 shows the time evolution of the VAN-LCC. We see growth in the monster from Q3 2007 to Q4 2007, followed by a rather dramatic breaking down of the LCC after that time. Hence we see indications that the service itself had the potential to form a real social monster and take off, but some change in the service and user conditions killed that takeoff—in this case, we have found that a new pricing model was introduced.

9.3.4 Comparison of the Social Network Monsters Over Time

Figure 9.6 sums up much of what we have seen in the visualizations of the last subsections. The figure shows the fraction of adopters in various components of the adoption network. Subscribers in the blue area are adopters which have no connection to other adopters. These users (termed isolates here, and referred to as singletons in [21]) have not been visible in our visualizations. The users in the green area correspond to the adopters in the social network monster (there is in every case only one component with >1,000 users).

We first consider Fig. 9.6a, the figure describing iPhones. Here we see that the growth of the monster (green), as a percentage of the total number of users, has not been monotonic. The monster has however grown monotonically in the absolute number of users—see again Fig. 9.2. We conclude from this that the number of isolated subscribers grew more rapidly than did the core. This implies that some change in the offering has induced a large growth in the number of new users in this period (Q2 2008–Q3 2008). One candidate explanation is the appearance of 3G handsets in this time period. Another likely explanation for many new users is the fact that "legitimate" iPhones were first available on the Telenor net at this time.

Figure 9.6b (Doro) simply confirms the picture seen in Fig. 9.3: no monster, essentially no large LCCs. At the same time we see an enormous dominance of isolates. This is consistent with the hypothesis that Doro users are elderly (which we can confirm), and that they speak mostly with other generations, i.e., non-Doro users. Again, it suggests that the adoption of this phone is not based on network influence, but on more ego-based considerations.

Figure 9.6c shows the VAN, while Fig. 9.6d shows the WVAN for the video product. Again we confirm the qualitative picture obtained from Figs. 9.4 and 9.5: the WVAN-monster decays slowly, while the VAN-monster collapses. In the case of the video service, the collapse corresponds to the initiation of payment for the system. Using the lingo of the iPhone example, this would be the same as turning of the "buzz". We also see in Fig. 9.6c a dominance of two-node components—not surprising for a transactional service—and a complete absence of isolates.

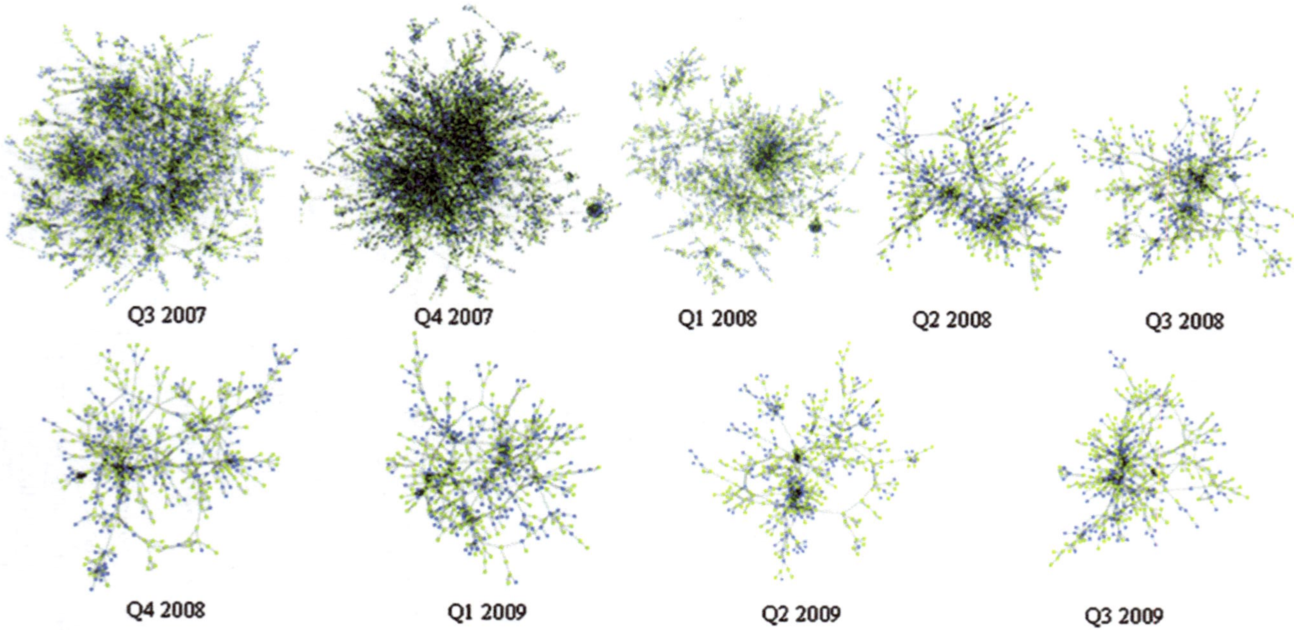

Fig. 9.4 Time evolution of the mobile video telephony adoption network. Links are real video links, where width represents duration of video conversations. Enterprise adopters have *blue* node color, while consumer adopters are tagged yellow

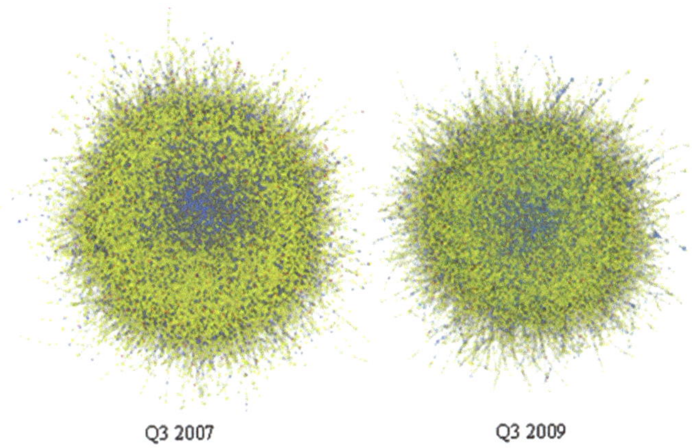

Fig. 9.5 Time evolution of mobile video telephony adoption network (WVAN-where the social links include all communication). Only two quarters are shown due to the fairly stable LCC. *Blue* node color represents enterprise subscribers, while *yellow* represents private subscribers

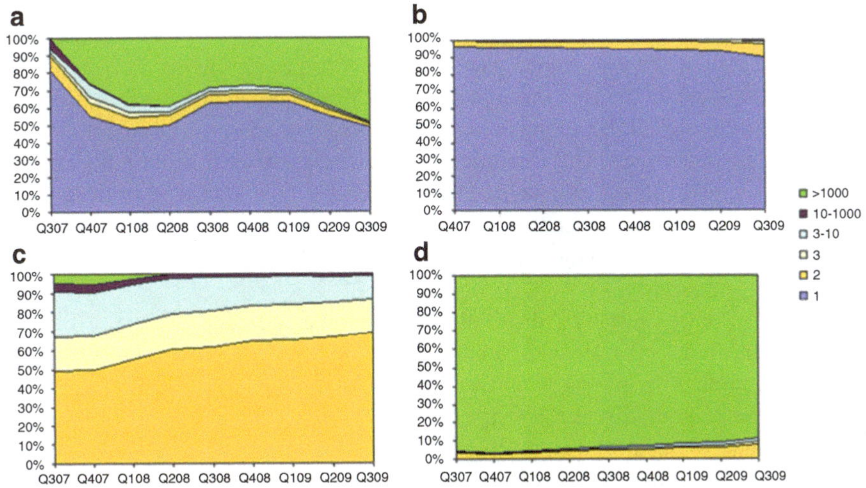

Fig. 9.6 Fraction of subscribers in components of various sizes in the adoption networks for: (**a**) iPhone. (**b**) Doro. (**c**) Video (video-links). (**d**) Video (W-links)

The latter result, while not surprising, is not in fact guaranteed (for WVAN) by our definitions: we will see two isolates in WVAN every time two subscribers use video transactions, but have no other (W) communication, and have no friends using video transactions. We see that this simply does not happen—primarily because every pair that uses video also uses voice, SMS, or both.

We offer some quantitative details illustrating the dynamics seen in Figs. 9.6c, d. We observe that 95.8 % of users are in the core of WVAN in Q3 2007, while only 5.7 % are in the VAN core. Two years later, the corresponding numbers are 88.7 % for WVAN and 0.76 % for VAN.

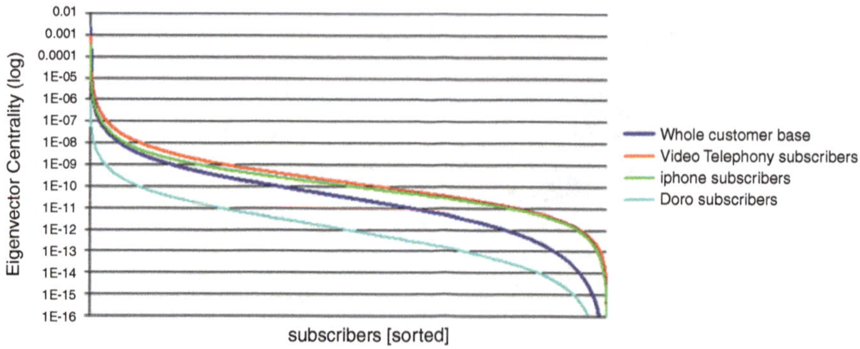

Fig. 9.7 Eigenvector centrality distributions for the whole customer base, Doro users, iPhone users, and video telephony users. Distributions are from Q3 2009. For ease of comparison, the x-scale is normalized so as to run from 0 to 100 % for all displayed distributions

9.4 Centrality of Adopters

We have seen how the iPhone and video adopters form a giant monster with respect to the W-links, while the Doro adopters do not. Motivated by this, we calculate the social centrality for all the adopters in each group, comparing it to the centrality of the whole customer base. Our expectation is that the involvement of highly central users is essential to the development of a large monster. To measure centrality we use the well-known eigenvector centrality (EVC). We believe high EVC will be strongly correlated with presence in the social monster, as it is already known to be correlated with strong spreading [7].

Figure 9.7 shows the EVC distributions for all the adopters. We see that video users are the most central, with iPhone just behind. We also see that the Doro adopters are rather peripheral socially, with their distribution falling well below that for the entire customer base. This supports our expectation that people in the giant monsters tend to be more central than the rest of the customer base. We believe that one may find, among these customers, the influential early adopters—those that adopt new products and services fairly early, and stimulate (or perhaps demand) others to do the same.

9.5 Kappa-Test

In all our results so far we see indirect evidence for social spreading effects (or their apparent absence, in the Doro case). As another test for social spreading, we introduce a simple statistical test, the kappa-test or κ-test.

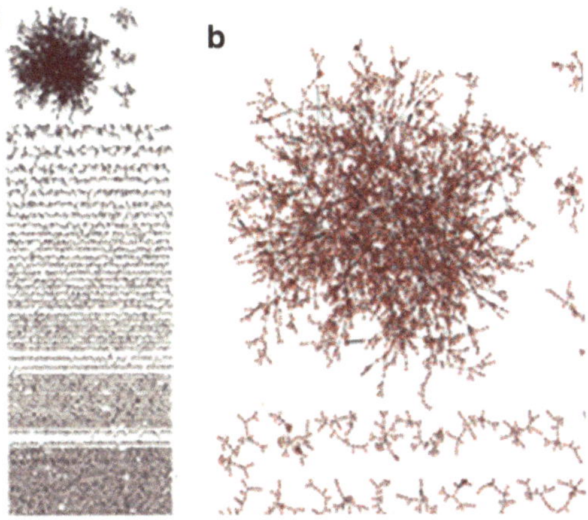

Fig. 9.8 (**a**) iPhone network from random reference model, Q1 2009. (**b**) LCC zoomed in

9.5.1 *Definition of the κ-Test*

We consider again the entire social network (as proxied by our communication graph) and define two types of links:

- A-links: links where neither, or only one, of the two connected nodes have adopted the product.
- B-links: links where the two connected nodes have both adopted the product.

We regard B-links to be the links which can indicate (but not confirm) social influence. We also recognize however that B-links can arise by other mechanisms, and even by chance. In order to evaluate the significance of the B-links that we observe in the empirical adoption data, then, we compare the empirical number of B-links (call it $n_{B,emp}$) with the number found by distributing at random the same number of adopters over the same social network, and then counting the resulting number of B-links $n_{B,rand}$.

We then define$\kappa \equiv n_{B,emp}/n_{B,rand}$. Clearly, if κgs significantly larger than 1, we have strong evidence for social spreading effects. More precisely, $\kappa > 1$ implies that people who communicate with each other tend to adopt together.

Figure 9.8 illustrates what happens when we scatter the iPhone adopters in Q1 2009 randomly over the empirical social network. The monster is still there, but it is smaller (by more than a factor 3) than the empirical monster seen in Fig. 9.2. Comparing the corresponding whole adoption networks of Figs. 9.2 and 9.8 by using the κ-test, we find that there are over twice as many links in the empirical adoption network compared to the random reference model—that is, κgs 2.18. We take this to be evidence that social spreading has occurred—more precisely, that people who talk together adopt together much more often than chance would predict.

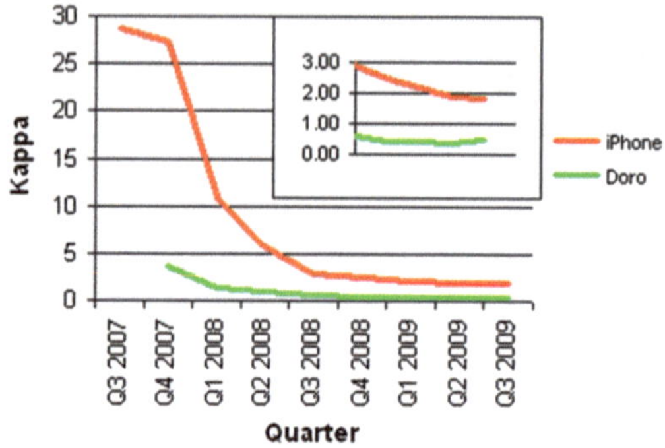

Fig. 9.9 Kappa for Doro and iPhone

Figure 9.8 illustrates an important point which gives insight into both monsters and social network structure. The point is that monsters arise even in the complete absence of social spreading effects. The monster seen in Fig. 9.8 is thus telling us something about the structure of the social network itself—that it has a "dense core" in which a dominating LCC arises even in the case of random adoption. At the same time, this dense core must include the set of users who give rise to the empirical monsters that we observe. The empirical LCC is simply larger than the random one (for the same number of adopters), due to social spreading (arising from mechanisms such as social influence or homophily).

Figure 9.9 shows the evolution of κ over time, both for the iPhone and for Doro. We notice that κ is very large in the early stages of product adoption (e.g., around 28.7 for the iPhone in Q3 2007). We find this to be typical: the first adopters are not randomly distributed, but rather tend to lie in a few small connected social groups. The large value for κ tells us that this observed distribution of the early adopters on a social network is extremely unlikely to have occurred by chance.

We notice also that κgs consistently less than 1 for Doro, after the early phase of adoption. While we argue that $\kappa > 1$ is evidence for social spreading effects, we do not believe that $\kappa < 1$ proves that such effects are not occurring. What $\kappa < 1$ does say is that adopting friends are found less often than a random model would predict. Our explanation for this is that the random model hits the dense core more often than the actual empirical adopters do. In other words, the empirical adopters are socially peripheral. This idea is in agreement with the EVC distribution seen in Fig. 9.6.

Finally we note that our κgest is not performed for the video adoption network in this chapter. The reason is that (as discussed in Sect. 9.3) the transactional nature of the video service constrains both VAN (exactly) and WVAN (empirically) such that there are no isolates. This constraint is not captured by the random reference model of the κgest. The purpose now is to introduce a link-based version of the node-based kappa-test.

9.6 Link Based Kappa-Test

The kappa-test defined in Sect. 9.5 considers products which are adopted nodewise, like e.g. the adoption of handset. In the case of transactional products like videotelephony, product adoption is defined in a pairwise manner: the nature of the product is *to activate links on the social network*. We consider videotelephony as a *link-based* product. The spreading process of a link-based product will be different compared to a node-based product, and hence the random spreading model in the kappa-test has to reflect this. In the node-based kappa-test the *nodes* are spread randomly and then the resulting links are compared to the empirical number of links between adopters. For link-based products, we suggest a random model where links in the social network are randomly activated.

We suggest the following for a link-based kappa-test: We start from the underlying social network, and track the time-evolution (adoption) of a link-based service; e.g. MMS or video telephony. In other words; a link-based service is a service in which the adoption requires both end-points of a link to adopt the service. Both nodes at the end-point of a link are mutually depending on each other in starting using the link-based service—communicating with each over the link. The link adoption of the network-based service, also gives rise to an adoption network.

Again, we are interested in measuring 'adopting together', so for links this is interpreted as meaning that two links have adopted together if they have a common node as end-point. In other words; two links are said to adopt together when the two links are adjacent. Figure 9.10 illustrates how we count adjacent links, two links A–C and A–D define an adjacent pair of links, since the node A is a common node for both links. Counting the number of open triangles in the adoption network then measures the occurrence of links adopting together. The random adoption network is generated through randomly choosing the links to adopt the link-based service from the set of possible links in the underlying social network, and the number of open triangles is then counted in the random case. We suggest then to define the link-based kappa test as;

$$\kappa = \frac{\#\ \textit{adjacent links in expirical network}}{\#\ \textit{adjacent links in random network}} \tag{9.1}$$

The above framework can now be used for generating kappa tests for comparing the empirical and random occurrence of links and adjacent links in the true adoption network and a randomly simulated adoption network, respectively. These adoption networks are considered relative to the underlying 'true' social network that can be measured. Summarizing, we have the following two kappa tests:

- Node based adoption, counting links: κg empirical number of links/random number of links
- Link based adoption, counting open triangles: κg empirical number of open triangles/random number of open triangles.

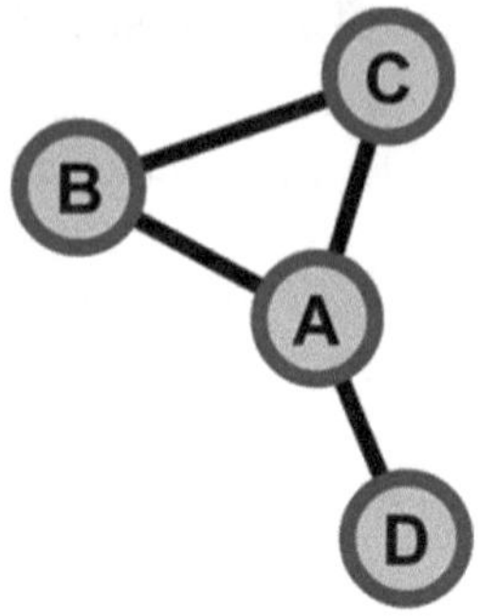

Fig. 9.10 Illustration of open and closed triangles. *A–C* and *A–D* are adjacent links since they share one common node and make an open triangle. *A–B*, *B–C* and *A–C* together make a closed triangle

We count the total number of open links in the network using the binomial coefficient and sum over all nodes i:

$$\begin{aligned}\sum_{i=1}^{n}\binom{k_i}{2} &= \sum_{i=1}^{n}\frac{k_2!}{2!(k_i-2)!}\\ &= \sum_{i=1}^{n}\frac{1}{2}k_i(k_i-1)\\ &= \frac{1}{2}\sum_{i=1}^{n}k_i^2-\frac{1}{2}\sum_{i=1}^{n}k_i \qquad (9.2)\\ &= \frac{1}{2}\sum_{i=1}^{n}k_i^2-L\end{aligned}$$

where k_i is node degree, n is the total number of nodes, and L is the number of links—all measured relative to the adoption network.

From the above discussion, it is also possible to consider other types of kappa-tests. For example, one can envision kappa-tests that compares;

- The number of closed triangles to the number of random triangles.
- The number of closed loops of some order to the number of random closed loops.

The idea is to consider local network structures, and how these local structures potentially 'adopt' together.

9.6.1 *Quarterly Development of the Link Kappa*

From Fig. 9.11 we see that the link kappa value defined in (1) is steadily increasing from around 15 to about 20. A kappa value of 15 means that there is 15 times as many adjacent links in the empirical data than in the random reference case! We can then conclude that the distribution of video usage on the social network is far from

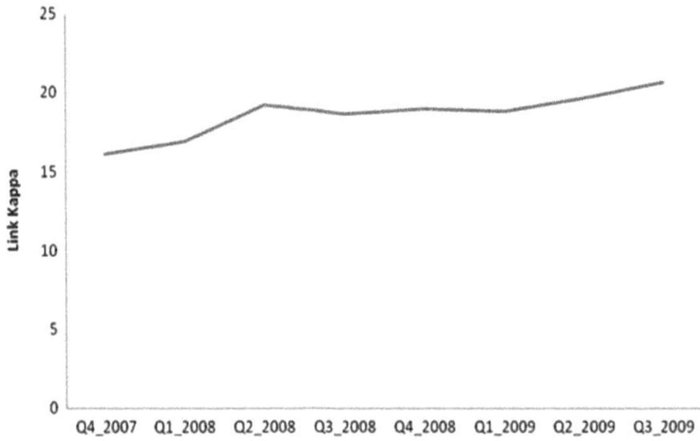

Fig. 9.11 Historical development of link kappa for video telephony. Link kappa is defined as the number of total adjacent links in the empirical data to the number of adjacent links in the random reference case. The random reference network is constructed by choosing an equal number of links randomly from the underlying social network and then count the number of adjacent links

a random process where social relations are randomly 'activated' to become video links.

The number of adjacent links is related to the node degree according to (2). Figure 9.12 shows the degree distribution for Q3 2009—both for the random 'link activation' model and for the real empirical video adoption network (VAN). As expected from the high link kappa value, the degree of the nodes in the empirical adoption graph is higher than in the corresponding random model (higher number of adopting neighbors means higher number of adjacent links). In the random case around 90 % of the nodes have degree 1—the least degree possible since the unit we use in this experiment is *links*. An isolated *link* will give both end nodes degree 1. This is expected, since the random model does not take into account that the videotelephony users, once they have started using the service, will use the service to communicate with more than one network neighbor. A more sophisticated random reference model could also take this into account. The simple random link activation model acts as basic reference and assigns the same activation probabilities to all links on the network. We reserve testing more advanced reference spreading models for future work.

Another way to measure clustering among adopters is to use the global clustering coefficient defined as total number of closed triplets divided by the total number of adjacent links. See e.g. reference [30] for a detailed discussion of the global clustering coefficient. Using the same 'kappa' logic as before, a completely random adoption process will also show some clustering. To compensate for this effect, we use the kappa test logic on the global clustering coefficient and define a new link kappa measure as C_{emp}/C_{rnd}, where C_{emp} is the clustering coefficient calculated from the empirical network and C_{rnd} is calculated from the random video adoption network. Figure 9.13 shows the development of the ratio C_{emp}/C_{rnd}.

In summary—measuring the social network dependence on video telephony is more difficult than measuring effect on node attributes like choice of handset. Video telephony is a link attribute involving choices of both end nodes. A simple

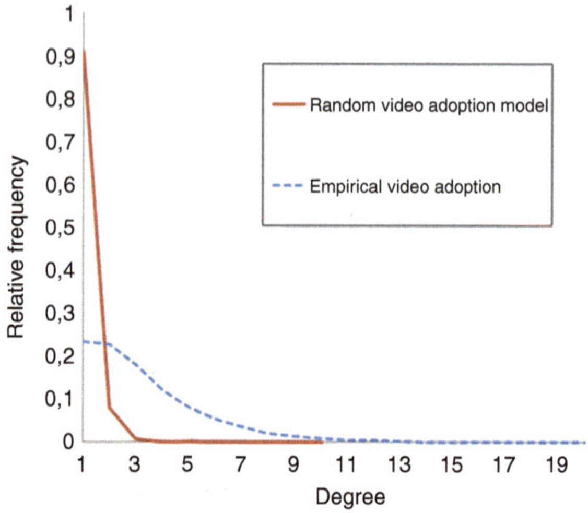

Fig. 9.12 Node degree distribution for the 'random link activation' reference model and the empirical video adoption network (VAN), Q3 2009

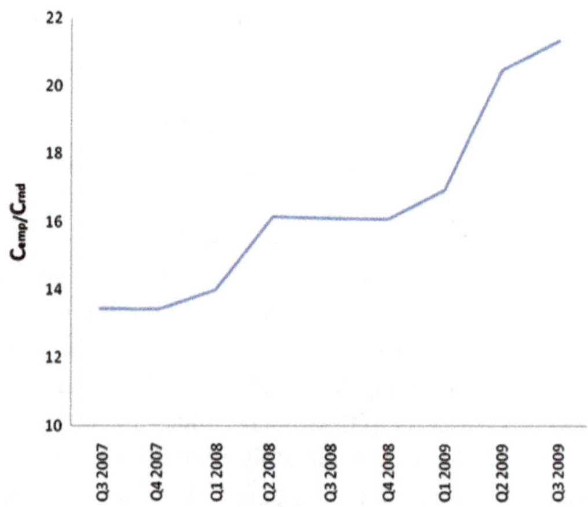

Fig. 9.13 Clustering coefficient kappa test defined as the empirical global clustering coefficient divided by the global clustering coefficient for the random network. The global clustering coefficient is defined as total number of closed triangles divided by the total number of adjacent links in the network

reshuffling of individual adopter status will not take this into account. Our simple link kappa test can be used for quantifying network dependent adoption for services of a transactional nature. In the case of video telephony we find that the empirical relations are clustered on the social network compared to a random link activation model.

9.7 Correlated Adoption Probability

Our final test for social spreading effects is to measure the probability p_k that a subscriber has adopted a product, given that k of the subscriber's friends have adopted the product. This conditional probability does not indicate causation, because it makes no reference to time order—it simply measures (again) how

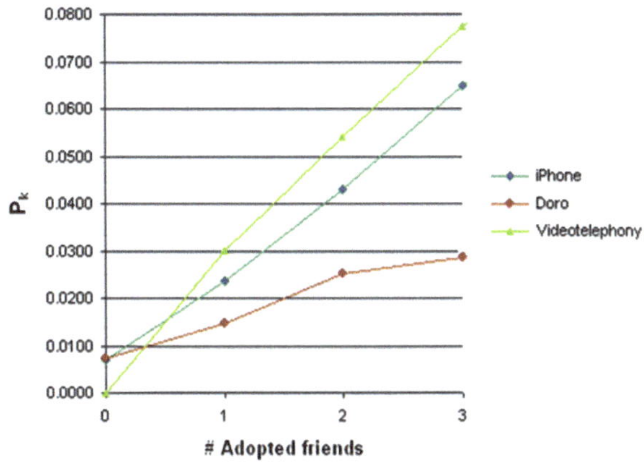

Fig. 9.14 Adoption probability pk vs. the number k of adopting friends, for three products. In each case we see a monotonic growth of pk with k-indicating that some kind of social spreading is occurring

strongly those that communicate together tend to adopt together. We measure p_k simply by first finding all subscribers with k adopting friends, and then finding the fraction of these that have themselves adopted.

Figure 9.14 shows p_k vs. k for the three products, for $0 \leq k \leq 3$. For higher k, the Doro data are too dominated by noise (a low n) to be useful. (The results for iPhone and video have better adoption profiles, and so are meaningful at least out to $k = 10$; but their qualitative behavior—monotonic increase, at roughly constant slope, with increasing k—is like that seen in Fig. 9.14.) Figure 9.14 supports our claim that there are some social spreading effects operating on Doro adoption—since we see a steady increase of p_k with k. Such effects are not visible from our κgest, for reasons given above; yet we see for example that, if we know that a subscriber has one friend using a Doro phone, that subscriber's probability of using one him- or herself is roughly *twice* the adoption probability for a subscriber with no adopting friends.

The iPhone and video p_k results lie, not surprisingly, considerably higher than the Doro curve. This is consistent with our claim that social spreading effects are much stronger for these products. For example, knowing that a person has one friend using an iPhone roughly triples the probability (compared to someone with no adopting friends) that this person also uses an iPhone. This comparison is however not possible to make for the video service, because the probability of using video telephony and having no (W-)friends who use video telephony is (as discussed above) empirically zero. Otherwise the video results are qualitatively the same as the iPhone results.

We also note that the p_k for video-telephony is consistent with the degree distribution for video adopters in Fig. 9.12, where we see that the nodes in the empirical VAN generally have a higher degree than expected from the simulated random link activation model. Since the adoption probability, p_k, increases with number of adopting neighbors, one will expect a higher number of activated neighbors in the adoption graph compared to a random model. A higher number of neighbors will again result in a higher number of adjacent links in the empirical data and thus the high link kappa value we see in Fig. 9.11.

9.8 Time Evolution of Computer Tablet Adoption Networks

Until now we have looked into the social interaction between users of different handsets, as well as video telephony. Recently, so called computer tablets, such as Apple iPad 3G and Samsung Galaxy Tab, have received increased attention. These tablet computers are particularly marketed as a platform for audio and visual media such as books, periodicals, movies, music and games, as well as web content. As a preview of current research we will show the social network of iPad 3G-adopters, and its time-evolution from its release date, as well as some early statistical results. We are not able to study uptake of WiFi-only tablets, since we depend on a SIM to map tablets to the social network. Computer tablet networks address some fundamental differences from the adoption networks already mentioned. An important difference from traditional handsets is that the SIM card placed in a tablet is not necessary the same SIM card which is being used for social interaction, It is typically a "twin SIM" solution, where a customer gets two SIMs on the same subscription. We use the SIM in the traditional handset as the node and map the social network. This will give us a picture of the social interaction among iPad 3G users. We will show that the 'non-pad' SIM cards are most often placed in an iPhone.

9.9 iPad 3G Adoption Network

As with the iPhone, the release date of iPad 3G varies with region—it was officially released in the US Apr 3rd 2010. In Telenor net it was released in November 2010. As the visualizations will show, thousands of users bought their iPad in the US and used it on Telenor net before they actually were officially released by Telenor in November 2010. Since such tablets are quite new in the given market, we have chosen to study the time evolution with a more fine-grained granularity—month by month.

Figure 9.15 shows the time evolution of the iPad 3G adoption network for the first 7 months. The structure reminds us of the iPhone evolution. We have here also included smaller social components, but for visualization purposes we have not included the isolates (iPad 3G-adopters with no iPad 3G friends), but we remind the reader that these are also part of the adoption network. From the visualization we see how the largest connected component gradually turns into a "monster" within a couple of months. When a specific iPad-user also uses an iPhone, the node is colored blue. Visually it is seen that the connected iPad-users have a high percentage of iPhone's. In general we find that 53.4 % of the users also are using iPhone for social interaction. We observe that in the cases where the iPad-user has at least one iPad-friend (adopters shown in Fig. 9.15) there are as many as 72.1 % also having an iPhone. The remaining users, which represent the disconnected users in the adoption network (isolates), there are only 38.6 % which have adopted an iPhone. This shows that iPhone is much more common phenomena in socially connected groups of iPad users. This also supports the idea of an Apple "tribe" of users.

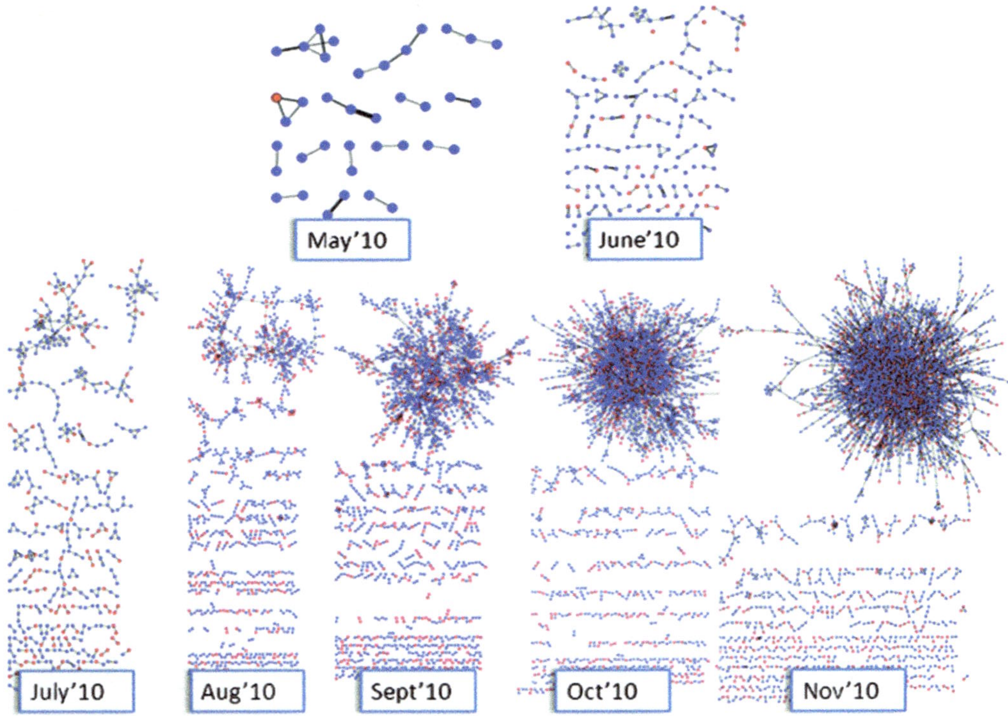

Fig. 9.15 Time evolution of iPad 3G adoption network. One node represent one subscriber. *Blue* node color represent an iPad 3G user which also uses an iPhone, while *red* color represent an iPad 3G user with another handset. Link width represents weighted sum of SMS and Voice traffic. Isolates are not included in the visualization

Fig. 9.16 Kappa for iPad 3G

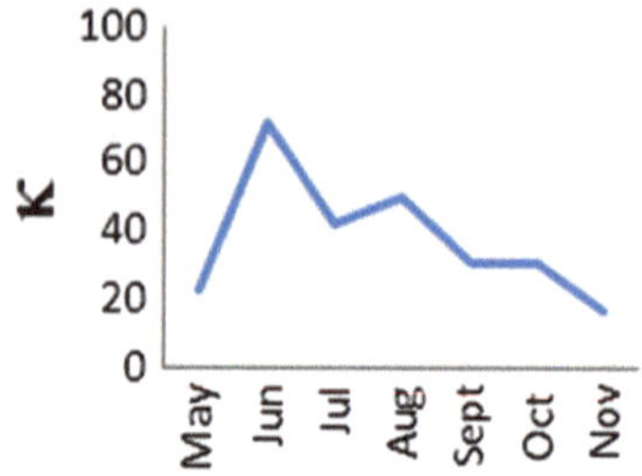

9.10 Kappa-Test for iPad 3G

As stated in Sect. 9.5, $\kappa >$ xgmplies that people who communicate together also tend to adopt together. Figure 9.16 shows the time evolution of κgor iPad 3G. We notice that it is significantly above 1, which indicate strong evidence for social network effects. κgaries between 16.9 and 72, which means that at most there are 72 times more empirical iPad-relations compared to the relations we find when spreading the adopters randomly on the whole communication network. We notice that the numbers are significantly higher than for iPhone—and from the perspective of κsghis trend supports that the spreading is stronger compared to iPhone, which is also reflected through the number of sales [16].

The rapid increase of kappa from May to June can be explained by the time it takes from the first adopters got their pads until friends are influenced and are able to get one. It is a product of how the individuals got their iPads since it involved travel to the U.S. or knowing a friend who was traveling there.

The decrease from june can be due to increased exposure of the product in the media which can lead to less dependence on social spreading, in combination with the increased number of sales. Due to the nature of κsgt will approach 1 if we have complete saturation of iPads in the market.

9.11 iPad 3G Adoption Probability

Figure 9.17 corresponds to the correlation adoption probability which we measured in Sect. 9.6. We measure the probability p_k that a subscriber has adopted iPad 3G, given that k of the subscriber's friends have adopted iPad 3G. The results shows that if you have one iPad friend the probability to adopt iPad is 14 times higher than with zero friends. If you have two friends the probability is 41 times higher, three friends 96 times. We observe a steep monotonic growth which should indicate strong social spreading effects. The adoption is highly dependent on the number of friends.

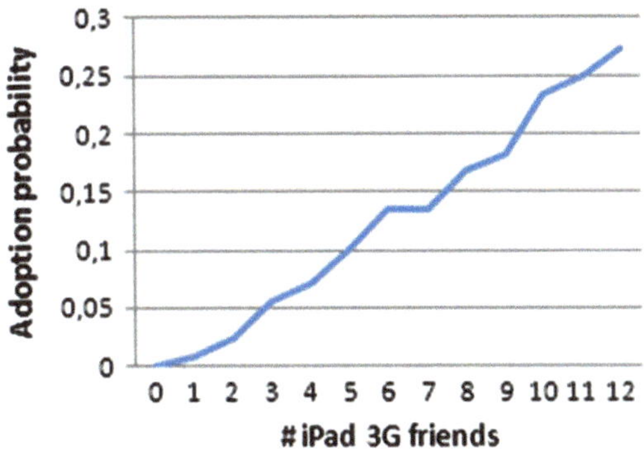

Fig. 9.17 Adoption probability pk vs. the number k of adopting friends, for iPad 3G. We observe a monotonic growth of pk with k-indicating that some kind of social spreading is occurring

9.12 Summary and Future Work

All of our results support a simple and fairly consistent interpretation:

- The iPhone has very strong social spreading, and has truly taken off
- The Doro handsets have only very weak social spreading. This device will probably never take off in the same sense as the iPhone.
- Video telephony use also has strong social effects, and started spreading very strongly; however its early takeoff was stopped by an external factor—here, a new price model.
- Preliminary results from studying the newly released iPad 3G reveals even stronger network-dependent adoption patterns than iPhone.

Standard whole-network measures, such as total number of users, or total traffic over time, can also give useful information on these same questions. We believe however that our measurement methods give new and useful insight into how and why these services have performed so differently.

We have also constructed two different link-based κ-tests for the VAN, because the VAN has a fundamental constraint—that adoption occurs only in pairs—that our simple κ-test does not capture. We conclude from these κ-tests that the remaining subscribers are well clustered due to the increase of κ over time—both for the test based on the clustering coefficient and κgased on adjacent links. These tests should be useful for any transactional graph with the pair constraint.

Also, we suspect that social spreading effects for the Doro handsets may be more visible at the two-hop level. A typical scenario might be an adult child would buy this type of phone for one or more of their elderly parents when, for example, use of a more traditional mobile phone becomes difficult because of the size of the display or keypad, or the complexity of the device. In such a scenario, it may well be there is little or no direct communication among the adopters, but a strong two-hop connection via the younger generation. We plan to test this idea in the near future.

Acknowledgements All of our visualizations were produced using the open-source visualization platform from cytoscape.org. We would also like to thank Dr. Ellen Altenborg at Telenor ASA, and professor Øystein D. Fjeldstad of the Norwegian School of Management, for fruitful discussions and inspiration related to network economy and network analysis.

References

1. Albert, R., Barabasi, A.-L.: Statistical mechanics of complex networks. Rev. Mod. Phys. **74**, 47 (2002)
2. Aral, S., Muchnik, L., Sundararajan, A.: Distinguishing influence-based contagion from homophily-driven diffusion in dynamic networks. Proc. Natl. Acad. Sci. **106**(51), 21544–21549 (2009)
3. Bearman, P., Moody, J., Stovel, K.: Chains of affection: the structure of adolescent romantic and sexual networks. Am. J. Sociol. **110**(1), 44–91 (2004)
4. Birke, D., Swann, G.M.P.: Network effects and the choice of mobile phone operator. J Evol Econ **16**, 65–84 (2006)
5. Bollobas, B.: Random Graphs. Cambridge University Press, Cambridge/New York (2001)
6. Bollobas, B., Riordan, O.: Mathematical Results on Scale-Free Random Graphs, pp. 1–37. Wiley, Weinheim (2002)
7. Canright, G.S., Engø-Monsen, K.: Spreading on networks: a topographic view. Complexus **3**, 131–146 (2006). doi:10.1159/000094195
8. Choi, H., Kim, S.-H., Lee, J.: Role of network structure and network effects in diffusion of innovations. Ind. Mark. Manag. **39**, 170–177 (2010)
9. Dasgupta, K., Singh, R., Viswanathan, B., Chakraborty, D., Mukherjea, S., Nanavati, A.A., Joshi, A.: Social ties and their relevance to churn in mobile telecom networks. In: Proceedings of the 11th International Conference on Extending Database Technology: Advances in Database Technology, EDBT '08, Nantes, vol. 261, pp. 668–677. ACM, New York (2008)
10. Dorogovtsev, S., Mendes, J.: Evolution of networks: from biological nets to the internet and WWW. Oxford University Press, Oxford (2000)
11. Dorogovtsev, S., Mendes, J.: Evolution of networks. Adv. Phys. **51**, 1079–1187 (2002)
12. Fetterly, D., Manasse, M., Najork, M., Wiener, J.: A large-scale study of the evolution of web pages. Softw. Pract. Exp. **34**(2), 213–237 (2004)
13. Eagle, N., Pentland, A., Lazer, D., Alex, P.: Inferring friendshop network structure by using mobile phone data. Natl. Acad. Sci. **106**(36), 15274–15278 (2009)
14. Erdös, P., Rényi, A.: On random graphs I. Publ. Math. Debr. **6**, 290–297 (1959)
15. Hill, S., Provost, F., Volinsky, C.: Network-based marketing: identifying likely adopters via consumer networks. Stat. Sci. **21**(2), 256–276 (2006)
16. http://www.apple.com/pr/library/2010/06/22ipad.html
17. http://www.doro.com/
18. Kleinberg, J.: Complex networks and decentralized search algorithms. In: International Congress of Mathematicians. European Mathematical Society, Zürich (2006)
19. Kumar, R., Novak, J., Raghavan, P., Tomkins, A.: Structure and evolution of blogspace. Commun. ACM **47**(12), 35–39 (2004)
20. Kumar, R., Novak, J., Raghavan, P., Tomkins, A.: On the bursty evolution of blogspace. Worldw. Web J. **8**(2), 159–178 (2005)
21. Kumar, R., Novak, J., Tomkins, A.: Structure and evolution of online social networks. In: KDD, Philadelphia. ACM, New York (2006)
22. Leskovec, J., Faloutsos, J.K.C.: Graphs over time: densification laws, shrinking diameters, and possible explanations. In: 11th KDD, Chicago, pp. 177–187. ACM, New York (2005)
23. Nanavati, A.A., Gurumurthy, S., Das, G., Chakraborty, D., Dasgupta, K., Mukherjea, S., Joshi, A.: On the structural properties of massive telecom call graphs: findings and impli-

cations. In: Proceedings of the 15th ACM International Conference on Information and Knowledge Management, CIKM '06, Arlington, pp. 435–444. ACM, New York (2006)
24. Newman, M.: The structure and function of complex networks. SIAM Rev. **45**(2), 167–256, 2003
25. Ntoulas, A., Cho, J., Olston, C.: What's new on the web? The evolution of the web from a search engine perspective. In: 13th WWW, pp. 1–12. ACM, New York (2004)
26. Onnela, J.-P., Saramäki, J., Hyvönen, J., Szabó, G., Lazer, D., Kaski, K., Kertész, J., Barabási, A.-L.: Structure and tie strengths in mobile communication networks. Proc. Natl. Acad. Sci. U.S.A. **104**(18), 7332–7336, 2007
27. Strogatz, S.: Exploring complex networks. Nature **410**, 268–276 (2001)
28. Sundsøy, P., Bjelland, J., Canright, G., Engø-Monsen, K., Ling, R.: Product adoption networks and their growth in a large mobile phone network. IEEE Advanced in Social Network Analysis and Mining (ASONAM 2010), Odense. IEEE, Los Alamitos (2010)
29. Van den Bulte, C., Wuyts, S.: Social networks and marketing. Marketing Science Institue, Cambridge (2007)
30. Wasserman, S., Faust, K.: Social network analysis: methods and applications. Cambridge University Press, Cambridge/New York (1994)
31. Watts, D.J., Strogatz, S.H.: Collective dynamics of small-world networks. Nature **393**, 440–442 (1998)

Chapter 10
Engagingness and Responsiveness Behavior Models on the Enron Email Network and Its Application to Email Reply Order Prediction

Byung-Won On, Ee-Peng Lim, Jing Jiang, and Loo-Nin Teow

Abstract In email networks, user behaviors affect the way emails are sent and replied. While knowing these user behaviors can help to create more intelligent email services, there has not been much research into mining these behaviors. In this paper, we investigate user engagingness and responsiveness as two interaction behaviors that give us useful insights into how users email one another. Engaging users are those who can effectively solicit responses from other users. Responsive users are those who are willing to respond to other users. By modeling such behaviors, we are able to mine them and to identify engaging or responsive users. This paper proposes four types of models to quantify engagingness and responsiveness of users. These behaviors can be used as features in email reply order prediction, which predicts the email reply order given an email pair. Our experiments show that engagingness and responsiveness behavior features are more useful than other non-behavioral features in building a classifier for the email reply order prediction task. When combining behavior and non-behavior features, our classifier is also shown to predict the email reply order with good accuracy. This work was extended from the earlier conference paper that appeared in [9].

B.-W. On (✉)
Advanced Institutes of Convergence Technology, Seoul National University, 864-1 Iui-dong, Yeongtong-gu, Suwon-si Gyeonggi-do 443-270, Korea
e-mail: on.byung.won@gmail.com

E.-P. Lim · J. Jiang
School of Information Systems, Singapore Management University, 80 Stamford Road, Singapore 178902, Singapore
e-mail: eplim@smu.edu.sg; jingjiang@smu.edu.sg

L.-N. Teow
DSO National Laboratories, 20 Science Park Drive, Singapore 118230, Singapore
e-mail: tloonin@dso.org.sg

T. Özyer et al. (eds.), *The Influence of Technology on Social Network Analysis and Mining*, Lecture Notes in Social Networks 6, DOI 10.1007/978-3-7091-1346-2_10,

10.1 Introduction

10.1.1 Motivation

Electronic mail (also known as email) despite its long history has remained to be the most popular communication tool today. Unlike other newer communication tools such as weblog, twitter, messenger, etc., email has been widely adopted in the corporate world and often seamlessly integrated with business applications. As users email one another within and outside the corporate boundaries, they form different kinds of email networks. Within each network, users demonstrate behaviors that also affect how emails are sent and replied.

In this paper, we study user interaction behaviors in email networks and how they are relevant to predicting future email activities. An email network is essentially a directed graph with nodes and links representing users and messages from users to other users respectively. Each email is assigned a timestamp and has other attributes including sender, recipients, subject heading, and email content. We focus on two user interaction behaviors that are closely related to how users respond to one another in email networks, namely **engagingness** and **responsiveness**.

We define *engagingness* behavior as the ability of an user to solicit responses from other users, and *responsiveness* behavior as the willingness of an user to respond to other users. A user at the low (or high) extreme of engagingness behavior are known as to be disengaging (or engaging). Similarly, a user can range from unresponsive to highly responsive. As suggested by their definitions, user engagingness and responsiveness have direct or indirect implications on the way emails are sent and responded, and the strength of relationships users may have with other users in the networks. Nevertheless, these implications have not been well studied. The use of interaction behaviors to enhance email functions has been largely unexplored.

This paper therefore aims to provide a fresh approach towards modeling the engagingness and responsiveness behaviors in email networks. These models are quantitative and assign to each user an engagingness score and a responsiveness score. The scores are within the [0,1] such that 0 and 1 represent the lowest and highest scores respectively. With the scores, we can rank all users by engagingness or responsiveness. Moreover, we derive new features from these behavior scores and use them in an example email activity prediction, i.e., email reply order prediction.

The engagingness and responsiveness behavior models can be very useful in several applications. In the context of business organizations, they help to identify engaging and responsive users who may be good candidates for management roles, and to weed out lethargic users who are neither engaging and responsive making them the bottleneck in the organization. For informal social email networks, engaging and responsive users could be the high network potential candidates for viral marketing applications. Engaging users may solicit more responses for viral messages while responsive users may act fast on these messages. By selecting these users to spread viral messages to targeted user segments by word-of-mouth, marketing objectives can be achieved more effectively.

In this paper, we specifically introduce the **email reply order prediction** task as an application, and show that engagingness and responsiveness behavior models contribute significantly to prediction accuracy. Email reply order prediction refers to deciding which of a pair of emails received by the same user will be replied first. This prediction task effectively helps an email recipient to prioritize his replies to emails. For example, if e_1 and e_2 are two emails sent to user u_k who plans to reply both. The outcome of prediction can either be e_1 replied before e_2 or vice versa. The ability to predict reply order of emails has several useful benefits, including helping users to prioritize emails to be replied, and to estimate the amount of time emails get replied. Here, our main purpose is to use the task to evaluate the utility of engagingness and responsiveness behavior models.

10.1.2 Research Objectives

This paper proposes to model engagingness and responsiveness behaviors quantitatively. In order to develop these quantitative behavior models, we first preprocess the emails so as to remove noises from the data and to construct the reply and forward relationships among emails. From the email relationships, we also derive email threads which are hierarchies of emails connected by reply and forward relationships. We then systematically develop a taxonomy of engagingness and responsiveness models using the reply relationships and email threads. These models are applied to the Enron email dataset, a publicly available dataset consisting of 517,431 emails from 151 ex-Enron employees. The email reply order prediction task is addressed as a classification problem. Our approach derives a set of features for a email pair based on the emails' metadata as well as engaging and responsive behaviors of their senders. As we evaluate the performance of the learnt prediction models, we would like to identify the interplay between behavior features and prediction accuracy. Our approach does not depend on email content or domain knowledge which are sometime not available and time costly to process. Given that there are only two possible order outcomes, we expect any method should have an accuracy of at least 50 %. In order for email reply order prediction to be useful, a much higher prediction accuracy is required without relying on content analysis.

Both behavior modeling and email reply order prediction are novel problems in email networks. Research on engagingness and responsiveness behaviors is a branch of social network analysis that studies node properties in a network. Unlike traditional social network analysis which focuses on node and network statistics based on static information (e.g., centralities, network diameter) of social networks, behavior analysis is conducted on networks with users dynamically interacting with one another.

In the following, we summarize the important research contributions of this paper.

- We define four of models for engagingness and responsiveness behaviors prevalent in email networks. They are (a) email based, (b) email thread based, (c) email sequence based, and (d) social cognitive model categories. For each model category, one can define different behavior models based on different email attributes. To the best of our knowledge, this is the first time engagingness and responsiveness behavior models are studied systematically.
- We apply our proposed behavior models on the Enron email network, analyze and compare the proposed behavior models. We conduct data preprocessing on the email data and establish links between emails and their replies. In our empirical study, we found engagingness and responsiveness are distinct from each other. Most engagingness (responsiveness) models of users are shown to be consistent with each other.
- We introduce email reply order prediction as a novel task that uses engagingness, responsiveness and other email features as input features. An SVM classifier is then learnt from the features of training email pairs and applied to test email pairs. According to our experimental results, the accuracy of our SVM classifier is about 77 % which is better than random guess (50 %). This indicates that user behaviors are useful in the prediction task.

Unlike most previous research on behavior analysis in email networks which focuses on mainly direct statistics of emails such as recipient list size, rate of emails from receiver to sender, and email size to characterize an email user [4, 13], our modeling of engagingness and responsiveness behaviors relies mainly on email reply and forward relationships not available directly in the email data. Previous research on email prediction tasks include the prediction of (a) social hierarchy of email users [12], (b) topics of emails [7], and (c) viral emails[13]. Email reply order prediction is thus a new task to be investigated. Although engagingness and responsiveness behaviors and reply order prediction task are defined in the context of email networks, our proposed approaches and results are also applicable to other form of information exchange networks such as messaging and blog networks.

10.1.3 Enron Email Dataset

Throughout this research, we use Enron email dataset in our empirical study of real data. This dataset is so far the only known publicly available email data with messages assigned with specific senders and recipients [6]. This dataset provides 517,431 emails for 151 Enron employees. Each email message has a unique message ID and contains header information such as the date and time when the message was sent, sender, recipients (To and Cc lists), subject and body in plain text format. We performed two data preprocessing steps on the email data, namely *duplicate elimination* and *email relationship identification*.

Duplicate elimination. As noticed by the previous studies on this corpus, there are many duplicate emails in either different folders of the same user (e.g., in computer generated folders such as all_documents, discussion_threads) or folders of different users (e.g., a message in sender's sent_mail folder often appears in some recipient's inbox or other folder). Message_IDs cannot be used to identify duplicate emails as such emails also have unique message IDs. We therefore use a strategy similar to [7] by computing the MD5 sum on email fields: Date/Time, Sender, To, Cc, Subject and Body. This will assign the same MD5 value (128 bit integer) to all duplicate emails that exactly match on these fields. After duplicate elimination, the dataset contains 257,044 unique emails.

Email relationship identification. To identify reply and forward relationships between emails, we first group all emails of each matching subject after ignoring the Reply and Forward prefixes (e.g., RE, FW, FWD, etc.) and order them by time. Each reply (or forward) email e_i in the group is then assigned a reply relationship (or forward relationship) with the most recent earlier email e_j such that e_i's sender is one of the e_j's recipients and that $t(e_i) - t(e_j) \leq 90$ days where $t(e)$ denotes the send time of e. With this approach,[1] we found 34,008 email relationship of which 27,730 and 6,278 are reply and forward relationships respectively. When a set of emails form a connected component by reply and forward relationships, we call it an email thread. From the email relationships identified, we derive 18,593 threads that connect 52,601 emails (about 20 % of all unique emails).

To evaluate our email relationship identification approach, we first compute precision that measures how many links are correct among the links detected by our method. For this, we selected a random sample of 100 link relationships from the total of 34,008 links. For every pair, we manually verified whether or not an email is sent and the other is the correct reply email. Our manual evaluation showed a precision of 91 %. To compute recall, we randomly selected 30 subject groups, each of which contains about five or ten emails. For each subject group, we manually created threads by connecting emails to their follow-up responses. This sample includes about 120 emails with 79 reply links and 21 forward links. For each link of two emails, we manually examined if the link is correctly found by our method. We found 79 % correct links which are actually present in the Enron dataset. This suggests that our identified relationships are quite accurate. In our subsequent experiments, we therefore use these identified email relationships.

10.1.4 Paper Outline

The remainder of this paper is organized as follows: In Sect. 10.2, we present engagingness and responsiveness behavior models. Subsequently, we discuss a

[1] We discuss the detailed description of this algorithm in Appendix.

challenging problem of predicting email reply order based on our behavior models in Sect. 10.3. The proposed models are evaluated and compared in Sect. 10.4 using a set of experiments on the Enron dataset. In particular, Sect. 10.4.3 describes experiments that evaluate the performance of email reply order prediction using different classifiers trained with different features including those based on email behaviors. In Sect. 10.5, we briefly introduce works related to our behavioral analysis problem. Finally, we offer our concluding remarks in Sect. 10.6.

10.2 Engagingness and Responsiveness Behavior Models

In this section, we describe our proposed behavior models for user engagingness and responsiveness. All the models assume that emails have been preprocessed as described in Sect. 10.1.3. We divide our models into the following categories:

- **Email based models**: These models consider emails as the basic data units for measuring user behaviors. Email attributes such as sender, recipient list, date, etc., are used.
- **Email thread based models**: These models consider email threads as the basic data units for measuring user behaviors. The models therefore use attributes of email thread to quantify behaviors.
- **Email sequence based models**: These models examine the sequence of emails received and replied by each user and derive the user behaviors from the gaps between emails received and their replies.
- **Social cognitive models**: These models consider social perception of user behaviors within the email network and measure behaviors accordingly.

Figure 10.1 shows the taxonomy of behavior models in the above categories to be further defined in the following sections. Each model (M) consists of a pair of engaging (E^M) and responsive (R^M) score formulas defined based on some principles. The E^M and R^M score values are in [0,1] range with 0 and 1 representing the lowest and highest values respectively. Table 10.1 shows a list of symbols and their meanings that we use in this paper.

10.2.1 Email Based Models

Email Count Model (EC)

The email count model is defined based on the principle that an engaging user should have most of his emails replied, while a responsive user should have most of his received emails replied. The engagingness and responsiveness formulas are thus defined by:

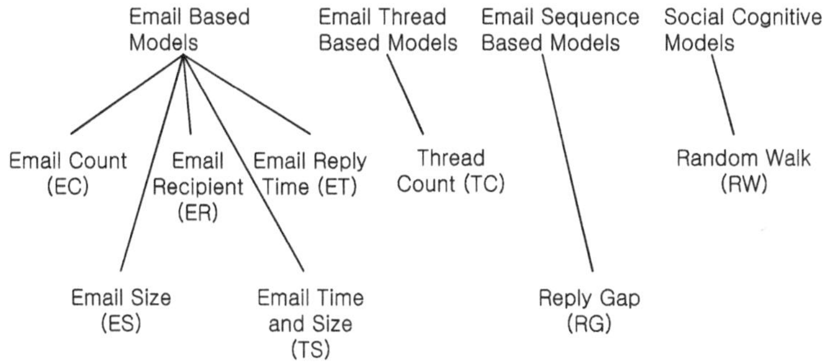

Fig. 10.1 Taxonomy of models

Table 10.1 Notations

$S(u_i)$	Emails sent by user u_i
$R(u_i)$	Emails received by u_i
$RB(u_i)$	Email replies sent by u_i
$RT(u_i)$	Emails replying to u_i's earlier emails
$SZ(e)$	Size of *e* added by the email sender excluding the forwarded content
$TH(u_i)$	Threads started by an email sent by u_i
$r(e)$	Reply to email *e*
$Sdr(e)$	Sender of email *e*
$Rcp(e)$	Recipients (in both To and Cc lists) of email *e*
$t(e)$	Sent time of email *e*
$E(u_i \rightarrow u_j)$	Emails from u_i to u_j
$E(u_i \leftrightarrow u_j)$	Emails between u_i and u_j
$rt(u_i \rightarrow u_j)$	Average response time from u_i to u_j
$rt(u_i \leftrightarrow u_j)$	Average response time between u_i and u_j
$RE(u_i \rightarrow u_j)$	Reply emails from u_i to u_j
$RE(u_i \leftrightarrow u_j)$	Reply emails between u_i and u_j

$$E^{EC}(u_i) = \frac{|RT(u_i)|}{|S(u_i)|} \tag{10.1}$$

$$R^{EC}(u_i) = \frac{|RB(u_i)|}{|R(u_i)|} \tag{10.2}$$

For users with empty $S(u_i)$ (or $R(u_i)$), $E^{EC}(u_i)$ (or $R^{EC}(u_i)$) is assigned a zero value.

Email Recipient Model (ER)

The intuition of this model is that an email with many recipients is likely to expect very few replies. Hence, an engaging user is one who gets replies from many recipients of his emails while an disengaging user receives very few or no reply when his emails are sent to many recipients. On the other hand, a responsive user is one who replies emails regardless of the number of recipients in the emails. A non-responsive user is one who does not reply even if the emails are directed to him only. The engagingness and responsiveness formulas are thus defined by:

$$E^{ER}(u_i) = \frac{1}{|S(u_i)|} \sum_{e \in S(u_i)} \frac{|\{u_j \in Rcp(e) \wedge r(e) \in RB(u_j)\}|}{|Rcp(e)|} \quad (10.3)$$

$$R^{ER}(u_i) = \frac{1}{|R(u_i)|} \sum_{\substack{e \in RB(u_i) \text{ s.t.} \\ \exists u_j, \exists e'' \in S(u_j), r(e'')=e}} \frac{|Rcp(e)|}{MaxRcpCnt} \quad (10.4)$$

where *MaxRcpCnt* (=291) denotes the largest recipient count among all Enron emails.

Email Reply Time Model (ET)

The reply time of an email can be an indicator of user engagingness and responsiveness. The email reply time model adopts the principle that engaging users receive the reply emails sooner than non-engaging users, while responsive users reply to the received emails quicker than non-responsive users.

Given an email e' which is a reply of email e, $e' = r(e)$, the *reply time* of e', $Rpt(e') = t(e') - t(e)$. The *z*-normalized reply time $\hat{Rpt}(e')$ is defined by $\frac{Rpt(e') - \overline{Rpt}}{\sigma_{Rpt}}$ where $\overline{Rpt}$ and σ_{Rpt} are the mean and standard deviation of reply time respectively. Now, we define the engagingness and responsiveness of ET model as:

$$E^{ET}(u_i) = \frac{1}{|S(u_i)|} \sum_{e \in S(u_i)} \frac{1}{|Rcp(e)|} \sum_{\substack{u_j \in Rcp(e), \\ \exists e' \in RB(u_j), e'=r(e)}} (1 - f(\hat{Rpt}(e'))) \quad (10.5)$$

$$R^{ET}(u_i) = \frac{1}{|R(u_i)|} \sum_{e' \in RB(u_i), e \in R(u_i), r(e)=e'} (1 - f(\hat{Rpt}(e'))) \quad (10.6)$$

where

$$f(x) = \frac{1}{1 + e^{-x}} \quad (10.7)$$

The function $f()$ is designed to convert the normalized reply time to the range [0,1] with 0 and 1 representing extreme slow and extreme fast reply times respectively.

Email Size Model (ES)

The email size model is analogous to the email reply time model except that we take the content size of emails into account rather than the reply time of emails.

The principle behind this model is based on the size of reply email roughly representing the amount of a recipient's effort. For instance, let us assume $SZ(e) = k$ and e' is a reply email of e. If $SZ(e') > k$, the engagingness score of the sender of e will be high. The amount of content in a reply email can be used to measure the amount of eagerness of the user sending the reply email. Let $\hat{SZ}(e)$ be the z-normalized $SZ(e)$. We then develop the engagingness and responsiveness measures based on email size as

$$E^{ES}(u_i) = \frac{1}{|S(u_i)|} \sum_{e \in S(u_i)} \frac{1}{|Rcp(e)|} \sum_{\substack{u_j \in Rcp(e), \\ \exists e' \in RB(u_j), e' = r(e)}} f(\hat{SZ}(e')) \tag{10.8}$$

$$R^{ES}(u_i) = \frac{1}{|R(u_i)|} \sum_{e' \in RB(u_i), e \in R(u_i), r(e) = e'} f(\hat{SZ}(e')) \tag{10.9}$$

Email Time and Size Model (TS)

This model combines both email reply time and size into a hybrid model as

$$E^{TS}(u_i) = \frac{1}{|S(u_i)|} \sum_{e \in S(u_i)} \frac{1}{|Rcp(e)|} \sum_{\substack{u_j \in Rcp(e), \\ \exists e' \in RB(u_j), e' = r(e)}} (1 - f(\hat{Rpt}(e'))) f(\hat{SZ}(e')) \tag{10.10}$$

$$R^{TS}(u_i) = \frac{1}{|R(u_i)|} \sum_{e' \in RB(u_i), e \in R(u_i), r(e) = e'} (1 - f(\hat{Rpt}(e'))) f(\hat{SZ}(e')) \tag{10.11}$$

Examples

To illustrate the behavior models in Sect. 10.2.1, suppose a simple email network as shown in Fig. 10.2. In Fig. 10.2a, u_i is a sender, while u_1, u_2, and u_3 are recipients. u_i sends email e_1 to u_1 and u_2, and then another email e'_1 is replied by u_1. However, u_2 does not respond to u_i. In the email network, the engagingness score of the user u_i is calculated as $E^{EC}(u_i) = \frac{3}{5} = 0.6$ and $E^{ER}(u_i) = \frac{\{\frac{1}{2} + \frac{2}{3}\}}{5} = 0.23$. In Fig. 10.2b, u_2, u_4, and u_i are recipients, whereas u_1 and u_3 are senders. u_3 sends email e_2 to u_2 and u_i. While u_2 does not reply to u_3, u_i replies to u_3 and to u_2 as Cc. In the figure, the responsiveness score of the user u_i is measured as $R^{EC}(u_i) = \frac{2}{2} = 1$ and $R^{ER}(u_i) = \frac{\{\frac{1}{4} + \frac{2}{4}\}}{2} = 0.38$, where we assume $MaxRcpCnt = 4$. In particular,

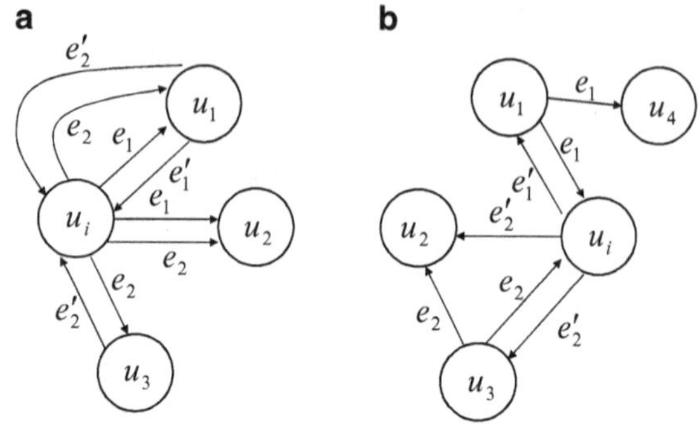

Fig. 10.2 An example for email based models. (**a**) Engagingness of u_i. (**b**) Responsiveness of u_i

Table 10.2 Distribution of reply times in the Enron email dataset

Reply time up to	1 h	5 h	10 h	1 day	5 days	10 days	90 days
# of email pairs	2,100	5,029	5,854	8,405	11,569	13,810	19,167

we order emails by the number of recipients in the ascending order, and then assign to *MaxRcpCnt* the number of recipients in an email at the 90 percentile. Recall that the email count model is a *macro* approach, while the email recipient model is a *micro* approach.

In the email reply time model, $E^{ET}(u_i) = \frac{\frac{1}{2}\cdot(x_1+\frac{1}{\infty})+\frac{2}{3}\cdot(x_2+\frac{1}{\infty}+x_3)}{2}$, where we compute x_i as follows:

- $x_1 = 1 - f(Rpt(t(e_1'(u_1,\{u_i\})) - t(e_1(u_i,\{u_1\})) = 5\,\text{s})) = 1 - 0.29 = 0.71$
- $x_2 = 1 - f(Rpt(t(e_2'(u_1,\{u_i\})) - t(e_2(u_i,\{u_1\})) = 10\,\text{s})) = 1 - 0.45 = 0.55$
- $x_3 = 1 - f(Rpt(t(e_2'(u_3,\{u_i\})) - t(e_2(u_i,\{u_3\})) = 20\,\text{s})) = 1 - 0.75 = 0.25$

where $e_v(u_x,\{U_y\})$ denotes email e_v sent by u_x to recipients U_y and e_v' denotes the reply of email e_v. To compute function $f(\hat{Rpt})$, we transform Rpt to z-scores. For instance, the z-score of $Rpt(t(e_1'(u_1,\{u_i\})) - t(e_1(u_i,\{u_1\})) = 5\,\text{s}) = \frac{5\,\text{s}-\bar{x}}{\sigma} = \frac{5-11.67}{7.64} = -0.87$, where $\bar{x}$ and σ denote the mean and standard deviation of reply times. According to our observation on reply times of Enron emails (see Table 10.2), the mean of reply times is much larger than the median. This indicates there are many outliers of reply times, and further most z scores can be negative. Thus we remove extreme reply times prior to computing z-scores. Then, $f(-0.87) = \frac{1}{1+e^{-(-0.87)}} = 0.29$. In particular, the term $\frac{1}{\infty}$ in $E^{ET}(u_i)$ indicates that u_i sends e_1 and e_2 to u_2 but u_2 does not reply to u_i. As a result, $E^{ET}(u_i) = \frac{\frac{1}{2}\cdot(0.71+0)+\frac{2}{3}\cdot(0.55+0+0.25)}{2} = 0.45$. The responsiveness of u_i is calculated in the same manner. In addition, the email size model computes engagingness scores in the same manner except that the length of email content is considered instead of the reply time of emails.

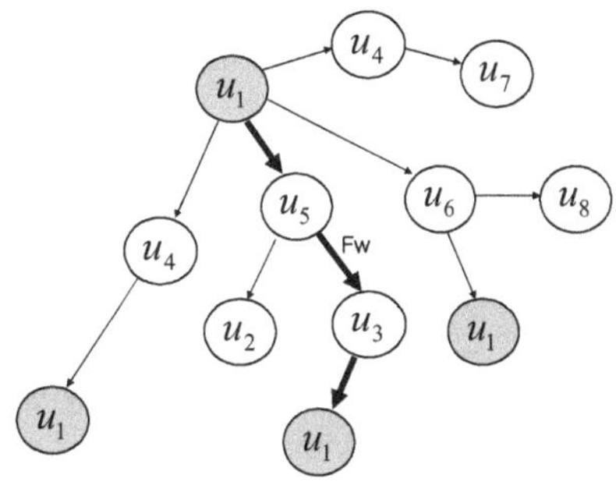

Fig. 10.3 An email thread example

Table 10.3 Distribution of emails per thread in the Enron email dataset

# emails	2	3	4	5	6	≥7	Total
# threads	11,302	3,925	1,614	732	404	616	18,593

10.2.2 Email Thread Based Models

Here, we define the **thread count model (TC)** as an email thread based model. In the email count model, engagingness is measured by emails sent by a sender and sent emails directly replied by some recipient(s). However, direct reply is not the only type of response to an email. Email may be indirectly replied in email threads due to forwarded emails. For example, as illustrated in Fig. 10.3, user u_1 advertises a job position by sending an email to professor u_5 who subsequently forwards it to his student u_3. If u_3 replies to u_1, we say that the original email is replied indirectly in an email thread.

Email thread is defined by a tree of emails connected by reply and forward relationships. Table 10.3 shows the distribution of threads by the number of emails per thread. As we can notice, the distribution follows Zipf's law. Majority of threads (11,302) contain only two emails. There are 3,925 threads that include three emails. The largest thread contains 37 emails.

Based on email threads, the thread count model includes indirect replies to emails forwarded between users using the principle: the user is highly engaging if he receives many of his emails replied directly or indirectly by recipients, and is highly responsive if he replies or forwards most emails earlier received. In the following, the engagingness and responsiveness of a user u_i are defined as:

$$E^{TC}(u_i) = \frac{1}{|S(u_i)|}|\{e \in S(u_i)|\exists t \in TH(u_i), \exists e', e \underset{t}{\twoheadrightarrow} e' \wedge u_i \in Rcp(e')\}| \tag{10.12}$$

$$R^{TC}(u_i) = \frac{1}{|R(u_i)|}|\{e \in R(u_i)|\exists u_j, e', t \in TH(u_j), e \underset{t}{\twoheadrightarrow} e' \wedge u_j \in Rcp(e')\}| \tag{10.13}$$

where $e \twoheadrightarrow_t e'$ returns TRUE when e is directly or indirectly connected to e' in the thread t, and FALSE otherwise.

10.2.3 Email Sequence Based Models

Email sequence refers to the sequence of emails sent and received by a user ordered by time. To derive engagingness and responsiveness from email sequences, we consider the principle that an engaging user is expected to have his sent emails replied soon after they are received by the email recipients, and a responsive user replies soon after they receive emails. As users may not always stay online, the time taken to reply an email may vary very much. Instead, we consider the number of emails received later than an email e but are replied before e by a user as a proxy of how soon e is replied.

The above principle is thus used to develop the **reply gap model (RG)**. Let seq_i denote the email sequence of user u_i. When an email received by u_i is replied before other email(s) received earlier, the reply of the former is known as an *out-of-order reply*. Formally, for an email e received by u_i, we define the *number of emails received* and *number of out-of-order replies* between e and its reply e' in seq_i, denoted by $n_r(u_i, e)$ and $n_{\overline{o}}(u_i, e)$ respectively, as

$$n_r(u_i, e) = \begin{cases} \text{\# emails received between } e \text{ and } e' \text{ in } seq_i, & \text{if } \exists e' \in RB(u_i),\ r(e) = e' \\ -1, & \text{otherwise} \end{cases} \quad (10.14)$$

$$n_{\overline{o}}(u_i, e) = \begin{cases} \text{\# emails received between } e \text{ and } e' \text{ in } seq_i \text{ and have been replied,} & \text{if } \exists e' \in RB(u_i),\ r(e) = e' \\ -1, & \text{otherwise} \end{cases} \quad (10.15)$$

The -1 value is assigned to n_r and $n_{\overline{o}}$ when e is not replied at all. The user engagingness and responsiveness of the RG model are thus defined as:

$$E^{RG}(u_i) = \frac{\sum_{e \in S(u_i)} \left(\frac{1}{|Rcp(e)|} \sum_{u_j \in Rcp(e)} \left(1 - \frac{n_{\overline{o}}(u_j, e)}{n_r(u_j, e)}\right)\right)}{|S(u_i)|} \quad (10.16)$$

$$R^{RG}(u_i) = \frac{\sum_{e \in R(u_i)} \left(1 - \frac{n_{\overline{o}}(u_i, e)}{n_r(u_i, e)}\right)}{|R(u_i)|} \quad (10.17)$$

For example, let $seq_i = \{e_1, e_2, e_3, e_4, e'_1, e'_4, e'_2\}$ be the email sequence of user u_i where $e'_k = r(e_k)$'s. Note that $\frac{n_{\overline{o}}(u_i,e_1)}{n_r(u_i,e_1)}, \frac{n_{\overline{o}}(u_i,e_2)}{n_r(u_i,e_2)}, \frac{n_{\overline{o}}(u_i,e_3)}{n_r(u_i,e_3)}$, and $\frac{n_{\overline{o}}(u_i,e_4)}{n_r(u_i,e_4)}$ are $\frac{0}{3}, \frac{1}{2}, \frac{-1}{-1}$, and 0 respectively. Hence, $R^{RG}(u_i) = \frac{\{(1-\frac{0}{3})+(1-\frac{1}{2})+(1-\frac{-1}{-1})+(1-0)\}}{4} = 0.625$. The engagingness of u_i can be computed in the same manner.

10.2.4 Social Cognitive Models

A social cognitive model is based on *social cognitive theory* which suggests that people learn by watching what others do [8]. Such kind of models thus measure a user's engagingness and responsiveness behaviors by observing what the other users react to emails sent from the user and observe the email interaction among one another. In this paper, we introduce a **random walk (RW)** social cognitive model.

For engagingness, each user u_k perceives a user u_i to be more engaging than another user u_j if more emails from u_i are replied ahead of emails from u_j based on the emails in the mailbox of u_k. For instance, suppose that u_k has an email sequence $seq_k = \langle e_1(u_1, \{u_k\}), e_2(u_2, \{u_k\}), e'_2(u_k, \{u_2\}), e'_1(u_k, \{u_1\})\rangle$, where $e_v(u_x, \{U_y\})$ denotes email e_v sent by u_x to recipients U_y and e'_v denotes the reply of email e_v. u_k receives e_1 before e_2 but the reply e'_1 comes after e'_2. This indicates that u_k considers u_2 more important than u_1. Furthermore, u_2 is more engaging than u_1 from u_k's standpoint. Based on the above observation, we say that u_k observes the engagingness superiority of u_2 over u_1.

Similarly for responsiveness, u_k perceives a user u_1 to be more responsive than another user u_2 if u_k observes reply emails from u_1 earlier than u_2 for the same emails sent to both u_1 and u_2 which can be from u_k or other users.

Formally, we represent an **engagingness weighted directed graph** $G^E = \langle U, L^E\rangle$ as follows:

- U represents the set of all users.
- L consists of directed edges. When in the mailbox of some u_k, u_i has x_k emails replied ahead of emails from u_j, we represent this by a directed edge $u_j \rightarrow u_i$.
- The weight of $u_j \rightarrow u_i$, $weight(u_j \rightarrow u_i)$, is the sum of x_k's for all u_k's. The larger is $weight(u_j \rightarrow u_i)$, the more users observe that u_i is more engaging than u_j.

In a similar manner, we can define a **responsiveness weighted directed graph** $G^R = \langle U, L^R\rangle$.

The engagingness (responsiveness) weighted directed graph will be further processed to derive the degree of engagingness (responsiveness) of users. Each directed graph so far captures the perceived relative difference between users in engagingness (responsiveness). It however does not immediately assign engagingness (responsiveness) scores to the users. We therefore propose to perform random walk on the engagingness (responsiveness) graph so as to determine the user engagingness (responsiveness) values as the stationary probabilities of visiting them.

The random walk process on the engagingness graph to obtain the engagingness of users denoted by $E^{RW}(u_k)$'s consists of the following steps:

1. Determine the largest node aggregated edge weight, $MaxWeight = Max_{u_j}\{\sum_{u_i} weight(u_j \rightarrow u_i)\}$

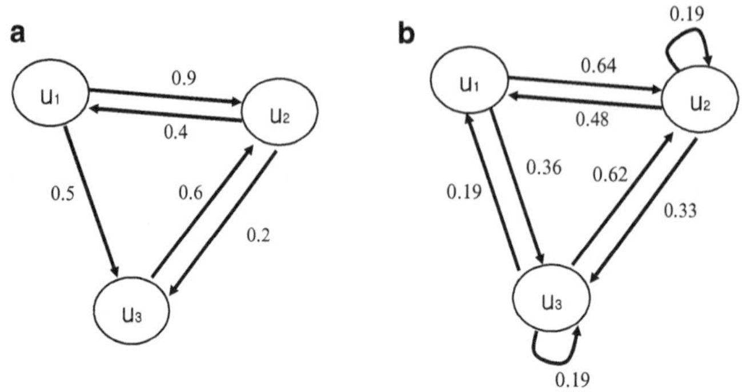

Fig. 10.4 Social cognitive model. (**a**) Engagingness weighted directed graph G^E. (**b**) Engagingness graph for random walks

2. For each user u_j,
   (a) $sum_j = 0$
   (b) For each edge $u_j \rightarrow u_i$,
      (i) Assign a transition probability to $u_j \rightarrow u_i$ as $p(u_j, u_i) = \frac{weight(u_j \rightarrow u_i)}{MaxWeight}$
      (ii) $sum_j = sum_j + p(u_j, u_i)$
   (c) Assign to the remaining weights to all users.
   Create an edge $u_j \rightarrow u_t$ for all u_t with $p(u_j, u_t) = \frac{1-sum_j}{|U|}$ if $u_j \rightarrow u_t$ does not exist;
   Increment $p(u_j, u_t)$ by $\frac{1-sum_j}{|U|}$ otherwise
3. For each user u_i, initialize $E^{RW}_{new}(u_i)$ randomly
4. Repeat the following steps:
   (a) For each u_i, $E^{RW}(u_i) = E^{RW}_{new}(u_i)$
   (b) For each u_i, $E^{RW}_{new}(u_i) = \sum_{u_j \rightarrow u_i} p(u_j, u_i) \cdot E^{RW}(u_j)$
5. Until $|E^{RW}(u_i) - E^{RW}_{new}(u_i)| \leq \epsilon^2$ for all u_i's

To illustrate the above algorithm, consider examples in Fig. 10.4. u_2 is more engaging than u_1 by $weight(u_1 \rightarrow u_2) = 0.9$. On the other hand, u_1 is less engaging than u_2 by $weight(u_2 \rightarrow u_1) = 0.4$. In Fig. 10.4a, the total engagingness weight of u_1 to all nodes u_2 and u_3 in G^E is $weight(u_i) = weight(u_1 \rightarrow u_2) + weight(u_1 \rightarrow u_3) = 1.4$. Similarly, the engagingness weight of u_2 and u_3 are 0.6 and 0.6 respectively. Then, the weight value of each edge is normalized by the maximum weight value, $MaxW = weight(u_1)$. For example, $weight(u_2 \rightarrow u_3) =$

[2]In our experiment, we used $\epsilon = .0000001$ and numbers of iterations required to compute E^{RW} and R^{RW} are 8 and 12 respectively.

$\frac{weight(u_2 \to u_3)}{MaxW} = \frac{0.2}{1.4}$. For nodes with total weight <1, the unused weight will be used to create edges with equal weights to all the nodes. For example u_2, it has unused weight of $\frac{\{MaxW - weight(u_2)\}}{weight(u_1)} = \frac{\{1.4-0.6\}}{1.4}$. As a result of the new edges for the unused weight, $weight(u_2 \to u_3) = \frac{0.2}{1.4} + \frac{\{1.4-0.6\}}{1.4} \cdot \frac{1}{3} = 0.33$. In this process, the engagingness graph is row-stochastic because its rows are nonnegative and the sum of each row is 1. This stochastic matrix can be viewed as a transition matrix associated to a family of Markov chains, where each entry (u_i,u_j) represents the probability of a transition from state u_i to state u_j.

10.3 Email Reply Order Prediction

We now consider the email reply order prediction which has the following setup. Given a pair of emails (e_i, e_j) sent to the same user (u) from users u_i and u_j respectively, we want to determine the order in which the two emails will be replied. Here, we assume that both e_i and e_j require some replies and u_i and u_j are not the same person. The outcome of prediction is either e_i or e_j first.

Our proposed method is to train a Support Vector Machine (SVM) classifier using labeled email pairs, and to apply the trained classifier on unseen email pairs. For each email pair, we can derive features directly from the emails themselves and their senders including the previous emails they have sent and received. There are three types of features used, namely: (a) *comparative email features* ($\mathbb{E}$), (b) *comparative interaction features* ($\mathbb{I}$) and (c) *comparative behavior features* ($\mathbb{B}$).

Table 10.4 lists the email features used in our classifier. For each email feature f_k, we derive a corresponding comparative feature f_k^c of an email pair (e_i, e_j) by

$$(e_i, e_j).f_k^c = e_i.f_k - e_j.f_k.$$

For email send time $t(e)$ feature, we further convert the positive and negative comparative feature values to 1 and −1 respectively. Interaction features refer to set of features derived from the sender of the email to the common recipient u_r as shown in Table 10.5. In the following sections, we will discuss the non-behavior features in more depth. The behavior features refer to the eight E^M and eight R^M behavior scores of email senders. The comparative interaction and behavior features are defined similar to that of email features.

For instance, we formulate our email reply order prediction as a binary classification problem. Each email pair is assigned a class label such that

$$\begin{cases} \text{Class} &= -1 \text{ if } t(e_i) - t(e_j) < 0 \\ \text{Class} &= 1 \quad \text{if } t(e_i) - t(e_j) > 0 \end{cases}.$$

The class label stands for u's preference to reply e_i before or after e_j with the assumption that e_i and e_j are received and replied by u. Now we suppose that $E^{ET}(u_i) = 0.8$ and $E^{ET}(u_j) = 0.4$. If we consider E^{ET} to be a feature (f_1),

Table 10.4 Email features $\mathbb{E}$

No	Description	No	Description
1	$t(e)$	9	$\|S(Sdr(e))\|$
2	$size(e)$	10	$\|R(Sdr(e))\|$
3	$size(r(e))$ (assuming we can determine the reply)	11	Avg. $\|S(Sdr(e))\|$ per day
		12	Avg. $\|R(Sdr(e))\|$ per day
4	$size(e) + size(r(e))$	13	$\frac{\|RB(Sdr(e))\|}{\|S(Sdr(e))\|}$
5	$Rcp(e)$	14	$\frac{\|RT(Sdr(e))\|}{\|R(Sdr(e))\|}$
6	$indegee(Sdr(e))$ (# users sending emails to $Sdr(e)$)	15	$\frac{\|RT(Sdr(e))\|}{\|S(Sdr(e))\|}$
		16	$\frac{\|RB(Sdr(e))\|}{\|R(Sdr(e))\|}$
7	$outdegee(Sdr(e))$ (# users receiving emails from $Sdr(e)$)	17	Avg response time for emails in $RT(Sdr(e))$
8	$indegree(Sdr(e))+ outdegree(Sdr(e))$	18	Avg response time for emails in $RB(Sdr(e))$

Table 10.5 Interaction features $\mathbb{I}$

No	Description	No	Description
19	$\|E(Sdr(e) \rightarrow u_r)\|$	27	$\frac{\|RE(Sdr(e) \leftrightarrow u_r)\|}{\|E(u_r \leftrightarrow Sdr(e))\|}$
20	$\|E(u_r \rightarrow (Sdr(e))\|$	28	$rt((Sdr(e) \rightarrow u_r)$
21	$\|E((Sdr(e) \leftrightarrow u_r)\|$	29	$rt(u_r \rightarrow (Sdr(e))$
22	$\|RE((Sdr(e) \rightarrow u_r)\|$	30	# threads involving $(Sdr(e)$, u_j as senders/recipients
23	$\|RE(u_r \rightarrow (Sdr(e))\|$		
24	$\|RE((Sdr(e) \leftrightarrow u_r)\|$	31	# threads involving $(Sdr(e)$, u_r as senders
25	$\frac{\|RE((Sdr(e) \rightarrow u_r)\|}{\|E(u_r \rightarrow (Sdr(e))\|}$		
26	$\frac{\|RE(u_r \rightarrow (Sdr(e))\|}{\|E((Sdr(e) \rightarrow u_r)\|}$		

the comparative feature of f_1 is $E^{ET}(u_i) - E^{ET}(u_j) = 0.8–0.4 = 0.4$. Furthermore, if we suppose $t(e_i) - t(e_j) < 0$, the feature vector used in SVM can be represented as $\{-1\ f_1{:}0.4\ldots\}$.

10.3.1 Non-behavior Features

10.3.1.1 Email Features $\mathbb{E}$

As shown in Table 10.4, Feature No. 1 represents the order in which emails e_i and e_j are received. For simplicity, let us denote by f_1 the feature value. $f_1 = -1$ if e_i arrived before e_j. $f_1 = 1$ if e_i arrived after e_j. $f_1 = 0$ if e_i and e_j arrived at the same time. Feature No. 2–4 measures the amount of effort required by a replier in terms of reading the content of a received email and writing the content of a reply email. The size of an email e represents the reading effort, while the size of the reply email $r(e)$ stands for the writing effort. Feature No. 5 counts the number of recipients in an email e, based on the fact that an email sent to many recipients is unlikely to be replied. Feature No. 6–8 measure indegree, outdegree, and total degree, respectively. Given a sender $Sdr(e)$ in an email e, the indegree of the sender is the number of users who send emails to the sender. The outdegree of the sender is the number of neighbors who receive emails from the sender. The total degree of the sender is the total number of users who exchange emails with the sender. Feature No. 9 and 10 are the total number of emails sent or received by a user. On the other hand, Feature No. 11 and 12 are the average number of emails sent or received by a user per day. Feature No. 13 and 14 estimate the proportion of reply emails in a user's sent and received emails. On the other hand, Feature No. 15 and 16 compute the proportion of emails that a user replies or receives a reply for. Feature No. 17 and 18 represent the average response time for the reply emails sent or received by a user.

10.3.1.2 Interaction Features 𝕀

Recall the framework of our email reply order prediction task, where u receives the emails from u_i and u_j, and then u will reply to either e_i or e_j first. Feature No. 19 counts the number of emails from u_i to u. We expect that u is likely to reply to e_i earlier than e_j if u_i usually sends more emails to u than u_j does. Similarly, Feature No. 20 counts the number of emails from u to u_i. Feature No. 21 counts the total number of emails exchanged between u_i and u. Feature No. 22 counts the number of reply emails exchanged between u and u_i and the total number of emails from u_i to u. Feature No. 23 counts the number of reply emails from u to u_i. Similarly, Feature No. 24 counts the total number of reply emails exchanged between u and u_i. Feature No. 25 estimates the proportion of emails replied. Feature No. 26 computes the proportion of emails replied out of the emails sent by u to u_i. We expect that u is likely to quickly reply to u_i who also responds to most of the emails received from u. Feature No. 27 measures the ratio of the total number of replies by the total number of emails exchanged between u and u_i. Feature No. 28 computes the average response time over all reply emails from u_i to u. Feature No. 29 also computes the average response time from u to u_i. Feature No. 30 counts the number of threads shared between u_i and u. It is because users who are involved in many threads are likely to be co-workers. Feature No. 31 counts the threads in which u and u_i actively participate. We define active participants to users who send at least one email in a thread.

10.4 Empirical Study

10.4.1 Set-Up

Dataset

For our task, we used the Enron email dataset that is publicly available at http://www.cs.cmu.edu/~enron. This dataset provides 517,431 emails for 151 Enron employees. Each email message contains a unique message_ID, header information such as the date and time when the message was sent/received, sender, recipients (To and Cc lists), subject and body in plain text format.

Using the email thread assembly algorithm (please see Appendix), we created a link database that stores a pair of emails linked via Reply or Forward relationships. The database consists of 34,008 links which includes 27,730 Reply links and 6,278 Forward links. These binary links make up a total of 18,593 threads that connect 52,601 emails.

Data Characteristics

We have conducted some analysis on the preprocessed email dataset to derive some statistics of Enron employees using and replying/forwarding emails. The interesting findings obtained include:

1. 52.6 K emails are involved in some threads.
2. Large majority (>90 %) of 18.5 K threads are short with two email messages each.
3. Large majority of threads last for at most 1 day.
4. Large majority of emails are replied within a day.
5. User response time is correlated with number of emails received, number of users he emails to, and number of users emailing him.

Evaluation Metric

To validate the effectiveness of our proposed models, note that we are not able to perform a direct evaluation on our behavior models because the ground truth is absent in the Enron dataset. Instead, we indirectly evaluate them, comparing the four types of behavior models on Enron dataset. To compare the ranked user lists produced by two models, we utilize the **Kendall τ distance measure**. In each ranked list, first and last ranked users represent the most and least engaging (or responsive) users respectively. Formally, we denote the rank of a user u_i in a ranked list L_k by $l_k(u_i)$. The Kendall τ distance between two ranked lists L_1 and L_2 is defined as $\frac{K(L_1,L_2)}{\frac{1}{2}n(n-1)}$ such that $K(L_1, L_2) = |(u_i, u_j) : u_i < u_j, (l_1(u_i) < l_1(u_j) \wedge l_2(u_i) > l_2(u_j)) \vee (l_1(u_i) > l_1(u_j) \wedge l_2(u_i) < l_2(u_j))|$. Note that Kendall τ distance is 0 if $l_1 = l_2$ for all users, and 1 if there is no correlation between l_1 and l_2 [3, 5].

10.4.2 *Analyzing Behavioral Models*

Correlation Between Engagingness and Responsiveness

We first show the correlation between engagingness and responsiveness in our proposed models. Table 10.6 illustrates the Kendall τ distance between two lists,

Table 10.6 Kendall τ distance between engagingness and responsiveness

Behavior model (M)	$\tau(E^M, R^M)$
M = EC	0.46
M = ER	0.52
M = ET	0.49
M = ES	0.47
M = TS	0.48
M = TC	0.46
M = RG	0.5
M = RW	0.11

where the Enron employees in one list are ordered by engagingness scores and the same employees in the other list are ordered by responsiveness scores in each model. By definition, if the Kendall τ distance is 0, the two lists stand for perfect match, while there is no correlation between the two lists in case of the Kendall τ distance is 1. Interestingly, our proposed models show that most τ distances range in between 0.4 and 0.5. These results indicate that engaging employees are not necessarily the same as responsive employees in the Enron email data.

Correlation Between Different Models

Tables 10.7 and 10.8 show the correlations of pairs of different models by engagingness and responsiveness respectively. For instance, we calculate the Kendall τ distance between two lists, where employees in one list are ordered by E^{EC} and the same employees in the other list are ordered by E^{ER}. The Kendall τ distance between E^{EC} and E^{ER} is 0.14 as shown in Table 10.7. In particular, our proposed models are more correlated by responsiveness rather than by engagingness. The email based models such as ER, ET, ES, and TS are highly correlated in both engagingness and responsiveness. On the other hand, the social cognitive approach is not highly correlated with the other models. For example, the Kendall τ distances between RW and the other models are 0.26 on average, while the distances between other models are considerably small. According to the results in Tables 10.7 and 10.8, the social cognitive approach shows low correlation with the other models. For example the Kendall τ distance between E^{ES} and E^{RW} is 0.24 and the Kendall τ distance between R^{RG} and R^{RW} is 0.27. In the social cognitive approach, each user u_k perceives a user u_i to be more engaging than another user u_j if more emails from u_i are replied ahead of emails from u_j based on the emails in the mailbox of u_k. Our further investigation reveals that most emails tend to be replied by the last-in-first-out principle. While some users may reply emails in the same order as they arrive (follow the first-in-first-out), most users exhibit a strong *recency bias* towards more recently received emails that appear higher in the inbox. Indeed, there are a few emails from u_i which are replied ahead of emails from u_j based on the emails in the mailbox of u_k. For instance, let us present that Sean Crandall (u_k), Fran Chang (u_i), and Alan Comnes (u_j) in the Enron dataset. u_i has a set of replied emails $\{e'_{126}, e'_{127}, e'_{15126}, e'_{15129}, e'_{15456}, e'_{15457}, e'_{15458}, e'_{15459}, e'_{27518}\}$, where subscripts stand for

Table 10.7 Kendall τ distance between two models by engagingness

	E^{ER}	E^{ET}	E^{ES}	E^{TS}	E^{TC}	E^{RG}	E^{RW}
E^{EC}	0.14	0.16	0.18	0.2	0.01	0.18	0.22
E^{ER}		0.12	0.14	0.16	0.14	0.15	0.24
E^{ET}			0.19	0.13	0.16	0.15	0.22
E^{ES}				0.09	0.18	0.19	0.24
E^{TS}					0.19	0.18	0.24
E^{TC}						0.18	0.22
E^{RG}							0.24

Table 10.8 Kendall τ distance between two models by responsiveness

	R^{ER}	R^{ET}	R^{ES}	R^{TS}	R^{TC}	R^{RG}	R^{RW}
R^{EC}	0.06	0.03	0.03	0.04	0.01	0.03	0.26
R^{ER}		0.07	0.07	0.07	0.06	0.08	0.25
R^{ET}			0.05	0.03	0.03	0.03	0.26
R^{ES}				0.03	0.03	0.05	0.26
R^{TS}					0.05	0.05	0.26
R^{TC}						0.03	0.26
R^{RG}							0.27

email ID. Similarly, u_j has a set of replied emails $\{e'_{400}, e'_{3065}, e'_{9321}, e'_{12248}, e'_{17495}, e'_{19143}, e'_{19144}, e'_{19672}\}$. Then, u_k has a sequence of emails ordered by time $\{e_{9321}, e_{19675}, e'_{19672}, e_{15126}, e_{15129}, e'_{15129}, e_{126}, e'_{126}, e_{127}, e'_{127}, e_{19144}, e'_{19144}, e_{19143}, e'_{19143}, e_{400}, e_{15495}, e_{3065}, e'_{3065}, e_{27518}, e'_{27518}, e_{15457}, e_{15456}, e_{15458}, e_{12248}, e_{17495}\}$. Some emails such as e_{15129} and e_{126} are replied right after the email arrives at a recipient. On the other hand, for each replied email of Alan Comnes (e.g., e_{3065}), there is no emails from Fran Chang that comes before an email from Alan Comnes and replies after the reply to Alan Comnes.

Interestingly, the email thread based model shows similar result to that of the email count model regardless of engagingness or responsiveness. This is because there are fewer number of forwarded emails among 151 Enron employees. For instance, from our email thread assembly, we obtained 7,291 email threads, each of which has more than or equal to three emails. In addition, we observed that an email sent by a sender is forwarded by recipients, and the sender finally receives reply emails by not the recipients but some other users. The total number of such emails is 313 among 151 Enron employees. For E^{TC}, only one thread contains eight forwarding emails, but most threads include at most one or two forwarding emails. Such small number of forwarding emails causes TC to be similar to EC.

Most Engaging and Responsive Users

Table 10.9 shows the top five engaging users and top five responsive users after averaging the ranks of our proposed models. The table shows that the two sets of

Table 10.9 Top-five users by engagingness and responsiveness. Note that we derive the overall engagingness and responsiveness of each user by averaging the engagingness and responsiveness of different models

	Engagingness		Responsiveness	
Rank	Enron employee	Position	Enron employee	Position
1	Ryan Slinger	Trader	John Lavorato	CEO
2	Larry Campbell	N/A	Monika Causholli	Employee
3	Joe Quenet	Trader	Jeff Dasovich	Employee
4	Mike Swerzbin	Trader	Kate Symes	Employee
5	Jeff King	Manager	Kay Mann	Employee

top users are different, consistent with our earlier results. It is interesting to note that most engaging users are traders. Other than CEO John Lavorato, the top responsive users are general employees. Interestingly, there exists no common actors between the two top-five employee lists by engagingness and responsiveness. In other words, there is no both high engaging and responsive actor among 151 Enron employees. This result is consistent with that in Table 10.6.

Role Analysis in Correlation

Figure 10.5 shows the scatter plot of engagingness and responsiveness scores of Enron employees with different roles. In the figures, we just present that 93 Enron employees among them are 3 chief executive officers, 9 directors, 35 employees, 3 house lawyers, 8 managers, 2 managing directors, 4 presidents, 12 traders, and 17 vice presidents. Since the job positions of the remaining employees from 151 Enron users are not known, we exclude them from Fig. 10.5. In particular, we show the engagingness and responsiveness scores of Enron employees with different roles in terms of the email reply time model. Note that most employees, managers, and traders tend to have higher engagingness scores than the other employees. In other words, employees, managers, and traders can effectively solicit responses from other actors. In contrast, vice presidents show wide range of engagingness scores. Unlike engagingness, we observed that responsiveness is not correlated to particular job appointments. Rather than actor roles, responsiveness is more related by actors' individual personality. Some actors are willing to respond to other actors, while other actors are not.

10.4.3 Email Reply Order Prediction

The goal of this experiment is to evaluate the performance of our proposed classification approach to predict email reply order. We also want to examine the usefulness of engagingness and responsiveness behaviors in prediction task.

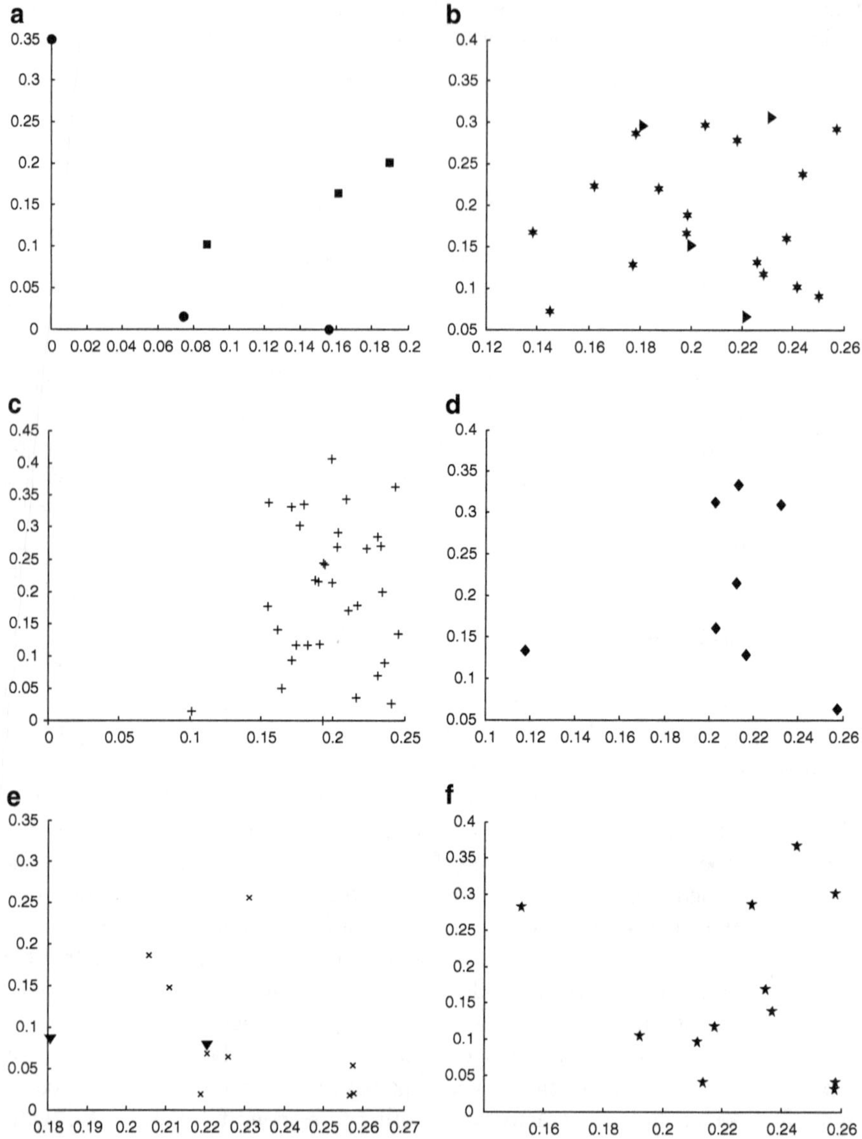

Fig. 10.5 Actor role in the email reply time model (X-axis and Y-axis denote E^{ET} and R^{ET}, respectively). Since the other models show similar results to the email reply time model, we omit those of the other models. (**a**) CEO and house lawyer. (**b**) President and vice president. (**c**) Employee. (**d**) Manager. (**e**) Director and managing director. (**f**) Trader

Table 10.10 Results of email reply order prediction

Features used in SVM	Average accuracy (%)
$SVM_{\mathbb{E}+\mathbb{I}}$	76.68
$SVM_{\mathbb{U}}$	77.3
$SVM_{\mathbb{B}}$	67.25
$SVM'_{\mathbb{E}+\mathbb{I}}$	65.33
$SVM'_{\mathbb{U}}$	69.31

There are five SVM classifiers trained, namely: (a) using comparative email and interengaging features (denoted by $SVM_{\mathbb{E}+\mathbb{I}}$); (b) using comparative behavior features only (denoted by $SVM_{\mathbb{B}}$), (c) using all features (denoted by $SVM_{\mathbb{U}}$), (d) using comparative email and interengaging features except $t(e)$[3] (denoted by $SVM'_{\mathbb{E}+\mathbb{I}}$), and (e) using all features except $t(e)$ (denoted by $SVM'_{\mathbb{U}}$). Classifiers (d) and (e) are included as earlier study [4] has shown that email replies often follow the last-in-first-out principle. $SVM'_{\mathbb{E}+\mathbb{I}}$ and $SVM'_{\mathbb{U}}$ allow us to find out if we can predict without knowing the email time information. From the 27,730 email reply relationships, we extracted a total of 19,167 email pairs for the prediction task. The emails in each pair have replies that comes after the two emails are received by the same user. For each email pair, we computed feature values based on only email data occurred before the pair. In addition, we used complement email pairs in training. The complement of an email pair (e_i, e_j) with class label c is another email pair (e_j, e_i) with class label $\bar{c}$. Fivefolds cross validation was used to measure the average accuracy of the classifiers over the fivefolds. The accuracy measure is defined by $\frac{\#\ correctly\ classified\ pairs}{\#\ email\ pairs}$.

Table 10.10 illustrates the results of all the five SVM classifiers. $SVM_{\mathbb{U}}$ produces the highest accuracy of 77.04 % due to the use of all available features. By excluding the email arrival order feature, the accuracy (of $SVM'_{\mathbb{U}}$) reduces to 68.97 %. This performance is reasonably good given that random prediction gives an accuracy of 50 %. The above results show that email arrival order feature is an important feature in the prediction task. We however notice that behavior features contribute to prediction accuracy especially when the email arrival order feature is not available.[4]

Table 10.11 depicts the top ten features for the $SVM_{\mathbb{U}}$ classifier. The table shows that engagingness based on the email reply time model *ET* is the most discriminative feature. This suggests that engagingness and responsiveness are useful in predicting email reply order.

[3]See Table 10.4.

[4]Recently, [4] reported that email replies often follow the last-in-first-out principle.

Table 10.11 Top-ten features for $\mathrm{SVM}'_{\mathrm{U}}$

Rank	Feature	Weight
1	$E^{ET}(Sdr(e_i)) - E^{ET}(Sdr(e_j))$	0.66
2	$R^{RG}(Sdr(e_i)) - R^{RG}(Sdr(e_j))$	0.59
3	$Indegree(Sdr(e_i)) - Indegree(Sdr(e_j))$	0.55
4	$E^{RW}(Sdr(e_i)) - E^{RW}(Sdr(e_j))$	0.54
5	Engaging threads xy	0.48
6	$R^{ES}(Sdr(e_i)) - R^{ES}(Sdr(e_j))$	0.37
7	$E^{ER}(Sdr(e_i)) - E^{ER}(Sdr(e_j))$	0.36
8	$E^{TC}(Sdr(e_i)) - E^{TC}(Sdr(e_j))$	0.32
9	emails y2x	0.27
10	$size(r(e_i)) - size(r(e_j))$	0.26

10.5 Related Work

We first review related work on engagingness and responsiveness behavior modeling. Engagingness and responsiveness behaviors have not been well studied in the past. There is one work on responsiveness [1] (even though it is not sufficient) but no work on engagingness. In [1], responsiveness behavior of a user (in the context of Enron email data set) was defined as the average deviation in response time of user from the other users. Users with positive deviations are known to be lethargic and those with negative deviations are responsive.

Since we are using the Enron dataset, we also review other research on the data set comparing their works with ours. These works can be divided into:

- **Knowledge extraction:** Rowe et al. present an automatic method for extracting social hierarchy data from user communication behavior on the Enron dataset [12]. Such communication patterns are captured by computing the social score based on a set of features: number of emails, average response time, number of cliques, degree centrality, clustering coefficient, mean of shortest path length from a specific vertex to all vertices in the graph, betweenness centrality, and Hubs-and-Authorities importance. Then, by performing behavior analysis and determining the communication patterns, their method ranks main users of an organization, groups similarly ranked and connected users to reproduce the organizational structure, and understand relationship strengths among users. Pathak et al. investigate socio-cognitive networks based on email communication in an organization [11]. Socio-cognitive network analysis involves understanding who knows who knows who in a social network. For analysis, the authors propose a model using probability distributions for communication probabilities, in which a Bayesian inference technique is used for updating the probabilities.
- **Email thread detection:** To exploit parent-child relationships from email messages, grouping messages together based on which messages are replies to which others, Yeh and Harnly propose email thread detection using undocumented

header information from the Microsoft Exchange Protocol and string similarity metrics [14]. Then, their method recovers missing messages from email threads.

- **Email label prediction:** Karagiannis and Vojnovic study various parameters including the email size, the number of recipients per email, role of the sender and recipient in the organization, information load on the user, etc., and their effect on reply probability and response time [4]. While their results shed some interesting insights into how these parameters affect users' replying behavior, further research is required to actually implement a learning model that can automatically prioritize emails based on these findings. Interestingly, through our experimental analysis, we found that email replies often follow the last-in-first-out principle which has been reported by Karagiannis and Vojnovic [4]. The study of [15] builds a supervised classifier to automatically label emails with priority levels on the scale of 1–5. Their model primarily focuses on graph-based metrics such as node degree, centrality, clique count, etc. derived from the underlying social networks of users. McCallum et al. present the author-recipient-topic model which learns topic distributions based on the direction sensitive messages sent between users [7]. In particular, this model works based on Latent Dirichlet Allocation and the author-topic model in which distribution over topics is conditioned distinctly on both the sender and recipient according to the relationships between users. Unlike our models, the authors have explored Enron dataset mostly from a Natural Language Processing (NLP) perspective. Recently, B. On et al. conducted preliminary study of behavior models on mobile social networks [10].
- **Email interaction prediction:** To predict whether emails need replies, Dredze et al. present a logistic regression model with a variety of features e.g., dates and times, salutations, questions, and header fields of emails [2].

10.6 Conclusion

In a nutshell, we study user engagingness and responsiveness behaviors in an email network. We have developed four types of behavior models based on different characterization principles. Using the Enron dataset, we evaluate these models. We also apply the models to email reply order prediction task.

The work is a significant step beyond the usual node and network statistics to derive node behavior measures for a given network. While our results are promising, there are still much room for further research. We will develop new behavior models based on probability and email content. We also plan to conduct a more comprehensive study of engagingness and responsiveness behaviors on a much larger and complete information exchange dataset (e.g., twitters, blogs, SMS, etc.). This will remove some shortcomings of the existing Enron dataset which does not have complete emails of each user. We will also expand our work to apply the behaviors to other interesting email prediction tasks.

Appendix

Email Thread Assembly The algorithm to identify reply and forward relationships among emails is as follows:

- Step 1: Group all emails with matching subjects after ignoring the prefixing Reply (RE, Re) and Forward (FW, Fw, FWD, Fwd) tags from the subject field. Emails with blank subject or subject matching *"no subject"* are ignored.
- Step 2: Sort emails in each subject group by date and time. We use the Perl module Time: Local to convert the message date and time into an integer number that indicates the number of seconds since the system epoch (Midnight, January 1, 1970 GMT).
- Step 3: For each email e_1 whose subject starts with one of the Reply or Forward tags (Re, RE, Fw, FW, Fwd, FWD)
  - Step 3a: Scan all the previous emails in its group
  - Step 3b: Find the most recent email e_2 such that the sender of e_1 is one of the recipients of e_2
  - Step 3c: If the subject of e_1 begins with a Reply tag, also check that the sender of e_2 is one of the recipients of e_1
- Step 4: Compute the time difference $t(e_1) - t(e_2)$
- Step 5: If $t(e_1) - t(e_2) \leq \xi$, add link $e_1 \rightarrow e_2$ to indicate that e_1 is a reply or forwarded email of e_2

Here, the parameter ξ specifies a time-window between emails e_1 and e_2 to consider it as a valid thread link. In our experiments, we set $\xi = 90$ days (3 months) and discard pairs that have a time difference larger than that.

References

1. Deepak, P., Garg, D., Varshney, V.: Analysis of Enron email threads and quantification of employee responsiveness. In: Workshop on Text Mining and Link Analysis (TextLink), Hyderabad (2007)
2. Dredze, M., Blitzer, J., Pereira, F.: Reply expectation prediction for email management. In: 2nd Conference on Email and Anti-Spam (CEAS), Stanford University (2005)
3. Fagin, R., Kumar, R., Sivakumar, D.: Comparing top K lists. SIAM J. Discret. Math. **17**, 134–160 (2003)
4. Karagiannis, T., Vojnovic, M.: Behavioral profiles for advanced email features. In: 18th International World Wide Web Conference (WWW), Raleigh (2009)
5. Kendall, M.: Rank Correlation Methods. Charles Griffin and Company Limited, London (1948)
6. Klimt, B., Yang, Y.: The Enron corpus: a new dataset for email classification research. In: 15th European Conference on Machine Learning (ECML), Pisa (2004)
7. McCallum, A., Wang, X., Coorada-Emmanuel, A.: Topic and role discovery in social networks with experiments on Enron and academic email. J. Artif. Intell. Res. **30**, 249–272 (2007)
8. Miller, N.E., Dollard, J.: Social Learning and Imitation. Yale University Press, New Haven (1941)

9. On, B.-W., Lim, E.-P., Jiang, J., Purandare, A., Teow, L.: Mining interaction behaviors for email reply order prediction. In: 2nd International Conference on Social Network Analysis and Mining (ASONAM), Odense, (2010)
10. On, B.-W., Lim, E.-P., Jiang, J., Chua, F., Nguyen, V., Teow, L.: Messaging behavior modeling in mobile social networks. In: Symposium on Social Intelligence and Networking (SIN) in conjunction with 2nd IEEE International Conference on Social Computing (SocialCom), Minneapolis (2010)
11. Pathak, M., Mane, S., Srivastava, J.: Who thinks who knows who? socio-cognitive analysis of an email network. In: 6th IEEE International Conference on Data Mining (ICDM), Hong Kong (2006)
12. Rowe, R., Creamer, G., Hershkop, S., Stolfo, S.: Automated social hierarchy detection through email network analysis. In: 9th WEBKDD and 1st SNA-KDD Workshop, San Jose (2007)
13. Stolfo, S., Hershkop, S., Hu, C., Nimeskern, O., Wang, K.: Behavior-based modeling and its application to email analysis. ACM Trans. Internet Technol. **16**(2), 187–221 (2006)
14. Yeh, J., Harnly, A.: Email thread reassembly using similarity matching. In: 3rd Conference on Email and Anti-Spam (CEAS), Mountain View (2006)
15. Yoo, S., Yang, Y., Lin, F., Moon, I.: Mining social networks for personalized email prioritization. In: 15th ACM SIGKDD Conference on Knowledge Discovery and Data Mining (KDD), Paris (2009)

Chapter 11
Efficient Extraction of High-Betweenness Vertices from Heterogeneous Networks

Wen Haw Chong, Wei Shan Belinda Toh, and Loo Nin Teow

Abstract Centrality measures are crucial in quantifying the roles and positions of vertices in complex network analysis. An important and popular measure is betweenness centrality, which is computed based on the number of shortest paths that vertices fall on. However, betweenness is computationally expensive to derive, resulting in much research on efficient computation techniques. We note that in many applications, it is the set of vertices with high betweenness that is of key interest and that their betweenness rankings rather than the exact values is usually adequate for analysts to work with. Hence, we have developed a novel algorithm that efficiently returns the set of vertices with highest betweenness. The convergence criterion for our algorithm is based on the membership stability of the high-betweenness set. Through experiments on various artificial and real-world networks, we show that the algorithm is both efficient and accurate. From the experiments, we also demonstrated that the algorithm tends to perform better on networks with heterogeneous betweenness distributions.

11.1 Introduction

In the real world, a variety of networks exist and their statistical, mechanical and temporal properties are the subject of much research, known broadly as complex network analysis. Networks of interest include social groups, collaboration networks, computer networks, food webs, etc.

In complex networks, centrality measures play an important role in quantifying how vertices and edges are positioned within the network. Popular concepts include degree centrality, which measures the number of neighbors a vertex has; closeness centrality, which measures the proximity of a vertex to all other vertices in the

W.H. Chong (✉) · W.S.B. Toh · L.N. Teow
DSO National Laboratories, 20 Science Park Drive, Singapore, 118230, Singapore
e-mail: cwenhaw@dso.org.sg; tweishan@dso.org.sg; tloonin@dso.org.sg

T. Özyer et al. (eds.), *The Influence of Technology on Social Network Analysis and Mining*, Lecture Notes in Social Networks 6, DOI 10.1007/978-3-7091-1346-2_11,

network; betweenness centrality [1, 9], which is based on the number of shortest paths that a vertex or edge sits on as an intermediary; and eccentricity centrality, which measures the distance from a vertex to the vertex furthest from it in the network.

This paper focuses on betweenness centrality. Amongst the various centrality concepts, betweenness centrality is well known to be computationally demanding. Despite recent advances, betweenness computation for large networks remains expensive. The fastest known algorithm was developed by Brandes [5] and computes exact betweenness for unweighted graphs in $O(mn)$ time and weighted graphs in $O(mn + n^2 \log n)$ time, where n is the number of vertices and m is the number of edges. It is based on computing the Single Source Shortest Path (SSSP) from every vertex in the network. Partial sums are accumulated over these SSSPs to derive betweenness values. In the process, closeness and eccentricity can also be derived. For application on large networks, the algorithm can be easily parallelized by distributing the SSSP computations amongst multiple processors. Building on this algorithm, an approximation technique was developed in [6]. This computes SSSPs from a subset of vertices chosen through some selection scheme. Since the subset can be chosen to be much smaller than the network size, computation savings can be achieved at the expense of accuracy. The authors referred to the selected source vertices as pivots. Henceforth, we shall refer to the approximation technique in [6] as the pivot method.

In this paper, we specify that instead of computing the exact betweenness for all vertices in the network, we merely need to extract the k highest ranking vertices, where k can be any number smaller than n. This is effectively a simpler problem. In many practical applications, $k \ll n$. In addition, many such applications do not require the actual betweenness values for analysis purposes. Hence complete and exact derivation expends computational resources to solve a much harder problem than necessary. Typically, it is the set of vertices with high betweenness that is of interest. These vertices have various practical purposes, e.g. corresponding to key nodes or gateways in computer networks. They may also be crucial vertices with a large impact on average shortest path length in a network upon elimination. In the case of a social network, high-betweenness vertices may be interpreted as having a strong middleman role. In designing our algorithm, we walk the line advocated by Tarjan [18]: "the most efficient algorithms are generally those that compute exactly the information relevant to the problem situation". It is rare that vertices with low betweenness are of interest. In any case, simply selecting vertices with one neighbor, or whose neighbors induce a clique will already extract many such vertices. In addition, our algorithm will terminate even though the betweenness rankings of vertices below the top k may not have converged.

Theoretical error bounds for the convergence of both closeness and betweenness centralities were derived in [6] based on Hoeffding's theorem [11] (See Appendix 2). It has also been shown that the computation of betweenness is more difficult and unreliable than that of closeness. In their conclusion, the authors in [6] proposed an approach for extracting k vertices of highest closeness. This was investigated in [16]. The strategy is to first use the approximation technique to obtain k' vertices with highest (estimated) closeness, where $k' > k$. k' is chosen such that it is guaranteed with a high probability that the k vertices (of highest exact closeness) is a subset of the k' vertices. Then, the exact closeness is computed for each of the k' vertices, to extract the final top-k vertices. To our knowledge, the problem of how to extract the highest ranking vertices in terms of betweenness has not been explored, nor has any strategy been proposed. Unfortunately, the framework in [16] is not extensible to extracting high-betweenness vertices due to the different nature of the metrics. While it is possible to obtain the exact closeness value of a single vertex via one SSSP computation with it as the root, it is necessary to compute multiple SSSPs for the betweenness of a single vertex. Another strategy is required for efficient extraction of high-betweenness vertices.

In Sect. 11.2, we formally describe betweenness centrality and the prior work that is directly relevant to this paper. We provide the basis for our algorithm design in Sect. 11.3, followed by a description of the algorithm itself. Section 11.4 presents our evaluation metrics and the various networks for experimentation. In Sect. 11.5, we compare our technique in terms of efficiency and accuracy against the exact algorithm and present the experimental results. In Sect. 11.6, we compare accuracies against another more recent competitive technique. We conclude in Sect. 11.7.

11.2 Preliminaries

Betweenness centrality is a metric based on the enumeration of shortest paths between vertex pairs in a network. Let σ_{st} denote the number of shortest paths between vertices s and t, and $\sigma_{st}(v)$ be the number that pass through the vertex v. Define the pair wise dependency as the fraction of shortest paths between s and t that pass through v:

$$\delta_{st}(v) = \frac{\sigma_{st}(v)}{\sigma_{st}}\,, \tag{11.1}$$

where $s \neq v \neq t$. The betweenness centrality of a vertex v accumulates the pair wise dependencies for all vertex pairs whose shortest paths pass through v:

$$\mathrm{BC}(v) = \sum_{st} \delta_{st}(v)\,. \tag{11.2}$$

Before describing the strategy for our algorithm, it is necessary to describe the workings of the exact algorithm by Brandes [5] and the pivot method [6].

11.2.1 Exact Algorithm

The one-sided dependency of a vertex s on another vertex v is derived by summation over the appropriate pair wise dependencies:

$$\delta_s(v) = \sum_{t} \delta_{st}(v)\,. \tag{11.3}$$

The betweennness of v can then be computed as

$$\mathrm{BC}(v) = \sum_{s} \delta_s(v) \, . \tag{11.4}$$

The algorithm is based on the following recursive relation for computing one-sided dependencies:

$$\delta_s(v) = \sum_{w:v \in P_s(w)} \frac{\sigma_{sv}}{\sigma_{sw}} (1 + \delta_s(w)) \, , \tag{11.5}$$

where $P_s(w)$ denotes the set of predecessors of a vertex w on the shortest path tree with s as the root. Essentially, an SSSP is computed for each vertex in the network, producing the shortest path tree from that vertex. For a given shortest path tree with s as the root, a backward pass then traverses through the vertices in order of non-increasing distance from s. During the traversal, the recursive relation in (11.5) is used to compute the dependencies of s on all other vertices in the tree. To compute the betweenness of any vertex, the appropriate dependencies arising from all SSSPs are summed up as in (11.4). For memory efficiency, a running sum can be maintained and updated for each vertex during the computations.

11.2.2 Pivot Method

The pivot method is very similar to the exact algorithm. The main difference is that instead of computing SSSPs for all vertices in the network, it selects a subset of vertices (pivots) to compute SSSPs and then extrapolates from the contributions of this smaller set to estimate betweenness values. Various pivot selection schemes have been tested [6] and it has been observed that random sampling of pivots consistently performs the best across different kinds of networks.

The efficiency and accuracy of the pivot method depends on the number of pivots used. Accuracy is largely monotonic with the number of pivots. Using fewer pivots leads to higher efficiency at the cost of accuracy. When all vertices in the network are used as pivots, the method is equivalent to the exact algorithm.

11.3 Proposed Algorithm

This section covers the basis for our algorithm design as well as its technical details.

11.3.1 Basis for Design

Through comprehensive experiments on various artificial and real-world networks [6], it was empirically shown that the following applies for the pivot method:

- Random selection of pivots is superior to more sophisticated selection schemes and performs consistently well on different kinds of networks;
- The inversion distance, i.e. the number of wrongly ordered pairs, decreases approximately monotonically with the number of pivots added.

The second point implies that as the number of pivots is increased, the ranking of each vertex approaches the true rank value. This observation forms the basis for our algorithm design. Given all the vertices in a network ranked in decreasing order of betweenness, we are only interested in the subset of k-highest ranked vertices. If a sufficient number of pivots is used to obtain the ranking, we expect that the membership of this subset would remain fairly consistent even if more pivots were added.

Formally, let S_k be the set of k vertices with highest exact betweenness. Denote $\hat{S}_k$ as the corresponding approximate set returned from the pivot method. Clearly, $\hat{S}_k$ is cheaper to compute than S_k. If the approximation is good, there is a large overlap between $\hat{S}_k$ and S_k. For discussion purpose, we introduce a subscript denoting the number of pivots such that $\hat{S}_{k,r}$ means that the estimated set is returned from the pivot method with r pivots. If q pivots are chosen in another trial of the pivot method, where $q > r$, it can be shown largely that $|S_k \cap \hat{S}_{k,q}| > |S_k \cap \hat{S}_{k,r}|$. Intuitively, this means that using a larger number of pivots leads to a more accurate approximation of S_k. Now consider the case where r is sufficiently large such that $|S_k \cap \hat{S}_{k,r}| = k$, i.e. the approximation is perfect. Note that r may be less than or equal to the network size n. Obviously, $r \ll n$ is desired and the smaller r is, the greater the computational savings. Given $r < n$, a larger set of pivots of size q can be selected such that $|S_k \cap \hat{S}_{k,q}| = |S_k \cap \hat{S}_{k,r}| = k$, i.e. $\hat{S}_{k,q} = \hat{S}_{k,r} = S_k$. Although we are not able to compute $|S_k \cap \hat{S}_{k,q}|$ and $|S_k \cap \hat{S}_{k,r}|$ since we do not have the ground truth S_k, we can directly and easily compare $\hat{S}_{k,q}$ and $\hat{S}_{k,r}$. This naturally leads to the design of an iterative algorithm where pivots are incrementally added to re-estimate $\hat{S}_k$, and convergence is formulated based on its membership stability across iterations. In accordance with the first observation, we use the random selection scheme for pivots. Next we describe the algorithm in detail.

11.3.2 Detailed Description

Our algorithm is essentially a modification of the pivot method. Instead of specifying an overall number of pivots at initialization, pivots are added incrementally in batches. At each iteration, we compute the SSSPs for the new batch of pivots, update all vertices' approximate betweenness values and extract the highest ranked set. Batches are made unique such that previously added pivots will not be re-added. Also note that normalization of the betweenness values is optional and does not affect the ranking. Let $\hat{S}_k(t)$ be the set of k highest ranked vertices extracted at iteration t. We compare it with the corresponding set extracted during previous iterations. If the membership of the sets remains largely stable according to some predefined criteria, the algorithm terminates.

```
Input: Network of vertices
Parameter: max_pivots
 1: t = 0 //iteration step
 2: num_pivots = 0 //number of pivots used so far
 3: counter = 0 //termination counter
 4: Order all vertices randomly into pivot_set(t)
 5: while num_pivots < max_pivots
 6:   pivot_batch = pivot_set(t) //pivot_set for iteration t
 7:   num_pivots = num_pivots + Δp //size of pivot_batch
 8:   Compute SSSPs for pivot_batch to update betweenness values for all vertices
 9:   Extract the k highest ranking vertices into Ŝ_k(t)
10:   if Ŝ_k(t) = Ŝ_k(t − 1) //current set is same as previous
11:     counter = counter + 1 //increment
12:   else
13:     counter = 0 //reset
14:   end if
15:   if counter = 3 //same set for 3 consecutive iterations
16:     Terminate with result set Ŝ_k = Ŝ_k(t)
17:   end if
18:   t = t + 1
19: end while
Output: Set of k highest betweenness vertices, Ŝ_k
```

Fig. 11.1 Proposed algorithm

The pseudo code for the algorithm is shown in Fig. 11.1. The final set of k highest betweenness vertices is saved in $\hat{S}_k$. The parameter max_pivots specifies the maximum number of pivots to be used in the event that convergence does not occur. It can be set to less than or equal to the network size. Lines 1–3 correspond to initialization. In line 4, the pivot_set is created by randomly ordering all vertices in the network such that consecutive batches of pivots can be easily added in iterations. This is in accordance with the random pivot selection scheme. Line 5 starts the algorithm iterations. At the start of each iteration t, we take a new batch of Δp pivots from pivot_set (lines 6–7). The value of Δp determines the amount of additional computations that is done in an iteration. A large value means that the algorithm takes larger steps across iterations, but achieves coarser resolution. We have arbitrarily set Δp to 10 in our experiments. Following the method based on (11.5), SSSPs are computed over the newly added pivots to obtain the latest betweenness approximations (line 8). The current set of k highest ranking vertices $\hat{S}_k(t)$ is then extracted (line 9). This can be done via sorting or by any efficient order statistics algorithm. In lines 10–17, we evaluate the convergence criteria. This is based on the membership stability of $\hat{S}_k(t)$ across consecutive iterations. If the membership of this set remains unchanged over some number of consecutive iterations (we have used three in our experiments), we deem convergence to have occurred and terminate the algorithm. The speedup of the algorithm is directly proportional to the number of pivots used. The running time is $O(mp)$, where $p = \sum_t \Delta p$, i.e. the total number of pivots added over all iterations. We also point out that the convergence criteria can be tweaked in many ways to achieve a tradeoff between efficiency and accuracy. A much stricter criterion would be to terminate only if the absolute order of vertex rankings in the sets are identical over multiple iterations. Another adjustment would be to increase the number of iterations for which the members of $\hat{S}_k(t)$ must remain unchanged. In our experiments, we have relaxed the convergence criterion somewhat to achieve greater computational efficiency. This has proven adequate to achieve good accuracy. One can think of special cases where the convergence criterion will not be met. For example, consider a network of vertices connected in a ring. All vertices have the same betweenness values and the membership of $\hat{S}_k(t)$ be unstable across iterations. However such contrived scenarios are generally rare in real networks. We deem it fruitful to investigate the performance of our algorithm on popular network models and real-world data.

11.4 Experiments

We describe our experiments, starting with the evaluation metrics and networks used, followed by an analysis of the results.

11.4.1 Evaluation Metrics

We term vertices in S_k as relevant vertices. Our estimated set $\hat{S}_k$ is also of size k. Accuracy is evaluated using precision, which measures the proportion of relevant vertices returned in $\hat{S}_k$:

$$\text{prec} = \frac{|\hat{S}_k \cap S_k|}{k} . \tag{11.6}$$

If all vertices in $\hat{S}_k$ correspond exactly to those in S_k, precision is 1. Where precision is less than 1, $\hat{S}_k$ contains irrelevant vertices. In such a case, it is desired that such vertices are ranked low in $\hat{S}_k$. We evaluate this using average precision, which is commonly used in document retrieval tasks and emphasizes returning relevant documents earlier. In our context, vertices from S_k are relevant and should be returned earlier, i.e. ranked higher. Average precision can be computed as

$$\text{ave\_prec} = \sum_{i=1}^{k} \text{prec}(i) \times \Delta\text{rec}(i) , \tag{11.7}$$

where prec(i) is the precision at a cut-off rank position i of $\hat{S}_k$, i.e. $\text{prec}(i) = |\hat{S}_i \cap S_k|/i$. $\Delta\text{rec}(i)$ is the change in recall from position $i - 1$ to i whereby recall measures the proportion of relevant vertices included in the result set, i.e. $\text{rec}(i) = |\hat{S}_i \cap S_k|/k$. Note that average precision is upper bounded by precision at position k.

Using the two measures above we only evaluate the extent that relevant vertices are included in $\hat{S}_k$ and if they are ranked above any irrelevant vertices that are also included. We do not directly compare the rankings of $\hat{S}_k$ with S_k using any rank correlation metrics, since $\hat{S}_k$ is not a closed list guaranteed to have the same set of members as S_k. The inversion distance is also not very meaningful since pairs of vertices can be ordered correctly in $\hat{S}_k$ even though one or both vertices in each pair may be irrelevant.

11.4.2 Heterogeneity Measure

We have implemented the entropy-based measure to quantify the heterogeneity of the actual betweenness distributions for our various tested networks. The motivation here is to check for any correlation between the performance of the algorithm and the heterogeneity of the underlying betweenness distribution. The entropy-based measure has previously been advocated by Wu et al. [20] to quantify the heterogeneity of degree distributions. To derive the measure for betweenness distribution, first construct a histogram of betweenness values. The histogram bins are uniform in width and cover the entire range of betweenness values from the distribution being evaluated. Let b_i be the probability that a randomly chosen vertex will have a betweenness value that is covered by the ith bin. The entropy-based measure H is then defined as

$$H = -\sum_{i=1}^{B} b_i \ln b_i \ . \tag{11.8}$$

Small H values are indicative of heterogeneous betweenness distribution. The maximum value of H occurs when $b_i = 1/B$ for all bins, which corresponds to a uniform distribution. In our experiments, we have used 1,000 bins across all networks for computing H.

11.4.3 Networks

We apply our algorithm on various artificial and real-world networks. For evaluation, it is necessary to compute exact betweenness and derive S_k for each network. This limits our experiments to networks of small to medium sizes. For all networks, we process them as undirected and unweighted networks. Loops and multiple edges between vertex pairs are excluded.

We examine three popular types of artificial networks. Each network generated is specified to have exactly 1,000 vertices and roughly 10,000 edges. The actual edge count depends on the generation scheme specific to each network type. Efficient generation schemes are described in [3]. The network types are:

Random Such networks [10] are defined by the edge probability θ, where $0 < \theta < 1$. For each pair of vertices, an edge is independently formed with probability θ. In our experiments, we use $\theta = 0.02$ such that each random network has around 10,000 edges.

Small world (SW) This model was introduced by Watts and Strogatz [19]. The model starts with an initial ring of n vertices, with each vertex connected to its nearest 2d neighbors. Depending on the generation variant used, shortcut edges are then obtained by randomly and independently rewiring existing edges or by adding new random edges [15]. We use the latter. Five thousand random edges are added to the initial ring in which each vertex is connected to its nearest ten neighbors, i.e. $d = 5$.

Preferential Attachment (Pref. A.) Barabási and Albert [2] formulated a model for generating networks with heavy tailed degree distributions. In this model, vertices are added one at a time. The newly added vertex connects a fixed number of edges to existing vertices with probability proportional to the degree of the latter. We implement the model of Bollobás et al. [4].

In addition to artificial networks, we select several real-world networks of various origins and sizes for our experiments. We feel that this is a good representation of the complex networks popularly analyzed in the literature. The selected networks are:

Protein This is the protein interaction network for yeast. The data originates from Jeong et al. [12]. Each vertex corresponds to a protein while the edges represent protein-protein interactions.

Enron Enron emails [17] are used to construct a network of email users. Email users correspond to vertices. Two users are linked if they have communicated by email at least once.

Ticker Following the September 11th terrorist attacks, Corman et al. [8] compiled and transformed Reuters ticker news articles into a network text representation. Words appearing in noun phrases are represented as vertices. Words appearing together in the same noun phrase or consecutively within a sentence are linked via edges.

Internet Autonomous Systems (AS) An AS is effectively a set of routers under a single administration. Routing in a network of ASes is coordinated by the Border Gateway Protocol. There are several types of ASes, e.g. ISPs, end-users; and relationships between ASes, e.g. provider-customer. AS networks can be obtained from [7]. We have used a sample network from 1 January 2007.

DBLP DBLP [13] is an on-line database of computer science publications with the authorship and publication details of hundreds of thousands of articles. The records

Table 11.1 Vertex and edge counts for the selected real-world networks

	Protein	Enron	Ticker	AS	DBLP
Vertices	1,458	5,312	13,308	24,013	75,207
Edges	1,993	15,578	148,034	49,332	202,291

span many years, with information in the recent years being more complete. We have constructed a collaboration network for the year 2006. Authors are represented as vertices while edges are formed between all authors who have co-authored publication(s). For each real world network, we extract the largest connected component to work on. This ensures that all pivots contribute properly to betweenness computation and that none fall in isolated small components. Generally, when processing a network with multiple components, the proper procedure is to extract the components and process each individually. Table 11.1 shows the number of vertices and edges corresponding to the largest component of each network.

11.5 Results

11.5.1 Artificial Networks

Two scenarios are considered: extraction of the 10 and 20 highest ranked vertices in terms of betweenness. We specify `max_pivots` to be 1,000 and add pivots in batches of 10. For each scenario in each artificial network type, we conduct 20 trials whereby each trial consists of a realization of the network type followed by the application of the algorithm. Results are averaged over the 20 trials to obtain the mean precision (MP) and mean average precision (MAP), shown in Table 11.2.

The best performance is observed on the preferential attachment networks, where the MP is higher than 0.9 for both scenarios with almost equally high MAP. It is remarkable that these results are achieved using relatively few pivots. For example, to extract the 10 highest ranked vertices of preferential attachment networks, the algorithm requires just an average of 11 % of the vertices as pivots. This is well below the network size of 1,000 and implies substantial savings in computation time.

The algorithm performs less impressively on the small world and random networks, although accuracy and computational savings are still reasonable. Performance on these two types of networks is very similar. We note that as k is increased from 10 to 20, MP and MAP improvement is in the range of 10–20 %. However, this is at a cost of using many more pivots. This can be explained as follows: with larger k for these two network types, it becomes more difficult for the membership of $\hat{S}_k$ to stabilize early. Convergence is only achieved at larger iterations when more pivots have been added. The larger number of pivots in turn results in higher accuracy. Compared to the preferential attachment networks, both network types require many more pivots for the algorithm to converge: more than three times as many when $k = 10$ and more than four times when $k = 20$.

Table 11.2 Results for each scenario ($k = 10, 20$) in each artificial network type, with standard deviations enclosed in brackets. The best results for each k are in bold

k	Network type	% of vertices used as pivots	MP	MAP
10	Random	38.9 (17.8)	0.71 (0.13)	0.64 (0.16)
	SW	38.4 (15.9)	0.68 (0.16)	0.62 (0.19)
	Pref. A.	**11.0 (0.041)**	**0.91 (0.07)**	**0.91 (0.07)**
20	Random	65.5 (19.9)	0.81 (0.12)	0.79 (0.14)
	SW	69.7 (20.5)	0.85 (0.07)	0.82 (0.09)
	Pref. A.	**16.1 (0.069)**	**0.92 (0.04)**	**0.91 (0.05)**

For further analysis, we investigate how the betweenness distributions of the networks affect the difficulty of the extraction task. Figure 11.2 shows the histograms of true betweenness values from three sample networks, one from each network type. For numerical comparison of heterogeneity, the average H values of the true betweenness distribution over each network type are shown in Table 11.3.

For better visual comparison, the top 20 betweenness values for the preferential attachment network have been excluded in its histogram. The distributions of the random and small world networks appear fairly similar and Gaussian-like, while that of the preferential attachment network is heavily skewed with a tiny portion of vertices taking on very high betweenness values. Compared to the first two networks, the range of betweenness values is much more extreme (by comparing the horizontal scales). Analogous to the fact that extreme outliers are more easily detected in outlier detection problems, the extremity of the high-betweenness vertices results in them being extracted more readily by the algorithm. We can also arrive at the same insight by considering the earlier example of a network comprising of a ring of vertices. In such a network, all vertices have the same betweenness, i.e. a uniform betweenness distribution. It is clear that even with the maximum number of iterations of the algorithm, i.e. using all vertices in the network as pivots, higher betweenness vertices will not be surfaced since there are no extremities.

Table 11.3 provides a numerical quantification for Fig. 11.2. H values are significantly smaller for preferential attachment networks, indicating their betweenness distributions are much more heterogeneous than random and small world networks. The current results are intuitive. A heterogeneous distribution may have more extreme values, which leads to greater ease of extraction. However note that H is computed over the entire distribution, rather than just over the large betweenness values of interest. Hence extremity and heterogeneity does not have a perfect correlation.

Finally, we have ruled out the power-law distribution for the betweenness values of the preferential attachment network after plotting the cumulative distribution function on doubly logarithmic axes. The distribution type is left for future investigation.

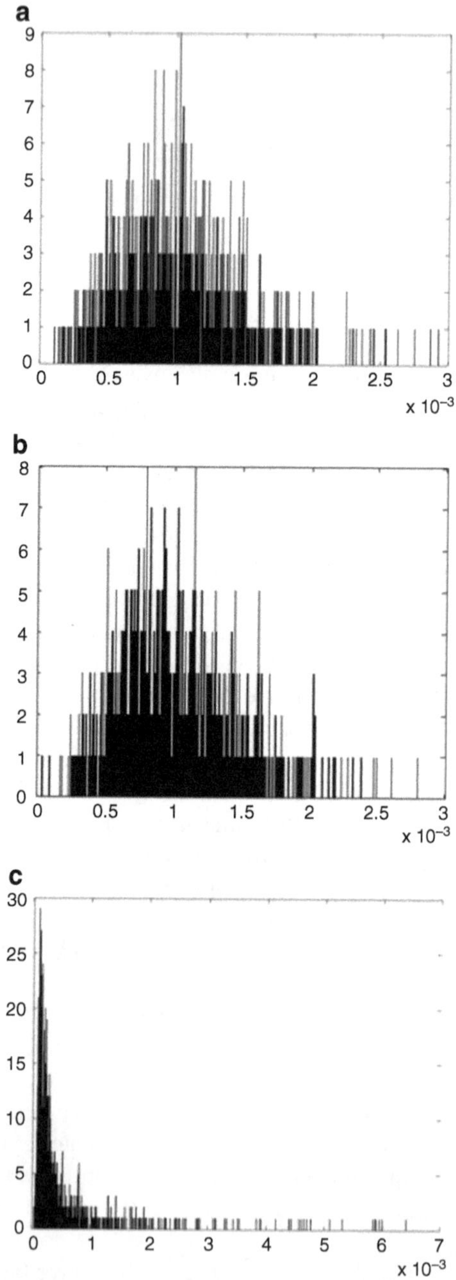

Fig. 11.2 Histograms of betweenness values for each artificial network type; that of the preferential attachment network appears significantly different. Networks: (**a**) Random, (**b**) Small world and (**c**) Preferential attachment

Table 11.3 Entropy-based heterogeneity values for each artificial network type (averaged over 20 trials) with standard deviations enclosed in brackets

Network type	H
Random	5.91 (0.067)
SW	5.93 (0.066)
Pref. A.	2.12 (0.13)

Table 11.4 Results for each scenario ($k = 10, 20$) in each real-world network, with standard deviations enclosed in brackets. The best results for each k are in bold

k	Network	% of vertices used as pivots	MP	MAP
10	Protein	6.79 (2.26)	0.96 (0.07)	0.96 (0.07)
	Enron	**1.62 (0.45)**	**0.98 (0.04)**	**0.97 (0.05)**
	Ticker	1.32 (0.34)	0.81 (0.10)	0.78 (0.13)
	AS	0.52 (0.32)	0.90 (0.05)	0.90 (0.05)
	DBLP	0.23 (7.31E−4)	0.73 (0.12)	0.69 (0.14)
20	Protein	15.43 (4.73)	0.90 (0.07)	0.90 (0.07)
	Enron	**2.56 (0.77)**	**0.92 (0.03)**	**0.92 (0.04)**
	Ticker	1.71 (0.59)	0.86 (0.05)	0.85 (0.06)
	AS	0.67 (0.20)	0.92 (0.03)	0.91 (0.04)
	DBLP	0.34 (9.57e−4)	0.83 (0.07)	0.80 (0.09)

11.5.2 Real-World Networks

We consider the same scenarios of extracting the top 10 and 20 vertices. For each network, ten trials of the algorithm are conducted whereby trials differ due to the random selection of pivots. Algorithm parameters are identical to those used for the artificial networks. Results are averaged over the ten trials and shown in Table 11.4. Excellent accuracies are obtained, with both MP and MAP above 0.8 for all network scenarios except the co-authorships network with $k = 10$. However, in this scenario the mean percentage of vertices used as pivots is extremely low compared to the network size, i.e. 0.23 %. More pivots can certainly be used to improve accuracy (this can be done by adjusting the convergence criterion). To illustrate this, we conduct separate experiments and plot the MP and MAP per iteration as the number of pivots is increased to 500. Figure 11.3 shows the plots for the DBLP co-authorships and Ticker news networks. All other networks exhibit fairly similar plots. The MP and MAP scores improve approximately monotonically as the number of pivots is increased. The approximate monotonicity is reflected in the kinks of the curves. The rate of improvement slows for larger number of pivots. At 500 pivots (0.66 % of network size), MP of 0.86 is achieved for the co-authorships network.

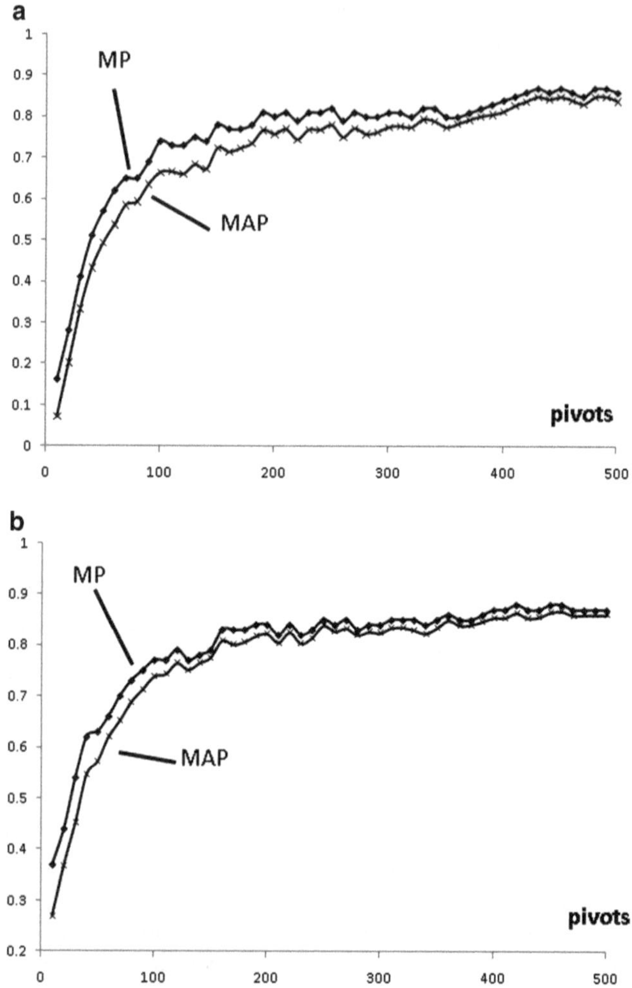

Fig. 11.3 MP/MAP of two real-world networks with increasing pivots, where $k = 10$. Each point is the respective MP/MAP score over ten trials. Networks: (**a**) DBLP and (**b**) Ticker

Returning to Table 11.4, it can be seen that for the protein interaction, Enron email and internet AS networks, the algorithm achieves MP and MAP scores of 0.9 and above. Across the board, these impressive results have been achieved at very low pivot counts relative to network size.

Similar to the case for the artificial networks, the number of pivots required for convergence increases at higher k, but the increase is generally less than linear, except for the protein interaction network. Further research can be conducted to explore the relationship between k and the number of pivots required for networks with different characteristics.

Table 11.5 Entropy-based heterogeneity values for each real-world network

Network type	H
Protein	2.57
Enron	1.26
Ticker	0.86
AS	0.38
DBLP	1.20

Table 11.5 indicates that the real world networks have various degrees of heterogeneity in their true betweenness distributions, although all H values are fairly low. Comparing Tables 11.4 and 11.5, there does not seem to be any obvious correlation between accuracies, efficiencies and heterogeneity measures. For example, while the protein network appears to have the least heterogeneous distribution, the algorithm still achieves good accuracies on it. However we note that the proportion of vertices required as pivots is the largest amongst all networks, with more than four times the proportion as the nearest competitor, the Enron network. Hence we are apt to conclude that the relative lack of heterogeneity is being compensated for with the use of more vertices.

11.6 Further Comparison

In previous experiments on each network, we have tabulated the percentage of vertices used as pivots by our algorithm. Implicitly, comparisons of both efficiency and accuracy are being made with the exact algorithm (akin to a baseline) described in Sect. 11.2.1. The baseline uses all vertices as pivots and achieves perfect accuracies at a high cost. For example, extracting the top 10 vertices from the Enron network requires just 1.62 % of vertices as pivots, and implies an efficiency improvement of more than 98 % over the baseline. This comes at a trade off of a 2 % drop in MP.

In this section, we conduct further experiments with real-world networks for explicit comparisons against a recent competitive method [14], which we term the sub-graph technique. This samples a large network greedily such that the extracted sub-graph contains the set of nodes with high betweennness and other centralities. To extract the high betweenness nodes, the exact betweenness computation algorithm is then applied on the sub-graph.

Denote n_g as the number of vertices and m_g as the number of edges in the sub-graph. For undirected networks, extracting S_k with the sub-graph technique then has a computational complexity of $O(g + n_g m_g)$ where the first term g represents the cost of sub-graph construction. Larger sub-graphs have higher probabilities of containing S_k and hence higher accuracies.

In this experiment, we compare the extraction accuracies given the same computation cost for our proposed and the sub-graph techniques. This is done by fixing the sub-graph size for each real world network such that the computational

Table 11.6 Average sub-graph sizes used

k	Network	n_g	m_g
10	Protein	403.1 (0.74)	489.9 (0.74)
	Enron	579 (0)	2,341.9 (2.85)
	Ticker	838 (0)	31,305.7 (27.77)
	AS	1,152 (0)	5,550.6 (0.7)
	DBLP	5,114 (0)	7,074.8 (3.71)
20	Protein	618.2 (0.42)	728.4 (1.26)
	Enron	780 (0)	2,719.5 (0.97)
	Ticker	998 (0)	33,993.4 (10.94)
	AS	1,344 (0)	6,077.7 (0.48)
	DBLP	6,091 (0)	8,510 (3.33)

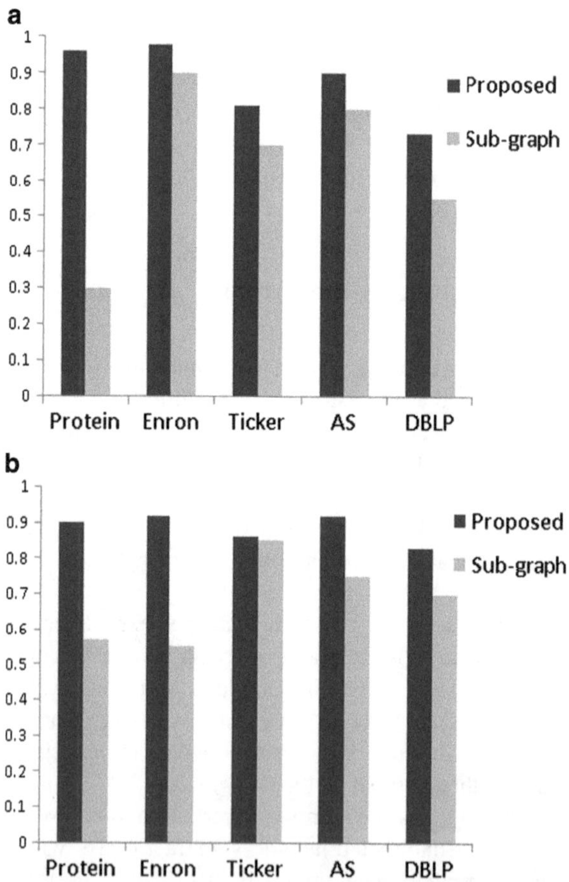

Fig. 11.4 Mean Precision (MP) over ten trials of our proposed and the sub-graph techniques given equal computation costs, for (**a**) $k = 10$ and (**b**) $k = 20$

cost equals that incurred by our algorithm in Sect. 11.5.2, i.e. $O(n_g m_g) = O(mp)$. We have ignored $O(g)$ which is small and hence given a slight advantage to the sub-graph technique. The average dimensions of the sub-graphs used are shown in Table 11.6 in Appendix 2. Figure 11.4 compares the mean precision over ten

Table 11.7 Detailed accuracy results for the sub-graph technique

k	Network	MP	MAP
10	Protein	0.3 (0)	0.3 (0)
	Enron	0.9 (0)	0.9 (0)
	Ticker	0.7 (0)	0.68 (2.3E − 3)
	AS	0.8 (0)	0.78 (0)
	DBLP	0.55 (0.05)	0.53 (0.03)
20	Protein	0.57 (0.05)	0.4 (0.04)
	Enron	0.55 (0)	0.4 (2.6E − 3)
	Ticker	0.85 (0)	0.79 (2.8E − 3)
	AS	0.75 (0)	0.74 (0)
	DBLP	0.7 (0)	0.58 (6.7E − 3)

trials for both techniques on each real world network. Detailed numerical results are shown in Table 11.7 in Appendix 2.

Figure 11.4 shows that our proposed technique consistently outperforms the sub-graph technique for each real-world network. We are apt to conclude that given the same computation cost, the former extracts S_k with higher precision. In particular, the difference in MP is largest for the protein network. For $k = 10$ on this network, the sub-graph technique performs poorly. Performance may have been impacted by the fact that the protein network is a much less heterogeneous network, as compared with the other networks.

Lastly, in terms of inclusion of high betweenness vertices, the sub-graph technique has been shown previously [14] to outperform sampling schemes based on depth-first search, breadth-first search and random walk. Hence by extension, our proposed technique outperforms these other techniques as well in terms of accuracy.

11.7 Conclusion

Betweenness computation is a notoriously expensive problem. Prior to the current work, it was not clear how the highest betweenness vertices of complex networks could be extracted accurately and efficiently in a systematic manner. Much work in the literature has focused on the efficient computation of betweenness values for vertices.

In this paper, we have developed a novel algorithm to accomplish the mentioned extraction task, using well known observations of the pivot method. The algorithm performs with excellent results on preferential attachment networks and various real-world networks. It performs less well, but still achieves reasonable results, on random and small world networks.

At the next stage, it is useful to investigate in detail the relationship between precision, number of pivots and the convergence criterion. The objective will be to provide hints to the potential user about the expected runtime and pivots required to obtain some required level of precision. This will enhance the utility of the algorithm in real applications.

Appendix 1: Hoeffding's Theorem

For independently identically distributed random variables $X_1, \ldots X_k$, where $0 \leq X_i \leq M$ for $i = 1 \ldots k$, and an arbitrary $\xi \geq 0$, the following probability bound applies:

$$\Pr\left(\left|\bar{X} - \mathrm{E}\left[\bar{X}\right]\right| \geq \xi\right) \leq \exp\left(-2k\left(\frac{\xi}{M}\right)^2\right), \tag{11.9}$$

where $\bar{X} = (X_1 + \ldots + X_k)/k$ and $\mathrm{E}\left[\bar{X}\right]$ is the expected value of $\bar{X}$.

Appendix 2: Detailed Results for Sect. 12.6

Table 11.6 shows the average number of vertices and edges (over ten trials) contained in the sampled sub-graph for each real-world network. Applying the exact algorithm on the sub-graph will incur a computation cost roughly equivalent to that incurred by our algorithm in Table 11.4. Standard deviations are enclosed in brackets. For each network, the required sub-graph dimensions increase with k as is intuitively expected.

Table 11.7 displays detailed MP and MAP results for the sub-graph technique. For each real-world network, ten trials are conducted. Standard deviations are enclosed in brackets.

References

1. Anthonisse, J.: The rush in a directed graph. Technical Reports BN 9/71, Stichting Mathematisch Centrum (1971)
2. Barabasi, A.L., Albert, R.: Emergence of scaling in random networks. Science **286**(5439), 509–512 (1999)
3. Batagelj, V., Brandes, U.: Efficient generation of large random networks. Phys. Rev. E **71**(3), 036113 (2005)
4. Bollobás, B., Riordan, O., Spencer, J., Tusnády, G.: The degree sequence of a scale-free random graph process. RSA Random Struct. Algorithms **18**, 279–290 (2001)
5. Brandes, U.: A faster algorithm for betweenness centrality. J. Math. Sociol. **2**(25), 163–177 (2001)
6. Brandes, U., Pich, C.: Centrality estimation in large networks. Int. J. Bifurc. Chaos **7**(17), 2303–2318 (2007)
7. CAIDA: The CAIDA AS relationship dataset. http://www.caida.org/data/active/as-relationships (2007)
8. Corman, S.R., Kuhn, T., Mcphee, R.D., Dooley, K.J.: Studying complex discursive systems. Hum. Commun. Res. **28**(2), 157–206 (2002)
9. Freeman, L.C.: A set of measures of centrality based on betweenness. Sociometry **40**(1), 35–41 (1977)
10. Gilbert, E.N.: Random graphs. Ann. Math. Stat. **30**, 1141–1144 (1959)

11. Hoeffding, W.: Probability inequalities for sums of bounded random variables. J. Am. Stat. Assoc. **301**(58), 713–721 (1963)
12. Jeong, H., Mason, S.P., Barabasi, A.L., Oltvai, Z.N.: Lethality and centrality in protein networks. Nature **411**, 41–42 (2001)
13. Ley, M.: The DBLP computer science bibliography. http://www.informatik.uni-trier.de/~ley/db
14. Maiya, A.S., Berger-Wolf, T.Y.: Online sampling of high centrality individuals in social networks. In: Zaki, M.J., Yu, J.X., Ravindran, B. Pudi, V. (eds.) Advances in Knowledge Discovery and Data Mining, 14th Pacific-Asia Conference, PAKDD 2010, Hyderabad. Proceedings. Part I, Lecture Notes in Computer Science, vol. 6118, pp. 91–98. Springer, Berlin (2010)
15. Newman, M.E.J., Watts, D.J.: Renormalization group analysis of the small-world network model. Phys. Lett. A **263**, 341–346 (1999)
16. Okamoto, K., Chen, W., yang Li, X.: Ranking of closeness centrality for large-scale social networks. In: Proceedings of the 2nd Annual International Workshop on Frontiers in Algorithmics, 2008, pp. 186–195. Springer-Verlag Berlin, Heidelberg (2008)
17. Shetty, J., Adibi, J.: Enron Dataset. http://www.isi.edu/~adibi/Enron/Enron.htm (2004)
18. Tarjan, R.E.: Data Structures and Network Algorithms. Society for Industrial and Applied Mathematics, Philadelphia (1983)
19. Watts, D.J., Strogatz, S.H.: Collective dynamics of 'small-world' networks. Nature **393**, 440–442 (1998)
20. Wu, J., Tan, Y.J., Deng, H.Z., Zhu, D.Z.: A new measure of heterogeneity of complex networks based on degree sequence. In: International Conference on Complex Systems. Springer, Berlin/New York (2006)

Chapter 12
Cross-Domain Analysis of the Blogosphere for Trend Prediction

Patrick Siehndel, Fabian Abel, Ernesto Diaz-Aviles, Nicola Henze, and Daniel Krause

Abstract In the recent years blogs became an important part of the web. New technologies like smartphones emerged that enable blogging at any time and make blogs more up-to-date than ever before. Due to their high popularity they are a valuable source of information regarding public opinions about all kind of topics. Blog postings that refer to products are of particular interest for companies to adjust marketing campaigns or advertisement. In this article we compare the blogging characteristics of two different domains: the music and the movie domain. We investigate how chatter from the blogosphere can be used to predict the success of products. We analyze and identify typical patterns of blogging behavior around the release of a product, point out methods for extracting features from the blogosphere and show that we can exploit these features to predict the monetary success of movies and music with high accuracy.

12.1 Introduction

In the last years weblogs or blogs evolved from being just online diaries to an important part of the web. The topics discussed in these blogs vary from politics to leisure time activities [26]. Today, the blogosphere is continuously growing and becoming more and more popular. New trends like the use of mobile devices enable bloggers to update their blogs every time. The content generated in the blogosphere is very valuable for a multitude of applications. The blogosphere follows its own

P. Siehndel (✉) · E. Diaz-Aviles · N. Henze · D. Krause
L3S Research Center, Leibniz University Hannover, Appelstr. 4, 30167 Hannover, Germany
e-mail: siehndel@L3S.de; diaz@L3S.de; henze@L3S.de; krause@L3S.de

F. Abel
Web Information Systems, Delft University of Technology, Mekelweg 4, 2628 Delft, The Netherlands
e-mail: f.abel@tudelft.nl

T. Özyer et al. (eds.), *The Influence of Technology on Social Network Analysis and Mining*, Lecture Notes in Social Networks 6, DOI 10.1007/978-3-7091-1346-2_12,

dynamics [8] and a deeper understanding of these dynamics promises advantages, for example, for marketing analysts who would like to study opinions on a particular product. Due to its actuality the blogosphere allows a real time tracking for the popularity or the sentiment related to a specific product. Specially online marketing campaigns which can be setup quickly would benefit from information about the popularity of a product close to the release date. Based on relations between the sales rank of products available at Amazon.com and the corresponding number of posts in the blogosphere [10] recent work shows that the analysis of blog data can potentially be used to predict the success of products [24]. However, previous studies focus on single domains and do not investigate how the corresponding approaches perform in other domains.

In this article, which details work presented in [1], we study and compare trend prediction based on blog analysis in the context of two different domains, the music and movie domain. We analyze how the blogosphere can be used to predict the success of movie and music products. In particular, we investigate the blog dynamics of both domains for certain time periods in the product life cycle such as the product release. We examine typical blogging behavior patterns for music albums and movies. Given more than 600,000 blog posts in the music and movie domain, we conduct experiments for predicting the blogging behavior within the blogosphere, i.e. we investigate whether it is possible to predict the amount of blog posts that talk about a certain product. Finally, we apply machine learning techniques to forecast the monetary success of music and movie products. Our main research questions are the following:

- Does the blogosphere show characteristic patterns within the domain of music and movies (Sect. 12.3)?
- Can identified characteristics be used to predict future posting behavior in the blogosphere (Sect. 12.4)?
- Is it possible to predict if a product is going to be a top or a flop product (Sect. 12.5)?
- Can identified characteristics be used to predict real world properties like monetary success of a music or movie product (Sect. 12.5)?

For all questions we elaborate the differences between the two considered domains. Further, we also partition the domains to see whether predictions for certain genres can be made more precisely or whether prediction is more precise for certain time periods within the life cycle of a product.

The article is organized as follows. In Sect. 12.2 we discuss related work. An analysis of the blog data set is presented in Sect. 12.3. The features used for our predictions are presented in Sect. 12.3.1. Section 12.3.2 outlines our evaluation framework for trend prediction in the blogosphere. The corresponding trend prediction experiments are presented in Sects. 12.4 and 12.5. Section 12.6 concludes our work and gives an outlook on future work.

12.2 Related Work

A challenge in blog data mining is the prediction of real world events from the behavior of the blogosphere. The first step towards this is to understand the characteristics and dynamics of the blogosphere. McGlohon et al. [20] point out that the temporal dynamics of blogs are very non-uniform and bursty. The blogging behavior depends on the network topology of the blogosphere, where some blog posting characteristics can be explained by cascading models [18]. Götz et al. [8] present a model that explains the topological and temporal characteristics of the blogosphere such as burstiness and power law like properties which can, for example, be observed for the popularity of posts and blogs over time. However, Götz et al. focus solely on the blogosphere itself, leaving the question open how the proposed models can be applied to draw conclusions on real world occasions.

Obradovic et al. [21] describe methods for identifying authorities inside the blogosphere and analyze how these evolve over time. Based on this, they present a methodology for gathering blog data of a specific domain. Glance et al. [7] present an approach for automated tracking of trends within the blogosphere and correlate these trends with real world events. Those findings are applied in *BlogPulse*,[1] a service that monitors popular news stories, text phrases, people, etc. based on recent blog posts available on the Web. The main focus of the platform and corresponding research work is automatic detection of events based on the blogosphere. Another example of a project monitoring the blogosphere is *blogscope*.[2] Blogscope allows users to analyze how specific topics are discussed inside the blogosphere.

The microblogging service Twitter[3] provides similar functionality and lists so-called trending topics,[4] a list of keywords which are most frequently used within the last hours, to support users in exploring discussions on these topics. With the advent of Twitter a variety of research activities started to investigate network structures and properties of the Twitter network [4, 16, 17]. Kwak et al. study how information spreads through the Twitter network [16] while Lerman and Gosh investigate how information spreads on Twitter in comparison to other social networking sites [17]. Furthermore, researchers start investigating the feasibility of Twitter-based early warning systems [25]. Weng et al. [28] describe how the link- and interaction structure on Twitter can be used to define communities. Based on these communities a model for the interestingness of hashtags is presented. Yang and Leskovec [29] use a time series clustering approach to study temporal patterns associated with social media content and how its popularity grows and fades over time. They uncover a small set of well defined shapes that the online content exhibit, after conducting a experimental evaluation on a huge collection of

[1] http://blogpulse.com

[2] http://www.blogscope.net/

[3] http://twitter.com

[4] http://search.twitter.com

microblogs from Twitter, blog posts and news media articles. Their contribution is a valuable exploratory analysis on the common temporal patterns in the attention and popularity of online content.

Compared to our contribution, all of the aforementioned approaches focus on detecting specific properties *within* the (micro-)blogosphere. None of the approaches focuses on predicting upcoming trends and relates them to monetary properties.

Gruhl et al. [9] formalize the notion of long-running *chatter* topics consisting recursively of *spike* topics generated by outside world events and show that there is a correlation between the number of posts related to some product and its sales performance at Amazon [10]. By using the posts about selected books and specifically spikes in the number of posts they forecast the trend of the corresponding *Amazon Sales Rank*.[5] Dhar and Chang [5] detect a correlation between social media chatter and the Amazon Sales Rank of music albums. However, in their analysis the authors do not only focus on features extracted from the blogosphere, but also include other sources such as reviews from mainstream news sites or MySpace friend connections of the music artists.

Recent work also considers opinions expressed in the blog postings. With *ARSA*, Liu et al. [19] describe a model for predicting the sales performance of movies based on the sentiment of blogs posts. They outline that the knowledge about the sentimental orientation of the blog posts has a positive effect on the precision of the predictions. The above mentioned previous works on trend prediction in the blogosphere focus on particular domains. Although the authors claim that approaches can be applied to other domains as well, a respective comparison of the trend prediction performance for different domains is missing. In this article, we close this gap. We analyze and compare blogosphere characteristics of two different domains and examine the trend prediction performance for both domains.

12.3 Characteristic Patterns in the Blogosphere

In this section we analyze the blogging behavior in the music and movie domain and reveal analogies and differences in the posting behavior of these domains. We mainly focus on characteristic patterns regarding the number of post per day related to a specific music album and movie respectively. The identified patterns further justify the features, which we will use in the forthcoming sections to predict the blogging behavior as well as the success of products.

As we are analyzing the correlation between the blogosphere with the success of music and movie products in the real world, we need some ground truth indicating the actual success of the products. In the music domain, we used the Amazon Sales Rank while the success of movies is measured by means of the daily box office

[5] http://www.amazon.com/gp/help/customer/display.html?nodeId=525376

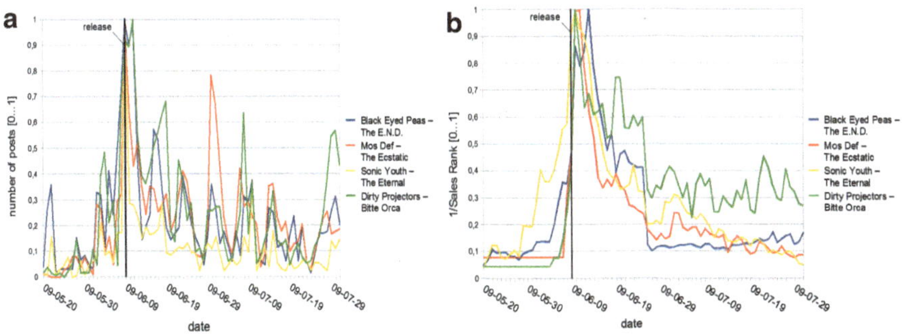

Fig. 12.1 Behavior of (**a**) number of blog posts about certain music albums and (**b**) the corresponding Amazon Sales Ranks over the time around the album releases

charts from *Box Office Mojo*.[6] In both domains we focused on the US market and thus considered only English blog posts.

An obvious feature for predicting the Sales Rank or the box office charts is the number of posts related to some specific movie or music product. In Fig. 12.1a, the number of posts related to four different music albums, all released on the 9th of June 2009, is plotted in the time period around the album release. For each album, the number of posts is normalized by the maximum number of posts related to the album. This was done in order to make the blogging characteristics of the different albums comparable. One can see that the daily number of posts related to the albums reaches a maximum around the release date of the albums. After the release of an album the number of posts becomes smaller with peaks that usually last for 1 or 2 days.

Figure 12.1b clarifies that there is a coherence between the number of posts and the Sales Rank evolution of the corresponding music albums sold by Amazon.com. The Sales Rank of albums reach a maximum a few days after the number of blog posts reached their maximum. This coherence leads to the idea, that the prediction of a product's sales rank based on the blogging behavior might be possible. Further, some of the peaks that appear in the blogosphere seem to occur in the plot of the sales rank evolution of the corresponding album as well. For example, on the 29th of June there is a peak in the number of blog posts related to the album "The Ecstatic" by Mos Def and 3 days after this peak in the blogosphere, the sales rank of the album improves as well.

Figure 12.2 shows the aggregated values of the number of posts and Sales Rank scores of 96 different music albums around their releases. The values for the Sales Rank and the number of posts have a daily temporal resolution. To consider each music album equally important, we normalized the number of posts and the Sales Rank scores before we calculated the average. The figure shows that the number of posts related to a certain music item and the Sales Rank of this music item

[6]http://boxofficemojo.com/

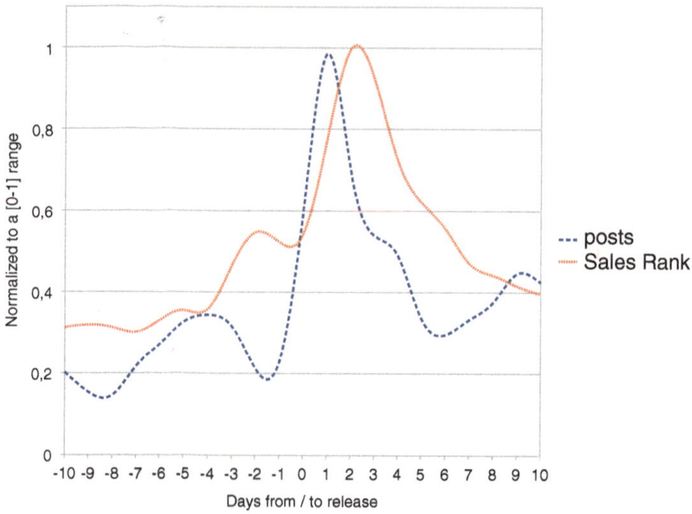

Fig. 12.2 Characteristic behavior of the Sales Rank and the number of blog mentions around release of music albums

are correlated. Both curves show a characteristic behavior around the release date. A monotonous increase of the number of blog posts and the Sales Rank can be observed before the release. In detail, the Sales Rank reaches the maximum 2 days after the release while the number of posts per day reaches its maximum 1 day after the release. Another characteristic within the music domain is illustrated in Fig. 12.3: the Sales Rank scores of different albums of the same artist rise if the artist releases a new album. For example, when the Dave Matthew Band released their album "Big Whiskey and the GrooGrux King", which was at the top of the Amazon sales ranking, also the old albums of the Dave Matthew Band improved regarding sales rank. We assume that an artist gains a lot of publicity around the release date of the new album which fosters the sales of other albums of that artist as well. Amazon, for example, bundles new and old albums as special promotion sets and sells them together.

The movie domain exhibits differences and similarities with the music domain regarding the coherence between blogging behavior and sales performance. Figure 12.4 shows how the average number of posts per day and the box office revenue of 23 movies around the release day of a movie. For the aggregation the number of posts and the box office values were normalized as done for Fig. 12.2. The curve shows that the number of posts related to the movies has two maximums: the first maximum is reached directly at the release day of the movie while the second maximum is reached 3 days after the release. The curve of the aggregated box office revenues for the movies shows a different characteristic around the release as the maximum is reached 1 day after the release. In the US, release days are usually Fridays.

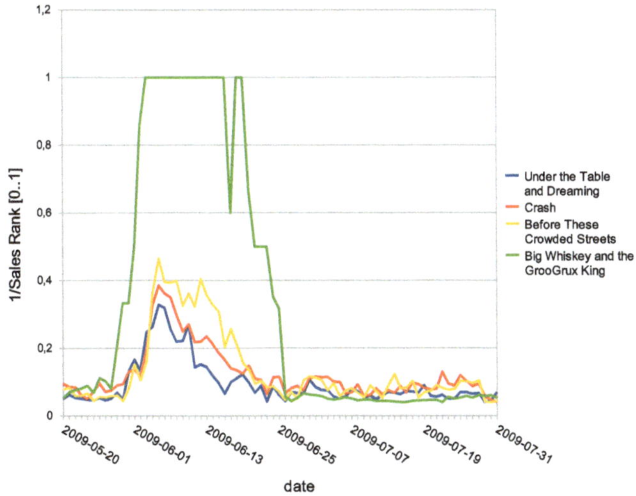

Fig. 12.3 Sales Rank of different albums from the Dave Matthew Band around the release of their new album

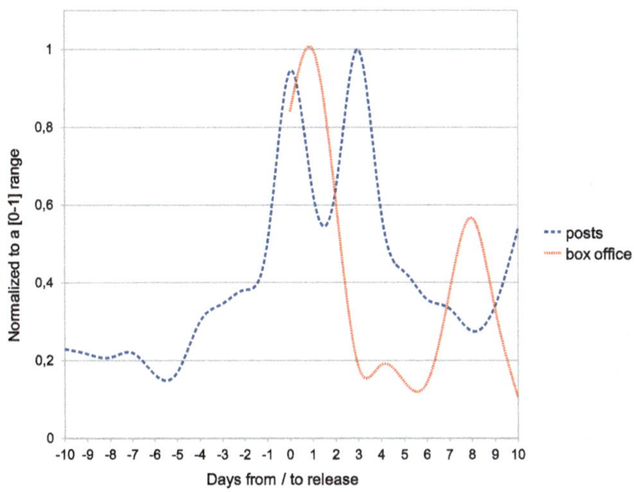

Fig. 12.4 Characteristic behavior of blog posts and box office revenues around release of movies

A comparison of the characteristics in the music domain (see Fig. 12.2) and movie domain (see Fig. 12.4) shows that both domains have a significant increase of blog posts (*spike*) shortly before the release. However, for the movie domain, there exists another spike after the release possibly caused by people who are writing reviews in their blog about the movies.

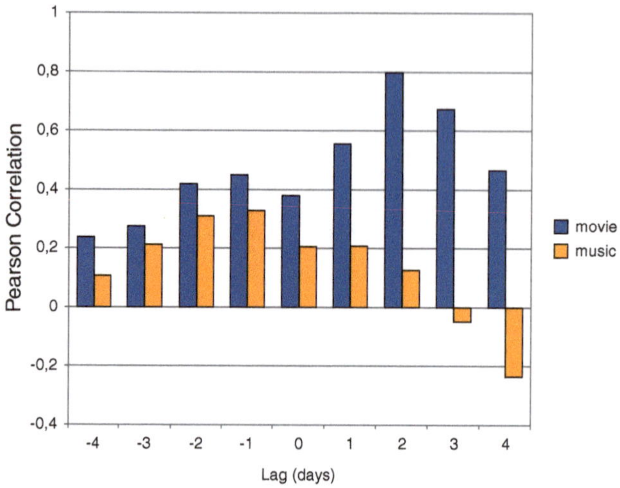

Fig. 12.5 Correlation between number of blog posts and box office revenue/Sales Rank for different lags of time

Figure 12.5 shows the average Pearson Correlation between the amount of posts per day related to some movie/album with the box office revenue/Sales Rank respectively. Within the music domain, the highest average correlation is reached with a lag of -1 day, i.e. the blogosphere is 1 day faster than the corresponding Sales Rank. For the movie domain, there is also a local maximum for the correlation with a time-lag of -1 day. However, the maximum correlation is obtained between box office revenue and the amount of posts per day with a lag of 2 days. Given the decreasing number of blog posts and increasing box office stats on the weekend depicted in Fig. 12.4, it seems that customers go to the cinemas on the weekend to watch the released movies and write about them on the forthcoming Monday as the number of posts shows a maximum after the weekend.

In summary, the time-lag between the sales performance and the (first) spike in the blogosphere motivates our idea to predict the sales performance of products in the music *and* movie domain based on the articles related to these products.

12.3.1 Features for Trend Prediction

The most promising features for trend predictions are based on the number of posts related to a specific product. For the identification of such posts we perform entity recognition by simple pattern matching, i.e. we identify blogs relevant to a given artist or music album by searching for blog posts that mention the artist name and album titles respectively. Hence, we only considered music albums and movies where the chance of ambiguity was very low. For example, we did not consider

Table 12.1 Number of posts for different methods to identify relevant posts for a period of 73 days and 275 albums

	Sum	Average	Max per day and artist
Artist in description	36,315,270	1,802	190,302
Artist in title	13,465,086	668	135,502
Title in description	214,030,858	10,622	521,525
Title in title	28,226,936	1,400	185,552
Artist and title in description	671,453	33.3	3,184
Artist and title in title	147,422	7.3	1,211

albums of the artist *Pink* as the chances to retrieve blog posts that mention the color *pink* are high. The number of relevant posts differs widely between the different albums. This is caused by the differences in the popularity of the artists. However, the name of the artist or the album has an impact on the number of identified posts. We reduced the impact of that problem by not looking at albums for which the number of posts was obviously too high and we also do not look at artists for which we found too little relevant posts. Table 12.1 gives an overview for the posts per day based on the different ways to identify relevant posts.

This table shows the results for 276 different albums which we analyzed. When just looking at the artist name or the title of a album we identify too many irrelevant posts. For example, some titles of music albums such as "back in business" are phrases that are likely to appear also in the description of blog posts which are not related to the music item. Nevertheless, even though the accuracy of such simple entity recognition strategies might be low, the number of posts identified via these different strategies are valuable features. For example, a peak regarding the number of blog posts that mention "back in business" might still be a good indicator and therewith an important feature for predicting the monetary success of the corresponding album.

12.3.1.1 Features for the Music Domain

We used the following features extracted from the blogosphere to characterize the music albums on a particular day:

- *F1:* number of posts where the *album title* appears in the main blog article or title of the blog post.
- *F2:* number of posts where the *artist name* appears in the main article or title of the blog post.
- *F3:* number of posts where the *artist name and album title* appear in the main article or title of the blog post.

Hence, for each music album and each day we extracted three types of lightweight blogosphere features. In addition to the features generated by counting blog posts that match a search query, we also extracted the following features of music albums:

- *F4:* (top level) *genre* as categorized by Amazon.com.
- *F5:* number of days when the music album will be or was released (*temporal distance to release date*).

The genre was applied as there might be differences between the blog posting behavior of bloggers who are listening to different kinds of music. As shown in Fig. 12.1b there are spikes for number of blog posts and the Amazon Sales Rank around the release date. Hence, we also modeled the temporal distance to the release of the music album as a feature. In some experiments, we also included the knowledge about the previous Sales Rank of a music item:

- *F6:* Sales Rank of Album for the last days.

12.3.1.2 Features for the Movie Domain

In the movie domain we generated features also by exploiting the metadata related to the popularity of a blog as well as the type of the blogs. Further, we computed, given the title of a movie, tf/idf scores for each post based on the Lucene scoring function.[7] The tf/idf score models the relevance of the blog post for the given query (the title of the movie). For the different features, we created *bins*, i.e. we discretized the popularity and tf/idf scores, assigned blog posts to these bins and counted how many posts were assigned to a specific bin on a specific day. In summary, we exploited the following features for the movie domain.

- *F7:* number of posts where the *movie title* appears in the main blog article.
- *F8:* number of posts where the *movie title* appears in the main blog article with specific indegree, i.e. number of incoming links. We discretized the indegree into five bins ranging from less than ten incoming links to more than 10,000 incoming links.
- *F9:* number of posts where the *movie title* appears in the main blog article of a blog with a specific popularity ranking. Given the Spinn3r (see Chap. 12.3.2) tier groups organized according to their internal *Weblog Influence Ranking*,[8] we assigned the blog posts according to the influence rank of the blog to six different groups.
- *F10:* number of posts where the *movie title* appears in the main blog article with some specific tf/idf score. We discretized the tf/idf into five bins ranging from less than 0.1 to more than 0.5.

---

[7] http://lucene.apache.org/java/2_4_0/scoring.html

[8] http://blog.spinn3r.com/2007/10/announcing-spin.html

In line with the music domain, we additionally exploited the temporal distance to the release of the movie as a feature (*F11*) and for some experiments also the precise box office scores (*F12*). For the features *F1–F3, F6, F7–F10 and F12* we used a sliding window technique: we applied not only the values of the most recent day, for which blog data is available, but we generated the features for a time span, the five most recent days.

12.3.2 Evaluation Procedure for Trend Prediction

The data set was obtained from *Spinn3r*.[9] For our analysis in the music domain we crawled blog posts published from May 20th to July 31st 2009 and for the experiments in the movie domain we gathered posts from October 1st to December 31st 2008. Overall the data set contains over 100 million blog posts from various sources releated to all kind of topics. For each post, Spinn3r provides the content and title of the post together with additional meta data like the source of the post, the language, and the number of ingoing links from other posts.

For the experiments, all posts where indexed using Lucene.[10] This index contains the text and the title of the post itself, and other metadata which could be used as features for predictions, like the ranking of the blog where the posts was published. Overall the size of the index is about 750 GB. After the indexing we filtered the posts and selected the ones which are relevant for our predictions and for further processing. The approach for the filtering is done in a lightweight way. For our experiments a post was counted as relevant, if it contains specific words. In Sect. 12.3.1 the features which were used to identify posts are described. In future work one could also use NLP techniques to improve the identification of relevant posts.

The complete procedure for the trend prediction task consists of the following steps:

- Crawling: The actual crawling is done by Spinn3r. We used the API provided by Spinn3r to download the blog posts and additional meta data such as timestamps.
- Indexing: We used Lucene to index the posts based on their textual content.
- Filtering: For the identification of relevant posts, we used Lucene queries to find posts which contain words related to specific products.
- Feature Extraction: Based on the identified posts we calculated features for trend prediction.
- Trend Prediction: The prediction task itself was done using different machine learning algorithms from Weka.[11]

---

[9]http://www.spinn3r.com/

[10]http://lucene.apache.org/

[11]http://www.cs.waikato.ac.nz/ml/weka/

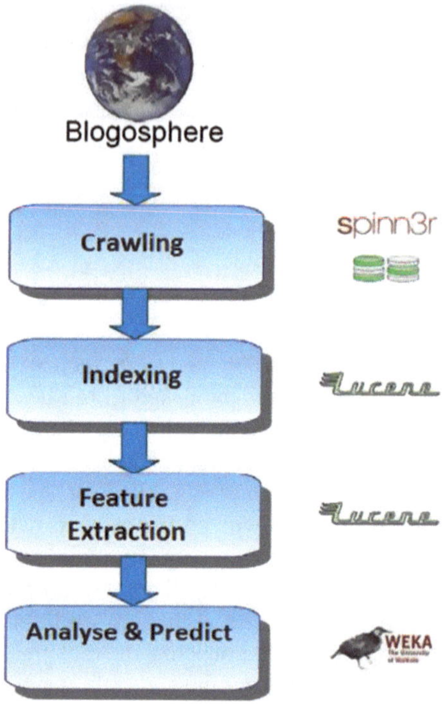

Fig. 12.6 Evaluation procedure used for trend prediction

Figure 12.6 shows the schematic design of our framework and the steps done for predicting trends.

12.4 Predicting Posting Behavior in the Blogosphere

In our first set of trend prediction experiments we focus on the posting behavior within the blogosphere. In particular, the main questions we answer in this section are the following: (1) is it possible to predict trends regarding the number of blog posts related to some item in the music or movie domain based on the related blog posts and (2) which features are most appropriate to predict these trends in the different domains?

12.4.1 Experimental Setup

We define the problem of trend prediction as a three class problem having the classes *raise*, *fall* and *stay*. We used three classes because, from our point of view, a relative small change in the number of posts per day should not be described as a *changed trend*. The trend class for a specific day is thus given as follows.

$$trend_x = \begin{cases} raise, & \text{if } post_x > post_{x-1} * \alpha, \\ fall, & \text{if } post_x < post_{x-1} * \frac{1}{\alpha}, \\ stay, & \text{else} \end{cases} \tag{12.1}$$

Where $post_x$ contains the number of posts on day x and $post_{x-1}$ contains the number of posts on day $x - 1$. With the value α we can adjust how changes regarding the number of posts per day are rated. For our experiments we set the weight α to 1.1.

For our predictions we focus on the number of posts around the release of the album or the premiere of the movie. This time period is the most interesting as it bears the highest dynamics: long time after or before the release the number of related posts is typically small and uniform so that for the majority of days the trend class would be *stay*.

For predicting the trend as described before we used different machine learning algorithms available in Weka, namely Naive Bayes [13], RBF Network [23], SMO [22], Decision Table [15], OneR [12], BFTree [6], LADTree [11] and SimpleCart [3].

The number of posts related to some movie or music item was represented using a sliding window. We choose to provide the normalized amount of posts for the last 10 days for the algorithms. The amount for each day was then used as a feature, i.e. the number of posts per day was normalized as follows.

$$post_{x,norm} = \frac{post_x}{\sum_{i=0}^{9} post_{x-i}} \tag{12.2}$$

Here, $post_x$ is the number of posts on day x. Due to the sliding window and normalization we rather focus on characteristic patterns than on absolute post counts. By using this sliding window technique we multiply the amount of provided features by the number of days we want to observer with the sliding window. We performed a ten-folded cross validation to evaluate the performance of the trend prediction algorithms.

12.4.2 Metrics

As metrics for measuring the performance of the trend prediction, we utilized precision and recall. In general, precision is the fraction of correct predicted instances for one class among those that the algorithm believes to belong to this class. The precision can be interpreted as percentage of correct predictions or the exactness of the used algorithm.

Table 12.2 Percentage of correct predictions. Period: 10 days before and after release (music domain)

Naive bayes	RBF network	SMO	Decision table	OneR	BFTree	LADTree	SimpleCart
44.24	48.24	53.76	61.90	54.88	58.52	56.64	60.65

Table 12.3 Precision and recall for predicting with the Decision Table algorithm whether the amount of blog posts related to a product will rise, fall or stay (music domain)

	Precision	Recall
Raise	0.638	0.656
Fall	0.607	0.785
Stay	0.000	0.000

$$precision = \frac{number\ of\ correct\ predictions}{number\ of\ predictions} \tag{12.3}$$

Recall is computed as the fraction of correct predicted instances among all instances that actually belong to the relevant class. Recall denotes the proportion of class instances that were identified correctly and describes the completeness of the prediction.

$$recall = \frac{number\ of\ correct\ predictions\ for\ class\ c}{number\ of\ class\ members\ in\ class\ c} \tag{12.4}$$

12.4.3 Results: Predicting Posting Behavior in the Music Domain

For the predictions within the music domain the machine learning algorithms exploit the same set of features, namely *F1–F3* as described in Sect. 12.3.1. By exploiting only features extracted from the blogosphere we can predict the future behavior of the blogosphere regarding music albums with a precision that goes beyond randomly guessing whether the number of posts will raise, fall, or stay at the same level.

The results are shown in Table 12.2. The best algorithm was Decision Table with a precision of 61.9 %. The most important feature was F3, and particularly the number of posts about the music album published 1 day before the day, for which the trend should be predicted. The results for precision and recall for the different types of trends are shown in Table 12.3.

Table 12.4 Percentage of correct predictions for the period of 10 days before and after the release of a movie

Naive bayes	RBF network	SMO	Decision table	OneR	BFTree	LADTree	SimpleCart
47.73	53.86	59.77	50.23	47.95	53.41	51.82	54.77

While precision for raise and fall does not differ significantly, the recall of instances classified as fall is higher which can be explained by the patterns observed in Sect. 12.3: an increase in the number of blog posts happens often as part of a sudden increase, for example, around the release of a music album, whereas a decrease evolves, on average, slower. The class *stay* is not predicted by the algorithm which is due to the fact that less than 10 % of the instances belong to this class. Due to the small amount of instances belonging to the class *stay*, the algorithm did not find characteristic patterns for this class. The Decision Table algorithm tries to optimize the overall performance of the predictions and therefore learned conditions/rules in a way that did not allow the algorithm to predict *stay* based on the given set of features. Hence, here we analyze the average performance of the algorithms over all classes and therefore aim to optimize the average performance rather than focusing on specific classes and certain characteristics such as predicting spikes as investigated by Gruhl et al. [9]. In other scenarios, a company might be just interested in special events such as spikes and therefore would need to optimize the accuracy for the class *raise*. Our results show that different algorithms might be useful when focusing on different tasks. One example is the overall performance of the Naive Bayes algorithm described in Table 12.2. Considering the overall performance this algorithm is the worst, but when just looking at the performance for the class *stay* this algorithms performs best with an Precision of 0.211 and a Recall of 0.214. When focusing just on one special event or class it would be also useful to treat the problem as a two class problem instead of three.

12.4.4 Results: Predicting Posting Behavior in the Movie Domain

The results for the prediction of the trend for the movie domain are shown in Table 12.4. The best algorithm for this setup was the support vector machine SMO with around 60 % correct predictions. All algorithms exploit features that are solely based on the blogosphere (namely *F7–F9*). The most important feature is the relative number of posts containing the title of the movie (*F7*).

The precision and recall of the different classes are displayed in Table 12.5. It is interesting to see that a *raise* in the number of posts is harder to predict than a decrease (*fall*) which can possibly be explained by spikes that raise fast and unpredictable but decrease rather slow and predictable.

Table 12.5 Precision and recall for predicting with the SMO algorithm whether the amount of blog posts related to a product will rise, fall or stay (movie domain)

	Precision	Recall
Raise	0.294	0.234
Fall	0.478	0.257
Stay	0.604	0.834

12.4.5 Synopsis

The results presented in this section show that (1) it is possible to predict trends within the blogosphere. By using only features extracted from the blogosphere as input for traditional machine learning algorithms such as Naive Bayes or Decision Tables, the precisions for predicting whether more, less, or a similar number of people will publish blog posts about a particular movie or music album is around 60 %. It is thus more than 20 % higher than if one would randomly guess the trend. Further, (2) for both domains the number of posts related to the movie or music album was the most important feature. In particular, regarding the music domain, the best strategy was to take the relative number of blog posts that mention the album title *and* artist name in the main article or title of the blog post. For the movie domain the most important feature was the relative number of posts containing the title of the movie at the actual day. This shows that the most important features for our predictions are the features which are timely very close to the day for which the trend should be predicted.

12.5 Predicting Sales Performance Based on Blogging Characteristics

In the previous sections we identified characteristic patterns in the blogosphere for the music and movie domains. We presented strategies for extracting features from the blogosphere that serve as input for machine learning algorithms to successfully predict the posting behavior within both domains. In this section we examine whether our trend prediction approaches are also applicable to forecast the actual sales performance of music and movie products.

We measure the sales performance by means of the Amazon Sales Rank and the box office revenue as described in Sect. 12.3. Figure 12.7 shows how both measures, on average, evolve over time after the release of a music album and movie respectively.

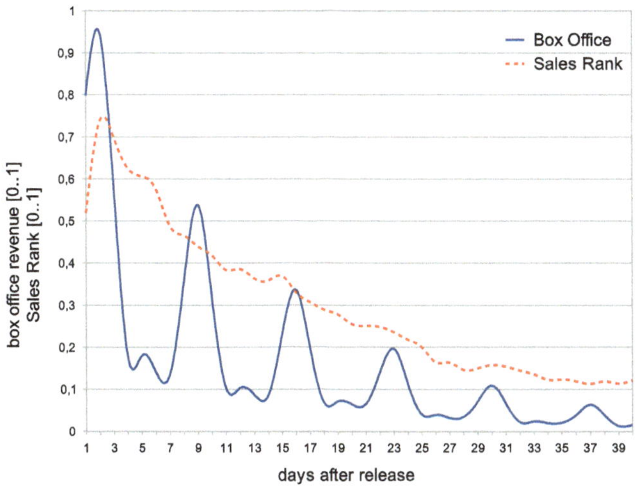

Fig. 12.7 Average box office revenue and Amazon Sales Rank after the release of a movie and music album respectively

The average sales performance of cinema movies drops clearly after the release. However, there exist regular peaks: people seem to go to the cinema rather on the weekends than weekdays. By contrast, the average sales performances of music albums decreases more slowly and does not follow regular patterns correlated with certain weekdays.

12.5.1 Experimental Setup

Given the data set as described in Sect. 12.3, the feature sets defined in Sect. 12.3.1 as well as the machine learning algorithms used in the previous section, we examine the quality of the trend prediction approaches with respect to three research questions.

1. Given two products and the corresponding features extracted from the blogosphere, can we predict which of the products will be more successful in the future regarding Amazon Sales Rank and box office income? Hence, can we predict a partial order between products?
2. Can we predict trends concerning how the sales performance of a product will evolve in the future, i.e. will it raise, fall, or stay on the same level (cf. Sect. 12.4)?
3. How accurately can we predict the actual Amazon Sales Rank and box office income for music albums and movies respectively by exploiting blogosphere features?

Regarding the second question, we used again a τ of 1.1 to determine whether a change of the box office is considered as raise/fall or stay (cf. Sect. 12.4). The setup for these experiments is based on the experiment in the last section. The features for the machine learning algorithms are extended by an additional feature containing the Amazon Sales Rank or the box office income.

12.5.2 Metrics

For our experiments, we again apply the precision to measure the percentage of correct predictions. Further, we use the *Pearson Correlation* to detect how strong, for example, the different features extracted from the blogosphere correlate with the sales performance. The higher the Pearson Correlation the higher the correlation (range: $1.. - 1$). A Pearson Correlation of $+1$ means that there is a perfect positive linear relationship between variables. To answer the first research question mentioned above, we further calculate the *Kendall tau Rank Correlation* [14], which is defined as follows.

$$\tau = \frac{n_c - n_d}{\frac{1}{2}n(n-1)} \tag{12.5}$$

n_c is the number of concordant pairs, for which the partial order was predicted correctly, and n_d is the number of discordant pairs. A τ of 1 means, that the partial order (ranking) was predicted without any error while -1 means that the predicted ranking is the reverse of the actual ranking. A τ of 0 means that the two rankings are completely independent.

12.5.3 Results: Predicting the Sales Performance of Music Albums

To answer the first question we predict the ranking of 50 randomly chosen music albums and analyze the Kendall Tau Rank Correlation of the prediction and the actual ranking. For this experiment we archive a correlation of 0.36. Figure 12.8 shows the percentage of correctly ordered music items based on the number of related posts. The prediction for music items with a very high and very low Sales Ranks is much better than for the ones with an intermediate Sales Ranks. It shows, that most of the successful albums have a relatively strong impact on the blogosphere. This results in many posts per day related to some album. For the music items with a Sales Rank between 500 and 1,200 this model produces a ranking which is slightly better than random. For these albums an ordering is very hard to do, because the amount of related posts is nearly the same for many of them. For the albums with a Sales Rank worse than 1,200 the number of correct predictions

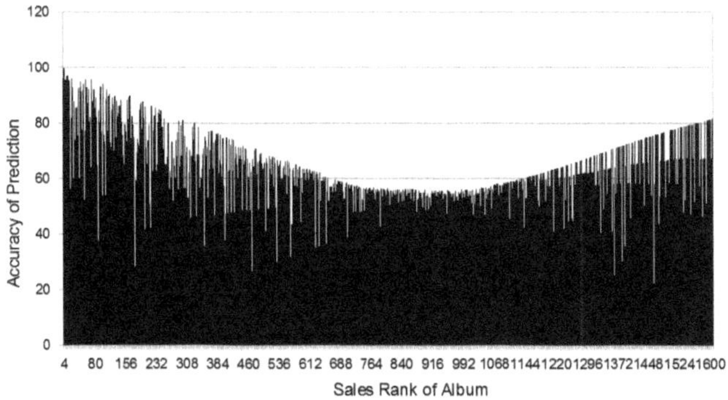

Fig. 12.8 Accuracy of predictions for the rank of an album, based on the number of posts

Table 12.6 Predicting the Sales Rank trend (raise, fall, stay): percentage of correct predictions for 50 randomly chosen albums

Bayes net	SMO	Meta bagging	Decision table	J48 tree
48.61	45.09	46.29	49.70	47.06

raises again, due to the fact, that most of these albums have only very little actual feedback in the blogosphere and therefore the rank is suggested to be little. On average the Top 100 albums have 68.45 posts per day while the worst 100 albums of the analyzed ones only get 4.1 posts per day on average. This leads to the idea of predicting whether an album will be a hit or a flop regarding the Amazon Sales Rank. To analyze this we took the top 100 and worst 100 albums and predicted, based on the number of posts per day within the last 4 days the class of the album (top 100, flop 100). For this experiment we archive 80.3 % correct predictions.

In the following experiments we aim to predict the trend of the Sales Rank or the box office revenue as well as their absolute values. We also analyze which features and methods are the best for a prediction of the trend, as well as for prediction of absolute values for both domains. In line with the previous sections, the prediction of the trend is again considered as a three class problem (raise, fall, stay). Table 12.6 lists the results for these trend predictions using the features *F1–F6*.

As seen in Sect. 12.4, lightweight machine learning algorithms show again high performance. For example, the Decision Table algorithm, which classifies in a rule-based manner achieves the best accuracy of 49.7 % which is significantly better than best guess or random predictions. In comparison to the movie domain, the performance of the trend prediction is approx. 30 % worse (cf. Sect. 12.5.4). However, the predictions are still better than if one would randomly select one of the three classes. In order to analyze whether the type of music album influences the trend prediction performance, we separated our data set according to the *genre* information. Hence, we randomly selected 50 music albums for each genre and repeated the trend prediction experiments for each set of albums. Figure 12.9 shows the results of the evaluation.

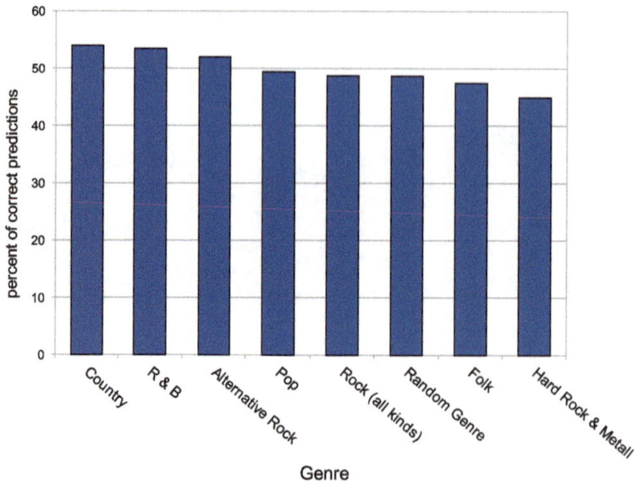

Fig. 12.9 Trend prediction performance of Decision Table algorithm for different genre

It is obvious that the trend prediction performance shows different precisions for the different genres. For the *Hard Rock & Metal* genre, the prediction is worst. This cannot be explained by the absolute number of blog posts related to the *Hard Rock & Metal* genre (approx. 64,000) which is less compared to the *Pop* genre (approx. 117,000) but more compared to *Country* (approx. 30,000). The trend prediction for music albums categorized as *Country* or *R&B* is best with 53.97 and 53.48 % respectively. These results are clearly better than if predictions are done without distinguishing the albums according to their genre (*random genre*) where the Decision Table algorithm has a precision of less than 50 %.

Additionally we analyzed whether the trend (raise, fall, stay) prediction is different for *new* album releases. For these albums the Amazon Sales Rank as well as the blogging behavior follows characteristic patterns (see above), in comparison to *old* music albums. Therefore, we randomly selected 50 new albums and 50 old albums and applied the same experimental setup as we did for Fig. 12.9.

Figure 12.10 highlights that the trend predictions for new album releases performs, on average, 34 % better than the trend predictions for old albums. Hence, the characteristic patterns of the blogosphere help to improve the precisions for predicting whether the Sales Rank will raise, fall or stay on the same level.

For the prediction of the absolute Sales Rank we considered all music albums (see Sect. 12.3) and the features *F1*–*F6* as described in Sect. 12.3.1.

The results for predicting the Amazon Sales Rank are listed in Table 12.7. The support vector machine, SMO regression, is the best algorithm having a relative error of just 16.41 %. As we will see in the next section, this performance for predicting the absolute monetary success is significantly higher for the music domain than for the movie domain.

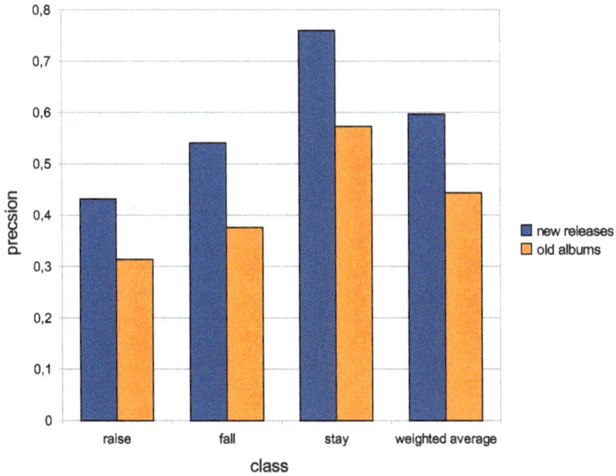

Fig. 12.10 Trend prediction performance for old and new albums

Table 12.7 Results for predicting the Sales Rank for 50 new released albums

	Linear regression	SMO regression	Bagging REPTree
Correlation	0.96	0.96	0.96
Mean absolute error	85.69	73.28	81.63
Relative error (%)	19.03	16.41	17.99

12.5.4 Results: Predicting the Sales Performance of Movies

To answer the questions above for the movie domain, we first analyze whether features extracted from the blogosphere are adequate for predicting the sales performance. Therefore, we compare the correlation of different features with the financial success of cinema movies. Generally one can expect, that the raw number of posts related to some movie or music item is a good indicator for the success of this product: the more people talk about some movie or album, the more likely they have seen the movie or bought the album. Another good indicator could be the user rating for the product.

Table 12.8 shows that the correlation of the overall number of blog posts and the gross income is much higher than the correlation between the IMDB[12] rating of a movie and its financial success. Moreover, as we are interested in predicting the success of a movie before it is launched and afterwards judged at IMDB, features

[12]http://www.imdb.com

Table 12.8 Pearson correlation between features and the reference data

	IMDB rating	Gross income	Votes at IMDB	Blog posts
IMDB rating	1	0.38	0.54	0.49
Gross income		1	0.81	**0.79**
Votes at IMDB			1	0.76
Blog posts				1

Table 12.9 Pearson correlation between different features describing the financial success of movies

	Worldwide	Domestic	Opening weekend
Worldwide	1	0.96	0.97
Domestic		1	0.97
Opening weekend			1

from the blogosphere seem to be more appropriate for the prediction of the financial success.

The Pearson Correlation between the worldwide total gross, the domestic total gross and the premiere weekend gross is very high as shown in Table 12.9.

Based on these numbers, it seems, that the influence of the user rating is small compared to the influence of the pure amount of posts related to some movie.

For the prediction of the financial success we focused on the first weekend after the release of a cinema movie as the first weekend is, for the 20 movies we considered in this experiment, crucial for the overall success of the movie: the Pearson correlation between the income of the movie at the weekend after the premiere and the overall gross income is 0.97.

Figure 12.11 depicts the results for predicting the opening weekend box office revenue for 20 different movies. The prediction is based on the number of posts related to each movie as feature (cf. *F7*, Sect. 12.3.1) using *additive regression*. Given the *actual* and *predicted* ranking, the Kendall tau Rank Correlation for this prediction is 0.509, i.e. more than half of all pairwise comparisons are correct. The prediction of the partial order seems to be less difficult compared to the music domain, where we archived a correlation of 0.36 in contrast to 0.509 for the movie domain.

If we take the budget of the movies as baseline we would just get a τ value of 0.312. A closer look at these predictions reveals that the movies with the titles "Madagascar Escape 2 Africa", "High School Musical 3", and "Beverly Hills Chihuahua" have the highest errors. These three movies are related to the genres "Comedy" and "Family" and the target audience of these movies seems to be underrepresented within the blogosphere [27]. In summary, we see that the prediction of an order between the movie products is working well even with rather lightweight blogosphere features.

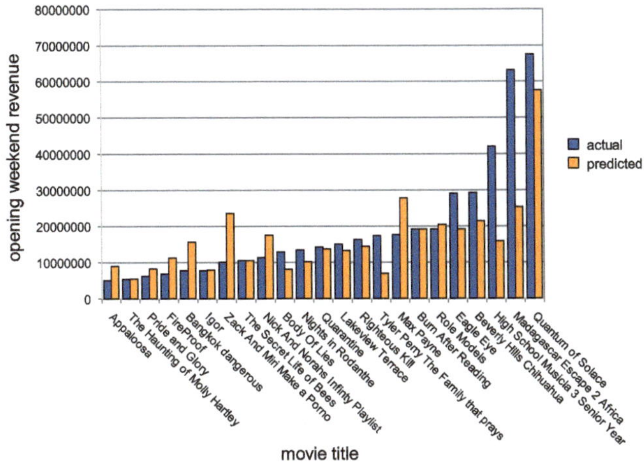

Fig. 12.11 Prediction of the opening weekend revenue for different movies based on the amount of related blogs

Table 12.10 Predicting the box office trend (raise, fall, stay): percentage of correct predictions for 20 movies

Bayes net	SMO	Meta bagging	Decision table	J48 tree
77.77	48.84	77.64	79.84	77.90

For predicting the trend regarding how the box office income will evolve over time, we included – in addition to features *F7–F12* – the actual day of week as a feature for the trend prediction as the box office follows characteristic temporal patterns as shown in Fig. 12.7. The results for different algorithms are listed in Table 12.10.

The precisions of the trend predictions are very high, e.g. 79.84 % for the Decision Table algorithm. Hence, for the movie domain we can predict trends concerning how the sales performance of a product will evolve in the future – will it raise, fall, or stay on the same level? – with a high precision as the box office itself follows characteristic pattern (see Fig. 12.7).

Figure 12.11 shows the results of the experiments for answering the last question: is it possible to predict the future absolute box office income? Therefore, we used the same setup as we applied for predicting the trend. While Fig. 12.11 indicates that such prediction task is possible for the first weekend after the release, the results of the experiment for the entire time period (see Sect. 12.3) are listed in Table 12.11.

The results are very promising: Using *Bagging [2]* together with a *REPTree* and the features *F7–F12*, we can predict the absolute box office revenue with a relative error of 26.21 % whereas the overall correlation of the predicted series of box office revenues with the real box office revenues is 0.88. In summary, we conclude that also the prediction of the absolute box office revenue is possible. However, as outlined

Table 12.11 Results for predicting the daily box office revenue of 20 movies

	Linear regression	SMO regression	Bagging REPTree
Correlation	0.87	0.86	0.88
Mean absolute error	\$434,228	\$362,107	\$258,478
Relative error (%)	44.02	36.71	26.21

in Table 12.11, the quality varies with the selected machine learning algorithm. A comparison of Tables 12.7 with 12.11 implies that the prediction of the absolute monetary success performs better for the music domain than for the movie domain.

12.5.5 Synopsis

In summary, we can answer the questions raised at the beginning of this section as follows.

1. Given just features extracted from the blogosphere, we can predict the future ranking (regarding the monetary success) of music and movie products with a Kendall tau Rank correlation of 0.36 and 0.51 respectively.
2. Trends (raise, fall, stay) of the box office revenue and Amazon Sales Rank can be predicted more precisely for the movie domain (79.84 % precision) than for the music domain (49.7 % precision). However, by distinguishing between genre or focusing on new album releases we are able to improve the precision in the music domain up to 59.7 %.
3. The absolute box office income of movies and absolute Amazon Sales Rank of music albums can be predicted with a relative error of 26.21 and 16.41 % respectively.

Our experiments thus showed that, given our trend prediction framework (see Sect. 12.3.2), we succeeded in predicting certain real-world characteristics in the music and movie domain based on the chatter in the blogosphere. Lightweight features that model the previous evolution of the number of blog posts about movies and music albums allow for forecasting trends regarding the monetary success of these items with high accuracy. In the movie domain, general trends (raise, fall, stay) can be predicted more accurately than in the music domain, because the music domain seems to be more dynamic than the movie domain: each week there are, for example, more new music album releases than cinema movie releases. However, when predicting the absolute monetary success we were able to forecast the sales ranks with high precision and a small relative error (less than 17 %). For the movie domain, we were further able to predict the gross salary income of movies with a relative error of less than 27 %.

12.6 Conclusion

This article shows how information gathered from the blogosphere can be used to predict the success of music and movies. We analyzed the characteristics of both domains within the blogosphere and the related sales performance, and figured out commonalities and differences between these two domains. For example, in the time period around the release date of a product, for both domains the number of blog posts about the product reaches a maximum signaling the maximum sales performance. However, in the domain of cinema movies there occurs a second *spike* possibly caused by customers writing reviews about the movie.

Motivated by the identified patterns, we predicted the future posting behavior within the blogosphere. Moreover, we forecasted the monetary success of music and movie products based on features extracted from the blogosphere. Our experiments showed that traditional machine learning algorithms such as Decision Tables successfully learn to predict the trends of movie box office revenues and Amazon Sales Ranks of music albums with a precision of 79.84 and 59.7 % respectively.

In this paper, we analyzed and discussed a variety of machine learning strategies for predicting different types of trends by monitoring the blogosphere. In our future work, we will investigate how different strategies can be combined in order to further optimize the performance of the trend prediction. We will moreover extend the set of features and apply SentiWordNet[13] to mine opinions expressed in the blog posts so that we can measure the impact of sentiment information on predicting the success of products in the in the music and movie domain. By analyzing the number of positive, negative or neutral posts about a product at a given point in time, we aim to find further evidence for estimating the success of products. Furthermore, we will analyze the performance of our trend prediction strategies on the basis of Twitter microblogs and will explore how the characteristic patterns that we detected in the traditional blogosphere will differ from patterns featured in the microblogosphere.

References

1. Abel, F., Diaz-Aviles, E., Henze, N., Krause, D., Siehndel, P.: Analyzing the blogosphere for predicting the success of music and movie products. In: Memon, N., Alhajj, R. (eds.) International Conference on Advances in Social Networks Analysis and Mining (ASONAM 2010), Odense, Denmark, pp. 276–280. IEEE Computer Society, Washington, DC (2010)
2. Breiman, L.: Bagging predictors. Mach. Learn. **24**, 123–140 (1996)
3. Breiman, L., Friedman, J., Stone, C.J., Olshen, R.A.: Classification and Regression Trees. Wadsworth International Group, Belmont, California (1984)
4. Cha, M., Haddadi, H., Benevenuto, F., Gummadi, P.K.: Measuring user influence in twitter: the million follower fallacy. In: Cohen, W.W., Gosling, S. (eds.) Proceedings of the Fourth

[13]http://swn.isti.cnr.it/

International Conference on Weblogs and Social Media (ICWSM '10). AAAI, Palo Alto, California (2010)
5. Dhar, V., Chang, E.: Does Chatter Matter? The Impact of User-Generated Content on Music Sales. Journal of Interactive Marketing, **23**(4), 300–307 (2009)
6. Friedman, J., Hastie, T., Tibshirani, R.: Additive Logistic Regression: A Statistical View of Boosting. Annals of Statistics, Vol. 28 (1998)
7. Glance, N.S., Hurst, M., Tomokiyo, T.: Blogpulse: automated trend discovery for weblogs. In: WWW 2004 Workshop on the Weblogging Ecosystem: Aggregation, Analysis and Dynamics, ACM (2004)
8. Goetz, M, Leskovec, J., Mcglohon, M., Faloutsos, C.: Modeling blog dynamics. In: International Conference on Weblogs and Social Media. AAAI, Menlo Park (2009)
9. Gruhl, D., Guha, R., Nowell, D.L., Tomkins, A.: Information diffusion through blogspace. In: WWW '04: Proceedings of the 13th International Conference on World Wide Web, pp. 491–501. ACM, New York (2004)
10. Gruhl, D., Guha, R., Kumar, R., Novak, J., Tomkins, A.: The predictive power of online chatter. In: KDD '05: Proceedings of the Eleventh ACM SIGKDD International Conference on Knowledge Discovery in Data Mining, pp. 78–87. ACM, New York (2005)
11. Holmes, G., Pfahringer, B., Kirkby, R., Frank, E., Hall, M.: Multiclass alternating decision trees. In: ECML '02: Proceedings of the 13th European Conference on Machine Learning, pp. 161–172. Springer, London (2002)
12. Holte, R.C.: Very simple classification rules perform well on most commonly used datasets. Mach. Learn. **11**(1), 63–90 (1993)
13. John, G.H., Langley, P.: Estimating continuous distributions in bayesian classifiers. UAI'95 Proceedings of the Eleventh conference on Uncertainty in artificial intelligence, pp. 338–345. Morgan Kaufmann Publishers Inc. San Francisco, CA, USA (1995)
14. Kendall, M.G.: A new measure of rank correlation. Biometrika **30**(1/2), 81–93 (1938)
15. Kohavi, R.: The power of decision tables. In: Lavrac, N., Wrobel, S. (eds.) Proceedings of the 8th European Conference on Machine Learning (ECML '95), Heraclion, pp. 174–189. Springer, Berlin/Heidelberg (1995)
16. Kwak, H., Lee, C., Park, H., Moon, S.: What is Twitter, a social network or a news media? In: Proceedings of the 19th International Conference on World Wide Web (WWW '10), pp. 591–600. ACM, New York (2010)
17. Lerman, K., Ghosh, R.: Information contagion: an empirical study of spread of news on Digg and Twitter social networks. In: Proceedings of 4th International Conference on Weblogs and Social Media (ICWSM '10), AAAI, Palo Alto, California, May 2010
18. Leskovec, J., Mcglohon, M., Faloutsos, C., Glance, N., Hurst, M.: Cascading behavior in large blog graphs. In: Society of Applied and Industrial Mathematics: Data Mining (SDM07), SIAM, Society for Industrial and Applied Mathematics, Philadelphia, April 2007
19. Liu, Y., Huang, X., An, A., Yu, X.: Arsa: a sentiment-aware model for predicting sales performance using blogs. In: SIGIR '07: Proceedings of the 30th Annual International ACM SIGIR Conference on Research and Development in Information Retrieval. ACM, New York (2007)
20. McGlohon, M., Leskovec, J., Faloutsos, C., Hurst, M., Glance, N.: Finding patterns in blog shapes and blog evolution. In: International Conference on Weblogs and Social Media, Boulder. Carnegie Mellon University, School of Computer Science, Machine, Pittsburgh (2007)
21. Obradovic, D., Baumann, S., Dengel, A.: A social network analysis and mining methodology for the monitoring of specific domains in the blogosphere. In: 2010 International Conference on Advances in Social Networks Analysis and Mining (ASONAM 2010), pp. 1–8. IEEE, Los Alamitos (2010)
22. Platt, J.C.: Fast Training of Support Vector Machines Using Sequential Minimal Optimization, pp. 185–208. MIT, Cambridge (1999)
23. Poggio, T. Girosi, F.: Networks for approximation and learning. Proc. IEEE **78**(9), 1481–1497 (1990)

24. Sadikov, E., Parameswaran, A., Venetis, P.: Blogs as predictors of movie success. Technical report, Stanford University (2009)
25. Sakaki, T., Okazaki, M., Matsuo, Y.: Earthquake shakes Twitter users: real-time event detection by social sensors. In: Proceedings of the 19th International Conference on World Wide Web (WWW '10), pp. 851–860. ACM, New York (2010)
26. Sussman, M.: Who are the bloggers? The what and why of blogging. Technical report, Technorati Media (2009)
27. Technorati: State of the blogosphere 2008. Technical report, Technorati Media (2008)
28. Weng, J., Lim, E.P., He, Q., Leung, C.W.K.: What do people want in microblogs? measuring interestingness of hashtags in twitter. In: Proceedings of the 2010 IEEE International Conference on Data Mining, ICDM '10, pp. 1121–1126. IEEE Computer Society, Washington, DC (2010)
29. Yang, J., Leskovec, J.: Patterns of temporal variation in online media. In: Proceedings of the Fourth ACM International Conference on Web Search and Data Mining, WSDM '11. ACM, New York (2011)

Chapter 13
Informative Value of Individual and Relational Data Compared Through Business-Oriented Community Detection

Vincent Labatut and Jean-Michel Balasque

Abstract Despites the great interest caused by social networks in Business Science, their analysis is rarely performed in both a global and systematic way in this field. This could be explained by the fact their practical extraction is a difficult and costly task. One may ask if equivalent information could be retrieved from less expensive, individual data (i.e. describing single individuals instead of pairs). In this work, we try to address this question through group detection. We gather both types of data from a population of students, estimate groups separately using individual and relational data, and obtain sets of clusters and communities, respectively. We measure the overlap between clusters and communities, which turns out to be relatively weak. We also define a predictive model, allowing us to identify the most discriminant attributes for the communities, and to reveal the presence of a tenuous link between the relational and individual data. Our results indicate both types of data convey considerably different information in this specific context, and can therefore be considered as complementary. To emphasize the interest of communities for Business Science, we also conduct an analysis based on hobbies and purchased brands.

V. Labatut (✉)
Computer Science Department, Galatasaray University, Çırağan Cad. No:36, 34357 Ortaköy/Istanbul, Turkey
e-mail: vlabatut@gsu.edu.tr

J.-M. Balasque
Business Science and Marketing Department, Galatasaray University, Çırağan Cad. No:36, 34357 Ortaköy/Istanbul, Turkey
e-mail: jmbalasque@gsu.edu.tr

T. Özyer et al. (eds.), *The Influence of Technology on Social Network Analysis and Mining*, Lecture Notes in Social Networks 6, DOI 10.1007/978-3-7091-1346-2_13,

13.1 Introduction

Bringing new insights in decision-making analysis, social networks have raised a great interest in the scientific community, including Business Science. However, in this field, they have a paradoxical position: on the one hand the interest of network analysis has been greatly emphasized years ago, but on the other hand this tool is not very widespread yet. In the first part of this section, we review previous works focusing on network analysis for Business and Marketing Sciences and try to find explanations to this observation. Then, in the second part, we explore more thoroughly one of these explanations, which is related to the nature of the data requested to extract social networks, and derive the problematics and core ideas of this paper.

13.1.1 Network Analysis in Business Science

In Marketing Science, and more generally in all the fields of Business Science, the strength of the concept of social network can be considered at different levels [1]. First, locally, by taking into account the interaction between a person and his precise relational context, it constitutes a good tool to better understand individual decisions. Second, at the level of a whole system, it provides a meaningful analysis basis and offers the necessary information to improve both global organization and individual activities management. The main point in both research and practice has been the possible benefits a person or a firm can get from social networks. Consequently, their analysis has been elaborated primarily in a utilitarian perspective, with a particular emphasis on their impact on the nature and efficiency of information dissemination. Their role was noticeably studied in the context of competitiveness in the construction sector [2], firm innovativeness [3], investors attraction for venture capital [4], effective use of their social capital [5] in the labor market [6], and administrative board decisions [7], among others. In Marketing Science, the focus has been put more on speed of information diffusion, with a major interest in word-of-mouth [8], changes of opinions and adoption of innovations inside groups of people (mainly consumers and potential consumers) [9–11] or diffusion of specific products [12].

In most of these studies, the analysis is centered on a single or a few persons, and consists in studying their most immediate connections in great details. Even if the investigation concerns a whole social system (e.g. group or firm), the focus remains local. Some works study the role these individuals of interest have in the network. Other works analyze the possible effects of the social network on these individuals, and generalize the resulting observations to the rest of the network, or to some subgroups of persons. This approach can be criticized in several ways. First, influence processes within social networks vary considerably depending on the nature, structure and strength of the links that connect the considered persons. For instance, Steyer et al. [10] showed the efficiency of information dissemination processes, used for viral marketing, depends on the whole network structure.

Van der Merwe [11] described its effect on the role of opinion leaders. According to various authors [13, 14], both opinion spreading and speed of innovation adoption depend on the considered network structure and density. Second, the interest of adopting a non-local approach is backed by several Marketing studies like [15], which, following a stream of Sociology studies, emphasized the necessity of taking sub-networks or cliques into account. These structures diffuse information faster: people belonging to them are more quickly and more deeply influenced, they rapidly adopt new products. So, from a managerial point of view, they are of higher interest. In the context of complex networks, this naturally leads to the notion of community, i.e. a group of nodes with denser relationships, compared to the rest of the network.

Burt [16] and Perry-Smith [17] showed structural holes improve the emergence of new ideas. In their analysis of firm innovativeness, Simon and Tellier [3] differentiated two kinds of innovativeness: exploitation and exploration. They showed groups with denser inner-connections were more efficient to diffuse ideas, but rupture innovations were less likely to happen in those parts of the firm. These denser groups can also be seen by people as stressful areas which constrain them too much, preventing any behavior opposed to the dominant one. In this context, people sometimes rely on persons not belonging to their community [18] or weakly connected [19]. Then, detecting communities can also, by contrast, reveal the zones of lower link density, or structural holes. It additionally allows a deeper study of the network structure by performing a centrality analysis. Indeed, people located in-between communities often play specific roles because of their central position [20]. Interestingly, this last point brings us back to the local approach, illustrating how complementary they are: a global approach can be used to locate persons of interest, which can then be studied more attentively.

Besides this complementary nature and the fact a global approach seems necessary to improve our understanding of social networks and their effects, it is rarely adopted in the fields of Marketing and Business Sciences. Moreover, when it is the case, authors generally do not use a systematic method. For instance, the works cited in the previous paragraphs [3, 17] do not use a precise definition of the concept of community and do not intend to identify all communities present in the studied network. We see two possible reasons for this. First, this kind of analysis is computationally far more demanding than local approaches. It relies on relatively new tools (both theoretically and practically speaking), making intensive use of modern computers. Because of this novelty, they do not have penetrated Business Science deeply yet. Second, and more importantly, practical extraction of social networks is a difficult and costly task [21, 22], because the information it requires is often difficult to access and thereby expensive.

13.1.2 Nature and Cost of Data

Let us consider data according to two axes: the cost axis and the individual vs. relational axis. In the latter, *individual* refers to data describing only one person, whereas *relational* points out data concerning two (or more) persons. On the first axis, we can distinguish three kinds of data, differing both by the nature of the information they convey and on how difficult and costly they are to obtain.

First, *factual* information is the most easily accessible; it corresponds to acknowledged, generally publicly available, facts. For individual data, we can cite for example social status, gender, age, etc. For relational data, it can take the form of communication streams such as email exchanges, lists of collaborations, etc.

Second, what we call *behavioral* information can either result from observations or be obtained directly by interrogating the persons of interest. For individual data, it describes how some person reacts to a given situation, whereas for relational data, the concern will be put on interactions between people, for instance by measuring the time workers spend together in a firm.

Third, *sentimental* information is related to feelings and thoughts. It is the most difficult to retrieve, since it cannot be accessed in other way than more or less direct questions, or very advanced physiological techniques [23, 24]. For individual data, it is for instance brands representations, firm image or products preferences. For relational data it corresponds to feelings (friendship, love, hate, admiration ...) people have for each other. Sentimental relational data can be estimated through questions of the sociometric form, where each person is asked to list his acquaintances and to quantify the strength and orientation of their relationships [25]. This so-called sociometric approach is considered to be both the most efficient, in terms of quality of the retrieved relationships, and the most difficult to apply [21]. Extracting a social network requires relational data, which is globally more difficult and costly to gather than individual data [26]. Indeed, most available factual data focus on single persons (resumés, archives, surveys ...); observing interactions in a whole population obviously requires more resources than concentrating on a single individual; and making people speak about others can be an even more sensitive task than making them reveal personal details.

From this data-related difficulty regarding social networks extraction, a question arises: can the information conveyed by social networks be retrieved by other, less expensive, means? In this work, we try to tackle this issue through the angle of group detection. We analyze data coming from a survey conducted on a population of university students. Its questions targeted both relational data, with a sociometric approach, and individual data, including factual, behavioral and sentimental-centered questions. However, in this chapter we present only the first stage of our work, which is concerned with the relational data and only a part of the individual data (mainly factual).

From the relational data, we extract a social network, in which we detect communities. We then analyze them from a Business-oriented perspective, and show their practical importance in this field of research. In parallel, we perform a classic cluster analysis on the factual individual data, in order to obtain clusters of students. The question is then to know if this analysis, which is standard in Business Science, gives access to the same information than community detection, which is much less employed. For this purpose, we first compare individual and relational information through an analysis of similarities and differences between the two kinds of groups.

We then use our results from the cluster analysis to design a predictive model able to estimate the community of an instance based on its individual attributes. This allows us to identify which attributes are the most important to characterize the communities, and therefore to tackle the problem of community composition by analyzing them in terms of individual data.

Our contributions are both practical and theoretical. First, we present and analyze some original data, and interpret the results of this analysis in the context of Business Sciences. Second, the problem of comparing the informative value of individual and relational data was not raised before, to our knowledge, and we propose an original method to tackle it. The rest of this chapter is organized as follow. In Sect. 13.2, we describe the survey we set to collect data, focusing on the parts used in the present work. We also give a short description of the tools used to analyze them: community detection, cluster analysis, and our predictive modeling approach. In Sect. 13.3, we present and comment our results regarding the identified communities and clusters, their characteristics and usefulness. In the conclusion, we highlight the original points of our study, discuss its limitations and explain how it can be continued.

13.2 Methods

We conducted two different analyses. The first is a comparison of groups estimated independently from the individual and relational data, resulting in so-called clusters and communities, respectively. The second is a study of the community composition in terms of individual factual data. In this section, we describe first how we gathered the data, and which part of them was used in this study. We then present the methods used to estimate and compare the groups of students, and finally the predictive analysis approach we applied to study community composition.

13.2.1 Data Collection

The data used in this chapter are a part of some results obtained from a larger survey. In this subsection, we first present the general survey and context of the study, and we then focus on the data selected to be used in this work.

13.2.1.1 Survey and Context

The Galatasaray University (GSU) is a small Turkish public institution of about 2,000 students, located in Istanbul, near the Bosphorus. It offers a wide variety of courses (sociology, economics, international studies, management, philosophy, computer science, engineering, law ...) taught mainly in French. In Turkey, students enter universities after having passed a national competitive examination called ÖSS. The ranking they get at this occasion is very important, because it has a direct effect on the set of universities and departments they can choose to study in. The GSU is one of the top universities in several fields, and as such it attracts students with very high rankings. For most students, the name of the university itself is more important than the actual standard of the department they are going to enter. This particular university can also recruit students directly from Turkish French-speaking high schools, thanks to a specific internal examination. Approximately two thirds of the students are undergraduates and will get a Lisans (i.e. License, or BS) diploma, the rest being Master and PhD students. Each department has a promotion of about 30 students per level. Community and cultural life is highly developed; the university counts 40 active sports clubs or cultural associations. There is a very strong feeling of belonging to a group, enhanced by the fact the name Galatasaray also refers to a prestigious high school, a popular association football club, and various other cultural and sporting structures. After the university, very strong ties remain between GSU alumni, which usually help each other professionally.

In this context, we have conducted a study on the social network of current GSU students. A university can be considered as a relatively close system for students, in the sense most of their friends also belong to it, making it an appropriate field of investigation. Accordingly to the previous description, this seems to be particularly true for the GSU. Our study is based on a survey taking place at several periods, in order to be able to study some of the network dynamics. The results presented here are limited to data obtained during the first phase of the overall research project, which took place during spring 2009 and involved 224 respondents, mainly at the Lisans level.

We designed a questionnaire focusing on social and personal attributes, social interactions (especially in the daily university environment), purchasing behavior and favorite brands. The questions can be distributed into three different thematic parts, although this separation does not appear in the questionnaire, voluntarily. The first one concerns factual data: age, gender, clubs or associations membership (inside and outside the university), school situation, previous high-school. The second part focuses on the student's behavior relatively to his friends: nature of the communication means he uses (cell phone, Facebook, Skype ...); and also concerning his shopping habits, information sources, buying behavior. The third part concerns his feelings about the university, his vision of his relationships with his friends, his desires, hobbies, goals and favorite brands. All questions were designed to gather individual data (i.e. information limited to the student himself), except one, which was dedicated to relational data (i.e. data involving two students). We adopted a classic sociometric approach, consisting in asking the student to name the peers he finds the most important in his everyday life, and to quantify these relationships on a scale ranging from -5 (hate) to $+5$ (love). A website was created to gather the responses. Part of the required information was very personal and sensitive, so a specific procedure was set to guarantee perfect anonymity, replacing all names by meaningless codes.

Table 13.1 Factual individual attributes used for both clustering and predictive analyses

Attribute	Type	Description
Gender	Dichotomous	Male vs. Female
Department	Nominal	The GSU has 22 departments
Class	Ordinal	Current year (Preparatory and Lisans): 6 different levels
Grade	Real	Current grade of the student, expressed from 0 to 4
Entrance	Dichotomous	Entrance examination: National vs. Internal
High-school	Nominal	High-school name
Category	Nominal	High-school type: 6 different categories
City	Nominal	High-school city: 55 different cities
Specialization	Nominal	High-school specialization: 17 categories
Clubs	Dichotomous	Forty activities inside and outside the GSU

13.2.1.2 Selected Data

As stated before, in this chapter we focus only on a part of the gathered data. First, the relational data (sociometric question) are used to build the social network, which means it is based on the feelings each student declares to have about his fellows. Each node in the network represents a student which either responded to the survey or was cited by a respondent (and sometimes both). Consequently, the network contains more nodes (622) than we had respondents (224), since some cited persons did not answer during this phase of the survey. Each link is directed from the respondent towards the cited student, and has a weight corresponding to the score the respondent associated to the relationship. The presence of a link between two nodes represents the fact the respondent considers the cited student as one of his most important fellows. Therefore, the communities identified in this network correspond to groups of people affectively bound inside the university.

Second, factual individual data are used to estimate clusters of students, in order to be subsequently compared to communities. The complete list of factual individual attributes is given in Table 13.1. In the rest of the document, we will refer to these data simply as 'the attributes'.

Third, three additional attributes were selected to illustrate how communities can be used in the context of Business Science. They correspond to behavioral information and concern the students' hobbies and the brands of mobile phone and digital player they own. All three attributes are nominal, and they are not used during the cluster analysis.

13.2.2 Analysis Tools

To identify groups (clusters and communities), we used a set of representative algorithms. We chose to apply several algorithms in order to be able to compare their results and ensure group stability. In other terms, our goal was not to compare the algorithms in terms of performance, but rather in terms of agreement, and to identify the most consensual groups. For this reason, we selected the algorithms by considering first the nature of the groups they detect and/or the process applied to perform this detection, so that a wide scope of approaches were represented. To ensure the reliability of the results, we favored proven algorithms, i.e. tools widely used in previous published works. Finally, we also chose the algorithms depending on whether their implementations were publicly available or not. All of the selected tools output a partition of the analyzed data, which means every instance belongs to exactly one group (groups are therefore mutually exclusive). Algorithmic complexity and scalability were not an issue, since the processing was performed completely off-line and on limited data.

Group detection algorithms differ mainly in the method they use for group identification. Some adopt a hierarchical approach, which can be either agglomerative or divisive. In the first case, each object is initially considered as a group, and the algorithm merges them iteratively until only a single group remains. In the second case, on the contrary, the process starts with a single group containing all objects, which is iteratively separated in subgroups until each of them contains only one object. In both case, the characteristic point is the criterion used to select the groups to be merged or divided. Other algorithms rely on the so-called partitional approach, which consists in defining an initial partition, randomly or according to some approximate method, and then iteratively improving it, relatively to some criterion, by moving objects from one group to the other. Finally, besides these general approaches, ad hoc methods exist, which we will describe in greater details in the following.

In this subsection, we first describe the cluster analysis and community detection algorithms we applied on our data. We then explain how we compared their results to assess their agreement. Finally, we formally define the model we used to predict community membership in function of the identified clusters.

13.2.2.1 Cluster Analysis

One of the most important points in the detection of clusters (based on the individual data) is the choice of an appropriate dissimilarity function, allowing to properly compare the instances. For some of our attributes (Gender, Class, Grade and Entrance), this choice was straightforward because their nature does not let much freedom: they are simple binary, ordinal and numeric values. But the remaining ones (Department, Clubs and Highschool-related attributes) have specificities requiring to make some methodological choices. For this reason, we defined and tested several functions, and present here only the one giving the best results.

The Department attribute has a nominal value, and we should consider two departments as different if they are not represented by the same symbol. However, a department belongs to a faculty, and can be considered as thematically closer to another department from the same faculty than to a completely unrelated one. For this reason, we chose to consider two departments as partially similar if they belong

Table 13.2 Summary of the cluster analysis algorithms applied to the individual data

Algorithm	Approach	Reference	R library
Agnes	Agglomerative	[28]	Cluster
DBScan	Density-based	[29]	fpc
Diana	Divisive	[28]	Cluster
Pam	Partitional	[28]	Cluster
TwoStep	Hybrid	[30]	Homemade

to the same faculty. The Clubs information is problematic because it actually is a very sparse vector of binary values, and we could not consider them as separate attributes, or their importance would be overstated. This is why we decided to use Jaccard's coefficient [27] to summarize all club memberships under the form of a single value. The problem of the Highschool-related attributes is they are highly correlated, which is why we also had to combine them under the form of a single value. Using our expertise of the context, we defined a synthetic nominal attribute corresponding to different highschool categories, by considering the highschool city, type of education, and teaching language, and the student highschool specialization.

To our knowledge, no previous work is supporting the fact some combinations of factual attributes would have a better predictive power than others relatively to the composition of the communities. Consequently, there is no a priori reason to favor a certain subset of attributes to perform the cluster analysis. We therefore opted for an exploratory approach, and considered all possible combinations of factual attributes during the cluster analysis.

The five algorithms we selected are summarized in Table 13.2. They are standard and proven tools, available in many data mining softwares and representative of the different families of cluster analysis methods. We used some implementations defined in two R language [31] libraries as indicated in Table 13.2, except for TwoStep, which we programmed ourselves.

Pam (Partitioning Around Medoids) [28] uses a partitional approach, and necessitates to know a priori the number of clusters. For each cluster, an instance is initially randomly selected and considered as its center. Each remaining instance is then assigned to the cluster whose center is the most similar. After this step, any instance in a cluster might become its new center if this allows reducing the sum of all instance-to-center dissimilarities. The process is repeated with these new centers until there is no more change in clusters and centers, leading to a stable partition.

Agnes (Agglomerative Nesting) [28] follows an agglomerative hierarchical approach. First, each instance is considered as a cluster. Then an iterative process is applied, which merges the least dissimilar clusters. Assessing this dissimilarity is straightforward if both clusters contain only one instance. Otherwise, the average linkage is used, i.e. the dissimilarity between the clusters is the average of all instance-to-instance dissimilarities. The process ends when only one cluster containing all instances remains.

Diana (Divisive Analysis) [28] is also hierarchical, but unlike Agnes it is divisive. It starts with a single cluster containing all instances, which will be split in two. First, the instance with the highest average dissimilarity to all other instances is identified and considered as the seed for a new cluster. The instances of the original cluster are then considered one by one, in a way similar enough to the process implemented in Pam, so that instances more similar to the new cluster are reassigned to it. The same splitting method is then iteratively applied to the largest cluster until all clusters contain only one instance. The largest cluster refers here to the cluster with higher diameter, i.e. maximal dissimilarity over all its pairs of instances.

TwoStep [30] is a very general method consisting in applying successively two different algorithms, with at least a hierarchical agglomerative algorithm as the second one. We used Diana for the first step and Ward's method [32] for the second. The first step can be considered as a preprocessing phase, consisting in identifying the dense areas of the data space in order to produce the smallest clusters of interest. During the second phase, larger clusters are built by merging these, in order to improve the quality of the partition.

DBScan (Density-Based Spatial Clustering of Applications with Noise) [29] is a density-based algorithm, which allows it to uncover non-convex clusters. The process starts by randomly selecting an instance, and considering its neighborhood. If it is dense enough, the instance is the seed of a new cluster, in which all its neighbors are also placed. Each neighbor is then considered: if its own neighborhood is dense enough, its own neighbors are added to the cluster and the process goes on with them. Once all possible nodes have been added to the cluster, one of the remaining nodes is selected randomly to start a new cluster using the same principle.

13.2.2.2 Community Detection

The selected community detection algorithms are summarized in Table 13.3. The interested reader will find a more detailed description of their functioning in this subsection. But before, we need to introduce Newman's *Modularity* measure [33], which is used by several of them. It estimates the quality of a network partition relatively to its topology. The original formulation is based on a normalized community adjacency matrix whose elements e_{ij} represent half the proportion of links between communities i and j [33]:

$$Q = \sum_i (e_{ii} - e_{i+}e_{+i}) \tag{13.1}$$

Where e_{i+} and e_{+i} are the sums over row and column i, respectively. The term e_{ii} corresponds to the observed proportion of links inside community i. The term $e_{i+}e_{+i}$ is an estimation of the same quantity for a network whose links are randomly distributed. The modularity consequently measures how much the considered network differs from a random network, in terms of number of intra-community links and relatively to the partition of interest. It can be considered as a chance-corrected measure. The theoretical maximum value is 1, but it is related to the network structure, and in practice it cannot be reached for all networks.

Table 13.3 Summary of the community detection algorithms applied to the data. The + signs represent the ability to process directed (D) or weighted (W) links (note these abilities depend on both the algorithm and the considered implementation). The last column displays the type of implementation we used: iGraph R library [38] or author's implementation

Algorithm	Approach	D	W	Reference	Implementation
CommFind	Laplacian, spectral, aglomerative	−	−	[39]	Author
EdgeBetweenness	Edge-betweenness, divisive	−	−	[40]	iGraph
EigenVector	Modularity, spectral, divisive	+	−	[41]	iGraph
FastGreedy	Modularity, greedy, hierarchical	−	+	[42]	iGraph
InfoMap	Compression, simulated annealing	+	+	[43]	Author
LabelPropagation	Information propagation	−	+	[44]	iGraph
Louvain	Modularity, greedy, hybrid	−	+	[45]	Author
MarkovCluster	Random-walk	+	+	[46]	Author
Radicchi	Link-transitivity, divisive	−	−	[47]	Author
SpinGlass	Modularity, simulated annealing	−	+	[48]	iGraph
WalkTrap	Random-walk, agglomerative	−	+	[49]	iGraph

When considering real-world networks, partitions whose modularity reaches 0.7 are considered to be very good [34,35]. Note numerous modularity variants exist, some of them allowing to process weighted [36] and directed [37] links.

Some algorithms are completely based on the modularity measure, and maximize it using various means. Exhaustive optimization is computationally intractable though, due to the number of possible partitions, so they perform an approximate processing. Modularity is also used in most hierarchical algorithms to select the best cut in the generated hierarchy of partitions, and therefore determine the optimal number of communities. Moreover, in Sect. 13.3 we use modularity to compare the various estimated community structures in terms of quality.

FastGreedy [42] is historically the first algorithm designed to maximize modularity. It relies on a hierarchical agglomerative approach to perform a greedy optimization. An iterative process takes place, starting with a partition containing as many communities as nodes. At each iteration, two communities are selected and merged to obtain a new partition. They are selected so that the modularity of this partition is maximal. The process ends when the merge leads to a single community containing all nodes. *Louvain* [45] also greedily optimizes modularity using a hierarchical agglomerative approach. The main difference with FastGreedy is the application of a partitional step at each iteration, allowing to merge several communities at once. This can affect the higher level communities, resulting in potentially different partitions.

EigenVector [41] is also a hierarchical algorithm, but unlike FastGreedy and Louvain, it is divisive. Moreover, it relies on a completely different optimization method inspired by spectral bisection [50]. This classic graph-partitioning approach takes advantage of some spectral properties of the Laplacian matrix, which is derived from the graph adjacency matrix. In the case of EigenVector, a so-called modularity matrix is used instead, which can be considered as an adjacency matrix undergoing the same chance-correction than the one used for the modularity measure. The algorithm then considers the eigenvector associated to the highest eigenvalue, and splits the network in two depending on the signs of its elements. This results in an approximate optimization of the modularity. This division is repeated iteratively until each community contains only one node. *CommFind* [39] also uses a spectral approach, but this one is based on the traditional Laplacian matrix. Instead of using only the best eigenvector, it selects the few best ones, which allows taking more information into account. It can then apply a cluster analysis on the resulting data, instead of iteratively performing bisections. For this purpose, CommFind uses a hierarchical agglomerative method, with the additional constraint of merging communities only if they are actually connected in the network.

SpinGlass [48] is another modularity optimization algorithm, which relies on an analogy between community structures and physical spin glass models. Each node is represented by a spin whose state corresponds to the node community index, whereas the network topology is represented by the couplings between spins. The energy level of the model is specified so that the absence of inter-community links and the presence of intra-community links are favored. Under certain conditions, the spin configuration leading to the minimal energy level for this system corresponds to the community structure of maximal modularity. To estimate this ground-state, SpinGlass uses simulated annealing [51], a Monte Carlo optimization method. The global aspect of this method and the non-hierarchical approach of the process are the main differences with the other presented modularity optimization algorithms.

A whole family of algorithms is based on link-centrality measures. The idea behind this approach is that inter-community links are the most central, in the sense one has to use them to go from any node in one community to any node in the other one. On the contrary, given the fact communities are by definition denser subgraphs, it is likely that a number of paths exist to connect any two nodes located in the same community, making intra-community links less central. In *EdgeBetweenness* [40], this idea is used to implement a hierarchical divisive approach. The process starts with the original network, and iteratively removes the most central links. The network is consequently split into smaller and smaller components, considered as communities in the original network. The process ends when no link remains. Note the centralities are updated at each iteration to take the last removal into account. The algorithm relies on the edgebetweenness centrality, which considers the number of shortest paths going through the link of interest. *Radicci* [47] applies the same process with a different measure called link transitivity. It focuses on triangles rather than shortest paths, considering links belonging to many triangles are more likely to be located inside communities, due to their higher density.

Another approach consists in first defining some function to measure the distance between nodes, and then applying a distance-based clustering approach to estimate communities by minimizing and maximizing intra- and inter-community distances, respectively. *WalkTrap* [49] uses a random walk-based distance, based on the probability to go from one node to the other in a fixed number of steps. Ward's method [32] is then applied to get the communities, which makes WalkTrap a hierarchical agglomerative algorithm. *MarkovCluster* [46] also relies on random walks, but does not include any clustering phase. It iteratively repeats a two-stepped process applied to the network transfer matrix, which contains the probabilities for a random walker to go from one node to another. First, this matrix is raised to some specified power, in order to get a transfer matrix containing probabilities for longer paths. Like for WalkTrap, pairs of nodes with a high probability are supposed to be in the same community. Second, each element in the matrix is raised to some specified power, in order to favor those higher probabilities. The resulting matrix is then normalized to get a new transfer matrix. Both steps are repeated until convergence. The final matrix is binary, and is interpreted as an adjacency matrix describing a network with multiple components. Each one of these components is considered as a community in the original network.

A different approach consists in adopting a data compression perspective and considering the community structure as a set of regularities in the network topology, which can be used to represent the whole network in a more compact way. The best community structure is therefore the one maximizing compactness while minimizing information loss. In *InfoMap* [43], the community structure is represented through a two-level nomenclature based on Huffman coding: one to distinguish communities in the network and the other to distinguish nodes in a community. The problem of finding the best partition is expressed as minimizing the quantity of information needed to represent some random walk in the network using this nomenclature. With a partition containing few inter-community links, the walker will probably stay longer inside communities, therefore only the second level will be needed to describe its path, leading to a compact representation. The authors optimize their criterion using simulated annealing [51].

LabelPropagation [44] relies on a completely different method, based on the simulation of a propagation mechanism. All nodes are initially assigned a different label. Then an iterative process is applied, consisting in giving a node the label which is majority amongst its neighbors (ties are broken randomly), if it is not already the case. The process converges and stops when this condition is verified for all nodes. Communities are then obtained by considering groups of nodes with the same label. By construction, one node has more neighbors in its community than in the others.

Besides the process they implement and the properties of the communities they identify, community detection algorithms also differ in the nature of the information they are able to process. Most of them are limited to unweighted and undirected links. As shown in Table 13.3, EigenVector can process directed links provided they are unweighted; five algorithms are able to process weighted links provided they are undirected; and only MarkovCluster and InfoMap have the ability to process both weighted and directed links. Gathering the data needed to extract weighted or directed networks is potentially more costly than for plain simple links. We selected algorithms with different abilities, in order to test if such a cost was justified and resulted in substantially different communities on our data.

All the selected implementations are open source and freely available. Table 13.3 shows which implementations we used: either the program available on the author's website, or the one provided with the R language [31] implementation of the iGraph library [38].

13.2.2.3 Partition Comparison

To compare the groups estimated by the previously described approaches, we chose the *adjusted Rand index* (ARI), which is widely used to measure similarity between two partitions of a given dataset. The original *Rand index* (RI) [52] is defined as $RI = (a+d)/(a+b+c+d)$, where a (resp. d) corresponds to the number of pairs whose elements belong to the same (resp. different) group(s) in both partitions, and b (resp. c) to the number of pairs whose elements belong to the same group in the first (resp. second) partition, whereas they belong to different groups in the second (resp. first) one. The adjusted version [53] is defined as:

$$ARI = (RI - E)/(1 - E) \tag{13.2}$$

Where E is the amount of similarity expected to be due to chance. The upper limit of this measure is 1 (the two partitions are exactly the same). The value 0 indicates a partial overlap, equivalent to what would be observed if both partitions were random (i.e. $RI = E$). Negative values indicate a strong divergence between the partitions.

The ARI was used to compare the partitions estimated by the various community detection algorithms and reach a reference partition, and to compare the partitions resulting from the cluster analysis with this reference partition.

13.2.2.4 Predictive Analysis

The second part of our analysis consisted in elaborating a predictive model of the composition of communities, on the basis of the factual attributes. A classic approach for this is to conduct a discriminant analysis, which allows estimating a model taking the form of a set of linear classification functions. Using the community partition as a reference, such a model would allow predicting the community of an instance thanks to its attributes. Its interest is also explicative, since it is possible to analyze the data used for the prediction to characterize the communities. However, this type of analysis was designed to handle numeric data, which is not our case. Extensions such as discriminant correspondence analysis and alternatives such as multinomial sigmoid regression (with Probit or Logit models) allow processing nominal data. But to our knowledge, no tool allows using heterogeneous data such as our factual attributes (some of which are real, ordinal, dichotomous and nominal). This would prevent us from applying the exhaustive exploration of the attributes we planned.

We propose an alternative approach based on the use of the partitions resulting from the cluster analysis. Let us consider a cluster C, and note $u(i)$ the community of one of its instances i according to the community detection result, and $\hat{u}(i)$ the estimation of this community according to our model. By setting $\hat{u}(i) = \text{argmax}_C\ (u(i))$, we assign all instances in C to the community which is prevalent in this cluster. By applying the same principle to all clusters, we can define a correspondence between each cluster and one of the communities, and consequently predict community membership for all instances.

Note it is possible to have the same community associated to several clusters, which means the clusters are considered as subgroups of this community. It is also possible for a community not to be associated to any clusters, which means its instances were diluted in several clusters having themselves a larger intersection with other communities. With this model, misclassifications appear when an instance belongs to a cluster whose associated community is not the correct one for this instance.

The quality of the model can be assessed by processing its success rate when predicting the communities of all the studied instances. One expects to get a high success rate when the clusters are similar to the communities, or when they form a subdivision of the community partition. Our assumption is the attributes used by the model to successfully predict community membership are characteristic of the considered communities. To explore the attribute space, we will build and evaluate a model for each partition identified during the cluster analysis phase, i.e. we will consider all possible combinations of attributes. The most discriminant one will be identified by selecting the model leading to the highest success rate. These attributes can then be ranked in terms of explicative power by considering the success rate associated to the models built on any subcombination. For instance, if the best predictions are obtained using three attributes, one can consider the prediction abilities of the models built using one or two of them.

13.3 Results and Discussion

Our presentation of the results follows the approach we presented in Sect. 13.2. First, we describe and compare the communities identified in our networks. In the following subsection, we explain how they can be used in the context of Business Science. Then, we perform a cluster analysis of the factual data and describe the obtained results. We use certain of these partitions in the following subsection to define our predictive model and identify the most discriminant attributes relatively to the communities. Finally, we use these attributes to interpret the communities.

13.3.1 Community Detection

Before performing community detection, we cleaned the social network extracted from our relational data by removing its isolated nodes. This is a classic procedure, because all algorithms consider separated components as distinct communities, leading to many meaningless communities when such nodes are present. We additionally removed the very small components to get a single giant component. These operations reduced the number of nodes to 552. We then applied all the appropriate

Table 13.4 Quality of the community detection results expressed in terms of modularity

	Unweighted		Weighted	
Algorithm	Undirected	Directed	Undirected	Directed
CommFind	0.8662	–	–	–
EdgeBetweenness	0.8754	–	–	–
EigenVector	0.7962	0.7823	–	–
FastGreedy	0.8780	–	0.8727	–
InfoMap	0.8441	0.0000	0.8384	0.0000
LabelPropagation	0.8165	–	0.7918	–
Louvain	0.8754	–	0.8733	–
MarkovCluster	0.6988	0.6805	0.7053	0.7323
Radicchi	0.7974	–	–	–
SpinGlass	0.8753	–	0.8667	–
WalkTrap	0.8549	–	0.8449	–

algorithms to four different versions of the network presenting (un)directed and (un)weighted links.

Table 13.4 shows the modularity values obtained on the unweighted undirected network. Most of the algorithms reach a very high modularity, close to 0.85. We can distinguish Radicchi, EigenVector and MarkovCluster, which are slightly below with a modularity under 0.8. This is still very high if we consider 0.7 as a high value for a real-world network, as previously mentioned.

Among the algorithms able to process weighted undirected networks, FastGreedy, Louvain, SpinGlass, InfoMap and WalkTrap are once again the top ones in terms of modularity. LabelPropagation performance decreases slightly (under 0.8), while MarkovCluster stays at the same level than before, clearly above the others.

On the unweighted directed network, InfoMap does not manage to find any meaningful partition and gets a zero modularity. EigenVector and MarkovCluster have modularities very close to those obtained on the unweighted undirected network. Only two algorithms are able to process the weighted directed networks. MarkovCluster obtains a modularity slightly higher than on the three other networks. Like for the previous network, InfoMap finds only one community and has a zero modularity. Interestingly, the additional information conveyed by the link direction seems to make it impossible for this algorithm to find a community structure suitable for compression.

To assess the effect of weights and directions, we compared the partitions estimated by each algorithm over the different networks. MarkovCluster, which was applied to all four networks, leads to very similar partitions with ARI values between 0.85 and 0.9. The same remark holds for most of the other algorithms which could be applied to several networks, although with slightly lower ARI values (between 0.78 and 0.9). Obviously, InfoMap is the exception because of its zero modularity for both directed networks. We can conclude from these results that, on our data, considering directions and/or weights during the community detection process does not seem to affect the identified communities. Yet, the selected algorithms are supposed to take advantage of this extra information, so we expected to observe a more significant difference. This might be due to the fact the unweighted undirected network is already highly modular, which means its topology conveys enough information to efficiently discover the community structure: in this case, there is not much to improve by including weights and directions in the process. Another explanation would be the tested algorithms are not able to efficiently take advantage of the extra information.

There is no clear improvement of the performance when considering extra information, so we decided to focus on the unweighted undirected networks, for which we obtained the highest modularity values. We concentrated our analysis on the top four algorithms, which have very close modularity values (above 0.875): EdgeBetweenness, FastGreedy, Louvain and SpinGlass. Interestingly, they lead to partitions with comparable sizes (number of communities): 22 for EdgeBetweenness, FastGreedy and Louvain, 28 for SpinGlass. By comparison, MarkovCluster and EigenVector (modularity bellow 0.8) found 85 and 48 communities, respectively. This is an important point, because for interpretation purpose, it is convenient to have a small number of relatively large communities compared to the size of the network and the number of available attributes.

We compared the partitions estimated by the top four algorithms using the ARI and obtained values between 0.73 and 0.82, which can be interpreted as a strong agreement between all four algorithms. Thanks to this high similarity between the optimal partitions, we can conclude the detected communities are relatively stable. FastGreedy is particularly interesting, because not only did it lead to the partition with the highest modularity and smallest number of communities, but it also has the highest ARI values when compared to the three other top algorithms. In other terms, it can be considered as a good compromise, which is why we will focus on this *reference partition* in the rest of our analysis. Fig. 13.1 gives a graphical representation of the trimmed network with the 22 communities identified by FastGreedy.

13.3.2 Business-Oriented Interpretation

As we mentioned in the introduction, previous works in Business Science have emphasized the role of social networks in information diffusion and purchase decision processes. These can be studied through the analysis of the network structure, and in this context community detection is particularly interesting. But communities are also potentially useful for they are groups of persons. Discovering this kind of groups and characterizing them in terms of purchase (or related) behavior appears as a major Business objective. The presence of such a property would increase even more the informative value of the communities, which is why we examine our results from a behavioral point of view in this section.

We selected three emblematic objects of our student population: its hobbies and two important purchases, i.e. mobile phones and digital players. Our goal was to

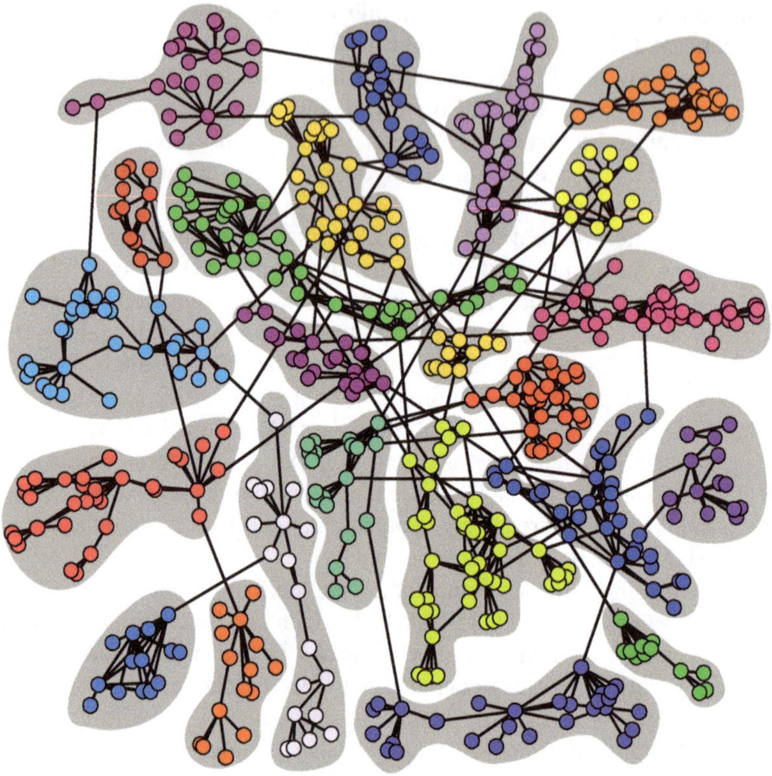

Fig. 13.1 Communities detected by FastGreedy using the relational data. The modularity processed for this partition is 0.88, i.e. a high value, which has two meanings: the network has a community structure and FastGreedy managed to identify it well. Isolated nodes were discarded for clarity

study the behavior related to these objects and to compare communities through this means. We analyzed the 22 communities to identify the two most widespread hobbies, the two most owned brands of mobile phones, and of digital players (Table 13.5) for each of them. Note it was not possible to find characteristic features for all communities.

The results we have in this first step of our study rely on too little data to be generalized (only 224 respondents). Nevertheless, clear differences between communities, concerning the hobbies and purchased brands, appear overall. There are globally two different kinds of communities for each or the three objects of study. In the first one, there is a unity of tastes and one, or sometimes two objects are clearly preferred. The nature of these objects depends on the considered communities. On the contrary, in the second kind, no clear trend appears, meaning there is no preferred object for this community (which can also be considered as a characteristic in itself).

Table 13.5 Characterization of the communities in terms of hobbies and purchase behavior

Community	Hobbies		Mobile phones		Digital player
1	Music	Sport	Nokia	–	Apple
2	Cinema	Sport	Nokia	Sony-Ericsson	Samsung
3	–	–	Nokia	–	–
4	Music	–	Nokia	Samsung	Creative
5	Sport	–	Samsung	Nokia	Apple
6	Reading	Music	Samsung	Sony-Ericsson	Apple
7	Cinema	Dance	Samsung	Sony-Ericsson	Apple
8	Sport	–	Samsung	–	Apple
9	–	–	Nokia	–	Apple
10	Cinema	Sport	Nokia	Samsung	Apple
11	Music	–	Nokia	–	–
12	–	–	Sony-Ericsson	–	Apple
13	Music	–	Nokia	Samsung	Sony
14	–	–	Nokia	–	–
15	–	–	–	–	–
16	Photo	–	–	–	–
17	Cinema	Sport	Nokia	Samsung	Philips
18	–	–	Nokia	Sony-Ericsson	–
19	–	–	Nokia	Samsung	–
20	Reading	–	Nokia	Samsung	Apple
21	Theater	–	Nokia	–	–
22	Cinema	Sport	Samsung	Nokia	Apple

If we focus on the hobbies, communities 3, 9, 12, 14, 15, 18 and 19 belong to the second kind. Among the remaining communities (first kind), we can regroup a majority of communities sharing the exact same interests, or very close ones. For instance, students in communities 2, 10, 17 and 22 are mainly interested in Cinema and Sport. Of course these are rough categories, and in reality a certain variance can exist: for example people probably do not practice the same sports nor like the same movies. Some communities have uncommon hobbies, for instance Dance and Theater are cited only by communities 7 and 21, respectively.

For the mobile phones, several tendencies can be highlighted. First of all, the brand Nokia is clearly the most widespread brand for the respondents. Nevertheless, important differences exist between Nokia-dominated communities. In communities 1, 9 and 14, nearly all the students own a Nokia mobile phone, whereas others have a second brand which is very often Samsung (4, 10, 13, 17, 19 and 20) and sometimes Sony-Ericsson (2 and 18). The second preferred brand is clearly Samsung, which is even dominant in a few communities (5–8 and 22). Interestingly, Apple does not appear, whereas it is largely dominating digital players. Only two communities do not have dominant mobile phone brand (15 and 16), which emphasizes the importance of brands in this sector, and the relevance of community detection.

Concerning the digital players, the most owned brand is by far Apple, which dominates in most of the communities. Interestingly, among the four communities interested primarily in music, Apple is dominant in only one (1), whereas Creative and Sony are prevalent in one community each (resp. 4 and 13). The remaining one (11) could not be characterized by any brand.

This raw analysis is just a first work on our data from a Business Science perspective. Further analyses need to be performed to uncover more meaningful information. For instance, one could be interested to know how hobbies correlate with the brands of purchased items. It is however perfectly illustrative of one of the interests of charactering communities in such a way: one can specifically select appropriate targets from a marketing perspective. Moreover, the structure of the network allows using more precise approaches, for instance by targeting a few persons depending on their connections.

Communities are valuable for Business Science analysis, but as mentioned before, obtaining them requires relational data, which are costly compared to the individual ones. For this reason, in the rest of this section we present our results regarding the identification of clusters based on factual individual data, and their usefulness to predict community membership.

13.3.2.1 Cluster Analysis

As we explained in the methods section, we decided to perform the cluster analysis in an exploratory way. For this reason, we applied all five selected clustering algorithms to all possible combinations of factual attributes. One could think a way of discriminating the numerous resulting partitions would be to select the few ones with the most separated clusters. However, this is not possible due to the nature of our data, which contains several nominal and dichotomous attributes. For some of these attributes, there was no other possibility to compare them than to define binary dissimilarity functions. Yet, when a clustering algorithm is presented a combination of nominal attributes compared via such a function, it will necessarily lead to a perfect partition, containing as many clusters as there are distinct combinations of values for the considered attributes. For instance, if we consider only the gender and entrance examination (both dichotomous attributes), we will obtain four perfectly separated clusters. Moreover, our goal is to use the clusters to predict community membership. These are the reasons why we selected cluster partitions depending on how much they fit the reference community partition.

Table 13.6 shows the results obtained for each algorithm over the best three combinations of attributes. The fit with the reference community partition was measured using the ARI. Other combinations lead to much lower ARI values (bellow 0.32 and mostly close to 0), which is why they are not presented here. For all five algorithms, clusters estimated using only the Department, Class and Grade attributes are the closest to the reference community partition, leading to ARI values close to 0.45. These values are intermediary, which seems to indicate the individual attributes used during the clustering process contain a part of the information underlying the network community structure. So on the one hand, we were able to use individual data to identify clusters which are relatively close to (or rather: not

Table 13.6 Three best combinations of attributes in terms of fitting of the cluster partition to the community partition. Values correspond to the fit quality expressed using the ARI

Attributes	Agnes	DBScan	Diana	Pam	TwoStep
Department, class, grade	0.457	0.444	0.450	0.456	0.448
Department, class, grade, highschool	0.433	0.223	0.424	0.422	0.429
Department, class, highschool	0.413	0.215	0.413	0.422	0.405

significantly different from) the communities estimated from relational data. But on the other hand, the corresponding partitions also have intermediate quality when considering how well they separate the space of attributes. This seems to confirm our previous observations regarding the difference in the nature of the information conveyed by the individual and relational data.

The partitions estimated by Agnes, DBScan, Diana, Pam and TwoStep for the first combination of attributes contain 25, 38, 21, 20 and 22 clusters, respectively. Except for DBScan, these sizes are very close to the 22 communities contained in the reference partition. The ARI values processed between the clustering algorithms are extremely high, ranging from 0.92 to 0.98, which means they identified almost the same clusters.

For the two other combinations of attributes presented in Table 13.6, the overlap with the reference partition is slightly lower. One can notice these combinations differ from the first one only by one attribute, which can be interpreted as a confirmation of the relevance of these attributes to discriminate the communities. The ARI values between the clustering algorithms are still very high, although slightly lower than for the first combination (close to 0.9). This is not true for DBScan however, which fails to detect any relevant clusters.

In summary, the various comparisons we conducted between the groups estimated by the cluster analysis approach and those identified by the community detection algorithms, generally lead to close to 0 ARI values, meaning the overlap between the corresponding partitions is very low. However, in some specific cases, appropriate combinations of attributes resulted in ARI values significantly different from 0. Thus, a link, even if a tenuous one, seems to exist between some individual attributes and the communities derived from the relational data. The next step in our study consisted in designing a predictive model to assess in which part the repartition of students in the different communities is determined by the attributes identified in this section.

13.3.2.2 Composition of the Communities

The work described in the previous section allowed us to identify the attributes which seemed to be the most relevant to discriminate the communities. In this section, we take advantage of the estimated clusters to design several models able to predict the community of an instance based on certain of its attribute values.

Table 13.7 Success rates obtained by applying our predictive approach to the previously described cluster partitions

Attributes	Agnes (%)	DBScan (%)	Diana (%)	Pam (%)	TwoStep (%)
Department, class, grade	75.5	81.9	72.3	72.3	73.4
Department, class, grade, highschool	69.7	47.9	64.8	69.0	68.3
Department, class, highschool	71.8	46.9	71.8	70.4	71.1

Our models are obtained by defining a correspondence between each cluster and a community, as explained in Sect. 2.2.4.

Table 13.7 presents the success rates for the previously presented cluster partitions, characterized here by the algorithm and combination of attributes used. The best performance is obtained with the DBScan partition on the first combination, with a 81.9 % success rate, but the results are also relatively high for the other algorithms (around 72–75 %). The ARI values we processed for this partition were clearly higher than zero, but not very high (around 0.45), so we expected success rates much lower than 82 %. However, this score has to be dampened. Indeed, with our approach, the number of clusters has an important effect on the prediction success rate. For instance, a partition in which all clusters contain only one instance each (which is a very bad clustering result) will necessarily lead to a perfect prediction. This explains why DBScan (38 clusters) has a higher success rate than the other algorithms (around 20 clusters) for the first combinations of attributes, when it has a lower ARI value. Moreover, the prediction can be applied only to students for which the considered attributes are available. Yet, the grade was a facultative question, and many students did not give any answer (only 96 responses). So, even if the success rate is high, it only concerns a few cases. Finally, the grade question is a delicate one, in the sense students with bad grades are less likely to answer it, which would bias our results.

For both other combinations of interest, the best results are obtained with the Agnes partition: 69.7 and 71.8 %, respectively. This means we obtain a success rate of more than 68 % on the basis of bigger samples, using combinations which still include Department and Class.

In order to understand how the attributes of interest compare in terms of explicative power, we additionally examined them separately using exactly the same method. The best result is obtained with Class (56.5 % for all five algorithms), followed by Grade (43.6 % with TwoStep) and Department (26.9 % for all five algorithms). The predictive rate of Highschool alone is very low: 9.7 % with all five algorithms. These scores allow us to rank these attributes of interest in terms of discriminant power.

13.3.2.3 Interpretation of the Discriminant Attributes

We a priori supposed the Department would be the most discriminant attribute, for the communities, because students from the same department spend most of their time together, making it easy to develop new relationships and strengthen older ones. However, the Class attribute happens to have the best predictive power, far beyond the department. This could be explained by a specificity of the GSU. Students integrating this university come from all parts of Turkey; they have very different skills and levels, both from the academic and linguistic perspectives. In particular, some of them have been speaking French since nursery school, whereas others never practiced this language before entering the GSU. For this reason, before starting the actual Lisans degree, they must follow a preparatory class for 1 or 2 years, including an intensive French course. Most students recruited via the national examination do not speak French and have to follow the 2-year-long preparation. All students which succeeded in the internal examination speak French and are prepared for only 1 year. During these preparatory years, all departments are mixed, because students do not follow specialized classes yet, but only French, methodological and common-core classes. We suppose this mixing make students develop cross-departmental relationships more easily. Moreover, this takes place during the first university years, and in a very new context for many students: they are far from home (Turkey is a large country), and family is very important in the Turkish society. For all these reasons, we think these relationships last even after the end of the preparatory program, when students enter specific departments and are separated from most of their preparatory fellows. Furthermore the university campus is very small, and there is therefore no major spatial obstacle to the persistence of interdepartmental relationships.

The Grade is the second best predictive attribute, which could be interpreted as the fact students with similar notes tend to get closer. However, as we stated before, this has to be interpreted carefully because of the scarcity of the responses concerning the corresponding question. The third discriminant attribute (Department) was also the most predictable, because spending daily hours together, working, interacting and sharing the same classroom make people closer and is favorable to the apparition of strong relationships (be it friendship or enmity). Moreover, students belonging to the same department are supposed to have the same academic interests, which can result in easier bounding and common club activity.

Some factors have surprisingly no influence on the repartition between communities. Gender, which could be supposed to have a central role in student interaction, especially in the case of young people evolving in a new environment, far from their home and family, does not seem to affect the way communities are formed. This is all the more surprising that stereotypes about Turkey often show some conservative part of the population considers gender separation as very important. Regarding the GSU students, this situation is not uncommon at all, although the majority of them come from a rather liberal background.

At a lesser degree, we expected high-school specialization (mathematics, literature . . .), and home city to have a noticeable effect. The life in Istanbul is clearly more cosmopolite, liberal, and culturally richer than in most parts of Turkey. For this reason, persons living in Istanbul sometimes have some sort of superior attitude towards people coming from rural environments, which can be aggravated by the differences of social status, and we expected this to appear in the composition of communities.

Of course, the scope of all these comments must be qualified, because they hold only for the students for which the mentioned discriminant attributes allow correctly predicting the community. For the rest of the population, we were not able to find a way to match communities and attributes, that is to find a link between the relational and individual data. This goes in the same direction than our results from the group comparisons, i.e. relational and individual data seem to convey different information, at least partially.

13.4 Conclusion

In this work, we gathered data from a population of university students, using a survey. From these data, we retained only the individual factual and relational information, and a part of the individual behavioral information, leaving the rest of the individual information for further exploration. We extracted a social network from the relational information, and detected 22 communities. Each community is characterized by a denser interconnection compared to the rest of the network. Using the individual behavioral information, we illustrated how these communities can be used to extract meaningful information in the context of Business Science. We characterized the communities in terms of hobbies and purchase behavior for two groups of products (mobile phones and digital players). We reached the conclusion that if most communities have heterogeneous tastes, it is nonetheless not the case for all of them. Detecting these communities and identifying their characteristics is a major asset for Business Science. Moreover, communities are supposed to have a strong effect on the buying process and decision making [12]. Consequently, any mean able to provide more information regarding potential client membership is extremely relevant and worthwhile.

For this purpose, in an attempt to predict communities from individual data, we then focused on the analysis of our individual factual information through classic cluster analysis. We considered all possible combinations of the factual attributes and compared the resulting partitions with the community partition, using the adjusted Rand index (ARI) [53]. This exploratory approach allowed us to identify the combinations of attributes leading to the best cluster partitions, in terms of similarity with the community partition. The corresponding ARI values are close to 0.45, which means although there is clearly more than random overlapping between clusters and communities, there is nevertheless a significant difference between them. Additionally considering these clusters were poorly separated, we concluded that, on these data, the information conveyed by the relational and factual individual data seems to differ significantly, at least in terms of groups of students. In other terms, the analysis traditionally performed in Business Science do not allow accessing the same information than what can be obtained through community detection. To our knowledge, this type of comparison was never performed before, especially in the domain of Business Science.

The third part of our analysis aimed at identifying the most discriminant factual attributes relatively to the communities. Our goal was to try giving an attribute-based interpretation to these groups formed only thanks to topological information. For this purpose, we took advantage of our results from the cluster analysis to build a predictive model, using the communities as reference groups. We found out the year of study (Class), the current grade (Grade) and the current department (Department) were the attributes of interest. We proposed some interpretations regarding why a community can be correctly predicted from these attributes.

13.5 Future Work

Our main result was to show the importance of community detection in a Business Science context. Indeed, not only are communities central in the information diffusion process, but they can also be characterized in terms of purchasing behavior. Further studies on other data and domains will show if they can be the basis of a new criteria for market segmentation. The perspectives for Business and Marketing Sciences seem very exciting and promising.

However, we consider this work as a first step in the analysis of our field results. Consequently, it suffers from some limitations we plan to solve quickly in the forthcoming articles. First, we mainly focused on the factual part of the individual information. The next step will consist in taking into account the rest of the behavioral and/or the sentimental individual data: maybe they convey the information necessary to define clusters exhibiting a better overlap with the communities. Second, we estimated mutually exclusive communities, which does not seem realistic, in the sense people often belong simultaneously to several groups. This could be solved by using an appropriate community detection algorithm [54] and fuzzy cluster analysis. Third, from a more general perspective, we plan to deepen our understanding of the way communities are constituted by proposing a dynamic model of community building.

Our work also suffers structural weaknesses, inherent to the context of the study. First, the survey was conducted in a small institution, with specific characteristics, which makes it difficult to generalize our results to another situation. This problem could be addressed by performing similar studies in other contexts, and for this purpose we are trying to start collaborations with searchers from other universities. Second, and more importantly, the data we analyzed is far from being complete, since it represents a relatively small part of the total number of students in the GSU. This response rate is normal for such a survey, especially considering the fact students participate on their behalf only. To improve this rate, we conducted our survey again, one semester later. This should both provide additional respondents, and add an interesting dynamic dimension for those who participated to both surveys.

Acknowledgements We would like to thank Günce Orman, who helped organizing and translating the survey, Siegfried Devoldère who also translated parts of the questions, and Taleb Mohamed El Wely who programmed the electronic form and designed the survey website. Our gratitude also goes to the reviewers, who provided us constructive comments and allowed us to improve the quality of this chapter.

References

1. Baret, C., Huault, I., Picq, T.: Management et réseaux sociaux: Jeux d'ombres et de lumières sur les organisations. Revue Française de Gestion **32**(163), 93–106 (2006)
2. Comet, C.: Productivité et réseaux sociaux: Le cas des entreprises du bâtiment. Revue Française de Gestion **32**(163), 155–169 (2006)
3. Simon, F., Tellier, A.: Créativité et réseaux sociaux dans l'organisation ambidextre. Revue Française de Gestion **187**, 145–159 (2008)
4. Ferrary, M.: Apprentissage Collaboratif et réseaux d'investisseurs en capital-risque. Revue Française de Gestion **163**, 171–181 (2006)
5. Ranie-Didice, B.: Capital social des dirigeants et performance des entreprises. Revue des Sciences de Gestion **231/232**, 131–135 (2008)
6. Fondeur, Y., Lhermitte, F.: Réseaux sociaux numériques et marché du travail. Revue de l'Ires **52**(3), 102–131 (2006)
7. Guieu, G., Meschi, P.-X.: Conseils d'administrations et réseaux d'administration en Europe. Revue Française de Gestion **185**, 21–45 (2008)
8. Dwyer, P.: Measuring the value of electronic word of mouth and its impact in consumer communities. J. Interact. Market. **21**(2), 16 (2007)
9. Goldenberg, J., Han, S., Lehman, D.R., Hong J.W.: The role of hubs in the adoption process. J. Market. **73**, 1–13 (2009)
10. Steyer, A., Garcia-Bardidia, R., Quester, P.: Modélisation de la structure sociale de groupes de discussion sur Internet: implications pour le contrôle du marketing viral. Rech. Appl. Market. **22**(3), 29–44 (2007)
11. van der Merwe, R., van Heerden, G.: Finding and utilising opinion leaders: social networks and the power of relationships. S. Afr. J. Bus. Manag. **40**(3), 65–73 (2009)
12. Hyunsook, K.: Comparing fashion process networks and friendship networks in small groups of adolescents. J. Fash. Market. Manag. **12**(4), 545–564 (2008)
13. Hartmann, W.R., Manchanda, P., Nair, H., Hosanagar, K., Tucker, C.: Modeling social interactions: identification, empirical methods and policy implications. Market. Lett. **19**, 287–304 (2008)
14. Watts, D.C., Dodds, P.S.: Influentials, networks and public opinion formation. J. Consum. Res. **34**, 441–458 (2007)
15. Iacobucci, D., Hopkins, N.: Modeling dyadic interactions and networks in marketing. J. Market. Res. **29**(1), 5–20 (1992)
16. Burt, R.: Structural Holes and Good Ideas. Am. J. Sociol. **110**(2), 349–399 (2004)
17. Perry-Smith, J.E.: Social yet creative: the role of social relationships in facilitating individual creativity. Acad. Manag. J. **49**(1), 85–101 (2006)
18. Rose, D., Charbonneau, J., Carrasco, P.: La constitution de liens faibles: une passerelle pour l'adaptation des immigrantes centro-americaines mères de jeunes enfants a Montréal Canadian Ethnic Studies **33**(1), 73–91 (1999)
19. Granovetter, M.: The impact of social structure on economic outcomes. J. Econ. Perspect. **19**(1), 33–50 (2005)
20. Sureh, C., Srividya, G., Swetha, K.: Viral distribution potential based on active node identification for ad distribution in viral networks. Int. J. Mobile Market. **4**(1), 48–56 (2009). (http://connection.ebscohost.com/c/articles/43884907/viral-distribution-potential-based-active-node-identification-ad-distribution-viral-networks)

21. Chollet, B.: L'analyse des réseaux personnels dans les organisations: quelles données utiliser? Revue Finance Contrôle Stratégie **11**(1), 105–130 (2008)
22. Doyle, S.: The role of social networks in marketing. J. Database Market. Cust. Strategy Manag. **15**, 60–64 (2007)
23. Droulers, O., Roullet, B.: Emergence du neuromarketing: apports et perspectives pour les praticients et les chercheurs. Décis. Market. **46**, 9–22 (2007). (http://www.afm-marketing.org/1-afm-association-francaise-du-marketing/126-afmnet/document.aspx?id=4123)
24. Ohme, R., Reykowska, D., Wiener, D., Choromanska, A.: Application of frontal EEG asymmetry to advertising research. J. Econ. Psychol. **31**(5), 785–794 (2010)
25. Parlebas, P.: Sociométrie, réseaux et Communication. PUF, Paris (1992)
26. Evrard, Y., Pras, B., Roux, E.: MARKET: Etudes et recherches en Marketing. Dunod, Paris (2000)
27. Jaccard, P.: Étude comparative de la distribution florale dans une portion des Alpes et des Jura. Bulletin de la Société Vaudoise des Sciences Naturelles **37**, 547–579 (1901)
28. Kaufman, L., Rousseeuw, P.J.: Finding Groups in Data: An Introduction to Cluster Analysis. Wiley, New York (1990)
29. Ester, M., Kriegel, H.-P., Sander, J., Xu, X.: A density-based algorithm for discovering clusters in large spatial databases with noise. Paper presented at the International Conference on Knowledge Discovery and Data Mining, Portland, USA, pp. 226–231 (1996)
30. Zhang, T., Ramakrishnon, R., Livny, M.: BIRCH: an efficient data clustering method for very large datebases. Paper presented at the International Conference on Management of Data, Montreal, Canada, pp. 103–114 (1996)
31. R Development Core Team: R: A Language and Environment for Statistical Computing. In. R Foundation for Statistical Computing, Vienna, Austria (2009)
32. Ward, J.H.: Hierarchical grouping to optimize an objective function. J. Am. Stat. Assoc. **58**(301), 236–244 (1963)
33. Newman, M.E.J., Girvan, M.: Finding and evaluating community structure in networks. Phys. Rev. E **69**(2), 026113 (2004)
34. Tasgin, M., Herdagdelen, A., Bingol, H.: Community Detection in Complex Networks Using Genetic Algorithms. arXiv:0711.0491 (2007). (http://arxiv.org/abs/0711.0491)
35. Newman, M.E.J.: Modularity and community structure in networks. PNAS USA **103**(23), 8577–8582 (2006)
36. Newman, M.E.J.: Analysis of weighted networks. Phys. Rev. E **70**(5) (2004)
37. Leicht, E.A., Newman, M.E.J.: Community structure in directed networks. Phys. Rev. Lett. **100**(11), 118703 (2008)
38. Csardi, G., Nepusz, T.: The igraph software package for complex network research. Int. J. Complex Syst. **695**)(2006)
39. Donetti, L., Munoz, M.A.: Detecting network communities: a new systematic and efficient algorithm. J. Stat. Mech. (10), P10012 (2004). (http://iopscience.iop.org/1742-5468/2004/10/P10012)
40. Girvan, M., Newman, M.E.J.: Community structure in social and biological networks. PNAS **99**(12), 7821–7826 (2002)
41. Newman, M.E.J.: Finding community structure in networks using the eigenvectors of matrices. Phys. Rev. E **74**(3), 036104 (2006)
42. Newman, M.E.J.: Fast algorithm for detecting community structure in networks. Phys. Rev. E **69**(6), 066133 (2004)
43. Rosvall, M., Bergstrom, C.T.: Maps of random walks on complex networks reveal community structure. PNAS **105**(4), 1118 (2008)
44. Raghavan, U.N., Albert, R., Kumara, S.: Near linear time algorithm to detect community structures in large-scale networks. Phys. Rev. E **76**(3), 036106 (2007)
45. Blondel, V.D., Guillaume, J.-L., Lambiotte, R., Lefebvre, E.: Fast unfolding of communities in large networks. J. Stat. Mech. P10008 (2008). (http://iopscience.iop.org/1742-5468/2008/10/P10008/)

46. van Dongen, S.: Graph clustering via a discrete uncoupling process. SIAM J. Matrix Anal. Appl. **30**(1), 121–141 (2008)
47. Radicchi, F., Castellano, C., Cecconi, F., Loreto, V., Parisi, D.: Defining and identifying communities in networks. PNAS **101**(9), 2658–2663 (2004)
48. Reichardt, J., Bornholdt, S.: Statistical mechanics of community detection. Phys. Rev. E **74**(1), 016110 (2006)
49. Pons, P., Latapy, M.: Computing communities in large networks using random walks. Proceedings of the Computer and Information Sciences – Iscis 2005, Istanbul, vol. 3733, pp. 284–293 (2005)
50. Barnes, E.R.: An algorithm for partitioning the nodes of a graph. SIAM J. Algebr. Discret Method **3**, 541–550 (1982)
51. Kirkpatrick, S., Gelatt, C.D., Vecchi, M.P.: Optimization by simulated annealing. Science **220**(4598), 671–680 (1983)
52. Rand, W.M.: Objective criteria for the evaluation of clustering methods. J. Am. Stat. Assoc. **66**(336), 846–850 (1971)
53. Hubert, L., Arabie, P.: Comparing partitions. J. Classif. **2**(1), 193–218 (1985)
54. Derenyi, I., Palla, G., Vicsek, T.: Clique percolation in random networks. Phys. Rev. Lett. **94**(16) (2005)

Chapter 14
Clustering Social Networks Using Distance-Preserving Subgraphs

Ronald Nussbaum, Abdol-Hossein Esfahanian, and Pang-Ning Tan

Abstract Cluster analysis describes the division of a dataset into subsets of related objects, which are usually disjoint. There is considerable variety among the different types of clustering algorithms. Some of these clustering algorithms represent the dataset as a graph, and use graph-based properties to generate the clusters. However, many graph properties have not been explored as the basis for a clustering algorithm. In graph theory, a subgraph of a graph is distance-preserving if the distances (lengths of shortest paths) between every pair of vertices in the subgraph are the same as the corresponding distances in the original graph. In this paper, we consider the question of finding proper distance-preserving subgraphs, and the problem of partitioning a simple graph into an arbitrary number of distance-preserving subgraphs for clustering purposes. We then present a clustering algorithm called DP-Cluster, based on the notion of distance-preserving subgraphs. We also introduce the concept of relaxation values to the distance-preserving subgraph finding heuristic embedded in DP-Cluster, and investigate this and other variations of the algorithm. One area of research that makes considerable use of graph theory is the analysis of social networks. For this reason we evaluate the performance of DP-Cluster on two real-world social network datasets.

14.1 Introduction

Cluster analysis is a technique for partitioning a dataset into groups of similar objects. It is often used as an exploratory data analysis tool to determine the underlying structure of a data set. A recent area of application is in the realm of social networks, where the goal is to find tightly-knit groups of people, also

R. Nussbaum (✉) · A.-H. Esfahanian · P.-N. Tan
Michigan State University, East Lansing, MI 48824-1226, USA
e-mail: ronald@cse.msu.edu; esfahanian@cse.msu.edu; ptan@cse.msu.edu

T. Özyer et al. (eds.), *The Influence of Technology on Social Network Analysis and Mining*, Lecture Notes in Social Networks 6, DOI 10.1007/978-3-7091-1346-2_14,

known as communities, based on their social relations. Communities are detected by partitioning the network into subgraphs in such a way that optimizes certain graph properties (e.g., minimizing the cut between clusters [9], or maximizing an edge-based modularity function [16]). In addition to these criteria, there are other graph invariants that are potentially applicable to clustering social networks. The motivation for our work is to explore the effect of alternative graph invariants on the process of community finding.

One of the difficulties with cluster analysis is that there is no strict definition of what a cluster is. This makes it more difficult to conjecture what sort of concepts might be usable in creating a clustering algorithm. In a social network, a vertex usually represents a person or small group of persons, while the edges represent the ties between them. We might wish to cluster participants according to family ties, peer groups, business relationships, and other personal attributes or common interests. For the graph of a social network, we expect to find higher connectivity between similar vertices than dissimilar ones. More importantly, we expect the centers of social groups to be quite dense, with fewer edges between communities. Since social networks tend to follow a scale-free distribution, we will not find large cliques. Still, we expect the shortest path between any two members of the same community in the network to involve other members from the same community rather than members from other communities. It is this last premise that gives us reason to explore the use of distance-preserving subgraphs as the basis of a clustering algorithm.

A distance-preserving subgraph is an induced proper subgraph that maintains the distances (lengths of shortest paths) as in the original graph. Consider the toy example of a social network shown in Fig. 14.1 which has 8 vertices and 13 edges. There are two natural communities in the network, one involving vertices (A, B, C, D) and the other (E, F, G, H). Clearly, both subgraphs are distance-preserving because the shortest path distance between any two vertices within each subgraph is identical to the one computed from the entire network. However, adding the vertex E to the subgraph (A, B, C, D) no longer preserves the distance between the vertex pair (E, B). Similarly, the addition of vertex F to (A, B, C, D) would make the subgraph non-distance-preserving because the distance between (F, C) is not the same as that in the original graph.

We face a number of challenges along the way to creating a useful clustering algorithm. As previously mentioned, we need to find distance-preserving subgraphs within a graph that represent clusters. While we generally cannot divide a given graph into an arbitrary number of distance-preserving subgraphs, we can always divide it into at least as many as desired, since isolated vertices are distance-preserving subgraphs. So we must devise a method of merging extra clusters such that we can always reach the desired number of clusters. We might also encounter graphs that can be divided into less than the desired number of distance-preserving clusters, in which case we will have to split them. Once we have addressed these challenges, we can use the heuristics found to develop a clustering algorithm.

This work is an extension of a previous paper of ours, *Clustering Social Networks Using Distance-Preserving Subgraphs* [17]. The bulk of the new material

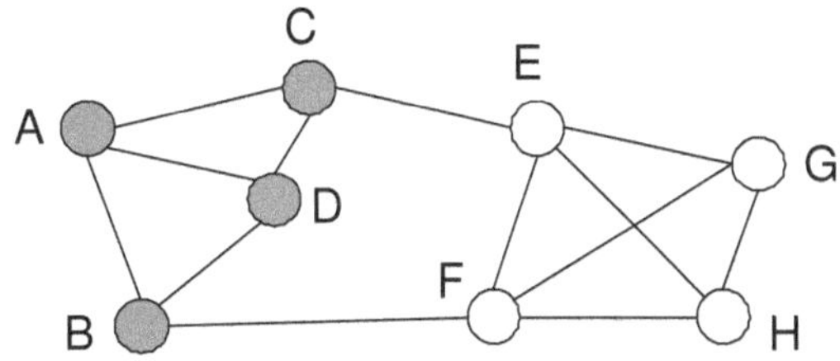

Fig. 14.1 A toy example of a social network

may be found in Sect. 14.4.4 and throughout Sects. 14.5 and 14.6. In the next section, we review related work in cluster analysis and give further background on distance-preserving subgraphs. In Sect. 14.3, we give a formal problem statement. In Sect. 14.4, we describe our algorithm, DP-Cluster, and variations on the basic algorithm. In Sect. 14.5, we present the results of applying the DP-Cluster algorithm on two social network datasets. We state our conclusions in Sect. 14.6.

14.2 Related Work

Many different clustering algorithms exist. Here we cover some of the more common ones, along with those based on the use of graph properties. We also provide some background into the topic of community finding. Finally, we give a more thorough explanation of distance-preserving subgraphs.

14.2.1 Clustering Algorithms

One of the better known methods of cluster analysis is k-means, whose name dates back to a paper by MacQueen [15]. k-means is a partitional algorithm that iteratively assigns objects to their nearest cluster centers, then recomputes the centers until they converge. Another important class of clustering methods is hierarchical clustering, which can be done in agglomerative or divisive fashion. Hierarchical clustering produces a dendrogram, which represents a series of clustering solutions, from all objects in one cluster to each object in a cluster of its own. Many variations of hierarchical clustering algorithms exist, including single-link, complete-link, group average, and Ward's method. An alternate approach is to define clusters as regions of high density objects separated by low density regions often populated by noisy observations. Two such algorithms are DBSCAN [8] and OPTICS [1].

A number of graph theoretic clustering algorithms have been developed. These algorithms are designed to optimize certain graph properties. For example, spectral clustering methods were developed to minimize variants of the graph cut property using the eigenvectors of the graph Laplacian matrix. Other heuristics have also been proposed based on minimizing diameter, p-centers, and other graph properties [4, 9, 18].

14.2.2 Community Finding

The technique of community finding, also called group detection [11], positional analysis [7, 21] or blockmodelling [21], is the process of placing vertices into groups in such a way that the vertices within a group are "similar" to each other and "dissimilar" to vertices in other groups. For example, Newman and Girvan [16] proposed an approach for discovering community structure in networks using modularity function as a measure of cluster quality. Scripps et al. [19] presented an overlapping clustering algorithm, taking into account the ill-effects of bridge vertices in a network. Liu et al. [14] gave an algorithm for building hierarchical communities using client-side web browsing history. More recently, there has been considerable interest in discovering dynamic communities in an evolving social network. For example, Zhou et al. [23] presented an algorithm for finding dynamic communities by combining the statically derived communities subject to certain constraints to ensure consistency of the clusters at different time periods. Tantipathananandh et al. [20] developed a community finding algorithm for dynamic networks using a graph coloring method.

14.2.3 Distance-Preserving Subgraphs

The topic of distance-preserving subgraphs is relatively unexplored. A subgraph of a graph G of order n is called a distance-preserving subgraph if the distances between every pair of vertices in the subgraph are the same as the corresponding distances between them in G, and the subgraph is a proper subgraph of G. A distance-preserving subgraph is necessarily induced if all edge weights in G are equal, since the omission of any edge would increase the distance between the endpoints of that edge. One can determine whether a given subgraph is distance-preserving by computing all-pairs shortest paths for the subgraph, and for G. If there are no negative cycles in G, then Floyd Warshall's algorithm [10] may be used to accomplish this, which has a time complexity of $O(n^3)$. If instead we have a subgraph $H \subseteq G$ that is known to be distance-preserving, and another vertex $v \in G$, determining whether $H \cup v$ is a distance-preserving subgraph of G is a single-source shortest path problem. This can be computed in $O(n^2)$ using Dijkstra's algorithm [6], or the Bellman-Ford algorithm [3] if G has negative edge weights.

A related concept is the distance-hereditary graph, first proposed by Howorka [13]. A graph G is distance-hereditary if every connected induced subgraph is distance-preserving. Distance-hereditary graphs are a subset of perfect graphs, and have been studied extensively [2, 5, 12].

14.3 Problem Statement

Let $G = (V, E)$ be a graph representing a connected social network of order $|V| = n$. Order refers to the number of vertices in a graph, and size refers to the number of edges. Our goal is to use the concept of distance-preserving subgraphs to partition $V(G)$ into k pairwise disjoint subsets $V_1, \dots, V_k$, such that $V_1 \cup \dots \cup V_k = V$, where V_i induces a distance-preserving subgraph. With n vertices and k clusters, on average a cluster must contain n/k vertices. Of course, the purpose of using cluster analysis is to find good clusters, not just ones of equal order. However, this fact hints at the fundamental question facing us: Given a graph G and integer m, does G contain a distance-preserving subgraph of order m? Answering this question raises several immediate issues.

14.3.1 Challenges

Our foremost concern is attaining clusters that are distance-preserving. Naturally, G will not always contain a distance-preserving subgraph of order m. So it will not always be possible to partition G into k distance-preserving clusters. Instead, we will seek to find clusters that are as close to being distance-preserving as possible. In the next section, we offer a way to quantitatively measure such almost distance-preserving subgraphs.

Even if G does have a distance-preserving subgraph of order m, we still have to find it. We suspect that this cannot be done for the general case in polynomial time. It definitely is computationally infeasible to do so in a naive fashion, so we resort to heuristics.

Since any distance-preserving algorithm is based off of distances between pairs of vertices, we have a problem if G is not connected. Our distance-preserving clustering algorithm assumes that G is a connected network. If the graph G is disconnected, we could apply our algorithm to each component separately.

14.3.2 Algorithmic Approach

Here we are at a crossroads. In the DP-Cluster algorithm presented in the next section, we partition G into as few properly distance-preserving clusters as we can find according to a heuristic, and proceed to merge them until we have k clusters. However, once we define a measure for how distance-preserving a subgraph is, we could instead construct an agglomerative hierarchical clustering algorithm. Specifically, we could start with G partitioned into n distance-preserving clusters, and repeatedly merge the two clusters whose union was most distance-preserving according to some metric, until we had k clusters left. It is less apparent how we might construct an efficient divisive hierarchical clustering algorithm. We proceed with our hybrid method in the interest of keeping larger parts of the clusters distance-preserving. It is not clear which path might lead to a better performing or less computationally expensive algorithm, although our algorithm seeks to minimize the number of times an all-pairs shortest paths algorithm is invoked.

14.4 DP-Cluster

Here we describe our heuristic for finding distance-preserving subgraphs, give a definition for an almost distance-preserving subgraph that we can use as a metric to merge these clusters, and present a simple clustering algorithm that combines the two, which we call DP-Cluster. The basic algorithm is covered in Subsect. C, and variations on the basic algorithm are discussed in Subsect. D. In the next section we compare DP-Cluster to the hierarchical clustering algorithm in Matlab's Statistics Toolbox (see *linkage* and *cluster*), along with random clustering for a baseline.

14.4.1 Finding Distance-Preserving Subgraphs

Finding large distance-preserving proper subgraphs in a graph is not an easy task. Clearly we cannot test each of the almost 2^n induced subgraphs of G to see whether or not it is distance-preserving. The best heuristic we have found so far is to start with a single vertex as a cluster C, which is trivially distance-preserving. At each step, we attempt to add each neighbor not in C to C in turn. If there is some non-empty set of neighbors such that the union of a single element with C leaves C distance-preserving, we choose one of them to permanently add to C according to some criteria, and continue. Once we reach a step where no neighbors can be added to C and have it remain distance-preserving, we are done.

14.4.2 Almost Distance-Preserving Subgraphs

We define the *average distance increase* for a subgraph of G as the sum of the distance increases between the subgraph and G, divided by the number of vertices in the subgraph. If the subgraph is distance-preserving, then this value is 0. The less distance-preserving the subgraph is, the higher this number will be.

14.4.3 The Algorithm

Our algorithm begins with each vertex from G in a separate cluster, all of which are trivially distance-preserving subgraphs of G. These clusters must be combined until there are only k clusters left. We pick one of these singleton clusters at random and use it as the start vertex to find a distance-preserving subgraph as described in the first part of this section. Random selection is used when there is more than one choice of vertices to add to the current cluster. Once this has finished, we set these vertices aside, pick another vertex at random, and repeat the process. Eventually, this will leave us with G partitioned into some number of distance-preserving clusters.

If we do not stop cluster growth at n/k vertices, we may end up with less that k distance-preserving clusters. In this case, we would have to break distance-preserving clusters apart to achieve k clusters. Since this has not happened with an actual dataset, we do not concern ourselves further with this possibility. Instead, we end up with a number of distance-preserving clusters larger than k. We then take each pair of clusters, and calculate how close to distance-preserving each potential merger is, according to the metric given in the second part of this section. The merge with the lowest value, i.e., the most distance-preserving, is made. This process is repeated until only k clusters remain.

Below is pseudocode for the basic versions of DP-Cluster. *clusters* is the set of clusters, whose members are sets of vertices. *unused* is the set of vertices that have not been placed into a cluster. *neighbors* is the set available vertices adjacent to some vertex in the current cluster. *usable* is the set of available vertices which can be added to the current cluster, and still have it be distance-preserving. RANDOM returns a random element from a set. NEIGHBORS returns the set of neighbors for a given vertex of a graph. RANDOMIZE returns a random permutation of a set. COUNT returns the number of elements in a set. ALMOST-DP returns how close a cluster is from being distance-preserving, according to the method described in the previous subsection.

14.4.4 Variations

Very often our distance-preserving subgraph finding heuristic will detect more than one neighbor whose addition leaves the resulting subgraph distance-preserving. In these cases, we must choose between them according to some criteria. Our default method is to do so randomly. This approach has the benefit that the search may be terminated after the first suitable vertex is found. The use of other metrics will affect subgraph generation in different ways. For reasons of efficiency, we prefer simple local measures that can be precomputed from G, rather than non-hereditary graph invariants that must be computed during execution. Unfortunately, this prevents us from using potentially useful graph invariants, such as diameter or girth, as tiebreak methods. Instead, we use the degree and clustering coefficient (CC) of vertices as

Algorithm 1 DP-Cluster

```
input  : A graph G = (V, E), and integer k.
output: A partition of V into k disjoint clusters.

unused ⟵ V
for i ⟵ 1 to n do
    v ⟵RANDOM(unused)
    unused ⟵ unused \ {v}
    clusters[i] ⟵ {v}
    neighbors ⟵NEIGHBORS(G, v) ∩ unused
    while unused do
        neighbors ⟵RANDOMIZE(neighbors)
        usable ⟵ {}
        foreach v ∈ neighbors do
            if IS_DP(G, clusters[i] ∪ v) then
                usable ⟵ usable ∪ v

            end
        end
        if usable ≠ {} then
            v ⟵RANDOM(usable)
            unused ⟵ unused \ {v}
            clusters[i] ⟵ clusters[i] ∪ v
            neighbors ⟵ neighbors ∪NEIGHBORS(G, v) ∩ unused
        else
            break
        end
    end
    c1, c2 ⟵ 0
    best ⟵ ∞
    while COUNT(clusters) > k do
        foreach i ∈ clusters do
            foreach j ∈ clusters \ {i} do
                if ALMOST_DP(clusters, i, j) < best then
                    c1 ⟵ i
                    c2 ⟵ j
                    best ⟵ALMOST_DP(clusters, i, j)
                end
            end
        end
        clusters ⟵ clusters ∪ {C1 ∪ C2} \ {C1, C2}
    end
end
return clusters
```

computed from the original graph. The clustering coefficient of a vertex v is the number of edges found between the neighbors of v divided by the total possible number of edges between the neighbors of v [22].

The DP-Cluster algorithm consists of two fairly independent parts, the distance-preserving subgraph finding heuristic, and the metric used to merge subgraphs. The first part partitions all vertices into distance-preserving subgraphs, and the second merges them as best it can. If we want more work done in the first part, we can relax the requirement that each subgraph found must be distance-preserving. Instead, we require that each distance in the subgraph found must be less than or equal to the corresponding distance in G, plus some constant. We call this constant the *relaxation value*. A relaxation value of 0 (and random tiebreaks) is equivalent to the basic version of DP-Cluster, i.e., each subgraph found in the first part of the algorithm must be distance-preserving.

14.4.5 Efficiency

Using distance-preserving subgraphs in any manner requires running an all-pairs shortest paths algorithm on G. Regardless of how we formulate our clustering algorithm, our running time must be at least $O(n^3)$. However, in generating distance-preserving subgraphs by adding one vertex at a time, we can use a single-source shortest paths algorithm in our distance-preserving subgraph finding heuristic. Variations that increase the size of the distance-preserving subgraphs found decrease the number of costly merges that must be performed.

14.5 Experimental Evaluation

In this section we compare and contrast DP-Cluster against a few existing hierarchical clustering algorithms, as well a random clustering algorithm, using different social network datasets. In each of our experiments, we test the basic algorithm, and examine the effects of using different tiebreaking methods and nonzero relaxation values. For clarity, we will continue to refer to the unmodified DP-Cluster algorithm as presented in Sect. 14.4.3, with random tiebreaks, and a relaxation value of 0, by using the adjective *basic*.

14.5.1 Datasets

The two datasets we use for testing are CiteSeer and Cora. They can be downloaded from the University of Maryland website at http://www.cs.umd.edu/~sen/lbc-proj/LBC.html. Vertices in these datasets are scientific publications, and edges represent citations, i.e., if the graph contains an edge (A, B), then either paper A cites paper B or paper B cites paper A. Although the papers represent authors, clustering in these datasets is closer to document classification than community finding in an ordinary social network. CiteSeer, which is composed of general topic computer science papers, contains 3,312 vertices, 4,536 edges, and 6 class labels: Agents, Artificial Intelligence, Database, Information Retrieval, Machine Learning, and Human-Computer Interaction. Cora, which consists entirely of

Table 14.1 Dataset properties – largest component

Dataset	Order	Size	Diameter	Number of classes
CiteSeer	2,110	3,668	28	6
Cora	2,485	5,069	19	7

machine learning papers, contains 2,708 vertices, 5,278 edges, and 7 class labels: Cased Based, Genetic Algorithms, Neural Networks, Probabilistic Methods, Reinforcement Learning, Rule Learning, and Theory. Since we want connected social networks for testing purposes, we extract the largest component from each dataset. For the remainder of this paper, we are referring to the largest component whenever we reference CiteSeer and Cora (Table 14.1).

14.5.2 Experiments

Before attempting to evaluate the full DP-Cluster algorithm, we want to look at results for each of the intermediate steps. Our first experiment is simply to find a single distance-preserving subgraph, using the incremental approach described in Sect. 14.4.1. When multiple vertices can be added to a cluster such that the cluster is still distance-preserving, we must choose between them in some fashion. We consider random selection, as well as the degree and clustering coefficient of the vertex as found in the original graph G. For vertex degree and clustering coefficient, we run two trials for each metric, one using ascending order, and the other with descending order. The goal in this experiment is to determine the effect of using different tiebreak methods and relaxation values on the clusters found, and to help choose which tiebreak methods to focus on going forward. We run 100 trials for each combination of dataset and method of breaking ties, and present statistics for the distance-preserving subgraphs found. We also run 100 trials for each combination of dataset and method of breaking ties with a relaxation value of 1. For each trial, we calculate the entropy of the final distance-preserving subgraph using the actual class labels. If G has k labels, then the entropy of the subgraph is given by the equation

$$entropy = -\sum_{i=1}^{k} \frac{m_i}{m} \log_k \frac{m_i}{m},$$

where m is the order of the subgraph, m_i is the number of vertices in the subgraph with label i, and $m_1 + \ldots + m_k = m$. Over all trials, we calculate the average order, standard deviation (σ) of the order, and the average diameter and entropy of the distance-preserving subgraphs found.

In the second experiment we examine the first part of the DP-Cluster algorithm, using random tiebreaks, as well as vertex degree and clustering coefficient in descending order only. That is, we run the algorithm as normal, but discard any clusters in excess of the number of class labels instead of merging them. As a result, each run of the DP-Cluster algorithm gives us a different subset of the vertices in G. The goal of this experiment is to give us some idea of the applicability of distance-preserving subgraphs to cluster analysis, without testing our definition of almost distance-preserving subgraphs as defined in Sect. 14.4.2. Here we run 100 trials on each dataset for each of the specified tiebreak methods, and calculate the average order and entropy over all trials. We run additional trials using random tiebreaks and nonzero relaxation values. In this experiment, the entropy for a given trial is the weighted average of the individual cluster entropies. For comparison, we calculate these same values using MATLAB's hierarchical clustering (HC) with various metrics, described in more detail below, and random clustering. Random clustering is exactly that, assigning each vertex to one of the k clusters with equal probability. As a different subset of vertices from G are used in each trial, the inputs to the hierarchical clustering and random clustering algorithms are only those vertices found by DP-Cluster in that particular trial.

The third experiment tests the full DP-Cluster algorithm as presented in Sect. 14.4.3, again using random tiebreaks, as well as vertex degree and clustering coefficient in descending order only. For each trial G is fully partitioned into distance-preserving subgraphs, which are then merged into k almost distance-preserving subgraphs. For this experiment, we run 20 trials on each dataset for each tiebreak method, and present the average entropy over all runs. Again, we run additional trials using random tiebreaks and nonzero relaxation values. We also consider cluster stability. For each run, we create an $n \times n$ incidence matrix, where entry i, j is 1 if i and j belong to the same cluster, and 0 if they do not. We then calculate the average correlation between these matrices for each pair of trials. Again, we calculate these same values using hierarchical clustering, and random clustering algorithms.

For evaluating MATLAB's hierarchical clustering algorithm, we use three different distance metrics. *Single linkage* (nearest neighbor) uses the minimum of all the distances between pairs of vertices in the two clusters. *Complete linkage* (furthest neighbor) uses the maximum of all the distances between pairs of vertices in the two clusters. *Average linkage* uses the average unweighted distance between all pairs of vertices in the two clusters. For each of these distance metrics, the pair of clusters with the minimum distance between clusters are merged at each step.

14.5.3 Results

In this subsection we give the results for our three experiments.

14.5.3.1 Finding a Single Distance-Preserving Subgraph

In Tables 14.2 and 14.3 we see that the average distance-preserving subgraph found was reasonably large, with considerable variation depending on the tiebreak method used. Even so, the average order is still much smaller than the average cluster needs

Table 14.2 Finding a single distance-preserving subgraph – CiteSeer

Tiebreak method	Relaxation value	Average order	σ(order)	Average diameter	Average entropy
Random	0	101	58	14	0.636
Degree, incr.	0	56	35	12	0.664
Degree, decr.	0	176	87	16	0.645
CC, incr.	0	86	51	14	0.657
CC, decr.	0	131	69	15	0.652
Random	1	223	112	17	0.684
Degree, incr.	1	131	87	16	0.666
Degree, decr.	1	416	184	19	0.720
CC, incr.	1	149	85	16	0.684
CC, decr.	1	334	182	19	0.667

Table 14.3 Finding a single distance-preserving subgraph – Cora

Tiebreak method	Relaxation value	Average order	σ(order)	Average diameter	Average entropy
Random	0	110	86	10	0.618
Degree, incr.	0	47	52	8	0.562
Degree, decr.	0	169	109	11	0.634
CC, incr.	0	64	57	9	0.590
CC, decr.	0	150	106	10	0.626
Random	1	188	140	11	0.642
Degree, incr.	1	91	99	11	0.624
Degree, decr.	1	339	166	13	0.707
CC, incr.	1	124	103	11	0.615
CC, decr.	1	298	189	12	0.666

to be, so we do not have to consider the problem of splitting excessively large distance-preserving subgraphs. The standard deviation (σ) of the order is also quite high, indicating that the heuristic is sensitive to the choice of initial vertex. More intelligent selection of starting vertices might not only reduce this, but improve the performance of the DP-Cluster algorithm as well. The average diameter found with the CiteSeer dataset is much higher than the one found for Cora, which corresponds to the fact that the original CiteSeer graph had a diameter of 28 compared to a diameter of 19 for Cora (Table 14.1).

It is clear from our results that the method of tiebreaking used has a significant effect on the order of the subgraph found. Specifically, using vertex degree and clustering coefficient in descending order both bias our heuristic towards using higher degree vertices earlier. This yields much larger subgraphs compared to selecting a vertex at random, along with an expected increase in diameter and entropy. We suspect what is happening here is that if higher degree vertices are not chosen sooner, they are likely never able to be used at all, limiting the pool of unused neighbors, and ultimately the size of the distance-preserving subgraph found. Notably, although using these metrics in ascending order produces clusters smaller than those found using random tiebreaks, entropy does not decrease. With

Table 14.4 Basic DP-Cluster, discarding excess clusters – CiteSeer

Algorithm	Average entropy
DP-Cluster	0.656
HC, single	0.815
HC, complete	0.627
HC, average	0.660
Random	0.888

Table 14.5 Basic DP-Cluster, discarding excess clusters – Cora

Algorithm	Average entropy
DP-Cluster	0.618
HC, single	0.795
HC, complete	0.589
HC, average	0.637
Random	0.811

the CiteSeer dataset, average entropy actually increases when using vertex degree and clustering coefficient in ascending order instead of random tiebreaks. Other methods of breaking ties might produce even larger subgraphs, or subgraphs of lower entropy. As previously mentioned, many graph invariants we would like to use are unfeasible for complexity reasons. Given the results here, subsequent experiments will focus on the use of random tiebreaks, as well as vertex degree and clustering coefficient in descending order only.

The effect of relaxing the distance-preserving requirement even by 1 is significant. Average cluster size is slightly less than double in most cases compared to the corresponding trial with a relaxation value of 0. Results using higher relaxation values continue the trend towards larger and larger clusters, and are omitted for brevity.

14.5.3.2 Partial Clustering With DP-Cluster

The basic DP-Cluster algorithm used approximately one quarter of the vertices from the largest component of the corresponding dataset on average. The hierarchical and random clustering algorithms used the same subset of vertices found by DP-Cluster in each trial as inputs, which is why the average order of these clustering algorithms is the same. We had some concern that the order of successive distance-preserving subgraphs would decrease rapidly after the first one. This was not observed in practice, and the average order for these trials was only slightly less than the average order for the corresponding trials in our first experiment times the number of class labels for that dataset (Tables 14.4 and 14.5).

The average entropy for all the clusters found by the basic DP-Cluster algorithm, while not as low as we might desire, did not increase appreciably from the previous

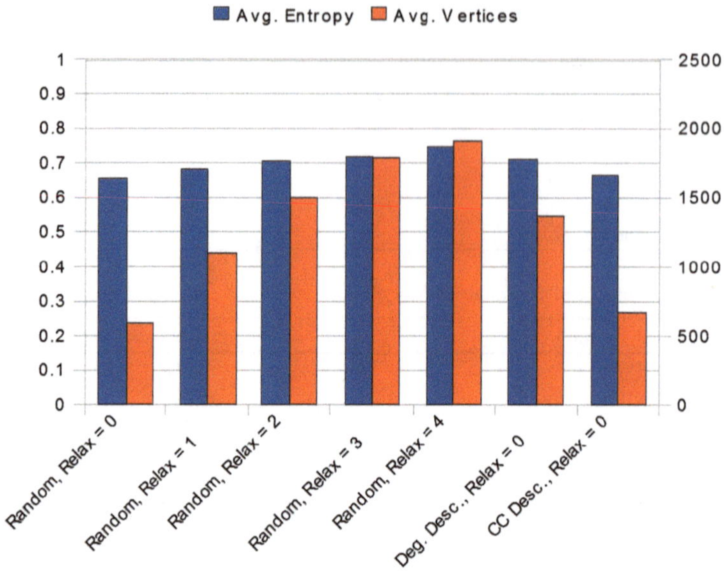

Fig. 14.2 DP-Cluster variations, discarding excess clusters – CiteSeer

experiment. For the CiteSeer dataset, DP-Cluster resulted in an average cluster order of 581, and it outperformed two of the three hierarchical clustering algorithms. With the Cora dataset, DP-Cluster resulted in an average cluster order of 633, and it outperformed the same two hierarchical clustering algorithms. Since the set of vertices used here varies from trial to trial, it is meaningless to consider correlation (Tables 14.4 and 14.5).

As seen in Figs. 14.2 and 14.3, variations in DP-Cluster drastically affect our results. Here we examine alternate tiebreak methods and nonzero relaxation values, without comparing each one back to the hierarchical clustering algorithm. In line with what we saw in the first experiment, the number of vertices used increases dramatically with each successive relaxation value. As we increase the relaxation value from 0 to 4, we go from using a quarter of the vertices in the dataset in each trial, to using nearly all of them.

The alternate tiebreak methods tested performed somewhat differently than we anticipated from the results of the first experiment. Using vertex degree resulted in much larger clusters as expected, and the average entropy of these trials did not show an improvement over random tiebreaks after taking into account the number of vertices used. With the clustering coefficient, the average number of vertices used in all clusters found was not that much higher than using random tiebreaks. This stands in contrast to the first experiment, where the average subgraph order found using the clustering coefficient metric was much higher than when choosing randomly. As with vertex degree, the entropy is again roughly in line with random tiebreaks after adjusting for the number of vertices used.

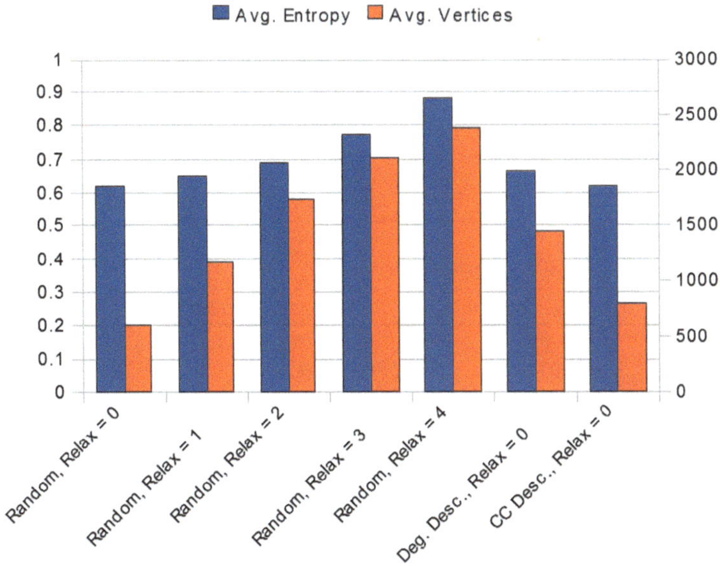

Fig. 14.3 DP-Cluster variations, discarding excess clusters – Cora

14.5.3.3 Full Clustering With DP-Cluster

For the CiteSeer dataset, performance of the hierarchical clustering algorithms range from somewhat better to much worse than basic DP-Cluster, depending on the distance metric used to create the hierarchical cluster tree. Unsurprisingly, random clustering led to much higher average entropies than all other clustering algorithms (Tables 14.6 and 14.7).

With the Cora dataset, basic DP-Cluster performs better than all but one of the distance metrics. It is not immediately clear why complete-link hierarchical clustering, which merges clusters according to the furthest distance between them, performs so well here. What is certain is that cluster entropy has significantly increased from the previous experiment. Also of concern is the relatively low correlation found between trials using DP-Cluster (Table 14.7).

We were less optimistic after the previous experiment that nonzero relaxation values would improve results using the full DP-Cluster algorithm. Here we see that for both datasets entropy decreases up to a relaxation value of 2, after which it increases again (Figs. 14.4 and 14.5). Correlation also increases along with the relaxation value, although this is probably due to the increase in variance of cluster order.

As with the previous experiment, using alternate tiebreak methods had mixed performance. Results using vertex degree and the clustering coefficient had entropies similar to DP-Cluster with a relaxation value of around 2. With both datasets, results using the clustering coefficient had higher correlations than those using vertex degree.

Table 14.6 Basic DP-Cluster, merging excess clusters – CiteSeer

Algorithm	Average entropy	Average correlation	Average clusters
DP-Cluster	0.778	0.264	102
HC, single	0.952	1.000	N/A
HC, complete	0.727	1.000	N/A
HC, average	0.898	1.000	N/A
Random	0.951	0.091	N/A

Table 14.7 Basic DP-Cluster, merging excess clusters – Cora

Algorithm	Average entropy	Average correlation	Average clusters
DP-Cluster	0.783	0.205	181
HC, single	0.937	1.000	N/A
HC, complete	0.748	1.000	N/A
HC, average	0.883	1.000	N/A
Random	0.937	0.077	N/A

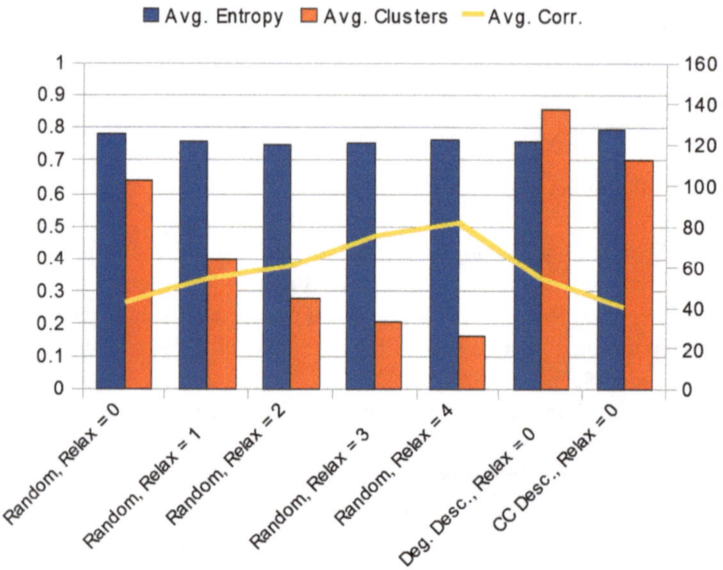

Fig. 14.4 DP-Cluster variations, merging excess clusters – CiteSeer

14.5.4 Discussion

Overall, the results of DP-Cluster compare favorably to hierarchical clustering methods. The algorithm has some obvious weaknesses, some of which may be due to the current implementation. Like many incremental algorithms, DP-Cluster is order dependent. It does find clusters of reasonably low entropy, even after "leftover" clusters are taken into account. However, complete-link hierarchical

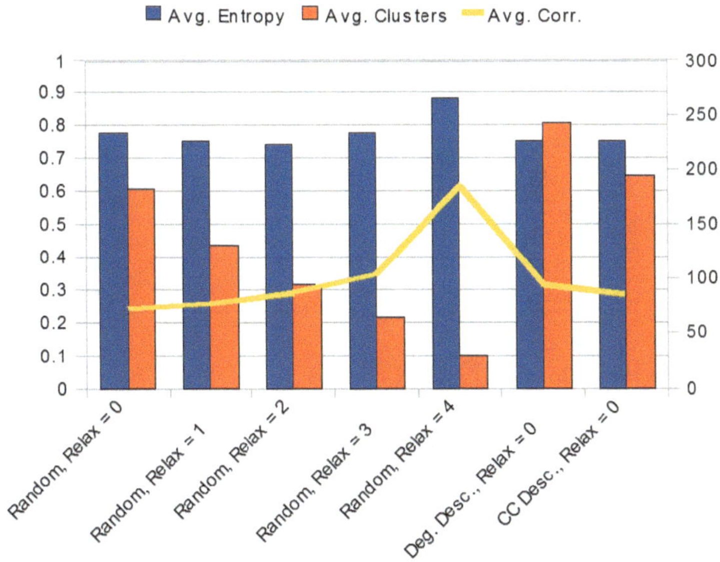

Fig. 14.5 DP-Cluster variations, merging excess clusters – Cora

clustering outperforms DP-Cluster on the CiteSeer and Cora datasets, although the gap is smaller with some of the DP-Cluster variations. This outperformance might disappear on other datasets depending on their structure. Also, DP-Cluster found clusters of fairly low stability given their low entropy. A better distance-preserving subgraph finding heuristic should reduce this effect. An algorithm with better time complexity would allow us to explore larger datasets as well. So far we have only tested DP-Cluster on datasets of modest size.

In this paper, we treat paper citations as undirected links, rather than directed arcs. One avenue of exploration would be to treat them as arcs instead. Alternately, we could investigate social networks in which links indicate a bidirectional relationship, rather than a unidirectional relationship like a citation or following another profile. An entirely different approach with the paper citation networks would be to treat authors as links instead of papers.

Our experimental results lead us to make the following conjecture.

Conjecture 1. Almost all graphs are distance-preserving, i.e., an arbitrary graph on n vertices has at least one distance-preserving subgraph for each order $m = 1, \ldots, n$.

If true, it underscores the need to develop heuristics for identifying distance-preserving subgraphs that better reflect actual communities in social networks. An exhaustive search of all connected graphs on up to 11 vertices provides some support for our conjecture, as seen in the table below (Table 14.8).

Table 14.8 A survey of distance-preserving graphs

n	# connected graphs	# connected, non-DP graphs	Proportion connected, non-DP graphs
5	21	1	0.04762
6	112	1	0.00892
7	853	4	0.00469
8	11,117	19	0.00171
9	261,080	183	0.00070
10	11,716,571	2,474	0.00021
11	1,006,700,565	107,176	0.00011

14.6 Conclusions and Future Work

The performance of the fairly simple DP-Cluster algorithm shows promise for the use of distance-preserving subgraphs in community finding. Nonetheless, further exploration is needed to develop a better performing algorithm. Along with finding better clusters, finding more consistent clusters is an issue. Possibilities here include improving the heuristic for finding distance-preserving clusters through intelligent selection of initial vertices, different tiebreak methods, or other variations in the same vein as our concept of relaxation values. Changing the manner in which the distance-preserving clusters are merged is also an option. Another approach is to create an agglomerative distance-preserving based hierarchical algorithm, which would combine the “finding” and “merging” processes into a single step. Our previously stated efficiency concerns regarding the use of all-pairs shortest paths versus single-source shortest path algorithms apply here.

References

1. Ankerst, M., Breunig, M., Kriegel, H., Sander, J.: OPTICS: ordering points to identify the clustering structure. ACM SIGMOD Rec. **28**(2), 49–60 (1999)
2. Bandelt, H., Mulder, H.: Distance-hereditary graphs. J. Comb. Theory B **41**(2), 182–208 (1986)
3. Bellman, R.: On a routing problem. Q. Appl. Math. **16**(1), 87–90 (1958)
4. Charikar, M., Chekuri, C., Feder, T., Motwani, R.: Incremental clustering and dynamic information retrieval. In: Proceedings of the Twenty-Ninth Annual ACM Symposium on the Theory of Computing, pp. 626–635. ACM, New York (1997)
5. Damiand, G., Habib, M., Paul, C.: A simple paradigm for graph recognition: application to cographs and distance hereditary graphs. Theor. Comput. Sci. **263**(1–2), 99–111 (2001)
6. Dijkstra, E.: A note on two problems in connexion with graphs. Numer. Math. **1**(1), 269–271 (1959)
7. Doreian, P., Batagelj, V., Ferligoj, A.: Positional analyses of sociometric data. Models and Methods in Social Network Analysis, pp. 77–97. Cambridge University Press, New York (2005)
8. Ester, M., Kriegel, H., Sander, J., Xu, X.: A density-based algorithm for discovering clusters in large spatial databases with noise. In: Proceedings of KDD, vol. 96, pp. 226–231. AAAI, Menlo Park (1996)

9. Flake, G., Tarjan, R., Tsioutsiouliklis, K.: Graph clustering and minimum cut trees. Int. Math. **1**(4), 385–408 (2004)
10. Floyd, R.: Algorithm 97: shortest path. Commun. ACM **5**(6), 345 (1962)
11. Getoor, L., Diehl, C.: Link mining: a survey. ACM SIGKDD Explor. Newsl. **7**(2), 12 (2005)
12. Hammer, P., Maffray, F.: Completely separable graphs. Discret. Appl. Math. **27**(1–2), 85–99 (1990)
13. Howorka, E.: A characterization of distance-hereditary graphs. Q. J. Math. Oxf. Ser. **2**(28), 417–420 (1977)
14. Liu, K., Bhaduri, K., Das, K., Nguyen, P., Kargupta, H.: Client-side web mining for community formation in peer-to-peer environments. ACM SIGKDD Explor. Newsl. **8**(2), 20 (2006)
15. MacQueen, J.: Some methods for classification and analysis of multivariate observations. Proceedings of the 5th Berkeley Symposium on Mathematical Statistics and Probability, vol. 1, pp. 281–297. Defense Technical Information Center, Ft. Belvoir (1966)
16. Newman, M., Girvan, M.: Finding and evaluating community structure in networks. Phys. Rev. E **69**(2), 26113 (2004)
17. Nussbaum, R., Esfahanian, A., Tan, P.: Clustering social networks using distance-preserving subgraphs. In: 2010 International Conference on Advances in Social Networks Analysis and Mining (ASONAM), pp. 380–385. IEEE, Washington, DC (2010)
18. Plesnik, J.: A heuristic for the p-center problem in graphs. Discret. Appl. Math. **17**(3), 263–268 (1987)
19. Scripps, J., Tan, P.: Constrained overlapping clusters: minimizing the negative effects of bridge-nodes. Stat. Anal. Data Min. **3**(1), 20–37 (2010)
20. Tantipathananandh, C., Berger-Wolf, T., Kempe, D.: A framework for community identification in dynamic social networks. In: Proceedings of the 13th ACM SIGKDD International Conference on Knowledge Discovery and Data Mining, p. 726. ACM, New York (2007)
21. Wasserman, S., Faust, K.: Social Network Analysis: Methods and Applications. Cambridge University Press, Cambridge (1994)
22. Watts, D., Strogatz, S.: Collective dynamics of 'small-world' networks. Nature **393**(6684), 440–442 (1998)
23. Zhou, D., Councill, I., Zha, H., Giles, C.: Discovering temporal communities from social network documents. In: Proceedings of the 2007 Seventh IEEE International Conference on Data Mining, pp. 745–750. IEEE, Washington, DC (2007)

Chapter 15
Extraction of Spatio-Temporal Data for Social Networks

Judith Gelernter, Dong Cao, and Kathleen M. Carley

Abstract It is often possible to understand group change over time through examining social network data in a spatial and temporal context. Providing that context via text analysis requires identifying locations and associating them with people. Our GeoRef algorithm too automatically does this person-to-place mapping. It involves the identification of location, and uses syntactic proximity of words in the text to link location to person's name. We describe an application using the algorithm based upon data from the Sudan Tribune divided into three periods in 2006 for the Darfur crisis. Contributions of this paper are (1) techniques to mine for location from text (2) techniques to mine for social network edges (associations between location and person), (3) spatio-temporal maps made from mined data, and (4) social network analysis based on mined data.

15.1 Introduction

Texts can help us answer the question "who is where?" Automatically identifying person–location pairs in texts requires understanding the text. This paper describes how to construct an artificially intelligent algorithm that "understands" which words are places with the help of an authoritative place list called a gazetteer. The algorithm associates entity-place pairs with one another as the basis of a two-mode, people-by-location network.

Social network analysis uses advanced mathematical techniques and statistical analysis to examine the relationships among group members. These members, or "entities," are represented by nodes, and the relationships among the nodes are

J. Gelernter (✉) · D. Cao · K.M. Carley
School of Computer Science, Carnegie-Mellon University, 5000 Forbes Avenue, Pittsburgh, PA 15213, USA
e-mail: gelern@cs.cmu.edu; dongcaocmu@gmail.com; kathleen.carley@cs.cmu.edu

T. Özyer et al. (eds.), *The Influence of Technology on Social Network Analysis and Mining*, Lecture Notes in Social Networks 6, DOI 10.1007/978-3-7091-1346-2_15,

represented by links (also called edges), that in a diagram are shown as lines between nodes. Nodes may be people, organizations, locations, events, resources, topics, etc.

Identifying locations. Location is particularly valuable in analyzing certain kinds of networks. For example, in epidemiology, geographic context proves more important than personal contact in understanding the spread of disease [1]. In disaster response, location of events and how they change over time can allow relief efforts to be coordinated efficiently [2]. In crime investigation as well as prevention, location is used to spot patterns and learn where to enforce preventive measures [3].

Identifying locations in a text is a complex problem. Named Entity Recognition typically includes identifying names of locations as well as people and organizations [4]. Named Entity Recognition can reach almost 80 % accuracy [5], but automatically identifying location accurately can be harder. For example, a group participant in GeoCLEF 2005, a conference devoted to geographic information retrieval (of which geospatial data mining is a part), had only 41 % of documents relevant to a query identified [6].

Time in networks. Newspaper articles often begin with month and day of writing, so mining the date is straightforward. Including time information in a network allows us to examine how a community evolved, and how a network can be viewed in a series [7]. Often this is shown visually with a series of diagrams or maps.

We are interested in the network measure known as centrality. According to the glossary of the social network analysis software, ORA, centrality is the nearness of an entity to all other entities in a network [8]. It has been shown that centrality measures may be robust in light of missing data [9]. Visualizations of data in time series allow us not only to see changes from one time period to another, but also they may allow us to make inferences about data that is missing. For example, if we have evidence of a foreign presence in Kassala in February, March and May, one may infer that foreign presence resident in Kassala in April as well.

In Sect. 15.2 below we describe related projects, and in Sect. 15.3 we discuss the types of difficulties involved in mining for location words. We describe the data in Sect. 15.4, and the GeoRef algorithm in Sect. 15.5. We provide several ways to evaluate our work in Sect. 15.6, both by demonstrating the accuracy of the algorithm's location-identification capabilities, and by dividing the data into spatio-temporal maps and giving network statistics for each of three time periods to show who was involved where. Discussion about algorithm optimization and generalizability follows in Sect. 15.7. We summarize in Sect. 15.8 what we believe are our main contributions.

15.2 Related Work

Earlier research has focused on the extraction of social networks from texts [10, 11]. As named entity identification has improved, so too has the extraction of social network data. Here we take the extraction of social network data as a given. Our interest is in extracting locations and in linking those locations to the social network.

Finding locations. Locations represent a particular challenge within named entity identification [12]. In addition to the standard approaches and heuristics, gazetteers are used. Gazetteers differ in entry scope, coverage, accuracy, and specificity. Choice of gazetteer by necessity will influence results. The gazetteer can supply additional background knowledge that is helpful in data analysis. Some researchers use existing gazetteers such as the National Geospatial Intelligence Agency gazetteer[1] or GeoNames,[2] while others generate them automatically [13] or derive them from Wikipedia [14]. Researchers have extended the problem of finding location names in text to identifying regions that signify places, such as "downtown" or "by the docks" [15, 16]. Such are not generally found in gazetteers.

Location-mining software has gone commercial. MetaCarta[3] will locate places named in a document or text stream. Yahoo! Placemaker[4] has a web service to do the same. These applications might use gazetteers that are not inclusive enough to find small towns named in a text. But using very large gazetteers can slow processing.

One way to improve the ability of a computer to recognize location is to use a specialized gazetteer. Wang et al. [17] devised a Location Aware Topic Model to discover topics and the location related to each topic. They extend the gazetteer by adding words with implied locations not found in a standard gazetteer. For example, they add leaders and connect leaders to their country (Barack Obama to the United States), events to countries (Olympics 2008 to Beijing, China), and groups to region (Sunni to the Middle East). Such a gazetteer, however, is difficult to prepare with any degree of thoroughness.

Techniques for spatiotemporal knowledge discovery have been described by Roddick and Lees [18]. Geospatial data mining begins with toponym resolution, or attaching a geographic location to a place named in a text [19]. The difficulty is that not all words that look like locations are associated with geographic locations, in what is called non-geo/geo ambiguity (is "Mobile" a phone or a town in Alabama?). The other problem in geospatial text mining is geo/geo ambiguity, introduced when there are several locations with the same name [20].

Linking people to location. Extracting relations between entities is substantially harder than entity recognition, and state-of-the-art systems perform less well on this task. Most relation extraction work assumes that entities have been identified correctly. Main methods for extracting relations between entities are to discover verb relations [21], construct concept graphs based on rules [22], or find syntactic proximity based on inference. The limitation of the syntactic proximity techniques is that they tend to miss links that are implied in the text but not close in a text, For

---

[1] National Geospatial Intelligence Agency gazetteer is at http://earth-info.nga.mil/gns/html/

[2] http://www.geonames.org

[3] http://www.metacarta.com

[4] http://developer.yahoo.com/geo/placemaker/guide

example, while they typically identify linkages in the same sentence, they less often find linkages that are expressed later in the paragraph.

15.3 Mining a Text for Location Words: Implications for the GeoRef Algorithm

Geoparsing is the identification of place names in a text; it is the backbone of the novel GeoRef algorithm. Geo-coding assigns latitude and longitude to a location [23].

We give examples of potential errors in mining locations from our data of the Sudan Tribune, and then describes what was done in coding the GeoRef algorithm to resolve these types of errors. We find errors of place names that are not recognized as places, and non-place names that are taken to be place names incorrectly. We show how each type of error is treated by our GeoRef algorithm. Then we conclude with a mention of the related problem of deciding which of multiple versions of the same place name in a gazetteer is the one referred to in a text.

15.3.1 Place Names Not Recognized as Places

Location words are recognized as places based on matches with the gazetteer. The types of errors of places not recognized – large places, small places, places with multiple spellings, and imprecise regions – result in type I error (omission of the correct response), and may all be improved by adjusting the gazetteer. This section illustrates in italics each difficulty in the context of our data.

Large places. These are regions which correspond to a geographical area larger than a country, which do not appear in standard gazetteers. We need to list countries that comprise the region in order to determine the geographic coordinates.

Examples:

…[T]he regime hopes to have a fig-leaf international presence with which to cultivate support among the *Arab and Islamic worlds*, and from stalwart economic partners Russia and China. wk35_4j

Algorithm solution:

1. Add Arab world and Islamic world to gazetteer
2. Resolve multi-country regions into those countries that comprise them
3. Enter geographic coordinates of the centroid of the multi-country region in the gazetteer

Small places. Towns or neighborhoods known locally may not appear in a world gazetteer. In the examples below, the reporter supposed even Sudan Tribune readers would not know the location of "Deleige" and "Tawilla", so the towns are followed in the same sentence with geographical descriptors in parentheses.

Examples:

The humanitarian organization Tearfund reported the death of a member of its relief team in *Deleige* (Wadi Saleh), West Darfur. wk 30_61

...Minawi and his soldiers deny responsibility for the violence in *Tawilla* (west of el-Fasher in North Darfur) and other towns in the region ... wk 30_61

Algorithm solution:

1. Add small towns to gazetteer
2. Enter geographic coordinates of each small town centroid to the gazetteer

Multiple spelling. In names transliterated from other languages, multiple spellings may be a problem. "Kordofan" appears as "Kurdufan" in the GeoNames gazetteer, for example. Also, punctuation might be lax. The U.S. without punctuation matches the pronoun "us," and so might not be found in a text.

Examples:

...a rally at Zeribah in *North Kordofan*, central Sudan." wk 30_61

"It is another disaster for *US* policy." wk 30_61

Algorithm solution:

1. Add multiple spellings of the same place to gazetteer
2. Recognize upper case "US" the United States. We cannot use lack of punctuation only, or else each predicate pronoun "us" will be resolved geographically

Imprecise regions. Many imprecise regions such as "north of the city" do not necessarily correspond to a precise geographic area. However, rather than lose a geographic reference, we bound these regions artificially. For example, the Upper Nile region in Sudan comprises three states: the Upper Nile (state 20), Jonglei (22), and Unity (19). We resolve "southeast Upper Nile region" as the state of Jonglei, although it might be more precise to use the centroid of the eastern portion of Jonglei (Fig. 15.1).

Examples:

.... between militias in the *southeast Upper Nile region* and the areas around Sudan's main oil fields which are in the south." wk 30_61

Many fled from *south and western Sudan* during a famine in the 1980s. wk 35_71

Algorithm solution:

1. Add to gazetteer the names of imprecise regions
2. Associate geographic coordinates with those imprecise regions

15.3.2 Non-place Names Mistaken for Places

All the words in italics in the examples below appear in the gazetteer as place names. In context, however, they do not refer to places.

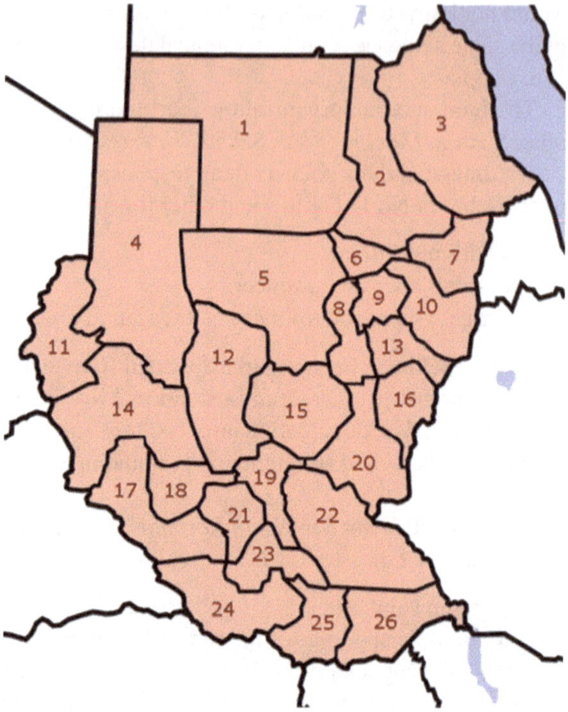

Fig. 15.1 States of Sudan (numbered) ©2010 Wikipedia

Common words. Ambiguities are created when country names are transliterated. For example, "Nor" and "Both," according to the GeoNames gazetteer, happen to be populated places in Sudan's Upper Nile. We surmount this problem by filtering the gazetteer for common words that are more likely to hold their common word meaning than be place names.

Examples:

With Chad's government neither willing *nor* able to protect rural populations, a massive increase in violence and civilian destruction seems *both* imminent and inevitable. wk 40_dd

Algorithm solution:

1. Create a separate list of geo-words that are also common words
2. For any geo-word found also on the list of common words (such as mobile, or nor), only attach geographic coordinates if that word is immediately preceded in the same sentence by another place name, or immediately followed in the same sentence by another place name.

Named Entities. Titles of books or periodicals as well as names of organizations might include geographical names that are a source of confusion in data mining.

Examples:

Those countries that have the required military assets must be ready to deploy them." ("Darfur Descending," The *Washington* Post, January 25, 2006) wk 28_av

'France is taking steps to stop the genocide as fast as possible,' he said on Radio *Monte Carlo* ... " wk35_4j

Algorithm solution:

1. List commonly-appearing phrases that contain geo-words, such as New York Times.
2. Do not attach geographic coordinates to geo-words found within those phrases

Metonymy. The literary conceit known as metonomy borrows the name of one thing to stand for another with which it is associated. Metonomy creates confusion especially in news articles because a capital city often indicates that country's government.

Examples:

... the inability of the donors conference to compel *Khartoum* to accept a robust UN force ... wk 28_av

"... to allow a UN mission into Darfur to replace an African Union force that has been unable to stem the violence *Washington* called genocide. wk 28_av

Algorithm solution:

1. Do not attach geographic coordinates to capital cities if followed by the words "regime" or "government". Example: In the phrase "Khartoum regime," Khartoum would not be considered a place.

Admittedly, this solution is inadequate in many cases of metonomy. Researchers are encouraged to work on this problem with Natural Language Processing techniques.

15.3.3 Which Is the Correct Match in the Gazetteer?

Confusion arises when there are two or more places with the same name. Leidner [12] relates rules that have been used by different researchers to resolve the problem of two places of the same name in the gazetteer that match a place named in the data. Examples of such disambiguation rules are: among same-named places in the gazetteer, choose the place that is higher in the geographical hierarchy (country above city), that is more populous, that is within the geographic domain of the data, or that is closer in distance to other non-ambiguous places named in the data.

15.4 Data and Resources for Data Processing

News article data. Our team decided that mining articles as the Darfur conflict escalated in 2006 would provide insight into the events of the time. Several thousand short pieces in the form of news reports, commentary, and an occasional published letter make up the full data set that was downloaded mostly from the Sudan

Tribune.[5] We selected 11 files randomly from among these for creating, refining and testing the GeoRef algorithm. File size differs because article length differs depending upon who wrote the article, the significance of week's events, and so on. One article might contain 500 words, while another's might have closer to 5,000. Locations in the 11 articles were annotated manually by coders guided by instructions in the Appendix. We divided the texts into three sets according to the time periods they represented: January 2006 (two files), March–April 2006 (four files), and May–July 2006 (five files). These divisions were made in order to balance the number of people's names found in the files, because the first two files were particularly rich in names.

Thesaurus of people's names. We manually created an external thesaurus for people's names that we used to automatically tag the names of people in the data. Very few of these people found in the data are political officials or foreign dignitaries, so our preliminary experiments with a thesaurus less well fit to the domain proved useless.

Gazetteers. GeoNames is attractive for our context because it includes alternate spellings, and many of our place names are transliterated from one of the official languages of Sudan, Arabic. We could not use the entire gazetteer since it would slow processing greatly. Instead, we limit the gazetteer to the GeoNames features of continent, first- and second-order administrative divisions, seat of a first-order administrative division, independent political entities and dependent political entities, territories, zones and buffer zones. Only for Sudan did we use entities in all feature classes. This serves the purpose of speeding processing without sacrificing resolution of location names in the data. Our gazetteer excerpt has 25,926 entries (8 % for the world, and 92 % for Sudan states, villages and topographical features).

15.5 The GeoRef Algorithm

The main tasks of the novel algorithm are to find location words in the data, identify locations with a precise area for which we can give latitude and longitude coordinates and a spatial hierarchy (for a city, for instance, it outputs also state and country). Also, the algorithm associates locations with other entities in text, such as topics or people. Figure 15.2 presents an overview, which is followed by an outline of the steps the algorithm follows. Plotting people-location pairs is a form of georeferencing, hence the algorithm name, GeoRef.

---

[5]Recall that in 2005, a separate government formed in southern Sudan in opposition to the dominating regime, and in early 2006, Sudan rejected United Nations peacekeeping efforts. Many died during the conflict between north and south in 2006. Sudan accepted African Union peacekeeping help in November 2006, and then accepted United Nations peacekeepers in early 2007.

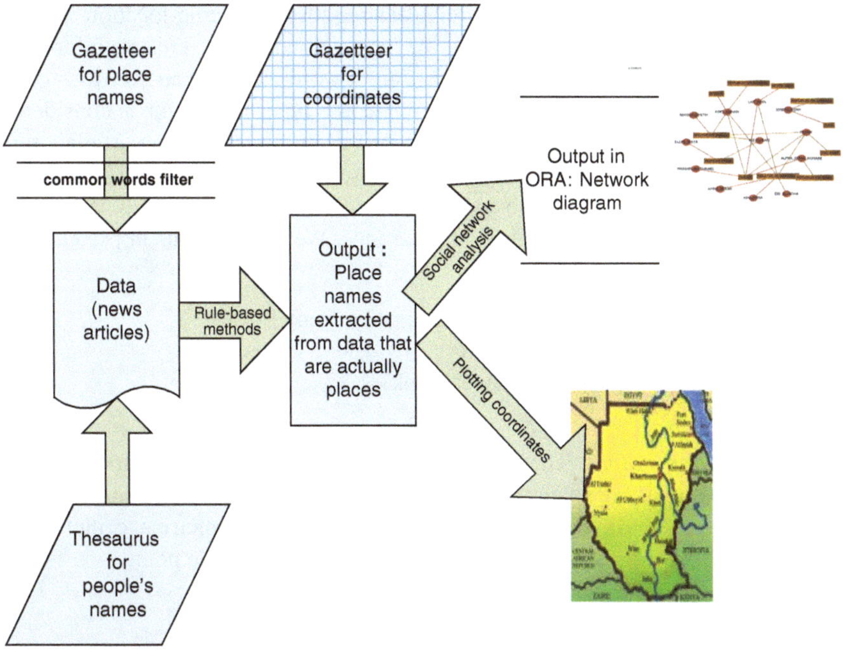

Fig. 15.2 The algorithm runs a thesaurus over the data to find people, and then a gazetteer to find potential geo-words to link to those people. Note that plotting topic-location pairs is a form of geo-referencing. The Sudan map is re-printed with permission Mill Hill Missionaries

Steps followed by the algorithm

1. *Mine for people's names.* The identification of the names in the given texts was done manually. These names were assembled into a list. Then this list was used to identify the people's names automatically in order to prepare the text for finding associated locations.
2. *Mine for location.* The process of mining for location was automated. We used the very large gazetteer GeoNames, with small city and town entries for Sudan only and the rest of the world at the level of country, state and major cities, and we filtered the gazetteer for common names. Then additional heuristics to disqualify place names in instances of metonymy and when the place name is embedded in other named entities are invoked.
3. *Associate each person's name with a location in text.* To find a location to match with a person, the program mines the geo-word closest to the person's name that is in the same clause. If the sentence contains two geo-words, it mines the geo-word that is before rather than after the person's name. If there is no geo-word in same sentence as the name, it looks in the same paragraph, first in the sentence immediately before, then immediately after, then anywhere in the paragraph. In cases in which no locations are found, it looks to the article title and first paragraphs for a geo-word.

4. *Determine link strength.* We assign relative strength to the name-location connection based on how certain we are that the connection is valid. This we infer from the distance in the document between linked words. If the geo-word is found anywhere in the same paragraph as the name, the link to the name is considered strong; if the program must find a geo-word in the title or in the article's first paragraph, the link is considered weak. In cases where no geo-word is found in any of the places suggested, we consider the connection to be invalid because no pair can be made with any degree of assurance. We describe this in pseudocode below.

   If geo-word occurs in same paragraph = 2 (strong link)
   Else if geo-word occurs in title or
   first paragraph of article = 1 (weak link)
   Else = 0

5. *Enrich location output.* The geo-word mined from the text is enriched with the upper levels of the spatial hierarchy. It is also associated automatically with the geographic coordinates of that region's centroid (the geometrical center of the region) so that the location can be plotted on a map as a single point.

15.6 Testing the GeoRef Algorithm

We describe separately a test for GeoRef location-identification, and a test for GeoRef associating locations with people.

15.6.1 Location Identification

An annotator was given 11 texts downloaded from the Sudan Tribune and asked to list every location found, following only a few guidelines (as reported in the Appendix). We wished to retrain validity by asking only one person to go through all the documents. But even this paid annotator could only tolerate only so much of a dull task without succumbing to fatigue and error. Our sample size, therefore, was limited by human attention constraints.

Procedure. We illustrate below an excerpt from the text, and examples of what the manual coder versus what the algorithm selected as location words from that text (Table 15.1). The manual coding was used as a benchmark to judge the degree of algorithm accuracy both at the corpus (collection) and at the document (text) level.

White Nile Petroleum and Dinka Bor Extinction [article title] **Tuesday 2 May 2006 23:30. By Deng Ajak Jongkuch** [file: week17]

May 1, 2006 On April 25 of 2005, the government of Southern Sudan signed a 10 year oil exploration licensing contract with a White Nile Limited owned by a former Middlesex and England cricket star Phil Edmonds. The agreement gave

Table 15.1 Comparison of one manual coder's decisions about what locations the "White Nile Petroleum" paragraph contains to the GeoRef output

Manual coding	GeoRef
Southern Sudan	Southern Sudan
England	White Nile
Block Ba	England
Junglei	White Nile
Southern Sudan	Junglei
Junglei	Southern Sudan
Bor	White Nile
	Junglei
	Bor

White Nile Limited a right to explore oil in Block Ba which covered an area of 67,000 km of State of Junglei. The area is believed to have about six billion of barrels oil in reserved. According to agreement, a government of Southern Sudan owned oil company Nile Petroleum Corporation will own 155 shares and 40 % in stakes while White Nile Limited will retain 60 % of stakes. According to CPA of wealth sharing modelity <sic>, 2 % of oil revenues will go to where oil exploration will take place. The government of Junglei is responsible for the 2 %, not the Bor County.

Scoring. We measure results at two levels – the corpus level and the document level.

At the corpus level, we identify the percent of location words identified manually that were also identified by GeoRef. For each document, we count the number of times GeoRef identified a location correctly, missed a location (type I error), and added a location not found in the manual benchmark (type II error).

We score a location correct if the place is an exact match with the manual coding or if the place is a subset of that found by the manual coder. So if, for instance, the manual location is Junglei, and the algorithm found Bor which is in Junglei, the GeoRef algorithm found Junglei too, so the output is correct. We also score a GeoRef location to be a match with that of the manual coder if it is higher in the hierarchy. So for example, if the coder found Southern Sudan and the algorithm found Sudan, we score the algorithm to be correct.

Results: Corpus level and document level accuracy in finding locations. At the corpus level, the GeoRef algorithm yielded 62 % accuracy, with a standard deviation (spread around the mean) of 18 %. We get this number by adding true positives, true negatives and false positives according to the formula below.

$$accuracy = \frac{true\,positives + true\,negatives}{true\,positives + false\,positives + false\,negatives + true\,negatives}$$

Table 15.2 Document level accuracy for finding locations by the GeoRef algorithm on the Sudan Tribune data sample

File name	Correct (TP)	Incorrect (type II) (FP)	Missing (type I) (FN)	Precision	Recall	Accuracy	F-measure
wk_1	24	3	1	89	96	86	92
wk_2	105	92	8	53	93	51	68
wk_9	19	0	3	100	86	86	93
wk_10	10	4	2	71	83	63	77
wk_11	9	3	2	75	82	64	78
wk_14	10	3	3	77	77	63	77
wk_17	31	33	16	48	66	39	56
wk_22cm	11	11	4	50	73	42	59
wk_22 3q	16	12	13	57	55	39	56
wk 22xs	31	7	1	82	97	79	89
wk 26	23	8	2	74	92	70	82
Mean	26.27	16	5	**71**	**82**	**62**	**75**
Std. deviation	27.34	**26.75**	**5.11**	/	/	**18**	/

This 62 % accuracy for finding locations represents a significant improvement over the 41 % accuracy reported by one of the participating groups in the 2005 GeoCLEF geographic information retrieval conference [6]. Document level results are arranged by file number in Table 15.2.

Table 15.2 shows the number of locations mined from text correctly (True Positive or TP), the number of locations found that are not actually locations (False Positive or FP), and the number of locations that should have been found that were not (False Negative or FN). Then we calculate precision and recall statistics as well as the combination of precision and recall called the F-measure. This is the standard information retrieval evaluation for whether all locations are found correctly (precision), and for whether all locations found should be found (recall). The F-measure combines the two.[6]

Limitations of experiment 1. This experiment based on manual coding as benchmark is limited by the sample size of the data. That sample size was limited in that asking a person to annotate too much data may introduce error from fatigue or carelessness. As it is, in our small data set, our coder missed numerous locations due to lapses in attention, especially in articles that are longer. The result is that many correct locations are marked wrong in the algorithm output. The accuracy of the algorithm, therefore, is somewhat higher than the statistics suggest.

Discussion of experiment 1. What accounts for the errors in Table 15.2? GeoRef identified place names that are not actually places (type II error), whether because they are within the names of organizations or companies, or because they are capitals

[6]On the standard means of evaluation for retrieval sets, see Manning, Raghavan and Schütz [25].

Table 15.3 Distributions of codes in each of the three time periods, with link statistics supplied by the ORA social network analysis software

	Time period 1	Time period 2	Time period 3
Number of people	12	12	7
Number of locations	11	10	6
Number of links	48	24	20
Total	71	46	23

that stand for countries as a form of metonymy. GeoRef omitted the names of villages too small to appear in the gazetteer (type I error). Type II error is far more common here that Type I error, both because metonymy and other errors of place name ambiguity occur regularly and are not well-managed by the algorithm, and because the data coder missed places that are legitimate.

15.6.2 People-Location Link Identification

We measure the people–location links using the same 11 files as in the location experiment.

Procedure. The people thesaurus was used to code for people and the GeoNames gazetteer excerpt was used to code for locations. The 11 files were separated into groups representing the three time periods, and each group was run independently.

Scoring. We measure the number of nodes and links first. The data was input into the social network analysis software ORA [8, 24] to find the number of links shown in Table 15.3.

Result: See links in Table 15.3

Result: See maps in Figs. 15.3, 15.4 and 15.5

The GeoRef algorithm attaches geographic coordinates to locations. To create a visualization, we associate the coordinates of the person with his paired location and then plot each location using Google Earth. We label each red site indicator with the number of occurrences of that entry in the data set. The color of label and the color of the tear drops are otherwise arbitrary. The maps for the three time periods (Figs. 15.3–15.5) give an idea of who were the actors in different phases, where they or their influence was, and how the situation changed as the year progressed.

Interpretation of maps. Data analysis is based on examination of Table 15.3, and the maps for each of the three time periods as shown in Figs. 15.3, 15.4 and 15.5. At the beginning of 2006, we see that influence was concentrated in the east and south of Sudan with dominant actors being Jan Pronk, UN-appointed special envoy to Sudan, and Kofi Annan, then Secretary General to the United Nations. The influence of the United Nations diminishes somewhat in the spring, according to the documents mined, with prominent actors being Sudanese. Abdallah

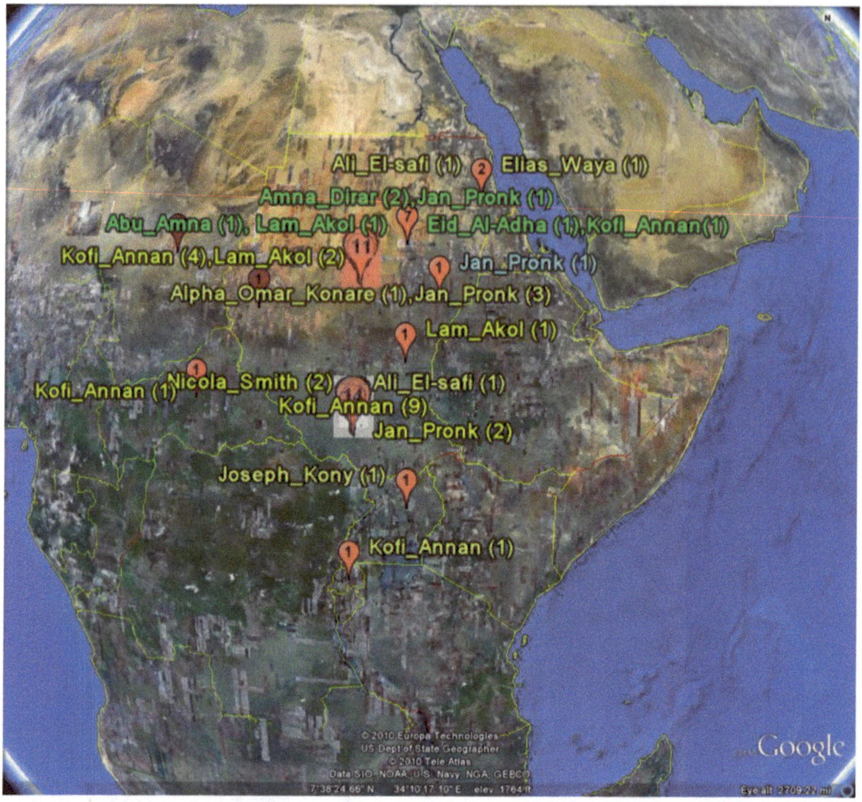

Fig. 15.3 (Above): Time Period 1: Jan 2006 (files wk1, wk2) (©2010 Google Map ©2010 Tele Atlas)

Moussa Abdalla, secretary-general of the Beja Congress Party in Port Sudan, and the Sudanese who were arrested in the Gadaref state, President al-Almin al-Hajj and Treasurer Hassan al-Masri, showed the center of the action moving to Sudan's north. Then by the late spring, Kofi Annan of the United Nations and Suliman Baldo who is the deputy director of the International Center for Transitional Justice return the foreign presence in Sudan to prominence, with the center of concern being Sudan's east. This interpretation is some reflection of actual happenstance since it derives from news articles. However, a more precise picture could be produced from a much larger data set. Also, there are errors that have been generated by the incorrect association of persons with locations. Other errors are caused by differences in precision due to the data mined such that some people are located by city while others are located to the level of Sudan only (and hence appear to cluster in the country's center).

Evaluation of maps. The utility of the maps will depend upon the map user's purposes. Historians, political scientists, and anthropologists, for example, might

Fig. 15.4 (Above) Time period 2: March-April 2006 (files for wk 9,10,11,14) (©2010 Google Map ©2010 Tele Atlas)

use our annotated map series to follow where people were acting over time. We could annotate maps based on historical documents as easily as current newspapers, as is done here.

Our annotations show a person's village, city, state or country, depending on what hierarchical level of location is named in the text. We could improve the utility of the maps in future by drawing a bounding box around the location being mapped to indicate the region indicated. This is not a present function of the software, however.

Network performance.

We are interested in calculating which people and which locations are most central to the group of people in the network constructed for each of the three time periods. To find network centrality, the people and locations mined and linked by GeoRef are input into the social network analysis software ORA. The set of people–location pairs for each time period is formed into a network and then reduced in

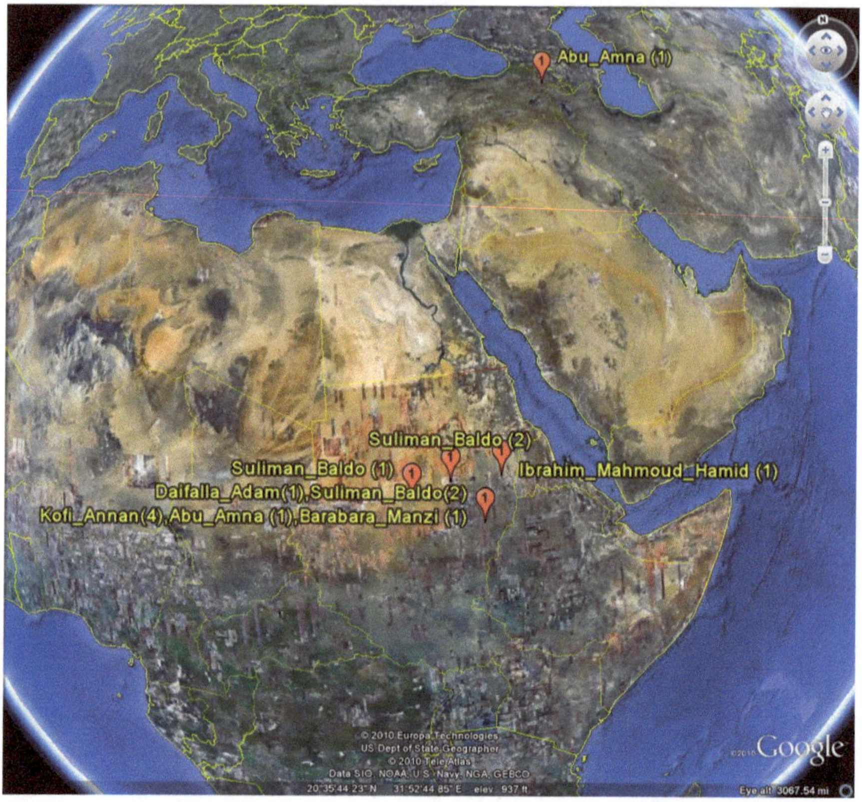

Fig. 15.5 (Above): Time period 3: May-July 2006 (wk 17, 22_1c, 22_3q, 22xs, 26) (©2010 Google Map ©2010 Tele Atlas)

order to calculate the statistics. Finally, we run the ORA "All Measures Report" on each network for each of the three time periods to produce tables 15.4 through 15.9 below.

We are interested in what places and what people are most central to the network in each of the three time periods. Degree centrality measures the number of direct links an entity has. Because links flow out from people and in to the locations, we are interested in the "Centrality-Out Degree" measure for people in tables 15.5, 15.7, 15.9, and the "Centrality-In Degree" measure for locations in tables 15.4, 15.6 and 15.8. The software calculates numerical scores for people and places based on the number of linkages they have. These raw values are then normalized on a scale between 0 and 1. We take only the top five results for each measure.

Time Period 1

Table 15.4 Period 1, centrality-in degree for locations

Rank	Location	Scaled value
1	Southern Sudan	1.000
2	Sudan	0.786
3	Wilayat al Khartum	0.500
4	Hamesh Khor	0.143
5	Africa	0.071

Table 15.5 Period 1, centrality-out degree for people

Rank	Agent	Scaled value
1	Kofi_Annan	1.000
2	Pronk	0.438
3	Lam_Akol	0.250
4	Amna_Dirar	0.125
5	Ali_el-Safi	0.125

Time Period 2

Table 15.6 Period 2, centrality-in degree for locations

Rank	Location	Scaled value
1	Port Sudan	0.455
2	Kassala	0.182
3	Al Qadarif	0.091
4	The East	0.091
5	Sudan	0.091

Table 15.7 Period 2, centrality-out degree for people

Rank	Agent	Scaled value
1	Abdallah_Moussa_Abdallah	0.500
2	Al-Amin_Al-Hajj	0.100
3	Hassan_al-Masri	0.100
4	Sulieman_Derar	0.100
5	Sima_Samar	0.100

Time Period 3

Table 15.8 Period 3, centrality-in degree for locations

Rank	Location	Scaled value
1	The East	1.000
2	England	0.091
3	Kassala	0.091
4	Wilayat al Khartum	0.091
5	Sudan	0.091

Table 15.9 Period 3, centrality-out degree for people

Rank	Agent	Scaled value
1	Kofi_Annan	0.833
2	Suliman_Baldo	0.667
3	Abu_Amna	0.500
4	Phil_Edmonds	0.167
5	Ibrahim_Mahmoud_Hamid	0.167

Interpretation of network performance results. We see from tables 15.4 through 15.9 above that the most central location in the first period is southern Sudan and the major actors are those associated with the United Nations, Kofi Annan and Jan Pronk. In the second period, the central actors are associated with Sudanese politics and the most central regions are northern Sudan. In the third period, the focus is more in eastern Sudan, in Kassala and also Khartoum.

The data used for the network centrality calculations are the same as the data as was used for the geographical maps, so it is not surprising that the top actors and locations resemble that in the three maps. This mathematical presentation validates the mapped visualizations.

15.7 Algorithm Optimization

In creating GeoRef, we have made two decisions that optimize processing time at the expense of gazetteer coverage and algorithm generalizability. We discuss both choices here.

GeoNames contains over ten million geographical names, with the main download file being 878 MB.[7] We suggest that those using GeoNames as an external referent use only a gazetteer excerpt unless other optimization methods such as parallel processing are used.

[7]The size quoted is as of November 2010.

The few rules in the algorithm for metonymy and for place names embedded in organization names are generalizable to other news domains. But these rules will be of limited value in other text domains. Other domains, however, such as business or history might have a fair number of place names embedded in titles or organization names. We recommend these as areas of further research.

In this paper, we have mined the date of the newspaper articles that appears in each article's beginning. This date mining will not generalize beyond news media. Extending temporal data mining to other sources can use natural language processing methods. For example, we could translate an event into a date (Thanksgiving), or to add time to an event ("a conference that occurred last week"). The algorithm would get the date of the event either by data mining or from a temporal thesaurus.

Another way we optimized in coding GeoRef is to allow a frankly superficial level of understanding of the people-location link. Deeper exploration of the people-location link remains for future work. Is the person travelling to the (linked) place? Does he start in the place? Is he in the place temporarily? Was he in the place at one time but no longer?

15.8 Contributions in Summary

This paper describes how to mine news articles for the names of people and locations using our novel GeoRef algorithm in preparation for social network analysis. We have offered heuristics for mining location, and for associating a person's name with a location. We use a spatio-temporal network approach and application with data from news articles. We map the data and also give network statistics to compare change over time in who and where are the network actors.

We present a network with node labels enriched beyond what is possible through data mining alone. The gazetteer supplies upper levels of the spatial hierarchy in additional to geospatial coordinates, so that for example, given city, the algorithm supplies state/province and country. Even so, non-optimal levels of accuracy imply that the spatiotemporal methods must be re-examined.

Acknowledgements Thanks are due to Michael Bigrigg for his insights into the network analysis. This work was supported in part by the Air Force Office of Sponsored Research (MURI: Computational Modeling of Cultural Dimensions in Adversary Organizations, FA9550-05-1-0388), the Army Research Institute W91WAW07C0063, and the Army Research Office ERDC-TEC W911NF0710317. Additional support was provided by the Center for Computational Analysis of Social and Organizational Systems (CASOS) at Carnegie Mellon University. The views and conclusions contained in this document are those of the authors and should not be interpreted as representing the official policies, either expressed or implied, of the Air Force Office of Sponsored Research, Army Research Institute, the Army Research Office, or the U.S. government.

Appendix

Excerpt from the instructions given to the data annotator to determine what constitutes a place name.

A. How to identify location in the text:

   * a noun
   * a city, state or country
   * a non-specific region (example: in the east)

B. How to annotate locations that appear in the text?

   * Record the geographic location that is meant rather than the exact words of the text
   * Example: text says "the West", you annotate "Europe and the U.S."
   * Example: text says "the east", you annotate "Eastern Sudan"
   * Example: text says "Eritrean capital", you annotate "Asmara"

C. What you find in the text may not be a place if

   * the place name appears within the name of a title or organization, Example: The New York Times
   * the location stands for its government in an instance of metonymy, Example: "Khartoum" in the text stands for the government of the Sudan

References

1. Chen, Y.-D., Tseng, C., King, C.-C., Wu, T.-S., Chen H.: Incorporating geographical contacts into social network analysis for contact tracing in epidemiology: a study on Taiwan SARS data. In: Zeng, D., et al. (eds.) Intelligence and Security Informatics: Biosurveillance, New Brunswick. LNCS, vol. 4506, pp. 23–36. Springer, Berlin/New York (2007)
2. Ashish, N., Eguchi, R., Hegde, R., Cuyck, C., Kalashnikov, D., Mehrotra, S., Smyth, P., Venkatasubramanian, N.: Situational awareness technologies for disaster response. In: Chen, H., Reid, E., Sinai, J., Silke, A., Ganor, B. (eds.) Terrorism Informatics: Knowledge Management and Data Mining for Homeland Security. Springer, New York (2008)
3. Skillicorn, D.: Knowledge Discovery for Counterterrorism and Law Enforcement. CRC, Boca Raton (2009)
4. Giuliano, C., Lavelli, A., Romano, L.: Relation extraction and the influence of automatic named-entity recognition. ACM Trans. Speech Lang. Process. **5**(1), 2:1–2:26 (2007)
5. Hassell, J., Aleman-Meza, B., Arpinar, I.B.: Ontology-driven automatic entity disambiguation in unstructured text. In: Cruz, I.F., et al. (eds.) ISWC 2006. LNCS, vol. 4273, pp. 44–57. Springer, Berlin Heidelberg (2006)
6. Gey, F., Larson, R., Sanderson, M. Joho, H., Clough, P., Petrasi, V.: GeoCLEF: the CLEF 2005 cross-language geographic information retrieval track overview. In: Peters, C., et al. (eds.) CLEF 2005. LNCS, vol. 4022, pp. 908–919. Springer, Berlin Heidelberg (2006)
7. Danowski, J.A., Cepela, N.T.: Automatic mapping of social networks of actors from text corpora: time series analysis. In: Memon, N., Alhajj, R. (eds.) International Conference on Advances in Social Network Analysis and Mining, 2009. ASONAM '09, Athens, 20–22 July 2009, pp. 137–142. IEEE Computer Society, Los Alamitos (2009)

8. ORA (Organizational Risk Analysis software), v. 2.0.8. Center for Computational Analysis of Social and Organizational Systems (CASOS), Institute for Software Research, Carnegie Mellon University. Copyright Kathleen Carley, 2001–2010. http://www.casos.cs.cmu.edu/projects/ora/
9. Borgatti, S.P., Carley, K.M., Krackhardt, D.: On the robustness of centrality measures under conditions of imperfect data. Soc. Netw. **28**(2), 124–136 (2006)
10. Carley, K.M.: Coding choices for textual analysis: a comparison of content analysis and map analysis. In: Marsden, P. (ed.) Sociological Methodology, vol. 23, pp. 75–126. Blackwell, Oxford (1993)
11. Carley, K.M.: Network text analysis: the network position of concepts. In: Roberts, C. (ed.) Text Analysis for the Social Sciences: Methods for Drawing Statistical Inferences from Texts and Transcripts, pp. 79–100. Lawrence Erlbaum Associates, Hillsdale (1997)
12. Leidner, J.L.: Toponym resolution in text: annotation, evaluation and applications of spatial grounding of place names. Unpublished doctoral dissertation, University of Edinburgh. Retrieved January 8, 2008 from http://hdl.handle.net/1842/1849 (2007)
13. Kozareva, Z.: Bootstrapping named entity recognition with automatically generated gazetteer lists. In: Proceedings of the Eleventh Conference of the European Chapter of the Association for Computational Linguistics, pp. 15–21. Association for Computational Linguistics, Morristown (2006)
14. Popescu, A., Grefenstette, G.: Spatiotemporal mapping of Wikipedia concepts. JCDL '10, Gold Coast, 21–25 June 2010, pp. 129–138. Association for Computing Machinery, New York (2010)
15. Purves, R., Clough, P, Joho, J.: Identifying imprecise regions for geographic information retrieval using the web. In: Proceedings of the GIS Research UK 13th Annual Conference, pp. 313–318 (2005). Retrieved April 11, 2010 from http://www.dcs.gla.ac.uk/$\sim$hideo/pub/gisuk05/gisuk05.pdf
16. Twaroch, F.A., Jones, C.B., Abdelmoty, A.I.: Acquisition of vernacular place names from web sources. In: King, I., Baeza-Yates, R. (eds.) Weaving Services and People on the World Wide Web, pp. 195–214. Springer, Heidelberg (2009)
17. Wang, C., Wang, J., Xie, X., Ma, W.-Y.: Mining geographic knowledge using location aware topic model. In: Proceedings of the 4th ACM workshop on Geographic Information Retrieval GIR'07, Lisbon, 9 Nov 2006, pp. 65–70. Association for Computing Machinery (2006)
18. Roddick, J.F., Lees, B.G.: Spatio-temporal data mining paradigms and methodologies. In: Miller, H.J., Han, J. (eds.) Geographic Data Mining and Knowledge Discovery, 2nd edn. pp. 27–44. CRC, New York (2009)
19. Buttenfield, B., Gahegan, M., Miller, H. Yuan, M.: Geospatial data mining and knowledge discovery. Retrieved April 7, 2010 from http://www.ucgis.org/priorities/research/research_white/2000%20Papers/emerging/gkd.pdf (2001)
20. Amitay, E., Har'El, N., Sivan, R., Soffer, A.: Web-a-where: geotagging web content. In: SIGIR'04, Sheffield, 25–29 July 2004, pp. 273–280. Association for Computing Machinery, New York (2004)
21. Pazienza, M.T., Pennacchiotti, M., Zanzotto, F.M.: Discovering verb relations in corpora: distributional versus non-distributional approaches. In: Ali, A., Dapoigny, R. (eds.) IEA/AIE 2006. LNAI, vol. 4031, pp. 1042–1052. Springer, Berlin Heidelberg (2006)
22. Xu, X., Mete, M., Yuruk, N.: Mining concept associations for knowledge discovery in large textual databases. In: Proceedings of the 2005 ACM Symposium on Applied Computing SAC'05, 13–17 March 2005, Santa Fe, pp. 549–550. Association for Computing Machinery (2005)
23. Roongpiboonsopit, D., Karimi, H.A.: Quality assessment of online street and rooftop geocoding services. Cartogr. Geogr. Inf. Sci. **37**(4), 301–318 (2010)

24. Carley, K.M., Reminga, J., Storrick, J. Columbus, D.: ORA user's guide 2010. Carnegie Mellon University, School of Computer Science, Institute for Software Research, Technical Report, CMU-ISR-10-120. Retrieved October 14, 2010 from http://www.casos.cs.cmu.edu/publications/papers/CMU-ISR-10-120.pdfTopic
25. Manning, C.D., Raghavan, P., Schütz, H.: Introduction to Information Retrieval. Cambridge University Press, Cambridge (2008)

Chapter 16
Detecting Communities in Massive Networks Efficiently with Flexible Resolution

Qi Ye, Bin Wu, and Bai Wang

Abstract Currently, community detection has led to a huge interest in data analysis on real-world networks. However, the high computationally demanding of most community detection algorithms limits their applications. In this chapter, we propose an iterative heuristic algorithm (called MMO algorithm) to extract the community structure in large networks based on local multi-resolution modularity optimization whose time complexity is near linear and space complexity is linear. The effectiveness of MMO algorithm is demonstrated by extensive experiments on lots of computer generated graphs and publically available real-world graphs. We also extend MMO algorithm to extract communities in distributed environment and use it to explore a massive call graph on a normal PC. The results show that MMO algorithm is very efficient, and it may enhance our ability to explore massive networks in real time.

16.1 Introduction

Nowadays, detecting communities in massive networks is still a big challenge to researchers. To overcome the high time complexity algorithm proposed by Hu et al. [10] whose time complexity is $O(|V|^2)$, we propose a novel community extraction algorithm based on local Multi-resolution Modularity Optimization (MMO). MMO algorithm is extremely fast and needs low memory storage requirements. Its time complexity is near linear and its space complexity is linear. To evaluate the effectiveness of our algorithm, we test MMO algorithm in both artificial benchmark networks and real-world networks. The results show that MMO algorithm is very fast and highly reliable, and it is better than many well known community extraction algorithms, such as the CNM algorithm [3] considering accuracy and speed.

Q. Ye (✉) · B. Wu · B. Wang
Beijing University of Posts and Telecommunications, Beijing, 100876, China
e-mail: yeqibupt@gmail.com; wubin@bupt.edu.cn; wangbai@bupt.edu.cn

T. Özyer et al. (eds.), *The Influence of Technology on Social Network Analysis and Mining*, Lecture Notes in Social Networks 6, DOI 10.1007/978-3-7091-1346-2_16,

We extend MMO algorithm to extract communities in distributed environment and use it to explore the structure of a massive call graph on a normal PC. The result shows that it may enhance our ability to explore massive networks interactively. We regard that MMO algorithm represents a good tradeoff between accuracy and speed for detecting node communities in massive real-world networks.

This chapter is structured as follows. In Sect. 16.2, we present previous related work. Section 16.3 contains details regarding the implementation of MMO algorithm. In Sect. 16.4, to verify the validity and utility of MMO algorithm, we run detailed experiments on a lot of networks. In Sect. 16.5, we will use MMO algorithm to explore a real-world call graph. Section 16.6 concludes this paper.

16.2 Related Work

Communities are important structures of many real-world networks. Conventionally, a community can be loosely defined as a subsets of nodes in which there are more edges between nodes within the set than to nodes outside. Currently, many community detection algorithms have been proposed such as divisive clustering algorithms [9, 16], modularity optimization algorithms [3, 13], label propagation algorithms [12, 17], etc. Newman and Girvan [14, 15] propose the well adopted concept of modularity to measure the quality of community detection. There are lots of algorithms based on the global modularity optimization [3, 13]. Clauset et al. [3] (CNM) propose an agglomerative hierarchical clustering algorithm based on the modularity optimization by incorporating several sophisticated data structures, and its time complexity is expected to be $O(|V|\log^2|V|)$ in sparse graphs. Blondel et al. [2] have introduced another greedy agglomerative clustering algorithm (BGLL) for the general case of weighted graphs based on the local modularity optimization. However, the modularity is not a scale-invariant measurement, and the modularity optimization algorithms may fail to identify communities smaller than a certain scale [8]. Hu et al. [10] propose a community detection algorithm by employing an attractive-force-based self-organizing process, however, its time complexity is $O(|V|^2)$. Raghavan et al. [17] design a simple and fast method based on label propagation whose time complexity is believed to be near linear. Leung et al. [12] study the dynamic of the algorithm and propose several methods to avoid the formation of giant communities in large graphs.

16.3 Community Definitions and Detection

16.3.1 Symbols and Definitions

Let a graph G be a triple consisting of a node set V, an edge set E, and a relation that associates with each edge two vertices. Each graph G can be represented mathematically by an adjacency matrix A with elements $A_{i,j} = 1$ if there is an edge from node i to node j and $A_{i,j} = 0$ otherwise. So the degree of node i can be defined as $k_i = \sum_j A_{i,j}$. Let a node set c be a community of graph G with $|c|$ nodes, and let C denote the community set in the graph. We define the internal and external degree of each node $v \in c$, let k_v^{int} and k_v^{ext}, as the number of edges connecting v to the nodes in c and the number of edges connecting v to the rest of the graph $V \setminus c$. In a similar way, we can also define the internal degree k_c^{int} of a community c as the sum of the internal degrees of its nodes, the external degree k_c^{ext} of a community c as the sum of the external degrees of its nodes. The total degree k_c of a community c is the sum of the degrees of its nodes. Let m_c be the number of edges in community c, and $2m_c = k_c^{int}$.

16.3.2 Linear Complexity Algorithm

16.3.2.1 Algorithm

Hu et al. [10] propose the definition of attractive force $F_{i,c}$ of community c to node i, and $F_{i,c}$ can be formulated as follows:

$$F_{i,c} = \sum_{j \in c} A_{i,j}. \tag{16.1}$$

As shown in Eq. (16.1), the community attractive force $F_{i,c}$ just depends on the number of neighbors of i in community c. As mentioned in the algorithm proposed by Hu et al. [10] whose time complexity is $O(|V|^2)$, each node will be moved into the community or communities with the largest attractive force, respectively. To get non-overlapping communities, we find this process could be modified into a near linear complexity one by only moving each node into the community with largest attractive force. We also note that the definition of the community attractive force in the algorithm proposed by Hu et al. [10] is very similar with the label selection strategy in the label propagation algorithm proposed by Raghavan [17] and it is different from the label score selection strategy proposed by Leung et al. [12].

Based on our previous work [22] to improve the time complexity of Hu's algorithm [10], we find that the quality of the community detection algorithm can be greatly improved by replacing the quality metric in Eq. (16.1) by the community modularity function [15]. However, the widely used modularity metric is not a scale-invariant measurement, and the modularity optimization algorithms may fail to identify communities smaller than a certain scale [8]. To get the multi-resolution modularity gain, we choose the modularity function proposed by Reichardt and Bornholdt [18] for a community c. The multi-resolution modularity based on the spin model can be described as

$$Q(c) = J(m_c - \gamma \frac{{k_c}^2}{4m}), \tag{16.2}$$

where J is a constant expressing the coupling strength and γ is a parameter expressing the relative contribution to the energy from existing and missing edges in the spin model. When $\gamma = 1$ and $J = \frac{1}{m}$, the value of spin coefficient of cohesion equals to the value of GN community modularity [18].

The resolution parameter γ enables us to span several community scales from very small to very large ones, where $0 \leq \gamma < \infty$. To get a multi-resolution modularity, we will let J be $\frac{1}{m}$ in Eq. (16.2). So the difference of the new multi-scale modularity $Q_{new}(c)$ and its original one is the gain of modularity $\Delta Q(c,v)$ of community c by inserting node v into the community c. The result can be described as the following equation:

$$\begin{aligned}\Delta Q(c,v) &= Q_{new}(c) - Q(c)\\ &= \frac{m_c + m_c^v}{m} - \gamma(\frac{k_c + k_v}{2m})^2 - \frac{m_c}{m} + \gamma(\frac{k_c}{2m})^2\\ &= \frac{1}{m}(m_c^v - \gamma(\frac{k_c k_v}{2m} + \frac{k_v^2}{4m})),\end{aligned} \tag{16.3}$$

where m_c^v is the number of links between node v and community c. As in Eq. (16.3) the term $\frac{1}{m}$ is the same for each community, we can simplify Eq. (16.3) as

$$\Delta Q(c,v) = m_c^v - \gamma(\frac{k_c k_v}{2m} + \frac{k_v^2}{4m}), \tag{16.4}$$

when comparing the multi-resolution modularity gains for different neighboring communities of node v. When $\gamma = 0$, Eq. (16.3) only shows link numbers to neighborhood communities, and our algorithm will perform as using Eq. (16.1). When $\gamma = 1$, Eq. (16.3) becomes the traditional GN modularity optimization gain. Changing γ allows us to find the communities at different resolutions, but we also believe that communities with broad size distribution cannot be found by a single value of γ.

Inspired by the algorithm proposed by Hu et al. [10] and other current fast local community detection algorithms, such as LPA algorithm [17] and BGLL algorithm [2], we now summarize our MMO algorithm as follows:

1. We initially set each node belong to a community, and set the iterative step $i = 1$.
2. For each node v remove it from the community C_v it belonged to. Calculate the multi-resolution modularity gain $\Delta Q(c,v)$ between node v to all the adjacent community C_v', where $v' \in N_v$.
3. Move node v into the adjacent community with largest multi-resolution modularity gain $\Delta Q(C_{v'}, v)$.
4. Repeat steps 2 to 3 and set $i = i + 1$ until the fixed sufficient I_{max} steps are reached or the multi-scale modularity $Q(C)$ dose not change obviously.

Algorithm 1 MMO algorithm

```
C = {{v}|v ∈ V}
for i = 1 to I_max do
    Q_old = Q(C)
    for v ∈ V do
        for v' ∈ N_v do
            c' = C_v'
            m^v_c' = m^v_c' + 1 {The default value of m^v_c' is 0}
        end for
        c_old = C_v
        c_best = c_old
        remove v from c_old
        Q_max = ΔQ(c_best, v)
        for v' ∈ N_v do
            Q' = ΔQ(C_v', v)
            if Q' is better than Q_max then
                Q_max = Q'
                c_best = C_v'
            end if
        end for
        insert v into c_best
    end for
    Q_new = Q(C)
    δ = Q_new − Q_old
    if δ < ε then
        break
    end if
    Q_old = Q_new
end for
for e_i,j in E do
    if C_i ≠ C_j then
        mark e_i,j as unlinked
    end if
end for
Find all the components as communities C
return C
```

5. Identify the community C_i for each node i, and for each edge $e_{i,j}$, if $C_i \neq C_j$ mark $e_{i,j}$ as unlinked. Find all the components as communities in the graph.

The pseudo code and more details about the MMO algorithm can be described in Algorithm 1.

16.3.2.2 Community Separation and Oscillation

When $\gamma = 0$, $\Delta Q(i, c)$ in Eq. (16.4) will be the same as the attractive force $F_{i,c}$ in Eq. (16.1), there are two cases may hinder our work on community detection. The first one is that a community may be unconnected, and this case may also arise in the algorithm proposed by Hu et al. [10]. The second one is the communities which

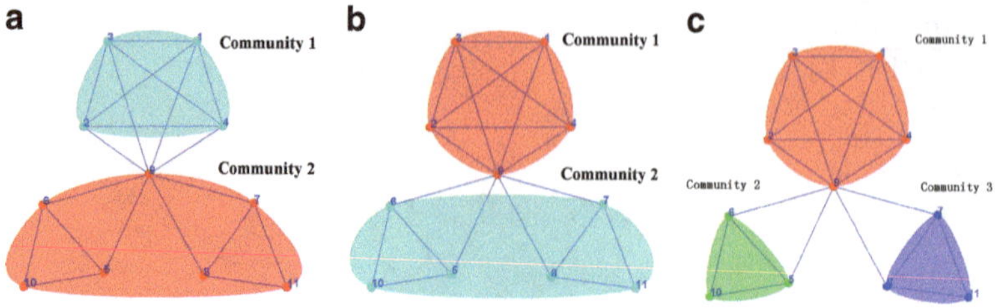

Fig. 16.1 The formation of unconnected communities during the community detection process. (**a**) Partition 1, (**b**) Partition 2, and (**c**) Partition 3

one belongs to may oscillate during the community detection process by our non-overlapping version. We will show these cases in more details as follows:

Community Separation

A required property of a community is connectedness that is there must be a path between each pair of nodes in the community, running only through vertices of c [7]. In Fig. 16.1, we use a toy network with three obvious communities to show the formation of unconnected communities during the community detection process. As shown in Fig. 16.1a, there are two communities linked to node 9, and node 9 has equal community force from these 2 communities. In Fig. 16.1b, the node 9 moves from community 2 to community 1. However, node 9 is a bridge in community 2 and his departure will cause community 2 become unconnected. To avoid this case, it is more reasonable to regard community 2 as two separated small communities as shown in Fig. 16.1c. When MMO algorithm is over, we mark all the edges between different communities as unlinked and find all the components as the final communities just as Raghavan et al. [17] did in their algorithm.

Community Oscillation

As shown in Fig. 16.2, node 10 has equal community force from the three communities, during each iteration it may randomly be selected by any neighboring communities, and this case leads to the community oscillation. To prevent this case, we will just remove a node from old community to a new one only when the community force in the new community is larger than the old one.

16.3.3 Iterations and Convergence

In this part, we will talk about the relations between iterations and the convergence state of MMO algorithm. When MMO algorithm does not yield an optimal result in terms of multi-resolution modularity, we call it achieve the convergence state.

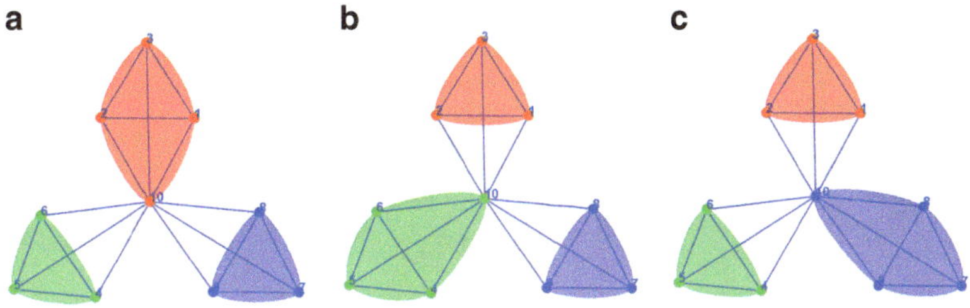

Fig. 16.2 The oscillation during the community detection process. (**a**) Partition 1, (**b**) partition 2, and (**c**) partition 3

Table 16.1 Experiment comparisons of the CNM(c), LPA(l), BGLL(b) and MMO(m) algorithms

Network	$\|V\|$	$\|E\|$	Q_c	D_c	T_c	Q_l	D_l	T_l	Q_b	D_b	T_b	Q_m	D_m	T_m
P-book	105	441	0.50	0.152	0	0.48	0.124	0	0.53	0.172	0	0.51	0.223	0
Word	121	425	0.29	0.052	0	0.00	0.049	0	0.29	0.054	0	0.27	0.085	0
Email	1,133	5,451	0.50	0.021	0	0.16	0.013	0	0.57	0.030	0	0.52	0.061	0
Jazz	198	2,742	0.44	0.253	0	0.28	0.212	0	0.44	0.252	0	0.44	0.273	0
E-neu	297	2,148	0.37	0.072	0	0.00	0.041	0	0.39	0.070	0	0.39	0.094	0
E-meta	453	2,025	0.40	0.044	0	0.06	0.032	0	0.43	0.041	0	0.40	0.086	0
P-blog	1,490	16,715	0.43	0.041	2	0.43	0.043	0	0.43	0.043	0	0.43	0.052	0
Net-sci	1,589	2,742	0.96	0.415	0	0.91	0.520	0	0.96	0.421	0	0.87	0.590	0
Power	4,941	6,594	0.93	0.000	0	0.80	0.041	0	0.94	0.000	0	0.53	0.073	0
CA-Gr	5,242	14,484	0.82	0.121	2	0.79	0.262	0	0.86	0.150	0	0.71	0.344	0
Hep-th	8,361	15,751	0.81	0.083	4	0.76	0.170	0	0.85	0.073	1	0.65	0.251	0
PGP	10,680	24,316	0.85	0.032	8	0.76	0.083	1	0.88	0.021	1	0.70	0.133	1
Gnu04	10,876	39,994	0.38	0.000	33	0.01	0.000	1	0.38	0.000	6	0.27	0.008	2
Gnu05	8,846	31,839	0.40	0.000	18	0.01	0.000	1	0.40	0.000	6	0.28	0.008	2
Gnu06	8,717	331,525	0.39	0.000	18	0.00	0.000	1	0.39	0.000	8	0.26	0.008	2
Gnu08	6,301	20,777	0.46	0.000	6	0.03	0.000	0	0.47	0.000	6	0.34	0.008	1
Gnu09	8,114	26,013	0.47	0.000	11	0.01	0.000	1	0.47	0.000	6	0.33	0.008	1
Astro-ph	16,706	121,251	0.63	0.040	139	0.27	0.183	2	0.73	0.053	6	0.64	0.276	5
Co-Mat	40,421	175,693	0.62	0.034	662	0.61	0.134	3	0.73	0.024	15	0.55	0.202	8
As06	22,963	48,436	0.64	0.000	121	0.29	0.000	2	0.66	0.000	9	0.47	0.002	6
Enron	36,692	183,831	0.51	0.025	680	0.32	0.042	5	0.61	0.017	53	0.56	0.066	14
EuIns	265,214	364,481	0.75	0.000	17,708	0.71	0.000	28	0.79	0.000	158	0.70	0.001	38
Epini	75,879	405,740	0.39	0.002	4,332	0.04	0.002	14	0.46	0.002	156	0.41	0.009	32
Slash8	77,360	469,180	0.31	0.001	6,553	0.01	0.000	18	0.34	0.000	152	0.31	0.004	28
Slash9	82,168	504,230	0.31	0.001	7,309	0.02	0.000	18	0.34	0.000	150	0.31	0.005	30
Amazon02	262,111	899,792	0.81	0.026	16,059	0.72	0.201	62	0.90	0.003	151	0.64	0.288	69
Amazon12	400,727	2,349,869	0.75	0.020	69,340	0.71	0.151	127	0.88	0.004	993	0.66	0.195	340
Amazon05	410,236	2,439,437	0.74	0.021	55,514	0.70	0.150	134	0.88	0.004	1,218	0.66	0.193	350
ND-Web	325,729	1,090,108	0.93	0.017	13,903	0.87	0.193	60	0.94	0.030	2,325	0.81	0.220	238
Google	875,713	4,322,051	–	–	–	0.82	0.164	232	0.98	0.006	1,971	0.77	0.205	655

To guarantee the effectiveness of MMO algorithm, the convergence iterations should be much less than I_{max} in most cases. We test MMO algorithm in four large real-world networks provided by Leskovec[1] as shown in Table 16.1. These networks include: a web graph provided by Notre Dame University (ND-Web); a web graph

[1] http://snap.stanford.edu

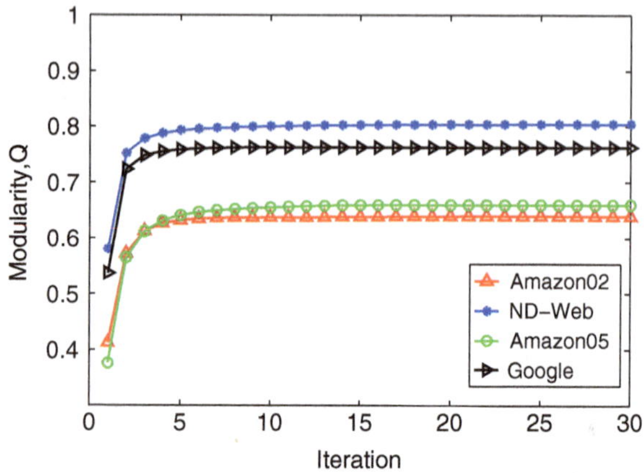

Fig. 16.3 Average iterations of our algorithm to achieve the convergence states. Values are averaged over five runs

provided by Google (Google); the Amazon product co-purchasing network from March 2 2003 (Amazon02); the Amazon product co-purchasing network from May 5 2003 (Amazon05). Figure 16.3 shows the iterations of MMO algorithm to achieve the convergence states in these large-scale networks by setting $\gamma = 1$. As shown in Fig. 16.3, it merely takes on average 5 iterations to achieve the convergence states in all these networks just like the convergence iterations of LPA algorithm [12].

16.3.4 Algorithm Complexity Analysis

In this part, we will discuss the data structures and complexity of MMO algorithm. In the iterative steps, we need to find out which community each node belongs to, and for each community we need to remove and add a node quickly. As MMO algorithm is non-overlapping and each node just belongs to one community, therefore we store the node community relations in a hash table. Furthermore, to speed up the MMO algorithm, we also store the community nodes in different hash tables. Under reasonable assumptions, the expected time to search, add and remove for a node in a community is $O(1)$ [4].

As shown in Algorithm 1 from lines 5 to 8, for each vertex v, we will first visit all its neighbors and record the links m_v^c of each neighboring communities, and this process will take $O(k_v)$ time complexity. By recording the k_c^{int} and k_c^{ext} in the community data structures, we can get the $\Delta Q(c, v)$ in $O(1)$ time. Therefore it will cost $O(2|V| + 4|E|)$ time to traverse the graph twice by broad first searching algorithm in an adjacency-list representation graph, and it takes $O(|V|)$ time to get the multi-resolution modularity Q at each iteration. It takes $O(3|V| + 4|E|)$ time each iteration. As the process at step 5 will take $O(|V| + 3|E|)$ time, the total time complexity of the MMO algorithm is $O((3I_{max} + 1)|V| + (4I_{max} + 3)|E|)$, where $|V|$ is the number of nodes, $|E|$ is the number of edges and I_{max} is the number of iterations in this algorithm. The space complexity of our algorithm is $O(2|V|+|E|)$.

As we have to store sparse graph G in an adjacency-list representation, the desirable property that the amount of memory it requires is $O(|V| + |E|)$. As we also have to maintain the communities, the amount of space it requires in the hash tables is $O(|V|)$. Comparing to the original algorithm proposed by Hu et al. [10] whose time complexity is about $O(|V|^2)$, MMO algorithm is much faster. Its time complexity is near linear, and its space complexity is linear.

16.4 Algorithm Comparison and Experiments

In this section, we present a number of tests on the community detection algorithms, e.g. GN algorithm [9], MCL algorithm [6], CNM algorithm [3], LPA algorithm [17] and BGLL algorithm [2], on widely used benchmark graphs and publically available data sets. First, we present experiments on artificial networks with built-in communities. Second, for our first examples of the algorithm performance in real-world network, we apply it to several small social networks with known communities. After that, to show the performance of MMO algorithm, we will use it to explore several real-world massive networks. As Hu et al. [10] do not mention the partition modularities for these networks, we do not compare the our results with theirs.

16.4.1 Environment and Data Set

All the community detection algorithms in Table 16.1 are integrated into *TeleComVis* [21], and all our Java algorithms are implemented in single threaded. We have implement all of these algorithms using Java platform: Java 6.0, Java HotSpot Server VM with 1.3 G heap size. The experiments are performed on an ordinary PC (CPU = Intel Core2 Duo 2.66 GHz, L2 Cache = 3,072 kB, RAM = 3 G) running Window XP operating system. In the following experiments, if we do not mention the value of γ, we will set $\gamma = 1.0$ for all the following experiments in accord with the GN modularity. In the following experiments, we also set $I_{max} = 30$ and $\epsilon = 0.00001$. We run detailed experiments on a lot of publically available network data sets as shown in Table 16.1. These networks vary greatly in topology structures and sizes from the smallest consisting 34 vertices to the largest of 0.87 million vertices including social networks, biological networks, Internet networks, etc. The networks are provided by Newman,[2] Arenas[3] and Leskovec.[4] Note that since these fast community detection algorithms are stochastic, different runs could

[2]http://www-personal.umich.edu/$\sim$mejn/netdata/

[3]http://deim.urv.cat/$\sim$aarenas/data/welcome.htm

[4]http://snap.stanford.edu

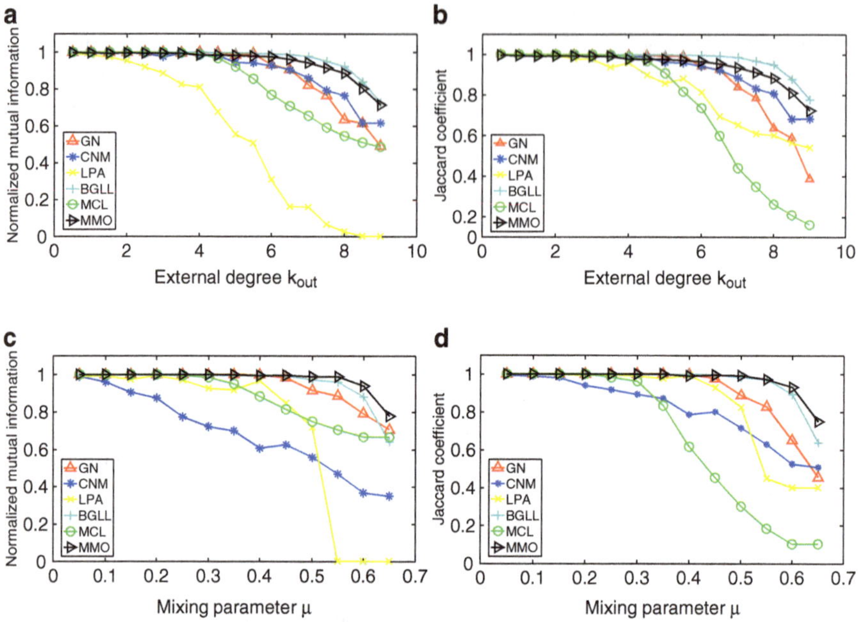

Fig. 16.4 Performance of community detection algorithms in the benchmark graphs. (**a**) NMI (GN graphs), (**b**) Jaccard (GN graphs), (**c**) NMI (LFR graphs), and (**d**) Jaccard (LFR graphs)

yield in principle different partitions. We have performed ten runs of each algorithm in different networks, and choose the average scores for each partition.

16.4.2 Computer-Generated Graph

First, to study the partition accuracy of MMO algorithm, we have studied a couple of social networks for which explicit knowledge about its communities is available. The most famous benchmarks for non-overlapping community detection are a class of benchmark networks introduced by Girvan and Newman(GN) [9] and a class of benchmark graphs proposed by Lancichinetti et al. (LFR) [11]. We will present tests in both of the GN benchmark graphs and the LFR benchmark graphs. In Fig. 16.4, each point is an average over 40 realizations of the networks. To compare the built-in communities with those delivered by different community detection algorithms, we use the normalized mutual information score (NMI) denoted as I [5, 7] and the Jaccard index (Jaccard) denoted as J [7] as the reliable measures of similarity.

In GN benchmark graph, each network is constructed with 128 nodes divided into 4 communities of 32 nodes each. Each vertex has on average k_{in} edges to vertices in the same community and k_{out} edges to vertices in other communities, keeping an average degree $k_{in} + k_{out} = 16$. Figure 16.4a and b show the performance of community detection algorithms in the GN benchmark graphs by using the normalized mutual information metric and Jaccard index metric, respectively. As shown in Fig. 16.4a and b, our algorithm performs perfectly when these communities are more fuzzy ($k_{out} = 8$) with the normalized mutual information $I = 0.857$ and the Jaccard index $J = 0.915$, comparing with the results got by BGLL algorithm $I = 0.924$ and $J = 0.940$. In this benchmark networks, BGLL algorithm performs slightly better than MMO algorithm.

Next, we use the LFR benchmark graphs to test MMO algorithm. In LFR benchmark graphs, all the graphs contains 1,000 nodes, and the exponents γ_{LFR} and β_{LFR} of degree distributions and community size distributions are 2 and 1, respectively. In LFR benchmark graphs, each node shares a fraction $1-\mu$ of its links with other nodes its community and a fraction u with other nodes of the benchmark network. As shown in Fig. 16.4c and d, MMO algorithm performs quite perfectly when these communities become more fuzzy ($\mu = 0.5$) with the normalized mutual information score $I = 0.989$ and the Jaccard index score $J = 0.993$, comparing with the results got by BGLL algorithm $I = 0.978$ and $J = 0.967$. The result shows that MMO algorithm is very robust in the artificial networks with built-in communities, and it has the best performance comparing with other the algorithms in the experiment.

16.4.3 Typical Social Networks

In this part, we present a number of experiments on some real-world networks with known communities. To show the quality of the node partitions in the networks without built-in communities, we use two metrics: one is the widely used modularity Q [15], and the other one is the newly proposed partition density D which will avoid the famous resolution limit problem [1]. The result shows that MMO algorithm performs comparably or better than past algorithm in this network with acceptable modularity, accuracy, and high partition density.

16.4.3.1 Zachary's Karate Club

First, we have investigated the classical social network of "Zachary karate club" [9]. The two smaller communities with the administrator and the teacher as the central persons are further divided into smaller ones. Today it is well accepted that the best partition in terms of modularity of the karate club network is partitioned into four communities with a value of $Q = 0.419$. As shown in Fig. 16.5a, we get six communities in the social network with $\gamma = 1.0$. The modularity Q is 0.3361 and the partition density D is 0.162. Comparing our partition with the known two community structure, the normalized mutual information I is 0.519 and the Jaccard score J is 0.652. To form larger communities, by setting $\gamma = 0.1$,

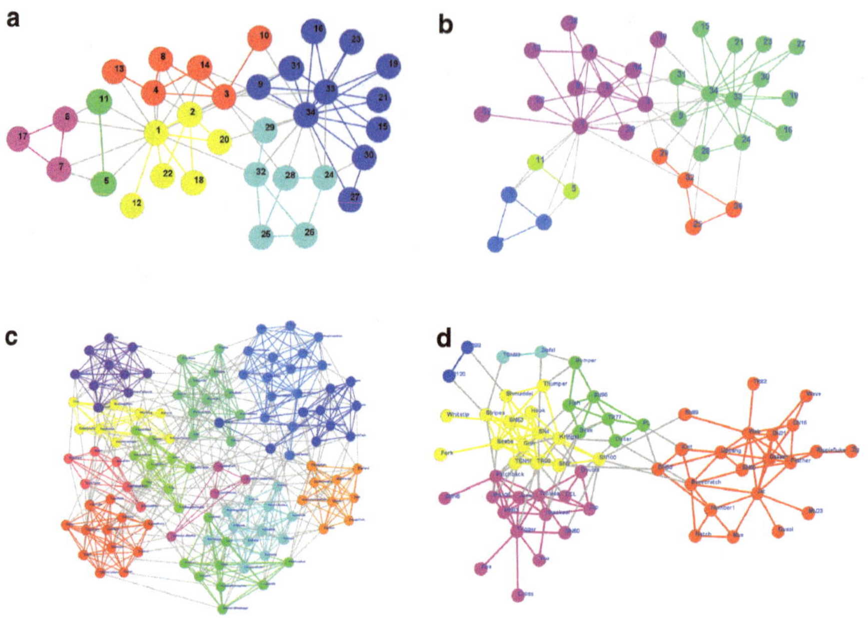

Fig. 16.5 Communities in some small real-world networks, and the node colors indicate the clustering. (**a**) Karate club $\gamma = 1.0$, (**b**) Karate club $\gamma = 0.1$, (**c**) Football $\gamma = 1.0$, and (**d**) Dolphin $\gamma = 0.1$

we get five communities with modularity score $Q = 0.395$ and partition density $D = 0.191$ as shown in Fig. 16.5b. The normalized mutual information I score of this partition is 0.573 and the Jaccard index is 0.812, respectively. There are five communities extracted by GN algorithm, and its modularity score Q is 0.401 with $D = 0.165$, $I = 0.579$ and $J = 0.742$. There are three communities extracted by CNM algorithm, and its modularity score Q is 0.380 and partition density $D = 0.132$ ($I = 0.692$ and $J = 0.841$). There are three communities extracted by MCL algorithm, and its modularity score Q is 0.374 and partition density $D = 0.160$ ($I = 0.852$ and $J = 0.926$). LPA algorithm is not very stable in this small network, and the largest modularity score Q is 0.374 and partition density $D = 0.157$. BGLL algorithm divides the network into four communities with $I = 0.586$ and $J = 0.811$. Its modularity Q is 0.419 and partition density D is 0.173. This example illustrates the advantage of our algorithm, which can give multiple different solutions by changing the parameter γ. The result also shows MMO algorithm performs comparably or better than past algorithm in this network with acceptable modularity and accuracy, and high partition density.

16.4.3.2 US College Football Team Network

We also apply MMO algorithm to the collage football network which represents the schedule of games between American college football teams in the 2000 season provided by Newman [9]. Nodes in the network represent teams and edges represent regular-season games between teams, and there are 115 nodes and 613 edges in the network. We have known the communities of the network and the teams are partitioned into 12 conferences [9]. As shown in Fig. 16.5c, we get 12 communities in the football team social network with $I = 0.927$ and $J = 0.916$. Its the modularity score is $Q = 0.601$ and D is 0.540. By setting $\gamma = 0.1$, we get 11 communities, and its modularity score is $Q = 0.603$ and $D = 0.518$. The normalized mutual information score of this partition is $I = 0.911$ and the Jaccard score is $J = 0.907$. By using the GN algorithm, we get ten communities with modularity $Q = 0.600$ and $D = 0.464$. Its normalized mutual information I is 0.878 and its Jaccard score J is 0.888. Using CNM algorithm, we get seven communities with $Q = 0.577$ and $D = 0.329$ ($I = 0.762$, $J = 0.795$). Using BGLL algorithm, we get seven communities with $Q = 0.604$ and $D = 0.483$ ($I = 0.885$, $J = 0.895$). The results also show that MMO algorithm works well considering both of the modularity score and partition accuracy in this network.

16.4.3.3 Bottlenose Dolphin Network

As a final example of small social network, as shown in Fig. 16.5d, we use MMO algorithm to explore the community structures of the bottlenose dolphin network [15]. It is a social network of a community of 62 bottlenose dolphins living in Doubtful Sound, New Zealand. The dolphin network splits into two as a result of the departure of a keystone individual SN100. The links between nodes are established by observation of statistically significant frequent associations, and the network contains 62 nodes and 159 edges. By setting $\gamma = 1.0$, we find nine communities, and its modularity Q is 0.501 and the Partition density D is 0.202. The normalized mutual information score I is 0.449 and its Jaccard Index J is 0.721. As shown in Fig. 16.5d, we get six communities by setting $\gamma = 0.1$ with $I = 0.524$ and $J = 0.780$. Its modularity Q is 0.520 and Partition density D is 0.153. Using GN algorithm, we get five communities with modularity $Q = 0.519$ and $D = 0.146$. Using CNM algorithm, we get four communities with modularity $Q = 0.495$ and partition density $D = 0.114$. The partition modularity got by MCL is 0.415, and the value extracted by LPA is only 0.341. Their partition density values are 0.175 and 0.158, respectively. By using the BGLL algorithm, we get four communities with $I = 0.636$ and $J = 0.830$. Its modularity Q is 0.526 and partition density D is 0.132. The result also indicates MMO algorithm performs comparably or better than most algorithms in this network considering partition density.

16.4.4 Algorithm Performance

To compare our algorithm with general modularity optimization algorithms, we run the experiments on the CNM algorithm, LPA algorithm, BGLL algorithm and MMO algorithm as shown in Table 16.1, and use the subscripts c, l, b and m to show the metrics got by these algorithms, respectively. In Table 16.1, for each algorithm we display the modularity Q of the communities, the currently proposed Partition Density D[1] and the computation time T (seconds). In Table 16.1 the hyphen character indicates the algorithm cannot solve the problem in 24 h. We find that MMO algorithm is extremely fast in massive networks, and we can get the communities in the Google web network (about 0.9 million nodes, 4.3 million edges) in about 10 min. The partition modularity values got by MMO algorithm are usually larger than those got by LPA algorithm in these networks, and they are usually less than those got by the CNM algorithm and the BGLL algorithm. However, the values of the newly Partition Density D got by MMO algorithm are always the best.

Furthermore, for sizes of all the communities extracted by MMO algorithm, the largest community found by MMO algorithm is smaller than the one found by LPA and CNM in most cases. The huge size "monster" community problem [12] is also a crucial problem in the community detection algorithms. For the sake of saving space, we do not show the size of the largest community in each network in Table 16.1. We can get that the largest community found by the CNM algorithm contains 117,088 nodes in graph $Amazon05$, while the largest community in the graph $Gnu04$ found by the LPA algorithm contains 10,653 nodes. These "monster" communities are too large, and it is hard to find real-world applications for these huge communities. However, the largest community found by MMO algorithm in $Amazon05$ contain 3,559 nodes and the largest one in $Gnu04$ contains only 893 nodes. Therefore, MMO algorithm performs well in avoid forming "monster" communities, and we can get the communities with proper sizes in massive networks.

16.4.5 Distributed Community Detection

The modularity gain in Eq. (16.4) is $\Delta Q = m_c^v$ when $\gamma = 0$. We can easily extend MMO algorithm to use the *MapReduce* programming model to extract communities by using quality gain $\Delta Q = m_c^v$. We use the Hadoop[5] distributed platform, an open-source Java implementation of *MapReduce* programming model. Our experiments are tested on a Hadoop environment with eight computing nodes (Intel Xeon 1.6 GHz × 4, 4,096 kB Cache, 4 GB RAM and Linux RH4 OS each). The algorithm is also implemented in Java language using Hadoop APIs.

[5] http://hadoop.apache.org

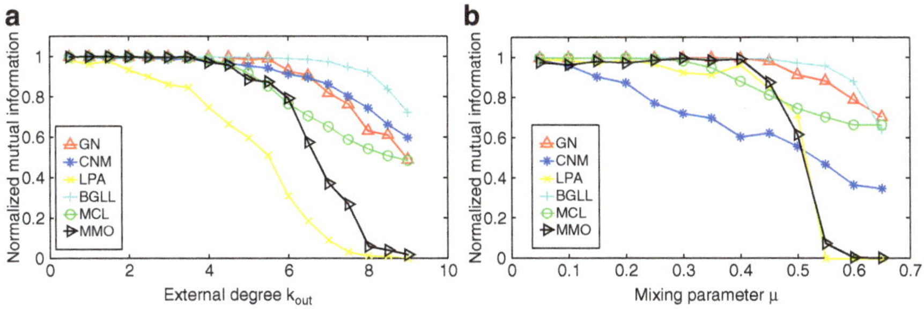

Fig. 16.6 Tests of different community detection algorithms with MMO distributed algorithm on the GN and LFR benchmark graphs

Given a graph G, we generally store it as adjacency lists in the Hadoop distributed file system. The adjacency lists of graph G can be described as:

$$\langle v, C_v, list\langle u, C_u \rangle \rangle,$$

where v is the ID of node v and C_v is the community ID which v belongs to, $u \in (N_v \cap \{v\})$. In the MapReduce task we use each node'ID v as the key and use the list of tuples $list\langle u, C_u \rangle$ as the value. The vertex-community mapping relations are stored in the tuple $\langle u, C_u \rangle$. In the Hadoop platform the adjacency list is generally split into several partitions and the information of a vertex may be stored in different computing nodes geographically. At each iteration, in the **Map** function, each node just need to be moved into the adjacent community with the largest in-degree gain m_c^v, and send it's new community ID to other adjacent vertices and to itself. The **Reduce** function collects new adjacent lists by the IDs of nodes and we can get new adjacent lists for the graph G which contains the new vertex-community relations.

To check the performance of MMO distributed algorithm in the distributed environment. Figure 16.6 shows the performance of MMO distributed algorithm by comparing with other community detection algorithms. Figure 16.6a and b show the similarities between the partitions and the built-in communities on the GN benchmarks and the LFR benchmarks using the normalized mutual information metric. As shown in Fig. 16.6a, in the GN benchmark graphs, MMO distributed algorithm performances better than LPA and MCL in most cases. As shown in Fig. 16.6b, in the LFR benchmark graphs, MMO distributed algorithm performances better than CNM and MCL in most cases. However, other community detection algorithms cannot run in the distributed environment.

Furthermore, we explore two massive real-world undirected networks, e.g., the U.S. patent citation network and LiveJournal social network provided by Leskovec on the Hadoop platform. Figure 16.7 shows the distributions of the community sizes of these two networks found by the distributed community detection algorithm. The patent citation network contains 3,774,768 vertices and 16,518,947 edges.

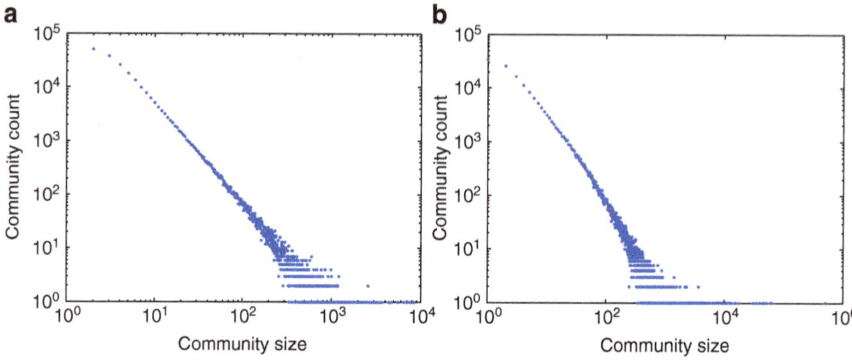

Fig. 16.7 The distributions of community sizes in the US patent citation network and LiveJournal social network

The LiveJournal social network contains 4,847,571 vertices and 4,285,123 edges. It takes 173 s to run our algorithm to extract the communities in the patent citation network. In this network, the largest community contains 8,396 vertices, and the modularity of this partition is 0.374. The distribution of community sizes are shown in Fig. 16.7a. It takes 1,873 s to extract communities in LiveJournal social network with the modularity $Q = 0.596$. The largest community contains 498,703 vertices and the distribution of community sizes are shown in Fig. 16.7b. As MMO algorithm can easily be implemented on the MapReduce programming model, it is scalable to very large networks in distributed environment.

16.5 Massive Network Exploring

Network exploring can provide multiple views of the networks at different levels of abstraction. After the experiments on the publically available networks, we will use MMO algorithm to explore a real-world call graph. The problem of discovering communities from large-scale sparse call graphs has a wide range of real-world applications, such as spam detection, telecom call group analysis and potential customer detection, etc. In this section, we will explore a massive phone call network using MMO algorithm. MMO algorithm has been integrated into our network analytical tool—*TeleComVis* [21] to get mesoscopic views for large networks based on communities, and users can zoom into the communities to find the relations between nodes in the communities and zoom out the communities to get the summarized overview of the relations between certain communities.

16.5.1 Call Graph Data

Call pairs in the fixed-line call graphs are gained from CDR (Call Detail Records) in the billing system of a telecom service provider in a city in 8 months. The data set has the following characteristics: the study is for intra-region calls, and does not include long distance or international calls; a Call Detail Record (CDR) contains the details of a call such as the time, duration phone number, origin phone number, destination, etc. We form these data sets into undirected graphs; to get the actual call graph of the acquaintances, we connect two phones with an undirected edge if there is at least one reciprocated pair of phone calls between them. The call graph contains all the call links over the observed months, and has 1,188,230 nodes and 9,251,228 edges.

Telecom service providers require an overview and even a deeper understanding of the customer relationships in massive call data. Currently, we are still lack of knowledge about what the massive networks look like and how the customer groups communicate. As there may be many incidental links such as wrong call numbers and telecom marking during the 8 months, to study the statistically significant local cohesive structures of the massive call graph, we first enumerate all cliques of size k and larger just as the method proposed by Spirin and Mirny [19] to study the structure of protein interaction network. As the call graph is sparse, we can exact enumerate all the cliques quickly by using the classical maximal clique enumeration algorithms [20]. To get a subgraph of the cohesive clusters, we also define the cluster addition subgraph G_C^+ of a set of node clusters C. The cluster addition subgraph G_C^+ is the union of all the induced subgraphs of each cluster c_i in C that is $G_C^+ = \bigcup_{c_i \in C} G[c_i]$. After that we will try to find out communities in these maximal clique additional subgraph $G_{C_k}^+$ to get overviews of the networks, in which each the clique contains at least k nodes. After the clique percolation, the subgraph $G_{C_{k=6}}^+$ contains 54,150 nodes and 243,946 edges, and the giant component of the subgraph contains 11,098 nodes. Figure 16.8a shows the communities in the subgraph and the modularity Q of the communities in the cohesive subgraph is 0.923. To make the picture we ever get the subgraph of all the cliques of size seven and larger. In the subgraph $G_{C_{k=7}}^+$ there are 14,962 nodes and 104,602 edges. We can extract all the communities in less than 1 s by our algorithm. Figure 16.8b shows the communities in the $G_{C_{k=7}}^+$ subgraph, and the modularity Q of the subgraph is 0.896. It shows we can use MMO algorithm to explore massive real-world graphs in real applications.

To compare the results of MMO algorithm and the global modularity optimization algorithm, in Fig. 16.9, we show the largest communities found by our algorithm and CNM algorithm. The largest community found by our algorithm in subgraph $G_{C_{k=7}}^+$ contains 774 nodes, however, the largest community by CNM algorithm in the subgraph contains 2,795 nodes. In Fig. 16.9a, we can find that the largest community extracted by the CNM algorithm can be divided into at least three smaller communities obviously. Comparing with the largest community found by MMO algorithm, as shown in Fig. 16.9b, our largest community is much smaller and more cohesive. In real telecom applications, after getting the communities

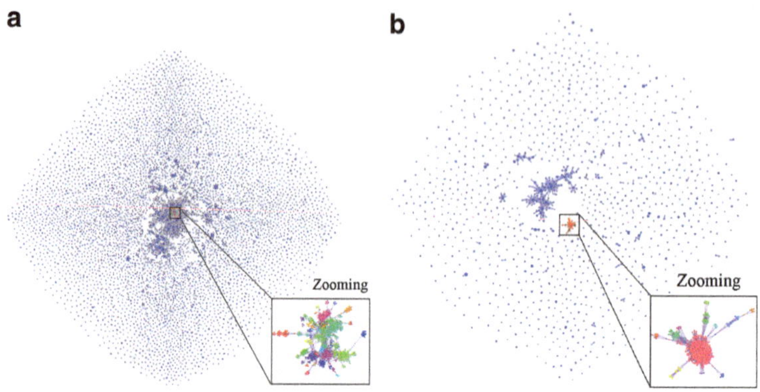

Fig. 16.8 The the community quotient graphs in the cohesive subgraphs $G^{+}_{C_{k=6}}$ and $G^{+}_{C_{k=7}}$ composed by maximal cliques

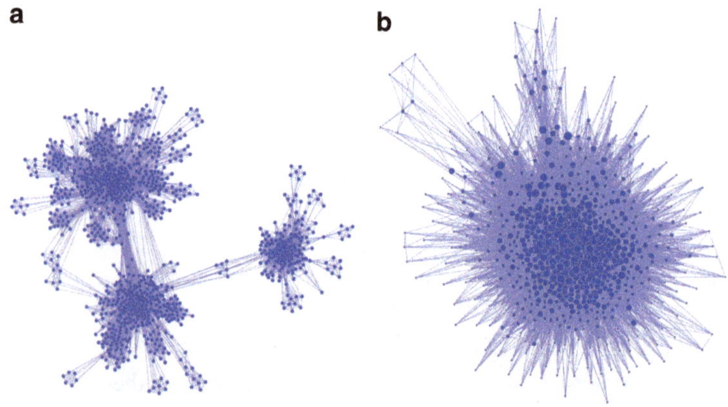

Fig. 16.9 The largest communities found by CNM algorithm and MMO algorithm in the cohesive subgraphs composed by maximal cliques

in call graphs, the telecom service providers may get the descriptions of these communities in more detail from the customer profiles. By incorporating the profiles of customers, we may be able to gain deeper insights into call graphs by examining the common properties in these communities.

16.6 Conclusions

The massive size of real-world networks makes the issue of the time complexity of community detection algorithms essential. Inspired by the algorithm proposed by Hu et al. [10] whose time complexity is $O(|V|^2)$, we propose a novel community detection algorithm called MMO algorithm. MMO algorithm is very fast and easily to implement. In our algorithm every node is initialized as an isolated community, and at every step each node adopts the neighboring community with the local multi-resolution modularity gain. As a result, the local densely connected nodes will be add into the local high quality communities quickly. Our algorithm has several advantages. First, it is intuitive and easy to implement for general case of unweighted networks. MMO algorithm is extremely fast, and we also show that its time complexity is near linear which is the same with LPA algorithm. However, its output is much better than those got by LPA algorithm, especially when the network becomes fuzzy. Second, the resolution parameter γ enables us to span several community scales from very small to very large communities to avoid the well resolution limit problem. Furthermore, we can show its space complexity is linear, and it is very suitable for detection communities in very large networks. We regard that MMO algorithm clearly performs better in computer time and gives acceptable modularity scores and community sizes. The values of the newly partition density D[1] got by MMO algorithm are always the best comparing with other algorithms.

At last, we extend MMO algorithm to extract communities in distributed environment and use it algorithm to explore the structure of a massive call graph. MMO algorithm is very efficient, and it can enhance our ability to explore massive networks interactively. It is possible to analyze the roles of nodes by the definition of community attractive force, and we can get the nodes which are shared in multi-communities. In the future, we will investigate how to extend MMO algorithm to an overlapping community algorithm to get soft partitions for massive graphs.

Acknowledgements We thank M. E. J. Newman, Alex Arenas and Jure Leskovec for providing us the network data sets. This work is supported by the National Science Foundation of China (No. 90924029, 60905025, 61074128). It is also supported the National Hightech R&D Program of China (No.2009AA04Z136).

References

1. Ahn, Y.Y., Bagrow, J.P., Lehmann, S.: Link communities reveal multiscale complexity in networks. Nature **466**, 761–764 (2010)
2. Blondel, V.D., Guillaume, J., et al.: Fast unfolding of communities in large networks. J. Stat. Mech. **10008**, 1-Ű12 (2008)
3. Clauset, A., Newman, M.E.J., Moore, C.: Finding community structure in very large networks. Phys. Rev. E **70**, 066111 (2004)
4. Cormen, T.H., Leiserson, C.E., et al.: Introduction to Algorithms, 2nd edn. MIT, Cambridge (2001)
5. Danon, L., Duch, J., et al.: Comparing community structure identification. J. Stat. Mech. **9008**, 09008 (2005)
6. Dongen, S.V.: Graph clustering by flow simulation. Ph.D. thesis, University of Utrecht (2000)
7. Fortunato, S.: Community detection in graphs. Phys. Rep. **486**, 75 (2010)
8. Fortunato, S., Barthélemy, M.: Resolution limit in community detection. Proc. Natl. Acad. Sci. **104**, 36–41 (2007)
9. Girvan, M., Newman, M.E.J.: Community structure in social and biological networks. Proc. Natl. Acad. Sci. **99**, 7821–7826 (2002)

10. Hu, Y., Chen, H., et al.: Comparative definition of community and corresponding identifying algorithm. Phys. Rev. E **78**, 026121 (2008)
11. Lancichinetti, A., Fortunato, S., Radicchi, F.: Benchmark graphs for testing community detection algorithms. Phys. Rev. E **78**, 046110 (2008)
12. Leung, I.X.Y., Hui, P., et al.: Towards real-time community detection in large networks. Phys. Rev. E **79**, 066107 (2009)
13. Newman, M.E.J.: Fast algorithm for detecting community structure in networks. Phys. Rev. E **69**, 066133 (2004)
14. Newman, M.E.J.: Modularity and community structure in networks. Proc. Natl. Acad. Sci. **103**, 8577–8582 (2006)
15. Newman, M.E.J., Girvan, M.: Finding and evaluating community structure in networks. Phys. Rev. E **69**, 026113 (2004)
16. Radicchi, F., Castellano, C., et al.: Defining and identifying communities in networks. Proc. Natl. Acad. Sci. **101**, 2658–2663 (2004)
17. Raghavan, U.N., Albert, R., Kumara, S.: Near linear time algorithm to detect community structures in large-scale networks. Phys. Rev. E **76**, 036106 (2007)
18. Reichardt, J., Bornholdt, S.: Statistical mechanics of community detection. Phys. Rev. E **74**, 016110 (2006)
19. Spirin, V., Mirny, L.A.: Protein complexes and functional modules in molecular networks. Proc. Natl. Acad. Sci. **100**, 12123–12128 (2003)
20. Tomita, E., Tanaka, A., Takahashi, H.: The worst-case time complexity for generating all maximal cliques. In: COCOON, pp. 161–170. Springer, Berlin (2004)
21. Ye, Q., Wu, B., et al: TeleComVis: exploring temporal communities in telecom networks. In: ECML PKDD, pp. 755–758. Springer, Heidelberg (2009)
22. Ye, Q., Wu, B., et al: Detecting communities in massive networks based on local community attractive force optimization. In: International Conference on Advances in Social Network Analysis and Mining, pp. 291–295. IEEE Computer Society, Los Alamitos (2010)

Chapter 17
Detecting Emergent Behavior in a Social Network of Agents

Mohammad Moshirpour, Shimaa M. El-Sherif, Behrouz H. Far, and Reda Alhajj

Abstract An effective and efficient approach in designing software systems to describe system requirements is using scenarios. A scenario, commonly shown as a message sequence chart or a sequence diagram, is a temporal sequence of messages sent between system components. Scenarios are appealing because of their expressive power and simplicity. Moreover due to the clear and concise syntactic of scenarios, they can be used to analyze the system requirements for general validity, lack of deadlock, and existence of emergent behavior. Emergent behavior or implied scenarios are specifications of behavior that are derived from compiling of all requirements together but are not explicitly specified in the set of scenarios. Although emergent behavior is not necessarily unwanted, nevertheless it is useful for system designers and engineers to be aware of its existence. Defining requirements using scenarios and conducting consequent analysis has been done for distributed systems as well as multi-agent system. In this research the requirements of a social network are described using scenarios. The scenarios are then used to detect emergent behavior using a systematic methodology. This is illustrated using a prototype of a social network of MAS for semantic search that blends the search and ontological concept learning.

M. Moshirpour (✉) · S.M. El-Sherif · B.H. Far
Department of Electrical and Computer Engineering, University of Calgary, 2500 University Drive NW, Calgary, T2N 1N4, AB, Canada
e-mail: mmoshirp@ucalgary.ca; smmelshe@ucalgary.ca; far@ucalgary.ca

R. Alhajj
Department of Computer Science, University of Calgary, Calgary, AB, Canada

Department of Information Technology, Hellenic American University, Manchester, NH, USA

Department of Computer Science, Global University, Beirut, Lebanon
e-mail: alhajj@ucalgary.ca

T. Özyer et al. (eds.), *The Influence of Technology on Social Network Analysis and Mining*, Lecture Notes in Social Networks 6, DOI 10.1007/978-3-7091-1346-2_17,

17.1 Introduction

Social networks have received enormous international interest in recent years, especially after the ubiquitous use of the internet as a communication medium [1]. Social network is a set of individuals and relationships between them. It can be represented as a set of actors (nodes or agents) that have one or more kind of relationships (ties) among them. The importance of the social network is due to its effect in diffusion of information among actors included within the network [2]. In this paper, when we use the term social network, we are referring to the abstract meaning of this term and not the social networks in popular culture such as Facebook or twitter. In other words, by social networks we mean a set of nodes that can communicate with each other via a network where they may have different types of relationships (ties) and different levels of strength of these relationships depending on several factors. The strength of ties represents how close the nodes are with respect to one another. We propose a semantic search framework that is based on a multi-agent system (MAS). Each MAS controls a document repository and each repository has a different ontology. The agents cooperate with each other to select the best subset of documents suitable for a semantic search query sent by a user. A query is in the form of searching for keywords in the context of one or more concepts. We use social networks in our system to communicate between agents from different MAS, which allows for proper handling of the concepts in the query. This allows agents to find peers that may have close but slightly different concepts in their respective ontologies.

Due to the integrated nature of social networks, gathering comprehensive and correct requirements for such software systems can be challenging. Scenario-based specification is an effective and efficient way to describe the behavior of a variety of software systems such as multi-agent systems (MAS) and distributed systems. Scenarios enable engineers and designers to describe system's functionality using the partial interactions of the system elements. In this research, the approach of scenario-based software engineering (SBSE) has been followed to represent the requirements of social networks.

There are two main ways of representing scenarios, namely, Sequence Diagrams (SD) developed by the object management group (OMG) [3] and Message Sequence Charts (MSC) which were developed by the International Telecommunications Union (ITU) [4]. In this paper MSCs are used to represent scenarios.

There are several advantages of using scenarios such as expressive power and simplicity. However, there are also several challenges such as weak partial ordering semantics that may result in missing some behavioral requirements particularly for software systems with distribution of control such as distributed systems, MAS and social networks. For instance, because each scenario gives a local and partial story of interaction between two or system components, the challenge is how the behavior of the whole system can be constructed from those scenarios and more importantly whether the derived behavior is acceptable or not. In the analysis of social networks, the interacting system components are individual nodes.

The model which describes the behavior of each system component (i.e. node for social networks) is usually called *behavioral model,* and the procedure of building the behavioral model from a scenario-based specification, is called *synthesis of behavioral models*, or simply, *synthesis process*. A commonly used model for behavioral modeling of individual components is the state machine. There are several reports on the procedure of converting a set of scenarios to a behavioral model expressed by state machines [5–10]. In the synthesis process, one state machine will be built for each node. The state machine includes all the interactions of a particular node based on the messages that it receives or sends. Theoretically, the behavior of the network can be described by the union (parallel execution) of all the state machines of the individual nodes.

One of the challenges during the synthesis process, is *implied scenarios* [11–14], also known as *emergent behavior*. An implied scenario is a specification of behavior that is in the synthesized model of the system but is not explicitly specified in the set of scenarios. This usually happens when several autonomous components need to handle a joint task as a group in a shared environment where control is also distributed. Although emergent behavior is not always unwanted, it is extremely useful for system designers and engineers to be aware of its existence. In this paper we use an example of a social network of MAS for semantic search to demonstrate the ideas.

The structure of this paper is as follows: in Sect. 17.2 some background on social networks, particularly about the relationships between nodes is presented. The case study for the social networks of MAS for semantic search is given in Sect. 17.3. In Sect. 17.4 system behavioural modeling is explained and the detection of indeterminism and emergent behaviour is discussed in Sect. 17.5. Finally conclusions and future work are presented in Sect. 17.6.

17.2 Social Networks

As mentioned previously, a social network is a set of individuals and relationships between them. Social networks are often shown using graphs which consist of several nodes representing actors of the network (such as agents) and arrows or lines representing the relationships between the actors [15] as shown in Fig. 17.1.

This section contains a brief overview on the structure of social networks and the measurement of tie strengths which of particular interest to this research.

17.2.1 Connection between Nodes

One of the most important features of a social networks is the connections between its nodes. It is necessary to identify the way the actors are embedded within a relation. There are many different types of relations. The most important types

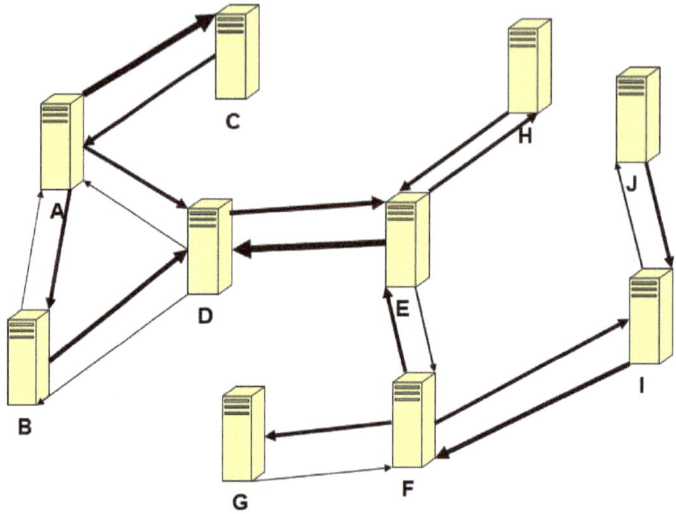

Fig. 17.1 Example of agents connected in a social network. The *arrow head* represents the direction of the relationship and the *thickness of the line* represents the strength of the relationship

of relation are the *dyad* relation (two actors involved in the relation) or the *triad* relation (three actors involved in the relation). In the dyad relation between A and B there are four possibilities; A has a relation with B, B has a relation with A, neither A nor B has relation with each other or both A and B has a mutual relation.

The *size* of the network is the number of nodes within the network. The *density* of the network is the ratio between the existing connections of the network to all possible connections. The number of possible connections within a network is $k(k-1)$, where k is the number of the nodes in the network in the case of the directed graph or the symmetric network. In the case of an asymmetric network, the number of possible connections equals $(k(k-1))/2$ because in this case the connection between A and B is the same as the connection between B and A. Note that when the number of the nodes increases linearly, the number of possible relations within the network increases exponentially.

The *degree* of a node is the number of connections in which this node is involved. In the case of a directed network, there are two types of degrees, *in-degree* and *out-degree* representing the number of relations towards and outwards from the node respectively. The degree of a node is a very important property of a node. The in-degree represents how powerful the node is. It corresponds to the amount of knowledge it has. The larger the in-degree the more knowledge it has. The out-degree represents how influential this node is. The larger the out-degree of a node the more it affects the surrounding nodes.

The *reachability* of an actor to another is the ability of one actor to reach another one by any sequence of steps. In directed graphs there may be a case that A can reach B but B cannot reach A. In symmetric data if two actors cannot reach each other so there will be a kind of division within the network.

The *distance* between two nodes is the number of steps required to exchange information between them. This is an important property of nodes in a social network because it specifies how effective a node is and how far knowledge at a node can propagate.

17.2.2 Tie Strength in Social Networks

Most social networks only consider if there is a relationship between two members or not. They do not consider the strength of the ties between members. Recently more attention has been paid towards this property (i.e. the tie strength). The strength of the tie is affected by several factors. Grannovetler [16–18] proposed four dimensions that may affect the tie strength:

- The duration of the relationship
- The intimacy between the two individuals participating in the relationship
- The intensity of their communication with each other
- The reciprocal services they provide to each other

In other literature, such as in the works of Wellman and Wortley [19], it is argued that emotional support strongly affect the strength of the tie between any two members in a social network. Other factors, such as socioeconomic status, educational level, political affiliation, race and gender are also considered to affect the strength of ties [20]. Moreover the structural factors, such as network topology and information about social circles may affect the tie strength [21].

17.3 Case Study: Social Networks of MAS for Semantic Search

Traditional search engines depend on the number of occurrence of given words in documents. Semantic search depends on understanding the meaning of the concepts used in the context of other words. It then tries to retrieve the related documents to these concepts. The backbone of semantic search is the semantic interoperability which is the main ingredient for notation extraction from the search phrase. Using social networks in this system provides great flexibility; especially in dealing with concepts in ontologies. It allows MAS to understand the meaning of the same concept even though its definition might be slightly different in each agent's ontology.

In our framework, we assume that in a society of n MAS (Mas_1, Mas_2, … Mas_n), each MAS (Mas_i) manages a repository R_i and consists of different agents, each with its own responsibilities. These repositories use different ontologies to represent their knowledge. The ontologies used within the repositories are not necessarily the same. Also, agents do not need to understand concepts in the same way. The most important concept here is the ability of agents to understand each other.

In our framework, we try to make agents from different MAS able to communicate with each other and to understand each other by interacting through a social network. In this social network, the strengths of relationships (ties) between agents are not the same.

The tie strength between agents is a good indicator of how close these agents are to each other. It helps in both semantic search and concept learning modules.

In the learning module, when the user sends a search query to a local agent, the local agent checks for new concepts that are not defined in the repository. If the local agent found new concepts, it asks its peers/neighbors for this new concept. These selected agents are now teacher agents. The choice of teacher agents depends on the tie strengths between the local agent and all its peers. The teacher agents teach the local agent the new concept by sending some illustrative examples representing this concept. If conflicts occur during the learning process, the local agent depends more on the examples sent by teachers with which it has stronger relationships (i.e. higher tie strengths).

The semantic search module starts when the local agent is sure that all new concepts in the search query are learnt correctly. The local agent annotates its own repository using keywords in the search statement. The annotation procedure re-categorizes the repository by conforming to concept hierarchy. Then the local agent searches the annotated repository for the search query and returns the results (called local results). At the same time the local agent sends the search query to all its neighbors (in this case they are called remote agents). Each of these remote agents searches its own repository by annotating it with the search keywords. Then each remote agent returns more results (called remote results). After gathering all the results of the search from all remote agents, the local agent tries to rank the results. The purpose of this ranking is to decide the order in which the local agent delivers the results to the user. The raking process depends also on the tie strength between the local agent and each of remote agents. The stronger the tie between them, the higher a rank is given to results returned from this particular agent.

17.3.1 Semantic Search Process

We have devised a spiral workflow to incorporate both search and concept learning in the semantic search process [22]. The spiral workflow and its suggested scenario are shown in Fig. 17.2. On one hand, search engines should be capable of responding to the requests according to agreements with the concept learning module. On the other hand, annotation procedures of search engines can be done on the fly based on the obtained concepts instead of depending on fixed predefined ontological concepts. This view exposes the intrinsic relationship between concept learning and semantic search in a heterogeneous environment. In such an environment, concept learning and semantic search are treated equally as basic roles, involved in the process which support each other to achieve their own goals by enriching the set of ontological concepts and reducing ambiguity of the search, respectively.

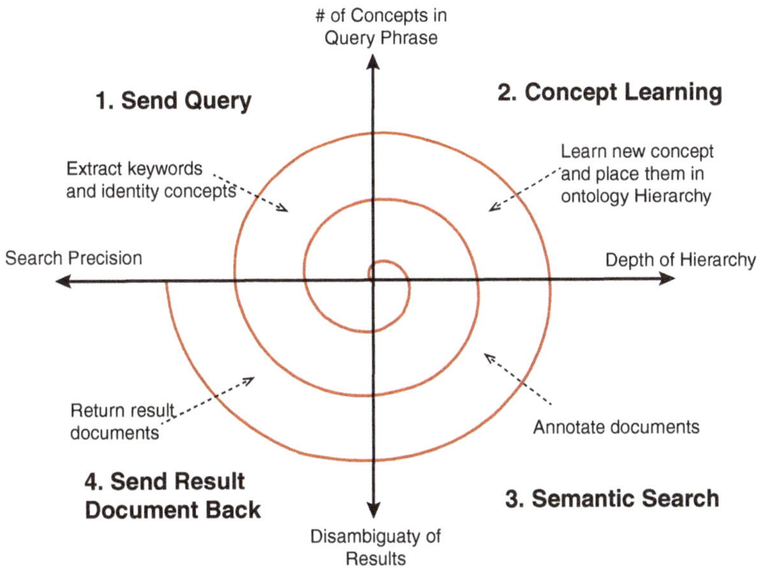

Fig. 17.2 Spiral workflow between semantic search and concept learning

Following the spiral process, concept learning module and semantic search take actions alternately.

The scenario of this process is as follow:

- The system is initiated by the user when he/she sends the search query to one agent (we call it local agent).
- Concepts are extracted from the search query.
- The concepts in the search query are compared by those defined with the ontology in the local repository. This comparison is essential to enable the local agent to find out the new concepts in the search query that are not defined in its local repository.
- If new concepts are found in the search query, the local agent requests the other agents (remote agents) to teach it these new concepts. (This step represents the initialization of the concept learning process.)
- The concept learning mechanism is continued until the local agent learns the new concepts adequately.
- After learning all new concepts, the concept hierarchy in local repository is reorganized to add the new concepts in their proper position.
- The annotation procedure is then performed on the fly on all the concepts in the local repository; old and newly learned concepts. UIMA [23] is used to enable search and classification within each document repository.
- In the same time, the local agent broadcasts the search query to all remote agents to search their local repository and send back the result documents.

The local agent collects the returned documents from remote agents and ranks them using social networks before retrieving them to the user.

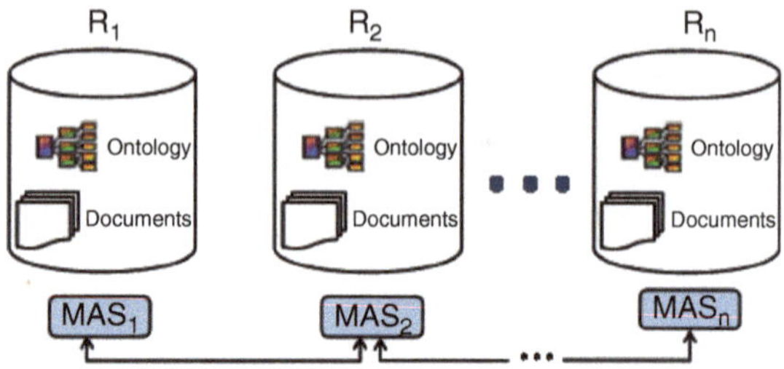

Fig. 17.3 The system architecture

17.3.2 Semantic Search Infrastructure

In the previous section, we describe the importance of the concept learning module in the semantic search system. The main obstacle in the concept learning system is the complexity of ontological heterogeneity solution. In order to solve this problem we propose to leverage of the power of a multi-agent system to use it in the infrastructure of our semantic search system. A great social network of MAS is used to set up the backbone elements that communicate with each other. As shown in Fig. 17.3, each MAS controls a repository that uses an ontology to cover a specific area of knowledge. Each repository contains some documents that are related to concepts defined within the ontology. Using MAS allows the system to hide the search complexity from the user.

17.3.3 Prototype System Architecture

Figure 17.4 shows different agent roles in each MAS in our prototype system. These roles are defined below.

Query Handler: This role involves accepting search query and processing it by extracting concepts from it. Also it is responsible for broadcasting the query statement to all the neighbor repositories.

Concept Manager: This role involves finding the new concepts in the search query and broadcast it to all neighbour agents in order to be learnt.

Concept Learner: This role involves maintaining and confirming newly learnt concepts; including creation of taxonomies of interested domain. It is also responsible of broadcasting these concepts to all group members to share searching for it. Moreover it rearranges local repositories with the newly learned concepts.

Document Annotator: This role involves annotating the documents in local repository and filtering them according to the search keywords, then returning back the filtered documents.

Peer Finder: This role involves detecting cooperative peers (agents) in the social network that communicate with the current agent with a relationship.

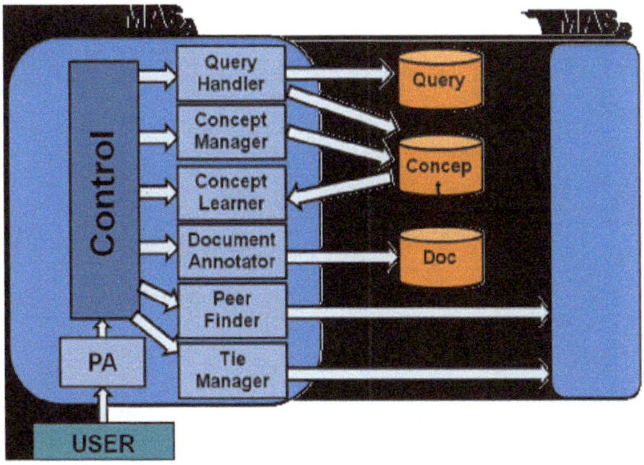

Fig. 17.4 Roles of different agents

Tie Manager: This role involves keeping track of common concepts between peers in the social network and the interactions which occur between those peers in the learning process. Tie manager is able to change the strength of tie between peers dynamically. It is also responsible for setting the initial strength of the relationship between agents.

17.4 System Behavioral Modeling

The requirements for the social network of MAS defined in the previous section are described using partial message sequence charts (pMSCs); defined formally in Definition 1.

This system consists of a large social network of multi-agent systems. Each MAS contains a repository and connects to other MAS on the network for concept learning purposes. The structure of the social network is ever-changing as MAS continue to strengthen or weaken the ties among them based on their commonalities. The managing of the ties is done by two agents of "peer finder" and "tie manager" which are part of each MAS in the network as shown in Fig. 17.4. For the purpose of this case study, it is assumed that the strength of ties between each two nodes in the network (i.e. each MAS) depends on the following criteria:

1. Number of times they have been able to successfully cooperate
2. Number of peers they have in common

Criteria (a) indicates that MAS which have the most concepts in common and continue to have a working relationship will have stronger ties. On the other hand (b) is derived from the social network concept that for node A to be balanced in its relationship (or friendship) with B and C, then A must believe that B and C are peers.

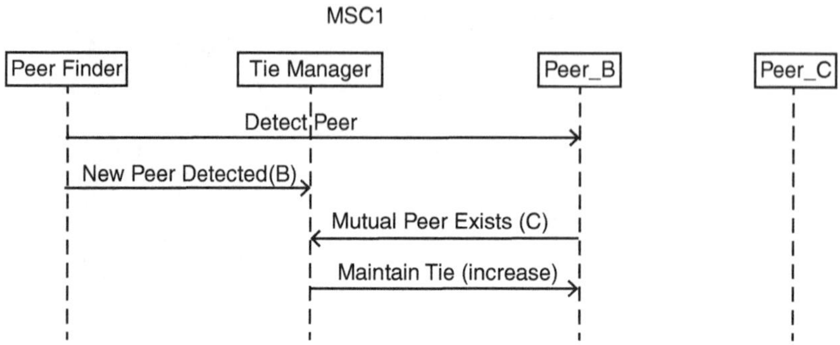

Fig. 17.5 The tie between MAS A and B are established based on their mutual peers

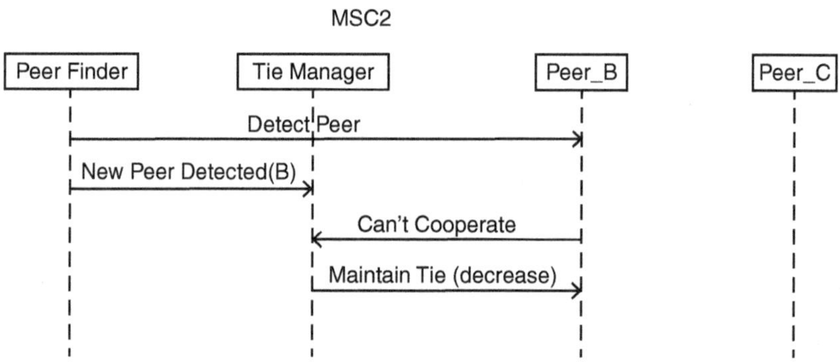

Fig. 17.6 The relation between MAS A and B is decided based on their ability to cooperate on a given query

In the following case study, three arbitrary MAS of A, B and C are selected from the social network. It is assumed that ties already exist between A and C as well as between B and C; however there are no relations between A and B. The following scenarios expressed using MSCs, define the behavior of the network in identifying peers. It is important to note that these scenarios have been devised from the perspective of MAS_A.

MSC1 shown in Fig. 17.5 illustrates a scenario where the ties between MAS A and B is established based on their mutual peer; Peer_C. Alternatively, MSC2 shown in Fig. 17.6, displays a scenario where the relations between MAS A and B are decided based on their ability to cooperate on a given query. The scenario shown in MSC1 (Fig. 17.5) typically occurs when each MAS attempts to update its ties with other nodes on periodic bases, whereas the scenario in MSC2 (Fig. 17.6) would occur when the ties with other MAS are updated as the result of a sent query.

However there could emerge a scenario where the periodic update of the ties of a MAS would coincide with the update of the ties triggered by sending a query. Such a scenario can be derived from the scenarios shown in MSCs 1 and 2 (Figs. 17.5 and 17.7 respectively) and is illustrated in MSC 3 (Fig. 17.7).

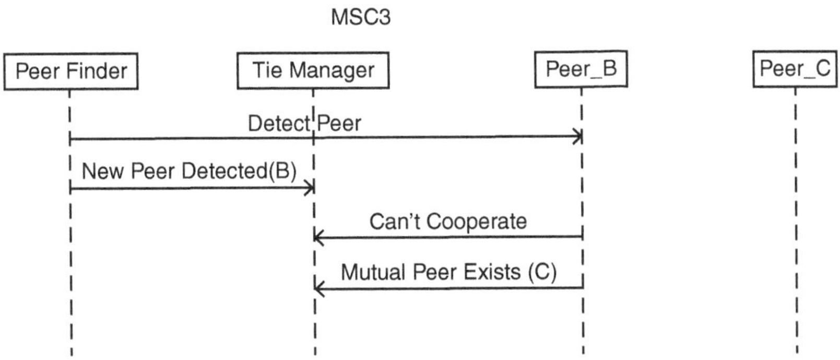

Fig. 17.7 Possible emergent behavior

17.4.1 *Definitions*

In this section, we give some definitions related to MSC notation based on a subset of ITU definitions for MSC [1,4,7].

Let P be a finite set of agents in a distributed system (with the total number of agents $p \geq 2$) and C be a finite set of message contents (or message labels) that are passed among the agents. Let $\sum_i = \{i!j(c),\ i?j(c) |\ j \in P\backslash\{i\},\ \ c \in C\}$ be the set of alphabet (i.e. events) for the agent $i \in P$, where $i!j(c)$ denotes an event that sends a message from agent i with content c to agent j, whereas $i?j(c)$ denotes an event that is received by agent i a message with content c from agent j. The set of alphabet will be $\Sigma = \bigcup_{i \in P} \Sigma_i$ and each member of Σ is called a message.

In the following, we try to capture a causal relationship between a message and its predecessors by defining partial Message Sequence Chart (pMSC).

Definition 1 (Partial Message Sequence Chart). A partial Message Sequence Chart (pMSC) over P and C is defined to be a tuple $m = (E, \alpha, \beta, \prec)$ where:

E is a finite set of events.

$\alpha : E\,\Sigma$ maps each event with its label. The set of events located on agent i is $E_i\ = \alpha^{-1}\,(\Sigma_i)$. The set of all send events in the event set E is denoted by $E! = \{e \in E \mid \exists i, j \in P,\ c \in C\ :\ \alpha(e) = i!j(c)\}$ and the set of receive events as $E? = E\backslash E!$.

$\beta :\ F!E?$ is a bijection mapping between send and receive events such that whenever $\beta\,(e_1) = e_2$ and $\alpha\,(e_1) = i!j(c)$, then $\alpha\,(e_2) = j?i\,(c)$.

$\prec$ is a partial order on E such that for every agent $i \in P$, the result of $\succ$ on E_i is a total order of its members and the transitive closure of $\{(e_1, e_2)\,|e_1 \prec e_2, \exists i \in P\,:\ e_1, e_2 \in\ E_i\}\ \cup\ \{(e, \beta(e))\,|e \in E\}$ is a partial order of the members of E.

The partial order $\succ$ captures casual relationship between the events of a pMSC. This causality basically represents two things. First, a receive event cannot happen without having its corresponding send event happened before. Second, a receive (or send) event, cannot happen until all the previous events, which are causal predecessors of it have already been accomplished. Obviously, if all the send events have their corresponding receive events (i.e. as defined by the function β), the structure is called a Message Sequence Chart or simply an MSC. In other words, an MSC has the same structural components as a pMSC, except that β is defined for $F! = E!$.

Definition 2 (Projection). The projection $m|_i$ for agent i in MSC m, is the ordered sequence of messages which correspond to the events for the agent i in the pMSC m. For $m|_i$, $\|m|_i\|$ indicates its length, which is equal to the total number of events of m for the agent i, and $m|_i[j]$ refers to jth element of $m|_i$, so that if e_j is the jth interaction event for agent i according to the total order of the events of i in m, then $\alpha_m(e_j) = m|_i[j-1]$, $0 \prec j \prec \|m|_i\|$. In $m|_i$, we call every element $i!j(c)$, $i, j \in P$, $c \in C$, a send message and every element $i?j(c)$, a receive message.

For example, the projection for the agent QH in MSC1 in Fig. 17.2 will be "QH!CL(send concept)".

Definition 3 (Equivalent Finite State Machine for a projection). For the projection $m|_i$, we define the corresponding deterministic finite state machine $A_i^m = \left(S^m, \Sigma^m, \delta^m, q_0^m, q_f^m\right)$ such that:

S^m is a finite set of states labelled by q_0^m to $q_{\|m|_i\|}^m$.

Σ^m is the set of alphabet

q_0^m is the initial state

$q_f^m = q_{\|m|_i\|}^m$ is the final state (accepting state)

δ^m is the transition function for A_i^m such that $\delta\left(q_j^m, m|_i[j]\right) = q_{j+1}^m$, $0 \le j \le \|m|_i\| - 1$. Thus the only word accepted by A_i^m is $m|_i$.

Note that scenarios can be treated as *words* in a formal language, which is defined over send and receive events in MSCs. Then, a *well-formed word* for an agent is one that for every receive event there exists a send event in that word, which in fact captures the essence of definition given for a pMSC (Definition 1). On the other hand, a *complete word* for a agent is the one that for every send event in it, its corresponding receive event also exists in it. In practice, a system designer must look for complete and well-formed words for each agent, which is not necessarily an easy task. For any MSC m in the set of MSCs M, any sequence ω of m, obtained from a sequence of events in m that respects the partial order of the events defined for m, is called a linearization of m, and is a word in the language *L(M)* of *M*.

17.4.2 Constructing Behavioral Models

As mentioned in the previous section, scenario based specification is an efficient and effective way to represent system requirements for software systems. However as each scenario only partially describes system's behaviour, scenario based

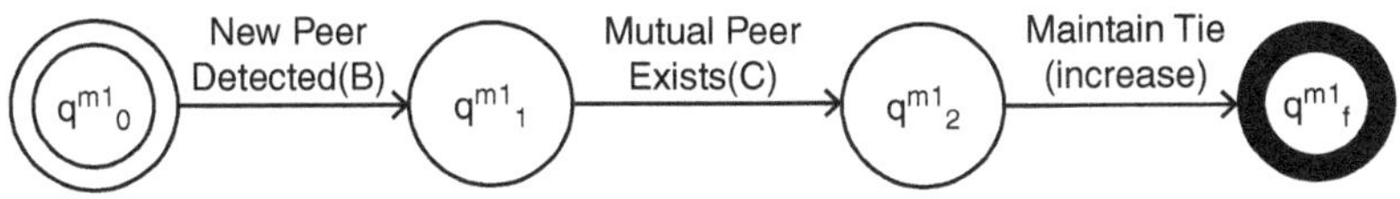

Fig. 17.8 eFSM for the Tie Manager agent of MAS_A in MSC1

Fig. 17.9 eFSM for the Tie Manager of MAS_A in MSC2

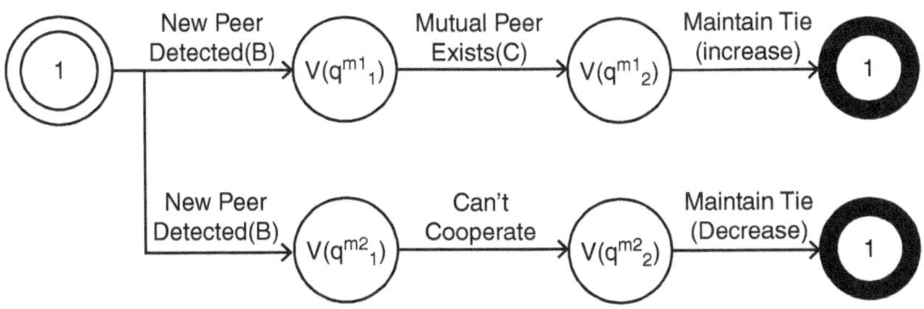

Fig. 17.10 The union of eFSMs built from MSCs 1 and 2

specifications are subject to deficiencies such as incompleteness and contradictions. Therefore having a methodology which can systematically discover system design errors before implementation will result in enormous savings in time and cost. The first part of this approach, which is the synthesis of state machines from message sequence charts is described in this section and is demonstrated using the example of the semantic search system.

The first step is to construct behaviour models for individual system component using finite state machines (FSMs). As explained earlier, the procedure of constructing FSMs from message sequence charts (MSCs) is referred to as behaviour modeling. For any system component *i* of a partial message sequence chart (pMSC) defined in Definition 1, an equivalent finite state machine (Definition 3) can be constructed. For the example of semantic search system, behaviour model of the tie manager (TM) agent of MAS_A is demonstrated. Figures 17.8 and 17.9 show the eFSMs that are constructed for the TM agent in MSC1 (Fig. 17.5) and MSC2 (Fig. 17.6) respectively.

To complete behavior model for the TM agent another FSM, which is the union of its corresponding eFSMs from different scenarios that contain TM is built and shown in Fig. 17.10.

17.5 Detection of Emergent Behavior

Emergent behaviour occurs when there exists a state, in which the component becomes confused as to what course of action to take. This happens when identical states exist in the union of eFSMs obtained through behavioural modelling. A definition for identical states is needed for detection of emergent behaviour. To achieve this we must first have a clear procedure to assign values to the states of the eFSMs. This is a very important step and is performed differently in various works. For instance, [9] proposes the assignment of global variables to the states of eFSMs by the system engineer. However the outcome of this approach is not always consistent as the global variables chosen by different system engineers may vary. Therefore to achieve consistency in assigning state values, the approaches of [24,25] which make use of an invariant property of the system called semantic causality is followed.

Definition 4 (Semantic causality). A message $m|_i[j]$ is a semantical cause for message $m|_i[k]$ and is denoted by $m|_i[j] \xrightarrow{se} m|_i[k]$, if agent i has to keep the result of the operation of $m|_i[j]$ in order to perform $m|_i[k]$.

For example, in MSC1 in Fig. 17.5, message "New Peer Detected (B)" is a semantic cause for message "Mutual Peer Exists (C)". As semantic causality is an invariant property of the system and is part of the system's architecture and the domain knowledge, it is independent of the choices made by the system engineers. In other words, we let the current state of the agent to be defined by the messages that the agent needs in order to perform the messages that come after its current states. Thus in order to evaluate state values of the resulting FSM, a domain theory which consists of the domain knowledge of the system must be constructed as defined formally in Definition 5.

Definition 5 (Domain theory). The domain theory D_i for a set of MSCs M and agent $i \in P$ is defined such that for all $m \in M$, if $m|_i[j] \xrightarrow{se} m|_i[k]$ then $(m|_i[j], m|_i[k]) \in D_i$.

Continuing with the above example, since the message "New Peer Detected (B)" is a semantic cause for message "Mutual Peer Exists (C)", both messages are part of the domain theory. However building the domain theory can be very time consuming. Therefore as a part of this systematic approach, building a light domain theory is introduced. The concept of light domain theory is closely tied to the calculated state values as defined in Definition 6. Using this definition, it becomes evident only states with the same incoming transitions have the potential to exhibit indeterministic behaviour which have the same incoming transitions. Assigning state values to states of eFSMs is done by making use of semantic causality as defined in Definition 6.

Definition 6 (State value). The state value $v_i|(q_k^m)$ for the state q_k^m in eFSM $A_i^m = \left(S^m, \Sigma^m, \delta^m, q_0^m, q_f^m\right)$ is a word over the alphabet $\Sigma_i \cup \{1\}$ such that $v_i|\left(q_f^m\right) = m|_i\,[f - 1]$, and for $0 < k < f$ is defined as follows:

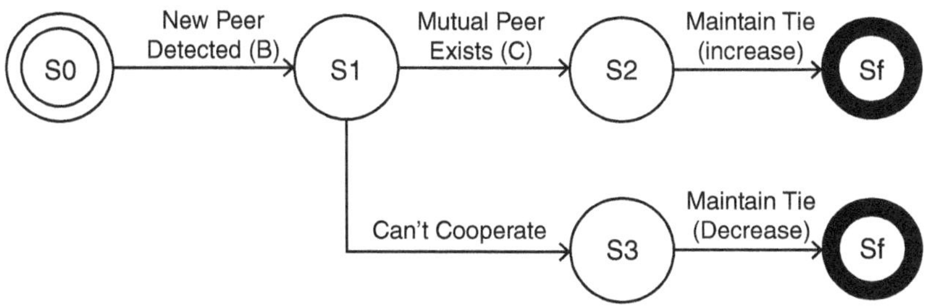

Fig. 17.11 Resulted FSM after merging identical states

1. $v_i|(q_k^m) = m\ |_i\ [k\ -\ 1]v_i|(q_j^m)$, if there exist some j and l such that j is the maximum index that $m|_i\ [j\ -\ 1] \xrightarrow{se} m|_i\ [l]\ ,\ 0 < j < k,\ \ k \leq l < f$
2. $v_i|(q_k^m)\ =\ m\ |_i\ [k\ -\ 1]$ if case (i) does not hold but $m|_i[k\ -\ 1] \xrightarrow{se} m|_i[l]$, for some $k \leq l < f$
3. $v_i|(q_k^m)\ =\ 1$, if none of the above cases hold

Getting back to our systematic approach to find emergent behaviour, by considering the resulting FSM in Fig. 17.10, we select pairs of states with the same incoming transitions and evaluate their state to look for identical states. Figure 17.11illustrates the constructed FSM as the result of the merging of identical states.

As it is shown in Fig. 17.11, state S1 is where the tie manager of MAS_A falls into confusion. That is, as it is illustrated in MSC3 (Fig. 17.7), TM will not be able to distinguish whether or not it should increase the tie with MAS_B or decrease it. Therefore as a result of the systematic approach in detecting emergent behavior in MAS, the system engineers is notified of such possible scenarios and is able to make modifications where necessary.

17.6 Conclusions and Future Work

Scenario based specification is an efficient and effective approach to illustrate the requirements of software system. Aside from their simplicity and expressive powers, scenarios can be used to analyze the requirements and design of software systems. Some of the failures in software systems can be directly attributed to their design. Research suggests that detection of failures and removal of faults during field use of a system is about 20 times more expensive than detection and removal in the requirement and design phase [26]. Unfortunately, manual review of the design documents may not efficiently detect all the design flaws due to the scale and complexity of the system. Therefore devising an automated and systematic methodology to analyze system requirements is greatly beneficial.

Furthermore, in this paper a method to identify the exact cause of implied scenarios is provided, so that by capturing it, implied scenarios can be detected and removed. This method is novel in the sense of formalization of the cause of implied scenarios. We believe that this is the main reason for some shortcomings and conflicts in the current works, as they have been revealed in [25, 27].

In this research we devised and demonstrated a method to detect and remove design flaws that may lead to emergent behaviors in social networks. These techniques were illustrated using a prototype of a social network of multi-agent systems for semantic search. Due to the lack of central control in social networks, the requirement gathering and design of such systems can be difficult. Thus the presented methodologies can be used to systematically validate the requirements of social networks.

In this research the requirements of social networks were analyzed with a component level perspective. For future work, the requirements of these systems can be analyzed with a system-level outlook. Furthermore since emergent behavior is not necessarily a negative quality of the system, the presented methodologies can be utilized to discover implied scenarios which do not cause problems for the system.

References

1. Scott, J.: Social Network Analysis: A Handbook, 2nd ed. Sage, London/Thousands Oaks (2000)
2. Hanneman, R.A., Riddle, M.: Introduction to Social Networks Methods. Sage, London/Thousand Oaks (2005)
3. Unified Modeling Language Specification. Version 2. Available from Rational Software Corporation, Cupertino (2006)
4. ITU: Message Sequence Charts. Recommendation, International Telecommunication Union (1992)
5. Harel, D., Kugler, H.: Synthesizing state-based object systems from lsc specifications. Int. J. Found. Comput. Sci. **13**(1), 5–51 (2002)
6. Kruger, I., Grosu, R., Scholz, P., Broy, M.: From mscs to statecharts. In: Rammig, F.J. (ed.) Distributed and Parallel Embedded Systems. Kluwer, Boston (1999)
7. Makinen, E., Systa, T.: MAS – an interactive synthesizer to support behavioral modeling in UML. In: ICSE 2001, Toronto (2001)
8. Uchitel, S., Kramer, J., Magee, J.: Synthesis of behavioral models from scenarios. IEEE Transaction on Software Engineering, Feb 2003, pp. 99–115
9. Whittle, J., Schumann, J.: Generating statecharts designs from scenarios. In: ICSE, Limerick (2000)
10. Whittle, J., Schumann, J.: Scenario-based engineering of multi-agent systems. In: Agent Technology from a Formal Perspective, 3d ed. Springer, London (2006)
11. Adsul, B., Mukund, M., Kumar, K.N., Narayanan, V.: Casual closure for MSC languages. In: FSTTCS, pp. 335–347. Hyderabad, India (2005)
12. Alur, R., Etessami, K., Yannakakis, M.: Inference of message sequence charts. IEEE Transaction on Software Engineering, July 2003, pp. 623–633
13. Muccini, H.: Detecting implied scenarios analyzing nonlocal branching choices. In: FASE 2003, Warsaw (2003)

14. Uchitel, S., Kramer, J., Magee, J.: Negative scenarios for implied scenario elicitation. In: 10th ACM SIGSOFT International Symposium on the Foundations of Software Engineering (FSE 2002), Charleston (2002)
15. Wasserman, S., Faust, K.: Social Network Analysis: Methods and Applications. Cambridge University Press, Cambridge/New York (1994)
16. Granovetter, M.S.: The strength of weak ties. Am. J. Sociol. **78**, 1360–1380 (1973)
17. Granovetter, M.S.: Getting A Job: A Study of Contacts and Careers. University Of Chicago Press, Cambridge (1974)
18. Granovetter, M.S.: The strength of weak ties: a network theory revisited. Sociol. Theory **1**, 201–233 (1983)
19. Wellman, B., Wortley, S.: Different strokes from different folks: community ties and social support. Am. J. Sociol. **96**, 558–588 (1990)
20. Lin, N., Ensel, W.M., Vaughn, J.C.: Social resources and strength of ties: structural factors in occupational status attainment. Am. Sociol. Rev. **46**, 393–405 (1981)
21. Burt, R.: Structural Holes: The Social Structure of Competition. Harvard University Press, Cambridge (1995)
22. Far, B.H., Zhong, C., Yang, Z., Afsharchi, M.: Realization of semantic search using concept learning and document annotation agents. In: Proceeding of Twenty-First International Conference on Software Engineering and Knowledge Engineering (SEKE), pp. 164–169. Boston, USA (2009)
23. Lally, A., Verspoor, K., Nyberg, E.: Unstructured Information Management Architecture (UIMA) Version 1.0 (OASIS, 2008) (2008)
24. Moshirpour, M., Mousavi, A., Far, B.: Detecting emergent behavior in distributed systems using scenario-based specifications. In: International Conference on Software Engineering and Knowledge Engineering, San Francisco (2010)
25. Mousavi, A.: Inference of emergent behaviours of scenario-based specifications. In: Department of Electrial and Computer Engineering, vol. PhD, University of Calgary, Calgary (2009)
26. Goldenson, D.R., Gibson, D.L.: Demonstrating the impact and benefits of CMMI: an update and preliminary results. CMU/SEI-2003-SR-009, Pittsburgh, Oct 2003
27. Mousavi, A., Far, B.: Eliciting scenarios from scenarios. In: Proceedings of 20th International Conference on Software Engineering and Knowledge Engineering (SEKE 2008), San Francisco, 1–3 July 2008

Chapter 18
Factors Enabling Information Propagation in a Social Network Site

Matteo Magnani, Danilo Montesi, and Luca Rossi

Abstract A relevant feature of Social Network Sites is their ability to propagate units of information and create large distributed conversations. This phenomenon is particularly relevant because of the speed of information propagation, which is known to be much faster than within traditional media, and because of the very large amount of people that can potentially be exposed to information items. While many general formal models of network propagation have been developed in different research fields, in this chapter we present the result of an empirical study on a Large Social Database (LSD) aimed at measuring specific socio-technical factors enabling information spreading in Social Network Sites.

18.1 Introduction

Social Network Sites (SNSs) constitute an efficient and effective platform to spread information, and can thus be seen as an alternative to traditional media. However in SNSs information flows are governed by different rules, because every user can (consciously or unconsciously) decide to facilitate information spreading. In this chapter we present the results of a research project aimed at investigating propagation paths in Friendfeed.

M. Magnani (✉)
Department of Computer Science, Aarhus University, Aarhus, Denmark
e-mail: magnanim@cs.au.dk

D. Montesi
Department of Computer Science, University of Bologna, Bologna, Italy
e-mail: montesi@cs.unibo.it

L. Rossi
Department of Communication Studies, University of Urbino Carlo Bo, Urbino, Italy
e-mail: luca.rossi@uniurb.it

T. Özyer et al. (eds.), *The Influence of Technology on Social Network Analysis and Mining*, Lecture Notes in Social Networks 6, DOI 10.1007/978-3-7091-1346-2_18,

Friendfeed, a microblogging service created in 2007 and acquired by Facebook in 2009, offers a very interesting case. On one side it can be considered as a classical microblogging service by allowing people to share short messages with a list of contacts. At the same time it allows users' contacts to comment directly under the original messages. While on Twitter conversations are spread through the network and traceable by the use of the reply sign @ and the re-tweet code RT [7] on Friendfeed conversations aggregate on fewer streams as comments on specific entries [6]: users spread conversations to a higher level of visibility simply by participating. A commented entry will be visible, in fact, to all the followers of the commenter in addition to all the followers of the original poster. In addition to these interesting and complex features, the majority of content produced inside this site is public and can be retrieved and analyzed, from the network of user contacts to most of the text entries and comments.

This large amount of user generated content by being persistent and searchable [1] allows us to access an unprecedented quantity of data to study the factors enabling or preventing information propagation. Even if the phenomenon appears to be of major interest when it involves breaking news such as the terror attack in Mumbai in 2008, that has been widely covered and reported live on Twitter, or the death of the pop star Michael Jackson, that created a massive amount of internet traffic both on Twitter and Facebook, the social web ceaselessly propagates information. Internet memes, units of cultural information able to spread through people retaining their informational content [4, 19], are an example of this on-line propagation of information.

The chapter is organized as follows. First, we discuss existing work on information propagation in social networks. In Sect. 18.3 we provide a brief description of the data used in our analysis, its acquisition and structure. In Sect. 18.4 we identify and classify a number of information propagation enablers, providing empirical data to highlight their role in the process. We conclude with a summary of the identified propagation patterns. This chapter extends our previous work [16] by applying our methodology to a new and larger dataset and by including additional analyses.

18.2 Related Work

The propagation of items through networks is a very abstract and general problem which has been studied in several fields. At the same time, different approaches have carefully exploited the specificities of their application fields according to the specific items traversing the network, e.g., viruses or Internet surfers, and developing specific solutions that worked well under those assumptions but are not meant to be general answers to this problem. Our goal here is not to explain in detail every approach that has been used but to highlight how previous researches and uses in different fields can provide insights into the topic. It is important to highlight that we are not going to move seamless ideas and concepts (such as *viral* or *propagation*) from a scientific field to another. Every discipline has its own specificity and moving concepts (and research methods) around would only generate greater confusion rather than real knowledge. Within this perspective being able to stress differences appears to be as important as stressing similarities.

Despite these necessary notes there is no doubt that contemporary studies on propagation are heavily related to the epidemiological studies. Epidemiology has tried to understand how *viruses* and other *pathogens* spread over the population. Although models assuming a standard rate of possible contacts have been used for a long time with overall good results [9, 10] assuming random contacts was not considered good enough to reproduce our everyday experience. Some contacts are more probable than others and our daily experience is mostly based on a fixed number of recurrent social interactions. This leads to the methodological challenge of being able to observe and trace only what is relevant from a specific point of view, and highlights the role of social networks in *pathogens* propagation. Nevertheless there are many crucial differences between the propagation of an epidemic and the spreading of information in a SNS, that can be grouped in two major areas: differences related to the *available data* and differences in the nature of the *network nodes*.

In a closed SNS the problem of identifying what constitutes a *meaningful connection* is solved by the nature itself of the socio-technical environment. If we stay with the classical boyd-Ellison article about Social Network definition and scholarship [2]: a SNS is defined also by its feature of articulating a set of connections between users. The explicit connection between users, the *meaningful link* is part of the SNS itself and its establishment appears to be an explicit choice of the user. We are not claiming that every connection has the same value to the user, we are well aware of the differences and the nuanced reality of signification often constructed within on-line friendship and we will later provide empirical data supporting this heterogeneity; what we are claiming is that when we are dealing with SNSs the *basic level* of social connection is available in the technical structure of the system itself. Within this perspective the definition of the network is an easier task requiring less work from the researcher and implying a minor level of ambiguity.

The second difference when we shift our focus from viral diffusion to information/cultural spreading is about the nature of the *virus* itself and the nodes of the network. The metaphor of media virus [19] had (and still has) great success among the large audience. According to Jenkins [8], who is investigating how cultural contents spread through our society, there are many crucial differences in the way viruses and cultural content spread. The epidemiological metaphor, even if it is very attractive, should not be used. Jenkins' point stresses the role of end users in the propagation process. While in virus spreading people are almost passive carriers of viruses (they cannot choose if they want to be infected or not and, if infected, they have no choice between spreading the virus as it is or changing it) memes[1] need some kind of collaboration to their propagation. If it is obviously possible that someone is unintentionally exposed to any kind of *unit of information* the choice between spreading it or not and the way in which it has to be done is definitely

[1]Memes are described [19] as units of information capable of retaining their informational content, inducing people to reproduce the meme itself and staying alive as long as they are able to be reproduced.

up to the single person. This means that the spreading of specific information can be done also to pursue specific personal interests, to enforce personal relationships between users or according to a personal definition of relevance [7]. Information spreading in a socio-technical context is not only matter of what has the major chance of being replicated but also of how this replication is used by the members of a specific cultural context. This is why exposition $\neq$ contagion $\neq$ spreading. Within this perspective the *nodes* of a social network involved in the spreading of information, as well as those involved in the spreading of any kind of cultural object, are substantially different from those involved in the spreading of a viral agent.

The active role of media audiences has been part of any media spreading theory since long time [18] and a theoretically founded research on propagation in SNSs should not try to simply show how information propagates through a SNS but also understand what is the role of SNS structures and connections in the larger process of propagation of cultural information.

Another large body of work related to the analysis of networks regards the Internet. Intuitively propagation depends on the influence of users on other users, and well known approaches like HITS and Google's PageRank [3, 12] have been studied to associate weights to Internet nodes. The two main similarities of these approaches with SNS analysis techniques regard the awareness that some nodes may be more influential than others and the fact that direct connections are not sufficient to compute node weights. However the complexity of the information items traversing the network and the fact that nodes (often) represent real people give rise to a significantly different scenario. In Sect. 18.4 we provide some empirical evidence to support this claim.

Similarly, approaches to emphasize hidden structures of the Internet can be re-thought to be applied to SNSs, like k-shell decomposition [5, 11]. Also in this case, as well as in works dealing with other kinds of social networks [13], the specificities of the social relationships may induce a hidden network structure very different from the network defined by base connections. Therefore, while these approaches may be useful, it is important not to over-simplify social models mapping them to simple networks. In the remaining of this chapter we analyze some of these details, which are shown to play a fundamental role in information propagation.

18.3 Data Extraction and Summary

In Friendfeed users may open a new discussion by posting an **entry**. Every post will be visible to all users *following* the poster, who can **comment** on the original entry or *like* it. Therefore, for what concerns the content of this chapter a discussion consists in an *entry* followed by a chain of *comments*. In the following, we will indicate with *post* any text entry or comment posted by a user, with *entry* a new conversation started by a user, and with *comment* a comment to an entry.

To perform our analysis, we monitored the activity of Friendfeed from August 1, 2010, 00:00 AM to September 31, 2010, 12:00 PM. The service was monitored at a rate of about 1 update every 3 s to retrieve public user posts. At the end of the monitoring period we computed the network of users starting from the users in the sample and retrieving all the connected graph of followers.

The resulting database contained about 12.5 million entries, 3.7 million comments, 800,000 likes, and 28 million subscriptions (following relationships). All the data can be downloaded from the project website.[2]

Global services such as Friendfeed can be used in many different ways according to the socio-cultural contexts we are observing. As we have claimed before [6] the role that a specific social medium plays within a specific media system can be properly understood only if it is framed within a specific cultural context. Therefore, from this database we extracted the portion of the social network concerning a single cultural context, specifically the Italian network.

Since geographical identification is not provided by Friendfeed we adopted an ad hoc solution to identify Italian users. We started from a set I_1 of users certainly Italian, obtained by running a language identifier on the last posts of every user. However, this procedure could not be used to identify all Italian users, because some of them had private accounts (therefore their posts were not available) and some of them produced a large majority of their content in other languages (usually English). However, the Italian network tends to be very dense: 95 % of these users had at least 30 % of their followers recognized as Italian users. Therefore, we generated a new set I_2 including also those users not recognized as Italian at the first iteration, e.g., because we could not access their conversations, but with more than 30 % of contacts inside I_1. At this point there were some other users whose contacts marked as Italian became more than 30 % of their contacts. As a consequence, we reiterated the computation until when the set I_n did not increase in size with respect to I_{n-1}.

This procedure used to find the Italian network as a fix point is exemplified in Fig. 18.1, were we use a 50 % threshold: the identification of a first set of Italian users, represented in black (second graph clock-wise), allows us to mark three additional nodes as Italian (third graph, gray nodes). When these new nodes are added to the set of Italian (black) nodes, a new node starts satisfying the condition of having at least half black nodes as neighbors (bottom left graph). The process continues until we cannot mark additional nodes (bottom right).

Filtering all posts made by Italian users we obtained a database with about 350,000 entries, 400,000 comments, 50,000 likes and 700,000 subscriptions, that will be used in most of the following analyses.

General information about Friendfeed can be found in [6], where we presented a statistical and sociological description of this SNS. However, before focusing on the topic of information propagation it is interesting to look at the distribution of sources of entries. Figure 18.2 represents the percentage of entries coming from the top 10 most active services, obtained after a semi-automated discretization of source indications. If we observe the most active services extracted from the Italian subset of data (Fig. 18.3) instead of the global data we are going to see a significantly

[2]http://larica.uniurb.it/sigsna

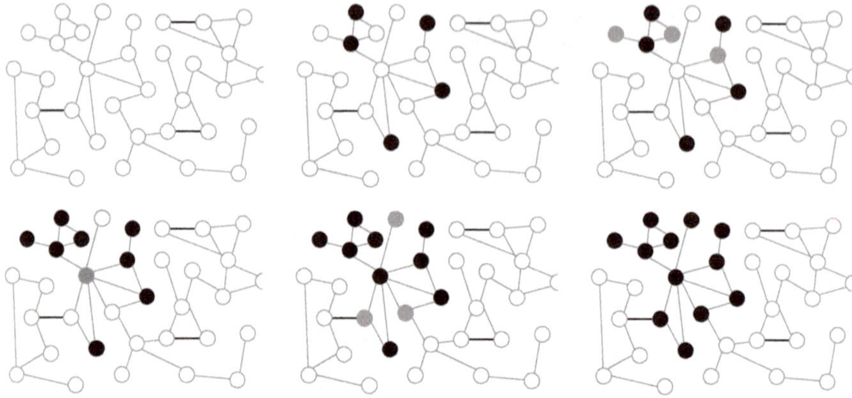

Fig. 18.1 Graphical explanation of the fix point procedure used to obtain the network of Italian users

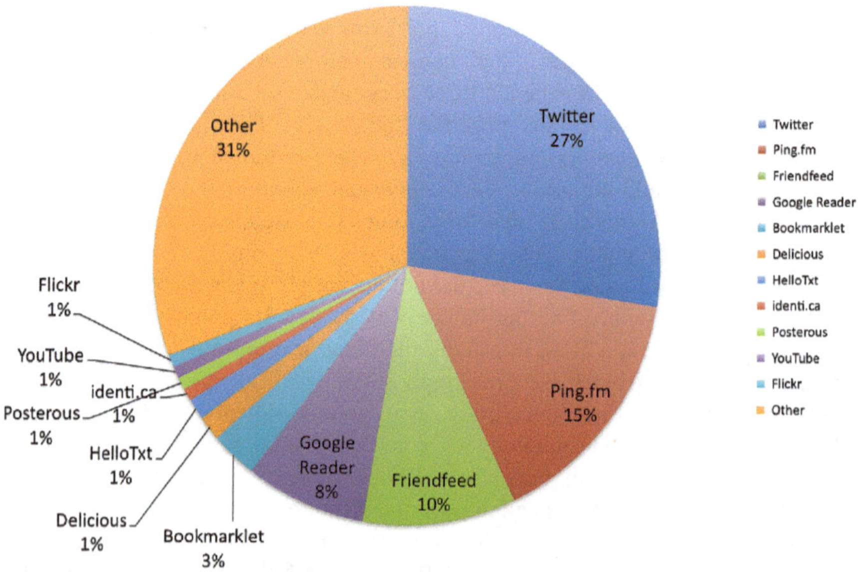

Fig. 18.2 Top 10 Sources of entries (all data set)

different picture. In Italy, where it exists a large online community of users that use Friedfeed as an online space for chat and discussion, the amount of entries produced directly in Friendfeed (and not imported into the system from an external service) increases from 10 % (global data) to 21 %. On the opposite side, due to the relatively small diffusion of Twitter in Italy entries imported from Twitter fall down from 27 % (global data) to 15 %. When we observe global online phenomena pointing out these local aspects is important because of their impact on more general processes like information propagation, that we are discussing in the following sections.

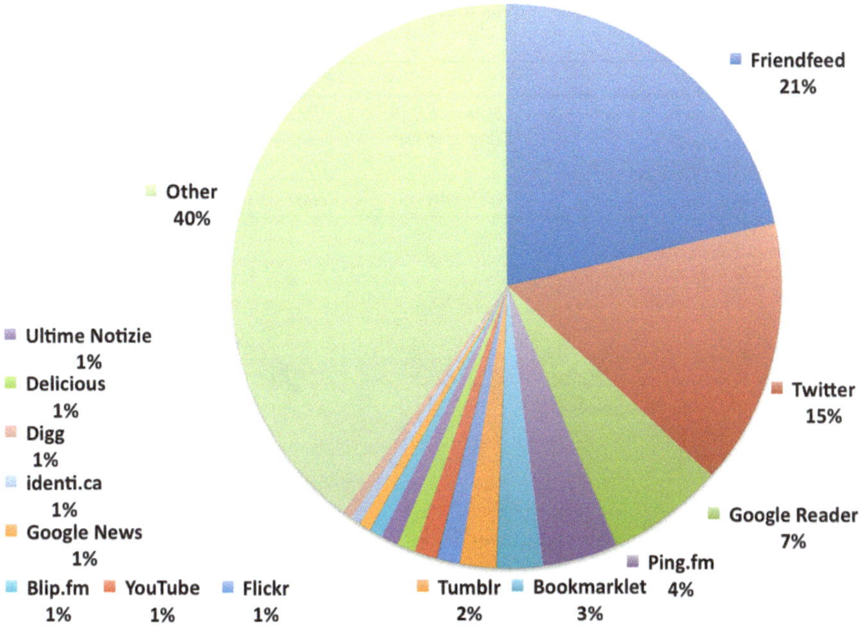

Fig. 18.3 Sources of entries (Italian data set)

18.4 Propagation Enablers

The discovery of factors enabling the spreading of memes and conversations should be based on a short list of well-defined metrics. In the following we focus on two main metrics: **number of interactions** (comments and likes), measuring the ability of a user or message to generate participation, and **audience**, counting the number of people exposed to a message.

In the following we discuss the factors influencing these metrics. These factors have been identified by analysing a large snapshot of the activity occurring inside Friendfeed. At a high level of abstraction a social data model is made of a *network* of *users* exchanging *messages*. We will organize the following discussion around these elements. This classification is only meant to simplify the complex picture drawn in the following, but does not indicate any independencies of these elements – on the contrary, we will see that they are strictly related one to the other.

18.4.1 User Modeling

The nodes of our network are not fixed entities, equal to each other. One important aspect differentiating them is their tendency to produce content.

Table 18.1 Basic statistics on entry production and comments received, Italian dataset, September 2010

	Min.	First qu.	Median	Mean	Third qu.	Max.
Entries (per day)	3,330	6,013	7,042	6,667	7,208	8,224
Comments (per day)	3,999	5,697	7,434	6,900	7,791	8,782
Daily Entries (per user per day)	0.03	0.07	0.2	0.79	0.60	116
Daily Comments (per user per day)	0.00	0.00	0.00	0.82	0.03	136

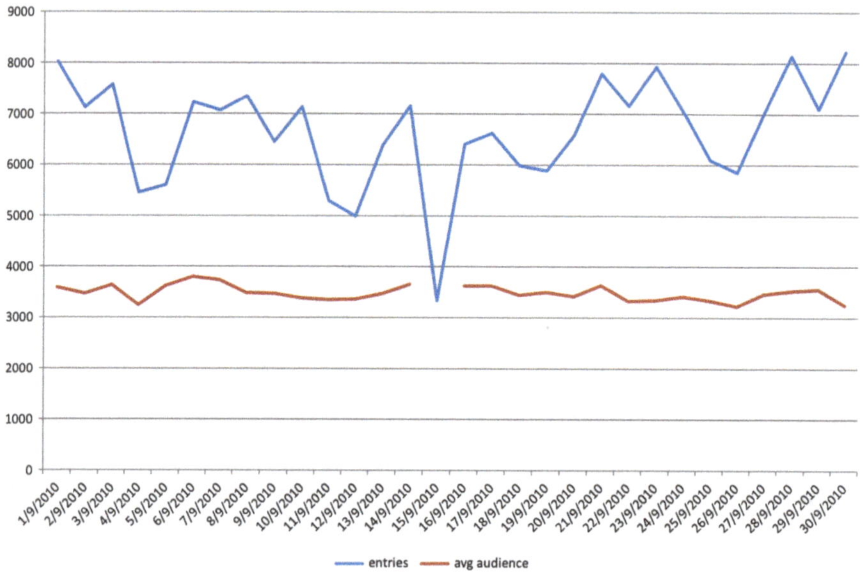

Fig. 18.4 Volume of daily activity (number of entries and comments per day, Italian subset), and average audience size

The entry production rate can be computed for each user and is indicated in Table 18.1. While these values approximate the long-term behavior (2 months) of each user, a more fine-grained analysis of the variations of this estimate highlighted that it can substantially vary depending on time and topic.

Observing the overall content production rate of the Italian community represented in Figs. 18.4 and 18.5 it is possible to describe a rather accurate time trend on a weekly base. As it clearly appears from the figure content production seems to have quite a cyclic behavior with lowest peaks during the weekend and a dull progression from Monday to Thursday.[3] The structural reason for that can be found in the high level of availability of Internet connections from most workplaces. On this point some sociological deduction is required. The weekly trend suggests a high

[3]On Sep. 15th the monitoring system had to be rebooted for maintenance, this explaining the missing values on that date.

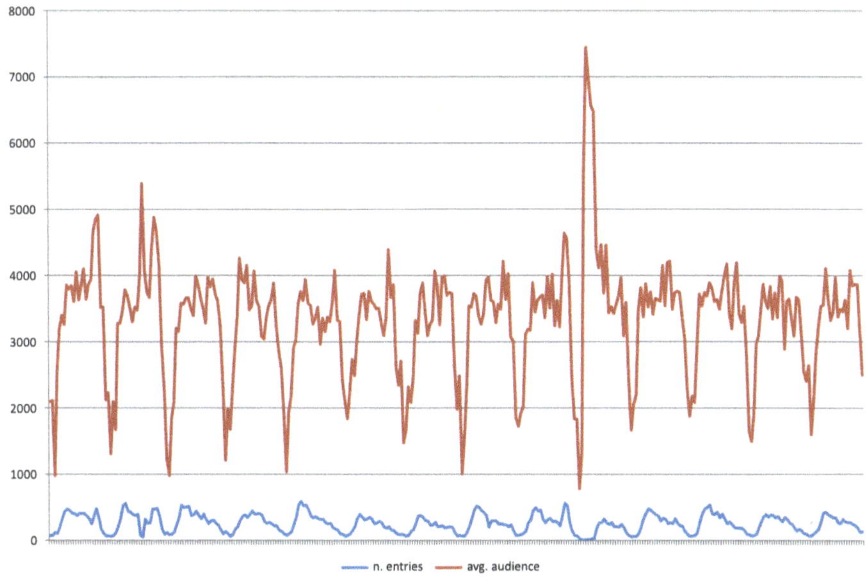

Fig. 18.5 Volume of hourly activity (number of entries and comments per hour, Italian subset, 2 weeks), and average audience size

level of routine with the social media use. These tools seem to be now part of a daily routine made of checking emails, browsing the Web and now updating and posting on social media. Within this routine daily issues can become topics of conversation and are often arisen by users. Weekends seem then, within the described scenario, points in time where the high level of connectivity and sharing is temporarily turned off or reduced.

The influence on propagation, and in particular the average number of users receiving an entry posted at a specific time, has been indicated at the bottom of Fig. 18.5 highlighting a daily trend similar to the one of entry and comment production.

Obviously contingency of life experience can induce a higher level of variability in average entry production rate. Even if, as we said, we can assume that social media use, and therefore content production, is part of daily routines of users, events can rapidly change them. This could be the case of a period of overwork that keeps users busy giving them less or zero time to share thoughts online, or – on the opposite side – it can be the case of an illness that forcing the users to stay at home would probably rise up his/her social media usage. A few examples taken from our qualitative observations should then be able to explain these points: during summer, when vacation time reaches its highs, many users post short entries to inform the community of their upcoming absence: [J.] *On monday I am leaving for summer holidays. No internet for two weeks.* ... In a similar way when user H. writes: [H.] *today I'm kind of sick ... May you sing me a little tune?* she is asking for some kind

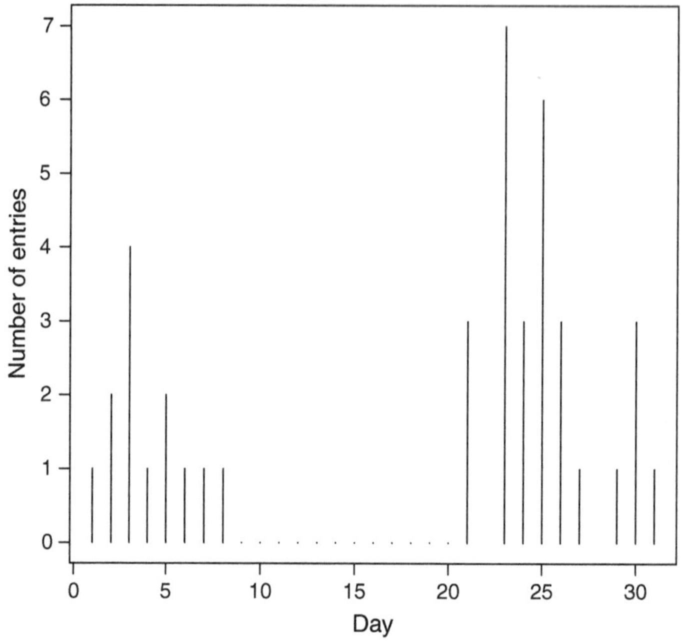

Fig. 18.6 Number of entries produced by user J. during August

of emotional support and alerting that she will be on-line and active in the social media context more that it is expected (or at different times).

Both examples suggest on one side the high level of contingency that can impact individual content production rate in a social media context and on the other side highlight the high level of relational use that social media have. Asking for emotional support during hard times or feeling the duty to inform people that you are not going to be available on-line because of vacation time shows, once more, the level of intimacy that social media can offer. In Fig. 18.6 we show the number of entries produced by the first user in August as one of many examples of specific entry production trends – in this case the message was posted at the beginning of the month.

18.4.2 Network Modeling

The analysis of how the network structure impacts on the propagation of messages can be described as the analysis of all the factors implied in the process that leads from the production of a message (exposition to a message on the network) to the choice, made by other users, to interact with that message and spread it.

Table 18.2 Connection network vs. communication network

Edges in connection network	692,668
Edges in communication network	52,913
Common edges	31,845

According to the final goal of this work we are assuming that aside the network made of established connections it is possible to observe a closer network made of most important connections that are technically equal to the others but much more used. Those connections can be established between off-line friends and then moved on-line but also between on-line friends that feel themselves very close. A link in this *communication* network indicates that the connected users exchanged at least one direct message, i.e., a comment.

The existence of a *communication network* alongside with the *connection network* can be proved by observing the existence, within the single user's network, of specific nodes much more active than others. As it can be observed in Table 18.2 not every existing connection is used in the same way. Some users seem to comment or interact with a far higher frequency than others and those two networks are only partially overlapping. This suggests that interaction here is not merely related to a simple exchange of information about specific topics but involves a more complex relational context made of friendship and empathy. Modeling network propagation should therefore keep into consideration the existence of such preferred paths and the existence of many of them can give to a single message a higher probability of being commented and having its visibility increased.

The relational aspect of *communication links* appears to be evident if we observe the relationship between the number of entries produced and the number of comments received. In fact, we could expect that the more entries a user posts, the more comments he/she will generate and those comments would spread the messages toward a larger audience. However, Fig. 18.7 shows an opposite behaviour. Automated programs or services that post on-line a large quantity of messages usually get zero or very few comments: there is no conversation or real interaction going on between those services and users. Those services can surely be used, with an informative purpose, by a large number of people but they do not seem to be able to generate any kind of conversation therefore, in a network such as Friendfeed, their messages will not propagate out of the first set of direct followers.

Even more interestingly the analysis of users with less than 20 entries posted per day shows that also for nodes plausibly representing real users and not *spammers* the correlation between number of posts and received comments is not evident. On the contrary, we can distinguish a large number of users whose entries are not commented ($y = 0$), and among commented users a positive correlation up to a certain posting rate, with the number of comments then diminishing again toward 0.

To conclude our analysis of the factors influencing the tendency of a connection to generate comments, consider Table 18.3 where we grouped all entries by their original sources. Entries coming from Friendfeed show an average comment rate higher than all other sources. This suggests that even if Friendfeed has the ability to

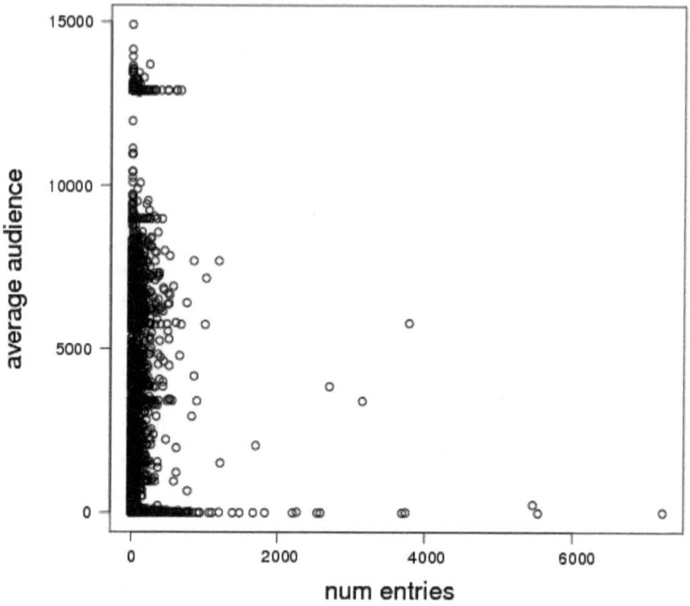

Fig. 18.7 Number of daily entries per user (x) and average audience (y)

Table 18.3 Number of comments received per posted entry, evaluated over different sources

	Twitter	Friendfeed	Facebook	Flickr	YouTube
AVG	0.49	3.41	0.22	0.28	0.18
MAX	197	787	2	163	75

aggregate many different sources the entries that have been created specifically for Friendfeed have a greater ability to induce conversations.

18.4.3 Conversation Modeling

Conversations in Friendfeed take place in a highly competitive environment. The technical structure of the service generates a social space where the visibility of published messages is defined by two opposite forces. Trying to describe how visibility happens in Friendfeed is important to stress once more that the probability for a message to be seen outside of the original network of followers is determined by the interactions (comments or likes) that it will be able to generate. Within this perspective the general visibility of a message seems to be related to the number of on-line users (belonging to the poster's network); if many of them are on-line there

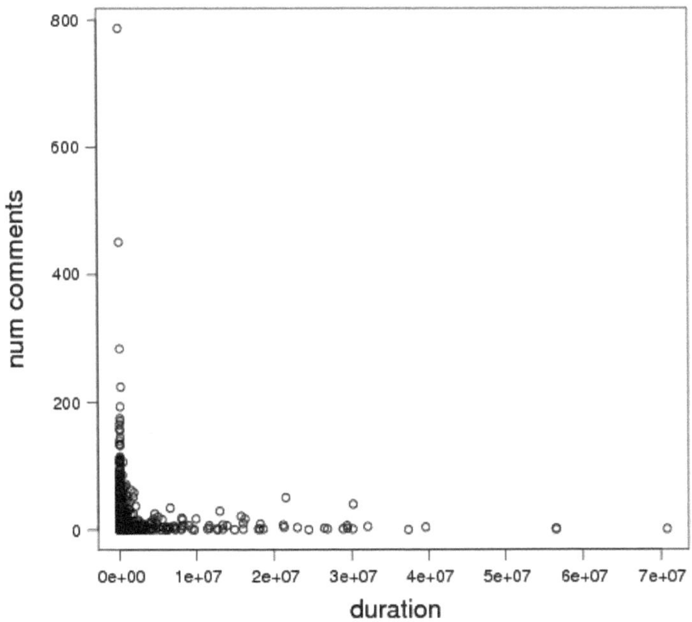

Fig. 18.8 Duration of discussions (x, minutes) and number of comments composing them (y)

will be a higher chance of visibility. At this level one could assume that a message sent while there are many on-line users has a higher probability to be commented and then propagated. Nevertheless at the same time users will produce, while they are on-line, concurrent messages that will move other messages out of the first page (where they would have had greater visibility).

The number of on-line users is therefore to be considered as a double direction force, able to push up the level of visibility of messages (and to spread them out of their original network) and to push down the same level of visibility by producing concurrent messages that will have the chance to move other messages out of the pages with the highest level of visibility.

The analysis of the average lifetime and of the lifetime distribution of conversations in Friendfeed gives us some additional insights on this issue. Observing Fig. 18.8 it is possible to see how on one side the largest part of conversation has a relatively short life span and on the other side there is no clear correlation between the number of comments in a discussion and its life time as it is shown in Fig. 18.9. This short life time indicates an average use of the service as a tool for informal conversation with no (or few) big topics addressed. Conversations seem to be made of interconnected comments that hardly have the ambition of creating more complex, structured and stable discussions. On the opposite of what one could think many of the most commented entries in our sample have an extremely short life time. This suggests that many of the most commented entries are due to a high emotional answer to the first original entry. This could be the case, as we suggested in recent

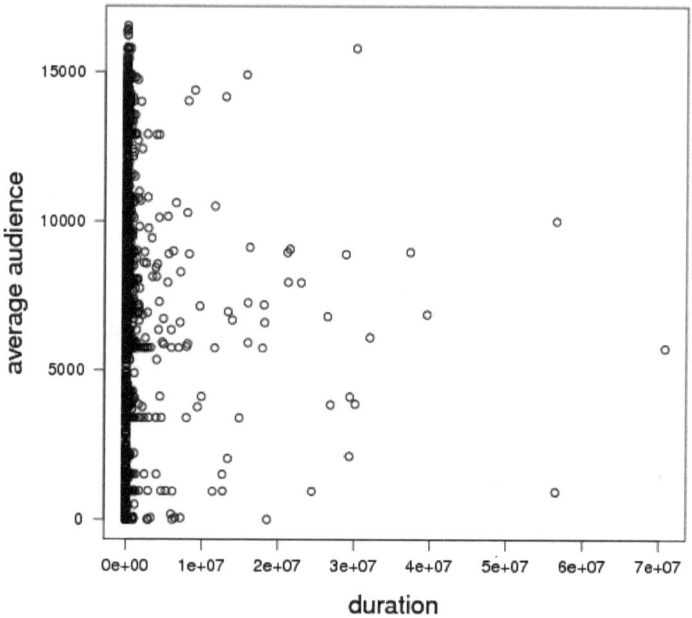

Fig. 18.9 Duration of discussions (x, minutes) and average audience (y)

work [17] of breaking news announcing something happened. In that case a highly emotional response will generate a massive amount of comments that will burst into the network but, at the same time, will be extinguished in a very short time (this relation between posting frequency and emotional involvement can also be used as a ranking parameter in search engines for social media [14, 15]). In addition to that, as illustrated in Fig. 18.9, the ability to reach a large audience is not directly related to the life time of the conversation. This is coherent to what we said in the introduction of this article and it confirms the ability of microblogging sites to spread messages to large audiences in a short time.

18.5 Summary and Concluding Remarks

In this work we provided an in depth description of the SNS Friendfeed and of some of its inner dynamics, investigating some major elements involved in the process of information propagation. The following is a list of our main findings:

- Users active inside Friendfeed generate much more comments than external users importing their messages into the service.
- Content production rate follows specific time-trends.
- These trends are locally affected by contingent events (both private and public).

- The average audience of an entry depends on its posting time with specifically identified trends.
- Information spreads on communication networks only partially overlapping the network of contacts.
- Automated users tend not to generate discussions.
- The number of comments received by users with more limited entry production rates increases only up to some threshold (what is often called *information overload*).
- Most conversations have a very quick growth and an evolution that usually ends within a few hours.
- This is particularly evident for highly commented entries – the presence of many comments often implies a shorter discussion.

These results show how the problem of information spreading in SNSs is influenced by many factors, and cannot be studied in depth reducing it to simpler network models – although this does not prevent simplified models from highlighting interesting features of these complex environments.

Acknowledgements This work has been partly funded by Telecom Italia, by PRIN project "Online social relations and identity: Italian experience in Social Network Sites", and by FIRB project "Information monitoring, propagation analysis and community detection in Social Network Sites".

References

1. boyd, d.: Taken Out of Context: American Teen Sociality in Networked Publics. Ph.D. thesis, University of California-Berkeley, School of Information (2008)
2. boyd, d., Ellison, N.B.: Social network sites: definition, history, and scholarship. J. Comput. Mediat. Commun. **13**(1), 210–230 (2007)
3. Brin, S., Page, L.: The anatomy of a large-scale hypertextual web search engine. Comput. Netw. ISDN Syst. **30**(1–7), 107–117 (1998)
4. Brodie, R.: Virus of the Mind. Hay House, Carlsbad (2009)
5. Carmi, S., Havlin, S., Kirpatrick, S., Shavitt, Y., Shir, E.: A model of internet topology using k-shell decomposition. PNAS **104**(27), 11150–11154 (2007)
6. Celli, F., Lascio, F.M.L.D., Magnani, M., Pacelli, B., Rossi, L.: Social network data and practices: the case of friendfeed. In: International Conference on Social Computing, Behavioral Modeling, and Prediction, pp. 1–8. Springer, Berlin (2010)
7. boyd, d., Scott, G., Gilad, L.: Tweet, tweet, retweet: conversational aspects of retweeting on Twitter. In: HICSS-43. IEEE, Kauai (2010)
8. Jenkins, H., Li, X., Krauskopf, A., Green, J.: If It Doesn't Spread, It's Dead: Media Viruses and Memes (2010). http://henryjenkins.org/2009/02/if_it_doesnt_spread_its_dead_p.html
9. Keeling, M.J., Eames, K.T.D.: Networks and epidemic models. J. R. Soc. Interface **2**(4), 295–307 (2005)
10. Kermack, W., McKendrick, A.G.: A contribution to the mathematical theory of epidemics. Proc. R. Soc. **115**(772), 700–721 (1927)
11. Kitsak, M., Gallos, L.K., Havlin, S., Liljeros, F., Muchnik, L., Stanley, H.E., Makse, H.A.: Identifying influential spreaders in complex networks. Tech. rep., Physics and Society, arXiv:1001.5285 (2010)

12. Kleinberg, J.M.: Authoritative sources in hyperlinked environments. J. ACM **46**(5), 604–632 (1999)
13. Leskovec, J., Backstrom, L., Kleinberg, J.: Meme-tracking and the dynamics of the news cycle. Proceedings of the 15th ACM SIGKDD international conference on Knowledge discovery and data mining – KDD '09, p. 497. ACM, New York (2009)
14. Magnani, M., Montesi, D.: Toward conversation retrieval. In: Agosti, M., Esposito, F., Thanos, C. (eds.) Italian Research Conference on Digital Libraries – Revised Selected Papers. Communications in Computer and Information Science, vol. 91. Springer Berlin Heidelberg (2010)
15. Magnani, M., Montesi, D., Nunziante, G., Rossi, L.: Conversation retrieval from Twitter [demo]. In: ECIR Conference. Lecture Notes in Computer Science Vol. 6611. Springer, Berlin/New York (2011)
16. Magnani, M., Montesi, D., Rossi, L.: Information propagation analysis in a social network site. In: International Conference on Advances in Social Network Analysis and Mining, pp. 296–300. IEEE Computer Society, Los Alamitos (2010)
17. Magnani, M., Rossi, L., Montesi, D.: Friendfeed breaking news: death of a public figure. In: Second IEEE International Conference on Social Computing, pp. 528–533. IEEE Computer Society, Los Alamitos (2010)
18. Morley, D.: The nationwide audience: structure and decoding. British Film Institute, London (1980)
19. Rushkoff, D.: Media Virus!: Hidden Agendas in Popular Culture. Ballantine Books (T), New York (1994)

Chapter 19
Learning from the Past: An Analysis of Person Name Corrections in the DBLP Collection and Social Network Properties of Affected Entities

Florian Reitz and Oliver Hoffmann

Abstract Many projects like the DBLP bibliography have to use names as identifiers for persons. Names however are neither unique nor is it guaranteed that a person is referred to by only one name. This causes inconsistencies which reduce the data quality of a collection. Though there are a large number of algorithmic approaches to solve this problem, little is known on the properties of the inconsistent entities. We show how to extract a large number of past name inconsistencies from the DBLP data set. We analyze the social network properties of these names and of the communities they belong to. We evaluate the usefulness of different properties to differentiate defective and none-defective names and present an approach which can predict the probability that a name will need correction in the future.

19.1 Introduction

There are many data sets which have to store information about persons who are only identified by their name. An example is the DBLP bibliographic project, a collection of publications in computer science and related fields. For each author there is a web page which lists the known publications of this person. If there are two authors with the same name and DBLP has not identified them yet, their publications will be listed on the same author page. We call this a *homonym* inconsistency as a single name refers to more than one real-world person. In October 2010 DBLP

F. Reitz (✉)
University of Trier, Universitätsring 1, Trier, Germany
e-mail: reitzf@uni-trier.de

O. Hoffmann
University of Trier, Universitätsring 1, Trier, Germany

Schloss Dagstuhl – Leibniz-Zentrum für Informatik GmbH, Wadern, Germany
e-mail: hoffmann@dagstuhl.de

T. Özyer et al. (eds.), *The Influence of Technology on Social Network Analysis and Mining*, Lecture Notes in Social Networks 6, DOI 10.1007/978-3-7091-1346-2_19,

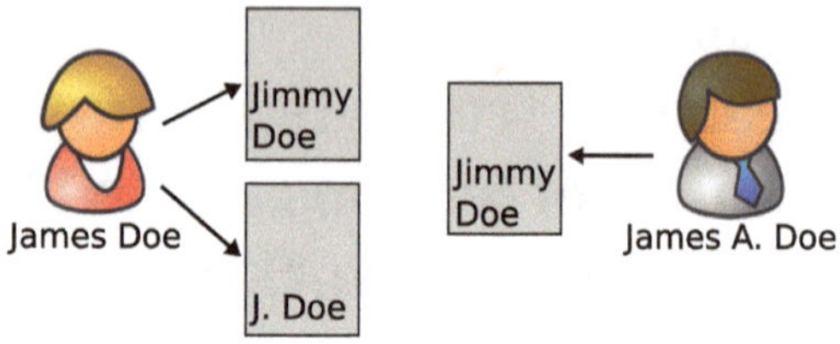

Fig. 19.1 Example of person-name inconsistencies

was aware of about 1,000 names which refer to at least two persons. Another problem occurs when one person uses varying names. The most common reasons for this are abbreviations of name parts or their casual omission, using of different transcription systems for non-Latin characters and simple typing errors. If the names are not properly matched with the author then we obtain multiple publication lists each representing a small part of the author's work. These partial names are called *synonyms*. A name can be homonym and synonym at the same time. In Fig. 19.1 the name *Jimmy Doe* is a homonym because is appears in publications of the real persons *James Doe* and *James A. Doe*. At the same time *J. Doe* and *Jimmy Doe* are synonyms for *James Doe*.

Homonyms and synonyms do not only reduce the usefulness of DBLP as a citation reference. In recent years, the collection has been used in a number of papers including studies on the structure of the computer science community (e.g. [9, 11]). Name inconsistencies can produce false or misleading results. A homonym for example can appear as a false bridge between two otherwise separate communities while in fact it represents two authors with distinct fields of interest. The problem of name inconsistencies is not limited to DBLP. Lee et al. [21] for example reported in 2005 that there are ten different name variations for the author *Jeffrey Ullman* in the ACM digital library.

Given the importance of the problem, it is not surprising that there have been many attempts to find and remove name inconsistencies. Most work is done on detecting defects which already exist in the data set. Traditional inconsistency detectors are limited to comparing attributes—usually the personal name. More recent algorithms use simple social network analysis, for example, the collaboration behavior of persons [27, 32]. Other approaches consider the publication behavior [18] or the thematic interest [25] of a person. The performance of these detectors depends on the social network properties of the inconsistent person entities. For example, a large number of names for which there is little information in the data set can decrease the quality of the candidates [18]. So far, there is little knowledge on these properties in real data sets mainly because it is extremely difficult to extract the ground truth—all defects—even for a small collection. Previous attempts have been limited to small parts of data sets or artificial collections. In Sect. 19.3 we present an approach to extract a large number of inconsistent names by analyzing past modifications of a collection. In Sect. 19.4, we apply this strategy to DBLP and analyze the properties of these names with respect to the requirements of inconsistency detectors. Knowledge on these properties can provide more realistic evaluations of detection approaches.

Usually, the inconsistencies reported by a detector are checked before the data set is modified. As for DBLP, these checks are still done by hand which is time consuming and expensive. This work is necessary as most detectors struggle with the small amount of information which is stored for each name entity. Searches in external data are often required. Because human resources are limited, only parts of a collection can be thoroughly checked. Not all names in a collection are equally prone to defects. For example, if a name is very common the chance it becomes a homonym is high. In most collections, we can find several of such negative conditions. If we know which names are influenced by these conditions we can concentrate our resources on them or warn users that this part of the data set cannot be entirely trusted. Similar strategies are used in the field of software engineering to detect and predict bugs in source code [8, 10]. Unfortunately, not all conditions are known nor is their area of influence. In Sect. 19.5, we propose a new algorithm which estimates the reliability of data by measuring the past influence of negative conditions. As a single name often provides insufficient information, we use communities instead which we extract from relational networks within the collection. We apply this approach to the DBLP collection and briefly discuss properties of conditions.

The central contributions of this paper are:

- We present a framework to detect past name inconsistencies in data sets.
- We apply the framework to DBLP and study network properties of defective names.
- We propose a new quality estimation approach based on communities and past defects.

In the following sections, we will use the term **person** to refer to a real-world person and **name** to refer to the respective entity (or entities) which represents this person in a data set.

19.2 Related Work

Our work is related to name-inconsistency detection or name disambiguation which is part of the more general entity resolution problem. Approaches to solve this problem are often optimized for specific applications, for example, name disambiguation in web site corpora (e.g. [34]) or data warehouses (e.g. [6]). In this work, we study the problem in the context of digital libraries—in particular DBLP—which is characterized by a small amount of available information for most name entities. However, this information is usually highly structured.

There is a number of approaches which attempt to overcome the insufficient data problem by including external data. Shin et al. [32] mine publishers web pages for abstracts of scientific publications from which they extract the thematic interest of the authors. Pereira et al. [27] send different queries to search engines to find web pages which contain publication lists of a person. Kang et al. [20] present a similar approach where they combine two names in a query for web pages. They search for co-occurrences of the names which they consider as implicit relations.

Name disambiguation algorithms can be categorized as *attribute based*, *attribute relational* and *extended relational*. *Attribute-based* approaches compare properties of names to find synonyms. For citation data bases, the personal name is the most important property. Elmagarmid et al. [12] published an extensive survey on comparing strings. Bilenko et al. [3] introduced a metric which adapts to the respective problem. Tejada et al. [33] presented a learning approach which computes similarities of several properties at once.

Most state-of-the-art approaches can be classified as *attribute relational*. They use relational information—like co-authors—as properties of a name entity. Han et al. [16] propose a Naive Bayes model and a Support Vector Machine. Both approaches use profiles of persons to determine if they authored a paper. A profile includes co-authors, paper titles and venues. For DBLP, they showed that using co-author names significantly improves the results. However, they used only a small subset of DBLP. Huang et al. [19] use a similar approach based on vector similarity which also includes co-author names. Han et al. [16] and Huang et al. [19] are called supervised because they require training information to generate the profiles. For large collections, it is often impossible to provide these sets for all names. Unsupervised approaches often apply clustering to group citations which belong to the same author. In this process, name entities are generated from scratch. Defects can be detected by comparing the proposed clusters with the structure in the collection. Han et al. [18] use k-way spectral clustering with paper title, venue and co-author name as similarity metrics and show that it outperforms arbitrary clustering algorithms as k-means. Pereira et al. [27] use a hierarchical clustering based on web information. Ferreira et al. [13] propose a citation clustering entirely based on common co-authors. These clusters are then used as a training set for a supervised detector. As an alternative to clustering, Han et al. [17] modified their Naive Bayes model so it can work unsupervised. On et al. [24] use co-author similarity for a preprocessing step called boxing which is intended to limit the number of name pairs which must be considered.

Extended relational approaches examine full relational network structures. Bhattacharya et al. [2] propose an iterative approach where synonyms in a network are successively merged. They consider changes in the neighborhood of a name for the next step of computation. Levin and Heuser propose two approaches for name disambiguation based on social networks. In [22] they introduce measures for name similarity in social networks. In [23] they present a genetic programming approach which dynamically selects from a number of similarity functions those which best fit. In both studies, they show that using social networks benefits the name disambiguation in DBLP. Shin et al. [32] examine longest circles in relational networks to detect names which belong to multiple persons. If a name is part of more than one circle the authors assume that it represents two or more persons. A similar idea has been proposed by Reuther et al. [31] but only for the direct neighborhood.

The aforementioned approaches aim at pointing out defects. Though experimental results indicate high precision and recall, intensive work is necessary to check the findings. Our approach points out names which are suspicious because of the communities they belong to. We do not provide the location of defects but can improve the deployment of resources to detect them. A similar idea can be found in the field of software engineering where past defects are used in attribute-oriented approaches to predict hidden or future bugs in software components [8, 10]. Our approach introduces previously unused external information, the past corrections. Implicitly, our approach is extended relational as it makes use of communities which are defined by complex network structures.

We also study properties of defective names. Prior work has used a number of test collections. The collection provided by Han et al. [16] is frequently used. Unlike our collection of defects, it represents the actual ground truth of a small portion of DBLP. The authors observe that the results of their approach change when properties are varied but refrain from a further analysis. Reuther et al. [30] compare different test collections but concentrate on size and available attributes. Bhattacharya and Getoor [2] extensively study the effect of properties on their approach. Though they also consider real data, a significant part of their work is done with controlled artificial collections. Several groups assume properties of defects when creating artificial test collections. On et al. [24], for example, test their approach with a collection where defective names have a high number of publications and provide a lot of information.

19.3 Obtaining Inconsistencies

In this study, we analyze defective name entities and use them to estimate the correctness of data. To this goal, we need a large number of names which are homonyms, synonyms or both. In this section, we propose a general framework which bases on detecting the correction of defects in the past. Our approach can be used for any collection which meets certain requirements. In Sect. 19.4, we apply it to the DBLP collection.

19.3.1 Inconsistency Detection

Let D be a data set which contains a set of name entities N and let A be a set of attached entities which usually appear in relation to a name. In a bibliographic collection, for example, the data entities could be publications and $a \in A$ would be attached to $n \in N$ if n authored a. Similar to the initial example, we call $n_1, n_2 \in N$ *synonyms* of a person p if both are attached to data entities which actually belong to p. We call n a *homonym* if it is attached to data entities from multiple persons. Finding homonyms and synonyms is difficult even if D is small. Han et al. [16] describe the cumbersome process of clearing a portion of DBLP which encompasses about 0.5 % of the total collection.

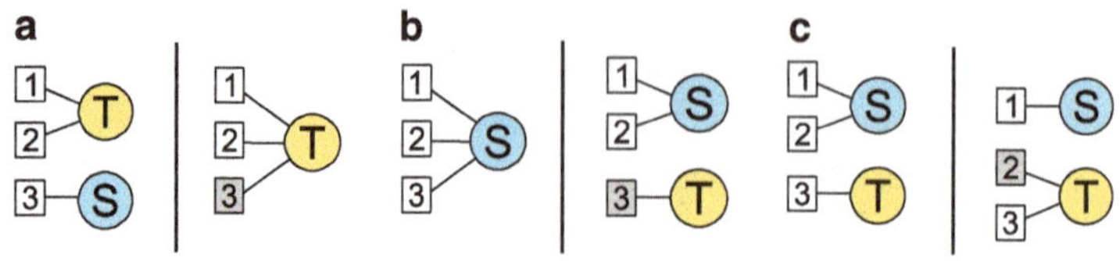

Fig. 19.2 Three types of corrections. Circles represent name entities (S: source, T: target) while rectangles represent data entities. *Left side*: before the modification. *Right side*: afterwards. (**a**) Merge. (**b**) Split. (**c**) Distribute

Assume that we can monitor modifications to D. In most collections there is attached information that, once attached to an entity, will never be removed. A publication, for example, is always attached to the same authors as an actor is to a movie. We call this information permanently attached. However, if a homonym or synonym is corrected some attached entities must be moved to another name. If we can detect moving permanently attached entities we can easily detect the corrections of name inconsistencies. We assume that a name was inconsistent before the modification and correct afterwards. To follow an attached entity, we must be able to identify it throughout the collection. We can monitor a collection for these changes but it is also possible to analyze past corrections provided they are available. The mining of modifications strongly depends on the application and the structure of the provided data.

19.3.2 Inconsistency Classification

Let m be a modification which removes a permanently attached entity a from name n_1 and reattaches it to name n_2. We call n_1 the *source* of this update and n_2 the *target*. By considering source and target before and after m we can tell if m corrected a homonym or a synonym. The correction of complex defects might require multiple similar modifications. We group all modifications with identical source names as well as identical target names if we register them within a defined period of time. We call these groups *corrections*. The time interval depends on the application. A correction is maximal, i.e., no other modification can be added without violating the definition of a correction. However, a correction can consist of only a single modification. There are three types of corrections which we consider in this paper. Figure 19.2 shows examples for all of them.

Merge: All data entities which were associated with the source name are reattached to the target name. The source name might disappear from the collection. A merge operation corrects a synonym inconsistency because all data entities listed for the source name should have been listed for the target name from the beginning. There are merge operations where multiple source names are integrated into a single target name in very short time. Based on the definition of a correction, we consider those as independent operations.

Split: Some data entities of the source name are reattached to the target name which was not listed in D before this correction. In this case, the source name was a homonym as it was attached to data entities for the different persons represented by source and target names.

Distribute: Like split, but there were data entities attached to the target name before the modification. Again, the source name was a homonym. Unlike split, source and target names were also synonyms for the person represented by the target name.

There are other types of corrections which alter personal names, for example the consistent renaming. Those are not relevant for our study because they are not directly related to the homonym/synonym problem.

19.3.3 Relation Between Corrections and Inconsistencies

The set of defective names we obtain is biased by the way name inconsistencies are detected in the underlying data set. Assume that a project applies an inconsistency detector which is good at finding defects with property $\mathcal{A}$ but can barely handle defects with property $\mathcal{B}$. In this case, defects with property $\mathcal{A}$ would be overrepresented and many defects with property $\mathcal{B}$ would be missing. It is also not possible to determine if a correction actually removes a defect or not. Corrections might be partial or simply wrong. Obviously, the sets of inconsistent names and corrected names are not identical. The degree of discrepancy depends on the underlying project and the significance of our results must be evaluated individually.

We cannot give a final answer to this problem. For our case study of DBLP, the following points are relevant. From our experience with other collections, we can tell that many points also apply to other projects. However, this has to be examined for the specific application. First of all, DBLP applies a set of algorithmic detectors which base on different principles. This includes detectors which base on attribute comparison only. It is unlikely that all approaches are subject to the same bias, i.e., defects missed by one approach might be detected by another. In particular, attribute-based approaches are less likely to prefer a relational property. Most detectors are applied to new data before it is added to the collection. This makes sense because preventing errors is better than detecting them later. If the detectors favor property $\mathcal{A}$ they will remove related errors in advance. This compensates the potential over-representation.

Usually, each correction is thoroughly checked before carried out. During this process many defects are discovered casually. If a collection is well known we can expect a high number of user-reported defects. For DBLP, about 6 % of the corrections are triggered by user input. Consider also that detection is not only applied to existing data but also to new information which is planned to be added.

As for the problem of false corrections: All corrections to DBLP are hand checked. This does not exclude errors but makes them less likely. In this study, we ignore all corrections which have later been reversed. For DBLP, this is a small amount.

19.4 Corrections in DBLP

In this section, we show how to apply the inconsistency-detection framework to the DBLP collection. To this goal, we use hDBLP[1] a historic version of DBLP. From this file, we can reconstruct all modifications which were done between 4th June 1999 and 8th October 2010. DBLP—more precisely: small portions of it—has been used as a test case for many inconsistency detectors. In this section, we analyze properties which are likely to influence the performance of these algorithms. We show how to extract three dynamic social networks from the data set and evaluate availability of relational information, network integration and similarity of *sources* and *targets*.

19.4.1 Data Source

The names in DBLP represent authors of papers in computer science. The publications are the attached entities. For each publication there is an XML file which contains the respective metadata. We use the unique file name as identifier for attached information. The file structure is similar to the BibTeX specification but is in XML syntax. For each day between October 1995 and October 2010 a snapshot of the files was stored. From these snapshots, we create a single set which contains a file for each publication and each version of the file, i.e., if a file has been modified two times in the period mentioned before there will be three files now, one for the original version and two for the modifications. Each file has a time stamp giving the date of modification. In 1999 some snapshots were damaged and we cannot reliably track modifications before this date. In June 1999 DBLP contained 120,000 publications which is less than 9 % of the current data set. So we lost only a small amount of information. For the period between 4th June 1999 and 8th October 2010, we detect 808,749 modifications.

By comparing the DBLP version of each day, we find 167,679 modifications to the author field of a publication record. We ignore modifications which alter the order of authors or just add or remove author elements. These changes fix

[1] http://dblp.uni-trier.de/xml/hdblp.xml.gz

errors which are not directly related to the name-inconsistency problem. Sometimes synonyms are not resolved by adjusting the differing names. In these cases, a special record is used to map the different names in the publication records. We include these *alternate name records* into our study.

We compute source and target names for each remaining modification. Usually, only one author of a citation is replaced. In this case, source and target are obvious. If more than one element is altered a clear mapping is more difficult. Assume that a modification changed the names listed for a publication from {Adam, Bob} to {Dave, Mike}. There are two possible source-target combinations: {Adam $\mapsto$ Dave, Bob $\mapsto$ Mike} and {Adam $\mapsto$ Mike, Bob $\mapsto$ Dave}. In many cases, source and target names are similar. For each possible name pair, we compare the names and pick the pairs which have the highest similarity. In 174 cases, we are not able to match name pairs. We ignore these modifications. There are also a number of modifications which were reversed later on. These attempts to fix the data were obviously defective themselves. We ignore those as well.

In the next step, we combine relevant modifications into corrections. We allow corrections to contain modifications from more than 1 day. This is necessary to capture time consuming corrections. However, if we set the time limit too high we risk the mixing of independent inconsistency corrections. For the historic collection, we obtained stable results by allowing time differences of up to 2 days. With our approach, we obtain 80,283 corrections consisting of 4,768 splits, 58,672 merges and 16,843 distributes. The number of merges includes 4,922 corrections we detected by analyzing the alternate name records. Sixteen percent of the sources and targets are affected by more than one correction. We consider these names multiple times in our study as a defect detector would also have to examine them more than once.

19.4.2 Social Networks in DBLP

We extract three types of social networks from the historic collection. A *collaboration network* describes the relation between name entities. Two names are related if there is at least one publication which lists both as an author. The weight $w_{n,m}$ of an edge between names n and m is given by the number of co-operations. For each day of the observed time frame, we create a collaboration network which reflects the data set of this day. The sequence of these static networks defines a dynamic collaboration network C. C is different from other dynamic collaboration networks like those used, for example, in [11] because it models the growth of DBLP rather than the evolution of relations. An extreme example is the relation between *L. Chwistek* and *W. Hetper*. They published a joint paper in 1938 [7] but this relation was not added to the dynamic collaboration network before 13th October 2003. Note that name inconsistencies can have a significant influence on C as they cause wrong edges and edge weights.

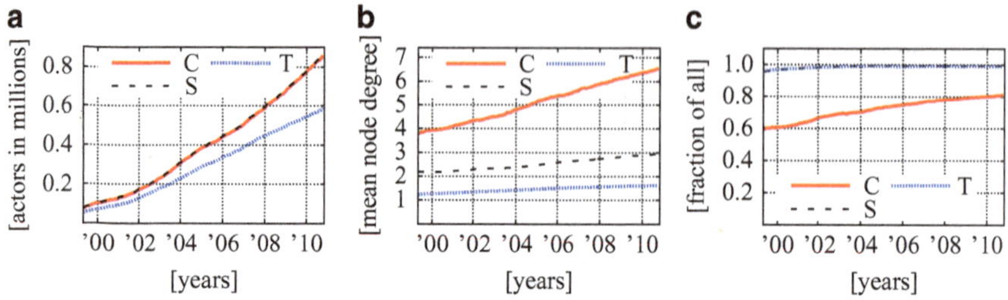

Fig. 19.3 Evolving aspects of the name entities in C, S and T between Jun. 1999 and Oct. 2010. (**a**) Number of actors. (**b**) Average node degree. (**c**) Giant component size

In a similar way, we define the dynamic two-mode network S which represents the relations between names and conferences or journals. DBLP uses the term *stream* to refer to all publications of a specific outlet. We consider a modification $\bar{S}$ of S where we add edges between streams that have a common community. These edges are weighted by the number of authors who published on both outlets. To prevent these edges from becoming too heavy we project their weight to an interval $[1 \ldots w_{max}]$ where w_{max} is the maximum edge weight in S.

We also want to consider the thematic relations of name entities. S can give us hints on this because if two authors regularly publish on the same conference we can assume that they work at least in related fields. However, there are many conferences on the same theme and two names might never publish in the same conference. In this case, we do not get the relation between these names. Pham et al. [28] provided us with a thematic clustering of DBLP streams which they used for their study. They obtained 23 clusters each representing a theme in computer science. We generate a dynamic network T in the same way we created S but with nodes for the clusters instead of the streams. We define $\bar{T}$ similar to $\bar{S}$.

Figure 19.3 shows how the number of actors, the average node degree and the giant component size of C, S and T developed over time. The size of C and S only differs by the small number of streams. T has less actors because not all DBLP streams are considered for the thematic clustering so some communities are missing. Because of the high degree of the stream and cluster nodes, the giant component in S and T almost contains all actors in the static networks.

In the following sections, we study the network integration of defective names. To this goal, we compare properties of defective names with the properties of all names in the most recent networks of C, S and T. But these networks also contain defective names which may bias the results. We already discussed this problem in Sect. 19.3.3. In DBLP, corrections are rare events. The expected waiting time for a specific name to be corrected is about 120 years. However, DBLP is considered a high quality data base which indicates that the number of defects is also low. Because of this, we assume that the number of defects is so small that influences on our baseline are not significant.

19.4.3 Local Properties

At first, we examine the node degree $d_R(n)$ where $R \in \{C, S, T\}$. $d_C(n)$ denotes the number of co-author names of n, $d_S(n)$ the number of streams which accepted papers from n and $d_T(n)$ the number of related theme clusters. The degree property is relevant for attribute relational inconsistency detectors because it determines the number of co-authors, streams and themes which can be used for comparing names. Figure 19.4a shows a cumulative distribution of the degree values in C. We obtained the values from the defective names at the moment before the correction. The y-axis shows the probability $p(d_C(n) \geq x)$. The cumulative distribution of all types—including the baseline—follows a power law with a long tail. Obviously, the sources of distribute and split corrections tend to have a higher degree than the baseline names. For the different types of sources we found $\langle d_C^{split} \rangle = 28.84$ and $\langle d_C^{dist} \rangle = 16.23$ while $\langle d_C^{baseline} \rangle = 6.55$. Merge sources on the other hand are less integrated ($\langle d_C^{merge} \rangle = 3.71$). This is not surprising because split and distribute sources represent data from several persons which makes it more likely that they have many co-authors. Merge sources on the other hand are lacking some information which reduces their degree. For S and T we find similar results. For example, for S we obtained $\langle d_S^{split} \rangle = 11.61$, $\langle d_S^{merge} \rangle = 1.3$ and $\langle d_S^{dist} \rangle = 7.85$ with a baseline of $\langle d_S^{baseline} \rangle = 2.94$. Figure 19.4b shows the degree distribution of the targets in C. Surprisingly, targets of merge operations have a higher degree than the baseline. We will discuss this disparity in Sect. 19.4.5. For the weighted degree $\hat{d}$ we found similar results. Figure 19.4c, for example, shows the situation in S.

The figures show that there is a significant number of corrected names which have a low degree. This is negative for all inconsistency detectors which work on neighborhood. The difference in degree between the types of corrections is also too small to use it as a classifier. However, we found a number of outlier rules for names with many publications. For example, 90.5 % of all names with $d_C(n) > 100$ were corrected at least once. These names are more likely to be defect because of the number of publications.

There is a number of approaches which are based on the idea that the neighborhood of a correct name in a social network is dense. Consider a name n in C. If we look at the co-authors of n we will find that many of them are also related with each other. This is because many authors work in small and stable groups where people regularly cooperate on publications. If n is a homonym, i.e., it represents two real-world persons p_1 and p_2, it is related to two different groups of co-authors. Given the size of the research field covered by DBLP, a cooperation between these two groups is very unlikely. We can use the local clustering coefficient on the stream and theme networks. This feature is mostly used in cluster-based algorithms but can also be used to detect homonyms. A measure for the density of the neighborhood is the local clustering coefficient

$$cc_R(n) = \frac{2 \cdot t_R(n)}{d_X(n) \cdot (d_R(n) - 1)} \tag{19.1}$$

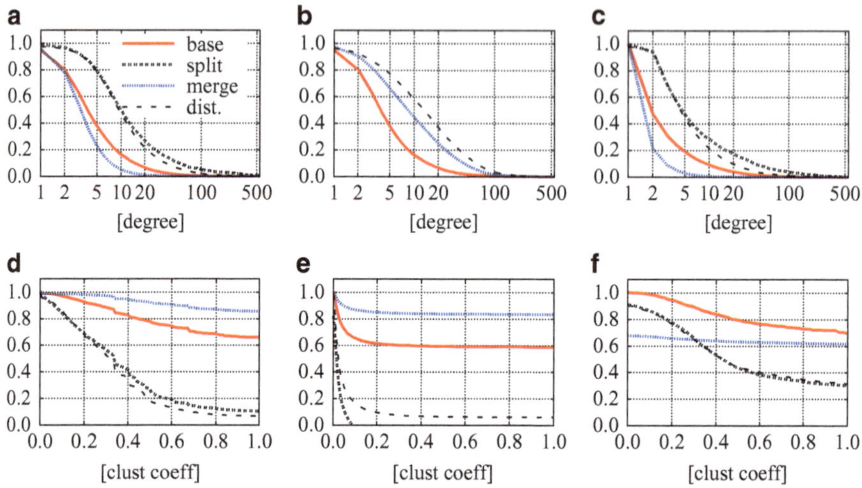

Fig. 19.4 Cumulative distribution of degree and clustering coefficient in C, S and T. Legend for all figures as in Fig. 19.4a. The y-axis shows $p(\text{degree} \geq x)$ or $p(\text{clusterCoeff} \geq x)$ respectively. (**a**) $d_C(n)$ sources. (**b**) $d_C(n)$ targets. (**c**) $\hat{d}_S(n)$ sources. (**d**) $cc_C(n)$ sources. (**e**) $\hat{cc}_S(n)$ sources. (**f**) $\hat{cc}_T(n)$ sources

where $t_R(n)$ is the number of triangles—closed circles consisting of three edges—which start and end in n. $cc_R(n) = 1$ if n and its direct neighbors form a complete sub-network. $cc_R(n)$ is only defined if there are at least two edges adjacent to n. Otherwise, it is not possible at all to construct triangles.

cc_R tends to be low for sources of split and distribute corrections which are both homonyms. For 84.3 % of all distribute sources and 78.6 % of all split sources cc_C is below 0.5 while only 23.7 % of the baseline names have this property. Figure 19.4d shows the cumulative distribution for $cc_C(n)$. Unlike $d_C(n)$, cc_C is less effective for names with a high number of publications. If the publication count is above 100, for example, the average clustering coefficient of split sources becomes 0.021 while the baseline value is 0.057 which is a less significant difference. This is because active names tend to cooperate with more than one group and remain active over a long time.

If we want to apply cc to stream and theme networks we must consider $\bar{S}$ and $\bar{T}$ instead, because we need the edges between the streams and the themes to complete the triangles. The theme nodes form a cluster in each static network of $\bar{T}$ and the sub-network defined by the streams is very dense. Without considering the uneven edge weights between the non-name actors we would mostly obtain 1 as a result. For $\bar{S}$ and $\bar{T}$ we apply the weighted clustering coefficient introduced by Zhang et al. [35]

$$\hat{cc}_R(n) = \frac{\sum_{j,k} \hat{w}_{nj} \cdot \hat{w}_{jk} \cdot \hat{w}_{nk}}{\left(\sum_k \hat{w}_{nk}\right)^2 - \sum_k \hat{w}_{nk}^2} \tag{19.2}$$

where $\hat{w}_{nj}$ is the weight of the edge between actors n and j normalized by the maximal edge weight in the network. Since we consider names from different static networks in C, $\bar{S}$ and $\bar{T}$, the normalization factor differs. Figure 19.4e shows the cumulative distribution of $\hat{cc}_{\bar{S}}$. The results are similar to those we obtained for cc_C but $\hat{cc}_{\bar{S}}$ is better at sorting out split sources. For 86 % of the split sources $\hat{cc}_{\bar{S}} < 0.1$. The results for $\hat{cc}_{\bar{T}}$ are less significant (see Fig. 19.4f). We assume that the 23 themes are too ambiguous, i.e., it is too likely that the persons behind a homonym are related to the same theme. This is particularly true for sources of merge operations.

19.4.4 Global Properties

We also considered the global closeness [1] and betweenness [14] centrality of defective nodes. Before this study, we expected significant differences for the different types of inconsistencies. A homonym, for example, should be more central because it might link to multiple co-author groups. We computed closeness and betweenness using the algorithm of Brandes [4]. Even with this fast approach, we were not able to handle the static networks of 2010 in reasonable time. In this section, we analyze the smaller collaboration networks till 30th September 2009 in their unweighted versions. We use normalized versions of the measures to compensate for varying component sizes. Let $A^{\infty}(n)$ be the set of names which are reachable from n. We compute

$$D_C(n) = \sum_{m \in A^{\infty}(n)} \frac{dist(n,m)}{a} \tag{19.3}$$

for closeness where $dist(n,m)$ returns the minimal distance between actors n and m in $A^{\infty}(n)$ and a is the size of $A^{\infty}(n)$ as well as

$$D_B(n) = \left(\sum_{\substack{s \neq n \neq t \in A^{\infty}(n) \\ s \neq t}} \frac{\sigma_{st}(n)}{\sigma_{st}} \right) \cdot \frac{1}{a(a-1)} \tag{19.4}$$

for betweenness. σ_{st} is the number of different shortest paths between actors s and t and $\sigma_{st}(n)$ denotes the number of those paths which pass actor n.

Despite our intuition, we found only extremely small differences between the inconsistency types. One reason is that D_B is 0 for more than 99 % of all nodes which includes almost all nodes with a small number of publications. For the rest we see that split candidates are more central than other names. For D_C as well, there is virtually no discrepancy. However, we found outlier rules. Table 19.1 lists the number of corrections which affected the 10^2, 10^3 and 10^4 actors with the highest closeness and betweenness centrality. On 30th September 2009, $D_B 10^4$ made up 1.4 % of the nodes but was affected by 38.7 % of all distribute corrections. However,

Table 19.1 Corrections of name entities with high global network centrality and share of the respective correction type

	Merge		Distribute		Split		All	
$D_C 10^2$	142	0.3 %	236	1.7 %	52	1.3 %	412	0.58 %
$D_C 10^3$	1,431	2.5 %	1,009	7.1 %	135	3.5 %	2,575	3.60 %
$D_C 10^4$	8,369	14.9 %	4,099	28.9 %	450	11.6 %	12,923	18.20 %
$D_B 10^2$	171	0.3 %	239	1.7 %	45	1.1 %	455	0.64 %
$D_B 10^3$	1,703	3.0 %	1,233	8.7 %	149	3.8 %	3,087	4.35 %
$D_B 10^4$	11,285	20.0 %	5,491	38.7 %	535	13.8 %	17,316	24.40 %

the share of the total number of publications is much higher as central names tend to have many publications. In general, the effect is less strong for actors with high closeness values but still significant. We assume that there are two reasons for this: Many nodes with a high centrality represent persons who are central in the computer science community. We think that these persons draw more attention from both the DBLP maintainer and the observing community so it is more likely that an inconsistency is detected. In addition, most central authors have a high publication count. With a growing number of papers the probability of errors grows as well.

19.4.5 Similarity and Relation of Source and Target

Some inconsistency detectors use network-related similarities to find pairs of names which qualify for a more intensive synonym check. In scholarly data bases we can assume that many authors publish repeatedly with the same co-authors [13, 16, 22]. So if there are synonyms n_1 and n_2 for a person p we can assume that n_1 and n_2 have some common co-authors. Similarities of conferences/journals [13] or themes [18] are used for the same reason. These approaches are less specific because it is much more likely that two distinct names are related to the same stream than to the same co-author. However, they are used as part of combined measurements which include the results from different metrics.

If we consider the source and target name pairs from all merge and distribute corrections directly before a correction we find that 57.9 % shared at least one common co-author. The average Jaccard distance of intersecting co-author sets is 0.14 with a standard deviation of 0.128. These results are significant. We compared both values for 100 million randomly selected name pairs from the collaboration graph of October 8th 2010 and found that only 3.4 % shared a co-author. Only 10 % of all pairs shared at least one stream. The probability of common neighbors in C increases if both source and target have many publications (Fig. 19.5a). However, the Jaccard distance drops by 50 % if there are more than ten publications associated with both names (Fig. 19.5b).

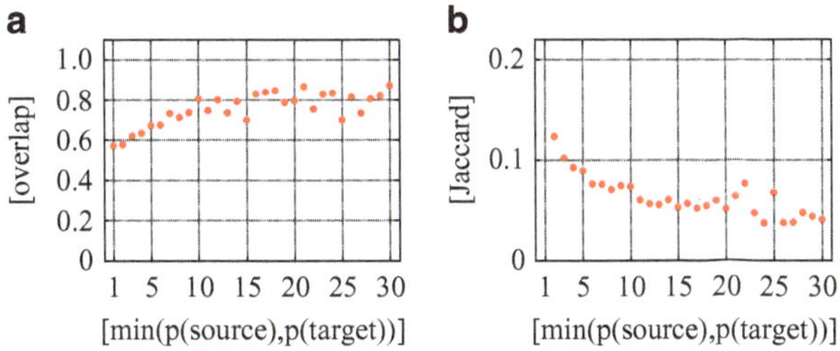

Fig. 19.5 Similarities of source and target in C by the amount of available publications p(source) and p(target). (**a**) At least one match. (**b**) Mean Jaccard distance

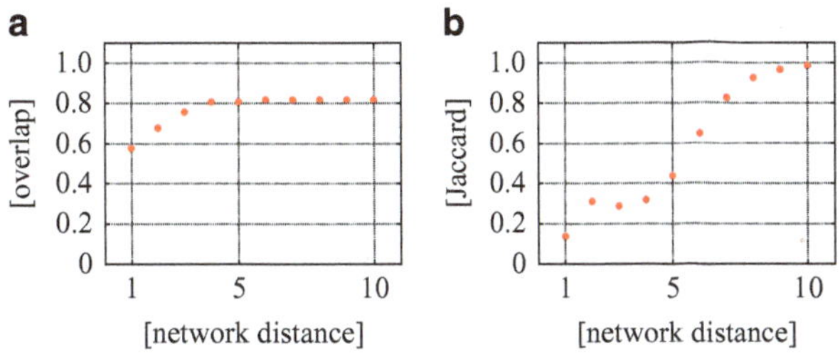

Fig. 19.6 Distance by co-authors of source and target by type of correction at different path lengths. (**a**) At least one match. (**b**) Mean Jaccard distance

We can extend the similarity to larger neighborhoods. Let $A_R^d(n)$ be a set of actors which can be reached in network R from n with paths that consist of up to d edges. We consider this extended adjacency for source and target. As all networks are small worlds, the size of A_R^d increases fast, especially for S and T. Figure 19.6 shows overlap occurrence and Jaccard distance for C for different values of d. We see that an increased neighborhood of sizes 2 and 3 can actually improve the number of reachable name pairs. The Jaccard distance rises accordingly. However, if we do not find the second name within a path length of 4 it is unlikely that both names are in the same connectivity component. This is contrary to the assumptions of Levin et al. [22] who stated that the maximum reasonable distance between names in DBLP is two. However, the possible improvement is small.

When we consider similarities we must be aware that there are significant differences between source and target names. On et al. [24] introduced a test collection based on DBLP where source and target always have the same number of publications. This is not realistic. Before a merge operation, the mean number of papers of the source is 5.56 while there are 83.01 papers for targets. Targets have more information attached to them because readjusting the smaller name of a synonym is cheaper. This explains the higher degree merge targets we found in Sect. 19.4.3. Merges where both source and target have many attached publications are rare because it is unlikely that two synonyms with that much information can

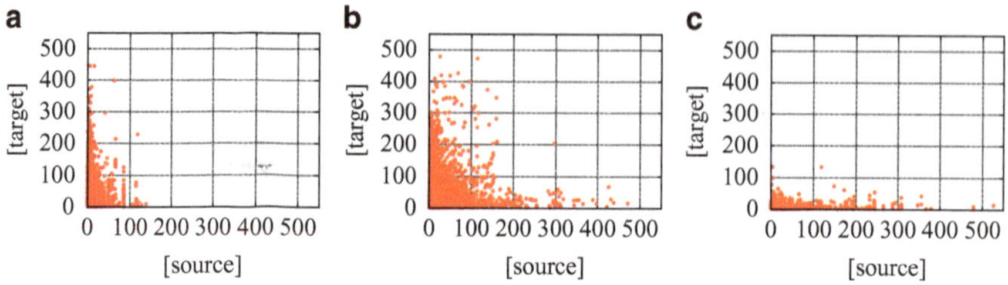

Fig. 19.7 Relation between properties of source and target names in the same pair. (**a**) Co-authors before merge. (**b**) Co-authors before distribute. (**c**) Co-authors after split

co-exist without being detected. This is not so much a problem for distribute pairs because it is possible that just a single publication was assigned wrongly. The mean number of publications for these sources is 30.3 and 57.22 for targets. Split operations have no target before the correction. After a split operation, sources have 62.0 publications attached to them and targets 7.51. For splits targets are modified so it is cheaper to choose the smaller part. We find the same situation for coauthors of sources and targets. Figure 19.7a, b plot the number of co-authors of merge and distribute sources respectively against their targets. Figure 19.7c shows the co-author count for split pairs after the correction.

19.5 Including the Context

In the previous section we saw that the amount of data we can use to assess the correctness of a name is often small. To compensate this, we propose a new approach which does not consider single names but communities which can provide more data. During our initial analysis, we noted that corrections to names are not evenly distributed in DBLP, i.e., there are areas in the relational graphs where we can find a high number of corrections. Many name-inconsistencies are singular defects. However, there are conditions which decrease the data quality of multiple names. Examples for negative conditions are low quality data sources or constellations where name disambiguation is particularly difficult. Conditions like this can be found in most data sets. Estimating strength and area of effect of these conditions can provide us with a mean to judge the correctness of data. For example, if a name n is closely related to names $m_1 \ldots m_k$ and we know that m_i have been frequently corrected in the past, we might become reluctant to trust the data attached to n even if n itself has never been corrected. This might lead to a closer investigation of this name and make users aware of possible problems. This information is also helpful if new information is attached to n (for example a new publication). This data can then be checked more thoroughly than usually. In the field of software engineering, this approach is known as bug prediction. It is used to identify software components with hidden defects based on prior corrections. This information is used to deploy resources for error detection.

The example shows that the estimation of negative conditions cannot rely on a single name. Name n itself has never been corrected so it does not cause suspicions. Instead we examine sets of nodes. The extraction of these sets is crucial as they must group names which are affected by negative conditions in the same way. In this study, we assume that this is true for closely related names and apply community extraction to relational networks. For each community, we compute a reliability score which determines our trust in the data correctness. In this section, we consider different approaches and test them on the DLBP data set.

19.5.1 Community Extraction and Reliability Estimation

To estimate the reliability of a name n, we determine the community to which it belongs. For this community we count the number of past corrections to its members. We obtain a function $r(n) \in [0, 1]$ which measures the reliability of n. For example, $r(n) = 0$ means that we do not have reason to believe that n is defective. If $r(n) = 1$ we assume that it is under massive influence of negative conditions.

At first we extract communities. Negative conditions change over time so we need to recompute the estimation periodically. We will see that $r(n)$ in DBLP changes very slow. However, this may not be true for other collections which then require frequent computation. From our experience we estimate that a computation time of 24 h is the upper limit for any approach which will be actually used. Many well established community extractors, like the edge-betweenness algorithm by Girvan and Newman [15], exceed this limit even for a small collection. The relational networks in DBLP—which is a small collection—contain about 840,000 actors. This is well out of reach for many approaches. In this study, we use three different extraction strategies: simple adjacency (A), Radicchi [29] (R) and Clique Percolation (CP) [26].

We already discussed the simple adjacency approach in Sect. 19.4.5. The algorithm is very fast but the resulting name sets barely resemble what is usually considered a community. As many relation networks are small worlds we obtain large—and overlapping—communities even for small distances.

To obtain more meaningful communities, we apply the algorithm of Radicchi et al. [29] in the version for weighted networks. We use this approach because the results are similar to the output of Girvan and Newman [15] for most graphs but it is much faster. The algorithm computes closed paths to determine whether an edge runs inside a community or connects two of them. Successively, edges between communities are removed till disjoint sets of names remain. The lengths of the circles can be configured. If the length is increased the algorithm needs more time, however the results might improve. Radicchi et al. also differentiate between a weak and a strong community definition.

Communities created by the approach of Radicchi are disjoint. For many data sets, this is not realistic as some names are part of two or more distinct communities. The number of approaches for overlapping community extraction is small. We apply the Clique Percolation method by Palla et al. [26]. Communities are defined as unions of k-cliques which share at least $k - 1$ nodes. The approach ignores edge weights but can handle the DBLP collection in less than 12 h. Clique Percolation ignores all nodes which are not part of at least one k-clique, for example, isolated nodes.

For each community $\mathcal{C}$, we compute the number of corrections which have affected its members. The raw frequency value $rf(\mathcal{C})$ is the sum of all corrections. rf depends on the size of a community because large sets of names have a higher correction count than small ones. Let $|\mathcal{C}|_N$ be the number of names which are members of $\mathcal{C}$ and $|\mathcal{C}|_A$ the sum of attached entities. To get comparable results, we define two normalized measures: $nf(\mathcal{C}) = \frac{rf(\mathcal{C})}{|\mathcal{C}|_N}$ and $af(\mathcal{C}) = \frac{rf(\mathcal{C})}{|\mathcal{C}|_A}$. Note that the normalized values can be higher than 1.0 if there is a very large number of corrections.

For the different measures we compute a reliability score $r(n)$ for each name in the communities. For (A) $r(n)$ is defined as the correction density of the community which is built around n. For (R) we define $r(n)$ as the density score of the community that contains n and for (CP) $r(n)$ is defined as the maximum density of all C which contain n.

19.5.2 Prediction Capabilities for DBLP

In this section, we apply the estimation approach to the DBLP data set. We are particularly interested in the number of corrections we can find for names labeled as reliable in comparison to those labeled as unreliable.

Data

We apply the community detectors to relational networks in C and S. It is not feasible to use T because these networks are extremely dense and the resulting communities comprise almost all names. Additionally, (R) and (CP) are too slow to handle S because of the high number of edges. We denote the communities obtained from (A) as $\mathcal{C}^{AC}$ and $\mathcal{C}^{AS}$ for C and S respectively. The communities computed by (R) and (CP) are named $\mathcal{C}^{RC}$ and $\mathcal{C}^{CC}$ respectively. To fulfill our runtime limitation we use (R) with a path length of 3. A path length or 4 requires significantly more computation time. The strong community definition failed to split the relational networks and a very large community remained. We assume that negative conditions do not affect such large groups at once so we use the weak definition. For (CP) we examine communities created with $k = 4$. Setting $k = 3$ includes 2-cliques (pairs)

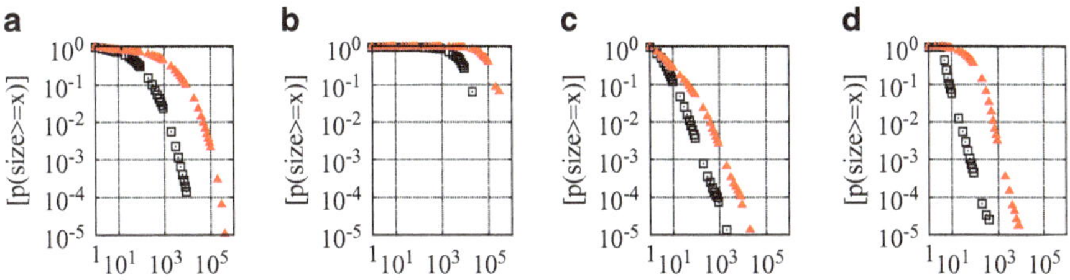

Fig. 19.8 Community sizes by number of names (*rectangle*) and publications (*triangle*) for the static networks in C and S of 8th October 2010. (**a**) $\mathcal{C}^{AC}$ sizes. (**b**) $\mathcal{C}^{AS}$ sizes. (**c**) $\mathcal{C}^{RC}$ sizes. (**d**) $\mathcal{C}^{CC}$ sizes

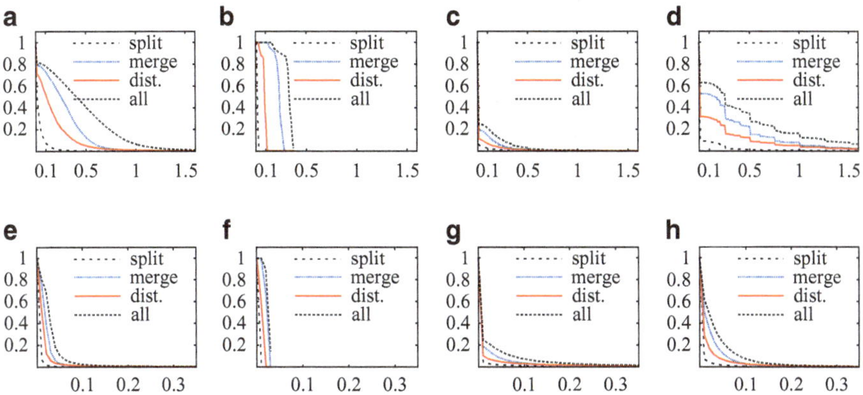

Fig. 19.9 Cumulative distribution of correction density in communities based on nf and af for the static networks in C and S of 8th October 2010. (**a**) $nf(\mathcal{C}^{AC})$. (**b**) $nf(\mathcal{C}^{AS})$. (**c**) $nf(\mathcal{C}^{RC})$. (**d**) $nf(\mathcal{C}^{CC})$. (**e**) $af(\mathcal{C}^{AC})$. (**f**) $af(\mathcal{C}^{AS})$. (**g**) $af(\mathcal{C}^{RC})$. (**h**) $af(\mathcal{C}^{CC})$

which are trivial. If k becomes too large, then we loose a number of nodes because they do not fit into a $k-1$-clique.

The communities differ in size (Fig. 19.8). The $\mathcal{C}^{AS}$ are by far the largest communities with a mean size of 5,524 and almost no small sub-networks. The $\mathcal{C}^{AC}$ follow with $\langle|\mathcal{C}^{AC}|_N\rangle = 132$. The Radicchi and Clique Percolation communities are much smaller ($\langle|\mathcal{C}^{RC}|_N\rangle = 5.77$ and $\langle|\mathcal{C}^{CC}|_N\rangle = 6.4$) but still provide more information than an average name. However, 72.2 % of the $\mathcal{C}^{RC}$ and 10.5 % of $\mathcal{C}^{CC}$ have less than ten publications in total.

Figure 19.9a–h show the cumulated distribution of the normalized values. For $\mathcal{C}^{AS}$, we see that there are few communities with a high correction density which indicates that these communities are of limited use for determining reliability. However, almost all communities experienced at least one split, merge or distribute operation. $\mathcal{C}^{RC}$ and $\mathcal{C}^{CC}$ create both more communities with zero corrections and communities with a high correction density.

Experiments

Our experiments are designed as follows: we select a point in time t—the 2nd October 2007 in this study—and extract the different sets of communities as described above. We then define times t_1 and t_2 with $t_1 < t < t_2$. For each community, we compute rf, nf and af based on the corrections we observed in $[t_1, t]$. We vary t_1 between 1 and 8 years before t. If t_1 and t are close only a small number of corrections is considered. If the distance is large we get more corrections including some which might not be relevant for future corrections any more. We call $[t_1, t]$ the *observation period* of the experiment. We compute $r(n)$ for each name and each community.

Based on $r(n)$, we place the names into loads $q_1, \ldots, q_k$ of approximately equal size. q_1 contains the names with the lowest rf, nf or af value while q_k contains those with the highest values. We make sure that names with the same correction density are placed in the same load. We vary k between four and ten. In a final step—the *evaluation period*—we count the number of corrections in the period $[t, t_2]$. We normalize those values in the same way we normalized the results from the observation period. We consider evaluation periods of 1–3 years. We compute rf, nf and af considering only the corrections from the evaluation period. If our assumptions are true the average correction densities in q_1 will be smaller than the correction densities in q_k. Many communities with no corrections are very young and usually small. Our experiments show that with this lack of data it is difficult to compute a reliable correction prediction. To get usable results, we ignore names with $r(n) = 0$. Depending on the experiment setting this step reduces the number of names for which we get an estimation.

We obtain only an estimation for names which are present at t. Given the constant growth of DBLP by about 10,000 names each month, we might lose a large number of names. However, this number is small compared to the total size of DBLP. During the evaluation period, structures within the networks might change in a way that we obtain different communities at the end of the evaluation period. Given the fact that there is no study on the stability of these special dynamic networks, this problem must remain open. Evolutionary clustering [5] might solve this problem provided that reasonably fast algorithms become available.

Results

In general, the experiments show that it is possible to get an estimation of a name's reliability. However, the results strongly depend on the experiment settings. Figure 19.10a shows the results without normalization. We give the fraction of corrections we found for each load. The differences between q_1 and q_4 for C^{AC} and C^{AS} are factor 3.19 and 2.36 respectively. For C^{RC} and C^{CC} the difference is small. However, if we take a closer look at the loads we obtained from C^{AC} and C^{AS} we see that the names in q_1 have less publications and a smaller activity than the names in q_4. Since the number of corrections is related to both values the result is not surprising. For $\mathcal{C}^{RC}$ and $\mathcal{C}^{CC}$, the number of publications and activity is about the same for all loads. The normalized results (Fig. 19.10b, c) are significant for all sets except for $\mathcal{C}^{AS}$ which seem to be too large to be used for predictions with normalization. We obtain the best result for a setting with four loads when using $\mathcal{C}^{RC}$ and af. The correction density in q_4 is 4.4 times as high as in q_1.

The prediction quality differs by the type of correction. Figure 19.10d shows the factor by which the correction density deviates from the baseline—the expected correction density if corrections are evenly distributed with respect to the number of attached publications. It is easier to predict split and distribute corrections than it is to predict merges. The figure depicts the results for $\mathcal{C}^{RC}$ and af but we find similar results for other combinations except for those which include $\mathcal{C}^{AS}$.

To our surprise, we found that observation and evaluation time have only a small influence on the results. Figure 19.10e shows the quotient q_k/q_1, i.e., the factor by which the correction density increases for an evaluation period of 1–3 years and an observation period between 1 and 8 years. Again, the results are for $\mathcal{C}^{RC}$ and af. We obtain the best results for an evaluation time of 1 year. However, increasing the evaluation time reduces the quality of the prediction only marginally. The best observation period is 4 years. For other communities the difference is even smaller. This means that we do not have to store all old corrections and that we can use a prediction for some time before we have to recompute it. The modification of the number of loads has a larger influence. If there are more loads our algorithm can sort out names with a bad prediction value and further differentiate names. Figure 19.10f shows the changes to q_k/q_1 for different numbers of loads. For $k = 1$, we obtain the baseline. Between $k = 2$ and $k = 4$, we see an increase in the result quality for all community sets except for $\mathcal{C}^{AS}$. After that, only $\mathcal{C}^{RC}$ can further increase the quotient to a maximum of 7.58. With a growing load number, the correction density of q_1 decreases from 0.0103 to 0.0073 while the density of q_k increases from 0.0254 to 0.0557 so the improvement comes from a better differentiation of the highly suspicious names.

A combination of different experiment settings can improve the results. At first we compute loads $q_1, \ldots, q_k$ for an experiment setting a. For each load q_i, we compute loads $q_{i1}, \ldots, q_{ik}$ with an experiment setting b. We obtain a $k \times k$ matrix Q where $Q_{1,1}$ contains the names which are rated best in experiment a and then best in experiment b. We obtain the best results for a combination of Radicchi and simple adjacency in S. For $\mathcal{C}^{RC}$ and $\mathcal{C}^{AS}$, the Jaccard distance of the respective q_1 loads is 0.224 which indicates that a combination can provide additional information. For a combination of $\mathcal{C}^{RC}$ and $\mathcal{C}^{AS}$ with three loads in each experiment, we get $Q_{3,3}/Q_{1,1} = 8.42$ which is better than any single result. With three loads in each experiment, we get nine loads which makes our result comparable to the data in Fig. 19.10f. Table 19.2 shows the results for the same experiment with a load number of four for each experiment. f_a and f_b show the factors between the correction density in the first and in the last load of the respective line or column. Obviously, experiment b can sort out names which were labeled as *likely correct* by experiment a but are nonetheless error-prone. Experiment a is better in separating defective and non-defective names because it is applied first. However, experiment b is better at

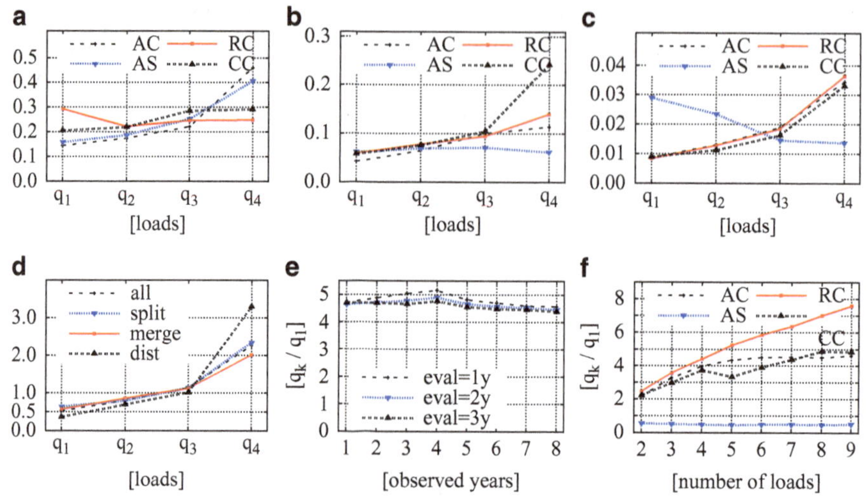

Fig. 19.10 Prediction results for different settings. (**a**) Fraction of rf. (**b**) Normalization by nf. (**c**) Normalization by af. (**d**) Deviation from baseline. (**e**) Influence of time settings. (**f**) influence of load number

finding very problematic names. In our experiments, the correction density in $Q_{\cdot,4}$ was often higher than the correction density in $Q_{4,\cdot}$. Table 19.2 also shows the results for the different types of publications. The predictability of distribute corrections is very high. When we compare the correction density in $Q_{1,1}$ and $Q_{4,4}$, we see an increase by factor 24.1. We could not predict split and merge as well. Because we exclude communities without past corrections, the split experiment considers only about 76,000 names so the results have limited significance.

19.5.3 Influential Factors in DBLP

To get an idea on the effects which reduce data quality in DBLP, we examine properties of communities with extreme reliability scores. We use the loads from the combined experiments shown in Table 19.2(d) in the previous section. Effects overlap and are difficult to measure directly so this list is not complete.

The name itself is an important factor. Many communities with low reliability consist of entities where names are abbreviated, like *F. Reitz* instead of *Florian Reitz*. The mean percentage of abbreviated names in reliable communities is 6.4 %. For not reliable communities the percentage is 44.6 %. If we only consider distributes the value goes up to 56.5 %. This is not surprising as the name is very important to distinguish persons. If only little information is given mistakes are more likely. Even if a name is given in full there are differences in the ambiguity as already noted by Bhattacharya et al. [2]. Names in unreliable communities tend to be shorter than

Table 19.2 Evaluation results for combined experiments based on $\mathcal{C}^{RC}$ ($q^a_\cdot$) and $\mathcal{C}^{AS}$ ($q^b_\cdot$)

	q^b_1	q^b_2	q^b_3	q^b_4	f_b
(a) All corrections					
q^a_1	0.00686	0.00535	0.00913	0.01309	**1.91**
q^a_2	0.00778	0.01159	0.01426	0.02021	**2.60**
q^a_3	0.01407	0.01682	0.01938	0.02870	**2.04**
q^a_4	0.02565	0.03306	0.04189	0.06276	**2.45**
f_a	**3.74**	**6.18**	**4.59**	**4.79**	
(b) Merge corrections					
q^a_1	0.00490	0.00338	0.00484	0.00821	**1.68**
q^a_2	0.00616	0.00642	0.00798	0.01137	**1.85**
q^a_3	0.00722	0.00867	0.01070	0.01705	**2.36**
q^a_4	0.01365	0.01522	0.02055	0.02867	**2.10**
f_a	**2.79**	**4.50**	**4.25**	**3.49**	
(c) Split corrections					
q^a_1	0.00030	0.00029	0.00106	0.00098	**3.27**
q^a_2	0.00050	0.00049	0.00130	0.00140	**2.80**
q^a_3	0.00095	0.00143	0.00065	0.00164	**1.73**
q^a_4	0.00189	0.00228	0.00354	0.00232	**1.23**
f_a	**6.3**	**7.86**	**3.34**	**2.37**	
(d) Distribute corrections					
q^a_1	0.00167	0.00176	0.00293	0.00508	**3.04**
q^a_2	0.00332	0.00411	0.00564	0.00815	**2.45**
q^a_3	0.00534	0.00784	0.00948	0.01113	**2.08**
q^a_4	0.01547	0.02112	0.02723	0.04024	**2.60**
f_a	**9.26**	**12.00**	**9.29**	**7.92**	

names in reliable ones. We examined randomly selected communities and found a large number of names which are of Chinese origin. In particular split and distribute operations show this property. Many Chinese names map to the same transcription in the Latin alphabet. This introduces ambiguity which favors homonyms. On the other hand, many merges are required because of persons omitting name parts. Partially, this has a cultural background as well. Authors with Spanish names, for example, have more name tokens than authors with British names. We cannot measure this effect directly as we found no way to automatically determine the cultural origin of a name.

Next we examine streams and themes for the density of corrections. For each stream s, we count the corrections which changed at least one of its publications. Corrections can affect many publications so we count each correction only once per stream. We normalize this value by the number of papers which were published on that stream. Table 19.3(a) shows the top five and the last five streams with more than 1,000 publications ordered to the correction density. In the same way we counted

Table 19.3 Number of corrections by stream and by theme

(a) Streams ordered by correction density. (J) indicates journals

	Stream	corr.	pub.	corr./pub.	...				
1	TCSV (J)	374	1,310	0.285	338	IT (J)	22	1,259	0.0174
2	CCGRID	319	1,168	0.273	339	CCE (J)	13	1,111	0.0117
3	IWANN	453	1,705	0.266	340	JEI (J)	14	1,274	0.0110
4	TSMC (J)	696	2,790	0.249	341	AFIPS	12	1,184	0.0101
5	TASLP (J)	259	1,081	0.240	342	MANSCI (J)	4	1,066	0.0038

(b) Themes ordered by correction density

	Theme	corr.	pub.	corr./pub.
1	Multimedia	6,401	45,734	0.140
2	Software engineering and prog. languages	6,954	51,956	0.134
3	Bioinformatics and computational biology	1,674	12,900	0.130
4	Real-time and embedded systems	655	5,081	0.129
5	Graphics	2,798	24,398	0.112
...				
19	Security and privacy	1,433	21,344	0.067
20	Natural language and speech	616	9,374	0.066
21	Hardware and architecture	940	14,667	0.064
22	Algorithms and theory	5,723	89,908	0.063
23	Scientific computing	519	10,105	0.051

the corrections of publications related to themes (Table 19.3(b)). For streams and themes the differences are significant. There is a correlation between abbreviated names and high correction count. However, we also find streams which provide full names but are nonetheless problematic. Please note that the number of corrections is in no relation to the quality of the publications of these streams. We assume that the publishers provide metadata of different structure or quality which causes the differences. We computed the average correction density of publications related to communities. If a community is labeled as reliable, the average correction density is 0.078. Otherwise it is 0.107. The difference is smaller than for name completeness which is because most communities are related to more than one conference.

The correction density of a community c is also influenced by its age and activity. We define the age of c by the average number of days since the attached publications of its members were added. The *activity* of c is defined as the average number of modifications to the publications associated to members. This includes the adding of new publications. In general, communities with low correction density are less active than other communities. In $\mathcal{C}^{RC}$ with $af = 0$ the average activity is 5.7 while for the communities with $af > 0$ the result is 121.6. Older communities are less likely to be corrected. If we consider the corrections between October 2008 and October 2010 we find a af of 0.016 if c is younger than 1,000 days and 0.005 if $age(c)$ >5,000. If a community has a high age and a low activity, we assume that it is not in the focus of interest which makes the detection of inconsistencies unlikely. There are other communities where there has been no time to do corrections because they are very young.

19.6 Conclusion and Future Work

In this paper, we presented a framework to extract a large number of inconsistent names from a data set by examining past modifications. Though we cannot get all defective names we showed that the framework is applicable for large collections—namely DBLP. We analyzed the properties of defective names and found that some of these properties differ from previous assumptions. We also introduced a risk estimator which uses knowledge on past corrections to estimate the likeliness that a name has hidden or future defects. This approach is based on communities instead of single names to provide more reliable results. For DBLP, we found that the estimation can predict areas with a high number of corrections in the future.

So far, we have applied our analysis only to the corrections in DBLP. This is because it is difficult to find data sets which provide the required information. In future work we must evaluate if other collections have the same properties and if the prediction heuristic can be used in the same way with the same experimental settings. We also plan to further evaluate the potential of combined predictions and intend to integrate evolutionary clustering. This might improve the information on names which were added during the evaluation period as we can assign them to one of the computed communities.

Acknowledgements We thank Manh Cuong Pham and Ralf Klamma for providing us with the thematic clustering data.

References

1. Bavelas, A.: Communication patterns in task-oriented groups. J. Acoust. Soc. Am. **22**, 725–730 (1950)
2. Bhattacharya, I., Getoor, L.: Collective entity resolution in relational data. TKDD **1**(1), 1–36 (2007)
3. Bilenko, M., Mooney, R.J., Cohen, W.W., Ravikumar, P.D., Fienberg, S.E.: Adaptive name matching in information integration. IEEE Intell. Syst. **18**(5), 16–23 (2003)
4. Brandes, U.: A faster algorithm for betweenness centrality. J. Math. Sociol. **25**(2), 163–177 (2001)
5. Chakrabarti, D., Kumar, R., Tomkins, A.: Evolutionary clustering. In: KDD, pp. 554–560. ACM, New York (2006)
6. Chaudhuri, S., Ganjam, K., Ganti, V., Motwani, R.: Robust and efficient fuzzy match for online data cleaning. In: SIGMOD Conference, pp. 313–324. ACM, New York (2003)
7. Chwistek, L., Hetper, W.: New foundation of formal metamathematics. J. Symb. Log. **3**(1), 1–36 (1938)

8. D'Ambros, M., Lanza, M., Robbes, R.: An extensive comparison of bug prediction approaches. In: MSR, pp. 31–41. IEEE, Piscataway (2010)
9. Deng, H., King, I., Lyu, M.R.: Formal models for expert finding on DBLP bibliography data. In: ICDM, pp. 163–172. IEEE Computer Society, Los Alamitos (2008)
10. Dimitrov, M., Zhou, H.: Anomaly-based bug prediction, isolation, and validation: an automated approach for software debugging. In: ASPLOS, pp. 61–72. ACM, New York (2009)
11. Elmacioglu, E., Lee, D.: On six degrees of separation in DBLP-DB and more. SIGMOD Rec. **34**(2), 33–40 (2005)
12. Elmagarmid, A.K., Ipeirotis, P.G., Verykios, V.S.: Duplicate record detection: a survey. IEEE Trans. Knowl. Data Eng. **19**(1), 1–16 (2007)
13. Ferreira, A.A., Veloso, A., Gonçalves, M.A., Laender, A.H.F.: Effective self-training author name disambiguation in scholarly digital libraries. In: JCDL, pp. 39–48. ACM, New York (2010)
14. Freeman, L.C.: A set of measures of centrality based upon betweeness. Sociometry **40**(1), 35–41 (1977)
15. Girvan, M., Newman, M.E.J.: Community structure in social and biological networks. Proc. Natl. Acad. Sci. U.S.A. **99**(12), 7821–7826 (2002)
16. Han, H., Giles, C.L., Zha, H., Li, C., Tsioutsiouliklis, K.: Two supervised learning approaches for name disambiguation in author citations. In: JCDL, pp. 296–305. ACM, New York (2004)
17. Han, H., Xu, W., Zha, H., Giles, C.L.: A hierarchical naive bayes mixture model for name disambiguation in author citations. In: SAC, pp. 1065–1069. ACM, New York (2005)
18. Han, H., Zha, H., Giles, C.L.: Name disambiguation in author citations using a k-way spectral clustering method. In: JCDL, pp. 334–343, ACM, New York (2005)
19. Huang, J., Ertekin, S., Giles, C.L.: Efficient name disambiguation for large-scale databases. In: PKDD. Lecture Notes in Computer Science, vol. 4213, pp. 536–544. Springer, Berlin (2006)
20. Kang, I.-S., Na, S.-H., Lee, S., Jung, H., Kim, P., Sung, W.-K., Lee, J.-H.: On co-authorship for author disambiguation. Inf. Process. Manag. **45**(1), 84–97 (2009)
21. Lee, D., On, B.-W., Kang, J., Park, S.: Effective and scalable solutions for mixed and split citation problems in digital libraries. In: IQIS, pp. 69–76. ACM, New York (2005)
22. Levin, F.H., Heuser, C.A.: Evaluating the use of social networks in author name disambiguation in digital libraries. JIDM **1**(2), 183–198 (2010)
23. Levin, F.H., Heuser, C.A.: Using genetic programming to evaluate the impact of social network analysis in author name disambiguation. In: AMW. CEUR Workshop Proceedings, vol. 619 (2010). CEUR-WS.org
24. On, B.-W., Lee, D., Kang, J., Mitra, P.: Comparative study of name disambiguation problem using a scalable blocking-based framework. In: JCDL, pp. 344–353. ACM, New York (2005)
25. On, B.-W., Elmacioglu, E., Lee, D., Kang, J., Pei, J.: An effective approach to entity resolution problem using quasi-clique and its application to digital libraries. In: JCDL, pp. 51–52. ACM, New York (2006)
26. Palla, G., Derenyi, I., Farkas, I., Vicsek, T.: Uncovering the overlapping community structure of complex networks in nature and society. Nature **435**, 814–818 (2005)
27. Pereira, D.A., Ribeiro-Neto, B.A., Ziviani, N., Laender, A.H.F., Gonçalves, M.A., Ferreira, A.A.: Using web information for author name disambiguation. In: JCDL, pp. 49–58. ACM, New York (2009)
28. Pham, M.C., Klamma, R.: The structure of the computer science knowledge network. In: ASONAM, pp. 17–24. IEEE Computer Society, Los Alamitos (2010)
29. Radicchi, F., Castellano, C., Cecconi, F., Loreto, V., Parisi, D.: Defining and identifying communities in networks. Proc. Natl. Acad. Sci. **101**(9), 2658 (2004)
30. Reuther, P., Walter, B.: Survey on test collections and techniques for personal name matching. IJMSO **1**(2), 89–99 (2006)
31. Reuther, P., Walter, B., Ley, M., Weber, A., Klink, S.: Managing the quality of person names in DBLP. In: ECDL. Lecture Notes in Computer Science, vol. 4172, pp. 508–511. Springer, Berlin (2006)

32. Shin, D., Kim, T., Jung, H., Choi, J.: Automatic method for author name disambiguation using social networks. In: AINA, pp. 1263–1270. IEEE Computer Society, Los Alamitos (2010)
33. Tejada, S., Knoblock, C.A., Minton, S.: Learning domain-independent string transformation weights for high accuracy object identification. In: KDD, pp. 350–359. ACM, New York (2002)
34. Yoshida, M., Ikeda, M., Ono, S., Sato, I., Nakagawa, H.: Person name disambiguation by bootstrapping. In: SIGIR, pp. 10–17. ACM, New York (2010)
35. Zhang, B., Horvath, S.: A general framework for weighted gene co-expression network analysis. Stat. Appl. Genet. Mol. Biol. **4**(1), 1128 (2005)

Chapter 20
Towards Leader Based Recommendations

Ilham Esslimani, Armelle Brun, and Anne Boyer

Abstract The development of Internet and the success of Web 2.0 applications engendered the emergence of virtual communities. Analyzing information flows and discovering leaders through these communities becomes thus a major challenge in different application areas. In this work, we present an algorithm that aims at detecting leaders through the use of implicit relationships with other users in behavioral networks in the context of recommender systems. This algorithm considers the high connectivity and the potentiality of propagating accurate appreciations so as to detect reliable leaders through these networks. This approach is evaluated in terms of precision using a real usage dataset. The results of the experimentation show the interest of our approach to exploit TopN leaders appreciations so as to generate accurate predictions through a behavioral network. Besides, our approach can be harnessed in different application areas caring about the role of leaders.

20.1 Introduction

With the heightened evolution of the Web, e-commerce applications and on-line social networks, understanding information flows and influence phenomena is crucial. Indeed, the success of Web 2.0 environments as social networks, blogs, wikis, etc. led to the emergence of virtual communities. Studying and analyzing leadership and detecting leaders or influencers through these communities becomes thus a major challenge.

Originally, leadership studies have been linked to the area of marketing. The objective consisted in the analysis of the "word-of-mouth" phenomenon and its

I. Esslimani (✉) · A. Brun · A. Boyer
KIWI Team-LORIA, Nancy University, 615 rue du Jardin Botanique,
54600 Villers-Lès-Nancy, France
e-mail: ilham.esslimani@loria.fr; armelle.brun@loria.fr; anne.boyer@loria.fr

T. Özyer et al. (eds.), *The Influence of Technology on Social Network Analysis and Mining*, Lecture Notes in Social Networks 6, DOI 10.1007/978-3-7091-1346-2_20,

impact on market trends. Indeed, usually, a small portion of a community has an important influence on opinion and decision making of the rest of the community [32]. This portion represents the opinion leaders.

Therefore, in the area of marketing, detecting opinion leaders allows the prediction of future decision making (about products and services), the anticipation of risks (due for example to negative opinions of leaders) and the follow-up of the corporate image (e-reputation) of companies.

Furthermore, studying leadership is also relevant in other application areas, such as: social network analysis and recommender systems. In the area of social networks analysis, detection of leaders represents a great perspective; it aims notably at analyzing influences between entities with the objective of studying social networks properties and predicting their evolution. Leaders can also be considered in the area of recommender systems based in particular on Collaborative Filtering (CF). CF is a recommendation technique which generates recommendations to an active user, based on his/her opinions on items and those of other users [17]. Leaders potentially represent reliable "neighbors"[1] that can provide relevant recommendations to the others about a Web page to visit, a product to purchase, a movie to watch, a restaurant to choose, etc. Generating recommendations based on leaders' preferences could improve user satisfaction and ensure his loyalty.

CF and recommender systems are widely implemented in many application areas thanks to their reliability for personalization. Some of the well known e-commerce applications integrating recommendation engines are Amazon[2] and LastFM.[3] However, some research questions still remain.

Some of these questions concern the new item cold-start problem or latency problem [2]. Indeed, when a new item is introduced in the system, the preferences (the ratings) relating to this item are not available because no user has assigned a rating yet. Thus, recommender systems based on ratings, as CF systems, are unable to recommend this new item to users.

In this work, we are interested in studying leader detection in the context of behavioral networks to alleviate the latency problem. In these networks, users are connected when they have similar navigational behaviors.

We propose to consider a behavioral leader as a user who is linked to many users with the same behavior and whose preferences can be propagated accurately towards these users. Thus, we propose an algorithm that aims at detecting leaders in behavioral networks. These leaders are identified by mining the relationships they have with the other users through similar navigational behaviors. These relationships are implicit relationships as they represent similar behaviors. We assume that the detection of a small segment of leaders can be considered when preferences about new items are not available. So, the recommender system can involve this

[1]Users that are similar to an active user, of which appreciations are combined to generate recommendations.

[2]http://www.amazon.com

[3]http://www.lastfm.com

segment of leaders, by asking them to rate the new items, so as to initialize the recommendation process and generate predictions to the other users based on the leaders' preferences.

Let us notice that our algorithm is not limited to recommender systems area, it can be involved in the frame of different application areas as marketing or social network analysis.

The remainder of this work is organized as follows. In the second section related works regarding latency problem and detection of leaders are presented. The third section focuses on the description of our proposed algorithm related to the selection and the detection of behavioral leaders. The fourth section is dedicated to the presentation of the experimentation we conducted so as to evaluate the performance of our approach. The results of this experimentation are presented in the same section. Finally, we summarize our research and conclude with some possible future directions.

20.2 Related Works

The issue regarding our research is to find a reliable method for detecting behavioral leaders. We propose to detect leaders based on implicit relationships with other users and exploit their appreciations to propagate recommendations to these users. As related works, we present here some research studies investigating the latency problem in the frame of recommender systems. We also focus on the problem of detecting leaders in different application areas.

20.2.1 Latency Problem

Recommender systems based on CF encounter the new item cold start problem, called also the latency problem. When a new item is introduced, it cannot be used in collaborative recommendations as users' evaluation about this item are not yet available in the system. Let us notice that in general users do not devote much time to express regularly their preferences about new items. This problem has in particular much impact on CF systems where new items are often incorporated such as CF systems recommending news articles [9,30]. To alleviate the latency problem, content-based filtering has been suggested as a solution in some research studies [7,22,23]. We present here an overview of these studies.

Content-based filtering relies on the analysis of the content of items so as to generate recommendations. Thus, a new item is recommended according to the similarity of its content with the other items. For example, a user who has already seen items about "genetics" will receive recommendations of new items related to this subject. This technique is often combined with CF in the frame of hybrid recommenders such as Fab [3] and Filterbots [15] and has been subject of many studies as [6, 25, 27]. Besides, probabilistic models for combining collaborative and content-based recommendations are suggested by Popescul et al. [28] and Schein et al. [29].

However, the problem of content-based filtering is the limitation of recommendation diversity and the overspecialization of recommendations as the recommended items are always similar and identical to those appreciated by the user before. Thus, the other items with a different content are neglected and are never integrated in recommendation lists suggested to this user.

20.2.2 Detection of Leaders and Influencers

Leadership and influence propagation have been subject of many studies in the area of marketing, social science and social network analysis [16]. Researchers tend to understand how communities start, what are their properties, how they evolve, what are the roles of their members and how influencers and opinion leaders can be detected through these communities. Katz and Lazarsfeld [12] defined opinion leaders as "the individuals who were likely to influence other persons in their immediate environment".

The earliest studies of influence and leadership focused on the analysis of the propagation of medical and technological innovations [10]. More recently, [31] also examined this question and proposed diffusion models of innovations in networks.

In the area of marketing (viral marketing), influence propagation is often linked to the word-of-mouth phenomenon and its effects on the success of new products [11]. The most important challenge in marketing is how to find a small segment of the population (influencers or leaders) that can influence the other segments by their positive or negative opinions regarding products and services [32]. Keller and Berry [20] confirm the importance of influencers as they guide the decisions of a community and predict market trends. According to their study, "one American in ten tells the other nine how to vote, where to eat and what to buy".

With the development of Internet, leaders and influencers do not use only traditional word-of-mouth, they can propagate their opinions based on interactive exchanges through blogs, forums, wikis and various social networks platforms. A social network represents a social structure between actors. It indicates the ways they are connected through various social relationships as friendship, co-working or information exchange [19]. Nowadays, social networks become the most important medium for propagating information, innovation and opinions.

Several recent studies have been interested in analyzing interactions and influences between entities and examining the impact of leaders in social networks. Kempe et al. [21] study approximation algorithms for influence maximization in co-authorship network. Agarwal et al. [1] show how to identify active and non active influential bloggers that can lead trends and affect group interests in the blogosphere. Goyal et al. [16] propose a pattern mining approach to discover leaders and to evaluate their influence in social networks. Actions such as tagging, rating, buying and blogging are considered in frequent pattern discovery. Goyal et al. [16] consider in fact that in a social network, a leader can guide the trends of performing actions. Thus, friends are tempted to perform the same actions than the ones the leader performed. An approach based on text mining and social network analysis is presented in [8]. This approach consists in detecting opinion leaders based on mining users' comments about products and mining communication relationships among them.

Other studies investigated the role of network structure on the propagation of information and opinions. Some of them [5, 26] emphasize the role of highly connected nodes in a social network, called also hubs, in information dissemination and evolution of collaboration in this network. Malcolm [24] confirm that highly connected nodes have an important influence on their neighbors. Keller and Berry [20] show also that users who influence others, have a relatively large number of social links.

Unlike the studies presented above, in this work we are interested in leadership detection by mining implicit relationships [4] between users based on behavioral information. Moreover, by considering social networks approaches, we aim at detecting leaders among users by taking into account the structure of users network. The following section describes our proposed approach.

20.3 Leader Detection and Preference Propagation in Behavioral Networks

Standard recommender systems and CF require a significant amount of rating data so as to evaluate similarities between users and compute recommendations. When a new item enters the system, ratings about this item are not yet available. Therefore, the system cannot incorporate it in any list of recommendations because no neighbor has rated this item.

In this work, we propose a novel approach of the recommendation process in a behavioral network: we substitute leaders for neighbors. The behavioral network is constructed based on implicit relationships between users exploiting behavioral information. Then, by considering highly connected users as potential behavioral leaders, their appreciations are propagated in the network. The more accurate the propagated appreciations are, the more effective the leaders are. This new approach has the advantage to alleviate the latency problem. Indeed, when a new item enters the system, the system asks the leaders to rate this item and propagate their ratings in the network.

In social networks leaders influence directly and explicitly their friends or collaborators by their opinions via social Web platforms. In our approach, influence or leadership is implicit since a leader is not involved himself in the propagation process. Indeed, leader opinions are propagated by the recommender system with the objective of predicting the future preferences of the other users.

The following subsections describe behavioral networks modelling and present the algorithm we propose to detect behavioral leaders.

20.3.1 Construction of the Behavioral Network

A behavioral network is constructed based on behavioral data, where users are linked as they share similar navigational patterns [14]. Behavioral data refers to usage traces capturing navigational activities and users interactions on a given Website. This approach exploits these data with the objective of assessing similarities between users.

We consider that two users u_a and u_b, who share common navigational patterns are similar. The longer the sequence of a common pattern is, the more the users are similar. Therefore, our goal is to identify for every pair of users (u_a, u_b), the maximum length $L_{Kmax}(u_a, u_b)$ of a navigational pattern among their navigational common patterns.

Then, the similarity of navigation between two users is computed by using formula (20.1) that takes into account common patterns between the active user u_a and the neighbor user u_b. This formula computes, for each pair of users u_a and u_b the similarity of navigation $SimNav_{(u_a,u_b)}$ as the ratio of the maximum length of a common frequent pattern $L_{Kmax}(u_a, u_b)$ and the minimum of maximum sizes of u_a and u_b sessions denoted $SessMax_{(u_a)}$ and $SessMax_{(u_b)}$.

$$SimNav_{(u_a,u_b)} = \frac{L_{Kmax}(u_a, u_b)}{\min(SessMax_{(u_a)}, SessMax_{(u_b)})} \tag{20.1}$$

We use the minimum of maximum sizes of sessions in the denominator so as to avoid to penalize a new user who has few sessions with short sizes. We note that the similarity value is normalized between 0 and 1. This metric emphasizes the importance of the longest frequent patterns to evaluate similarities of users. The higher the length of a navigational pattern is, the more the users are similar.

Once navigational similarities are evaluated, we build the behavioral network by using a non directed graph $G = (N, E)$ where nodes N represent users, edges E represent the links between users and the navigational similarities are the weights of the edges. The more two users are similar in terms of navigational behavior, the higher the weight value of the edge. This approach is detailed in [14].

20.3.2 Detecting Leaders in the Behavioral Network

In the frame of the constructed behavioral network, we aim at discovering reliable users: the leaders. We propose an algorithm that considers users' connectivity to select potential leaders that propagate, in a following step, their preferences in the network. Then, by assessing the quality of these propagated preferences, actual leaders are detected.

In social networks, the detection of leaders relies on the analysis of the social links through the network. Here, we emphasize the role of behavioral links to identify behavioral leaders in a network.

According to [5,20,24,26] mentioned in Sect. 20.2, we define a behavioral leader as a user who is not only highly connected in the behavioral network. He has also a high potentiality of predicting the preferences of the other users. We assume in fact that behavioral leaders' preferences can be propagated in the network. We propose to propagate appreciations with an attenuation factor. This factor is directly related to the similarity of navigation between users (the weights of the links). Indeed, when users are very similar, there is a high probability that they share the same appreciations about items.

Moreover, we assume that the appreciations on items that a behavioral leader can propagate, are related to the items he prefers. Since our model relies on usage traces, the estimation of user appreciations ("like" or "dislike" an item) is required. To distinguish preferred items from non preferred ones, we take into account two implicit parameters: frequencies of visiting an item and duration of visiting an item that we can compute based on extracted information from web server log files [13].

Algorithm 1 is our proposed algorithm for detecting behavioral leaders. This algorithm uses as input the graph $G = (N, E)$ modelling the behavioral network where nodes N represent users and edges E are the links between them. Our algorithm includes two main steps. Each step considers a distinct set of items denoted I_{tr} and I_{ts}. I_{tr} refers to the items used (at the training step) to assess behavioral similarities and construct the behavioral network and I_{ts} represents the set of items considered to validate the actual behavioral leaders (the test step), they are the new items.

20.3.2.1 First Step of Algorithm 1

This step ("function SelectPotentialLeaders") aims at detecting potential leaders. For each node u_a in the graph G, the connectivity (degree centrality) is computed as the number of links (neighbors) incident upon u_a. Then, TopN potential leaders U_{PL} are selected based on their high connectivity in the behavioral network.

20.3.2.2 Second Step of Algorithm 1

This step ("function DetectLeaders") selects the leaders of highest quality. For each potential leader $u_{pl} \in U_{PL}$ from the previous step, the items they liked are identified $I_{prf}(u_{pl}) \subset I_{ts}$. Then, as presented in formula (20.3), potential leaders' appreciations $apr(u_{pl}, i_j)$ on items i_j ($i_j \in I_{prf}(u_{pl})$) are propagated to their direct neighbors. The propagated appreciation, denoted $papr(u_{pl}, i_j)$, from a leader u_{pl} to the neighbor node u_a about an item i_j is weighted by the coefficient $\alpha_{(u_a, u_{pl})}$. As presented in Fig. 20.2, the weights α range from 0 to 1 according to the similarity between u_{pl} and u_a computed by formula (20.1).

Once the appreciations are propagated to a neighbor u_a, they are evaluated in terms of precision using formula (20.4). This precision is calculated as the ratio

Algorithm 1 Detection of behavioral leaders

function SELECTPOTENTIALLEADERS
  for each node u_a over the graph G **do**
    Evaluate "Degree centrality" $D_{(u_a)}$ ▷ denoted $|\Gamma_{(u_a)}|$

$$D_{(u_a)} = |\Gamma_{(u_a)}| \quad (20.2)$$

  end for
  Sorting Degrees D of all nodes N in a descending order
  return TopN potential behavioral leaders U_{PL} with high Degrees of centrality
end function

function DETECTLEADERS
  for each potential behavioral leader $u_{pl} \in U_{PL}$ **do**
    Select preferred items $I_{prf}(u_{pl}) \subset I_{ts}$
    Select neighbor nodes
    for each selected neighbor u_a **do**
      for each item $i_j \in I_{prf}(u_{pl})$ **do**
        Propagate appreciations $apr(u_{pl}, i_j)$ to u_a such as:

$$papr(u_a, i_j) = \alpha_{(u_a, u_{pl})} * apr(u_{pl}, i_j) \quad (20.3)$$

        Evaluate precision of each $papr(u_a, i_j)$ ($papr(u_a, i_j)$ is relevant or not for u_a)
      end for
      Evaluate precision of all propagated appreciations to u_a

$$p(u_a) = \frac{N_{rl}}{N_r} \quad (20.4)$$

    end for
    Evaluate precision of the potential leader u_{pl} as the average of precisions p computed over all his neighbors

$$P(u_{pl}) = \frac{\sum_{u_a=1}^{m} p(u_a)}{m} \quad (20.5)$$

  end for
  return TopN actual behavioral leaders U_L with the best ratios of precision
end function

between N_{rl} representing the number of propagated items that are relevant for u_a (that are really appreciated by him) and N_r representing the number of all propagated items (relevant and irrelevant). Then, as presented in formula (20.5), for each potential behavioral leader we evaluate the precision $P(u_{pl})$ as the average of precisions computed over all his neighbors u_a. We note that m represents in formula (20.5) the number of u_{pl} neighbors.

Precision ratio highlights finally the actual behavioral leaders over the network. The higher the precision ratio is, the more reliable the behavioral leader is.

Fig. 20.1 Example of usage data extracted from the web server log file of the Credit Agricole Intranet

<stat ip=127.0.0.1 startDate=1205854948962 endDate=1205854949067
port=8080 urid=ca801 method= GET referer=j6/home scheme=http
serverName=127.0.0.1 uri=/jcms/display.jsp qs=j193
sessionId=F87C360D2B3 locale=fr userAgent=Mozilla/5.0
id=j193 type=generated.PortletPortal
pub=j193 mid=j2 workspace=j4 gids=ca8015133 ccat=j5
pcat=j5 portal=j193 zone=Public name=Identification/>

20.3.2.3 Recommendation Generation

Once behavioral leaders are detected, we propose to use them as the first raters on new items. When a new item enters the system, they are asked to consult this new item. As these leaders are representative users, if they have liked this new item, the system propagates the ratings in the network and recommend them to the other users if the estimated ratings are high.

20.4 Experimentation

20.4.1 Dataset

So as to evaluate the performance of our approach, we use a real usage dataset extracted from the Extranet of Credit Agricole Banking Group, in particular the usage data relating to the Department of Strategies and Technology Watch. All the users are members of the Group and can access numerous resources such as: news, articles, faq, special reports, etc.

Thus, we exploit the usage data that represents the navigational activities of users on the Intranet. This data has been stored in Web server log files. Figure 20.1 presents an example of this usage data in XML format. The log files contain mainly information about user-ids, item-ids, session-ids and time of starting and ending the consultation of items. The studied dataset is related to 748 users and 3,856 items. The average size of a user session in this dataset is about 6. The dataset has been split into 80 and 20 % corresponding respectively to training and test datasets.

So as to evaluate the quality of the propagated appreciations through the network, we extracted leaders' preferences about items denoted $I_{prf(u_l)}$ from the test set I_{ts}. As mentionned in Sect. 20.3.2, we considered only positive appreciations of these leaders (the items they like). Besides, the weights from formula (20.1) and presented in Fig. 20.2 are used as the attenuation factor at the propagation step. For example, similarity values in the range $[0.8 - 1.0]$ have a corresponding α weight equal to 1.0. We note that the assignment of α weights considers here the distribution of similarities between users over to the studied dataset.

To illustrate this propagation process, we present an example in Fig. 20.3 that represents appreciation propagation about "news articles". Considering her high connectivity in the behavioral network ($D_{(Rose)} = 5$), Rose is a potential

Fig. 20.2 Attenuation factor depending on similarities

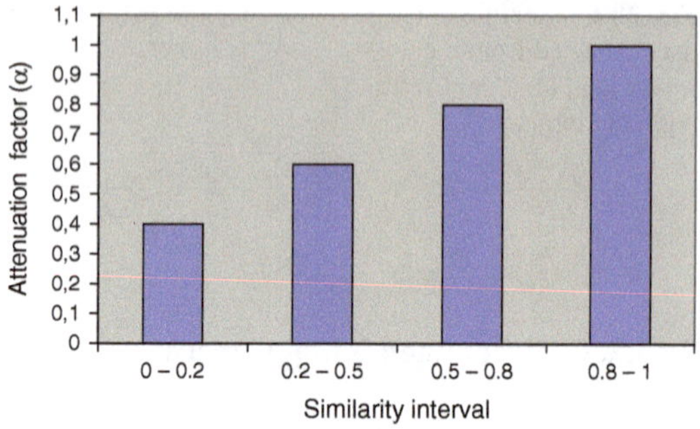

Fig. 20.3 Propagation of a potential behavioral leader appreciation

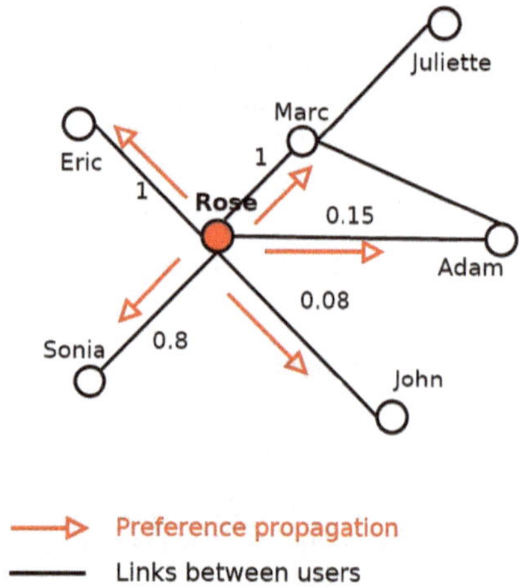

behavioral leader among all the other users. When propagating her appreciation about her preferred article "Web 2.0 applications", similarity weights are considered. Therefore, Marc, Eric and Sonia will receive a recommendation of "Web 2.0 applications" article, because $SimNav_{(Rose,Eric)} = 1.0$, $SimNav_{(Rose,Marc)} = 1.0$ and $SimNav_{(Rose,Sonia)} = 0.8$. At the opposite, Adam and John will not receive this recommendation because the corresponding similarity weights are weak: $SimNav_{(Rose,Adam)} = 0.15$ and $SimNav_{(Rose,John)} = 0.08$.

20.4.2 Evaluation

The evaluation of the precision can rely on statistical or decision support measures [18, 33]. When it is statistical, an accuracy measure evaluates the deviation between propagated appreciations and the real preferences that are actually assigned by users to items. When it is a measure of decision support, it evaluates the relevance of a set of propagated appreciations by computing the proportion of items that the user consider actually useful and relevant [2]. Precision is widely used as a measure

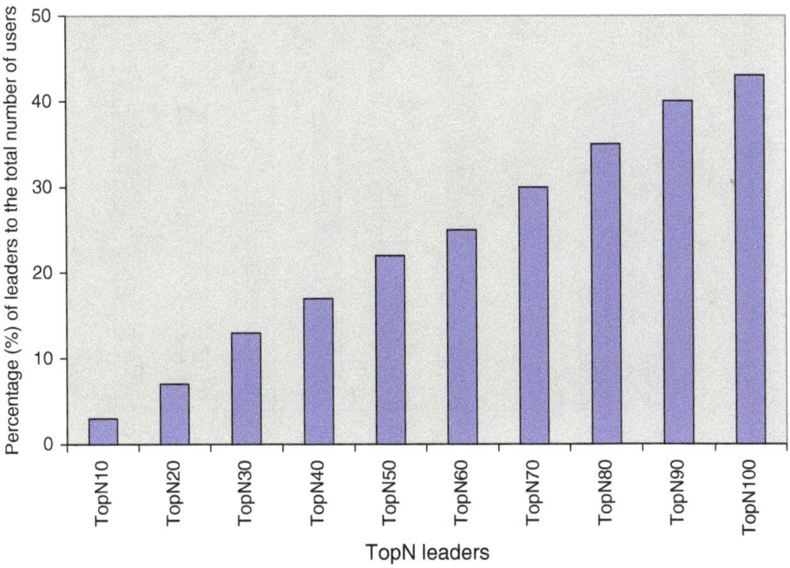

Fig. 20.4 Percentage of leaders in the studied dataset

of decision support. Let us notice that here binary preferences are considered to distinguish relevant items from non relevant ones.

20.4.3 Results

This evaluation aims at examining the effectiveness of our approach for detecting behavioral leaders in the behavioral network. Thus, in this experimentation, we evaluate the precision of the propagated appreciations regarding each potential leader based on formulas (20.4) and (20.5).

Figure 20.4 presents the percentage of TopN potential behavioral leaders from the total number of users in the studied dataset. Let us recall that users are considered as potential leaders when they are highly connected in the behavioral network.

We can observe from Fig. 20.4 that TopN10 behavioral leaders represent about 3 % of users compared with the total number of users in the dataset, whereas TopN100 leaders involve about 43 % of users to the total number of users. The percentage of leaders from TopN10 to TopN100 does not evolve linearly because some potential leaders are not represented in Fig. 20.4 as the corresponding precision can not be evaluated due to one of the following reasons:

- The items propagated by potential behavioral leaders have not been viewed yet by the neighbors (the similar users linked to them in the network). Thus, we can not examine if the concerned potential leaders are actual or not.

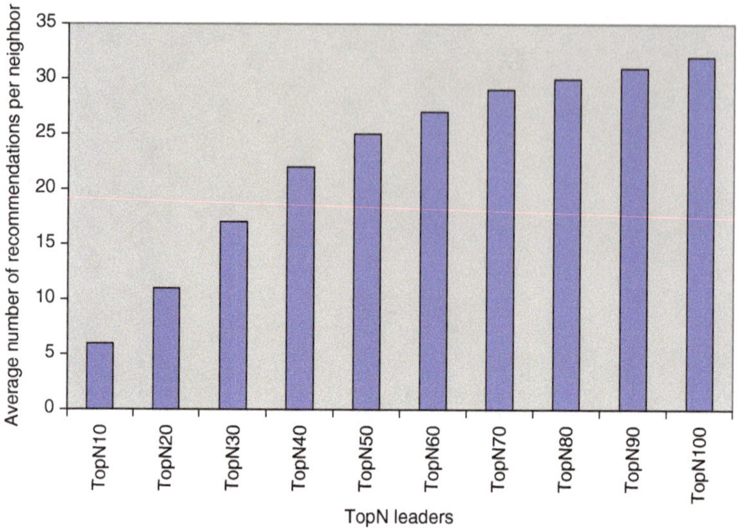

Fig. 20.5 Average number of propagated recommendations by TopN leaders

- The potential behavioral leaders did not appreciate the items (in the test set I_{ts}). So, the system can not propagate their preferences to the neighbors.

We note that in the results presented in this section, this category of behavioral leaders is not considered.

Figure 20.5 presents the number of propagated recommendations per neighbor based on TopN leaders appreciations. We observe that the number of propagated recommendations increases as the number of leaders increases also. Thus, the higher the number of leaders involved, the higher the coverage (the number of predictions generated by leaders). Indeed, we can see from Fig. 20.5 that considering TopN100 leaders leads to the propagation of about 33 recommendations per neighbor on average, whereas TopN10 generate only about 7 recommandations per neighbor on average.

With the objective of evaluating the performance of our approach for recommending relevant items, we compared the precision of recommendations to the standard CF [17]. We note that the standard CF exploits here the Pearson Coefficient as a similarity function to detect neighbor users, that are involved in the prediction process.

Figure 20.6 presents the precision averages corresponding to our approach (Leaders based preference propagation) and to the standard CF. These precisions have been computed over the same pairs of $< user, item >$ considered at the propagation step by TopN leaders. By observing the evolution of the results in Fig. 20.6, we can notice that for both models the precision average corresponding to propagated recommendations deteriorates as the percentage of TopN leaders increases. Besides, we can see that, on the set of items predicted by the leaders, our approach outperforms the standard CF as a higher accuracy is attained. Indeed, our

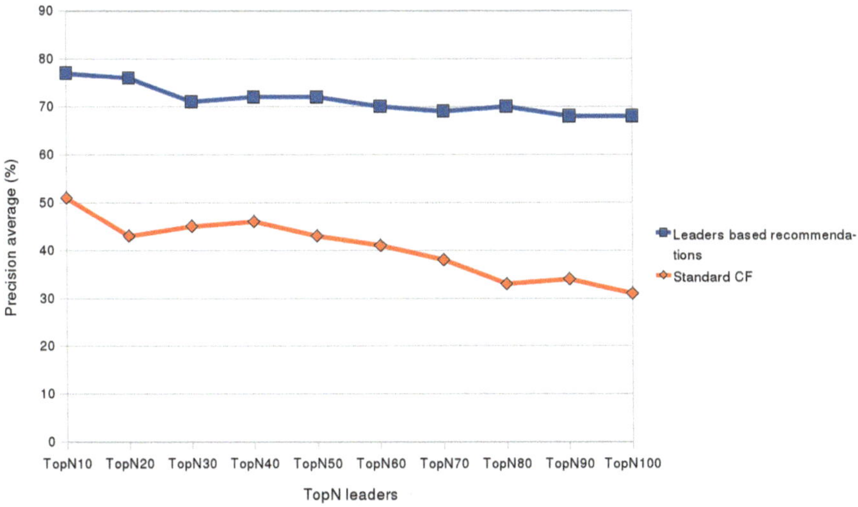

Fig. 20.6 Precision average of leaders based recommendations compared to standard CF

model reaches about 77 % of precision when TopN10 leaders are considered at the propagation step. At the opposite, the standard CF is less accurate as the precision average reaches at best 51 % when TopN10 leaders are considered.

Thus, these results confirm the effectiveness of behavioral leaders regarding the proposition of relevant items to the other users. Moreover, these results converge with our initial objective which consisted in the detection of a small segment of users having an important potentiality of prediction. Indeed, even if the number of recommendations propagated to every neighbor increases as the number of leaders rises, it turns out that generating few recommendations by reliable leaders contributes to the better performance.

So, overall, the results presented here show the interest of our approach to detect reliable behavioral leaders in behavioral networks. These leaders have in fact an important potentiality of proposing relevant items, as a high accuracy is reached by most of them (in particular by TopN10 and TopN20 leaders). Thus, they represent the entry nodes in the behavioral network that can be considered by the system to initialize the recommendation of new items so as to alleviate latency problem. Nevertheless, the performance of our approach remains a tradeoff between the improvement of recommendation accuracy and the enhancement of the coverage.

20.5 Conclusion and Future Work

In this work we presented a new approach that aims at detecting leaders within the framework of behavioral networks so as to alleviate latency problem. In these networks, users are connected when they have similar navigational behaviors. The detection of leaders relies on their high connectivity in these behavioral networks and their potentiality of propagating accurate appreciations.

This approach is evaluated in terms of precision using a real usage dataset. The experimentation highlights the importance of considering a small segment of TopN behavioral leaders through the network so as to propagate accurately the preferences to the other users. Indeed, a high accuracy of propagated preferences is reached compared to the standard CF. However, the performance of the leader based recommendations remains a tradeoff between the improvement of recommendation accuracy and the enhancement of the coverage.

In this work, we experimented our approach in the area of recommender systems. This approach can be harnessed in other application areas, attaching importance to the role of leaders, as marketing and social network analysis.

As a future work, we plan to experiment additional datasets so as to validate the generalization of our approach. Moreover, we plan to solve the problem of coverage in the frame of our approach. Besides, we plan to investigate other methods for detecting leaders and analyze their performance.

References

1. Agarwal, N., Liu, H., Tang, L., Yu, P.S.: Identifying the influential bloggers in a community. In: Proceedings of the International Conference on Web Search and Web Data Mining (WSDM'08), pp. 207–218. ACM, New York (2008)
2. Anand, S., Mobasher, B.: Intelligent techniques for web personalization. Lect. Note Artif. Intell. **3169**, 1–36 (2005)
3. Balabanović, M., Shoham, Y.: Fab: content-based, collaborative recommendation. Commun. ACM **40**(3), 66–72 (1997)
4. Bao, H., Chang, E.: Adheat: an influence-based diffusion model for propagating hints to match ads. In: WWW'10: Proceedings of the 19th International Conference on World Wide Web, pp. 71–80. ACM, New York (2010)
5. Barabasi, A.L., Jeong, H., Neda, Z., Ravasz, E., Schubert, A., Vicsek, T.: Evolution of the social network of scientific collaboration. Phys. A **311**(3–4), 590–614 (2002)
6. Basilico, J., Hofmann, T.: A joint framework for collaborative and content filtering. In: Proceedings of the 27th Annual International ACM SIGIR Conference on Research and Development in Information Retrieval (SIGIR'04), pp. 550–551. ACM, New York (2004)
7. Billsus, D., Pazzani, M.: User modeling for adaptive news access. User Model. User Adapt. Interact. **10**(2–3), 147–180 (2000)
8. Bodendorf, F., Kaiser, C.: Detecting opinion leaders and trends in online social networks. In: Proceedings of the 2nd ACM Workshop on Social Web Search and Mining (SWSM'09), pp. 65–68. ACM, New York (2009)
9. Burke, R.: Hybrid recommender systems: survey and experiments. User Model. User Adapt. Interact. **12**(4), 331–370 (2002)
10. Coleman, J., Menzel, H., Katz, E.: Medical Innovations: A Diffusion Study. Bobbs-Merrill, Indianapolis (1966)
11. Domingos, P., Richardson, M.: Mining the network value of customers. In: KDD '01: Proceedings of the Seventh ACM SIGKDD International Conference on Knowledge Discovery and Data Mining, pp. 57–66. ACM, New York (2001)

12. Elihu, K., Lazarsfeld, P.F.: Personal Influence; the Part Played by People in the Flow of Mass Communications. Free Press, Glencoe (1955)
13. Esslimani, I., Brun, A., Boyer, A.: A collaborative filtering approach combining clustering and navigational based correlations. In: Proceedings of the 5th International Conference on Web Information Systems and Technologies (WEBIST), Lisbon, pp. 364–369 (2009). INSTICC
14. Esslimani, I., Brun, A., Boyer, A.: From social networks to behavioral networks in recommender systems. In: Proceedings of The 2009 International Conference on Advances in Social Networks Analysis and Mining (ASONAM), Athens, pp. 143–148. IEEE Computer Society, Los Alamitos (2009)
15. Good, N., Schafer, J.B., Konstan, J.A., Borchers, A., Sarwar, B., Herlocker, J., Riedl, J.: Combining collaborative filtering with personal agents for better recommendations. In: Proceedings of the Sixteenth National Conference on Artificial Intelligence and the Eleventh Innovative Applications of Artificial Intelligence Conference Innovative Applications of Artificial Intelligence (AAAI'99/IAAI'99), pp. 439–446. American Association for Artificial Intelligence, Menlo Park (1999)
16. Goyal, A., Bonchi, F., Lakshmanan, L.V.: Discovering leaders from community actions. In: Proceeding of the 17th ACM Conference on Information and Knowledge Management (CIKM'08), pp. 499–508. ACM, New York (2008)
17. Herlocker, J., Konstan, J., Borchers, A., Riedl, J.: An algorithmic framework for performing collaborative filtering. In: Proceedings of the 22nd Annual International ACM SIGIR Conference on Research and Development in Information Retrieval (SIGIR'99), pp. 230–237. ACM, New York (1999)
18. Herlocker, J.L., Konstan, J.A., Terveen, L.G., Riedl, J.T.: Evaluating collaborative filtering recommender systems. ACM Trans. Inf. Syst. **22**(1), 5–53 (2004)
19. Jamali, M., Abolhassani, H.: Different aspects of social network analysis. In: Proceedings of the 2006 IEEE/WIC/ACM International Conference on Web Intelligence (WI'06), pp. 66–72. IEEE Computer Society, Washington, DC (2006)
20. Keller, E., Berry, J.: The Influentials. Simon and Schuster, New York (2003)
21. Kempe, D., Kleinberg, J., Tardos, E.: Maximizing the spread of influence through a social network. In: Proceedings of the Ninth ACM SIGKDD International Conference on Knowledge Discovery and Data Mining (KDD'03), pp. 137–146. ACM, New York (2003)
22. Krulwich, B., Burkey, C.: Learning user information interests through extraction of semantically significant phrases. In: Proceedings of the AAAI Spring Symposium on Machine Learning in Information Access, Stanford (1996)
23. Lang, K.: Newsweeder: learning to filter netnews. In: Proceedings of the 12th International Conference on Machine Learning (ICML95), pp. 331–339. Tahoe City, USA (1995)
24. Malcolm, G.: The Tipping Point: How Little Things Can Make a Big Difference. Little Brown, New York (2000)
25. Melville, P., Mooney, R.J., Nagarajan, R.: Content-boosted collaborative filtering for improved recommendations. In: Proceedings of the Eighteenth National Conference on Artificial Intelligence, pp. 187–192. American Association for Artificial Intelligence, Menlo Park (2002)
26. Newman, E.: Clustering and preferential attachment in growing networks. Phys. Rev. Lett. **64**, 025102 (2001)
27. Pazzani, M.J.: A framework for collaborative, content-based and demographic filtering. Artif. Intell. Rev. **13**(5–6), 393–408 (1999)
28. Popescul, A., Ungar, L., Pennock, D.M., Lawrence, S.: Probabilistic models for unified collaborative and content-based recommendation in sparse-data environments. In: Proceedings of the 17th Conference in Uncertainty in Artificial Intelligence (UAI'01), pp. 437–444. Morgan Kaufmann, San Francisco (2001)
29. Schein, A., Popescul, A., Ungar, L.H., Pennock, D.M.: Methods and metrics for cold-start recommendations. In: Proceedings of the 25th Annual International ACM SIGIR Conference on Research and Development in Information Retrieval (SIGIR'02), pp. 253–260. ACM, New York (2002)

30. Sollenborn, M., Funk, P.: Category-based filtering and user stereotype cases to reduce the latency problem in recommender systems. In: Proceedings of the 6th European Conference on Advances in Case-Based Reasoning (ECCBR '02), pp. 395–420. Springer, London (2002)
31. Valente, T.W.: Network Models of the Diffusion of Innovations. Hampton, Cresskill (1995)
32. Watts, D.J., Dodds, P.S.: Influentials, networks, and public opinion formation. J. Consum. Res. **34**(4), 441–458 (2007)
33. Ziegler, C., McNee, S., Konstan, J., Lausen, G.: Improving recommendation lists through topic diversification. In: Proceedings of the 14th International Conference on World Wide Web (WWW'05), pp. 22–32. ACM, New York (2005)

Chapter 21
Enhancing Child Safety in MMOGs

Lyta Penna, Andrew Clark, and George Mohay

Abstract This paper presents a method for improving child safety in Massively Multiplayer Online Games (MMOGs). The focus is to monitor and detect relationships forming with a child in online games, and to alert if the relationship indicates that an offline meeting with the child has been arranged or has the potential to occur. The research problem involves determining contextual meaning of messages in MMOGs which is addressed by use of a ranking system. The paper extends previous work (Penna L, Clark A, Mohay G (2010) A framework for improved adolescent and child safety in MMOs. In: Memon N, Alhajj R (eds) 2010 international conference on advances in social network analysis and mining (ASONAM 2010), IEEE Computer Society, University of Southern Denmark, Odense, pp 33–40; Penna L, Clark A, Mohay G (2005) Challenges of automating the detection of paedophile activity on the internet. In: Proceedings of Systematic Approaches to Digital Forensic Engineering (SADFE'2005), Taiwan, pp 206–222) by providing a systematic and comprehensive evaluation using World of Warcraft as a case study MMOG and a prototype of the design.

21.1 Introduction

Massively Multiplayer Online Games (MMOGs or commonly named MMOs) are of the genre of online games that involve a high degree of social interaction, a virtual economy, and provide an alternative online reality that continues to exist regardless of whether anyone is playing. MMOGs are not available in an offline or independently played environment and therefore offer a large social element making it difficult to avoid interaction with others online if the game is played as intended.

L. Penna (✉) · A. Clark · G. Mohay
Information Security Institute, Queensland University of Technology, Brisbane, QLD, Australia
e-mail: l.penna@student.qut.edu.au; a.clark@qut.edu.au; g.mohay@qut.edu.au

T. Özyer et al. (eds.), *The Influence of Technology on Social Network Analysis and Mining*, Lecture Notes in Social Networks 6, DOI 10.1007/978-3-7091-1346-2_21,

MMOGs have items and places of value within the game that can be bought and sold creating an online economy.

MMOGs may be used as tools for meeting, socialising and forming relationships with otherwise unknown persons [2]. The MMOG medium offers an opportunity for children to meet new individuals with whom they can interact for game based achievements. In addition to social interaction, MMOGs offer community experiences whereby the child is subject to group dynamics, status building roles and virtual economies. As childrens' use of online MMOGs for game play and other enticing social experiences grows, so too does the potential for paedophiles to use the medium for finding children to molest. Online grooming may potentially lead to a dangerous offline encounter.

Numerous arrest cases exist whereby a paedophile has located and groomed a child online. A growing percentage of these arrest cases involve relationship formation specific to MMOG environments leading to an offline encounter, for example, World of Warcraft (WoW) related cases [6, 11, 13]. Child predators are migrating from traditional methods to alternative media where children are accessible. Police are now working undercover in online interactive games in order to detect a variety of illegal activities including grooming of children [11].

Currently there is scientific debate [12] as to whether or not online paedophiles are a new type of offender [16] or if those with a pre-disposition to offend are responding to the opportunities afforded by the new forms of social media [4]. Empirical evidence points to the problem of Internet-based paedophilia as endemic [10]. Internet-based paedophiles are often highly technology-savvy, using a range of tactics to groom victims and to mask the trail of their activities. For example, masquerading as young persons to gain the trust of potential victims, using multiple online personas, use of an evolving specialised vocabulary to share child abuse materials, and use of encryption and anonymisation technologies or private networks which are harder to monitor and police [17].

There is no publicly available set of complete online grooming detection methods or techniques. Existing research to detect components of online grooming include deception detection research [19] and methods for detecting MMOG formed relationships that have potential to result in offline contact [14]. NetModerator, a proprietary ISP based implementation, uses heuristics and is aided by human monitors to improve online child safety [5]. Habbo [7] is an example MMOG that uses filtering of the exchange of phone numbers, addresses, and other personal information. The Australian Government released the NetAlert Internet content filter [1]. The use of this type of filter has many advantages, particularly for young children, however the list of sites and materials to be banned is enormous and constantly changing and, in addition, the filter can be easily bypassed [8].

This paper summarises research and the proposed design from previous works [14] and offers additional materials by providing a systematic evaluation of the design using the prototype built. The paper offers a method of evaluation that uses an extended set of labeled data (see Sect. 21.3.2) to demonstrate how the alert system performs with various suspicious message and conversation types and durations (see Sect. 21.4). The experiments presented in the paper demonstrate the negative ranking concept within the proposed design, the sensitivity of token ranking, the impact of different message window sizes used to determine contextual meaning, and the results of quantitative synthetic scenarios.

Our research differs to other approaches as it focuses on determining contextual meaning in MMOG messages to determine if a meeting has potential to occur outside of the MMOG (this includes locations that are not specific to the child) by use of a ranking system. The research design also considers if the game based relationship has evolved to include other alternative online communications. The design proposed from this research aims to provide an automated tool without human moderators that is adaptable to multiple users and does not store sensitive data external to the users PC. The research concept can also be used to aid existing cybercrime units [9] and for producing forensic evidence for court if required. Methods identified in this research are applicable to automating the detection of criminal relationship formation, grooming, and sharing of offline contact information and/or meeting arrangements. Inappropriate communications and adult profiling are outside the scope of this research.

21.2 Architecture and Software Design

This section summarises the design concept of a monitoring and analysis tool that detects where a relationship has the potential to escalate to an out of game environment. More specific detail can be found on the design and prototype in previous works [14].

Over time and via a variety of online communication modes a communicator may gather sufficient information to physically locate another person. The threat is where a communicator locates a child offline or the child seeks out and locates the communicator. The aim of the design is to detect and alert the parent of potential for these scenarios. Hence the general design concept is for a parent to place the software at the end-user position (host-based) by choice. However, the design concept is applicable to alternative placements, such as covert methods used by authorities to place the software at a known criminal's PC and feedback alerts to the authorities where required.

Our proposed design logs data in real time then parses and analyses the data post-hoc, it does not impact gaming performance. It makes use of a database for storing communications and event data. The data set is searched for indicators of physical locations, meetings being arranged or precursors to an offline meeting. We call these indicators tokens. Individual tokens have preset ranks defined in the database; ranks are relative to either the constant token value or are defined by the rules and regular expressions that generate the token. The analysis and output stage of the design involves ranking messages and communicators with a level of suspicion based on the tokens found in the message and their ranked contextual meaning in a conversation. The ranking system involves the use of a message

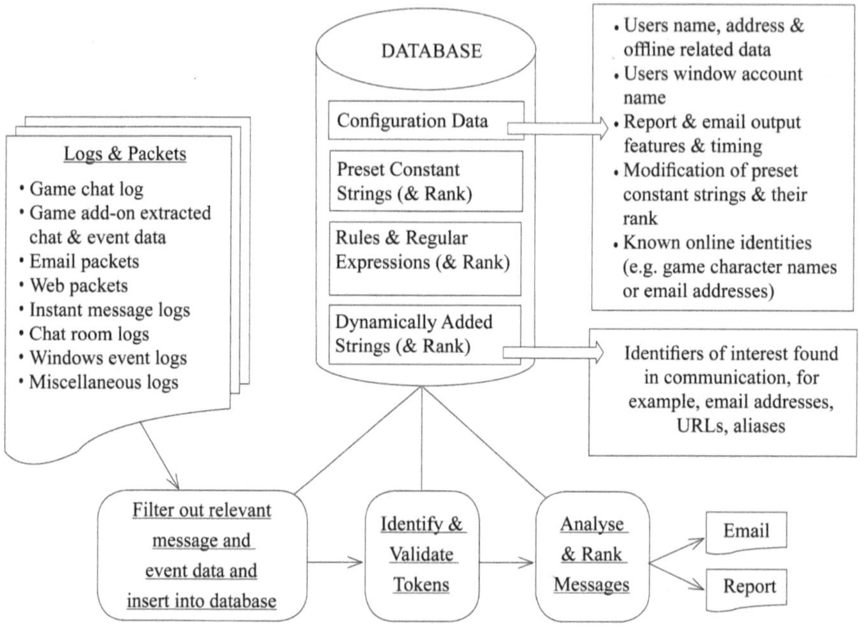

Fig. 21.1 The design concept

window (set of messages surrounding the original message within a predefined time frame) to determine contextual meaning. Messages deemed suspicious are alerted via email or other report output. The output method and analysis required for output are configurable. Figure 21.1 illustrates this design.

21.2.1 Key Design Concepts

21.2.1.1 Scenarios and Tokens

Synthetic scenarios include sequences of messages that indicate the potential for communication in a MMOG to move to an offline context or move outside of the MMOG in which case the scenario indicates further monitoring and analysis outside the context of the game is required. A non-exhaustive example set of scenario types are used in this paper for evaluation of the design and are as follows:

1. Arranging an offline meeting.
2. Sharing of contact information for offline communications.
3. Child or communicator sharing physical locator information.
4. Sharing of online alternative communication to the MMOG.

Each scenario type is identified by one or multiple components of information related to the scenario type within one or multiple messages. We term these identifiable components *tokens*. Tokens can be found using a rule, regular expression, or constant string match. Rules define how matches with constants or regular expressions may be combined. Tokens include group token types and base token types. Base token types include rudimentary components of information of interest, for example, a suburb. Group token types include groupings of base tokens, for example, an address consists of multiple base tokens in a valid format. Therefore the term *token* is used to express either a group token type with multiple joined and possibly validated base tokens or individual base tokens. Tokens are discarded if they do not comply with validity checks for their type. Some validation methods are variable dependent on the country, region or language the user defines as their own.

A non-exhaustive set of example group token types used for categorising output alerts includes: Address, Day/Time, Phone/Mobile, User Constants (configurable set of user related locator information), Place/Meeting, Non-Game Communications Devices (online alternative methods of communications for example, email), and Game Specific Communications (negative ranked group token type).

21.2.1.2 Token Ranks Relative to Semantic and Contextual Meaning

Tokens are provided a rank as a measure of confidence that the token is a true indicator of offline physical location content (or other offline contact information), out of game online communications (which indicate other online environments to monitor data for), or an offline meeting being arranged. Our method of creating specific ranking values has evolved as a trial and error development process and is similar to Spam ranking methodologies in software like the SpamAssassin system [18]. The design involves positively ranking suspicious tokens and negatively ranking tokens commonly used in the context of the MMOG. For example, in the prototype using WoW as an example MMOG, the method of ranking involved creating an initial list of commonly used WoW strings from our large sample of "normal game play" data (see Sect. 21.3.2 Dataset) along with existing online WoW word and phrase dictionaries. The most commonly used WoW specific strings from this dataset were assigned a negative ranking. An example of positive ranking tokens is whereby our prototype uses regular expression matches to recognise various time and address formats.

The token rank is affected by the degree to which the token matches a regular expression and the possible multiple meanings of the matched constants. For example, a phone number matching both the prefix (area code) and number would have a higher rank than a phone number without the prefix. Another example (from WoW chat), the message *"this quest is sick... I have to collect tunnel rat ears!"* contains the token string *"tunnel"*. *"Tunnel"* is a commonly used English word, suffix, suburb, meeting place and a WoW game related word. The semantics of each such string are addressed by storage in the database of an extractable indicator of the various meanings of each string. Hence, the various meanings of the word *"tunnel"* are taken into consideration and the overall rank is deemed slightly positive. The token *"quest"* while sharing other meanings, is a heavily used word in the WoW game with game meaning and is therefore ranked very negative.

21.2.1.3 Configuration/Alerting/Reporting Facilities

The design allows configuration of the user's personal information related to their physical address, frequented places such as schools and clubs, contact phone numbers, email addresses and other methods of contact. The more information provided the better however, this information is not required for the system to function.

Configuration of the user's country, region and main language used allows the system to use appropriate modules that tailor the rules, regular expressions and constants to the user's location to result in better analysis.

Other online identities that are previously known and safe for the child to interact with can be entered into the system by choice. In addition, a facility to change ranks for constant strings, rules and regular expression matches is available to assist in the reduction of common false positives.

The design allows the option of profiling for specific information to gain an overall picture of the child's online experiences. An example of this is a level of suspicion for each online communicator (and their various aliases) that the child user communicates with. A list of aliases is automatically updated as the child meets online identities and aliases are linked together. Other output options include output of analysis of a particular communicator, of the child's main contacts communicated with, the game play style of the child (for example, listing the main players the child groups with during game play), and so on.

21.2.1.4 Message Analysis, Message Windows and Contextual Ranking

Each message containing a token is subjected to a ranking process. This can be performed in stages by group token type. For each group token type, messages with tokens of these group token types are investigated, a *message rank* is assigned to the message under investigation by calculating the sum of the token ranks the message contains. Having assigned a message rank, each message is then assigned a *contextual message rank*. A contextual message rank involves calculating the sum of the message rank of the message under investigation with the message ranks of the surrounding messages (within a *message window* of a preconfigured time frame). Only messages with a positive contextual message rank are alerted.

Figure 21.2 illustrates the ranking process and message window. The messages are illustrated as the large boxes where the smaller internal boxes are the tokens with a numerical rank. The darker grey tokens illustrate the potential for two tokens to overlap, for example, where one string token contains another string token. The message rank for each message is shown as the sum of the token ranks in the

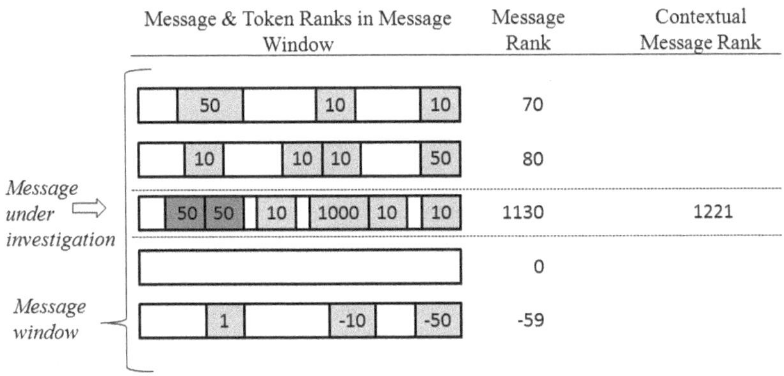

Fig. 21.2 Contextual ranking

message. The contextual rank of the message under investigation is illustrated as the sum of the message ranks within the message window.

In summary three levels of ranking exist, level 1 is the individual token rank, level 2 is the message rank, level 3 is the contextual message rank. The message window time frame can be configured.

21.2.2 Other Design Concepts and Design Limitations

Similar to a virus protection system, the design incorporates automated updates (for example, changes to rules and token ranking, addition of new modules, etc.) via Internet connection to a main server to maintain an up-to-date database and analysis process. It also requires security of database data and user logs including encryption options, requirements for strong user passwords, methods to ensure child users do not turn off the software, and various software and data integrity checks.

The processing speed of the token identification and ranking stage depends on the amount of rules, regular expressions and constants to be matched against. While the inclusion of further standard rules would increase the processing speed, the inclusion of exclusion rules (for example pattern matching that excludes messages with certain properties from further investigation) would reduce the processing speed. It is also subject to the amount of communications data used in the process. The processing speed of analysis is dependent on both the amount of online communications the user has and the configuration of the analysis and output.

Limitations of the design include the assumption that detecting and linking aliases of each player's various MMOG characters is achievable. Existing research demonstrates some methods of detecting aliases between two different pseudonyms (for example [3]). However MMOGs have different environmental properties to chat rooms, newsgroups and other online communities due to the high probability that one user is only logged on as one pseudonym at a time.

Alternative online communications to the game are used within the design to detect if the child is potentially communicating using them. Therefore, for example, should there be a known email address in the database, then email packets related to this email address will be identified and stored in the database for analysis and alerting, while all other unrelated packets will be discarded. The downside of this is that if online alternative communication methods are discussed during the game, and the child then receives/sends information via this alternative communication method in parallel to the game (and hence prior to any database updates), these alternative communication messages will be overlooked. To resolve this it is suggested that after the design analysis stage, if newly acquired alternative communications indicators are found, the design should iterate over the processes again with the new information (and hence, collect and analyse packets related to this alternative communication).

21.3 Evaluation Methodology

This section outlines the method for evaluation of the design including discussion of the data sets and the alert tally methods used to evaluate the design. The evaluation addresses the research aim to assess the proposed design for its ability to distinguish and alert to relationships forming in a MMOG that result in the possibility of out of game communications or meetings.

21.3.1 Alerting Definitions

The central consideration in determining what should and should not trigger an alert to the parent/guardian or authority is the answer to the question "what alerts or kinds of alerts would they like to see (and not see) in monitoring the child's activities?" As a result this research has adopted the following approach. We use three terms to define the nature of the alert triggered by a message or conversation: true positive, false positive and warning.

Synthetic scenarios are defined in Sect. 21.2.1.1 as a message or conversation that has definitive indicators of an offline meeting being arranged. This is precursored by the sharing of offline contact information (such as phone, postal address), physical locator information, or the sharing of online alternative communication to the MMOG they formed the relationship in (for example a web site or email address). The alerts triggered on detection of activity matching these scenarios types are classified as *true positives*.

Alerts triggered by conversations or messages that do not appear to contain useful information are classified as *false positives*. For example, a message that asks *"where will we meet?"* is evaluated as a false positive if this message has clear meaning to discuss an online WoW game meeting.

However there are instances in the 'clean' database (that is, the database before insertion of the injected scenarios) of partially or potentially suspicious messages or conversations and these also need to trigger an alert: these alerts we consider to be separate from true positives or false positives and we classify these as *warnings*. That is, a *warning* indicates a message or conversation which contains some components of information (for example a base token) of interest yet does not adhere to the definition of a true positive as described earlier. For example, a message that states *"I live in Berwick, Melbourne"* clearly states physical locator information and is of significance yet without further messages containing additional locator information such as the street name this message is not a complete true positive.

Due to the size of the data set used for evaluation it is not practical to label and assess every message for evaluation. Therefore, for the experiments presented in this paper, we assess only the alerts that result from the experiment. False negatives are considered to have occurred if a known suspicious message does not alert, such as an injected synthetic scenario message or suspicious message from the sample real data set.

21.3.2 Dataset

21.3.2.1 Real Data

Real data is used from the researchers WoW game play. This consists of data from over 1,191 game play hours during the course of 3.5 years data collection. The real dataset contains 118,159 game chat messages (of various game chat communication types) with 2449 game player aliases related to these messages. Some Hotmail, SMTP mail, and Microsoft Messenger Instant Messages are contained within the real data set to ensure this alternative data source was equally applicable for the design.

The real data has been used to assist in the creation of the design and also was a component to the creation of the WoW word/phrase list for negating matches to WoW specific context. This data has been used to highlight any specific issues/intricacies to the concept that otherwise would not have been identifiable using synthetic data. The data does not and is not intended to contain any unlawful activities; synthetic data was created for that purpose.

From the real data, a sample set of ten MMOG chat communications were selected and labeled A-J and includes the following message types:

- Suggestions of meeting arrangements that exclude any details. For example a conversation discussing the idea of meeting offline yet not providing evidence that these communicators could actually meet. These are messages A, D, H all of which should result in warnings.

- Discussing communication in alternative online mediums. These messages are B, C, G, and I. Messages B, C and G are three straightforward true positives (email addresses). Message I should trigger.
- Online game based meeting arrangements, messages E, and J. Both message E and J are not suspicious.
- Generalised locator information, message F. Message F should result in a warning.

An ideal design would alert to each message in the sample of real data messages with varying ranks with the exceptions of messages E and J. It is acceptable if the design only alerts to messages B, C, and G as these are the only definitive suspicious messages in the sample of real data messages.

21.3.2.2 Synthetic Scenarios

Synthetic data was created to demonstrate the central abilities of the design that otherwise are not addressed by the sample set of real data messages (71 synthetic messages were injected). Various real cases (cited in Sect. 21.1) involved persons meeting online in the WoW game, after which activities escalated to offline meetings or attempts to meet and resultant arrests. One case implied a child had provided information related to their home address. Another case implied the phone number of either the child or another player was disclosed. These two cases were used as a starting point for constructing scenario types which are expected to be alerted by the design when amongst large masses of other benign data. Additional scenario types were created to demonstrate further scenario scope and other design abilities. The resultant four scenario types are used as a guide to the creation of our synthetic scenarios and are as follows:

1. Scenario Type 1: Arranging an offline meeting (e.g. address/place and time shared)
2. Scenario Type 2: Sharing of offline alternative communication contact information (e.g. phone number)
3. Scenario Type 3: Child or communicator discloses sufficient personal information to be located (e.g. school name)
4. Scenario Type 4: Sharing of online alternative communication contact information (e.g. email address)

The design allows for various communication methods, therefore the scenario types alone do not test the boundaries of the design. For this reason the following sample of communication methods have been selected (a selection thought most exemplary of functioning) and used in the evaluation:

(a) WoW whispers (demonstrates private communication in game)
(b) WoW party chat (demonstrates grouped communication in game)
(c) WoW in-game mail (demonstrates mail service in game)
(d) Email (demonstrates alternative communications to game based communications)

Table 21.1 Synthetic data distribution

		Implementation timing				
Scenario type	Communication type	3 minutes stand-alone	3 minutes amongst other chat	10 minutes amongst other chat	>24 hours, amongst other chat	N/A
(1) Meeting	(a) WoW whispers	(i)	(ii)	(iii)		
	(b) In-game mail				(i)	
(2) Offline communication	(c) WoW party chat	(i)	(ii)	(iii)		
(3) Child's location	(d) WoW party chat	(i)	(ii)	(iii)		
(4) Alternative online communication	(e) WoW whisper					(i)
	(f) Email (with dynamically added email address constant)				(i)	

In addition to the various scenario types and communications methods, it is important to consider how these will be injected into the database in terms of timing of communications. The following sample of communications timings were used:

- 3 minutes conversation in a standalone context (no other surrounding messages occurring at the time)
- 3 minutes conversation amongst other messages
- 10 minutes conversation amongst other messages
- conversation spanning over 24 hour period amongst other messages

A total of 12 synthetic scenarios were injected (71 messages overall) amongst the real data. Table 21.1 displays how these injected scenarios apply to the scenario types, communication types, and injection implementation timings. For example, Scenario 1(a)(i) will be injected into the database as a communication between the child and one other person in the form of a WoW game whisper in a conversation that is separate to other communications (that is, there are no other whispers, group chats or channel chats occurring at the time) where the child and other communicator attempt to arrange an offline meeting. In another example, Scenario 2(c)(iii) represents a communication via a grouped chat (party chat) with the child where the communication suggests an offline communication (e.g. phone, PO Box, etc) over the course of a 10 minute communication while various other communications occur (e.g. guild, channel, whisper, or grouped chat). As a final example, Scenario 4(e)(i) is a one line whisper indicating an email address, and Scenario 4(f)(i) is an email sent/received with the to/from address the same as the email address from Scenario 4(e)(i) at least 24 hours later.

A successful result is these synthetic messages being distinguished as suspicious from amongst non-suspicious real data (and hence alerted), as well as the involved communicators being distinguished as particularly suspicious communicators comparatively to non-suspicious communicators amongst the researchers real data.

21.3.3 Examples

This section provides examples of our synthetic and real scenarios. The example real WoW messages correspond to a subset of those described and labeled in Sect. 21.3.2.1. The synthetic data labeling for the synthetic examples corresponds to that in Table 21.1 in Sect. 21.3.2.2 (hence there are 12 injected synthetic scenarios to demonstrate scope). Further examples of synthetic scenarios can be found in previous work [14].

Three example messages found in the real WoW data set are provided in Table 21.2 (with anonymised naming) to illustrate a message that is a suspicious (message C), a message that warrants a warning as it discusses partial locator information (message F) and a message that is of game context and is therefore not suspicious (message J).

Our synthetic Scenario 3(d)(i) is one example of a typical scenario to be alerted and the messages involved in the conversation are displayed in Table 21.3. This scenario includes sharing of child user information including a day and rough estimate of time that the child will be at a specific location. With some basic analysis and a phone book, a predator could locate the child given this scenario.

Table 21.4 illustrates one scenario that has been shown to be more difficult to detect. This is due to the unfamiliar locator information surrounded with suggestions that the intention of the meeting is WoW related in addition to the conversation being conducted over 10 minutes surrounded by messages of game context.

21.3.4 Tally Methods

A base experiment has been designed for a point of reference to provide a comparison to each of the alternative experimental configurations. Each additional experiment is shown in an evaluation table and is compared to the base experiment. For each experiment the paper also discusses which sample real messages were alerted, the synthetic scenarios alerted during the experiment, and the impact on communicator suspicion positions and ranks for involved members of each scenario.

Group token types are used to categorise alerts in the main evaluation tables. Group token types contain cross-overs where message alerts may be contained in more than one group token type category (due to base token cross-over) and therefore many alerts may be repeated across groupings. For a consistent evaluation duplicate alerts were removed and were counted in the first group they occurred in, in order of the group token types shown in the evaluation tables. The reduction of duplication is limited to the same chat ID, that is, if a person repeats the same message multiple times this is still counted as multiple messages.

The process of selecting false positives is subject to human interpretation. A script was written and used so that once an alert had been classified by expert

Table 21.2 Example real WoW game messages labeled for experiments

Message label	Event type	Instigator	Recipient	Chat message
C	game_whisper	Ogrange	Suzie	Plz send mail to ogrange@hotmail.com
F	game_guild_chat	Howard	Guild	I would rather work atm i want money i work at pizza hut as a delivery driver and dont even earn enough to save for rego or anything it all goes on petrol
J	game_whisper	Mike	Suzie	Love it if you could, Ill meet you at the jetty?

Table 21.3 Scenario (3)(d)(i)

Instigator	Recipient	Chat message
S3di_comm1	Party	So are you coming to tomorrows 4pm raid *Child*?
Child	Party	Nah I have dance class
S3di_comm2	Party	Really? are you good?
Child	Party	I'm ok
S3di_comm1	Party	Do you do that every Thursday?
Child	Party	Yup
S3di_comm1	Party	Is it a good dance school, like one that's hard to get into?
Child	Party	Not really, its just a local one
S3di_comm1	Party	What's it called?
Child	Party	BusyBee dance studio

Table 21.4 Scenario (1)(a)(iii)

Instigator	Recipient	Chat message
S1aiii_comm	Child	Do you want to come to a WoW session with a few others at GameHouse in town?
Child	S1aiii_comm	Sure, when is it?
S1aiii_comm	Child	8pm Saturday
Child	S1aiii_comm	Cool, I'll be there

human evaluation as a true positive, false positive or warning this alert was consistently classified the same throughout each experiment.

The experiments initially involved configuring various user constants including their school, hobbies, address and various other details. One interesting occurrence, due to the configured hobbies being dance and cricket, is the resultant false positives for those regularly talking about dance (in WoW context, that is, dancing in WoW) and about cricket (such as discussions of T.V. hosted cricket games).

21.4 Experiments

This section discusses the experiments that were used to evaluate the design concept. A prototype of the design has been implemented for experimental purposes running under Windows XP and uses the WoW game as an example MMOG. Evaluation of computational feasibility was conducted by timing experiments on an AMD Phenom 8450 2.10 GHz PC.

The experiments assess the negative ranking method used in the design, the token ranking sensitivity, and the impact of different message window sizes when used for determining contextual meaning. To analyse each experiment, we measure the following results compared to the base experiment:

(i) change in overall alert count;
(ii) change in false positives;
(iii) change in alerts to researcher's injected synthetic scenarios and sample real data messages; and
(iv) change in suspicious communicator ranking and positions;
(v) change in computational processing time.

21.4.1 *Base Experiment*

The base experiment of the program involved completing the design, inserting real data into the database, collecting and implementing the constants and regular expressions into the database, determining the ranking for individual tokens, creating a window size to use for determining contextual meaning of a message and then, having completed this, creating and inserting experimental scenarios into the database, configuring the user constants and then running the program. The window size is set to 4 minutes.

The results of the base experiment are displayed in Table 21.5. The results of the evaluation indicate that the amount of alerts is a small percentage (1.27 %) of the overall dataset. While the amount of false positives alerted compared to the total records is very low (at 1.01 %) the amount of false positives compared to the amount of overall alerts is high (1,193 out of 1,504 alerts, 79 %). The overall analysis of this base experiment is that the resultant small amount of alerts is a good result, and the amount of false positives within this alert set is acceptable as the preference is to err on the side of false positives. The contextual message rank for alerts from the base experiment is between 50 (being the floor for an alert rank) and 4,933.

The rank of suspicion for online communicators has been created to demonstrate a possible output using the design. The *suspicious communicator rank* was created by connecting the communicator aliases and ranking these communicators based on alerted message ranks related to the communicator. The suspicious communicator rank is the sum of positive message ranks for messages alerted that are either from or to the communicator. The communicator suspicion ranks from the base experiment range between 0 and 136,419 (with 0 as the floor).

Table 21.5 Base experiment evaluation

Group token types	Messages alerted (includes warnings)	False positives
Address	1,006	872
Day/time	161	120
Phone/mobile	22	14
User constants	68	23
Place/meeting	143	133
Non-game communication devices	104	31
Total for 118,230 records	1,504 (1.27 %)	1,193 (1.01 %)

Table 21.6 Base experiment: sample real messages alerted

Chat ID	Should alert?	Does alert?	Contextual message rank
A	Yes	Yes	100
B	Yes	Yes	1,301
C	Yes	Yes	999
D	Yes	Yes	136
E	No	Yes	110
F	Yes	Yes	53
G	Yes	Yes	1,406
H	Yes	Yes	116
I	Yes	Yes	545
J	No	Yes	56

Table 21.6 illustrates the sample real messages and their alert status. This dataset is used to assess individual messages rather than scenarios of communication. The overall suspicion rank of the communicators involved in this real data is subject to other real communications the identities may have had and therefore is not used for assessment.

The result of the real messages showed two exceptions to the expectations, messages E and J. Message E discusses meeting at a WoW location and results in a false positive. Analysis of message E could be enhanced by the addition of the WoW contextual phrase *"Rebel Camp"* to the constant string list as this indicates a WoW game based location in the message that has been shown to be overlooked in the constant string creation. The rank assigned at approximately −50 would be appropriate as this is a standard WoW game specific location token rank. The context of message J (shown in Sect. 21.3.3) and surrounding messages was WoW game based (the word *"jetty"* was intended as the WoW game jetty location) yet this message also alerted. Again, the addition of a few negative ranked tokens for WoW context phrases in the surrounding messages would have achieved a better result.

Table 21.7 Base experiment: scenarios alerted

Scenario	Scenario alerted?	Highest contextual message rank
1(a)(i)	Yes	2,821
1(a)(ii)	Yes	2,063
1(a)(iii)	No	N/A
1(b)(i)	Yes	423
2(c)(i)	Yes	3,025
2(c)(ii)	Yes	458
2(c)(iii)	Yes	446
3(d)(i)	Yes	1,140
3(d)(ii)	Yes	1,037
3(d)(iii)	Yes	1,015
4(e)(i)	Yes	3,490
4(f)(i)	Yes	4,861

That is, the surrounding messages with WoW locations *"Feralas"* and *"Thousand Needles"* plus the WoW level indicator acronym *"lvl"* would have a better effect on the contextual analysis process if these locations were added and altered to a rank of −50. The rank results of the remainder of the messages appeared reasonable.

Table 21.7 illustrates the synthetic scenarios and alerts. The synthetic scenarios included groups of up to eight messages to form a conversation. The result was that except for one scenario, all synthetic scenarios were alerted and related communicators were highlighted as suspicious. The exception case Scenario 1(a)(iii) (shown in Sect. 21.3.3) did not show sufficient indicators to be identified. The place *"GameHouse"* is unknown in the database (and represents a relatively realistic occurrence) and does not highlight a place. The phrases *"do you want to come to"*, *"I'll be there"*, could be added to the database however, this would be a limited overall solution. It may be more useful to consider adding some regular expressions with enhanced pattern matching for these types of phrases.

Table 21.8 shows communicators involved in the synthetic scenarios, their suspicious communicator position and their rank. Only identities involved in synthetic scenarios are highlighted when assessing suspicious communicator positions and ranks as other identities (such as real data identities) have positions and ranks that are dependent on other real data messages. The overall positioning of each synthetic entity is subject to the positioning of real entities and the data involved in their communications however, the positioning and ranking table is both indicative of whether the synthetic communicators are identified as suspicious and useful for comparison to alternative experiments. The result of the suspicious communicator analysis shows scenario communicators with relevant ranks, *communicator S2aiii_comm* has a 0 rank as Scenario 1(a)(iii) did not alert.

The base experiment token update processing time is 4 hours, 2 minutes and 8 seconds. The base experiment analysis processing time is 7 hours 46 minutes and 56 seconds. Note that the processing time is for a substantial amount of data and a typical weekly run of the system of would process drastically faster. For example,

Table 21.8 Base experiment: suspicious communicators

Alias(es)	Position	Communicator rank
S1ai_comm	7	25,389
S1aii_comm	17	8,242
S1aiii_comm	N/A	0
S1bi_comm	111	1,281
S2ci_comm	12	18,150
S2cii_comm	200	458
S2cii_other	200	458
S2ciii_comm1	110	1,293
S2ciii_comm2	110	1,293
S2ciii_comm3	110	1,293
S3di_comm1	34	4,643
S3di_comm2	34	4,643
S3dii_comm	33	5,095
S3diii_comm1	54	3,045
S3diii_comm2	54	3,045
S4ei_comm, S4ei_comm@hotmail.com	14	16,702

based on the researchers normal game play, 3,000 messages per week would occur taking approximately 8 minutes to process using the unoptimised prototype on the above said machine. Using this example and the percentages shown for the base experiment as a rough guide, this would result in around 38 alerts per week. This estimate differs from that in previous works due to extensions to the rule base in the prototype. Further enhancements to the prototype such as incorporating exclusions rules for messages with specific properties would see these estimates altered.

21.4.2 Negative Ranking Removed

The concept of using both positive and negative ranks for tokens evolved from attempting to find contextual meaning in the messages. Tokens that indicate WoW context are ranked negatively. The desired impact of negative token ranks is negating messages that are of WoW context. The impact of using negative ranking is shown by comparing the base experiment to Table 21.9 which shows the result of only positive token ranks (that is, all negative ranks are replaced with the zero value).

Removing negative ranking adds a great deal more alerts and false positives. Overall, there was a 236 % increase in alerts, a 285 % increase in false positives, and there was a 18.76 % decrease in the processing time for the token updates component and a 31.76 % decrease in processing time for the analysis and output stage. The processing time decrease demonstrates the computational impact of the negative ranking usage.

Table 21.9 Negative ranking removed: evaluation

Group token types	Messages alerted (includes warnings)	Messages alerted compared to base experiment	False positives	False positives compared to the base experiment
Address	3,623	+2,617	3,411	+2,539
Day/time	456	+295	382	+262
Phone/mobile	138	+116	127	+113
User constants	116	+48	65	+42
Place/meeting	589	+446	558	+425
Non-game communication devices	138	+34	59	+28
Total for 118,230 records	5,060 (4.28 %)	+3,556 (+236.44 %)	4,602 (3.89 %)	+3,409 (+285.75 %)

The messages alerted from the sample of real messages were the same as the base experiment except for a higher rank for message F. Message F was ranked lower in the base experiment due to WoW contextual surrounding messages. The discussion is about a communicator working at Pizza Hut (see Sect. 21.3.3) yet contains no suburb information related to their workplace, therefore the lower rank in the base experiment was more appropriate. In addition, message J was ranked higher due to the contextual ranking (negative ranking) being removed. Message J is not suspicious and results in a false positive alert, an increase in it's rank demonstrates the use of negative ranking in the design as better alternative.

Of the synthetic scenarios, Scenario 1(a)(iii) alerts whereas it did not in the base experiment. The difference being only a small amount at a rank of 57 whereas in the base experiment the rank was under 50 (where 50 is the floor rank for an alert). Scenario 1(a)(iii) is not an easily detectable scenario, while it is good that this experiment detected it, it would be better to find a general method to introduce to detect this particular type of scenario rather than to endure the substantial increase in false positives.

The suspicious communicator list resulted in lower positioning for communicators yet similar ranks compared to the base experiment. This occurs due to many more communicators being alerted based on false positives. *S1aiii_comm* ranked higher due to the scenario alert being slightly higher, having said that, it was a very low position (of 832).

One anomaly found in this dataset was the addition of alerts of a few messages indicating a certain player attended TAFE (Technical and Further Education) and gave indication of what time they would be attending. No name of the TAFE was provided, even so, the lack of alerting in the base experiment suggests that the ranking for *"TAFE"* would need adjustment as this message is relevant to a child being able to physically locate an adult game player.

The experiment demonstrates that with no major improvement to the true positive and warnings alert count there was a major increase in the false positives. Therefore the experiment of removing the negative ranking showed that the negative ranking is an effective method of differentiating contextual meaning in the messages.

21.4.3 Ranking Sensitivity

Token ranking is a sensitive component to the design. The next experiment is designed to evaluate the impact of token ranking values. One example that demonstrates the design to be sensitive to token ranks is the case of ranking an address street format. An example address format is *"Number Street-Name Suffix"* such as *"20 Margaret St"*. The design regular expression matches on this format and then validates the suffix to determine if real locator data is being shared. The WoW game has many examples where similar text is expressed with different meaning. The following are examples of components of WoW comments that match a valid address street format: (Note that Av, Pts, Run, St are valid suffixes)

- *10 fresh run* (suggests ten people are needed for a new run of a WoW raid)
- *3 skill pts* (message discusses three WoW game skill points)
- *3 more AV* (message meaning three more marks are required from the WoW Alterac Valley battleground)
- *5 at ST* (meaning five players are positioned at Stables in WoW Arathi Basin battleground)
- *10 achievement run* (message meaning Naxx 10 player raid was about to run as a WoW achievement gaining process)

Careful consideration should be taken in matching the address street format tokens to a rank. The base experiment of the program showed results where the address street format is ranked 500. As an example, Table 21.10 illustrates the evaluation results where the address street format is ranked with the lower rank of 100. The results are less overall alerts and less false positives.

The real message alerts and contextual message ranks were identical to that of the base experiment. In this experiment, of the synthetic scenarios, Scenario 1(b)(i) is not alerted. This scenario is a clear example of an offline meeting being arranged and hence should alert. It has not been alerted due to the low rank of the street format and other scenario tokens being outweighed by the surrounding WoW based contextual messages.

The positions and ranks of suspicious communicators are similar to the base experiment however the rank was substantially lower for *S1bi_comm* which is expected due to Scenario 1(b)(i) not alerting. The communicator is still given a rank in this instance due to the configuration of the suspicious communicator rank floor being lower than that configured for the contextual message rank floor for alerts/output.

Overall there was a 32.58 % decrease in the alerts and a 39.15 % decrease in false positives. The token update stage processing time was increased by 1.03 % and the processing time for the analysis and output was decreased by 11.54 %. Suspicious messages from Scenario 1(b)(i) did not alert. This experiment shows the design is sensitive to ranking. It is preferable to have more false positives (as in the base experiment) in preference to a false negative. An alternative to the base experiment is to have the lower address format rank (to reduce false positives) yet incorporate

Table 21.10 Lower rank for street format: evaluation

Group token Types	Message alerted (includes warnings)	Messages alerted compared to base experiment	False positives	False positives compared to the base experiment
Address	625	−381	506	−366
Day/time	109	−52	73	−47
Phone/mobile	17	−5	9	−5
User constants	65	−3	20	−3
Place/meeting	95	−48	88	−45
Non-game communication devices	103	−1	30	−1
Total for 118,230 records	1014 (0.86 %)	−490 (−32.58 %)	726 (0.61 %)	−467 (−39.15 %)

into the WoW list an alternative check to determine if the address street format is more likely to have WoW game meaning so as to detect scenarios like Scenario 1(b)(i), however this would be game specific.

21.4.4 Window Size Experiments

The concept of a message window is explained and illustrated in Sect. 21.2.1.4. The message window is used as a guide to determine contextual significance within a configurable time frame, the size of the window is flexible. The base experiment uses 2 minutes either side of the message under investigation to determine contextual ranking. We have also evaluated the use of alternative window sizes to the base experiment to determine how precision varies with window size and the results are displayed in Fig. 21.3.

Figure 21.3 shows a spike of alerts, false positives, true positives and warnings when using a 4 minute message window. The true positives and warnings improves by 11 % from a 1 minute window size to a slight peak at the 4 minute window size then remains relatively constant. This trend would suggest that to capture the most true positives and valid warnings the message window would remain at 4 minutes yet the spike in false positives is pronounced (increases by 36% over same time period). The best choice for a conservative parent is a window size of 4 minutes. We now discuss alternative window size experiments to identify their main impact when compared to the base experiment window size of 4 minutes.

21.4.4.1 Twenty Minute Window Size

The overall alert count and false positives are slightly reduced compared to the base experiment with a 5.39 % decrease in the alert count, a 6.29 % decrease in false

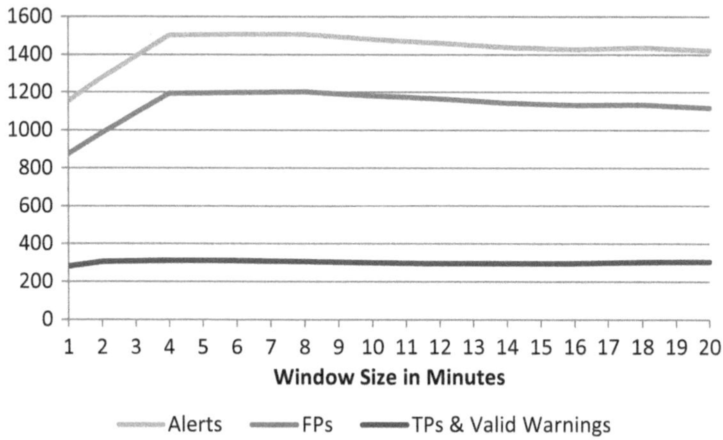

Fig. 21.3 Window size trend

positives. The processing time for the analysis and output stage was increased by 64.96 % (the token update stage is unaffected by the window size for analysis).

Sample real messages A and F did not alert due to 20 minutes of surrounding WoW contextual data to influence the assessment of the contextual meaning of the messages. The absence of these two messages in the alerts is not of high significance as they both of should result in a warning alert only. Non-suspicious messages E and J do not alert in this experiment which is a good result. Other sample real messages have either higher or lower ranks based on the additional surrounding messages.

Synthetic scenarios alerted for this experiment are the same as for the base experiment and contain reasonably similar contextual rankings however some ranks where subject to the assessed contextual meaning of surrounding messages. There was a mixed change in positions and ranking for suspicious communicators again due to dependence on the additional surrounding messages.

Overall the changes compared to the base experiment were insignificant, not alerting to two of the sample real messages A and F while not major (given their type) with only a marginal reduction in false positives would suggest the base experiment a better alternative.

21.4.4.2 One Minute Window Size

For this experiment the overall alert count reduced by 23.2 %, false positives reduced by 26.66 % and processing time of the analysis and output stage decreased by 24.48 %.

The experiment showed the same real data message alerts and similar ranks with the exception of a warning for message F. The experiment showed that same synthetic scenarios alerted as in the base experiment however Scenario 1(a)(ii) had only half the base experiment rank. This scenario was conversed over 3 minutes where the message window was 1 minute, therefore while individual messages where all alerted correctly, the contextual message rank was only calculated for those within a 1 minute time frame, showing multiple alerts with lower ranks and a highest contextual rank lower than the base experiment.

Suspicious communicator positions and ranks were similar to the base experiment, with the exception of those involved in conversations spanning greater than 1 minute. This experiment, when compared to other experiments, indicated the context of the surrounding messages to have little impact, it was the time frame of scenario communication combined with the shorter contextual window time frame that had an impact on the contextual message ranks along with associated communicator ranks and positions. The experiment does not distinguish suspicious message from more trivial alerts as effectively as the base experiment had achieved using rank values.

21.4.4.3 Four Minute Alternative Window Size

This experiment showed a slight reduction in alerts of 4.81 % and reduction of false positives by 6.68 %. The processing time was reduced by 1.68 %. The experiment shows some very minor improvement in alerts, false positives and processing time over the base experiment. The experiment shows similar scenario alerts and suspicious communicator ranks and positions, yet does not give an alert for message F. While this is an acceptable result it is better to make the alert and accept the additional few false positives.

In summary the message window time frame does not significantly impact on the design as much as the negative ranking method and the token ranking. The time frame experiments highlight the need to determine and to distinguishes between a "typical WoW conversation time frame" compared to a "typical general conversation time frame in WoW". Applying the design to alternative MMOGs would require this assessment for all game types therefore a general framework for determining this in MMOGs would be useful.

21.4.5 Quantitative Scenarios

In addition to the previous experiments and the use of synthetic scenarios as described earlier, we conducted some further experiments using the real communication of adults and children. To do so, we called for volunteers of diverse culture, age (children and adults) and backgrounds to offer further synthetic scenarios so as to demonstrate the capabilities of the design in both an objective and more quantitative manner. This further experimentation used conversations from adults of various age generations and school children aged 12–14. The school children created communication scenarios as part of a paired activity with other students which was prepared and monitored by their teachers as a component of their education on cyber-awareness and cyber-bullying during the National Day of Action Against Bullying and Violence.

The volunteers were asked to each craft one scenario with one of the following properties:

(i) The scenario indicates an offline meeting is being arranged; or
(ii) The scenario provides sufficient locator information for one communicator to be located.

In total 34 scenarios (277 messages) were injected into the database amongst other data within 4 minute conversation time frames. The result was that 30 of these scenarios had messages alerted and were detected (88 %). Those that were not detected were shown to be surrounded with significant WoW contextual messages which out-ranked that of the scenarios.

To verify the cause of unalerted scenarios a new experiment was conducted. The prototype contextual analysis was refined to only include those surrounding messages that involved one of the communicators from the message under investigation (this includes individual or group communicators). 100% of the volunteer scenarios were then detected due to synthetic scenarios having no surrounding messages that alter the contextual message rank of the message under investigation when this rule is applied. This experiment demonstrates that the prototype identifies the scenarios with accuracy yet the contextual analysis is the area to be focused on for refining the prototype. The use of such a rule assumes alias detection is accurate for instances when a MMOG player uses more than one account (uncommon) or changes their character use within a conversation (more common). The use of the rule reduces false positives by 12.83 % when compared to the base experiment. The contextual analysis can be further improved in the prototype by expanding it to incorporate more complex analysis, such as, rules that gather information over time.

21.5 Conclusions

This paper has discussed a design for the detection of potentially hazardous relationships being formed with a child playing a MMOG. A design was outlined and then evaluated using a prototype to conduct experiments to demonstrate the design. The evaluation included experiments to assess the following design components: the negative ranking method; the token ranking sensitivity and; the message window size. Further experiments used a larger set of volunteered data created by impartial volunteers so as to further assess the design reliability using a quantitative approach.

The evaluation showed the negative ranking system within the design to be a highly effective technique for determining message contextual meaning. The design was shown to be subject to token ranking sensitivity which suggests fine tuning token ranks would improve the overall results. Message window size was assessed as having a peak of true positives and valid warnings where the size was 4 minutes. The message window was demonstrated to have less impact on overall reliability when compared to other design components. The quantitative experiment showed a 88 % detection rate and demonstrated the contextual analysis method to be an area that would most benefit from improvement. Overall, the evaluation showed the design to be effective and feasible.

One area of further research we propose involves altering the design to first analyse whether the communicator is an adult talking to the child. Achievements have been made in this direction for example that by Walkerdine et al. [19] who have shown it possible to determine the age and gender of a chat room user. Methods used during their and other related research may be useful for incorporating into the ranking approach used to detect suspicious messages in this research for MMOG environments.

References

1. Australian Government: NetAlert. Last accessed September 2007: www.netalert.gov.au
2. Caplan, S., Williams, D., Yee, N.: Problematic Internet use and psychosocial well-being among MMO players. Comput. Human Behav. **25**(6), 1312–1319 (2009)
3. Chen, H., Goldberg, M., Magdon-Ismail, M.: Identifying multi-ID users in open forums. In: Proceedings of the 2nd NSF/NIJ Symposium on Intelligence and Security Informatics (ISI 04), Tucson. Springer (2004)
4. Cooper, A.: Sexuality and the internet: surfing into the new millennium. Cyberpsychol. Behav. **1**, 187–193 (1998)
5. CRISP Thinking: NetModerator. Last accessed May 2010: www.crispthinking.com
6. GamePolitics.com: FBI: Pedophile Met Would-be Victim in World of Warcraft (World of Warcraft), 25 Jun 2008. Last accessed December 2010: http://www.gamepolitics.com/2008/06/25/fbi-pedophile-met-would-be-victim-world-warcraft
7. Habbo: Last accessed December 2010: www.habbo.com
8. Higginbottom N. and Packham B.: Student cracks Government's $84m porn filter, Aug 2007. Last accessed September 2007: http://www.news.com.au/dailytelegraph/story/0,22049,22304224-5005941,00.html
9. Hinduja, S., Schafer, J. A.: US cybercrime units on the world wide web. An International Journal of Police Strategies & Management **32**(2), 278–296 (2009)
10. Hughes, D., Gibson, S., Walkerdine, J., Coulson, G.: Is deviant behaviour the norm on P2P file sharing networks? IEEE Distrib. Syst. Online **7**(2), 1–11 (2006)
11. Koch W.: Predators use gaming consoles to 'get foot in the door'. USA Today, 7 Feb 2008. Last accessed December 2010: http://www.usatoday.com/tech/news/2008-07-01-porn_N.htm
12. Middleton, D.: Internet Sex Offenders. In: Beech, A.R., Craig, L., Browne, K.D. (eds.) Assessment and Treatment of Sex Offenders: A Handbook, Wiley, NY, pp. 199–215 (2009)
13. National News: World of Warcraft pedophile stole teen girl, 30 June 2008. Last accessed January 2009: http://www.news.com.au/story/0,23599,23944622-421,00.html?from=public_rss
14. Penna, L., Clark, A., Mohay, G.: A framework for improved adolescent and child safety in MMOs. In: Memon, N., Alhajj, R. (eds.) 2010 International Conference on Advances in Social Network Analysis and Mining (ASONAM 2010), IEEE Computer Society, University of Southern Denmark, Odense, pp. 33–40 (2010)
15. Penna, L., Clark, A., Mohay, G.: Challenges of automating the detection of paedophile activity on the internet. In: Proceedings of Systematic Approaches to Digital Forensic Engineering (SADFE'2005), Taiwan, pp. 206–222 (2005)
16. Quayle, E., Holland, G., Linehand, C., Taylor, M.: The internet and offending behaviour: a case study. J. Sex. Aggress. **6**, 78–96 (2000)

17. Rashid, A., Rayson, P., Greenwood, P., Walkerdine, J., Duquenoy, P., Watson, P., Brennan, M., Jones, M.: Isis: Protecting Children in Online Social Networks. In: At the International Conference on Advances in the Analysis of Online Paedophile Activity, Paris, June 2009
18. Spam Assassin: Last accessed May 2010: www.spamassassin.com
19. Walkerdine, J., Greenwood, P., Rashid, A., Rayson, P., May-Chahal, C., Duquenoy, P., Watson, P., Jones, M., Brennan, M.: Forensics Software for Detecting Online Paedophile Activity. in ICT that makes the Difference, Brussels (2009)

Chapter 22
An Adaptive Framework for Discovery and Mining of User Profiles from Social Web-Based Interest Communities

Nima Dokoohaki and Mihhail Matskin

Abstract Within this paper we introduce an adaptive framework for semi- to fully-automatic discovery, acquisition and mining of topic style interest profiles from openly accessible social web communities. To do such, we build an adaptive taxonomy search tree from target domain (domain towards which we are gathering and processing profiles for), starting with generic concepts at root moving down to specific-level instances at leaves, then we utilize one of proposed Quest schemes to read the concept labels from the tree and crawl the source social network repositories for profiles containing matching and related topics. Using machine learning techniques, cached profiles are then mined in two consecutive steps, utilizing a clusterer and a classifier in order to assign and predict correct profiles to their corresponding clustered corpus, which are retrieved later on by an ontology-based recommender to suggest and recommend the community members with the items of their similar interest. Focusing on increasingly important digital cultural heritage context, using a set of profiles acquired from an openly accessible social network, we test the accuracy and adaptivity of framework. We will show that a tradeoff between schemes proposed can lead to adaptive discovery of highly relevant profiles.

N. Dokoohaki (✉)
Software and Computer Systems (SCS), School of Information and Telecommunication Technology (ICT), Royal Institute of Technology (KTH), Stockholm, Sweden
e-mail: nimad@kth.se

M. Matskin
Computer and Information Science (IDI), Norwegian University of Science and Technology (NTNU), Trondheim, Norway
e-mail: misha@kth.se

T. Özyer et al. (eds.), *The Influence of Technology on Social Network Analysis and Mining*, Lecture Notes in Social Networks 6, DOI 10.1007/978-3-7091-1346-2_22,

22.1 Introduction

As web of interrelated content is gradually giving its place to web of interpersonal content, classical problems of information retrieval continue to persist. Much of this content lies within the heart of social web. At the same time publication means are becoming more and more easily available to both human and machine publishers. As these publication mediums increase their production pace day by day, it becomes harder for human readers to find and retrieve the exact content which they are looking for.

Adaptive Web and its myriads of approaches, specifically recommendation techniques and approaches have proven to be good candidates in dealing with retrieval of relevant information, by providing users with suggested contents of their taste. One infamous problem for recommendation techniques to function properly is the sparsity of the usage data. One might want to build a recommender at the top of a content library already available, to provide users with suggestions while lack of enough user data hinders the functionality of the system. To deal with this problem, one can propose for discovery of interested users, acquisition of their explicit interests and processing their profiles for generating suggestions of items that might be of their interest to buy or view. As lots of such users document and share their daily activities within social networks these days, social web can be a possible repository to discover such users. At the same time users utilize topic style profiles to express their interests. While individual profiles might contain topics of different and sometimes conflicting topics. Some social networking sites and services, such as LiveJournal [1], provide means for community formation, where individuals of same interest gather to share information items of same interest. As a result, community profiles seem to be more suitable for our task as they provide a rather focused type of topic terms, as of compared to individual profiles. To build such a framework, we propose for a semi- to fully- automatic framework mainly composed of a crawler and a learner, in which the crawler harvests the source repository for profiles and caches them. After data normalization and dataset preparation, miner reads and analyzes raw profiles and applies clustering to gathered data to generate clusters of interrelated topics and their corresponding profiles. To increase the accuracy of the overall learning, clusters are stored and fed into a classifier to evaluate and assess the correct assignments of clusters to topics and their corresponding profiles. Second learning process also helps creating an initial probability distribution over all interrelated topic set, which could be used later on by a semantically enhanced recommender or a simple topic recommender as initial point to generate recommendation for the corresponding members of the communities. For the crawler to be able to discover relevant profiles, we need to build a taxonomy tree with leaves containing terms of the domain for which we are discovering profiles for. For instance, if were looking for communities of art, then crawler needs to formulate queries with terms around or related to domain of art. Consequently, we use the tree to formulate queries that are used eventually by the crawler to cache the discovered profiles. To be able to intelligently and effectively formulate these queries heuristics can be proposed toward which queries are formulated.

As a matter of fact, we have defined three schemes (or schemes), namely: depth-based, allowing for discovering and crawling for topics on a certain taxonomy tree-depth at each time, n-split, allowing iterative discovery and crawling of all topics while at each iteration gathered data is split for n-times, and finally greedy, which allows for discovery and crawling the network for all topics and processing the cached data altogether. We study this framework in the context of discovering possible interested communities of individuals from LiveJournal, an openly accessible social blogging journal and network. To focus the task of the framework onto a certain domain, we hypothesize gathering and processing data for two on-line museums that are seeking communities and individuals of related interest to recommend information items pertaining to their artifacts to. We evaluate the effectiveness of framework from the two perspectives: firstly, accuracy of the mining steps and secondly, the adaptivity of the outputs of learner from the perspective of lexical relevance to the query. To accomplish the former, we study the accuracy of the miners clustering and classification performance with respect to each scheme proposed. To justify the latter, a basic lexical parser is used to assess the relevance of the top terms in each cluster groups with respect to each scheme.

The rest of this manuscript is structured as follows: first a background overview will be given, and then approach is introduced, followed by introduction of three mining schemes proposed. This is followed by introduction of the framework, which contains the description of the learners, while last section describes the experiment with two museums followed by evaluation results. And finally a conclusion and future work section brings this manuscript to its end.

22.2 Related Work

User profiles play a crucial role in the context of adaptivity enabled, and personalization empowered information systems.

Availability of profiles is vital for these systems to function properly. As a result, we can see the problem from two perspectives: firstly, discovering the users and acquiring the knowledge pertaining to their profiles, and secondly, mining these gathered data to find useful patterns that can be consumed by a recommender for personalized recommendation generation. Focusing on the former, discovering and sharing interest profiles across websites has been under focus by many researchers. Ghosh and Dekhil [2] argue that profile construction and discovery on the web can be augmented to address the sparseness of the profile data, as well as improving the content of the profiles. Teevan et al. [3], study heuristics for discovering and processing the prior interactions (profiles) of users for the task of search personalization on behalf of the users. This problem becomes more important when personalization is cross-platform and cross-domain [4]. To profile users across multiple domains, ontology-driven user profiles [5, 6] are utilized. As a result many researchers have discussed the issue of discovering and retrieving profiles across multiple domains within the context of ontological user profiles [7–12]. Gauch et al. [13], give a complete overview of different models of discovery and retrieval for ontology-based user profiling. Problem with these models are that most of these models are either focused on modeling the user profiles rather than discovery or harvesting them, or they are focused on generic web context while we are more interested in social web context.

When harvesting and acquiring profiles becomes trivial, problem of dealing with sparse data becomes the most important issue under focus. To address this problem, researchers approach different methodologies to gather, analyze and generate user profiles. This is usually done through applying machine learning techniques to web data [14]. Utilizing these techniques has been very appealing for personalization tasks [15–17]. For instance, techniques such as clustering of user transactions [18], data mining techniques such as clustering [19] and web usage mining techniques [20], were proposed to support personalization needs. This field is collectively referred to as web mining for personalization [16]. Mining web content for personalization has been attractive to addressing inherent problems of recommender systems [21]. More specifically two types of recommenders have been dependant on myriads of machine learning techniques for their functionality, namely content-based [22] and collaborative filtering recommenders [23]. Agent-assisted personalization has been a target domain for applied user profiling. Soltysiak and Crabtree [24] describe the architecture for an agent- based approach for user profiling and automatic generation of profiles using machine learning techniques. In a similar work, Billsus and Pazzani [25] utilize the same heuristics for learning Web user profiles. They use a nave Bayesian classifier for discovery and identification of interesting websites for supporting the personalization task of users on whose behalf the profiles are created and maintained. With respect to second problem mentioned, it seems that most of the literature at hand is focused on generating aggregate usage history from an already cached and stored usage experience. This is while not much attention has been paid to addressing the problem of formulating profiles when no experience data is available. Thats why discovery of users has become crucial to assist the task of profile generation [26].

If explicit interests of the users are already at hand, one can propose for utilization of these interest descriptions for creation of possible user profiles. While such data can be found nowadays in social web context, then social web can serve as a novel or complementary source for discovery and harvesting of profiles of relevant interest. Users tend to often express such interests in the form of bag-of-words [27] or simply topics [28]. As a result scientists are proposing new methodologies for generating profiles for users from these topics and utilizing them for supporting recommender systems. These methods are often utilizing text classification schemes [29], or more recently topic modeling techniques [30]. While speaking of data mining in social networks, current literature points out to applying statistical analysis for uncovering network structures [31], rather than content. Most related work to our work is presented by Liu and Maes [32]. Focusing on the social networking services context, Liu and Maes propose for building models out of interests and tastes which are harvested out of Orkut, and leveraging it for addressing the sparsity of recommendation software. Inspired by Liu and Maes, within this paper, we have proposed for Quest [33], a framework for harvesting and mining topic-based interest profiles from online social networks. This framework combines web mining architecture and profile generation techniques, but we put more emphasis on the actual profile generation process. While the former part helps for harvesting the profiles from the network, the latter part helps mining and learning groupings of profiles according to their shared interest topics. We use a two step miner (similar to e.g. work of Soltysiak and Crabtree [24]), through which first we cluster the profiles according to their common topics, while the second step assesses the assignment of profiles to their correct categories and clusters using a classifier. We focus our experiments on data acquired from social blogging site, LiveJournal [1].

22.3 Quest-Driven Social Web Mining Architecture

In this section we outline the architecture of the miner as well as the detailed process of learning phase. Many social networking sites are paving the path for ease of publication and sharing of users content within their boundaries. At the same time ease of publication and open expression of interests [28], allow for adaptive technologies to spot and attract customers to on-line libraries of materials or goods, which could be eventually purchased by interested customers. To exploit this feature we design a framework (Fig. 22.1) at the top of a source social network, which allows for a semi-automatic supervised approach utilizing taxonomy assisted crawler and a two-step learner to first of all gather, then process and finally generate what we refer to as initial user profiles.

Through the knowledge flow created across this framework, we harvest the crawled interest topics from the source repositories, and cache them. Then following the normalization process we prepare them to be fed into the input of the mining process. Using the two step learner, we group them into clusters of profiles and their interrelated topics. The clusters are consecutively fed into the classifier. Classifying learner assesses and evaluates correct assignment of profiles to their corresponding clusters for further precision. After clusters resulting from previous step are classified, a predictive model of clusters along with their probabilistic weights, are generated as output of classifier. We refer to the output in this step as initial user profiles. Using classified clusters of profiles along with the weights generated by the classifier the semantic recommender can create a predictive recommendation set. As designing the mining process has been the main focus of this work, we leave the recommendation generation for the future work. In the following section we focus on structure of the taxonomy tree, followed by the descriptions of our schemes and how they affect the overall knowledge flow.

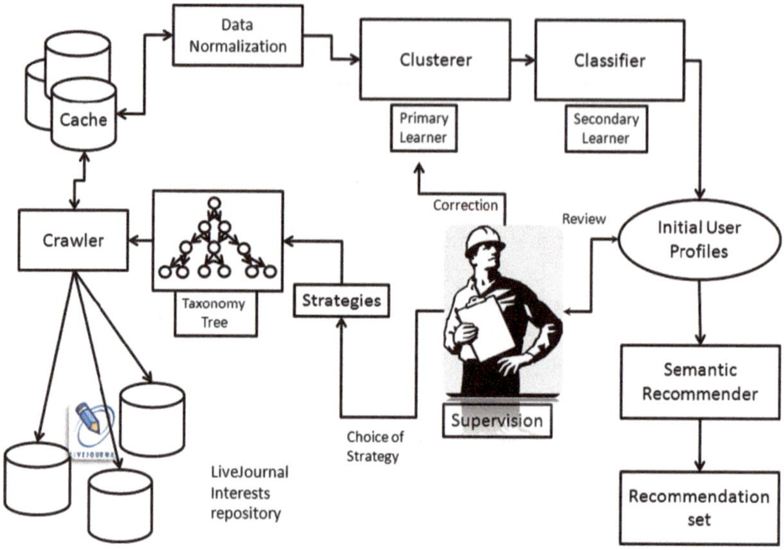

Fig. 22.1 Quest component architecture and knowledge flow

22.3.1 Utilizing Concept Taxonomies for Automating Profile Discovery Process

In order to specify those topics which are used for discovering and acquisition of relevant data for mining segment to work on, we should have a partial to rather complete knowledge of which topics are needed to query for. This knowledge could be described semantically utilizing a taxonomical hierarchy comprising of topics surrounding the target domain, towards which were gathering and processing data for [34, 35]. We have adopted this idea as the solution to the problem at hand and designed a basic taxonomy tree composed of an isa relationship in addition to a hierarchy, where the deeper the topics lie, the more specific the topics become while the root of the tree is the central topic to the domain at hand. Taxonomy is formulated as a tree consisting of nodes representing distinguished topics. In a general case taxonomy could be derived or constructed from an ontological presentation of the domain. In such taxonomy edges represent the subtopic relationship [36].

In our experiment, we focused on the context of cultural heritage in main and further focus was given to two specific museums, one maintaining artifacts of the art, historical paintings, and the other maintaining artifacts of science, scientific historical instruments such as physics. Further detail regarding the taxonomy and concepts incorporated in it is presented in the experiment part. Topics are chosen from general topics corresponding to cultural heritage domain (root topic), and as we move to lower levels we see the branches towards each museum, while museum itself forms a concept and the leaves present the exhibits corresponding to the

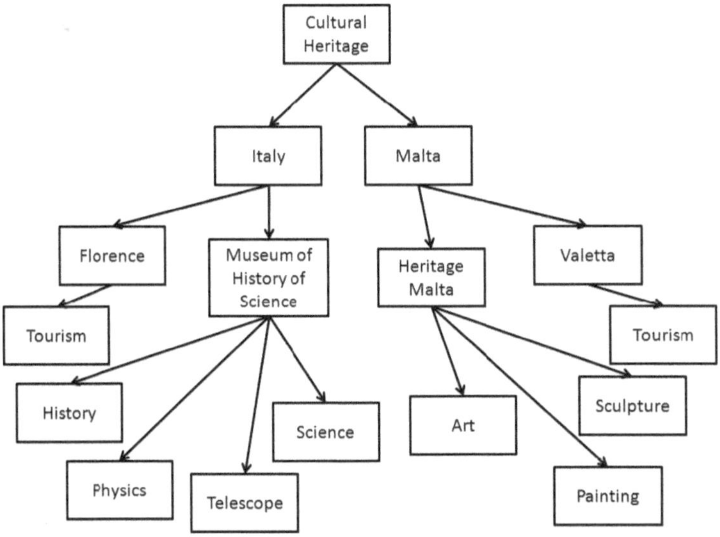

Fig. 22.2 Primary taxonomy tree constructed from cultural heritage domain under study

museums, so for the artistic museum we can observe topics related to art such as sculpture, while in the case of scientific exhibit, we observe topics such as telescope. It is worth mentioning that this taxonomical classification could be more complete and at the same time more complex. But this poses a tradeoff to search: the more detailed the tree becomes, the less probable it becomes to actually find interested people, as the terms they use to express their interests are very broad. As mentioned earlier, its arguable that If granularity of the knowledge of domain exceeds a partial set of topics, as taken into account in our case, then a full ontology can be considered instead [36]. This poses a tradeoff where the more detailed the topics become the less probable becomes to actually find any interested individual or community in that certain topic becomes. Experiments presented later justify this matter to some extent. At the same time if partial knowledge of the domain needs to be extended, one can consider mining semantically relevant topics surrounding the topics of the existing topic and expanding the tree along the depth and width with interrelated topics. This has been taken into account for extension of the experiments in future work (Fig. 22.2).

22.3.2 *Intelligent Query Formulation Using Quest Schematics*

To study the effectiveness of the approaches proposed for discovering and retrieval of possible matches across the network, we have proposed for a set of schemes among which depending on the need for effectiveness or efficiency, scheme designer or mining supervisor can make a choice.

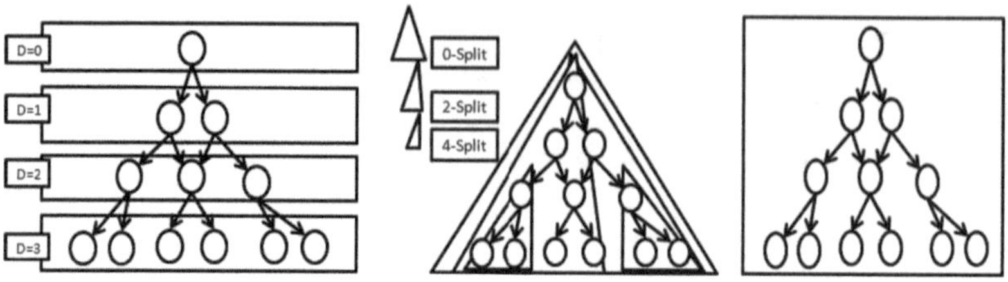

Fig. 22.3 Visualized schematics for depth-based (*top*), N-Split (*middle*) and greedy quest (*bottom*); each boundary visualizes the concepts that formulate the queries

To do so, we define Φ as a query set as $\Phi = \{T_1, T_2, T_3, \ldots, T_n\}$ in which Φ is a query that consisting of n topics T_i. Taken into account this assumption we define the quest schematics in following sections.

22.3.2.1 Depth-Based Quest

Depth-based quest is an iterative decremental scheme. When working within the framework of this scheme in each iteration, starting from the root, topics are taken from a certain depth of taxonomy tree (depth d), and are used to fill the query Φ to harvest the network for matching interest results. On the next iteration next depth $d + 1$ is taken into account, and the same step is repeated, and this mechanism iterates until the leaves of the taxonomy tree are reached. For example, in Fig. 22.3 taxonomy tree has depth $d = 4$, and scheme iterates four times, accordingly. As a result:

$$\Phi_{depth} = \{\lceil T_1 \rceil_{d=0}, \lceil T_1, T_2 \rceil_{d=1}, \ldots, \lceil T_n, T_{n-1} \rceil_d\}$$

Where Φ_{depth} is the query formulated according to depth-based scheme and $\lceil T_n, T_{n-1} \rceil_d$ is a set of n topics taken from depth d of the taxonomy tree.

22.3.2.2 Split-Based Quest

N-Split (Split) is an iterative scheme through which a subset (a split) of the taxonomy tree is digested into the query formula to be executed. We iterate over and over the query topics, until the size of split becomes lower or equal to a single topic. Returning results are incrementally cached. In this schematics, it is important which number of splits is chosen. Figure 22.3 depicts the geometry of splits. For instance, in Fig. 22.3, three splits are displayed as triangles of different size. Even splits. As a result:

$$\Phi_{split} = \{\lceil T_1 \ldots T_3 \rceil, \lceil T_4 \ldots T_8 \rceil, \ldots, \lceil T_{n-4}, T_n \rceil_d\}$$

Where Φ_{split} is the query formulated according to split-based scheme, $\lceil T_{n-4}, T_n \rceil_d$ is a split topic set, divided by the size of n, e.g. $n = 4$.

22.3.2.3 Greedy-Based Quest

Greedy or all-at-once strategy is an incremental strategy, in which all topics within the tree are taken incrementally and are utilized to fill the query formula. As a result:

$$\Phi_{greedy} = \{\lceil T_1 \ldots T_n \rceil\}$$

In which, Φ_{greedy} is the query formulated according to Greedy strategy, and $\lceil T_1 \ldots T_n \rceil$ is a set on n topics that exist in the taxonomy tree.

22.3.3 *Mining for Quest*

While quest strategies allow for intelligent query formulation against the interest topics available in the profiles, retrieved matches need to be processed in the next step accordingly to generate profiles consumable by recommender system. To deal with interest topics gathered from the social network, we have proposed for a two-step mining process. In this process we reduce dimensionality of topic attributes through a clustering methodology, and we form centroid around the topics which are originally taken from taxonomy tree. Clusters are respectively fed into a function, typically a classifier, which eventually generates our initial profiles.

22.3.3.1 Clustering of Profiles

For a query Φ, containing t_i topics we retrieve a set of profiles. We define p_l as the set of l profiles that have been retrieved with respect to our query as follows:

$$p_l = \{p_1, p_2, \ldots, p_l\}$$

If t_i' is the retrieved topic set corresponding to the latter query. We can take t_i' as an observation set, where each observation can be seen as n-dimensional vector in a vector space as follows;

$$t_i' = \left\{ t_1', t_2', \ldots, t_n' \mid \forall p \in p_l, p = \bigcup_{n=1}^{k} t_n', |p| > k \right\}$$

In which t_i' is the set of all n topics retrieved from a profile p, in which profile p contains at least k topics of all combinations topics that we have queried for. Taken this set as our observation, we can use a generic k-means clustering algorithm [37] to partition these n observations into k sets of non-empty non-overlapping sets referred to as clusters ($k < n$), as $t'_{clustered}$;

$$t'_{clustered} = \{t_1', t_2', \ldots, t_n'\}$$

In which $t'_{clustered}$ represents the partitioned or clustered set of profiled topics. The clustering algorithm takes the set of n topics, and tries to divide the n topics into the

Schemes	*Depth 2*	*Greedy*	*8-Split*
Centroid1	art	art	culture
Centroid2	museum	politics	culture
Centroid3	design	history	multiculturalism
Centroid4	artists	museum	America
Centroid5	art	sculpture	culturalheritage
Centroid6	painting	science	Europeans
Centroid7	film	art	culture
Centroid8	sculpture	design	travel

Fig. 22.4 Sample centroid formation for interest topics with respect to schematics used

k set of $t'_{clustered}$ topics. If each profile contains m attributes, or features in the feature space *(here k=1, 2, 3 k)* then each cluster is spread surrounding centroids $c_{t'}$;

$$c_{t'} = \{c^1_{t'}, c^2_{t'}, c^3_{t'}, \ldots, c^n_{t'}\}$$

An example of centroids formation is presented in Fig. 22.4, where green topics are relevant matches, while red ones are either least relevant. We can observe that centroids of the clustering learner are formed around those topics which are exactly matching topics to our original query topics, or are semantically close to those topics. We take advantage of this obvious effect to eliminate the centroids which are either irrelevant or less-relevant to the task at hand. With respect to this, the centroid formations are observed and supervised to make sure that the correct centroids are chosen for the clusters being formed. At the same time, number of clusters affects the centroid formation.

By taking cluster size and distance metrics as control factors, we can measure the performance of the clustering step in the experiments later on.

22.3.3.2 Classifying Clustered Interest Topics

In general, clustering is utilized to reduce the dimensionality of an input data, especially if the number of input attributes is high. While clustering in single step can be configured to group a stack of profiles, but still assignments need to be verified in a single further step for improved accuracy. This is essential if the framework is desired to be automated [33].

At the same time clustering allows for a set of instances to be treated as a single (clustered) instance during each step in algorithm. Taken into account these two facts, we can increase the effectiveness of the miner by feeding existing groupings of clusters of profiles and their topics to a classifier. Classification techniques [38] are very appealing where a predictive outcome based on a set of input observational

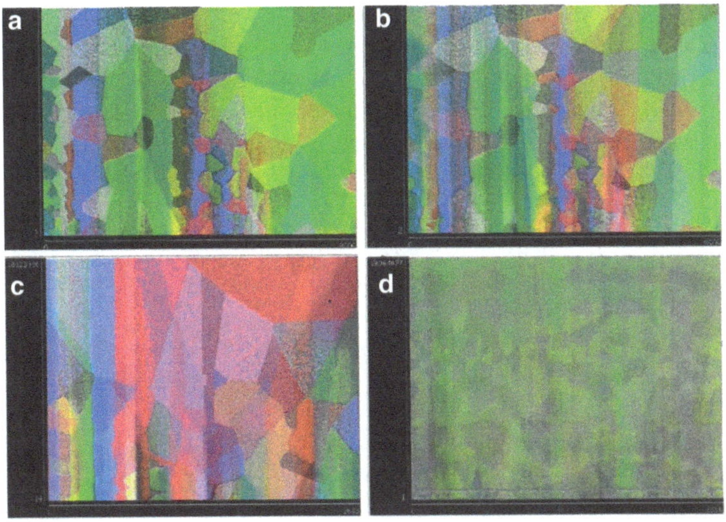

Fig. 22.5 Boundary visualization for generated profiles: (**a**) and (**b**) Class probability estimators for N-split n = 2 and n = 6. (**c**) and (**d**) Class probability estimators for depth d = 1 and greedy

data is needed. Taken into account this background, we take a classifier as a function, where it can take the set of our clustered observations as an argument, while the output would be, a probabilistic model created from the clustered interest topics of respective profiles. This predictive output will become our generated profiles, favorable to recommendation step. Our function should assign higher predictive probabilities to more appealing topics, which are the topics we have queried for and now form the centroids of the clusters. In our experiments we have used three classifiers; a *Bayesian classifier*, a *kNN classifier*, and a *pruned decision tree*. At this point supervisor (see Fig. 22.1) observes the predicted model and if needed refines the prediction output. Supervisor observes the accuracy and precision of the experiments to make sure the classification step was successful. Predicted model is stored for recommendation service to take as input and generate recommendation accordingly. Utilizing existing data for extended experiments we can either use a full ontological recommender system [39], or a topic-based recommender engine [40]. In the case of the former recommendations can be created based upon their lexico-semantic distance from user interests to predefined item annotations [41], while in the case of the latter we can use the existing set of topics along with their weight distributions for inferring new topic sets [30]. A visualization of boundary of output profiles subjective to our experiment lateron, can be seen in Fig. 22.5.

22.3.4 Measuring Adaptivity of Quest Schemes

As presented earlier a generic k-means clusterer spreads centroids surrounding the highly weighted topics within the profile documents. Exact matches rank highest naturally since they are the most frequent among all profiles. One of the most effective approaches used for increasing the chance of getting most relevant topics, is probabilistic topic models [40] that use Latent Dirichlet Allocation (LDA) [42]. An LDA model aims at finding a combination of topic set for each profile, such as $z \mid p$, with each topic described by terms using another probability distribution, such as $P\,(t' \mid z)$, described as follows:

$$P\left(t' \mid p\right) = \sum_{i=1}^{n} P\left(t_i' \mid z_i = 1\right) P\left(z_i = j \mid p\right)$$

In which $P(t_i')$ is the probability of topic i for a given profile and z_i is the latent topic. $P(t_i' \mid z_i = 1)$ presents the probability of t_i' within topic j, while $P(z_i = j)$ is the probability of picking a term from topic j in the document. To do so first we can derive a probability distribution P_1 where the frequency of topic per each matching profile is high. As a result:

$$P_1\left(t' \mid p\right) = \frac{freq\left(t', p\right)}{\sum_{t_i}^{n} freq\left(t_i', p\right)}$$

In which $P_1\,(t' \mid p)$ is the measure of the probability of topic t given a profile p. This gives us the ability to put a threshold on the quality of profiles that we retrieve to avoid gathering empty or very sparse profiles. Now we can combine this measure with $P\,(t' \mid z)$ with $P(t_i')$ to derive $P_2\,(t' \mid p)$ as follows:

$$P_2\left(t' \mid p\right) = \rho P_1\left(t' \mid p\right) + (1 - \rho) P_1\left(t' \mid p\right)$$

Taking into account the discussion so far we formalize the adaptivity in the context of our experiments as follows:

Adaptive Quest. A Quest scheme is referred to as adaptive if we can derive a probabilistic distribution where the frequency and relevance of centroids topics are comparatively high. The method is said to converge if the increasing relevancy and frequency of profile topics are feasible.

We use P_1 to measure the frequency of topics among the resulting centroids, while we utilize P_2 to derive the relevance of topics with respect to clustered set of profiles. We will demonstrate how this concept holds during the experiment using both machine learning process as well as probabilistic method proposed.

22.4 Evaluating Quest Schematics: A LiveJournal Experiment

In this section we layout the details of our experiment followed by analysis of results.

22.4.1 Crawling LiveJournal Community Profiles

LiveJournal [1] is a social networking website empowering the users who create, share and maintain journals. Users within this website can keep a journal, diary or simply a blog [43]. LiveJournal has about two million active users per month. When users create profiles on this website, they emphasize their interests[1] using a set of topics. There are in general two types of accounts on this website: users and communities. A LiveJournal community is a journal where users can share items, information and posts about a similar subject. Since communities are focused on a subject of interest, interest topics expressed for these communities creates this opportunity to study and analyze these communities for discovering interested customers, which turn out to be the members of the respective communities. We managed to discover, crawl and cache about 1,000 community profiles with in total more than 11,000 topics, among which each profile contains at least eight topics corresponding to existing topics in our domain taxonomy tree. First raw gathered topics are normalized using an unsupervised filter. We used porters word tokenizer and stemming algorithm [44] before hand to respectively tokenize the topics into words and map the terms within profile documents to their base linguistic forms. Subsequently, we fed the data into the miner. At each pace clusterer slices the data, while supervisor observes the clustering output and accuracy and then clustering results are saved and loaded into classifier to be processed for predicting the initial user profiles. At the end of this step supervisor observes the accuracy and resulting predictions before submitting it to recommender engine. The experiments at hand, we have focused the context on cultural heritage and museum domains. In this case we are aiming at discovering on-line or on-site visitors of website or physical exhibitions of museums. To increase the heterogeneity of results, we took into account two museums of different nature, one a collection of scientific instruments,[2] focusing on science and physics sub-domain, while the other museum is an art collection, focusing on paintings and statues of religion sub-domain.[3]

22.4.2 Evaluation and Comparison of Quest Schematics

In order to study the effectiveness and accuracy of the process, we study two main aspects of the framework proposed: *mining accuracy* and *adaptivity*.

Since our focus is more on evaluation of the quest schematics, which enable adaptive discovery of communities as well as processing and transforming them into tangible recommendation input, we focus the first evaluation part of this manuscript

[1]LiveJournal interests. http://www.livejournal.com/interests.bml

[2]Museum of History of Science at Florence, Italy. http://www.museogalileo.it/en/index.html

[3]Museum of Fine Arts, Malta. http://www.heritagemalta.org/museums/finearts/fineartsinfo.html

into effectiveness of miners, and the second part onto measuring the adaptivity by taking a look at empirical results comparing frequency of relevant topics within the clusters formed.

22.4.2.1 Clusterer Evaluation

Per each strategy we ran the miner with the following configurations: depth-based approach with depth configuration $d = 0,\ 1,\ 2$, n-split approach with splits size $n = 2,\ 4,\ 6$ and finally greedy approach with a complete dataset. To cluster the interest topics gathered we have utilized *Lloyds algorithm* [45] for simple k-means clustering. We have used two distance measures as our control factors; *Euclidean* and *Manhattan* distances. Results are compared with respect to cluster size increase and variation of schematics used. We compare these results with respect to their *wcss (within cluster sum of squares)*:

$$wcss = arg_{t'}min \sum_{i=1}^{k} \sum_{t_i}^{n} \|t_i - \vartheta_i\|$$

In which t' is the set of partitioned topics, t_i is the set of input topics, and ϑ_i is the mean of points in the partition [45]. Given a set of observation algorithm tries to choose the mean and partition the input set in a way that error of *wcss* becomes minimal. As a result we utilize this metric to compare and show the effectiveness of the clusterer. To study the effectiveness and accuracy of the clusterer we have gathered and plotted *wcss* error per each scheme. To demonstrate effectiveness of each strategy, we have tested different sizes of clusters, e.g. *2, 4, 6, 8, 16 and 32*. Results are depicted in Fig. 22.6. The plot is stacked to depict deviations more clearly.

We perform the tests using a training set. In these results, missing values are replaced with mean/mode in the case of Euclidean and in the case of Manhattan component-wise median is used. At first glance, it is clearly visible that clustering algorithm using Euclidean distance performs more accurately than using Manhattan distance. We can clearly see in the case of greedy result-set the larger the cluster size the higher the error and at the same time we can observe the considerable difference between error using Manhattan and Euclidean distances. One of the reasons greedy errors are quite high is the size of the final dataset, as the larger the data more iterations and splitting are required by algorithm, which in turn increases the error. Observing depth-driven schemes, we can observe that error accumulated during clustering experiment is less than greedy opposite to greedy increasing size of clusters decreases the error. What is interesting is that the lower we move on the tree, the more considerable the resulting error becomes.

This gradual increase in error is visible starting at the root of the tree, e.g. *depth 0*, moving towards the lower depth of the tree, e.g. *depth 2*. Finally moving to n-split experiment, we observe that split-based approach yields way less errors among all strategies, and at the same time it degrades more gracefully by increasing the size of

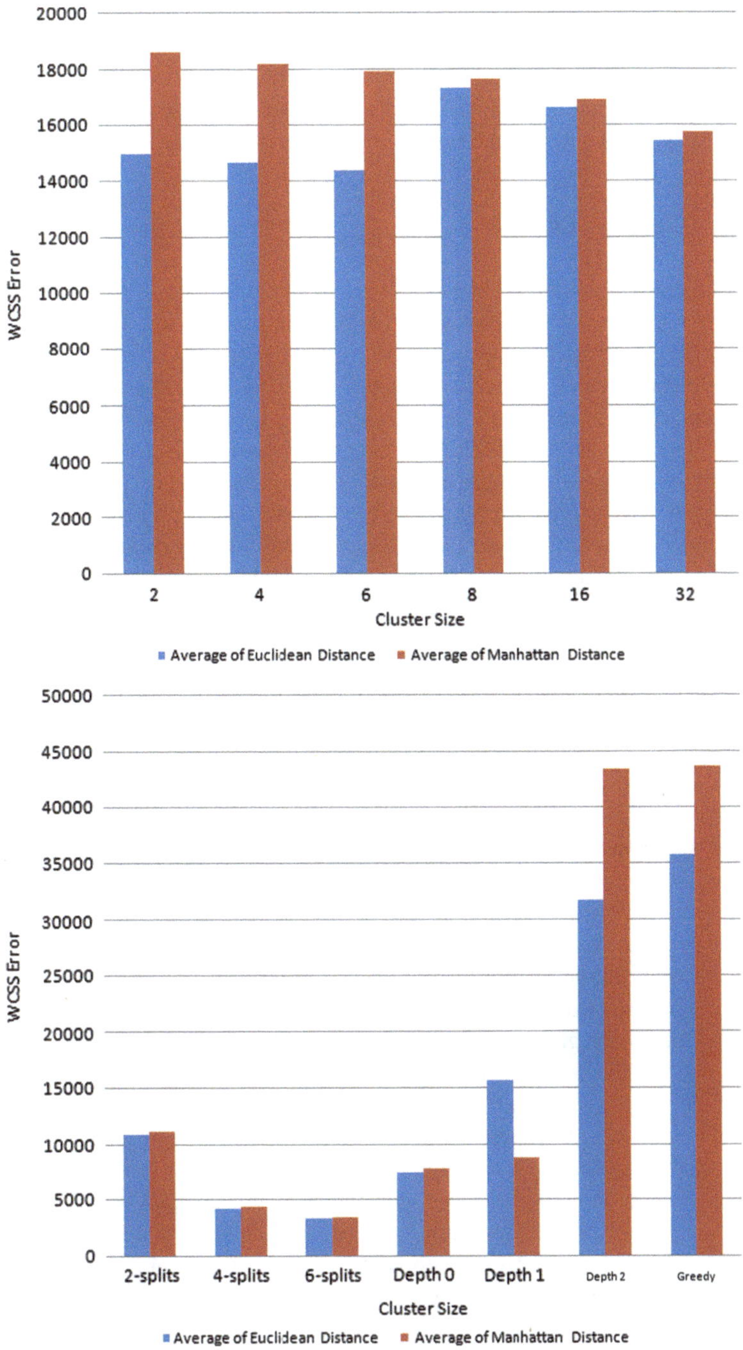

Fig. 22.6 Stacked plot of average clustering accuracies with Manhattan and Euclidean distances, visualizing errors per cluster size (*top*) and per schematics (*bottom*)

n (size of splits at each iteration), as well as increasing size of clusters. At the same time changing distance does not change the error between the results that much as this difference is totally insignificant. So far we observe that split-driven schemes yield least errors among schemes proposed, as well as clustering with Euclidean distance is more accurate in the case of the dataset we have used.

22.4.2.2 Classifier Evaluation

We have experimented with three classifiers; a Bayesian classifier, a lazy classifier, and a tree classifier. For the Bayesian classifier we used a *Nave Bayesian classifier* [46], for the lazy classifier we used *k-Nearest Neighbor (kNN) classifier* [47], and for the tree classifier we used *Ross Quinlans pruned decision tree* [48].

To evaluate the accuracy of the classifier, accuracy and precision of the profiles generated are analyzed. For evaluating the classification step, we have used *f-score (f-measure)* with respect to three classifiers being tested. F-measure considers both the precision and the recall of the test to compute the score. In general f-measure is calculated as the weighted harmonic mean of precision and recall where precision is the count of correct values divided by the count of all returned values and recall is the number of correct values divided by the number of values that should have been returned. We have used $f_1 measure$ which is calculated as follows:

$$f_1 = \frac{2.precision.recall}{(precision + recall)}$$

Results are visualized in Fig. 22.7. As of before, results are stacked to distinguish deviations more clearly. The former plot presents the average f-measure for each classifier with respect to increasing input cluster size. The latter on the other hand visualizes the f-measure with respect to each scheme utilized. Plots are presented separately to ease readability of results. As expected, we can observe that kNN classifier performs more accurately than two other classifiers at hand, as it scores highest f-scores among all three. This is while tree classifier comparatively exhibits less error than the Bayesian classifier.

We can easily see gradual decrease of scores in both resulting plots. In the case of first plot, results do show deviations at large cluster sizes, which is expected due to increasing calculations at each point, as they tend to converge the larger the cluster size becomes. With respect to second plot, starting with greedy experiment set, f-score seems to be the lowest among all of other schemes. And while observing depth- driven schemes we can see slow increase in accuracy and recall, when moving down the root of the taxonomy tree. This is natural due to the fact that the lower depth of taxonomy tree contains more focused topics, as well as more number of leafs to enrich a query. When moving to n-split approach, it is notable to see that f-measures for $n = 2, 4, 6$ are almost similar and the increase in the scores with respect to increase of n is almost linear. As a matter of fact, we can see that lazy classifier as well as split schemes yields most suitable results in the context of our work.

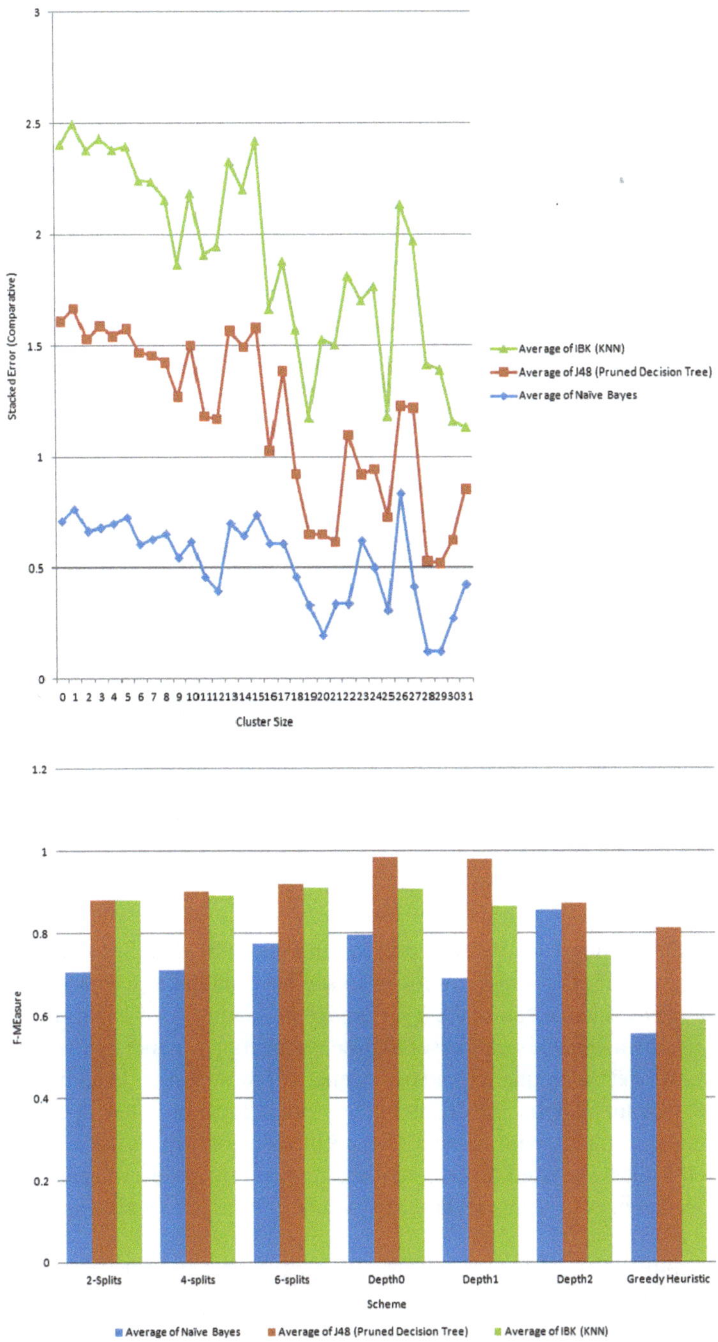

Fig. 22.7 Stacked plot of average classification accuracies, visualizing f-score per size of clusters (*top*) and per schematics used (*bottom*)

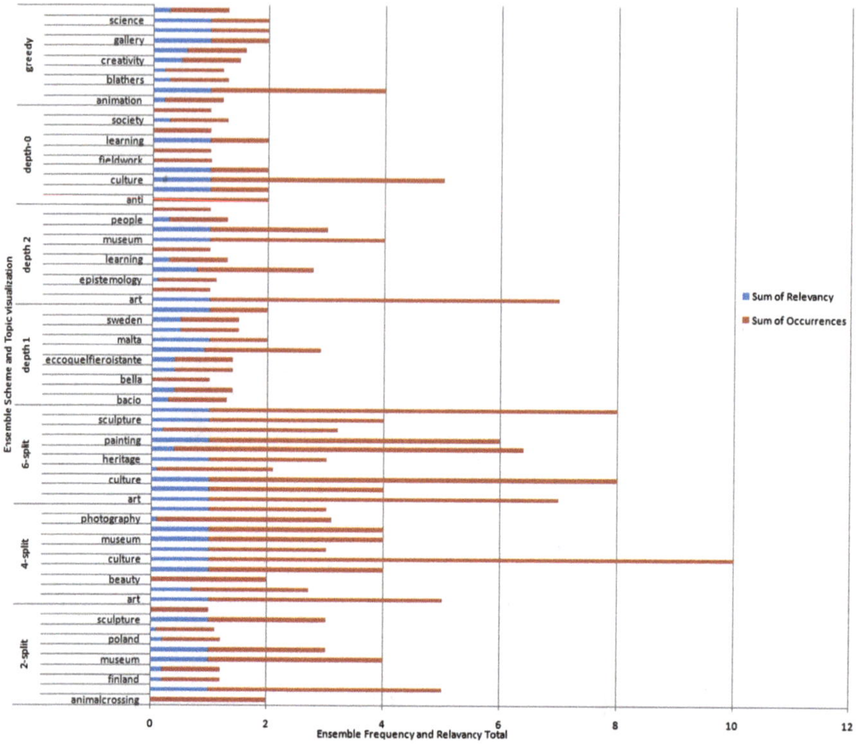

Fig. 22.8 Empirical comparison of the frequency and relevancy of centroids spread of topics

22.4.2.3 Adaptivity Evaluation

In addition to mining the stream of profiles and grouping them into topics tangible by a recommender, it is important for us to see how much these topics are relevant and if choice of scheme can make a difference in adaptivity of our framework. We evaluate this by using a lexical parser to process the topics associated with centroids and in turn we get the frequency and occurrences of these topics. In addition we used the toolkit to train a Gibbs LDA (Latent Dirichlet Allocation) [49] model to help us to infer relevant topics with respect to current collection of profiles. The new set of inferred topics was used to filter out less-relevant or irrelevant centroids topics. Sum of occurrences of terms together with sum of relevance weights are plotted in Fig. 22.8.

To generate these results we have fixed the size of clusters. Observing the results presented in the plot we can see that the most relevant and maximum occurring topics are associated with centroids found for n-split schemes. With respect to occurrence times, depth schemes show increasing frequency of topics as the depth increases, so frequency and depth and frequency of topics are associated directly.

This is while greedy scheme holds the least frequency among all. Increasing frequency is completely visible in the split schemes, as n becomes larger the frequency of topics increases sharply. At the same time, combined with the frequency, we can compare the relevance of centroids topics.

We can observe that the most relevant topics are associated with split-schemes as well, and this relevance increases with increasing number of splits; for instance, in two-split we can see the centroids topic *animalcrossing* with a relatively high frequency but with low relevance, and this is the case with four-split with centroids topic beauty with same frequency, but as it is observable that six-split centroids are highly relevant and are at the same time highly frequent. As compared with depth schemes, we can observe that relevance increases but it is not associated with frequency: in the case of depth 0, we can see centroids formed around fieldwork and anti, in the case of depth 1, we can see *eccoquelfieroistante* or *bella*, and *epistemology* and *learning* in the case of depth 2. This is while greedy shows more improved relevance than depth scheme. As a matter of fact, among all the schemes proposed n-splits seems to be most adaptive one and it is evident that the higher the value of *n* the faster the results will converge.

22.4.3 Discussion on Experiments Results

Taking into consideration results presented in the previous section, we discuss some of the qualitative and quantitative issues that can affect the result of ours, as well as similar experiments below:

1. **Size and semantics of the taxonomy tree:** We have experimented with a rather small to average taxonomy tree in this work. The main reason for this choice is the fact that, across the social network subject to this experiment, the more focused the topics get on the low level concepts, such as actual scientists like *Galileo* or instruments like *Telescope*, the less probable it gets that we might actually find any community or individual being directly interested on the matter. So one might suggest that a full rich taxonomy be learned from the target domain and utilize that to formulate the queries. But if instead of increasing the size of the tree, e.g. the depth, the length of tree, e.g. number of concepts at each level increases, the hit ratio for profiles discovered increases drastically. We have proven this using query expansion technique, which has led to discovering more than 17,000 community profiles, as of compared to 1,000 profiles subjected to experiment in this work.
2. **Availability of interested people within the social network:** One of the significant experiences with gathering profiles for the experimented domain at hand, e.g. Museums of Science or Visual Arts, is the fact that finding people on the social web, who have explicitly expressed their interests about certain topics and concepts surrounding this domain, seems pretty hard. It is obvious that people tend to express very generic topics and at the same time most of the

attention of people is on media, music, books or movies [28] rather than their specific interest in limited areas like visual arts or physics. At the same time, if we analyze their individual profiles, we see that the keywords in the profiles are very scattered around different matters and subjects, which led us to focus on community profiles in the first place, since communities are actual places that people share their idea about a certain subject or topics relevant to these topics. As a matter of fact, it is important to know first if within the target social domain exist people who are actually interested on the target domain at hand. Perhaps this points out to extension of this work on how to discover multiple sites and domains where context-focused interested individuals gather and socialize.

3. **Quality of the keywords documenting and presenting peoples interests:** One of the problems with systems that utilize the user asserted keywords (such as LiveJournal) is the quality of these keywords. LiveJournal utilizes user created or asserted keywords for describing their interests. This becomes important when a machine learning algorithm processes the data cached from these keywords. If not supervised normalized and filtered correctly during creation, these keywords could become problematic and their quality can affect the result of learning process. To deal with this problem, as stated previously we have managed to use the adaptive tree to cluster those keywords which are important and less importance will be given to keywords less relevant or irrelevant to the process. This can also be measured by measuring distance to cluster centroids. Another approach is treating keywords as tags. In this case quality of these keywords can be measured and possibly filtered [50].

22.5 Conclusions and Future Work

In this work we introduced a machine-learning equipped architecture which utilizes a set of semi- to fully- automated schemes and strategies for adaptive discovery and mining topic-based user profiles, to support the task of mining for personalization, in order to support a recommendation generation later on. We have experimented with interest profiles gathered from a popular social network to assist us with evaluating the accuracy and adaptivity of framework. Results present a trade-off between strategic approaches which could guide effective query formulation, expansion and analysis of profile data from social web. According to current state of results, split-driven technique seems to be the most accurate and adaptive among all three proposed. This is while depth-based technique shows average performance while it takes a bit time and data to converge when it comes to adaptivity. Among all greedy technique shows poor performance although when it comes to adaptivity it can present more adaptivity as it shows average relativity of profile selection and categorization. To deal with larger proportions of data, a combination of split and depth techniques can provide reasonable results for an automated framework. As a future work the framework should be used with further social data, gathered possibly from multiple heterogeneous domains, as well as using the resulting processed profiles for actual recommendation generation to see if the accuracy of recommendation can be drastically improved.

References

1. LiveJournal (2010). http://www.livejournal.com/, last accessed 2010
2. Ghosh, R., Dekhil, M.: Discovering user profiles. In: Proceedings of WWW 2009, pp. 1233–1234. ACM, New York (2009)
3. Teevan, J., Dumais, S., Horvitz, E.: Personalizing search via automated analysis of interests and activities. In: Proceedings of the 28th Annual International ACM SIGIR Conference on Research and Development in Information Retrieval, p. 456. ACM, New York (2005)
4. Liu, H., Maes, P., Davenport, G.: Unraveling the taste fabric of social networks, Int. J. Semant. Web Inf. Syst. **2**, 42–71 (2006)
5. Pretschner, A., Gauch, S.: Ontology based personalized search. In: Proceedings, 11th IEEE International Conference on Tools with Artificial Intelligence, pp. 391–398 (1999). http://dx.doi.org/10.1109/TAI.1999.809829
6. Trajkova, J., Gauch, S.: Improving ontology-based user profiles. Proc. RIAO **4**, 380–389 (2004)
7. Dokoohaki, N., Matskin, M.: Personalizing human interaction through hybrid ontological profiling: cultural heritage case study (2008). http://eprints.ecs.soton.ac.uk/15451/
8. Cantador, I., Szomszor, M., Alani, H., Fernández, M., Castells, P.: Enriching ontological user profiles with tagging history for multi-domain recommendations. In: 1st International Workshop on Collective Semantics: Collective Intelligence & the Semantic Web (CISWeb 2008). CEUR-WS (2008). http://ceur-ws.org/Vol-351
9. Razmerita, L., Angehrn, A., Maedche, A.: Ontology-Based User Modeling for Knowledge Management Systems. Lecture Notes in Computer Science, pp. 213–217. Springer, Berlin/New York (2003)
10. Felden, C., Linden, M.: Ontology-based user profiling. Business Information Systems, 314–327. doi:10.1007/978-3-540-72035-5_24
11. Sieg, A., Mobasher, B., Burke, R.: Ontological user profiles for representing context in web search. In: Proceedings of the 2007 IEEE/WIC/ACM International Conferences on Web Intelligence and Intelligent Agent Technology-Workshops, pp. 91–94. IEEE, Los Alamitos (2007)
12. Szomszor, M., Alani, H., Cantador, I., O'Hara, K., Shadbolt, N.: Semantic modelling of user interests based on cross-folksonomy analysis. In: International Semantic Web Conference, pp. 632–648. Springer, Berlin/New York (2008)
13. Gauch, S., Chaffee, J., Pretschner, A.: Ontology-based user profiles for search and browsing. Web Intell. Agent Syst. **1**, 219–234 (2003)
14. Sebastiani, F.: Machine learning in automated text categorization. ACM Comput. Surv. **34**(1), 1–47 (2002). doi:10.1145/505282.505283
15. Cooley, R., Mobasher, B., Srivastava, J.: Web mining: information and pattern discovery on the world wide web. In: Proceedings of the 9th IEEE International Conference on Tools with Artificial Intelligence (ICTAI-97), vol. 1, pp. 558–567. IEEE, Los Alamitos (1997)
16. Eirinaki, M., Vazirgiannis, M.: Web mining for web personalization, ACM Trans. Internet Technol. **3**, 1–27 (2003)
17. Mobasher, B.: Data mining for web personalization. In: Brusilovsky, P., Kobsa, A., Nejdl, W. (eds.) The Adaptive Web: Methods and Strategies of Web Personalization. Lecture Notes in Computer Science, pp. 90–135. Springer, Berlin/Heidelberg (2007). doi:10.1007/978-3-540-72079-9_3
18. Mobasher, B.: A web personalization engine based on user transaction clustering. In: Proceedings of the 9th Workshop on Information Technologies and Systems (WITS'99), Charlotte (1999)

19. O'Connor, M., Herlocker, J.: Clustering items for collaborative filtering. In: The Proceedings of SIGIR-2001 Workshop on Recommender Systems, New Orleans. ACM, New York (2001)
20. Srivastava, J., Cooley, R., Deshpande, M., Tan, P.: Web usage mining: discovery and applications of usage patterns from web data, ACM SIGKDD Explor. Newsl. **1**, 23 (2000)
21. Middleton, S.E., Shadbolt, N.R. De Roure, D.C.: Ontological user profiling in recommender systems. ACM Trans. Inf. Syst. **22**, 54–88 (2004)
22. Pazzani, M., Billsus, D.: Content-based recommendation systems. In: Brusilovsky, P., Kobsa, A., Nejdl, W. (eds.) The Adaptive Web: Methods and Strategies of Web Personalization. Lecture Notes in Computer Science, pp. 325–341. Springer, Berlin/Heidelberg (2007)
23. Herlocker, J.L., Konstan, J.A., Borchers, A., Riedl, J.: An algorithmic framework for performing collaborative filtering (1999). http://portal.acm.org/citation.cfm?id=312682
24. Soltysiak, S.J., Crabtree, I.B.: Automatic learning of user profiles: towards the personalisation of agent services. BT Technol. J. **16**, 110–117 (1998)
25. Pazzani, M., Billsus, D.: Learning and revising user profiles: the identification of interesting web sites. Mach. Learn. **27**, 313–331 (1997)
26. Wulf, V., Reichling, T.: Expert recommender systems in practice. In: Proceedings of the 27th International Conference on Human Factors in Computing Systems CHI 09, p. 59. ACM, New York (2009)
27. Wallach, H.M.: Topic modeling: beyond bag-of-words, Language 977–984 (2006)
28. Banerjee, N., Chakraborty, D., Dasgupta, K., Mittal, S., Joshi, A., Nagar, S., Rai, A., Madan, S.: User interests in social media sites: an exploration with micro-blogs. In: Proceeding of the 18th ACM Conference on Information and Knowledge Management, pp. 1823–1826. ACM, New York (2009)
29. Sebastiani, F.: Machine learning in automated text categorization. ACM Comput. Surv. **34**, 1–47 (2002)
30. Krestel, R., Fankhauser, P., Nejdl, W.: Latent dirichlet allocation for tag recommendation. In: Proceedings of the Third ACM Conference on Recommender Systems RecSys 09, vol. 61. ACM, New York (2009)
31. Jensen, D., Neville, J.: Data mining in social networks. In: National Academy of Sciences Workshop on Dynamic Social Network Modeling and Analysis. National Academies Press (2002)
32. Liu, H., Maes, P.: Interestmap: Harvesting social network profiles for recommendations. In: Beyond Personalisation (2004). http://web.media.mit.edu/~hugo/publications/papers/BP2005-hugo-interestmap.pdf
33. Dokoohaki, N., Matskin, M.: Quest: an adaptive framework for user profile acquisition from social communities of interest. In: International Conference on Advances in Social Network Analysis and Mining, pp. 360–364. IEEE, Los Alamitos (2010)
34. Novak, B.: A survey of focused web crawling algorithms. In: Proceedings of SIKDD, pp. 55–58. ACM, New York (2004)
35. Ester, M., Grob, M., Kriegel, H.P.: Focused web crawling: a generic framework for specifying the user interest and for adaptive crawling strategies. In: Proceedings of 27th International Conference on Very Large Data Bases, pp. 321–329. Morgan Kaufmann, Orlando (2001)
36. Chakrabarti, S., Van Den Berg, M., Dom, B.: Focused crawling: a new approach to topic-specific Web resource discovery. Comput. Netw. **31**, 1623–1640 (1999)
37. Hartigan, J.A.: Clustering Algorithms. Wiley, New York (1975)
38. Baharudin, B., Lee, L.H., Khan, K.: A review of machine learning algorithms for text-documents classification. J. Adv. Inf. Technol. **1**, 4–20 (2010)
39. Ruotsalo, T.: Methods and Applications for Ontology-Based Recommender Systems (2010). lib.tkk.fi
40. Krestel, R., Fankhauser, P.: Tag recommendation using probabilistic topic models. In: Eisterlehner, F., Hotho, A., Jäschke, R. (eds.) ECML PKDD Discovery Challenge 2009 (DC09), vol. 497, p. 131. CEUR-WS (2009). http://sunsite.informatik.rwth-aachen.de/Publications/CEUR-WS/Vol-497/

41. Ruotsalo, T., Mäkelä, E., Kauppinen, T., Hyvönen, E., Haav, K., Rantala, V., Frosterus, M., Dokoohaki, N., Matskin, M.: Smartmuseum: personalized context-aware access to digital cultural heritage (2009). http://citeseerx.ist.psu.edu/viewdoc/summary?doi=10.1.1.164.9014
42. Blei, D.M., Ng, A.Y., Jordan, M.I.: Latent dirichlet allocation. J. Mach. Learn. Res. **3**, 993–1022 (2003)
43. Marwick, A.: LiveJournal Users, New York (2008)
44. Porter, M.: The porter stemming algorithm (2001). http://tartarus.org/~martin/PorterStemmer/
45. Kanungo, T., Mount, D.M., Netanyahu, N.S., Piatko, C.D., Silverman, R., Wu, A.Y.: An efficient k-means clustering algorithm: analysis and implementation. IEEE Trans. Pattern Anal. Mach. Intell. **24**, 881–892 (2002)
46. John, G., Langley, P.: Estimating continuous distributions in Bayesian classifiers. In: Proceedings of the Eleventh Conference on Uncertainty in Artificial Intelligence, pp. 338–345. Morgan Kaufmann, San Francisco (1995)
47. Aha, D.W., Kibler, D., Albert, M.K.: Instance-based learning algorithms. Mach. Learn. **6**, 37–66 (1991)
48. Quinlan, J.R.: C4.5: Programs for Machine Learning. Morgan Kaufmann Series in Machine Learning. Morgan Kaufmann, San Mateo (1993)
49. Wei, X., Croft, W.B.: LDA-based document models for ad-hoc retrieval. In: Proceedings of the 29th Annual International ACM SIGIR Conference on Research and Development in Information Retrieval SIGIR 06, vol. 54, p. 178. ACM, New York (2006)
50. Krestel, R., Chen, L.: The art of tagging: measuring the quality of tags. In: Domingue, J., Anutariya, C. (eds.) Proceedings of the 3rd Asian Semantic Web Conference, pp. 257–271. Springer, Berlin/Heidelberg (2008)

Chapter 23
DB2SNA: An All-in-One Tool for Extraction and Aggregation of Underlying Social Networks from Relational Databases

Rania Soussi, Etienne Cuvelier, Marie-Aude Aufaure, Amine Louati, and Yves Lechevallier

Abstract In the enterprise context, People need to visualize different types of interactions between heterogeneous objects (e.g. product and site, customers and product, people interaction (social network)...). The existing approaches focus on social networks extraction using web document. However a considerable amount of information is stored in relational databases. Therefore, relational databases can be seen as rich sources for extracting a social network. The extracted network has in general a huge size which makes it difficult to analyze and visualize. An aggregation step is needed in order to have more understandable graphs. In this chapter, we propose a heterogeneous object graph extraction approach from a relational database and we present its application to extract social network. This step is followed by an aggregation step in order to improve the visualisation and the analyse of the extracted social network. Then, we aggregate the resulting network using the k-SNAP algorithm which produces a summarized graph.

R. Soussi (✉) · E. Cuvelier
Ecole Centrale Paris, MAS Laboratory, Business Intelligence Team, Grande Voie des Vignes 92 295 Chatenay-Malabry, France
e-mail: rania.soussi@ecp.fr; etienne.cuvelier@ecp.fr

M.-A. Aufaure
Ecole Centrale Paris, MAS Laboratory, Business Intelligence Team, Grande Voie des Vignes 92 295 Chatenay-Malabry, France

INRIA Paris-Rocquencourt, Axis Team, Domaine de Voluceau 78150 Rocquencourt, France
e-mail: Marie-Aude.Aufaure@ecp.fr; Marie-Aude.Aufaure@inria.fr

A. Louati
ENSI, RIADI-GDL Laboratory, Campus Universitaire de la Manouba, 2010, Tunisia

INRIA Paris-Rocquencourt, Axis Team, Domaine de Voluceau 78150 Rocquencourt, France
e-mail: Amine.louati@riadi.rnu.tn; Amine.Louati@inria.fr

Y. Lechevallier
INRIA Paris-Rocquencourt, Axis Team, Domaine de Voluceau 78150 Rocquencourt, France
e-mail: Yves.Lechevallier@inria.fr

T. Özyer et al. (eds.), *The Influence of Technology on Social Network Analysis and Mining*, Lecture Notes in Social Networks 6, DOI 10.1007/978-3-7091-1346-2_23,

23.1 Introduction

The data manipulated in an enterprise context are structured data as well as unstructured data such as e-mails, documents, etc. Graphs are a natural way of representing and modeling such data in a unified manner (structured semi-structured and unstructured ones). The main advantage of such structure relies on (or resides in) its dynamic aspect and its capability to represent relations, even multiple ones, between objects. It also facilitates data query using graph operations. Explicit graphs and graph operations allow a user to express a query at a very high level of abstraction.

People need to visualize different types of interactions between heterogeneous objects (e.g. product and site, customers and product, people interaction like social networks, etc.).

In order to analyze these interactions and facilitate their querying using graph query languages and social network analysis methods, it is relevant to modulate such interaction by using a graph structure.

Indeed, these different graphs can help enterprises sending product recommendations (using the graph of Products and client), finding experts (using social network), etc.

Nevertheless, in a business context, important expertise information is stored in files, databases and especially relational databases. Relational database pervades almost all businesses. Many kinds of data, from e-mails and contact information to financial data and sales records, are stored in databases. Also, databases used in business contain information about all people, objects and processes related to the enterprise. This data source is a rich one to extract object interaction.

However, a relational database is not the most suited data structure to store the "graph-like" information about a social network. By nature, a graph database is more preferable, because its structure is close to the structure of a social network.

Then, this chapter presents a new approach of social network extraction from relational database which allows discovering hidden relationships between entities. This approach has been generalized to extract different kind of heterogeneous objects graphs: such graph contains several kinds of relations and objects. Each object owns a set of characteristics which can be different from object to another. In order to facilitate the visualization and data interpretation, it seems interesting to aggregate the extracted graphs. This aggregation should use not only the relations between nodes but also the characteristics of each one and very few algorithms do that. In this context, we use the aggregation algorithm K-SNAP.

Then, the structure of this chapter is the following. First, we propose in Sect. 23.2, as a pre-treatment, to migrate the social network information stored in a classical relational database towards a graph database model. Starting from this new representation of the social network information contained in the original databases, we extract the social network structure, but it would be a pity to lose a lot of information using the classical graph representation of a social network. Indeed, in the graph theory used to model such networks, all nodes are of the same type, and all relationships

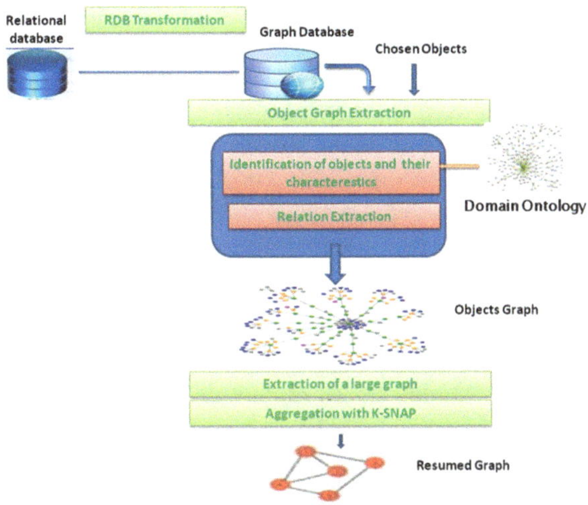

Fig. 23.1 Graph extraction approach

are of the same kind. But, in real life, all people in a social network do not play the same role, and all relationships dot not necessary share the same type. In other words, we are not all friends, or only friends, with our neighbors or colleagues. The enterprise framework is a perfect example for this: accountants do not have the same relationship with their accountant colleagues, with the salesmen, with the workers and, finally with their manager. And all these people play, of course, different roles in the business of their enterprise. That is why we propose in Sect. 23.3 to use heterogeneous graphs to model and extract such complex social networks, by working directly on the resulting graph database. The extraction of the social network is made using graph transformations. In a last step, we propose a visualization process because the "raw data" of a network can have, in general, a huge size which makes its difficult to analyze and visualize. In order to ease the latter tasks we propose to use an aggregation process in Sect. 23.4. After a study of the existing graph aggregation methods, we propose to use an existing technique which takes into account the heterogeneity of our networks. A global view of our all-in-one solution is given in Fig. 23.1. Finally, we conclude and give some perspectives to this work.

23.2 Graph Database Models and Graph Aggregation Algorithm

23.2.1 Graph Database Models

A graph database is defined [2] as a "database where the data structures for the schema and/or instances are modeled as a (labeled) (directed) graph, or generalizations of the graph data structure, where data manipulation is expressed by graph-oriented operations and type constructors, and has integrity constraints appropriate for the graph structure. There is a variety of models for a graph database (for more details see [2]). All these models have their formal foundation as variations of the basic mathematical definition of a graph. The structure, used for modeling entities and relations, influences the way that data is queried and visualized. In this section, we compare existing models in order to find the one most suitable one for storing and representing a social network. We will focus on the representation of entities and relations in these models. In the following, we present some models classified according to the data structure used to model entities and relations.

23.2.1.1 Models Based on Simple Node

Data are represented in these models by a (directed or undirected) graph with simple nodes and edges. Most of these models (GOOD [10]), GMOD [1], etc.) represent both schema and instance database as a labeled directed graph. Moreover, LDM [12] represents the graph schema as a directed graph where leaves represent data and whose internal nodes represent connections between the data. LDM instances consist of two-column tables, one for each node of the schema. Entities in these model are represented by nodes labeled with type name and also with type value or object identifier (in the case of instance graph). Some models have nodes for explicit representation of tuples and sets (PaMaL [7], GDM [11]), and n-ary relations (GDM). Relations (attributes, relations between entities) are generally represented in these models by means of labeled edges. LDM and PaMaL use tuple nodes to describe a set of attributes which are used to define an entity. GOOD defines edges to distinguish between mono-valued (functional edge) and multi-valued attributes (nonfunctional edge). Nevertheless, these models do not allow the presentation of nested relations and are not very well suited for complex objects modeling.

23.2.1.2 Models Based on Complex Node

In these models, the basic structure of a graph (node and edge) and the presentation of entities and relations are based on hypernodes (and hypergraphs). Indeed, a hypernode is a directed graph in which nodes themselves can be graphs (or hypernodes). Hypernodes can be used to represent simple (flat) and complex objects (hierarchical, composite, and cyclic) as well as mappings and records. A hypergraph is a generalized notion of graph where the notion of edge is extended to hyperedge, which relates to an arbitrary set of nodes. The Hypernode Model [13] and GGL [9] emphasize the use of hypernodes for representing nested complex objects. GROOVY [14] is focused on the use of hypergraphs. The hypernode model is characterized by using nested graphs at the schema and instance levels. GGL introduces, in addition to its support for hypernodes (called Master-nodes), the notion of Master-edge for the encapsulation of paths. It uses hypernodes as

Table 23.1 Graph database model comparison

	Entity		Relation		
	Complex	Dynamic	Nested	Neighborhood	Visualization
Hypernode	+	+	+	+	+
Groovy	+	+	+	+	−
GGL	+	+	+	+	−
GOOD	−	+	−	−	+
GMOD	−	+	−	−	+
PaMaL	+	+	−	+	+/−
GDM	+	+	−	−	+
LDM	+	+	−	−	−

an abstraction mechanism consisting in packaging other graphs as an encapsulated vertex, whereas, the Hypernode model additionally uses hypernodes to represent other abstractions like complex objects and relations. Most models have explicit labels on edges. In the hypernode model and GROOVY, labeling can be obtained by encapsulating edges, that represent the same relation, within one hypernode (or hyperedge) labeled with the relation name.

23.2.1.3 Discussion

The purpose of this review of graph database models is to find the most suited one to model many complex data objects and their relationships, such as social networks. Social Network is an explicit representation of relationships between people, groups, organizations, computers or other entities [3]. As other networks, it can be represented as a complex graph [32].

Indeed, the social network structure can contain one or more types of relations, one or more types or levels of entities and many attributes over the entities. This structure is dynamic due to growth of the volume, change of attributes and relations.

Then, we compare the previous graph database models using some characteristics related to social network: the ability to present dynamic and complex objects, nested and neighborhood relations and the ability to give a good visualization of social network. We resume the comparison on Table 23.1 where "+" indicates the graph model support, "−" indicates that the graph model does not support and "+/−" partial support. From this comparison, we have concluded that models based on hypernodes can be very appropriate to represent complex and dynamic objects. In particular, the hypernode model with its nested graphs can provide an efficient support to represent every real-world object as a separate database entity. Moreover, models based on a simple graph are unsuitable for complex networks where entities have many attributes and multiple relations.

23.2.2 Graph Aggregation Algorithms

When graphs of extracted social networks are large, effective graph aggregation and visualization methods are helpful for the user to understand the underlying information and structure. Graph aggregations produce small and understandable summaries and can highlights communities in the network, which greatly facilitates the interpretation.

The automatic detection of communities in a social network, can provide this kind of graph aggregation. The community detection is a clustering task, where a *community* is a cluster of nodes in a graph [8, 20], such the nodes of the cluster must be more connected with inside nodes, than with nodes outside of the cluster (see [23, 24] for extended reviews).

The first class of clustering algorithms are the *partitional algorithms*, which try to find a partition of a set of data, with a given number of clusters, using jointly, most of the times, similarity or a dissimilarity **measures** and a quality criterion of the found partition. The most popular partitional algorithm (with several variants), the *k-means clustering* [15], tries to find a partition of the set of objects which minimizes the *sum-of-square* criterion which adds the dissimilarities from each object to the centre of its own cluster. Several (di)similarity measures can be defined in the social network context, like those based on the *Jaccard index*, which measures similarity between the sets of *neighbours* of the two nodes, but other measures can be defined [23, 24].

Hierarchical clustering algorithms try to organize data into a hierarchical structure, and are divided into *agglomerative* and *divisive* algorithms, depending on whether the partition is coarsened, or refined, at each iteration. The basic idea beyond *agglomerative algorithms* is simple: at the starting point, the objects to cluster are their own classes, and then at each stage we merge the two more similar clusters. Of course a dissimilarity measure between two clusters is mandatory, and for a given dissimilarity measure d between objects, several cluster-dissimilarities exist. The result of the clustering process is a *dendrogram*, which can be cut to give one single partition. *Divisive clustering algorithms,* split the dataset iteratively or recursively into smaller and smaller clusters, with respect to a quality criterion. The most popular method for divisive hierarchical clustering of social networks uses the notion of edge betweenness [6], because finding the connecting edges between communities is also finding these communities. The algorithm given in [8] splits the network into clusters by removing, step after step, the edge with the higher betweenness value. The use of a stopping criterion which measures the improvement at each step should permit to stop when no improvement is gained with an iteration. In most cases the *modularity* [19] is used. SuperGraph [27] employs hierarchical graph partitioning to visualize large graphs.

Specially designed for graphs, *spectral algorithms* [29] are based on the notion of connected components. These algorithms work with a Laplacian, matrix based onthe adjacency (or weight) matrix [21, 25]. If the graph of the social network contains k, completely disjoints communities (i.e. without any link between them), called *connected components*, then the k *eigenvectors* associated to the eigenvalue 0 are indicator vectors of the k connected components. If the clusters of the social network do not contain "clean" connected components (i.e. if there are links between existing communities), then a simple clustering on the k *eigenvectors* associated to the k least eigenvalues, can retrieve the k communities.

Some other algorithms works on graph aggregation use statistical methods to study graph characteristics, such as degree distributions [18], hop-plots [4] and clustering coefficients [31]. The results are often useful but difficult to control and especially to exploit. Methods for mining frequent graph patterns [33] are also used to understand the characteristics of large graphs. Washio and Motoda [30] provide an elegant review on this topic.

However, all the previous algorithms use only on links between nodes of the graph of the network, and do not take into account the internal values contained in each node, while classical clustering algorithms applied on tables of values, work only on these values ignoring completely the possible link between individual. An algorithm which can take into account both kind of information would be very valuable. Designed for graphical graph aggregation the k-SNAP algorithm [28], in its divisive version, begins with a grouping based on attributes of the nodes, and then tries to divide the existing groups thanks to their neighbours groups, trying minimizing a loss information measure.

23.3 Social Network Extraction from Relational Databases

In this section we describe our approach of graph extraction which is based on two steps. The first step to perform is to transform relational databases into graph databases according to a graph model.

This transformation allows the extraction of all the entities in the relational database on the form of nodes and outlines the relations between them which facilitate, in further steps, the selection of the desired entities. Also, nodes in graph database are more complex than a simple graph which can encapsulate all the attribute of entities in the same node and give us a simple graph of entities.

The second step is to define a method to transform the graph according to chosen entities. This method has to deal with the identification of entities of interest for a particular user and to reorganize the graph – nodes and relationships – according to this point of view. Then, we applied this approach to extract social network.

23.3.1 Graph Extraction

The graph extraction approach is based on two main steps: (1) converting the relational database into graph database and (2) Extracting the heterogeneous graph (with chosen entities) from the graph database.

23.3.1.1 Converting Relational Database into Hypernode Database

Having a graph database instead of a relational database will provide a clearer view of existing objects in the initial database. Indeed, all these objects will be presented in the form of nodes, and the relations between them will be outlined thus facilitating the selection of the desired objects of interest in a further step. In addition, nodes in a graph database can encapsulate all the attributes of objects in the same node and give us a simple graph of objects.

Using the comparison between existing graph database models (Table 23.1), we have chosen to work with the hypernode model [13] because the hypernode database with its nested graphs can provide an efficient support to represent each real-world object as a separate database entity.

The transformation of a relational database into a graph database includes schema translation and data conversion [16]. The schema translation can turn the source schema into the target schema by applying a set of mapping rules. In our work, we propose a translation process which directly transforms the relational schema into a hypernode schema. A data conversion process converts data from the source to the target database based on the translated schema. Data stored as tuples (rows) in the relational database are converted into nodes and edges in the graph database. This involves unloading and restructuring relational data, and then reloading them into a target database in order to populate the schema generated during the translation process. The main advantages of this transformation are (1) to discover underlying graphs of objects from relational databases, taking into account the implicit relations expressed by the means of primary and foreign keys and (2) to model data in a more flexible way (objects can easily be added or removed in a graph). The reader interested by details about this approach can refer to [26]. The resulting hypernode database schema (Fig. 23.3) is composed by two sets H_b and R_b built from the sets of hypernodes H and relations R. The first set $H_b := \{(h, N_h), h \in H\}$is defined by:

- h denotes the name of H,
- N_h denotes a set of nodes $N_h := \{n_h | n_h := \langle n, t \rangle\}$ where n is the node name, t is the type. t is a predefined type (Integer, String,. . .) or a H element.

The second one $R_b := \{\langle r, h_s, h_d \rangle, r \in R, h_s, h_d \in H\}$:

- r denotes the name of R,
- h_s denotes the hypernode source name
- h_d denotes the hypernode destination name

From the relational database tables (Fig. 23.2), we extract six hypernodes (Fig. 23.3):
Thesis, *Laboratory*, *Thesis_hasStudent*, *Student*, *Director_thesis* and *Foreign_Student*.

The table *Thesis_hasLab* is transformed into a relation because it contains only foreign keys. The hypernode Thesis:

Director thesis

Dir_id	St_id#	lab_id#	Grade	Dir_lastname	Dir_name
27	05	12	Prof	Norman	Lochan
38	03	12	HDR	jean	Weber
56	03	16	Prof	Alain	Dupont

Thesis_hasLab

Lab-id#	th_id#
12	102
12	106

Thesis_hasStudent

St_id#	th_id#	supported
03	102	False
05	106	True

Laboratory

Lab_id	Lab_name	Lab_adresse
12	INSA	Lyon, France
16	MAS	Paris, France

Thesis

th_id	Dir_id#	Th_name	Topic
102	38	logic	Electronic
106	27	Fuzzy set	Computer
102	56	logic	Electronic

Student

St_id	st_name	st_lastname
03	Mohsen	Ali
05	jack	Pierre

Foreign_Student

St-id#	country
03	Egypt

Fig. 23.2 Relational database

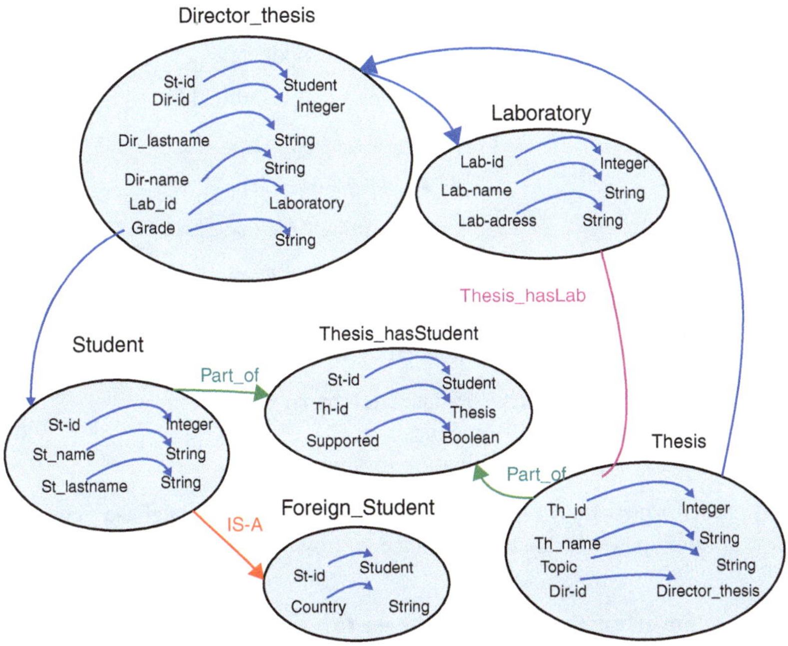

Fig. 23.3 Hypernode database schema

$$
\begin{aligned}
Thesis = (\text{“}Thesis'' ,\{ &< Th\_id, Integer >,\\
&< Th\_name, String >,\\
&< Topic, String >,\\
&< Dir\_id >,\\
&< Director\_thesis >\})
\end{aligned}
$$

has three nodes (*Th_id*, *Th_name*, *Topic*), with predefined types and one node *Dir − id* having *Director_thesis* as type because it is a foreign key exported from *Director_thesis* hypernode. Thesis has the relation

$$< \text{“}Part\_of'', Thesis, Thesis\_hasStudent >$$

with the hypernode $Thesis\_hasStudent$.

Then, for each hypernode in the hypernode database, a set of instances hypernode *HI* is extracted from the relational tuples.

The set of instances hypernode $\mathscr{H}$ is defined by $\mathscr{H} = \{h_i | h_i := \langle h, l_i, N_i \rangle\}$ where:

- h_i denotes the instance hypernode,
- h denotes the hypernode source name,
- l_i denotes the name of H_i,
- N_i denotes a set of nodes $N_i := \{n | n := \langle l_n, t_n, val_n \rangle\}$ where l_n is the label of the node, t_n is the type, and val_n mentions the node value.

For example, *Thesis_1* is an instance of *Thesis* and is defined by:

$$\begin{aligned} Thesis\_1 = \langle Thesis, Thesis\_1\ , \{ &< Th\_id, Integer, 102 >, \\ &< Th\_name, String, ''Logic'' >, \\ &< Topic, String, ''Electronic'' >, \\ &< Dir\_id, Director\_thesis, Director\_thesis\_1 > \} \rangle \end{aligned}$$

For each relation in R_b, a set of instance relations R is extracted using the value of keys on the relational tables. RI is defined by $R := \{r_i | r_i := \langle r, h_{s_i}, h_{d_i} \rangle\}$ where:

- r denotes the relation which is instanciated by r_i,
- h_{s_i} denotes the hypernode source instance,
- h_{d_i} denotes the hypernode destination instance,

Finally, transformed data are loaded into the hypernode database schema. An excerpt of the hypernode database instance is shown in Fig. 23.4.

23.3.1.2 Converting the Graph Database to a Graph Containing *Objects of Interest* (from a User Point of View)

The Hypernode database represents the graph of objects. From this graph, we may apply transformation rules according to the user's interest (the set of objects the user would like to see their interaction).

The graph containing the objects of interest is defined by: $GO = (O_I, R_O)$ where:

- O_I is a finite set of object such $O_I = \{o_I | o_I \in \mathscr{H}\}$,
- R_O is a finite set of relations between objects such $R_O := \{r | r := \langle l, o_{I_1}, o_{I_2} \rangle, o_{I_1}, o_{I_2} \in O_I\}$ where l is the relation name.

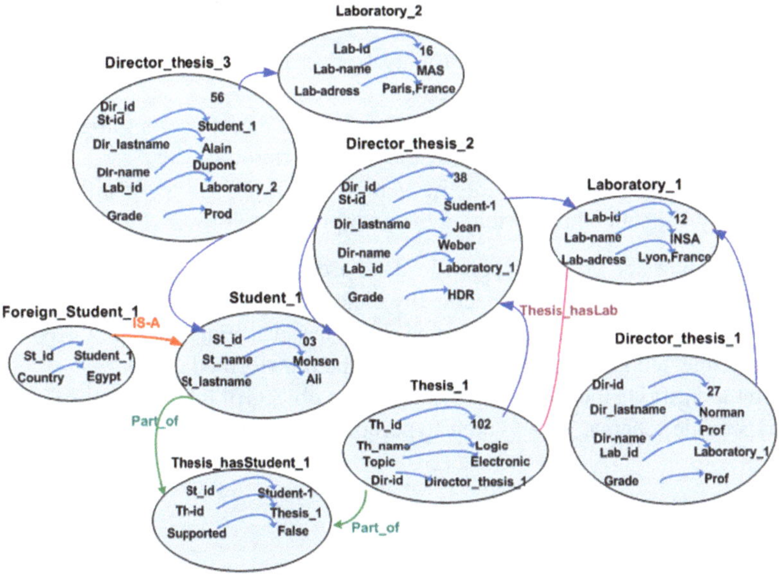

Fig. 23.4 Part of the *Hypernode* database instance

Transforming the graph leads to cope with two main problems: objects of interest (named *objects* in the following) identification and relations extraction and transformation.

23.3.1.3 Objects Identification

Object identification is the process used to identify hypernodes that contain the elements of interest for the user (for example Laboratory or Student). These objects will constitute the nodes of the transformed graph according to the user's point of view.

The identified objects have the type chosen by the user, e.g. persons, organization, process, etc.

Many problems occur at this step. First, an object can be described by the mean of different tables in the relational database, and then many hypernodes can represent the same object. Second, the names of the hypernodes are not all the time significant.

Each object has a number of characteristics which help to identify it. In order to identify the chosen objects in the graph database, a domain ontology is used. In fact, ontology contains concepts and relationships that describe a domain.

Then, we use an ontology having the same domain than the initial database. For instance, we use an enterprise ontology if the initial relational database is an enterprise database. This ontology, which describes the objects and their relations, is built semi-automatically by using information collected from domain documents.

The proposed approach is based on three main phases:

- Building minimal enterprise ontology from scratch (manually) using existing enterprise models and pattern,
- Learning ontology from web document: Global enterprise ontology is learned from enterprise websites and using the minimal ontology,
- Population and enrichment of the generic ontology: more specific enterprise ontology is obtained by enriching the enterprise ontology.

The hypernode set in the hypernode database schema is analyzed, considering ontology concepts, and more specifically concepts related to the objects chosen by the user. If the hypernode contains some characteristics related to the desired object, it will be selected to be one of the objects in the transformed graph.

After identifying the hypernodes that contain objects of interest for the user, from the hypernode schema, we add their hypernodes instances to O_I.

23.3.1.4 Relation Construction

After the objects identification step, we define relations (edges) between identified entities. The identified objects are instance hypernodes. In the hypernode database, instance hypernodes can share relations. Then, we try to use the existing relations and find hidden ones.

In our process to transform the relational database into a hypernode database [26], we have defined four types of relations: *IS-A*, *Part-of*, *dependency with known name* (using the initial relational tables containing only foreign keys), *dependency with unknown name*.

Identified objects can be related by these exiting relations. In this step we try to find other hidden relations between these objects.

In order to facilitate this task, we define a set of relation patterns (Table 23.2) using the schema of the hypernode database. These patterns are used to create the objects relations. A pattern relation P_r is defined by $P_r = \langle n, o_{I_1}, o_{I_2}, o_m \rangle$ such as n is the name of the relation, o_{I1} and o_{I2} the entities which share the relation, o_m a mediator for this relation (the hypernode used to find the new relation).

Indeed, these patterns will be used to find relations between the identified objects: existing relations objects already share in the hypernode database and new relations (build using key value and mediator objects). A mediator is an object facilitating the communication between two other objects (acting as a router). After having identified relations and objects (of interest), we build the transformed graph corresponding to chosen objects. In the next section, we present a use case experimentation corresponding to a social network perspective extracted from an actual relational database.

Table 23.2 Pattern used to extract relations

Initial Relation	Pattern	Process and description
$R_1 := \langle$"$IS - A''$, $h_s, h_d\rangle$ where h_s or h_d instances $\in O_I$	——	h_s or h_d instances are added to O_I
$R_2 := \langle r, h_s, h_d\rangle$ where h_s and h_d instances $\in O_I$	$\mathrm{Pr}_1 := \langle r, h_s, h_d, null\rangle$	Find all the existing relations between h_s and h_d instances then add them to R_O
	$Pr_2 :=< Same\_(h_d.name), o_{Ii}, o_{Ij}, hd >$ where $o_{Ii} = h_{is}$, $o_{Ij} = h_{is}$ and $i! = j$	Find all the h_s instances which have relations with a same h_d instances and link them with a new relation "$Same\_(hd.name)$"
$R_3 := \langle r, h_s, h_d\rangle$ where h_s instances $\in OI$ (finite set of entities) and $h_d \notin O_I$	$Pr_3 :=< Same\_(h_d.name), o_{Ii}, o_{Ij}, h_d >$ where $o_{Ii} = h_{is}$, $o_{Ij} = h_{is}$, $i! = j$ and $r! =$ "Part-of"	Find all the h_s instances which have relations with a same h_d instances and link them with a new relation
	$Pr_4 :=< Same\_h_j.name, o_{I1}, o_{I2}, h_j >$ where $o_{I1} = h_s$, $o_{I2} = h_s$, $r =$"Part-of" and $h_j \in \{h \| h$ has the relation $R_h :=<$ "Part-of", $h_j, h_d >\}$	- Find all the hypernodes h_j having a "Part-of" relation with h_d such as R :=<"Part-of", h_j, h_d > - Add new node to hs containing the name of h_j - Then the pattern Pr_4 is applied: Find all the h_d instances which have relations with a same h_j instances and link them with a new relation
$R4 := \langle r, h_s, h_d\rangle$ where $h_s \notin O_I$ and $h_d \in O_I$	$Pr_5 :=< Same\_hs.name, o_{I1}, o_{Ij}, h_d >$ where $o_{I1} = h_d$ and $o_{I_j} \in \{o_I \| o_I$ has relation with $\mathrm{h}_s\}$.	- Add a new node on h_s containing h_d - If h_s have relations with other entities h_j :we link each h_j with each h_d instance if they are in relation with the same h_s.

23.3.2 *Social Network Extraction Using Graph Transformation*

In this section, we present an experiment to transform a graph extracted from a relational database into another one according to a social network perspective. A social network can be represented as a graph [32], where the nodes represent people and the edges represent relationships among people, such as values, visions, idea, financial exchange, friends, kinship, conflict, trade, web links, airline routes, etc.

As a consequence, the resulting structures are often very complex. Choosing the right methods and techniques of information extraction requires having a rich and high quality source of information.

The existing approach of social network extraction uses just web data like: e-mail messages [5], Friend-of-a-Friend (FOAF) documents [17], and observing face-to face communications [22].

For example, Flink [17] uses four different types of knowledge sources: HTML pages, FOAF profiles, public collections of emails and bibliographic data. Flink employs a co-occurrence analysis technique to extract the social network from this data. However, these existing approaches are designed only to extract social network from web data and are not able to use other rich sources like relational databases.

Indeed, in the context of enterprise and business data are principally stored into a database. Enterprise databases contain information about people, objects manipulated in the enterprise and the associated processes. The objective is to highlight all this information and the relationships between people, objects and processes for a better performance in the enterprise.

We have applied our approach to extract an underlying social network from a relational database. In this section, we describe this process using the Hypernode database depicted in Figs. 23.3 and 23.4.

23.3.2.1 Person Identification

The chosen objects in this case are the hypernode representing persons. Then, in this step, we describe the process to identify people. The hypernode database schema is used to extract candidate hypernodes (those which may represent persons). Then, the instances are used to deeply analyze the candidates and detect those containing people.

Hypernodes candidates detection. A person has a number of characteristics like name, surname, birthday, address, email, etc. Some of these characteristics are used when designing databases containing persons. Based on characteristics from various ontologies such FOAF ontology and person ontology (schemaWeb), we have manually designed a person ontology (PO) containing all these characteristics and their synonyms (collected from WordNet). Figure 23.5 shows an excerpt of this ontology. Using the person ontology, the set of nodes related to each hypernode in the hypernode database is analyzed.

- If the node's name is one of the PO concepts, the number of characteristics for this hypernode is incremented.
- If the number of characteristics for the hypernode $>=1$ and one of them contains a name, the hypernode h is a candidate to contain persons.

Candidate hypernodes Analysis. Each candidate hypernode has a set of instance hypernodes h_i. In order to analyze the name found in each instance (we take just the 10 first instances), the name is sent to a web search engine. The top 10 returned documents are downloaded and form the set D_i of the considered instance, and this

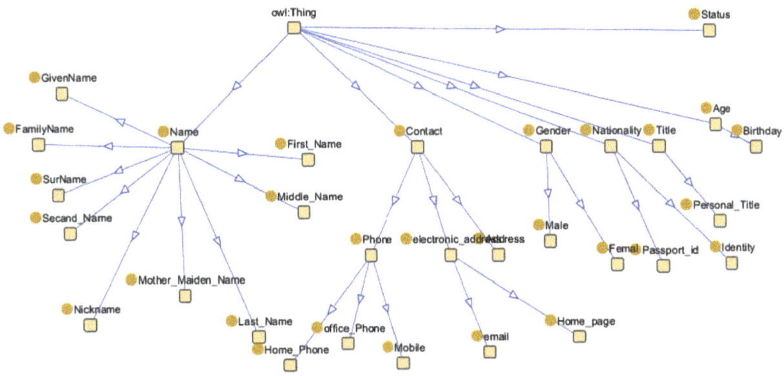

Fig. 23.5 Part of the person ontology

set is parsed using DOM.[1] Each document in D_i is analyzed using the NER tool (Named Entity Recognition) developed in Stanford[2] and which is able to put three kinds of tags (Person, Location or Organization). We give for each document d, a weight w_d. If the name is tagged in the document by Person, the document is weighted by $w_d = 1$, otherwise $w_d = 0$. The mean assigned to the name found in the hypernode instance h_i ($\overline{h_i}$) counts how many times it is considered as a person name in the documents (where the tag of this name is Person):

$$\overline{h_i} = \frac{\sum_{d \in D_i} w_d}{|\mathrm{D_i}|} \tag{23.1}$$

The mean assigned to the hypernode ($\overline{H}$) calculates the mean where the names found in its instances are considered as a person name:

$$\overline{H} = \frac{\sum_{h_i} \overline{h_i}}{|\{h_i\}|} \tag{23.2}$$

NER has a precision around 90 % for finding Person entities; so, a hypernode is considered as representative of a person if more than 60 % of its instances contain a person name (we take only 60 % as a threshold due to problems such as wrongly written names, use of abbreviations, etc. which lower the precision of NER).

[1] http://www.w3.org/DOM/

[2] http://nlp.stanford.edu/ner/index.shtml

Table 23.3 Relation R_{h1} pattern

<table>
<tr><th>Relation and identified pattern</th><th>Example of extracted relations</th></tr>
<tr><td>

Relation:
$R_{h1} :=<'''', Director\_thesis, Student, >$
Patterns:
$Pr_1 :=<'''', Director\_thesis, Student, null>$

</td><td>

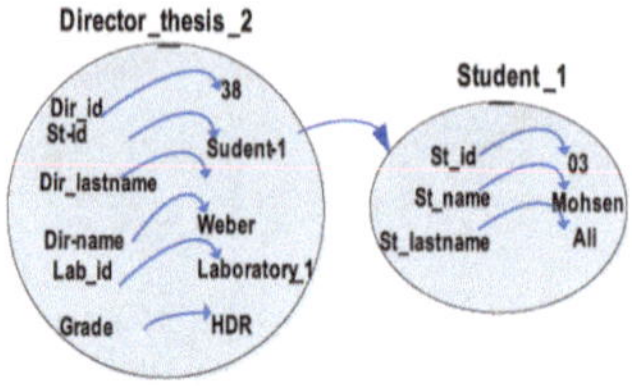

</td></tr>
<tr><td>

$Pr_2 :=< Same\_Student, Director\_thesis_i, Director\_thesis_j, Student >$

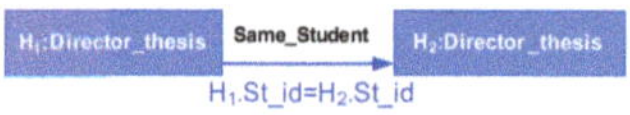

</td><td>

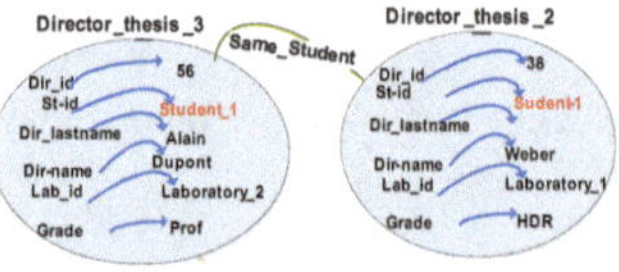

</td></tr>
</table>

23.3.2.2 Relation Construction

From the previous step, the entities identification process identifies the Hypernodes “Student “and “Director_thesis” as person entities. Then, all their instance hypernodes are added to the entities set.

The relation construction process is then performed using the identified entities. We start by identifying the relation R_1 in order to search hidden entities.

In our example, the process identifies “*Foreign-Student*” as an entity due the relation $R_1 =<'' IS - A'', Foreign - Student, Student >$.

We will detail the identified relation in what follows using the set of pattern described in Table 23.2.

From the relation $R_{h1} :=< “'', Director\_thesis, Student >$, we identify two patterns (Table 23.3):

- $Pr_1 :< “'', Director\_thesis, Student, null >$: in the database schema, $Student$ and *Director_thesis* share the relation R_{h1}. Using Pr_1 and the value of the foreign key $St - id$, we search on the instance hypernode database for each *Student* the corresponding *Director_thesis*. R_{h1} relates directly *Student* and *Director_thesis* then we have no mediator (null).
- $Pr_2 :=< Same\_Student, Director\_thesis_i, Director\_thesis_j, Student >$: two thesis director may have the same *Student* (same value of $St - id$). Then, we search on the instance hypernode database all the instances of *Director_thesis* which have the same *Student* (mediator for this pattern) in order to add between them the relation Same_ Student.

From the relation $R_{h2} :=<'''', Director\_thesis, Laboratory >$, we identify one pattern (Table 23.4): *Laboratory* is not an entity (of interest) then its instances are not included in the final graph:

Table 23.4 Relation R_{h2} pattern

Relation and identified pattern	Example of extracted relations
Relation: $R_{h2} :=<'''', Director\_thesis, Laboratory >$ **Pattern:** $Pr_3 :=< Same\_Laboratory, Director\_thesis_i, Director\_thesis_j, Laboratory >$ 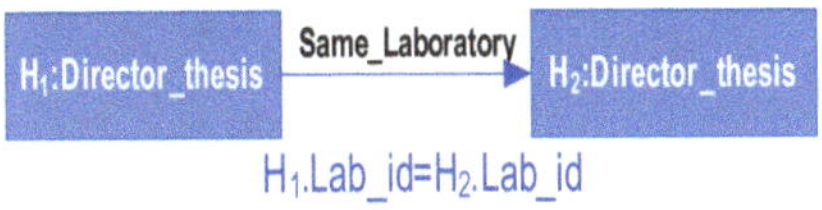 *Laboratory* is not connected to other entities	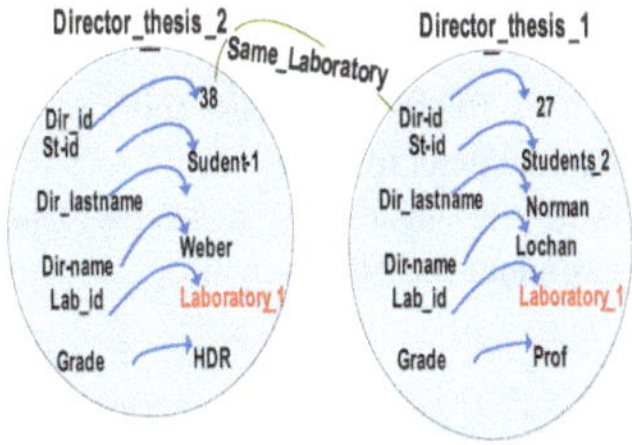

Table 23.5 Relation *Rh*3 pattern

Relation and identified pattern	Example of extracted relation
Relation: $R_h :=<'' Part-of'', Student, thesis\_hasStudent >$ **Pattern:** – *Thesis_hasStudent* shares two relations "Part-of" with *Student* an *Thesis* – Add the node n :< *Thesis*, *Thesis_i* > to each instance of *Student* – $Pr_4 :=< Same\_Thesis, Student_i, Student_j,$ $Thesis\_hasStudent >$ 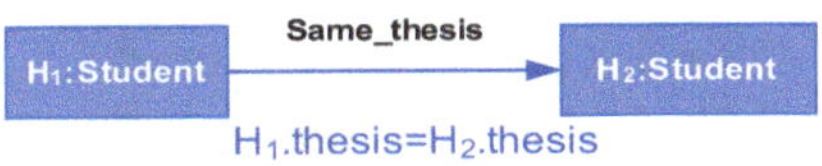 	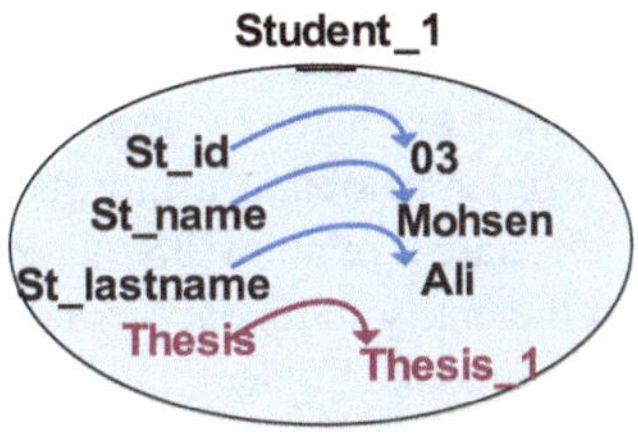

- $Pr_3 :=< Same\_Laboratory, Director\_thesis_i, Director\_thesis_j, Laboratory >$: using the value of the foreign key *Lab_id* in each hypernode instance of the entity *Director_thesis*, we will link those having the same value of *Lab_id* by the relation *Same_Laboratory*.

From the relation $R_{h3} :=<'' Part-of'', Student, thesis\_hasStudent >$, we identify one pattern (Table 23.5) and we add some information:

- *Thesis_hasStudent* shares two relations "Part-of" with *Student* and *Thesis*. We add a new node on the hypernode *Student* < *Thesis, Thesis_i* >, corresponding to his Thesis. Then, we can apply the pattern Pr_4.
- $Pr_4 :=< Same\_Thesis, Student_i, Student_j, Thesis\_hasStudent >$, by this pattern we search all the students which share the same thesis. We did not find such relation which is semantically inexact.

Table 23.6 Relation R_{h4} pattern

Relation and identified pattern	Example of extracted relation
Relation: $R_{h4} :=<'''', Thesis, Director\_thesis>$ **Pattern:** – Thesis has no relations with other entities then no pattern detected. – Add the node n :< *Thesis*, *Thesis_i* > to each instance of Student	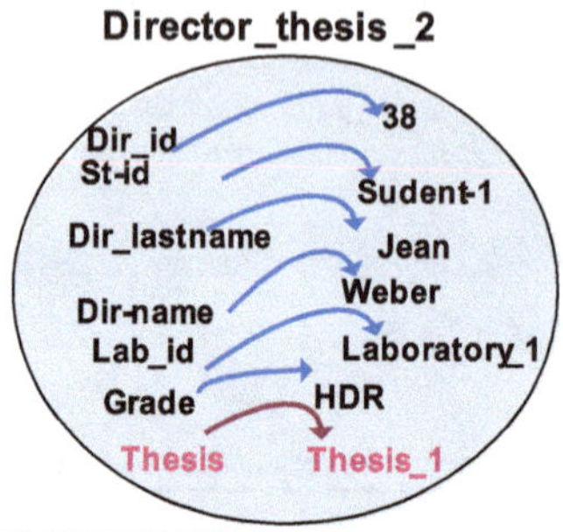

From the relation $R_{h4} :=<'''', Thesis, Director\_thesis>$, there are no identified patterns because *Thesis* is not related to other entities (Table 23.6). Considering the identified patterns and the hypernode database instance (Fig. 23.4), a first social network is extracted by applying the set of patterns to the instance hypernodes.

In order to obtain a more sophisticated social network, we merge the entities which share a relation "IS-A". For example, we merge the entity "Foreign-student" with the entity "Student" by adding all the information found in this hypernode to the hypernode "Student". Additionally, if "Foreign-student" has relations with other entities, these relations will be added to "Student". Finally, we obtain the social network depicted in Fig. 23.6. In the previous steps, we have extracted a social network from a relational database. However, a relational database can contain hundreds or thousands of tuple then we will obtain a very large social network.

From the resultant social network in Fig. 23.6, a graph composed with homogeneous hypernodes has been extracted. The type of the selected hypernode is specified by the user (for example Director-Thesis) in order to perform K-SNAP algorithm. Then we will have an aggregated view of this graph which will facilitate its visualization and analysis.

The extracted graph has the hypernode instances of "Director_thesis" as vertex and their relations as edges.

23.4 Visualizing the Social Network Using the K-SNAP Graph Aggregation

In the previous section, we were able to extract a social network from a graph database. However, as the actual relational databases contain hundreds or even thousands of records, we obtain as a result, the large social network seen in Fig. 23.7. An efficient graph aggregation will be valuable to visualize such graph in

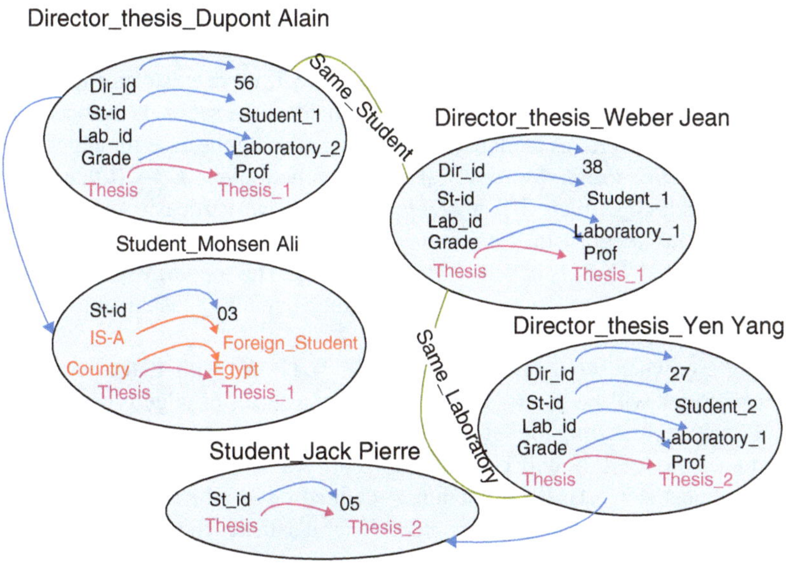

Fig. 23.6 The corresponding social network

Fig. 23.7 The complete graph

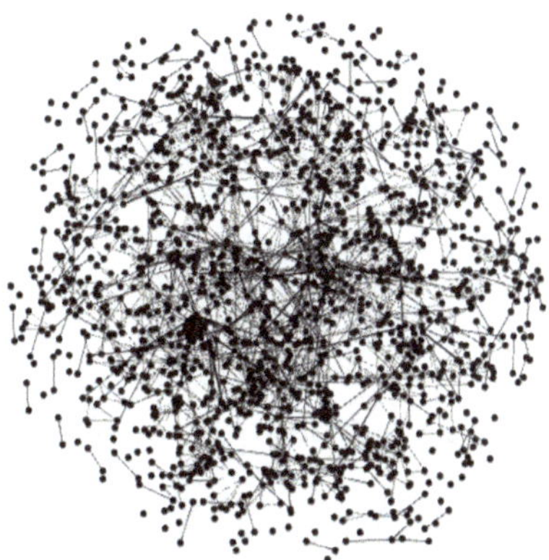

highlighting its underlying structure. And even if any classical community detection could be used to aggregate such a graph, do not use the inner values of the extracted nodes would be a wasting of efforts and information. Then we chose to aggregate our graphs with the k-SNAP algorithm because it permits an aggregation on the both kind of information: links and attributes.

Let use recall here the basic concepts of graph theory. A *graph* G is defined as a pair of sets: $G = (V, E)$, where V is the set of *vertices* or *nodes*, and E the set of *edges* or *links* which connect vertices. The two vertices connected by an edge are called *endpoints* of this latter. Conversely, the edges connecting a vertice to the other vertices are called *incident* edges of the node. A graph can be *directed* or *undirected*.

In the first case, also called *digraph*, an edge is denoted as pair (v, w), where v is the origin and w the target, and in the social networks framework it means: "v is in relation with w", the opposite being true if and only if there exists an edge (w, v). If the graph G is undirected, then an edge is denoted as the set of its vertices: $\{v, w\}$. Most of the times, vertices are labelled, but it can also be the case for edges, then G is called a *labelled graph*. Moreover, if exists a function $\omega : E \rightarrow$ R that assigns a weight for each edge, then G is a *weighted* graph. Two vertices v and u are called *neighbors* or *adjacent*, if they are connected by an edge. The set of neighbors of a node v, denoted $\Gamma(v)$, is called its *neighborhood*. The topology of the graph can be captured in the *adjacency matrixA*, where the element $a_{i,j}$ is equal to one when $(v_i, v_j) \in E$, and zero otherwise.

From here, when we denote a graph by $G = (V, E)$ with V the set of nodes, the set of edges will be $E = \{E_1, E_2, \ldots.., E_r\}$ the set of edge types, with each $E_i \subseteq V \times V$ representing the set of edges of a particular type.

And each node of V will be characterized by a set of attributes $\Lambda(G)$. For a set of attributes $A \subseteq \Lambda(G)$, a function Φ defined on V which is called *Attributes Compatible Grouping* or simply *A-compatible*, if it satisfies the following condition: $\forall u, v \in V, if\, \Phi(u) = \Phi(v)$ then $\forall a_i \in A, a_i(u) = a_i(v)$, it will be simply denoted by Φ_A. This function induce a partition $\{g_1, g_2, \ldots g_k\}$ on V where in each group g_i, every node has exactly the same values for the set of attributes A.

In fact, The *A-compatible* Φ_A only considers the node attributes. However, nodes do not just have attributes, but also participate in pairwise relationships represented by the edges.

For that, we consider now relationships when grouping nodes. For a grouping, we denote the neighbor-groups of node v in E_i as $NeighborGroups_{\Phi,E_i}(v) = \{\Phi(u)|(u, v) \in E_i\}$ which represents the set of groups on the partition associated with Φ where at least one element is connected to v by the relation E_i.

23.4.1 Attributes and Relationships Compatible Grouping

For a set of attributes $A \subseteq \Lambda(G)$ and a set of relations R, a grouping is compatible with the set of attributes A and relationship types R or simply (A, R)-*compatible*, if Φ satisfies the following conditions:

1. Φ is *A-compatible*,
2. $\forall u, v \in V$ if $\Phi(u) = \Phi(v)$,

then $\forall E_i \in R, NeighborGroups_{\Phi,E_i}(u) \equiv NeighborGroups_{\Phi,E_i}(v)$.

In each group of an (A, R)-*compatible* grouping, all the nodes are homogeneous in terms of both the set of attributes A and the set of relations R. In other words, every node inside a group has exactly the same attributes of A, and is adjacent to nodes in the same set of groups for all the relations in R.

Now, we can formally define the graph aggregation algorithm k-SNAP. Note that all calculations will be made from the incidence matrix $A_t = (a^t_{i,j})_{1<i,j<n}$ associated with the relation E_i.

23.4.2 K-SNAP Algorithm

First of all, we must mention that k-SNAP has been introduced to improve SNAP by relaxing the homogeneity requirement for the relations, i.e., for all relationships between two groups for example, there is no requirement that all nodes in these two groups are involved, however we want to maximize the ratio of participation while maintaining the homogeneity requirement for the attributes (the grouping remains *A-compatible*).

For this, we propose the evaluation measure Δ that allows to determine for each iteration the best group to be split until the size of the grouping is equal to k.

But first, we define N_{E_t} the participation matrix of rank $|\Phi_A|(|\Phi_A|$ is the cardinal of the partition of V induced by Φ_A) corresponding to the relation E_t by:

$$(n^t_{i,j})_{1<i,j<|\Phi_A|} = \sum_{k=0}^{|g_i|}(1 - \prod_{l=0}^{|g_j|}(1 - a^t_{kl})) \tag{23.3}$$

Then, we define P the matrix of rank $|\Phi_A|$ which contains the ratios of participation of different groups with respect to the relation E_t:

$$(p^t_{i,j})_{1<i,j<|\Phi_A|} = \frac{n^t_{ij} + n^t_{ji}}{|g_i| + |g_j|} \tag{23.4}$$

For a given graph G, a set of attributes A and a set of relations R, the evaluation measure Δ of a *A-compatible grouping* Φ_A is defined as follows:

$$\Delta(\Phi_A) = \sum_{1\leq i,j\leq|\Phi_A|} \sum_{E_t\in R} \delta^t_{ij} \text{ avec } \delta^t_{ij} \begin{cases} n^t_{ij} & if \ \ p^t_{ij} \leq 0.5 \\ |g_i| - n^t_{ij} & otherwise \end{cases} \tag{23.5}$$

This measure is based on determining the difference in participation of each pair of groups with respect to the relationship E_t, i.e., Δ-measure counts the minimum number of differences in participations of group relationships between the given *A-compatible grouping* and a hypothetical (A, R)- *compatible grouping* of the same size. According to equation (23.5) we have two possible cases:

1. If this group, the relationship is weak ($p^t_{i,k} \leq 0.5$), then it counts the participation differences between this weak relationship and a non-relationship ($p^t_{i,k} = 0$).
2. On the other hand, if the group relationship is strong ($p^t_{i,k} > 0.5$), it counts the differences between this strong relationship and a 100 % participation-ratio group relationship ($p^t_{i,k} = 1$).

Finally we define a matrix $W_{E_t} = (\delta^t_{ij})_{1\leq i,j\leq|\Phi_A|}$ from equation (23.5), that evaluates the part of the Δ value contributed by a group g_i with one of its neighbors g_j in a group relationship of type E_t.

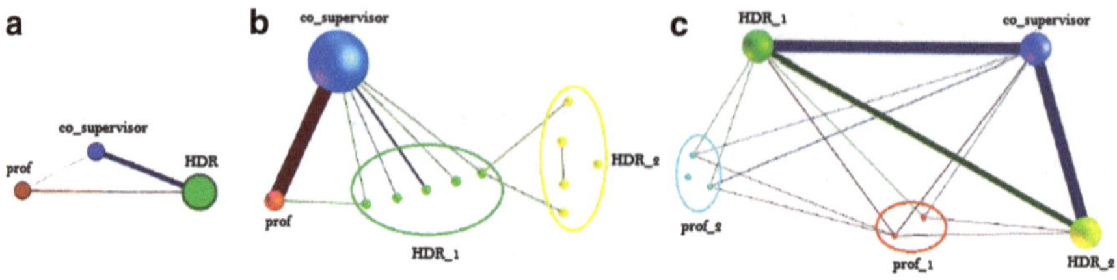

Fig. 23.8 The *A-Compatible Grouping and the 2 first iterations*

Given k the desired number of groups, the k-SNAP operation produces an (A, R)*-compatible grouping* with the minimum Δ value, starting from a *A-compatible grouping* and Δ initialized to zero, the procedure is to look for each iteration the group to split. For this, we introduce a heuristic that chooses the group that makes the most contribution to Δ with one of its neighbour groups. More formally, for each group g_i, we denote $CT(g_i)$ as follows: $CT(g_i) = max\left\{\delta_{ij}^t\right\}$.

Then, at each iterative step, we always choose the group with the maximum CT value to split, based on whether nodes in this group g_i which have relationships with nodes in its neighbour group g_t, where: $g_t = \arg\max_{g_j}\{\delta_{ij}^t\}$ and then split it into two sub-groups according to the following strategy: one of these groups contains all nodes participating in the relationship with the group g_t and the other contains the rest, i.e. the nodes that have no relation with the group g_t.

Now we will apply the algorithm on the graph extracted from the social network of thesis director (Fig. 23.7). In this experiment, we are interested in analysing how thesis directors in the database interact with each other based on two relations *Same_Laboratory* and *Same_student*. Each node in this graph has one attribute called *grade*, a direct visualization highlights our inability to interpret this graph without further treatment.

In order to explain the process of classification of k-SNAP, we will analyze the result of this classification on a sample of the real graph.

At first, k-SNAP generates a summary formed by three groups (*A-Compatible Grouping*) in accordance with the modalities *HDR, co-supervisor* and *prof* of the attribute *grade* as shown in Fig. 23.8a. The first iteration (Fig. 23.8b) leads to the subdivision of the HDR group into two subgroups according to the relationship *Same_Student*, because it maximizes the contribution of Δ. This iteration gives rise to two groups: *HDR_1* group consists of the HDRs that supervise a student with at least one professor or "co-supervisor".

However, *HDR_2* group consists of the HDRs who supervise students that have only as director, HDRs. After the second iteration (Fig. 23.8c), the group of professors is divided into two subgroups according to the relationship *Same_Laboratory* (Fig 23.9); the professor of *prof_1* group shares the lab with at least one of the other groups (HDR and co-supervisor), i.e., the laboratory to which they belong has members with various degrees. Even if our aggregation algorithm is rather of a semantic nature (takes into account the contents of the node), it's interesting to

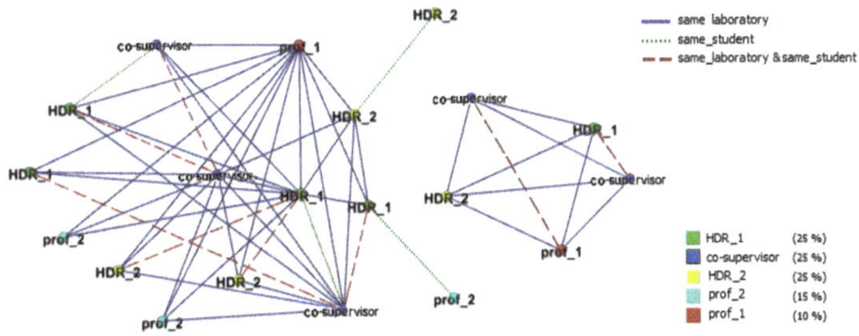

Fig. 23.9 Overview of the graph after the second iteration

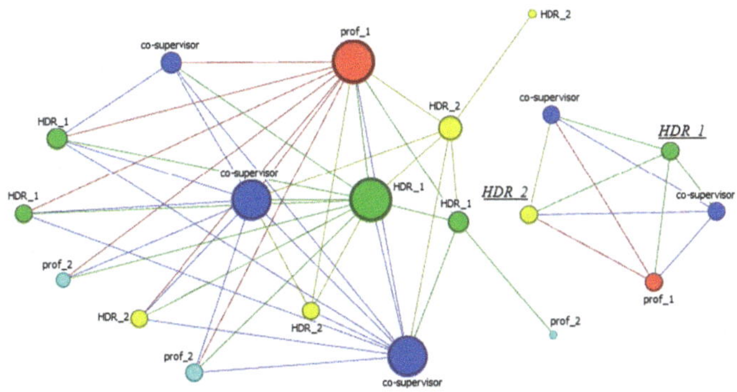

Fig. 23.10 Degree centrality of the graph

apply some of SNA metrics and try to compare its results with our criterion. We have chosen degree centrality as a measure and it distribution within the network is shown in the figure below (Fig. 23.10). According to the subdivision of the HDR group (Fig. 23.8b), we can notice that nodes belonging to the *HDR*_1 group have globally a high degree of centrality. This is in accordance with our principle of division. In fact, all nodes of *HDR*_1 group supervises a student with at least one professor or "co-supervisor" thus, this creates a link which consequently increases the degree of centrality. It's the same interpretation for professors in the second iteration (Fig. 23.8c).

We can say that our results are consistent with the centrality measure.

However, if two nodes (highlighted and written in italic (Fig. 23.10)) have the same median index of centrality, they may do not belong to the same group because their relationships with others are of different types. In this case, the measure of centrality is not adequate to our criterion; it depends on the nature of the relationship.

By changing the resolutions of summaries, users can better understand the characteristics of the original graph data and also explore the differences and similarities across different iterative steps.

23.5 Conclusion

In this paper, we have presented an approach to extract a social network from a relational database, then the aggregation method of the resulted social network using K-SNAP algorithm.

The social network extraction process is an application of the graph extraction approach from a relational database. This process allows having different graphs using as input the same relational database and the type of entities chosen by the user. The extraction approach is based on two steps: (23.1) translation of a relational database into a graph database, and (23.2) graph transformation which is realized after a process of objects identification then a graph rearrangement (nodes and relations). We have applied our approach using a real database.

The main interest to use K-SNAP was to show that algorithms designed for being applied on other kind of data sources can be use without any adaptation after applying our method for extracting social networks.

In our future work, we will focus on how to improve the extracting method by the use of an automatically built ontology describing the relations between the entities on the relational database. Then, we will try to define a storage system based on the hypernode model and a graph query language better suited to the social network structure. We will also improve the aggregation method by combining it with conceptual clustering.

Acknowledgements This work is partially financed by the ARSA project (Social Networks Analysis for Public Administrations) and by the STIC INRIA-Tunisia project "Social network exploration for recommender systems". The Academic chair in Business Intelligence is funded by SAP.

References

1. Andries, M., Gemis, M., Paredaens, J., Thyssens, I., Bussche, J.D.: Concepts for graph-oriented object manipulation. In: Proceedings of the 3rd International Conference on Extending Database Technology: Advances in Database Technology, vol. 580, pp. 21–38. Springer, London (1992)
2. Angles, R., Gutierrez, C.: Survey of graph database models. ACM Comput. Surv. **40**, 1–39 (2008)
3. Barnes, J.A.: Class and committees in a Norwegian island parish. Hum. Relat. **7**, 39–58 (1954)
4. Chakrabarti, D., Faloutsos, Zhan, C.Y.: Visualization of large networks with min-cutplots, a-plots and r-mat. Int. J. Hum. Comput. Stud. **655**, 434–445 (2007)
5. Culotta, A., Bekkerman, R., McCallum, A.: Extracting social networks and contact information from email and the web. In: First Conference on Email and Anti-Spam, Computer Science Department Faculty Publication Series, Mountain View, California (2004)
6. Freeman, L.C.: A set of measures of centrality based upon betweenness. Sociometry **40**, 35–41 (1977)
7. Gemis, M., Paredaens, J.: An object-oriented pattern matching language. In: JSSST, vol. 742, pp. 339–355. Springer, Berlin (1993)
8. Girvan, M., Newman, M.E.J.: Community structure in social and biological networks. Proc. Natl. Acad. Sci. U. S. A. **99**, 7821–7826 (2002)

9. Graves, M., Bergeman, E.R., Lawrence, C.B.: Graph database systems for genomics. IEEE Eng. Med. Biol. **14**, 737–745 (1995)
10. Gyssens, M., Paredaens, J., Gucht, D. V.: A graph-oriented object model for database end-user interfaces. SIGMOD Rec. **19**, 24–33 (1990)
11. Hidders, J.: Typing graph-manipulation operations. In: Proceedings of the 9th International Conference on Database Theory (ICDT), pp. 394–409. Springer, Berlin (2002)
12. Kuper, G.M., Vardi, M.Y.: The logical data model. ACM Trans. Database Syst. **18**, 379–413 (1993)
13. Levene, M., Loizou, G.: A graph-based data model and its ramifications. IEEE Trans. Knowl. Data Eng. **7**, 809–823 (1995)
14. Levene, M., Poulovassilis, A.: An object-oriented data model formalized through hyper-graphs. Data Knowl. Eng. **6**, 205–224 (1991)
15. MacQueen, J.: Some methods for classification and analysis of multivariate observations. In: Proceedings of the 5th Berkeley Symposium on Mathematical Statistics Probability, University of California 1965/66, Berkeley, vol. 1, pp. 281–297 (1967)
16. Maatuk, A., Akhtar, M., Rossiter, B.N.: Relational database migration: a perspective. In: DEXA'08, Turin, pp. 676–683 (2008)
17. Mika, P.: Flink: semantic web technology for the extraction and analysis of social networks. J. Web Semant. **3**, 211–223 (2005)
18. Newman, M.E.J.: The structure and function of complex networks. SIAM Rev. **45**, 167–256 (2003)
19. Newman, M.E.J.: Detecting community structure in networks. Eur. Phys. J. B **38**, 321–330 (2004)
20. Newman M.E.J, Girvan, M.: Finding and evaluating community structure in networks. Phys. Rev. E **69**, 026113 (2004)
21. Ng, A., Jordan, M., Weiss, Y., Dietterich, T., Becker, S., Ghahramani, Z.: Advances in Neural Information Processing Systems. Chapter on Spectral Clustering: Analysis and an Algorithm, vol. 14. MIT Press, Cambridge (2002)
22. Pentland, A.: Socially aware computation and communication. Computer **38**, 33–40 (2005)
23. Santo, F.: Community detection in graphs. Phys. Rep. **486**, 75–174 (2010)
24. Schaeffer, S.A.: Graph clustering. Comput. Sci. Rev. **1**, 27–64 (2007)
25. Shi, J., Malik, J.: Normalized cuts and image segmentation. IEEE Trans. Pattern Anal. Mach. Intell. **22**, 888–905 (2000)
26. Soussi, R., Aufaure, M.A., Baazaoui, H.: Towards social network extraction using a graph database. In: Proceedings of Second International Conference on Advances in Databases, Knowledge, and Data Applications, Menuires, pp. 28–34 (2010)
27. Rodrigues Jr., J.F., Traina, A.J.M., Faloutsos, C., Traina Jr., C.: Supergraph visualization. In: ISM '06: Proceedings of the Eighth IEEE International Symposium on Multimedia, pp. 227–234. IEEE Computer Society, Washington, DC (2006)
28. Tian, Y., Hankins, R.A., Patel, J.M.: Efficient aggregation for graph summarization. In: SIGMOD '08: Proceedings of the 2008 ACM SIGMOD International Conference on Management of Data, pp. 567–580. ACM, New York (2008)
29. von Luxburg, U.: A tutorial on spectral clustering, vol. 149. Technical Report, Max Planck Institute for Biological Cybernetics (2006)
30. Washio T., Motoda, H.: State of the art of graph-based data mining. SIGKDD Explor. Newsl. **5**, 59–68 (2003)
31. Watts, D.J., Strogatz, S.H.: Collective dynamics of 'small-world' networks. Nature **393**(6684), 440–442 (1998)
32. Xu, X., Zhan, J., Zhu, H.: Using social networks to organize researcher community. In: Proceedings of the IEEE ISI 2008 Paisi, Paccf, and SOCO International Workshops on Intelligence and Security Informatics, pp. 421–427. Springer, Heidelberg (2008)
33. Yan X., Han J.: gSpan: Graph-based substructure pattern mining. In: Proceedings of ICDM'02, Maebashi City, pp. 721–724 (2002)

Chapter 24
Extending Social Network Analysis with Discourse Analysis: Combining Relational with Interpretive Data

Christine Moser, Peter Groenewegen, and Marleen Huysman

Abstract Online occupational communities are a rapidly growing phenomenon and will become increasingly important to firms in the future. This growth has been mirrored by scientific innovations: major advances have been made with regard to technology, software development and statistical modeling. However, we are often left with only partial information: although we might be able to gather very detailed and massive relational data from for example online communities, we often overlook information on the ties that bind. While we are provided with an increasingly detailed topology of a network this does not allude to what content is at stake. We therefore propose to combine Social Network Analysis (SNA) and Discourse Analysis (DA) in order to reach a deeper understanding of the community. Data from an ongoing study of an online occupational community were analyzed as an example using SNA and DA. We present findings from SNA and are able to complement this relational information with interpretive findings from DA. We contribute to the methodological literature on online communities, in particular in the fields of SNA and DA.

C. Moser (✉) · P. Groenewegen
Department of Organization Science, Faculty of Social Science, VU University Amsterdam, Amsterdam, The Netherlands
e-mail: c.moser@vu.nl; p.groenewegen@vu.nl

M. Huysman
Department of Information, Logistics and Innovation, Faculty of Economics and Business Administration, VU University Amsterdam, Amsterdam, The Netherlands
e-mail: m.h.huysman@vu.nl

T. Özyer et al. (eds.), *The Influence of Technology on Social Network Analysis and Mining*, Lecture Notes in Social Networks 6, DOI 10.1007/978-3-7091-1346-2_24,

24.1 Introduction

In response to the mushrooming developments around the Internet in general and social media in particular, we recently see major advancements in tools and technology that facilitate data collection for social network analysis (SNA) and mining. One might even argue that approaches toward social network research are technology-driven. The ability to be able to 'data-crunch' seduces many researchers to do exactly that. However, sometimes this abundance in information leads to false hopes: although enormous data-sets can be studied in a certain way, this does not automatically improve our knowledge about the phenomenon under study. For example, when investigating networks it is of course necessary to investigate the network topology. For this, advanced technology in the field of data mining is of the essence and it needs to be combined with SNA tools. Nevertheless, whenever the researcher is interested in the actual content of the network as well, these advanced methods often fall short of expectations. We have a lot of information on the nodes and the structure connecting them, but we fail to spot the content of ties. In this article, we propose that it is sometimes useful to complement advanced approaches toward the collection and analysis of social network data with an interpretive approach, for which we chose discourse analysis (DA). By doing so, we are able to offer additional explanations to what we see when performing SNA. Furthermore, we might be able to interpret already existing explanations about the network structure more accurately. We argue that it can often be beneficial to not only rely on a single method, when the combination of methods potentially yields valuable insights.

Recently, scholars called for more use of mixed methods in social research [1]. Often, the execution of only statistical analyses is perceived as not sufficiently covering the field of research, or leading to neglect of relevant information from the empirical data. On the other hand, qualitative studies are often experienced as too detailed, too diverse, and findings are thought of not to be generalizable [2]. In this study, we combine two methods. Specifically, Social Network Analysis in combination with Discourse Analysis is used, thereby responding to calls for research in this direction, in particular in the field of information systems [3]. Data stem from a case study of an online occupational community. Publicly available message board postings are used as indicators of network ties for Social Network Analysis (SNA), and the content of the postings as data for Discourse Analysis (DA).

Network research focuses on relations and patterns of relations rather than on (single) actors and their attributes [4, 5]. It can incorporate data from different sources (e.g., qualitative, quantitative, graphical data, [5]). The structure of a network is important, as is the embeddedness of actors within the network. Calculations of various network parameters, such as density, centrality and brokerage shed light on the position, activity and influence of actors in the network. Within discourse research, the focus is on language use. A discourse is defined as 'a particular way of talking about and understanding the world (or an aspect of the world)' [6:1]. Language is seen as a web of meaning and sensemaking. Within discourse analysis this web is traced, and the meaning that actors ascribe to words is investigated.

This article is structured as follows. First, we provide a short review of research into online communities. Next, in the approach section we describe in detail how we applied the two approaches in the present study, and why they complement each other. We illustrate how the two approaches can fruitfully be combined in methods and analyses. We conclude with a discussion, where we point out future research directions.

24.2 Research into Online Occupational Communities

A growing number of communities mainly interacts online [7], due to the rise of the global Internet and improved technology [8–10]. Within online communities, computer-mediated communication plays a prominent role: language is the main channel of expression and social interaction. Computer-mediated discourse is 'the communication produced when human beings interact with one another by transmitting messages via networked computers' [11:612]. Online communities differ from actual communities due to their restriction of social interaction to online communication. Despite this restriction, complex social interaction takes place in online communities [12]. Communication as the main way of social interaction in online communities can therefore provide unique rich data: discourse manifests itself in written and spoken text, and can be accessed through the analysis of message board postings, as several studies have shown [13, 14].

Studies of online communities typically employ a variety of data analytical methods but pay scant attention to the variegated manner in which content of the communication can be analyzed. A new research stream uses community data as input for analysis and increasingly includes content analysis [15], but also here various mathematical models, survey research and statistical methods prevail. For example, Bagozzi and Dholakia [16] conducted research into an open source software community, employing a survey and analyzing it using structural equation modeling. Franke and Shah [17] also use a survey in order to investigate how community users share among and assist each other. Similarly, a community around Apache software has been studied by Franke and von Hippel [18] by means of a survey. Often, motivations to contribute to community knowledge are investigated, such as in the case of the Linux kernel community [19], a community about library software [20], a community about computer-controlled music instruments [21], firm-hosted communities in general [22] or different virtual communities [23]. Other research was interested in behavior of community members [24], or sharing among members [25]. There are some studies that employ qualitative methods. Case studies [26–31] and ethnographies [7, 32, 33] are dominant in that domain. However, studies that combine approaches are scarce. For example, Fauchart and von Hippel [34] combine a grounded theory approach with a survey; but the findings from the grounded theory part serve as input for the survey, and are not actually combined in the analysis. Similarly, O'Mahony and Ferraro [35] develop a theoretical model using an ethnographic approach, and later develop a survey that highlights one part of the theoretical model. They also limit their analysis to these two different parts.

The above review by far does not mention all research that has been conducted in the field of online communities; nevertheless, these studies represent the methodological approaches that are typically used, and the problems that are addressed. However, many studies could profit from a more in-depth analysis of the ongoing conversation in communities, especially since many of the mentioned studies into online communities are positioned within or touch upon the field of computer-mediated communication. This type of communication lends itself to be studied from a social network perspective, as well from a more content-oriented or discourse perspective: all necessary information is often at hand, as we will see in our illustrative analysis. Thus, we believe that an integration of social network analysis and discourse analysis is a fruitful approach to study computer-mediated communication in online occupational communities. In the next section, we illustrate how this depth could be reached. We do so by first computing degree centrality of community members and explain what this measure expresses. Next, we will continue by analyzing the same data in a different way, using discourse analysis. We will then show that the combination of methods leads to a much deeper understanding of the problem under study.

24.3 Providing Networks with Meaning

Network research is interested in the topology of a network – the structure – and the position of individuals in this structure. There are two main streams of research: one focuses on the structural side of networks, and accordingly presumes that individuals are influenced by this structure. On the other hand, the position of the individual can be studied: depending on the number of social ties, the kind of ties, length of paths and such measures, an individual can access the network and surrounding individuals, and is therefore able to tap into her social capital [36]. To illustrate the point we want to make in this study, we conduct a straightforward analysis of our data and compute degree centrality of community members, based on message board postings. In social network analysis simple indicators such as degree centrality are frequently employed. Centrality is a critical concept which has led to an increasingly finely tuned set of centrality measures to cater for specific theoretical aims [37,38]. In this case study the degree centrality suffices; our goal is not to make claims about prominence, status or brokerage in this online occupational community, but rather to show that any social network measure – in this case degree centrality – can potentially profit from the combination with an interpretive method – in this case discourse analysis.

Discourse analysis provides a strong analytical tool for the study of text since it 'focuses on how social relations, identity, knowledge and power are constructed through written and spoken texts in communities (. . .)' [39]. Within discourse analysis, important words are traced in conversations. In addition, use of words that are central to the dominant discourse can be traced back to individual actors. The focus lies on the analysis of the structuration of meaning within a network. Here, structure is formed by language, in the form of written text. Adopting elements of Laclau and Mouffe's discourse theory [40], language is believed to be socially constructed: 'Language use is a social phenomenon: it is through conventions, negotiations and conflicts in social contexts that structures of meaning are fixed and challenged' [6:25]. Discourse is structured around nodal points: a sign, or word, around which other signs are organized. The signs around this nodal point derive meaning from their relation to it, but the nodal point also transfers meaning upon the surrounding signs.

24.4 Setting and Methods

The case study that is described in this article has been conducted among the community of Dutch cake decorators. The community operates independent of a firm or organization, membership is voluntary and free of charge. The website was launched by a number of Dutch cake enthusiasts in 2004. At the time of writing, the website has about 10,000 registered members (with daily newcomers) and about 500 regularly active members (members who post several times a month, and posted in the past more than 150 messages). Members differ in age, gender, education and background, and left a total of more than 1.3 million postings. Postings are linked to topics; any registered member can open a topic or post about an existing topic. The top ten users are responsible for more than 12 % of the total number of postings. The average number of messages posted daily is more than 600. Data for this article were collected from a single day on one sub-forum of the website. Following Fairclough [41], data were selected according to the identification of *cruces,* which are defined as moments of crisis. This conceptualization is slightly modified as moments of crisis are called events. Not only moments of crisis trigger what Fairclough had in mind: 'such moments of crisis make visible aspects of practices which might normally be naturalized, and therefore difficult to notice; but they also show change in process, the actual ways in which people deal with the problematization of practices' [41]. It is argued that other, non-crisis events may also visualize social practices, simply through above average frequency of social interactions. Events in this manner are therefore defined as the days with most forum postings. We selected one such day and extracted our data from the online community web site.

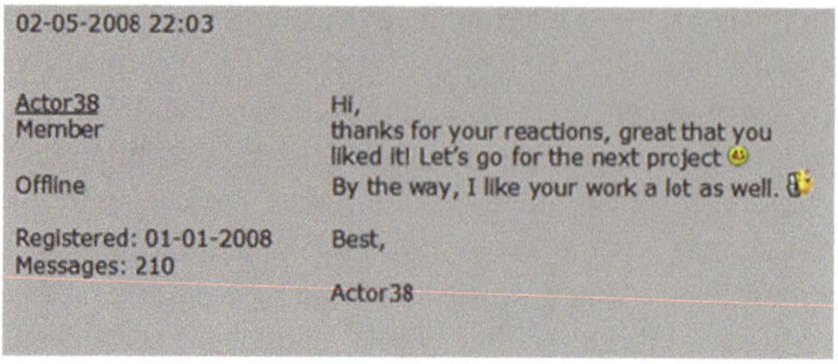

Fig. 24.1 Example of a typical message

Table 24.1 Two-mode matrix of message board postings

	1	2	3	4	5	6
38	1	0	0	0	0	0
39	0	1	0	0	0	0
40	1	0	1	0	0	0
41	0	0	0	0	1	1
42	0	0	0	0	1	0
43	0	0	0	0	0	1

24.4.1 Social Network Analysis

For the SNA part of our analysis, 636 postings were analyzed, posted by 106 different members. A posting contains several pieces of information: text, time stamp, and source. Figure 24.1 shows an example of a typical message.

As a first step of the social network analysis, data was entered into a 2-mode matrix. This means that we entered actors in rows, and events in columns. An event was defined as a topic on the forum. A network tie was defined as the simultaneous presence of postings at the same topic. Table 24.1 shows an example of such a matrix.

In the rows, we can find the actors (actors 38, 39, 40, 41, 42 and 43). The columns represent events, defined as topics: shown are topics 1, 2, 3, 4, 5 and 6. We see that actor 38 and 40 both are present at topic 1, which from our perspective means that they have a tie. The same goes for actor 41 and 42 and topic 5, and actor 42 and 43 at topic 6. The 2-mode matrix was then projected to a 1-mode, so that the matrix presented only actors. Projection followed Bonacich [42] and was executed in Ucinet [43].[1] The projected network from the example in Table 24.1 then looks like this (Table 24.2):

[1] 'Given a binary incidence matrix A where the rows represent actors and the columns events, then the matrix AA' gives the number of events in which actors simultaneously attended. Hence AA' (i,j) is the number of events attended by both actor i and actor j. The matrix A'A gives the number of events simultaneously attended by a pair of actors. Hence A'A(i,j) is the number of actors who attended both event i and event j' [43].

Table 24.2 Projected 1-mode matrix of message board postings

	38	39	40	41	42	43
38	0	0	1	0	0	0
39	0	0	0	0	0	0
40	1	0	0	0	0	0
41	0	0	0	0	1	1
42	0	0	0	1	0	0
43	0	0	0	1	0	0

Table 24.3 Normalized degree centrality

Actor	Normalized degree centrality
25	17.534
61	17.421
33	15.894
38	14.593
40	14.310

This step led to a valued network which was dichotomized at the level of co-presence in postings, using Ucinet [43]. That is, all values above '1' were transformed into '1'.

Having prepared the data for the most important part of our analysis, we computed degree centrality [38] in Ucinet [43]. Analysis is based upon the following: 'The number of vertices adjacent to a given vertex in a symmetric graph is the degree of that vertex. For non-symmetric data the in-degree of a vertex u is the number of ties received by u and the out-degree is the number of ties initiated by u.' [43]. The underlying formula is expressed as

$$\Sigma(\mathrm{cmax} - \mathrm{c(vi)})$$

divided by the maximum value, where c(vi) is the degree centrality of vertex vi, given vertices v1. . . vn and maximum degree centrality cmax.

We then normalized the data, in order to show their relative values. The normalized degree centrality is the degree divided by the maximum possible degree expressed as a percentage [43]. We present the results from this calculation in Table 24.3. Actors 25, 61, 33, 38 and 40 appear to be most central in this network.

In this section, we explained in detail what kind of data we used to calculate a normalized degree centrality measure. In the next section, we will describe how we implemented the next step of our analysis: discourse analysis.

24.4.2 Discourse Analysis

At this point, we have gathered information on the network topology: we know that the network features a core-periphery structure. Furthermore, we identified the most

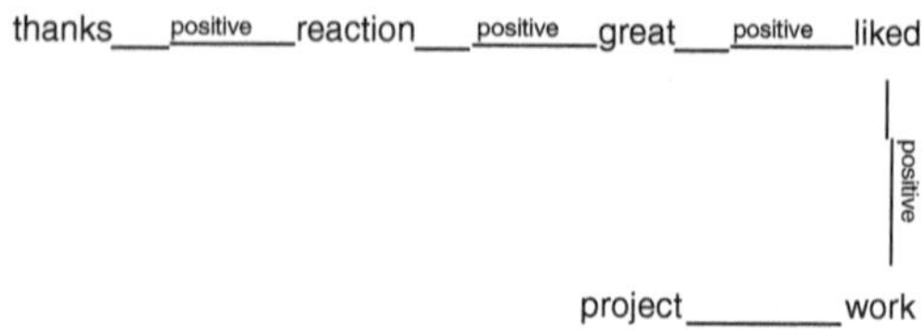

Fig. 24.2 Example of mini-discourse analysis

central actors, at least in terms of normalized degree centrality. The next step will be to supplement this network with meaning: what is it that circulates in this network, in terms of content and meaning? In order to fill in the picture, a combination of discourse theory [40] and critical discourse analysis [41] was adopted. Discourse analysis is an interpretive approach, and is considered a qualitative method [44]. Therefore, analysis relies on the interpretation of the researcher, instead of formulas. Discourse analysis differs significantly from other approaches that use text as data, such as content analysis [45, 46] or NLP techniques. These approaches tend to categorize text, assign numbers to categories or portions of text, and then calculate statistics. However, discourse analysis is concerned with the actual *meaning* of a message, rather than values assigned to it. That is, when looking at the message as shown in Fig. 24.1, the number of words is irrelevant. The important aspect is the meaning of the message: Actor38 is grateful, expresses confidence in the next project, and reciprocates compliments. Discourse analysis thus delivers categories of meaning rather than numbers, and tries to explain how actors attach meaning to their messages.

A discourse is defined as 'a particular way of talking about and understanding the world (or an aspect of the world)' [6:1]. Within discourse theory, words form a web of meaning that can be traced through the analysis of language. Discourses are arranged around *nodal points,* or *floating signifiers.* Floating signifiers are 'signs that different discourses struggle to invest with meaning in their own particular way' [6:28]. This entails that different meanings are attached to some words in the dominant discourse, or that their meaning is not yet fixed. The meaning of a word is thought to be fixed by *key signifiers.* Key signifiers are words that in themselves are less significant, but become important through the combination with other signifiers. This discursive struggle takes place within frames of reference within which meaning is attached to words, through the combination of key signifiers. For example, the message of Actor38 (Fig. 24.1) only is filled with meaning when combined with surrounding messages. The word 'reactions' is meaningless, until we know that 'reactions' refers to messages of other actors, who complimented Actor38 on her cake. Thus, the word 'reactions' carries a positive meaning (because the reactions were compliments), and is also associated with 'cake' (because the reactions were about a cake). However, the analysis of a message only takes into account the words that were actually used in that message. A mini-discourse analysis of this example could look like the example in Fig. 24.2.

Table 24.4 Use of discursive elements of actor 38

	We-them	Compliments and empathy	Competition	Advice and criticism
Actor38	17 %	47 %	15 %	21 %

However, more than one message is needed to conduct a useful analysis in order to be able to say anything meaningful about the actual discourse. We thus carried out a discourse analysis of the messages that we earlier used for the social network analysis. Based upon detailed analyses as shown in Fig. 24.2, we sorted and categorized data. We arrived at the following overarching categories: *we-them, compliments and empathy, competition,* and *advice and criticism*. (Table 24.5 offers some examples of messages that represent the categories.) Discourse analysis provided us with something we lacked: information about the content of the network. We now can put together a picture of how the dominant community discourse might look like: it comprises four different categories.

After having conducted network as well as discourse analysis, we now know how the structure of the network looks like in terms of degree centrality, and also what the prevailing elements of the dominant discourse are. The dominant discourse, in this article, is reflected in the four categories that we found in our messages. In other words, the discourse that is dominant in the community of cake bakers, consists of messages that mainly are concerned with the categories *we-them, compliments and empathy, competition,* and *advice and criticism*. As a last step in this illustration, we want to bring together the two. We argue that it is not only significant to find out what constitutes the dominant discourse, but also how central actors use this discourse. Therefore, we investigated one of the central actors closer. We coded all of the messages that Actor38 left on the message board that day into one of the four categories. Table 24.4 shows the results of this analysis.

In this section, we discussed in detail which methods we used in which way. In the following section, we will report the results of this analysis.

24.5 Findings

After having analyzed our data, we now report our findings. The network graph, a visualization of the earlier calculated degree centrality (Fig. 24.3), shows that the central actors not only feature the highest degree centrality as in number of postings, but are also embedded in the network: they form the very core. This core-periphery structure is typical for online communities, as it also reflects the tendency toward the small world phenomenon [47].

In Table 24.5, we present the four categories that emerged from discourse analysis: they represent the dominant discourse that prevails within the community

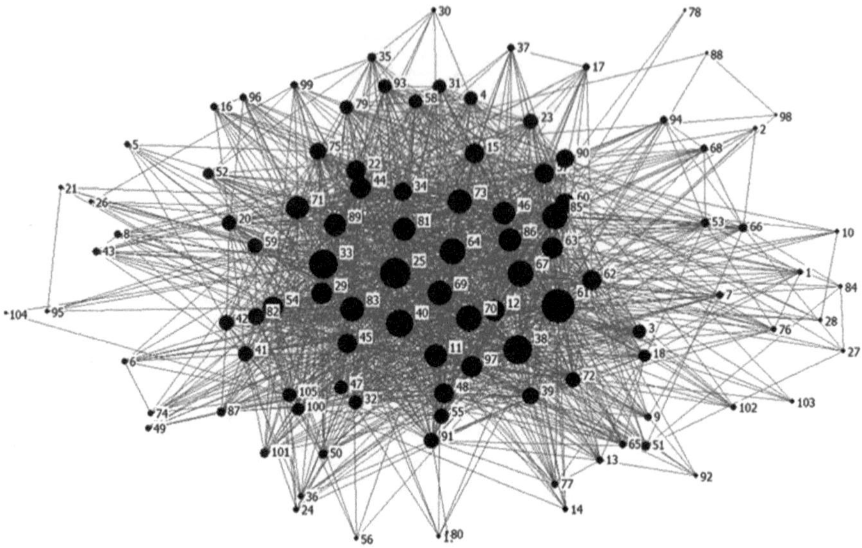

Fig. 24.3 Degree centrality

Table 24.5 Four categories that represent community discourse

Category	Explication and illustration
We-them	Use of abbreviations/jargon; use of real names instead of avatars; references to personal, offline contact; references to we vs. them (we, henhouse, professionals, cake ladies, cake enthusiasts, hunks, dames vs. you, the rest of the forum, the not-Xers, pupils); attributes of we vs. them (make you jealous, have insider stories, won't unveil the mystery, won't post everything on the forum, have capital, can buy stuff vs. we get the picture, are curious, as if I were there, want to come, am sorry, don't know so many people, we are nice too, save money, get a job);
Compliments and empathy	Demonstrations of empathy and emotions (what a relief, next time better, big hug, I know how much it means to you, you can do it, what a misery, you learn from your mistakes, you need to get over it, come on, I saw how sad you were, great, wow, luckily, happy for you); wishes of success and congratulations;
Competition	Use of competitive vocabulary (won a competition, 1st place, you're on 1, top 5, nr. 1, winner, great haul, fun of scoring, passed, challenge, want to have that, jealous); curiosity about other peoples results;
Advice and criticism	Advice as positive support that is sought among community members (great, beautiful, leave it that way, go ahead, perfect, sweet, professional, stylish, smart, will succeed); objective advice in form of questions (is it compulsory?, maybe at home?) criticism dampened by use of smilies or apologies (don't do it, sorry; if I were you ;)

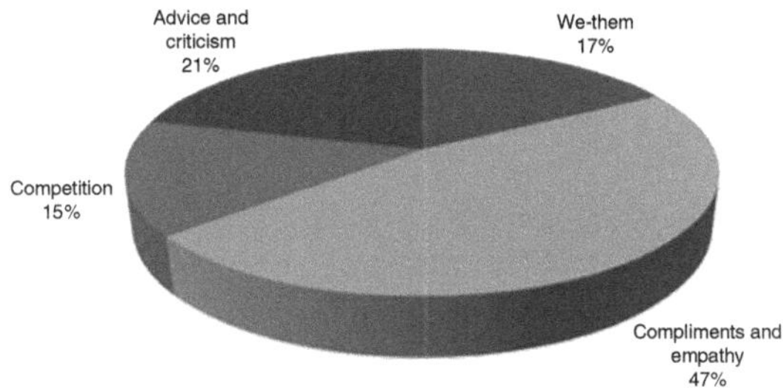

Fig. 24.4 Distribution of messages of actor 38 across four categories

of cake bakers. We add quotes and typical expressions to illustrate the categories. The first category, *we-them*, is about the way community members refer to each other in day-to-day communication. It is very clear that they differentiate between at least two different groups. Second, *compliments and empathy* play an important role in the community discourse. Third, *competition* is related to the former category: although members readily compliment each other, they do also compete for attention, reputation and even more flattering comments. Finally, members engage in *advice and criticism*.

Clearly, a large portion of Actor38's messages belong to the category 'compliments and empathy'. The remainder of her messages is almost evenly distributed across the other three categories. Figure 24.4 visualizes this distribution.

At the end of this analytic illustration, we are able to make claims about the network topology in terms of degree centrality, the content of the network in terms of the dominant discourse, and the use of this discourse of Actor38. Obviously, this last step could be repeated for any actor. In Fig. 24.5, the combination of findings of our illustrative analysis is presented.

Using social network analysis in combination with discourse analysis, we provided our network with meaning. We not only mapped out the topology of the network, but were also able to describe the dominant discourse of the network, and analyzed discourse usage of one individual actor.

24.6 Discussion

The combination of results from social network analysis and discourse analysis yields insights into the topology as well as the content of an online community. Social network analysis provides data about the network and the relations among its actors, whereas discourse analysis allocates meaning within the network. By combining these two methods, we aim to bridge a gap that often separates scientific approaches that might profit from each other. We showed that social network analysis is useful to map out the topology of an online community. This topology is valuable to for example identify central actors in a network. On the other hand,

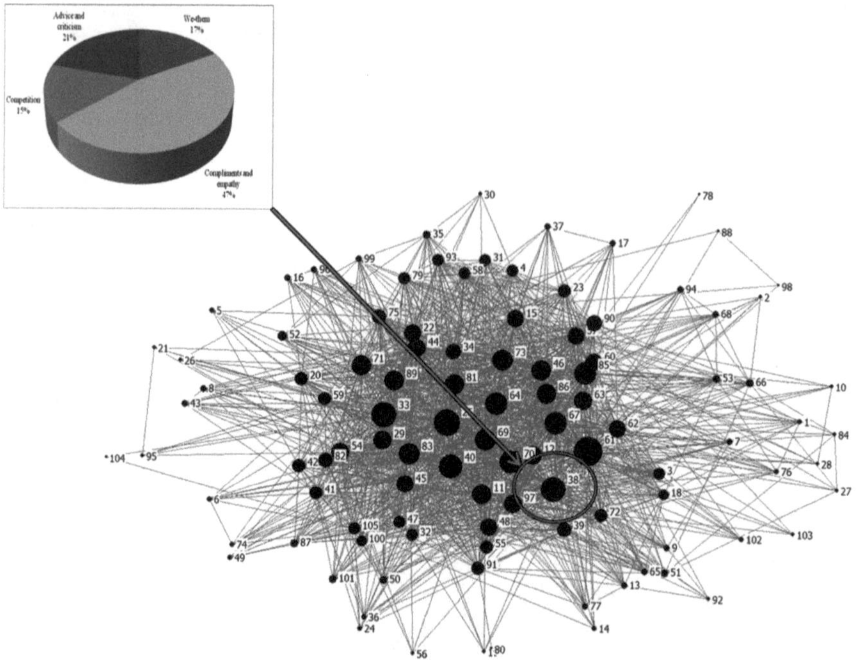

Fig. 24.5 Combination of findings of illustrative analysis

discourse analysis provides the network with meaning: when we know what the community is all about, we can interpret the findings from network analysis more thoroughly. The combination of social network analysis and discourse analysis integrates knowledge about actors' position in a given network with their use of the dominant community discourse. Thus, position can be linked to content, and vice versa.

One of the disadvantages of discourse analysis is that some form of text is needed in order to extract meaning from it. In addition, it takes time to analyze data properly. Furthermore, discourse analysis produces 'soft' data instead of numbers that can be statistically computed, urging some scholars to comment on its low generalizability [2]. However, we have shown that it is possible to conduct discourse analysis and nevertheless transform it into output that is for some more feasible than words. Visualization or statistically expressed numbers sometimes help to make interpretive results more accessible, and therefore enhance the quality of the research. In accordance with the illustration presented in this article, discourse analysis is possibly most valuable when complemented with other methods, as is reflected by researchers calling for more use of mixed methods [1]. Accordingly, future research should be interested in other combinations of discourse analysis with other approaches. For example, different measures of social network analysis might complement findings from discourse analysis [3]. Moreover, when combining the interpretive qualities of discourse analysis with more descriptive content analysis techniques [46], insights might be gained regarding the semantic network within the community.

Future research should take into account the advantages that a combination of methods yields. There are several directions that are as yet unexplored, but promise fruitful results. One possibility is to repeat the analysis we performed in this article several times. This way, results could be interpreted over time and thus reveal network evolution, both in a structural as well as discursive way. Second, it might be interesting to compare the discursive profile of several actors. For example, do profiles of central actors differ significantly from the ones of peripheral actors? Do central actors feature similar profiles? Does a profile predict network position in the future? These are all compelling questions, and answers could help us understand online communities much better than we do now.

References

1. Hollstein, B.: Qualitative Methoden und Netzwerkanalyse – ein Widerspruch? In: Hollstein, B., Straus, F. (eds.) Qualitative Netzwerkanalyse. Konzepte, Methoden, Anwendungen, pp. 11–35. VS Verlag für Sozialwissenschaften, Wiesbaden (2006)
2. Graziano, A.M., Raulin, M.L.: Research Methods. A Process of Inquiry. Pearson, Boston (2004)
3. Vidgen, R., Henneberg, S., Naude, P.: What sort of community is the European conference on information systems? A social network analysis 1993–2005. Eur. J. Inf. Syst. **16**(1), 5–19 (2007)
4. Wasserman, S., Faust, K.: Social Network Analysis. Methods and Applications. Cambridge University Press, New York (1994)
5. Kilduff, M., Tsai, W.: Social Networks and Organizations. Sage, London (2003)
6. Phillips, L., Jørgensen, M.: Discourse Analysis as Theory and Method. Sage, London (2002)
7. Füller, J., Jawecki, G., Muhlbacher, H.: Innovation creation by online basketball communities. J. Bus. Res. **60**(1), 60–71 (2007)
8. Baym, N.K.: Interpreting soap operas and creating community: inside a electronic fan culture. In: Kiesler, S. (ed.) Culture of the Internet, pp. 138–163. Lawrence Erlbaum Associates, Mahwah (1997)
9. Reid, E.: Virtual worlds: culture and imagination. In: Jones, S.G. (ed.) CyberSociety. Computer-Mediated Communication and Community. Sage, Thousand Oaks (1995)
10. Cox, A.M.: An exploration of concepts of community through a case study of UK university web production. J. Inf. Sci. **34**(3), 327–345 (2008)
11. Herring, S.C.: Computer-mediated discourse. In: Schiffrin, D., Tannen, D., Hamilton, H. (eds.) Handbook of Discourse Analysis, pp. 612–634. Blackwell, Oxford (2003)
12. Baym, N.K.: The emergence of community in computer-mediated communication. In Jones, S.G. (ed.) CyberSociety. Computer-Mediated Communication and Community, pp. 138–163. Sage, Thousand Oaks (1995)
13. Brandes, U., Corman, S.R.: Visual unrolling of network evolution and the analysis of dynamic discourse. Inf. Vis. **2**(1), 40–50 (2003)
14. Malouf, R., Mullen, T.: Taking sides: user classification for informal online political discourse. Internet Res. **18**(2), 177–190 (2008)
15. Rosen, D., Woelfel, J., Krikorian, D., Barnett, G.A.: Procedures for analyses of online communities. J. Comput. Med. Commun. **8**(4) (2003)

16. Bagozzi, R.P., Dholakia, U.M.: Open source software user communities: a study of participation in Linux user groups. Manag. Sci. **52**(7), 1099–1115 (2006)
17. Franke, N., Shah, S.: How communities support innovative activities: an exploration of assistance and sharing among end-users. Res. Policy **32**(1), 157–178 (2003)
18. Franke, N., von Hippel, E.: Satisfying heterogeneous user needs via innovation toolkits: the case of Apache security software. Res. Policy **32**, 1199–1215 (2003)
19. Hertel, G., Niedner, S., Herrmann, S.: Motivation of software developers in open source projects: an internet-based survey of contributors to the Linux kernel. Res. Policy **32**, 1159–1177 (2003)
20. Morrison, P.D., Roberts, J.H., von Hippel, E.: Determinants of user innovation and innovation sharing in a local market. Manag. Sci. **46**(12), 1513–1527 (2000)
21. Jeppesen, L.B., Frederiksen, L.: Why do users contribute to firm-hosted user communities? The case of computer-controlled music instruments. Organ. Sci. **17**(1), 45–63 (2006)
22. Wiertz, C., de Ruyter, K.: Beyond the call of duty: why customers contribute to firm-hosted commercial online communities. Organ. Stud. **28**(3), 347–376 (2007)
23. Dholakia, U.M., Bagozzi, R.P., Klein Pearo, L.: A social influence model of comsumer participation in network- and small-groupbased virtual communities. Int. J. Res. Market. **21**, 241–263 (2004)
24. Huffaker, D., Wang, J., Treem, J., Fullerton, L., Poole, M.S., Ahmad, M.A., et al.: The social behaviors of experts in massive multiplayer online role-playing games. Paper presented at the International Conference on Computational Science and Engineering, Vancouver (2009)
25. Lakhani, K.R., von Hippel, E.: How open source software works:"free" user-to-user assistance. Res. Policy **32**(6), 923–943 (2003)
26. Hemetsberger, A., Reinhardt, C.: Learning and knowledge-building in open-source communities: a social-experiential approach. Manag. Learn. **37**(2), 187–214 (2006)
27. Piller, F., Schubert, P., Koch, M., Möslein, K.: Overcoming mass confusion: collaborative customer co-design in online communities. J. Comput. Med. Commun. **10**(4), article 8 (2005)
28. Ross, D.A.R.: Backstage with the knowledge boys and girls: Goffman and distributed agency in an organic online community. Organ. Stud. **28**(3), 307–325 (2007)
29. Van Oost, E., Verhaegh, S., Oudshoorn, N.: From innovation community to community innovation user-initiated innovation in wireless leiden. Sci. Technol. Human Value **34**(2), 182–205 (2009)
30. Müller-Seitz, G., Reger, G.: Is open source software living up to its promises? Insights for open innovation management from two open source software-inspired projects. R D Manag. **39**(4), 372–381 (2009)
31. Fang, Y., Neufeld, D.: Understanding sustained participation in open source software projects. J. Manag. Inf. Syst. **25**(4), 9–50 (2009)
32. Goodsell, T.L., Williamson, O.: The case of the brick huggers: the practice of an online community. City Community **7**(3), 251–271 (2008)
33. O'Mahony, S.: Guarding the commons: how community managed software projects protect their work. Res. Policy **32**, 1179–1198 (2003)
34. Fauchart, E., von Hippel, E.: Norms-based intellectual property systems: the case of French chefs. Organ. Sci. **19**(2), 187–201 (2008)
35. O'Mahony, S., Ferraro, F.: The emergence of governance in an open source community. Acad. Manag. J. **50**(5), 1079–1106 (2007)
36. Borgatti, S.P., Foster, P.C.: The network paradigm in organizational research: a review and typology. J. Manag. **29**(6), 991–1013 (2003)
37. Bonacich, P.: Power and centrality: a family of measures. Am. J. Sociol. **92**(5), 1170–1182 (1987)
38. Freeman, L.: Centrality in social networks. Conceptual clarification. Soc. Netw. **1**, 215–239 (1979)
39. Luke, A.: Theory and practice in critical discourse analysis. In: Saha, L. (ed.) International Encyclopedia of the Sociology in Education, pp. 50–56. Elsevier, Oxford (1997)

40. Laclau, E., Mouffe, C.: Hegemony and Socalist Strategy. Towards a Radical Democratic Politics. Verso, London (2001)
41. Fairclough, N.: Discourse and Social Change. Polity Press, Cambridge (1992)
42. Bonacich, P.: Techniques for analyzing overlapping memberships. Sociol. Methodol. **4**, 176–185 (1972)
43. Borgatti, S.P., Everett, M.G., Freeman, L.C.: Ucinet for Windows: Software for Social Network Analysis. Analytic Technologies, Harvard (2002)
44. Miles, M.B., Huberman, A.M.: Qualitative Data Analysis. Sage, Thousand Oaks (1999)
45. Carley, K.M., Diesner, J.: AutoMap: Software for Network Text Analysis. CASOS (Center for Computational Analysis of Social and Organizational Systems), ISRI, CMU (2005)
46. Van Atteveldt, W.H.: Semantic Network Analysis. Techniques for Extracting, Representing, and Querying Media Content. Vrije Universiteit, Amsterdam (2008)
47. Uzzi, B., Spiro, J.: Collaboration and creativity: the small world problem. Am. J. Sociol. **111**(2), 447–504 (2005)

Chapter 25
How Latent Class Models Matter to Social Network Analysis and Mining: Exploring the Emergence of Community

Jaime R.S. Fonseca and Romana Xerez

Abstract This article introduces latent class models (LCM) into the framework of social networks. We suggest ways of bridging both fields to broaden the debate on the effects of social networks on the community. It discusses the advantages of reducing complex data to a limited number of typologies from a theoretical and empirical perspective. Instead of using data that originated from inaccurate sources, we focused our study around the concept of homophily; some first-hand data was obtained for the study and the latent class model applied to identify the clustering patterns of the social network as represented by the data. The findings show three-latent class typologies for social networks. We discuss each one in terms of: (1) network structure, (2) trust and reciprocity, (3) resources, (4) community engagement, (5) the internet and (6) years of residence. We discuss the implications of the results and suggest new directions for the community debate on SNA.

25.1 Introduction

Nowadays, people share information and communicate through social relations with others, such as friends, family, coworkers, employees, and business partners, and so social networks play important roles in our daily lives. Our lives are profoundly influenced by social networks without our knowledge of the implications, [1]. A social network is a set of actors (points, nodes, or agents) that may have relationships (links, arcs, edges, or ties) with one another. It may have few or many actors, and one or more kinds of relationship between pairs of actors. In social networks, each actor represents a person or social group, and each link represents the presence or strength of a relationship between two actors. Nodes can be used to represent larger social

J.R.S. Fonseca (✉) · R. Xerez
Univ Tecn Lisboa, ISCSP, P-1349055 Lisbon, Portugal
e-mail: jaimefonseca@iscsp.utl.pt; rxerez@iscsp.utl.pt

T. Özyer et al. (eds.), *The Influence of Technology on Social Network Analysis and Mining*, Lecture Notes in Social Networks 6, DOI 10.1007/978-3-7091-1346-2_25,

units (groups, families or organizations), objects (airports, servers, or locations) or abstract entities (concepts, texts, tasks or random variables), [2].

Different perspectives defended the emergence of social networks in the 1930s, with Moren's sociometry, [3, 4]. However, almost all the authors seem to agree that the enlargement of this area of study, which only took place after 60 years, was due to the development of certain basic empirical tools for understanding the graphical component to which sociologists did not have access until then. There are three main traditions in social network analysis, based on: (1) sociometric analysis, with work in small groups and graph theory methods, (2) research by scientists at Harvard University from the early 1930s with studies on interpersonal relations and the formation of cliques, and (3) investigation into community structure by anthropologists at the University of Manchester [5].

Thus, in the 1960s the analysis of social networks started to progress methodologically and freed itself from the structural perspective. "Between 1960 and 1975 twenty articles about social networks were listed. Between 1990 and 2005 the number exceeded three thousand [6]. It can therefore be viewed as "a broad intellectual perspective and not as a narrow set of methods".

Social studies have been conducted from the 1930s, observing and modeling the network structure, its influence and dynamics, and information flow from tribal and village societies on to global corporate and industrial societies, [1].

The use of social networks to discover "roles" for people (or nodes) in a network goes back over four decades to the work of [7], which is based on the hypothesis that nodes in a network that relate to other nodes in "equivalent" ways must have the same role, [8]. This equivalence is given a probabilistic interpretation by Holland et al. [9]: nodes assigned to a class/role are stochastically equivalent if their probabilities of relationships with all other nodes in the same class/role are the same.

Mullins [10] analysis of "theories and theory groups" is perhaps the most extensive and historically grounded study of social networks in sociology. While yielding important insights into the evolution and internal structure of theory groups, he leaves open the question of how the groups fit together to form a larger whole, [11].

Almost all kinds of social interaction are more likely to occur between near neighbors in social spaces, [12]. Distance in socio-demographic space stands as a proxy for social distance in general, and people at extremes of distance do not share the same social world. They interact with different others, they are exposed to different views and interests, they have different lifestyles and tastes, and so forth, [12].

A social network is actually a union (i.e. overlapping) of networks from family, friends, church and work, for instance, [13], and social network data typically consist of a set of n actors and a relational tie $y_{i,j}$, measured in each ordered pair of actors i, j $=$ 1,..., n. In the simplest cases, $y_{i,j}$ is a dichotomous variable, indicating the presence or absence of a relationship of interest, such as friendship, collaboration or transmission of information or disease. The data are often represented by an n $\times$ n sociomatrix, Y.

Marsden [14] has shown that the vast majority of the network structure in the 1985 General Social Survey can be accounted for by *homophily*. The likelihood of a tie usually depends on the actors' attributes. For example, for most social relations the likelihood of a relationship is a function of the age, gender, geography, race and status of individuals. In addition, ties are often more likely to occur between actors who have similar attributes than between those who do not, a tendency that we call homophily by attributes [15, 16]. Another feature of most social networks is *transitivity* of relations whereby two actors who have ties to a third actor are more likely to be tied than actors who do not, [2]. Transitivity has been extensively studied both empirically and theoretically, [17], and it can lead to some clustering of relationships within the network.

In this study we have investigated the issue of SNA from a novel perspective, and the original contribution of this study stemmed from our reasonable skepticism about the traditional way of obtaining and processing network data. Instead of using data that originated from inaccurate sources, we focused our study around the concept of homophily; some first-hand data was obtained for the study and the latent class model applied to identify the clustering patterns of the social network as represented by the data.

25.2 Social Network Analysis

Social network analysis (SNA) is a set of relational methods for systematically understanding and identifying connections between actors, thus providing a set of tools to empirically extend our theoretical intuition of the patterns that construct social structure. Modern social network analysis is part of a research paradigm that is based on four aspects: (1) social network analysis motivated by structuralism intuition based on the social actors' links of social actors, (2) the systematization of empirical data, (3) strongly built from graphic imagery and (4) dependent on the use of computational and/or mathematical models [18].

To build a useful understanding of a social network, a complete, meticulous description of a pattern of social relationships is a necessary starting point for analysis, because ideally we will find out about all of the relationships between each pair of actors in the population. The key questions in a social network analysis often revolve around the identification of clusters, but conclusions about clustering are usually drawn by informal visual examinations of the network rather than by more formal inference methods, [19]. In order to get a more detailed description of the patterns, we propose a typology of actors based on the variables used to characterize them (social characteristics for searching for ideal clusters, and demographic characteristics, for instance, for better cluster characterization) in networking, by applying latent class models. Latent class models based on associations between the clustering base variables are used to uncover patterns by finding a latent categorical variable X consisting of S categories (clusters or groups), [20].

25.2.1 Bridging LCM to SNA

For a better understanding of the actors' characteristics, assuming that actors can be characterized into a group of typologies that can be considered as resulting from combinations of observed variables, we propose to use clustering through latent class models, which have a long tradition in the social sciences, after being introduced by Lazarsfeld and Henry [21] and successively applied by McCutcheon [22] and Clogg [23], among others, to evidence the underlying structure of data.

This methodology has several advantages over more traditional clustering methods. For example, (1) it automatically selects the best number of clusters, basically by using likelihood ratio tests or theoretical information criteria; (2) it deals well with different levels of clustering base variables (all categorical, all continuous, and mixed case); (3) it works well with large datasets; (4) it allows us to handle randomly missing data in almost trivial ways; and (5) it allows us to handle covariates and detects a non-cluster structure when it really exists. This technique reduces complex data into a limited number of typologies by shrinking diversities in networks into homogeneous clusters of respondents with similar response patterns, to characterize it adequately and use it in further analysis.

Latent class models are designed to justify associations between two or more observed variables, using the structural relationships of these variables with an underlying latent variable, with two or more classes, according to [14]. These probabilistic/statistical models allow us to test whether a group of unobserved classes (latent variable) properly justifies the association between the variables observed. In this context, a specific solution, formed by a group of latent classes, is reasonable when it leads to the minimization of the association between observed variables inside each class. This minimization is the result of the basic assumption of independence or conditional independence.

Social network analysis (SNA) is a set of methods and theories widely used to examine relationships in fields like sociology or business, and it takes the focus off individual attributes and puts it instead on relationships, such as who-talks-to-whom and who-sleeps-with-whom, [24]. Postulating a heterogeneous population made up of S groups or homogeneous sub-populations (latent classes), the latent class model is defined by the variable Y with S categories or latent types of actors, described through the observed variables, $X_1, X_2, \ldots, X_P$, with $I_1, \ldots, I_P$ categories, respectively. Let $\lambda_{i_1 i_2 .. i_p}$ be the probability of a certain individual belonging to categories $(i_1, i_2, \ldots, i_P)$, in relation to the conjoint variable $(X_1, X_2, \ldots, X_P)$, with $i_1 = 1, \ldots, I_1, \ldots, i_P = 1, \ldots, I_P$. In these conditions, supposing the existence of a latent variable Y, with S categories, explaining the relationships between the observed variables, probability $\lambda_{i_1 i_2 .. i_p}$ can be defined by the model

$$\lambda_{i_1 i_2 .. i_p} = \sum_{s=1}^{S} \lambda_Y(s) \lambda_{X_1|Y=s}(i_2) \ldots \lambda_{X_p|Y=s}(i_p),$$

in which

$-\lambda_Y(s)$ represents the probabilities of Y = s, probabilities that an individual belongs to latent class s (s = 1. . . ,S), that is, the probabilities of the latent classes, also designated by relative sizes or mixture proportions, which estimate the likelihood that individuals belong to each one of the classes.

$-\lambda_{X_p|Y=s}(i_p)$ $p = 1, \ldots, P$ represents the conditional probability that variable X_p is in the category i_p, knowing that the latent variable Y is on level s.

In estimating latent class models, the estimates of the probabilities of latent classes or relative sizes and certain individuals' conditional probabilities are of fundamental importance in their structure, to take values in certain categories of the observed variables, given that they are members of a class of the latent variable. The proportions of latent classes describe the distribution of probability of the latent classes or typologies. They are useful in describing the prevalent typologies inside the population and comparing prevalence among sub-populations. As for the variables that we used in this study, all the categorical variables were modeled through multinomial distribution. For a more complete description of estimation of latent class models using the maximum likelihood method, through the EM (expectation-maximization) algorithm, see [25, 26]. Concerning the methodologies used to select the appropriate model, we proposed traditional information criteria. Especially, because the observed variables were all categorical, we used the AIC_3 information criterion, more suited to this situation according to [20], and [27]. The process began with an estimate of the model base, or homogeneity model, which supposes the hypothesis of a single latent class to obtain an appropriate description of the actors. Next we estimated the models that needed two latent classes to describe the individuals properly and so forth, in order to increment the unit in relation to the value of S, the number of latent classes, until the inclusion of a new latent class was not relevant. This value of S was detected by minimizing the AIC_3, because clustering base variables are categorical, [20] and [27], or, otherwise, when the graphic representation of their values (for the various models) shows an "elbow."

25.3 Data and Methods

25.3.1 Traditional Network Data

A social network consists of a set of entities (actors), together with a relationship between those entities, [28]. The great interest in social networks can be explained by important theoretical and intuitively appealing research questions connected to social networks and challenging methodological problems associated with the collection and analysis of social network data, [29].

Following [30], social network data can be viewed as a social relational system characterized by a set of actors and their social ties (some types in Table 25.1), and the aim of social network analysis is to understand the network structure through description, visualization, and (statistical) modeling, [29].

Table 25.1 Social network data types

Social network data type	Collection
Ego-centered or personal networks	From a sample of actors (egos) reporting on the ties with and between other people (alters).
Complete or one-mode networks	On a well-defined group of actors who report on their ties with all other actors in the group.
Relational system	Assumed to be composed of the sampled egos and reported alters and their ties, as well as possible additional actor and tie information, and the ties reported by actors can usually not be assumed to be independent.
Social relations	Defined on a set of *n* social actors or individuals, and *measures how these actors are related to each other*.

But a variable on a relationship between actors may be incomplete or erroneous because of insufficient knowledge on the part of one actor about all the others. This may be even more so as the number of actors increases. Based on a self-monitoring network, [31] concluded that informants were extremely inaccurate, i.e. contrary to expectations, informants' reports of their behavior bear little resemblance to their actual behavior.

Bernard and Killworth [32] confirm these results on informants' ability to report their communication accurately. By using a kind of self-monitoring or nearly self-monitoring, network, they concluded again that people did not know those with whom they communicated with any accuracy, those with whom they communicate.

Concerning the conclusion that people do not know the people that they talk to with any accuracy, [33] ask the following question: What structure are we uncovering when we subject such data to analysis? They partly answered this question as follows. There are two distinct networks, at least in communicative cognitive and behavioral structures. Essentially, who people think they talk to and who people really talk to are different networks, and should be treated as such.

Again, [34] consider that social networks are usually based on behavior, communication, exchange, etc, and that the obvious thing to observe when studying a network is behavior. This is because behavior must be correlated with other important things about the network. However, in repeated experiments, they have been unable to show (at least for the question "Who do/did you talk to?") that cognition is related to behavior in any meaningful way and so they concluded that cognitive data might not be used for drawing any conclusions about behavioral social structure.

Bernard et al. [35] mostly concluded that their informants could not recall with acceptable accuracy who they communicated with in a group over a period of time. For example, informants claimed to have talked to people they had never actually talked to and said they had never talked to people they did talk to. They were unable to rank or scale their communications accurately even when referring to

Table 25.2 Power of homophily

Reasons why homophily is a powerful force in cultural dynamics	Description	Authors
Value homophily (Psychologically)	We often feel justified in our opinions when we are surrounded by others who share the same beliefs	[15]
Status homophily	We feel more comfortable when we interact with others who share a similar cultural background	[14, 15]
Induced homophily	Emerges from influence dynamics that make individuals more similar over time	[16]

the people with whom they communicated the most. This reality is also true for services, and [36] states that the lack of symmetry in ties of the stored matrix is due to the fact that some services (especially bigger or older ones) might not remember all the collaborations they activated in the past, while smaller or newer services will probably recall more outgoing ties.

25.3.2 *Homophily Principle*

This suggests that other forms of data gathering, based on questions that require informants to recall their behavior, may well be suspect. But, as is well known, the phenomenon of perceived similarity between two people is referred to as homophily, the degree to which pairs of individuals who interact are similar with respect to attributes, such as beliefs, values, education, social status, etc, [37]. As for [38], homophily, the principle that "likes attract", is a prominent explanation for the persistence of cultural diversity, that is to say the tendency of people with similar traits (physical, cultural – a set of individual attributes that are subject to social influence – and attitudinal characteristics) to interact with one another more than with people with dissimilar traits (Table 25.2).

According to [39], homophily is the tendency for friendships and many other interpersonal relationships to occur between similar people.

Information on individual attributes, contextual variables, and social processes can and should be combined with network data in drawing conclusions regarding social phenomena, [28]. In this context, we require relations to be based on pairs of actors and to admit a dichotomous qualitative distinction between relationships that are present and absent.

Tie variables are often, though not necessarily, dichotomous, indicating the presence or absence of a relationship. The accompanying mathematical representation is an adjacency matrix with 0s and 1s, where the diagonal is usually not defined (actors do not indicate ties with themselves). If the graph is *undirected* (for instance when relations between actors are observed instead of self-reported), the adjacency matrix is symmetric, [29].

A social relation is defined on a set of *n* social actors or individuals, and *measures how these actors are related to each other*, [40]. Conventional social science data consist of a rectangular array of measurements, in which the rows of the array are the cases, or subjects, or observations, and the columns consist of scores (quantitative or qualitative) on attributes, or variables, or measures, [41].

Because of all of this, we argue that the basic actors' relationship will include several important actors' attribute measurements that characterize them accurately, not a simple question about the presence or absence of a relationship.

25.3.3 Research Strategy

Our dataset was obtained from a questionnaire in a survey of actors, with the variables shown in Table 25.3. We used traditional network questions, or clustering base variables, and some socio demographic variables, in order to characterize the neighbors better. In our research, the methodology mix began with designing a questionnaire, combining closed-ended and open-ended questions in a single data collection procedure – mixed survey instrument – (by letting respondents determine their own frame of reference for the answers) in order benefit from both quantitative and qualitative data collection and analysis. In the qualitative collection methods, we also included interviews, focus groups and participant observation, to explore new topics and assist in theory building, providing a context for quantitative data, and explaining or clarifying quantitative findings.

Thus, we intended to investigate the same underlying phenomenon by conducting mixed-method research involving collecting, analyzing, and interpreting qualitative and quantitative data in a single study, thereby providing a bridge between qualitative and quantitative paradigms. The goal was to merge knowledge by using qualitative (quantitative) conclusions to update quantitative (qualitative) conclusions. Our sample was obtained in a questionnaire, with a short description of the study and information about confidentiality and incentives. A total of 402 respondents completed the survey, yielding a response rate of 75.8 % (see Table 25.3 for sample demographics). The instrument basically included two types of measure, nominal and ordinal. We collected information about *structure*, *trust and reciprocity* between neighbors, *resources, community engagement*, *internet* and *years of residence*, and some demographic variables (Table 25.3). Our main goal was to identify *structure, trust and reciprocity* in neighbors and *resources*, and *community engagement* as social capital dimensions. Secondly we examined the *internet* and *years of residence* as two possible new dimensions.

Table 25.3 Variables and their goals

		Variables
Social capital	Network structure	• How many people live in your home besides you? • Regarding your neighbors in the building or street, we can say that • How many neighbors in the building or street do you know by name? • Where do the relatives that you relate to most live? • Where do the friends that you relate to most live? • Where do the coworkers that you relate to most live?
	Trust and reciprocity in neighbors	• Regarding trust, we can say that • In the last 6 months you have done/received a favor from a neighbor
	Resources	• With how many of the people who do not live with you do you discuss personal matters or ask for help or advice? • To whom do you usually turn in the event of illness? • To whom do you usually turn if you need money? • To whom do you usually turn in a personal crisis? • In the last year I have offered to house sit when neighbors are away • In the last year I have greeted neighbors whenever I see them • In the last year I have been accompanied someone or been accompanied to the doctor • In the last year I have given or received a gift • In the last year we have done leisure activities together • In the last year when going shopping I have asked if they need anything
	Community engagement	• In recent years, have you done any of the following to solve a problem in the neighborhood or city?

(continued)

Table 25.3 (continued)

	Variables
Internet	• Talking to relatives by e-mail • Talking to relatives over the internet • Talking to friends by e-mail • Talking to friends over the internet • Talking to coworkers by e-mail • Talking to coworkers over the internet • Talking to coworkers over the internet • Talking to neighbors by e-mail • Talking to neighbors over the internet
Years of residence	• How long have you lived in Alvalade?
Covariates	• Gender • Marital status • Job situation • Religion • Education • Age

25.4 Data Analysis and Results

Firstly, we estimated latent class models, from the 1-latent class model to 4-latent class model, in order to uncover the true data pattern, and we selected a 3-latent class model, by using the AIC_3 information criterion for model selection, [27]. In this solution we have the first class with 39 % of cases, the second with 37 % and the third with 24 %. The other probabilities in the table represent conditional probabilities. For instance, 0.2375 is the probability of the answer *I live alone*, given that s/he belongs to cluster 1, 0.0537 is the probability of the answer *I live alone*, given that s/he belongs to cluster 2, and 0.0920 is the probability of the answer *I live alone*, given that s/he belongs to cluster 3. The highest probability (0.2375) tells us that the answer *I live alone* belongs to cluster 1.

These results were obtained from the assumption that social capital has a six-component construct, with the three more traditional dimensions (*network structure*, *trust and reciprocity*, *resources*), and the other three proposed dimensions (*engagement, internet*, and *years of residence in Alvalade*).

We have displayed the results of the parameter estimates of the selected model separately in Tables 25.4–25.10 for a better understanding of each component, though we estimated the models jointly with all the information.

Table 25.6 shows the three-class model parameter estimates for resources. We have also displayed the profiles separately for the same reasons. We used additional information given by the covariates for a better understanding of the three latent classes: gender, marital status, professional situation, religion, education, and age.

Table 25.4 Three-latent class model parameter estimates for network structure

	Cluster size		
Variables	Cluster1 (39 %)	Cluster2 (37 %)	Cluster3 (24 %)
Home			
I live alone	**0.2375**	0.0537	0.0000
1	**0.3150**	0.1777	0.2278
2–3	0.3842	0.5110	**0.5486**
4–5	0.0622	**0.2187**	0.1568
6–7	0.0010	**0.009**	0.0048
Neighbors			
Doesn't know people	0.0131	6,20E-03	**0.0929**
Knows few people	0.1970	0.1279	**0.4949**
Knows a lot of people	**0.2816**	0.2498	0.2512
Knows most of the people	0.5083	**0.6160**	0.1610
Knows			
None	0.0119	0.0087	**0.1735**
1–3	0.1503	0.1219	**0.538**
4–7	**0.2544**	0.2288	0.2245
8–12	**0.2441**	0.2435	0.0531
13–19	0.1584	**0.1752**	0.0085
More than 20	0.1809	**0.2219**	0.0024
Family			
Alvalade	**0.2514**	0.2418	0.0646
Near Alvalade	0.1182	**0.2081**	0.1248
Lisbon	0.2778	**0.2778**	0.1722
Lisbon metropolitan area	0.1841	0.1015	**0.2268**
Other part of country	0.1428	0.1312	**0.3086**
Abroad	0.0258	0.0396	**0.103**
Friends			
Alvalade	**0.4765**	0.1960	0.0224
Near Alvalade	0.0389	**0.1972**	0.104
Lisbon	0.2428	**0.4570**	0.2786
Lisbon metropolitan area	0.2151	0.1097	**0.4324**
Other part of country	0.0266	0.0401	**0.1009**
Abroad	0.0001	0.0001	**0.0617**
Coworkers			
Alvalade	**0.3318**	0.0151	0.0009
Near Alvalade	0.0945	**0.2459**	0.0831
Lisbon	0.3052	0.4063	**0.5256**
Lisbon metropolitan area	0.1522	0.2929	**0.3502**
Other part of country	**0.0906**	0.0265	0.0195
Abroad	**0.0257**	0.0132	0.0207

We then used this information to complement the knowledge about each latent class (Table 25.7). In Table 25.4 we have the three-latent class model parameter estimates for network structure. In Table 25.5 we display the three-class model parameter estimates for trust and reciprocity.

Table 25.5 Three-latent class model parameter estimates for trust and reciprocity

	Cluster size		
	Cluster1 (39 %)	Cluster2 (37 %)	Cluster3 (24 %)
Trust			
Don't trust people in Alvalade	0.0247	0.0091	**0.0287**
Trust few people in Alvalade	0.2407	0.1413	**0.2594**
Trust many people in Alvalade	**0.4419**	0.4124	0.4413
Trust most people in Alvalade	0.2894	**0.4292**	0.2677
Don't know people	0.0034	**0.0079**	0.0029
Chat			
Yes	**0.9868**	0.9474	0.6702
No	0.0132	0.0526	**0.3298**
Favor			
Yes	0.6561	**0.7732**	0.3384
No	0.3439	0.2268	**0.6616**

Table 25.7 displays the three-class model parameter estimates for engagement. In Tables 25.4–25.10 parameters' estimates consist of two kinds of probability: firstly, we have the probabilities of belonging to clusters 1, 2 and 3, respectively 0.39, 0.37 and 0.24; secondly, we have conditional probabilities, probabilities of answering in a certain way, given that they belong to a cluster: for instance, 0.0884 is the probability of answering *signed a petition*, given that s(he) belongs to cluster 1, 0.1604 is the probability of answering *signed a petition*, given that s(he) belongs to cluster 2, and 0.2264 is the probability of answering *signed a petition*, given that s(he) belongs to cluster 3; because of 0.2264 is the great one, individuals with this answer are allocated to cluster 3.

Table 25.8 shows the three-class model parameter estimates for years of residence.

Table 25.9 displays the three-class latent model parameter estimates for the internet, with all the clustering base variables.

Based on the estimated parameters in Tables 25.4–25.10, we can profile the three latent classes, as shown in Tables 25.11–25.17. In Table 25.11 we characterize typology by *network structure*, in accordance with the variables used, and we name the three classes.

Table 25.10 shows the three-class model parameter estimates for all the covariates used. In Table 25.11 we display the uncovered typology by network structure in accordance with parameters' estimates of Table 25.4.

Medium structure (cluster 1) with 39 % of the respondents, where we have people who live alone but know a lot of neighbors, and have family and friends in Alvalade.

Higher structure (cluster 2), with 37 % of the respondents, in which we have people who live with many people, four to seven, know almost all their neighbors, and have family and friends near Alvalade.

Table 25.6 Three-latent class model parameter estimates for resources

	Cluster size		
	Cluster1 (39 %)	Cluster2 (37 %)	Cluster3 (24 %)
Family persons			
0	0.0820	0.0539	**0.1969**
1–3	0.6584	0.5953	**0.6953**
4–6	0.2159	**0.2686**	0.1003
7–10	0.0322	**0.0551**	0.0066
11 or more	0.0115	**0.0271**	0.0010
Kinship persons			
0	0.7626	0.4719	**0.8033**
1–3	0.2201	**0.4079**	0.1854
4–6	0.0151	**0.0837**	0.0101
7–10	0.0022	**0.0366**	0.0012
Friend persons			
0	**0.1546**	0.0375	0.1266
1–3	**0.4991**	0.3041	0.4774
4–6	0.3025	**0.4633**	0.3379
7–10	0.0393	**0.1513**	0.0513
11 or more	0.0045	**0.0438**	0.0069
Neighbor persons			
0	0.4852	0.4620	**0.8720**
1–3	0.4239	**0.4359**	0.1241
4–6	0.0792	**0.0879**	0.0038
7–10	0.0118	**0.0142**	0.0001
11 or more			
Colleague persons	**0.5526**	0.1268	0.4211
0	0.3769	0.3984	**0.4437**
1–3	0.0636	**0.3096**	0.1156
4–6	0.0068	**0.1525**	0.0191
7–10	0.0001	**0.0127**	0.0005
11 or more			
Other persons	**0.9404**	0.8814	0.8684
0	0.0560	0.0989	**0.1063**
1–3	0.0019	0.0064	**0.0075**
4–6	0.0011	0.0067	**0.0085**
7–10	0.0006	0.0067	**0.0093**
11 or more			
Illness persons	0.4187	**0.7167**	0.5395
Husband, wife, partner	**0.3031**	0.2295	0.2691
Close relative living separately	**0.0897**	0.0002	0.0002
Distant relative living separately	0.0348	0.0534	**0.1496**
Friend	**0.0384**	0.0001	0.0001
Neighbor	0.0000	0.0000	**0.0206**
Coworker	**0.0384**	0.0001	0.0001
Charitable institution, volunteers	**0.0769**	0.0002	0.0208
Prefers not to ask for help			

(continued)

Table 25.6 (continued)

	Cluster size		
	Cluster1 (39 %)	Cluster2 (37 %)	Cluster3 (24 %)
Money	0.2418	**0.4383**	0.3712
Husband, wife, partner	**0.3131**	0.2950	0.2538
Close relative living separately	**0.0892**	0.0646	0.0240
Distant relative living separately	0.0130	0.0659	**0.1030**
Friend	**0.0128**	0.0000	0.0206
Coworker	**0.0256**	0.0000	0.0001
Charitable institution, volunteers	**0.2531**	0.136	0.2272
Prefers not to ask for help	**0.0513**	0.0001	0.0001
Personal Crisis			
Husband, wife, partner	**0.3139**	0.2716	0.2065
Close relative living separately	**0.2891**	0.1377	0.1874
Distant relative living separately	**0.0513**	0.0264	0.0002
Friend	0.1427	0.4842	**0.5204**
Neighbor	**0.0513**	0.0264	0.0002
Coworker	0.0001	0.0397	**0.0409**
Charitable institution, volunteers	**0.0128**	0.0000	0.0000
Prefers not to ask for help	**0.1131**	0.0139	0.0442
Never needed to ask for help	**0.0256**	0.0000	0.0001
House-Sitting			
Never	0.5408	0.5632	**0.9134**
Once a year	**0.1927**	0.1919	0.0717
2–6 times a year	**0.1754**	0.1671	0.0144
7–12 times a year	**0.0203**	0.0185	0.0004
Once a week	**0.0069**	0.0061	0.0000
More than once a week	**0.0639**	0.0532	0.0001
Greeting			
Never	0.0006	0.0000	**0.0609**
2–6 times a year	0.0013	0.0000	**0.0185**
7–12 times a year	0.0089	0.0000	**0.0475**
Once a week	0.0788	0.0010	**0.1608**
More than once a week	0.9103	**0.9858**	0.7123
Doctor's appointments			
Never	0.7037	0.8171	**0.9979**
Once a year	**0.1595**	0.1253	0.0021
2–6 times a year	**0.0677**	0.036	0.0000
7–12 times a year	**0.0476**	0.0171	0.0000
Once a week	**0.0104**	0.0025	0.0000
More than once a week	**0.0111**	0.0018	0.0000
Invitations			
Never	0.4851	0.3652	**0.7345**
Once a year	**0.1792**	0.1713	0.1461
2–6 times a year	0.2146	**0.2606**	0.0943
7–12 times a year	0.0922	**0.1422**	0.0218
Once a week	0.0215	**0.0422**	0.0027
More than once a week	0.0074	**0.0185**	0.0005

(continued)

Table 25.6 (continued)

	Cluster size		
	Cluster1 (39 %)	Cluster2 (37 %)	Cluster3 (24 %)
Gifts			
Never	0.2828	0.2243	**0.9699**
Once a year	**0.2927**	0.2749	0.0292
2–6 times a year	0.3207	**0.3566**	0.0009
7–12 times a year	0.0789	**0.1038**	0.0000
Once a week	0.0204	**0.0318**	0.0000
More than once a week	0.0046	**0.0085**	0.0000
Leisure			
Never	0.6226	0.4754	**0.8368**
Once a year	**0.0741**	0.0706	0.0597
2–6 times a year	0.1413	**0.1677**	0.0682
7–12 times a year	0.0883	**0.1307**	0.0255
Once a week	0.0310	**0.0572**	0.0054
More than once a week	0.0428	**0.0985**	0.0044
Need shopping?			
Never	0.5768	0.6970	**0.8736**
Once a year	0.0566	**0.0575**	0.0463
2–6 times a year	**0.0975**	0.0834	0.0432
7–12 times a year	**0.0695**	0.0500	0.0166
Once a week	**0.1078**	0.0653	0.0139
More than once a week	**0.0918**	0.0468	0.0064

Table 25.7 Three-latent class model parameters estimates for engagement

	Cluster size		
	Cluster1 (39 %)	Cluster2 (37 %)	Cluster3 (24 %)
Engagement			
Signed a petition	0.0884	0.1604	**0.2264**
Participated in discussions	0.0354	**0.0955**	0.0003
Organized or participated in boycotts or protest marches	0.0001	**0.0395**	0.0001
Contacted a politician to solve a problem	**0.0517**	0.0391	0.0004
Contacted a radio station, TV channel or newspaper	0.0257	**0.0527**	0.0002
Was involved with neighbors to defend	**0.1154**	0.0924	0.0211
Other initiatives	**0.1538**	0.0791	0.0008

Lower structure (cluster 3), with 24 % of the respondents, where we have people who live with two to three people, know a few neighbors, and have family and friends in other places in Portugal or abroad.

Table 25.8 Three-latent class model parameter estimates for time in Alvalade

Living	Cluster size Cluster1 (39 %)	Cluster2 (37 %)	Cluster3 (24 %)
Less than 1 year	0.0173	0.0457	**0.2103**
1–5 years	0.0873	0.1778	**0.4278**
6–10 years	0.0581	0.0913	**0.1148**
11–20 years	0.1967	**0.2388**	0.1570
21–30 years	**0.1642**	0.1540	0.0529
31–40 years	**0.1584**	0.1146	0.0206
Up to 40 years	**0.3179**	0.1777	0.0167

In Table 25.12 we characterize the typology by *trust and reciprocity*, in accordance with the variables used.

Middle trust (cluster 1), with 39 % of respondents, where we have persons that trust many neighbors, and they stop at the street to talk with them.

Higher trust (cluster 2), with 37 % of the respondents, where people trust almost all neighbors and have already done/received a favor.

Lower trust (cluster 3), with 24 % of the respondents, with people who do not trust their neighbors in Alvalade, do not stop to talk to them in the street and have not done/received a favor.

Table 25.13 displays the characterization of typology by resources and again we have in *cluster 1* (*medium resources*) people who live far away from close and distant relatives, friends, neighbors, coworkers and other people.

In situations of need, like illness or money, they may be helped by close or distant relatives who do not live with them, a neighbor, a charity or a volunteer, prefer not to ask for help, or have never needed to ask for help. In times of personal crisis they may be helped by their spouse, partner or a close or distant relative who does not live with them, a neighbor, a charity, a volunteer, or prefer not to ask for help or have never asked for help. With regard to house-sitting or going to the doctor's with a neighbor they rarely do so (once a year or more than once a week), while they frequently run shopping errands (twice to six times a year or even more than once a week).

In *cluster 2* (*higher resources*) we have people who live near to close or distant relatives, friends, neighbors, coworkers and other people and may be helped by their spouse or partner. They frequently engage with neighbors, such as saying hello, having dinners/parties, exchanging gifts and spending time together.

Cluster 3 (*lower resources*) is characterized by being helped by friends and coworkers in situations of poor health, needing money and personal crises, and hardly ever by neighbors.

In Table 25.14, we show typology by engagement and in *cluster 1* (*middle engagement*) we have people who have contacted the police to solve a problem, been engaged with neighbors for defense and other initiatives. In *cluster 2* (*higher engagement*), we have people who have participated in activities to discuss issues, organized or participated in boycotts or protest marches and have contacted a radio station, TV channel or newspaper. Finally, in *cluster 3* (*lower engagement*) we have people who have signed a petition.

Table 25.9 Three-latent class model parameters estimates for internet

	Cluster size		
	Cluster1 (39 %)	Cluster2 (37 %)	Cluster3 (24 %)
Talk with family by e-mail			
Never	**0.765**	0.0943	0.3786
Rarely	0.1023	**0.4349**	0.2292
Few times a week	0.1062	0.3266	**0.3301**
Everiday	0.0265	**0.1442**	0.0622
Talk with family by Internet			
Never	**0.9734**	0.4878	0.8114
Rarely	0.0133	**0.2885**	0.1261
Few times a week	0.0004	**0.1842**	0.0624
Everiday	0.0129	**0.0395**	0.0001
Talk with friends by e-mail			
Never	**0.7907**	0.0017	0.2137
Rarely	0.1312	**0.2208**	0.0427
Few times a week	0.0767	0.3964	**0.5985**
Everiday	0.0014	**0.3811**	0.145
Talk with friends by Internet			
Never	**0.9857**	0.2773	0.7081
Rarely	0.0134	**0.2354**	0.1058
Few times a week	0.0004	**0.1715**	0.1234
Everiday	0.0006	**0.3158**	0.0627
Talk with colleagues by e-mail			
Never	**0.8131**	0.0968	0.2149
Rarely	0.1305	0.1037	**0.1444**
Few times a week	0.0554	**0.3911**	0.3522
Everiday	0.001	**0.4085**	0.2885
Talk with colleagues by Internet			
Never	**0.9986**	0.3038	0.7491
Rarely	0.0005	**0.2764**	0.0419
Few times a week	0.0004	0.1429	**0.1474**
Everiday	0.0005	**0.2769**	0.0616
Talk with neighbors by e-mail			
Never	**0.9483**	0.7893	0.9377
Rarely	0.0387	**0.1185**	0.0209
Few times a week	0.0001	**0.0658**	0.0002
Everiday	0.0129	**0.0263**	0.0001
Talk with neighbors by Internet			
Never	0.9484	0.7891	**0.9585**
Rarely	0.0386	**0.0924**	0.0206
Few times a week	0.0129	**0.0527**	0.0002
Everiday	0.0001	**0.0658**	0.0002

Concerning the internet (Table 25.15), we have in *cluster 1* (*lower e-neighborhood*), people who never contact family, friends, coworkers or neighbors by e-mail or internet.

Table 25.10 Three-latent class model parameter estimates for covariates

Covariates	Cluster size Cluster1 (39 %)	Cluster2 (37 %)	Cluster3 (24 %)
Genre			
Female	**0.5725**	0.557	0.4388
Male	0.4275	0.443	**0.5612**
Marital status			
Married	**0.4466**	0.2801	0.1656
Single	0.1789	**0.516**	0.4956
Living together	0.0258	0.0516	**0.1877**
Divorced	0.0698	0.0564	**0.0888**
Separated	0.0391	**0.0528**	0.0403
Widow	**0.2398**	0.0167	0.022
Job situation			
Employed	0.3855	0.4571	**0.6273**
Looking for first job	0.0128	**0.0396**	0
Unemployed	0.0319	**0.046**	0.042
Retired	**0.4428**	0.1123	0.0625
Other	0.0884	**0.3054**	0.2475
Religion			
Catholic	**0.6601**	0.5715	0.5851
Ortodox	**0.0385**	0.0264	0.0207
Protestant	**0.0514**	0.0132	0
Jewish	0	**0.0264**	0
Muslim	0.0128	**0.0132**	0
No religion	0.1218	0.2963	**0.3321**
Other	**0.0775**	0.0526	0.0617
Educational level			
1–3	**0.3356**	0.0132	0.0801
4	0.1503	**0.1842**	0.1104
5–6	0.2346	**0.3786**	0.2905
7–9	0.2666	0.3449	**0.4363**
Age			
15–19	0.0384	**0.2638**	0.1657
20–39	0.0922	0.2754	**0.5777**
40–49	0.0795	**0.2034**	0.1323
50–69	**0.3703**	0.2276	0.1019
70 or more	**0.4068**	0.0166	0.0223

In *cluster 2* (*higher e-neighborhood*), we have people who frequently make contact by e-mail or the internet. In *cluster 3* (*midle e-neighborhood*), we have people who rarely contact family, friends, coworkers or neighbors by e-mail or the internet.

Table 25.11 Typology by network structure

	Size		
Variables	***Middle structure*** **(39 %)**	***Higher structure*** **(37 %)**	***Lower structure*** **(24 %)**
Home	Lives alone; 1	4–7	2–3
Neighbors	Knows a lot of people	Knows most of the people	Doesn't know anyone; knows a few of people
Acquaintances	4–12	13 or more	Up to 3
Relatives	Alvalade	Close to Alvalade; Lisbon	Greater Lisbon; other part of the country or abroad
Friends	Alvalade	Close to m Alvalade; Lisbon	Greater Lisbon; other part of the country or abroad
Coworkers	Close to; other part of the country	Greater Lisbon; abroad	Alvalade; Lisbon

Table 25.12 Typology by trust and reciprocity

	Clusters size		
Variables	***Middle trust*** **(39 %)**	***Higher trust*** **(37 %)**	***Lower trust*** **(24 %)**
Trust	Trust many people in Alvalade	Trust majority of the people in Alvalade	Don't trust people in Alvalade, trust few people in Alvalade
Chat	Yes	–	No
Favor	–	Yes	No

Where years of residence are concerned (Table 25.16), we have in *cluster 1* (*old neighbors*) people who have lived in Alvalade for more than 21 years, in *cluster 2* (*medium neighbors*) people who have lived in Alvalade for 11–20 years, and in *cluster 3* (*young neighbors*) people who have lived in Alvalade for less than 11 years.

As for covariates, we wanted to characterize the three clusters in more detail. In *cluster 1* (*oldest/female*) we have a majority of retired, married or widowed females who are Catholic, orthodox or protestant, have had fewer than 3 years' education and are aged over 50.

In *cluster 2* (*middle age/male and female*) we have people who are single or separated, looking for their first job or unemployed, are Jewish or Muslim, have had between 4 and 6 years' education and are aged under 20 or between 40 and 49. In *cluster 3* (*younger/male*), we have a male majority, who are separated or in a common law union, have jobs, no religion, have a college degree and are aged between 20 and 39.

Table 25.13 Typology by resources

Variables	Cluster size		
	Middle resources (39 %)	*Higher resources* (37 %)	*Lower resources* (24 %)
Close relatives RELATIVES	–	4 or more	Up to 3
Distant relatives ISTANT RELTIVE	–	1 or more	None
Friends	Up to 3	4 or more	–
Neighbors	–	1 or more	None
Coworkers	None	4 or more	One to 3
Other people	None	–	1 or more
Illness	Close relative living separately; distant relative living separately; neighbor; institution, solidarity, volunteers; prefers not to ask for help; never needs for help	Spouse, wife, partner	Friend or colleague
Money	Close relative living separately; distant relative living separately; institution, solidarity, volunteers; prefers not to ask for help never needs for help	Spouse, wife, partner	Friend or colleague
Personal crisis	Spouse, wife, partner; close relative living separately; distant relative living separately; neighbor; institution, solidarity, volunteers; prefers not to ask for help; never needs for help	–	Friend or colleague
House-siting	From once a year to more than once a week	–	Never
Greeting neigbbors	–	More than once for a week	Never to once a week
Going to Doctor	From once a year to more than once a week	–	Never
Inviting over	Once a year	From 2 to 6 times a year to more than once a week	Never
Giving or receiving gifts PRESENTE	Once a year	From 2 to 6 times a year to more than once a week	Never
Leisure activities	Once a year	From 2 to 6 times a year to more than once a week	Never
Need shopping	From 2 to 6 times a year to more than once a week	Once a year	Never

Table 25.14 Typology by engagement

	Cluster size		
Indicators	*Middle engagement* (39 %)	*Higher engagement* (37 %)	*Lower engagement* (24 %)
Civic participation	Contacted a politician to solve a problem; was involved with neighbors to defend; other initiatives	Participated in discussions; organized or participated in boycotts or protest marches; contacted a radio station, TV channel or newspaper	Signed a petition

Table 25.15 Internet

	Cluster size		
Indicators	*Lower e-neighborhood* (39 %)	*Higher e-neighborhood* (37 %)	*Middle e-neighborhood* (24 %)
Talk with family by e-mail	Never	Rarely; everiday	Some time a week
Talk with family by Internet	Never	Rarely; everiday; some time a week	–
Talk with friends by e-mail	Never	Rarely; everiday	Some time a week
Talk with friends by Internet	Never	Rarely; everiday; some time a week	–
Talk with colleagues by e-mail	Never	Some time a week; everiday	Rarely
Talk with neighbors by Internet	Never	Rarely; everiday	Some time a week
Talk with neighbors by e-mail	Never	Up to everiday	–
Talk with colleagues by Internet	–	Up to everiday	Never

25.5 Conclusions and Perspectives

The aim of latent class models is to identify the latent classes required to explain the associations between a set of observed variables (clustering base variables) and to allocate observations to these segments. The latent class model was applied to identify the clustering patterns of the social network as represented by the data and these results have demonstrated the effectiveness of the statistical method in the analysis of social networks, thus telling us why latent class models matter in social network analysis. Jointly, the four components of social capital used uncover a data pattern based on latent class model, and reveal a three-cluster latent structure, which is a real, interpretable solution.

Table 25.16 Years of residence

	Cluster size		
Indicators	*Highest years of residence* (39 %)	*Middle years of residence* (37 %)	*Lower years of residence* (24 %)
How long do you live in Alvalade	21 years or more	Between 11 and 20 years	Up to 10 years

Table 25.17 Covariates

	Cluster size		
Covariates	*Oldest/female* (39 %)	*Middle age/both male and female* (37 %)	*Younger/male* (24 %)
Genre	Women	–	Men
Marital status	Married; widow	Single; divorced	living together
Ocupation	Retired	Looking for a first job; unemployed; other	Employed
Religion	Catholic; orthodox; prostestant; other	Jewish; Muslim	No religion
Education	Up to 2° cicle	3° cicle; full degree	Master; PhD
Age	50 or more	15–19; 40–49	20–39

We can call these social capital classes *medium social capital* (cluster 1), *higher social capital* (cluster 2), and *lower social capital* (cluster 3). For a better characterization from the covariates used, we reached following conclusions. The actors in the first class are the oldest, mostly female, retired, and have the lowest education. The actors in the second class are looking for a job, have had a mid-level education and are middle aged. The actors in the third class are mostly male, have jobs, have a college degree and are aged between 20 and 39.

This perspective is in accordance with the works of scholars who emphasized modern public policies and programs (e.g. early retirement) which result in the devaluation of older adults [42], and point out that older adults have denser social networks (39 %). But these actors are also retired, thus reducing contact with non-family, and kinship ties are more likely to last as older adults' health declines, out of a sense of obligation. They are also widows, and widowhood eliminates access to perhaps the most rewarding of all social ties.

The social capital pattern is supported by structure, trust and reciprocity, resources, and engagement, not by years of residence or the internet. First, where years of residence are concerned, we have *older neighbors* corresponding to *medium social capital*, and *medium neighbors* corresponding to *higher social capital*. It can be an indicator that years of residence are not relevant to social capital. Second, the internet can be not understanding as relevant to social capital, in this context.

Now, from the new variable (latent variable) *social capital*, with three categories, which social capital categories are more related to the categories of *how frequently*

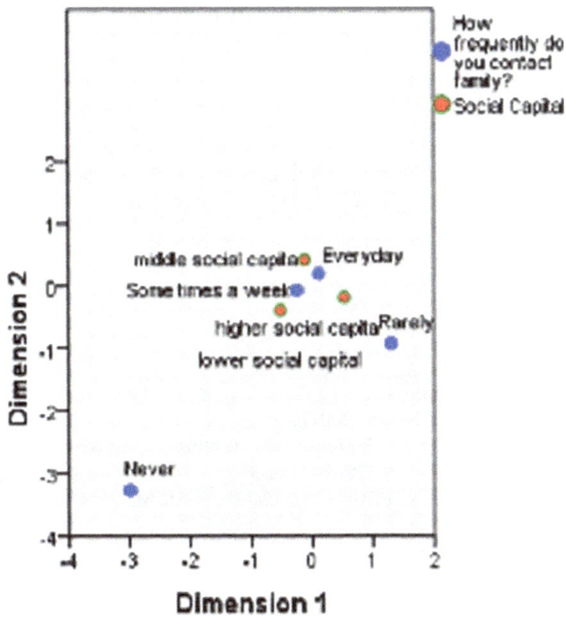

Fig. 25.1 Social capital vs. frequency of contact with family

do you contact family? We can use correspondence analysis to get answers to these questions.

Figure 25.1 displays the correspondence analysis biplot for categories of *social capital* and *how frequently do you contact family*? We can see that the category of the variable *how frequently do you contact family* that contributes most to *higher social capital* is *everyday* (Fig. 25.1).

25.6 Policies Implications

While this article explores the research carried out in Alvalade, it is useful to draw attention to the important role that communities play in cities and neighbourhoods. This neighborhood's social capital score provides sociologists, planners and policy-makers with arguments that demystify the decline of community social capital.

The research results show the importance of strong social networks among family, friends, coworkers and neighbors. These networks are an important source of emotional and financial support, in sickness and in many everyday activities.

More than half of the respondents have, at least, one neighbor who asks for help in a crisis. The network of neighbors' resources indicated a source of capital in this case. Social networks in the Alvalade neighborhood are a strong component of community life.

Finally, our research into Alvalade suggests several contributions to the discussion of the empirical and theoretical relevance of the result. We propose to address the four components of social capital and its effects on neighboring. The results confirm that: (1) network structure; (2) resources; (3) trust and reciprocity; and (4) community engagement shapes the community. We suggest the maintenance of *bairros* through social ties towards sustainable cities and communities. We recommend further investigation to ascertain community theory and practice.

References

1. Cross, R., Borgatti, S.P., Parker, A.: Beyond answers: dimensions of the advice network. Soc. Netw. **23**, 215–235 (2001)
2. Handcock, M.S., Raftery, A.E., Tantrum, J.M.: Model-based clustering for social networks. J. R. Stat. Soc. A **170**, 1–22 (2007)
3. Wasserman, S., Faust, K.: Social Network Analysis. Cambridge Universisty Press, Cambridge (1999)
4. Borgatti, S.P., et al.: Network analysis in the social sciences. Science **323**(5916), 892–895 (2009)
5. Scott, J.: Social Network Analysis: A Handbook. Sage, Londres (2001)
6. Bernard, R.H.: The development of social network analysis: a study in the sociology of science. Soc. Netw. **27**, 377–384 (2005)
7. Lorrain, F., White, H.C.: Structural equivalence of ondividuals in social networks. J. Math. Soc. **1**, 49–80 (1971)
8. McCallum, A., Corrada-Emmanuel, A., Wang, X.: The author-recipient-topic model for topic and role discovery in social networks: experiments with enron and academic email. Technical report UM-CS-2004-096, Department of Computer Science, UMASS at Amherst, 2004. Presented at the NIPS'04 Workshop on 'Structured Data and Representations in Probabilistic Models for Categorization' (2004)
9. Holland, P.W., Laskey, K.B., Leinhardt, S.: Stochastic blockmodels: first steps. Soc. Netw. **5**, 109–137 (1983)
10. Mullins, N.C.: Theories and Theory Groups in Contenmporary Sociology. Harper and Row, New York (1973)
11. Ennis, J.G.: The social organization of sociological knowledge: modeling the intersection of specialities. Am. Soc. Rev. **57**, 259–265 (1992)
12. McPherson, J.M., Popielarz, P.A., Drobnic, S.: Social networks and organizational dynamics. Am. Soc. Rev. **57**, 153–170 (1992)
13. Watts, D.J., Dodds, P.S., Newman, M.E.J.: Identity and search in social networks. Science **296**, 1302–1305 (2002)
14. Marsden, P.V.: Latent structure models for relationally defined social classes. Am. J. Soc. **90**, 1002–1021 (1985)
15. Lazarsfeld, P., Merton, R.K.: Friendship as a social process: a substantive and methodological analysis. In: Berger, M., Abel, T., Page, C.H. (eds.) Freedom and Control in Modern Society, pp. 18–66. Van Nostrand, New York (1954)
16. McPherson, M., Smith-Lovin, L., Cook, J.M.: Birds of a feather: homophily in social networks. Annu. Rev. Soc. **27**, 415–444 (2001)
17. White, H.C., Boorman, S.A., Breiger, R.L.: Social-structure from multiple networks: I, blockmodels of roles and positions. Am. J. Soc. **81**, 730–780 (1976)
18. Freeman, L.C.: The Development of Social Network Analysis. Empirical Press, Vancouver (2004)

19. Liotta, G.: Graph drawing. Lect. Notes Comput. Sci. **2912**, 202–213 (2004)
20. Fonseca, J.R.S., Cardoso, M.G.M.S.: Mixture-model cluster analysis using information theoretical criteria. Intell. Data Anal. **11**, 155–173 (2007)
21. Lazarsfeld, P.F., Henry, N.W.: Latent Structure Analysis. Houghton Mifflin, Boston (1968)
22. McCutcheon, A.L.: Latent class analysis. In: Sage University Paper. Sage Publications, Newbury Park (1987)
23. Clogg, C.C.: Latent class models. In: Arminger, G., Clogg, C.C., Sobel, M.E. (eds.) Handbook of Statistical Modeling for the Social and Behavioral Sciences, pp. 311–359. Plenum, New York (1995)
24. Luke, D.A. and Harris, J.K.: Network analysis in public health: history, methods, and applications. Annu. Rev. Public Health **28**, 69–93 (2007)
25. McLachlan, G.F., Peel, D.: Finite Mixture Models, 1st edn. Wiley, New York (2000)
26. Fonseca, J.R.S., Cardoso, M.G.M.S.: Retail clients latent segments. In: Bento, C., Cardoso, A., Dias, G. (eds.) Progress in Artificial Intelligence. Lecture Notes in Computer Science, pp. 348–358. Springer, New York (2005)
27. Fonseca, Jaime R.S.: On the performance of information criteria in latent segment models. Presented at International Conference on Mathematical Science and Engineering, Rio de Janeiro (2010)
28. Butts, C.T.: Social network analysis: a methodological introduction. Asian J. Soc. Psychol. **11**, 13–41 (2008)
29. Marijtje, A.J.v.D. Vermunt, J.K.: What is special about social network analysis? Methodology **2**, 2–6 (2006)
30. Wasserman, S., Faust, K.: Social network analysis: methods and applications. Cambridge University Press, New York (1994)
31. Killworth, P.D., Bernard, H.R.: Informant accuracy in social network data. Hum. Organ. **35**, 269–286 (1976)
32. Bernard, H.R., Killworth, P.D.: Informant accuracy in social network data II. Hum. Commun. Res. **4**, 3–18 (1977)
33. Killworth, P.D., Bernard, H.R.: Informant accuracy in social network data III: a comparison of triadic structure in behavioral and cognitive data. Soc. Netw. **2**, 10–46 (1979/1980)
34. Bernard, H.R., Killworth, P.D., Sailer, L.: Informant accuracy in social network data IV: a comparison of clique-level structure in behavioral and cognitive network data. Soc. Netw. **2**, 191–218 (1979/1980)
35. Bernard, H.R., Killworth, P.D., Sailer, L.: Informant accuracy in social-network data V: an experimental attempt to predict actual communication from recall data. Soc. Sci. Res. **11**, 30–66 (1982)
36. Bellotti, E.: Brokerage roles between cliques: a secondary clique analysis. Methodol. Innov. Online **4**, 53–73 (2009)
37. Torres, I.M.: A tale of two theories: sympathy or competition? J. Bus. Res. **60**, 197–205 (2007)
38. Centola, D., González-Avella, J.C., Eguíluz, V.C., Miguel, M.S.: Homophily, cultural drift, and the co-evolution of cultural groups. J. Confl. Resolut. **51**, 905–929 (2007)
39. Thelwall, M.: Homophily in MySpace. J. Am. Soc. Inf. Sci. Technol. **60**, 219–231 (2009)
40. Anderson, C.J., Wasserman, S., Crouch, B.: A $p*$ primer: logit models for social network. Soc. Netw. **21**, 37–66 (1999)
41. Hanneman, R., Riddle, M.: Introduction to social network methods. Self-published to the web at, http://faculty.ucr.edu/~hanneman/nettext/ (2005)
42. Cornwell, B., Laumann, E.O., Schumm, L.P.: The social connectedness of older adults: a national profile. Am. Soc. Rev. **73**, 185–203 (2008)

Chapter 26
Integrating Online Social Network Analysis in Personalized Web Search

Omair Shafiq, Tamer N. Jarada, Panagiotis Karampelas, Reda Alhajj, and Jon G. Rokne

Abstract With the emergence of high speed internet applications and advanced Web 2.0 based Rich Internet Applications (i.e., blogs, wikis, etc.), it has become much easier for the users to publish data over the Web. This brings a challenge for the Web search solutions to let individual users find the right information as per their preferences, because traditional Web search engines have been built on "one size fits for all" concept. Different users of the Web may have different preferences. Search results for the same query raised by different users may differ in priority for individual users. In this book chapter, we present the extended version and results of our proposal on community-aware personalized Web search. It is quite challenging to know the preferences of the users by the search engines. We have designed and developed our unique approach of finding the preferences of users from the relevant parts of the user's social network and community. We believe that the information related to the queries posed by the users may have strong correlation with the relevant information in their social networks. In order to find out personal

O. Shafiq (✉) · J.G. Rokne
Department of Computer Science, University of Calgary, Alberta, Canada
e-mail: moshafiq@ucalgary.ca; rokne@ucalgary.ca

T.N. Jarada
University of Calgary, Calgary, Alberta, Canada
e-mail: tjarada@gmail.com

P. Karampelas
Department of Information Technology, Hellenic American University, Manchester, NH, USA
e-mail: pkarampelas@gmail.com

R. Alhajj
Department of Computer Science, University of Calgary, Alberta, Canada

Department of Information Technology, Hellenic American University, Manchester, NH, USA

Department of Computer Science, Global University, Beirut, Lebanon
e-mail: alhajj@ucalgary.ca

T. Özyer et al. (eds.), *The Influence of Technology on Social Network Analysis and Mining*, Lecture Notes in Social Networks 6, DOI 10.1007/978-3-7091-1346-2_26,

interest and social-context, we find (1) activities of users in their social-network, and (2) relevant information from user's social networks, based on our proposed trust and relevance matrices. We have further developed a mechanism that extracts from user's social network information to be used to re-rank search results from a search engine. We also have discussed the implementation and evaluation details of our proposed solution.

26.1 Introduction

The amount of information available over the Web is increasing rapidly. Through the use of high-speed internet, high capacity network, and upcoming advanced interactive websites, like facebook, YouTube and blogging, it has become even easier for the internet users to publish data over the Web. With this information flooding, it becomes hard for a user to find out right information over the Web. Search engines like Google, Altavista, Yahoo, Bing, etc. bring thousands of search results for a particular search query. It is almost impossible and mostly frustrating for a human user to go through the content of all the search results manually. With the increase of information over the Web, scalability of Web search engines became important, e.g., [13]. Search engines, like Google, even provide manual mechanisms to rank up and down search results. But for each and every search result, it is not possible for a user to adjust the ranking manually in advance; as a result categorization and personalization of search results become an important issue [24]. Different efforts are being made in order to enable community and social network aware [1], user-terminology-aware [2] and group-aware [4,16] search engines that may help in bringing results closer to the user's interest. After providing the personalized version [9] of Web search by Google, researchers still seem to feel the need to move towards social network-aware search [17]. Not only Web search, but the personalized search has been explored in other real-life scenarios, e.g., medical and digital libraries [15].

Our goal is to find out a way to prioritize search results based on the interests, activities and community of users. There are different ways that exist in order to find out contextual information, i.e., location etc. But this information is most of the time not enough or limited to find out the right search results for the right user at the right time. Different users searching over the Web for the same thing may have different preferences. An executive going for a business meeting would probably be interested in a hotel closer to the meeting place; however a back-packer searches for a hotel in the same city might want to search for, rather cheaper hotel regardless of the location.

We propose to exploit user's social network in order to find out the interests, activities of the users and their community, i.e., friends in the social network. This information can help in bringing word-of-mouth recommendation system from trusted friends in the social network. Every group of users may have certain set of activities over the social network, i.e. postings, public profile information, tagging, blogging, etc. Similarly different friends of the user may also have similar activities. Most of the times, friends of a user in a social network have to some extent similar interests and therefore could help in finding out the right information the user needs. The information about the related search query from friends in a social network, or activities of a user in social network could help in finding out the relevant information over the Web and prioritize it for the user. It could help the user to find out the right information at the right time. Such kind of community-aware personalized Web search utility could be used in many different ways and in many applications involving Web Intelligence and Business Intelligence, i.e., for summarizing important search results, caching of important search results, as well as collaboration techniques.

We have developed methodology to find out activities of users over a social network as well as their friends/community. Secondly, we find out how to use this information to prioritize relevant information over the Web. This way, we are able to use social networks for finding relevant information over the Web in a personalized way. There are different kinds of friends and communities in a social network based on which we can find out the relevant information. Same as in real-life, a user can have different trust matrices for different friends in a social network. This means, information collected from a more trusted friend is more important than that of the one from lesser trusted one. As a part of this research, we have found out metrics based on which the trust can be built and used in a social network. Similarly, different metrics to rank the results over the Web have also been sought.

The rest of the chapter is organized as follows. Section 26.2 provides an overview of the related work together with the pros and cons. Section 26.3 describes our proposed solution of community-aware personalized Web search and discusses how to model the information based on user's individual preferences as well as trusted and relevant friends of the users in their social network. Section 26.4 describes the details implementation and evaluation, followed by conclusion.

26.2 Related Work

Various approaches have been developed for personalized Web search based on contextual information, i.e., interests and preferences of users [20, 23]. A number of approaches are based on modeling and collecting contextual information. For example, context-aware search methods [18] use special ontology that is constructed from the table of contents of the book, to help formulating the query for efficiency and to refine query search results that are relevant to the user's interests. Location-awareness is another form of context-awareness that is used to filter out search results based on the current location of the users. There are different ways in which clients access the services over the Internet. With the advancements of requirements and complexity in consumer applications, consumers expect the services to be aware of their current environment and situation, i.e., the type of device through which consumers are communicating, their preferences, locations, etc. The context information can be used by services to provide their clients with a customized and personalized behavior. Chen et al. [6] describe an ontology for supporting pervasive context-aware systems. An ontology is developed as a part of the Context Broker Architecture (CoBrA), a broker-centric agent architecture that provides knowledge sharing, context reasoning, and privacy protection supports for pervasive context-aware systems.

Other approaches take context into account one way or the other. For instance, Almeida and Almeida [1] propose an algorithm for search results ranking based on community-based evidence; they call it query contextualization which is obtained from user's interactions. First, the algorithm identifies interest-based community using session interest graphs followed by community identification in the graphs. Based on community identification, search results are ranked. This way, community information is used as a way to provide context for the query specified by the user. Authors claim to improve the search results up to 48 %.

Computing word-of-mouth recommendations is another form of context-awareness that has been introduced recently. The idea is to identify who knows what in the social-network of a user, and based on that some information is brought up. Not only this, the process also includes finding out who is trustworthy source of information. For example, Granovetter [10] proposes how social networks can serve as a source of new information to which an individual may not otherwise have access and Sugiyamaet et al. [21] proposes adaptive Web search based on automatically created users profiles. This is especially useful in use-cases like job-hunting where weak social ties might be better than strong social ties to bring some new and interesting information. Heath [11] proposes algorithms to compute trust metrics in his developed system based on social-network. The information is collected from tags used in the system to comment on and recommend some information. Another algorithm helps in calculating the prevalence of an individual in the reviews of items that have been tagged with a particular tag, thereby providing a relative measure of their experience with the topic. Calculation of affinity score between one individual and another is based on the analysis of reviews where the information is provided to the algorithm in the form of FOAF (Friend of a friend) description.

With the evolution of Semantic Web [3] over the last decade, several approaches for personalized Web search from social networks based on Semantic Web have also been initiated. For example, Carminati et al. [5] propose the usage of tags as a basis to enforce advanced personalization policies for Web based search. A multi-layer framework has been proposed where data collected by social tagging communities is complemented with additional services that provide users the ability of expressing their agreement or disagreement with existing tags, denoting the members that they trust based on their characteristics and relationships, or specifying policies enforcing the criteria adopted by a given end user to access the resources based on the associated tags and ratings. The framework helps in representing the tagging information as well as the user policies based on Semantic Web standards so that its expressivity could be exploited easily. The layers include data layer which consists of services in-charge of managing social network data, Web metadata as well as ratings by the users. Second is Rule layer that consists of modeling user-preferences and trust policies specified by the users. This is the key of the information that helps in identifying contextual information based on social network. Last is Application Layer where the output of data and rule layers is used by a set of agents corresponding to the application layer, for a variety of purposes, i.e., social network data represented in Semantic Web is used by semantic search engines in order to find users and resources matching given queries.

Zeng et al. [25] first introduce user interest models which are then used to build a social network to track the group interest related to the given user. The authors then refine the search task based on the semantic dataset using the acquired group interest. The search refinement is carried out based on the interest of the individual user, as well as interest of the group which the user is part of.

After covering the related approaches, in the next section, we present our methodologies for contextualizing users' interest based on the information from their social network and use it to refine Web search results. The novelty of our approach is that our methodologies are generic enough and can be customized for any social network and any Web search engine. Secondly, the proposed methodologies prescribe the usage of Semantic Web technologies to make the modeling of user preferences more expressive that could be used during the search refinement process.

The key problems observed in the related works as described above could be articulated as follows. Most of the related works consider location information as the only important part of context [6]. However, in case of user-based customized Web search, location is not the only important factor that should be taken into account. Therefore, most of the related work approaches have not considered user context to its full potential. Secondly, several user based context calculation techniques are computation exhaustive. For example, the work described in [1] proposes to generate interest graphs and then tries to identify community, which makes the whole approach highly computational extensive, and hence causes high resource consumption and hence not cost effective with respect to time. Further, most of the approaches are limited to the interest represented in the form of keywords only. Considering keyword based approaches, this is a quite straight forward, simple and cost effective method. However, it imposes a limitation because complex information about user's preferences cannot be modeled using simple keywords; therefore, we have taken into account the modeling of complex preferences of users using semantic expressions.

Most of the approaches blindly take into account the information from social-network of a user, regardless of its relevance. There could be some information in the social network which might be relevant from syntactic point-of-view, however, might be quite different from semantic point-of-view. Therefore, most of the approaches are unable to identify relevant and irrelevant information from the social network of a user. We have introduced the use of relevance metrics to take into account only information which is relevant to users' interests.

26.3 Community Aware Personalized Web Search

Currently available Web search solutions treat users mostly the same, in a "one size fits all" manner. Web search engines give same search results for the same queries by different users. However, in reality it is very likely that different users may have different preferences. Therefore, we believe that the search mechanisms need to be aware of the contextual information, preferences and interests of the users. In this section, we describe our proposed solution to tackle this problem.

Figure 26.1 depicts our solution in a layered manner that acts as a middleware between the user and the Web search engine. The first layer takes the information from the social network of users, and finds out the activities of the users in their social network, e.g., what kind of postings a user is doing, tagging, and keywords from user's own profile. It helps us in knowing the current state of personal interests of the user him/herself. Secondly, we have built a similar mechanism to find out the activities and information posted by the community or friends of the user in the social network; it can be tagging, posting a video, blogging and information from friends' public profile, etc. This may help us in finding out what kind of information and interest does members of the community of a user have. We believe that the information collected from the community of the user may be of direct interest to the user, and hence may serve as preference of the user. However, there may be several cases where some part of the community is not relevant for some information for the user (e.g., a user searching for computer science material might not find as relevant information from his/her friends belonging to the medical field). In order to tackle this, we have developed trust and relevance schemes to find out the relevant information from the user's social network. This mechanism allows users to specify trust relationship with their friends or community in the social network. For example, there can be some friends who are most close or trustworthy, from whom the user might want to use more information whereas some of the friends may be of lesser trust, i.e., not close enough, from whom a user might not want to consider the information, similar to what happens in real-life.

We allow users to assign weights, which describe the level of trust, to the friends and other related communities in a social network. This helps in finding out what information from the community is more trustworthy than others. The trust mechanism allows to pullout trustworthy information from user's social network, which is then used to re-rank Web search results. Similarly, users are also provided with mechanisms to specify the level of relevance of their friends in their social network, with respect to different search topics. This allows the personalized mechanism to consider only relevant subset of the user's social network, and hence avoid irrelevant information.

Our approach is to build our proposed solution in a generic manner, such that it is not dependent on any particular social-network or Web search engine. Our solution can be customized for any search scenario, and hence can be applied on any kind of known social networks (e.g., facebook, youtube, blogs, etc.) as well as any kind of Web search engine (i.e., Google, Yahoo, Alta Vista, etc.). Our Social-Network

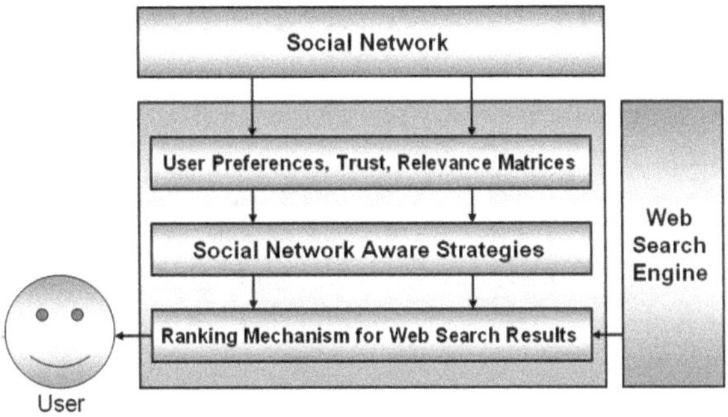

Fig. 26.1 Layered model for community-aware personalized Web search

Analysis based contextual mechanism does not require any change or interference in the Web search engine because it acts as a search-engine front-end for users searching information over the Web; it helps them in ranking and reordering of Web search results according to their preferences obtained from their social-network.

Figure 26.1 provides an overview of our proposed solution in the form of layered model architecture. Each user and his/her friends have their activities on the social network from which the preferences and the trust are identified. Based on the trust and relevance schemes, preferences of a user and his/her community from the social-network are obtained. Certain standard social-network analysis based techniques are used to select relevant subset preferences from the user's community. The Social Network Aware Strategies are applied to Web search data with the information coming from the user's social network, and Web search results are ranked accordingly. While ranking the search results, our solution does not hide or change any results from the user. It just re-ranks and re-orders Web search results for the user based on his/her social-network information, which might be interesting for the user. We define the social network, in a generic way, as follows:

Definition 1 (Social Network SN). Let SN be a social network that shows connectivity between different members in the social network. It can be represented as a two-dimensional matrix of n rows and n columns.

$$\textit{Social Network} := SN\ (n\ ,\ n)$$

where, SN is the two-dimensional matrix. Each of the entries in SN is referred to as, $SN_{i,j}$, where $1 \leq i \leq n$ and $1 \leq j \leq n$. The value of each entry $SN_{i,j}$ in the matrix describes the connectivity between two particular members of the social network, namely i and j. Null values refer to no connectivity, whereas, positive values indicate the existence of some connectivity between the members.

In the subsections below, the sub-modules of the community-aware personalized Web search model shown in Fig. 26.1 are described in detail.

26.3.1 User Preferences and Trust Model

In order to know user's preferences in a social network, activities of users and their friends in the social-networks are to be modeled in a systematic way. This information could be used for the purpose of ranking and re-ordering Web search results. The design methodology behind our solution is generic. Therefore, our solution is not restricted or dependent on any particular type of social network. In any social network, a user has certain activities which can be postings of certain information, doing some activities, attending some events, tagging and commenting on photos of the users, etc. The same holds for the friends of the considered user in the social-network; they are expected to have similar kind of activities. We have adopted a simpler way to model user preferences by having this information as key-pair values. This is a practical approach where all the activities of a user are summarized in the form of a set of keywords. For example, if a user is blogging on the topic of soccer in his/her social network about the upcoming FIFA World Cup in 2010 in South-Africa, in that case a simple set of keywords mentioning interests of the user may be listed as {FIFA, World Cup, soccer, 2010, South Africa}. Similar sets of keywords are collected for each of the users performing their activities on the social network.

26.3.1.1 User Preferences Metric

A sample list of keywords of interest for users is given in Table 26.1 that shows the id of the users against the important keywords collected based on their activities in the social network.

Based on the activities of the users, the keywords provided in Table 26.1 represent their interests. These keywords, once collected, can be taken into account for ranking Web search results for the users. Similarly, keywords of other users (which may be friends of each other) could be taken into account while ranking based on the interest of a group of people.

Definition 2 (Preference List). Let PL be the list of preferences of a member in the social network, which may also be a user searching for information over the Web. PL can be represented as tuple:

$$PL\ (index,\ keywords\ (m))$$

where, index is a numeric item that corresponds to the user ID in the social network SN, and keywords is a one dimensional array of keywords, having each item $keywords_i$ as preference of the user, with length $1 \leq i \leq m$.

26.3.1.2 User Trust Matrix

Each user in a social network has his/her friends. However, as in real-life, there are different ties with different friends. These ties may also vary with time. Close

Table 26.1 List of keyword sets for users in a social network

User ID	Set of keywords
1	FIFA, World Cup, soccer, 2010
2	Cricket, World Cup, Australia, 1992
3	Politics, North America
4	Programming, Java, Web, Enterprise
5	Traveling, Airline tickets, holidays
6	Electronics, Boxing day, sales
7	Movies, Hollywood, Bollywood, Avatar

friends or important friends normally have closer ties and hence higher trust factor than that of others. Our approach takes into consideration the social ties and trust of users with their friends in the social network. This information is necessary and is required in ranking the information. For some of the searches, friends of a user with closer ties and high trust metric might be of more importance than others, e.g., while buying a computer. However, there might be cases where weak social ties are more important for a user than stronger social ties, e.g., in case of job search. Our approach is to represent the social ties based on trust in a numerical scale from 0 to 10, ranging from 0 as the no/weakest ties to 10 as the strongest ties. Such information is calculated for each user with each of his/her friends in the form of a matrix; it is taken into account while performing social network aware personalized Web search ranking.

Definition 3 (Trust Matrix TM). Let TM be the social network (as described in Definition 1) that shows connectivity between different members in the social network. The value of each entry $TM_{i,j}$ in the matrix describes the level of trust between the two connected members.

$$TM\ (n, n)$$

As described in Definition 1, null values mean no connectivity; whereas, positive values describe connectivity between members, with its value ranging from 1 to 10 as the level of trust (i.e., 1 as for lower level of trust and 10 as for higher level of trust). We describe standard representation of a social network as follows:

1. Vertex v represents a user in social network n
2. Edge e represent connection between two particular users in social network n
3. Weight w of each edge represents the level of trust between the two connected users in social network n
4. Preferences p denote the list of preferences/interest values or logical expressions for each of the users in the social network

Table 26.2 shows a one-mode adjacency matrix of a sample social network. Rows and columns show users A to G and each of the cells shows the weight of the connecting edge, i.e., the strength of trust relationship between the users.

Table 26.2 TM – Trust matrix for a simple social network

	A	B	C	D	E	F	G
A	X	9	9	9	4	2	3
B	2	X	7	6	6	5	1
C	6	2	X	4	9	6	8
D	4	5	3	X	8	1	4
E	0	8	4	4	X	7	6
F	8	5	7	2	2	X	2
G	2	4	6	5	5	2	X

The diagonal of the matrix shows the highest weight as we assume that a user may have his/her own interests at highest priority.

26.3.1.3 User Relevance Matrix with Respect to Topics

As described in the previous section about user trust matrix, where the level of trust between different users in a social network is quantified with numbers, in a similar way, we represent the relevance of user or user-groups relationship with each other, with respect of a particular topic, in a quantifiable manner. For example, the user is interested in sports (particularly football), however, there are couple of friends in the user's social network relevant to football as well as cricket. Now, in order to perform group-level preference calculation, it will be important to include the information obtained from friends relevant to football, rather than cricket. In order to represent this level of relevance, we propose the use of relevance matrix.

Definition 4 (Relevance Matrix RM). Let RM be the relevance matrix that shows the level of relevance between different members in a social network, with respect to a particular topic.

$$RM\ (n,\ n,\ topic)$$

where, RM is the two-dimensional matrix,. Each of the entries in RM is referred to as, $RM_{i,j}$, where $1 \leq i \leq n$ and $1 \leq j \leq n$. The value of each entry $RM_{i,j}$ in the matrix describes the level of relevance between members i and j, with respect to a particular topic, with the value ranging from 1 to 10 (i.e. 1 as for lower level of relevance and 10 as for higher level of relevance).

Tables 26.3a and b shows two relevance matrices that show relationships between various users in a social network, based on different topics.

After representing the level of relevance as well as the trust between the different users, we calculate balance between the trust and relevance matrices, and hence identify the most relevant and trust friends of a user in his/her social network to find the list of preferences. The balance between trust and relevance is calculated using the expression given as follows:

Table 26.3 RM – Relevance matrix of users based on topics 'Football' and 'Cricket'

	A	B	C	D	E	F	G
(a) Topic: Football							
A	X	5	7	2	5	3	2
B	5	X	6	8	2	6	6
C	3	2	X	5	6	5	3
D	8	5	3	X	2	4	1
E	0	8	4	4	X	2	2
F	1	5	7	2	2	X	4
G	2	4	6	5	5	2	X
(b) Topic: Cricket							
A	X	7	3	5	8	9	2
B	5	X	7	6	4	6	6
C	4	2	X	4	7	5	5
D	7	5	3	X	2	3	3
E	3	8	4	4	X	2	7
F	4	5	7	2	2	X	6
G	2	4	6	5	5	2	X

Table 26.4 Calculated measures based on relevance and trust

	A	B	C	D	E	F	G
A	X	0	0	0	0	6	4
B	10	X	**42**	**48**	12	**30**	**36**
C	18	4	X	20	**54**	**30**	9
D	**32**	25	9	X	16	4	1
E	0	**64**	16	16	X	14	4
F	0	25	**49**	4	4	X	16
G	4	16	**36**	25	25	4	X

$$\alpha TM_{i,j} + \beta RM_{i,j} = P_{i,j} \tag{26.1}$$

where TM is the trust matrix and RM is the relevance matrix. Moreover, α and β have been introduced as two threshold measures, which can be fine tuned by the user to reflect whether he/she gives more preference to trust, relevance or both.

Table 26.4 shows the calculated measures between different users in a social network, based on the relevance as well as trust. Once the balance of trust and relevance between a user and his/her friends is calculated, most trustworthy as well as highly relevant part of the social network is selected to deduce preference information from the relevant part of user's social network. This way, we manage to focus on the key and required part of the social network of the user, rather than performing calculation for whole network, and hence avoid non-trusted and irrelevant information.

26.3.2 Social Network Analysis Strategies

Once the important part of the social network (with higher relevance and trust) is selected, social network analysis (SNA) strategies [8] constitute the next important step of our proposed solution. They further help in narrowing-down the required members of the user's social network, for whom the preferences are to be collected in order to re-rank Web search results. SNA measures help in analyzing the social network in terms of network and graph theory consisting of nodes and ties. Nodes are individual actors in social networks. For example, betweenness centrality of a node calculates the extent to which the node lies between other nodes in the network. This measure takes into account the connectivity of the node's neighbors, giving a higher value for nodes which bridge clusters. An edge that is said to be a bridge, if deleted, would cause its endpoints to lie in different components of the social network. Closeness measure shows the degree to which an individual is near all other individuals in a network (directly or indirectly). Degree measure counts the number of direct ties to other actors in the network. This is also known as the "geodesic distance". We have used such SNA measures to identify for a given user his/her friends whose preferences and interests can help in better ranking Web search results. Below we list a couple of general purpose strategies which could be effective by employing SNA measures:

Strategy 1: A user may want to get preferences from his/her friends to rank Web search results.

Technique: Preferences of friends with higher value of *betweenness* centrality should be taken into account while ranking Web search results. List of preferences would be calculated by considering Eq. (26.1) and Definition 2 as:

From Eq. (26.1) ... α *TMi,j* + β *RMi,j* = *Pi,j and based on Definition 2 ... PL(index, keywords(m))*

Betweenness Centrality is calculated as

$$C_B(v) = \sum_{s \neq v \neq t \in V} \frac{\sigma_{st}(v)}{\sigma_{st}}$$

where σ_{st} *is the number of shortest paths from s to t, and* $\sigma_{st}(v)$ *is the number of shortest paths from s to t that pass through vertex v.*

$$PL(Max\ (C_b(P)))$$

where P is the sub-part of the social network that was identified after calculating members with higher relevance and trust. Preference list of members with maximum betweenness centrality in the identified P sub-social network would be considered for re-ranking Web search results.

Strategy 2: A user may want to get preferences from his/her friends having higher degree of dependence within the social network; this is to be used in ranking Web search results.

Technique: Preferences of the friends connected with *Bridge edge* should be taken into account while ranking Web search results.

The bridge measure is computed as B(SN); its deletion increases the number of connected components within the social network SN. The algorithm follows from Tarjan [22].

$$PL\ ((B(P)))$$

where P is the sub-part of the social network that was identified after calculating members with higher relevance and trust. Preference list of members in the Bridge vertex in the identified P sub-social network would be considered for re-ranking Web search results.

Strategy 3: A user may want to get preferences from his/her friends, who are found closely related in the social network, to rank Web search results.

Technique: Preferences of the friends with higher *Closeness* measure should be taken into account while ranking Web search results.

Closeness is calculated as

$$C_C(v) = \sum_{s \neq v \neq t \in V} \frac{1}{\sum_{t \in V/v} d_G(v,t)}$$

which is the reciprocal of the sum of geodesic distances to all other vertices in the social-network.

$$PL(Max(C_c(P)))$$

where P is the sub-part of the social network that was identified after calculating members with higher relevance and trust. Preference list of members with the highest Closeness, in the identified P sub-social network, would be considered for re-ranking Web search results.

Strategy 4: A user may want to get preferences from his/her friends, who are found receiving higher degree of connections in the social network, to rank Web search results.

Technique: Preferences of the friends, with higher *In-degree* measure, should be taken into account while ranking Web search results.

In-degree is calculated as $\text{indeg}^{-}(v) =$

$$\sum_{v \in V} \deg^{-}(v)$$

$$PL(Max(indeg^{-}(P)))$$

where P is the sub-part of the social network that was identified after calculating members with higher relevance and trust. Preference list of members with the highest in-degree value, in the identified P sub-social network, would be considered for re-ranking Web search results.

Strategy 5: A user may want to get preferences from his/her friends who are found actively communicating with other friends in the social network, to rank Web search results.

Technique: Preferences of the friends, with higher *Out-degree* measure should be taken into account while ranking Web search results.

Out-degree is calculated as out$\deg + (\mathrm{v}) =$

$$\sum_{v \in V} \deg^{+}(v)$$

$$PL(Max(outdeg + (P)))$$

where P is the sub-part of the social network that was identified after calculating members with higher relevance and trust. Preference list of members with the highest out-degree, in the identified P sub-social network, would be considered for re-ranking Web search results.

Strategy 6: A user may want to get preferences from his/her close friends to rank Web search results.

Technique: Preferences of the friends in the social network that are directly connected to the user should be taken into account while ranking Web search results.

Directly connected friends D are the ones at distance d=0

$$PL(Max(D(d = 0)(P)))$$

where P is the sub-part of the social network that was identified after calculating members with higher relevance and trust. Preference list of members with the friends connected at distance d = 0, in the identified P sub-social network, would be considered for re-ranking Web search results.

Strategy 7: A user may want to have recommendation for ranking search results based only on his/her own interests.

Technique: Only preferences of the user him/herself should be taken into account while ranking Web search results.

PL (user) shows the Preference list of the user him/herself only, and does not take into account the social-network of the user.

Strategy 8: A user may want to have recommendations for ranking search results based on the interest of closely connected friend in his/her community.

Technique: Preferences of the friends forming a *Clique*, should be taken into account while ranking Web search results.

Clique is calculated as Cl = subset of at least three members in the social-network, such that every two members in the subset are directly connected.

$$PL(Cl(P))$$

where P is the sub-part of the social network that was identified after calculating members with higher relevance and trust. Preference lists of members who are part of the clique, in the identified P sub-social network, would be considered for re-ranking Web search results.

The above mentioned strategies use standard SNA measures to help the user getting preference list from the members of his/her social network in different possible ways, while performing Web search. These measures are generic and can be applied to any kind of social network and any Web search engine. These strategies help the user to know the preferences as a set of recommendations that are taken into account while performing re-ranking of Web search results.

26.3.3 Ranking Mechanism for Web Search

In this section, we provide the details of our next key component of the social-network aware personalized Web search solution. It takes into account the preferences list which is retrieved as described in the previous sub-sections, uses the preferences to re-rank Web search results. This way, Web search results are re-ordered, based on the information obtained from the social network of a user, to help in displaying more relevant and interesting Web search results at the top of the retrieved list.

Ranking of information is carried out on individual as well as group basis. In case of individual basis, the user performing the search is the point of reference and all the calculations from the social network measures are carried out accordingly. However, in case of group-based ranking, the calculations from the social network measures are carried out with reference to all users taking part in the group.

26.3.3.1 Individual Ranking

Ranking of Web search results based on the preferences of an individual user is carried out while taking the user as the point of reference and all the calculations from the social network measures are carried out accordingly. Preferences of the users, after performing the calculations from the social network measures, are taken

Algorithm 1 Individual Ranking of Web search results

Input: User Query Q, Social-Network SN represented as the adjacency matrix
Output: List of re-ranked Web Search results
begin

1. *TM (SN)* is the adjacency matrix of the user's social network representing the trust level as described in the previous sub-sections
2. *RM (SN, topic)* is the adjacency matrix of the user's social network representing the level of relevance with respect to a topic, as described in the previous sub-sections
3. $P = \alpha\ TM + \beta\ RM$ is the subpart of the social-network, as specified in Eq. (26.1)
4. *PL = (index , keywords (m)) P,* where PL is the list of preferences from the members of the sub social-network P
5. *List R' = Re-ordered (R, PL),* where R' is the re-ordered list of Web search results based on the list of preferences PL

end

into account while ranking Web search results. Listing 1 is proposed for ranking Web search results based on individual ranking.

Listing 1. Algorithm for individual ranking of Web search results Source Codewww

Algorithm 1 is described below step-wise.

Step 1: Calculate the sub-social network based on higher level of trust and relevance matrices as P
Step 2: Calculate the list of members from the sub-social network P from the social network analysis strategy selected by the user
Step 3: Retrieve the preferences/interest keywords of all the users identified by the calculation in Step 1 and Step 2
Step 4: Take top 100 search results from the search engine based on the search query provided by the user
Step 5: Match the list of preferences/interest keywords obtained in Step 3 with the Web search results
Step 6: Re-order the Web search results in descending order to show the most relevant Web search results on the top, with respect to the selected social-network

There might be the possibility of having thousands of Web search results for most Web search queries; therefore, matching the list of preferences with each of the returned Web search results is not feasible. Hence, we propose to perform the matching of the preference/interest keywords for the top 100 Web search results.

26.3.3.2 Group Based Ranking

Ranking Web search results based on a certain group in the social network is carried out while taking into account all users who are part of the group. Calculations for

Algorithm 2 Group Ranking of Web search results

Input: User Query Q, Social-Network SN, represented by the adjacency matrix
Output: List of re-ranked Web Search results
begin

1. *SN (n, e) is the network with n vertices and e edges*
2. *SN' = Social Network SN with vertices merged into one for the members identified in a group*
3. *TM (SN')* is the adjacency matrix of the user's social network representing the trust level among members, as described in the previous sub-sections
4. *RM (SN', topic)* is the adjacency matrix of the user's social network representing the level of relevance among members, with respect to a topic, as described in the previous sub-sections
5. $P = \alpha\ TM + \beta\ RM$, is the sub part of the social-network, as described in Eq. (26.1)
6. *PL = (index, keywords(m)) P*, where PL is the list of preferences from the members of the sub social-network P
7. *List R' = Re-ordered (R, PL)*, where R' is the re-ordered list of Web search results based on the list of preferences PL

end

the social network strategies are done for each of the user in the group. Then for a particular social network strategy, preferences of the users identified by the group in the social network are taken into account while ranking Web search results. Listing 2 is proposed for ranking Web search results based on group ranking.

The key difference between the two algorithms for individual ranking and group-based ranking is the additional step in the group-based ranking algorithm, where the calculations are carried out for all users taking part in the group in the social network.

Listing 2. Algorithm for group ranking of Web search results

The algorithm is described below step-by-step.

Step 1: Retrieve the social network of the members belonging to a particular group.

Step 2: Merge vertices representing the group as one node in the social network, and calculate the sub social-network based on higher level of trust and relevance matrices as P

Step 3: Calculate the list of members from the sub social-network P derived by applying selected the social network analysis strategy, with respect to the group

Step 4: Retrieve the preferences/interest keywords of all the users identified by the calculation in Step 3

Step 5: Take the top 100 search results from the search engine based on the search query provided by the user

Step 6: Match the list of preferences/interest keywords obtained in Step 4 with the Web search results

Step 7: Re-order the Web search results in descending order to show, with respect to the selected social-network, the most relevant Web search results on top

26.3.3.3 Fractional Cascading for Ranking Search Results

After calculating the preferences based on personal and group level information from the user's social network, the final step is to rank the relevant Web search results based on the best matches with the preferences obtained. However, looking at the huge size of Web search results, this task can become very cumbersome and time-consuming to do (i.e., if we start matching each Web search result with each of the preferences and then calculate and rank them in the order of best match). Especially if the list of preferences is higher, the ranking process can take a significantly large amount of time, in comparison to the time in which the results are obtained from the Web search engines. Therefore, we employ the techniques of orthogonal range search to perform the ranking of Web search results for ordering the best match.

Orthogonal range searching formalizes the search based on multiple dimensions (from one to n dimensions). We take each preference item as one dimension. So, if we have three items in the calculated preference list, then we have a three-dimensional match/ranking mechanism. Similarly, if there are 4, 5 or n items in the preference list, the dimensions will be 4, 5 or n, respectively. In order to keep our solution as generic as possible, we have chosen to use a dynamic data structure for matching the search results based on n dimensions. In this case, we use fractional cascading mechanism, which takes into account each dimension, and calculates the match with the first dimension; if a good match is found with the first dimension, only then proceeds to the other dimensions, otherwise it drops the calculation for the rest of the dimensions (i.e., preference items) for the particular search result, and then proceeds to the next search result accordingly. In this case, we save the time, by calculating the necessary dimension match only, and drop the search results where no good match is found with any of the dimensions.

The Listing 3 sketches the fractional cascading based algorithm for ranking Web search results based on the preferences mentioned as dimensions. It calculates the match of each Web search result R with each dimension D. As soon as a Web search result R does not match any of the dimensions, the algorithm stops calculating the further matches for that Web search result and continues to the next search result; hence it saves time by calculating only for the required dimensions. Once dimension match check is performed for each Web search result D, the counter array items having count equal to the number of dimensions is the answer, i.e., it ranks those Web search results as the highest ones; they matches with every dimension, and vice versa. Web search results are then re-ordered based on the ranking obtained from this mechanism.

Listing 3: Fractional-cascading based Ranking algorithm

As already described by fractional cascading technique [19], cost estimation of the algorithm is $O(k) + n$, where n is the time spent in matching dimension D with a Web search result.

Algorithm 3 Fractional cascading for ranking search results

```
Counter [1.... D] ⇓ 0
For each Web search result R
For each Preference as dimension D
if (D matches R)
counter[D] ++
else
break and continue to next Web search result
```

Evaluation and Discussion

Ranking algorithms are the ones that involve maximum processing in re-ordering the Web search results based on the preferences of the user's community. As described in Chap. 3, the complexity and cost estimation of our ranking algorithm, as being based on fractional cascading technique [19], is $O(k) + n$, where n is the time spent in matching dimension D with a Web search result. The increase in the cost of the algorithm, with increasing dimension is linear, therefore, the approach is sustainable, as the list of preferences increases or extends. Moreover, we have limited the re-ordering of only top 100 results, rather than attempting to re-order all of the search results. This is because, after analyzing click-through and click-stream datasets, we found that, although many of the Web search engines provide millions of the search results. However, users mostly visit the top range of the Web search results, and do not normally visit the results going beyond certain initial range, normally in terms of hundreds. Therefore, re-ordering of the top 100 search results is beneficial for the users.

From implementation point-of-view, we have evaluated our solution using a real-life data set of social network, based on wikipedia where different users posted information, and compared the personalized Web search results with the original search results in many different ways. One way to evaluate was the comparison of ranked search results with original search results from a search engine, through user feedback, i.e. by first allowing the users to build a sample social network of web blogs through a wiki, and then using the community information collected from wiki pages, to rank the search results. We assumed that different users posting on same wiki page, were taken as connected to each other as "friends" in the social network.

For this purpose, we used the history of wiki page updates, to find out which users have been posting and sharing information of different wiki pages. In order to evaluate the usability of personalized search results, each participant was required to issue a certain number of test queries and determine whether each result is relevant to his/her interest or not. Users compared the original search results from a search engine versus ranked search results, and rated the usefulness of the personalized Web search results in different aspects. The important observation was that, not only users found a significant number of re-ranked Web search results more relevant, and also did not find our results irrelevant as compared to the original search results.

Search Query: Football
Original Search Result titles: 1. NFL.com – Official Site of the National Football League 2. BBC SPORT | Football 3. FIFA.com – Fédération Internationale de Football Association (FIFA) 4. CBC.ca Meyer's all-in approach a theme among college football coachesý 5. Official Site of the Premier League – Barclays Premier League News 6. The Official Website of Arsenal Football Club | Arsenal.com 7. AFL – The official site of the Australian Football League – AFL.com.au 8. Manchester United Football Club 9. American football – Wikipedia, the free encyclopedia 10. Sky Sports | Football News 11. Chelsea Football Club – Official Site for News, Tickets & Fixtures

Search Query: Football
Personal Preferences: FIFA, American Football, Chelsea
Re-ordered Search Results: 1. FIFA.com – Fédération Internationale de Football Association (FIFA) 2. American football – Wikipedia, the free encyclopedia 3. Chelsea Football Club – Official Site for News, Tickets & Fixtures 4. NFL.com - Official Site of the National Football League 5. BBC SPORT | Football 6. CBC.ca Meyer's all-in approach a theme among college football coachesý 7. Official Site of the Premier League – Barclays Premier League News 8. The Official Website of Arsenal Football Club | Arsenal.com 9. AFL – The official site of the Australian Football League – AFL.com.au 10. Manchester United Football Club 11. Sky Sports | Football News

This is because, our approach does not hide any search results, but only shows the same search results, but in a re-ordered fashion. Therefore, the risk of bringing any irrelevant search results goes almost to none. The advantage of this evaluation approach, based on user feedback, was that the relevance of the search results was explicitly judged by the participants, and hence, there was no compromise on calculating the rating for the relevance of a Web search result, as per user needs.

Given below are the listings that show the search results obtained from Web search engine against the reordered search results based on the preferences of the user in its social network. Listing 4 shows the re-ordered search results based on the preferences of the user itself. Listing 5 shows the re-ordered search results based on the preferences of the user. While Listing 6 shows the re-ordered search results based on the preferences computed from the friends in the user's social network.

Listing 4. Original search results for a sample query

Search Query: Football
Community Preferences: FIFA, American Football, Australian Football, Chelsea, Arsenal
Re-ordered Search Results: 1. FIFA.com – Fédération Internationale de Football Association (FIFA) 2. American football – Wikipedia, the free encyclopedia 3. Chelsea Football Club – Official Site for News, Tickets & Fixtures 4. AFL – The official site of the Australian Football League – AFL.com.au 5. The Official Website of Arsenal Football Club | Arsenal.com 6. NFL.com – Official Site of the National Football League 7. BBC SPORT | Football 8. CBC.ca Meyer's all-in approach a theme among college football coachesý 9. Official Site of the Premier League – Barclays Premier League News 10. Manchester United Football Club 11. Sky Sports | Football News

Listing 5. Reordered search results for a sample query based on individual user's interests

Listing 6. Reordered search results for a sample query based on interests of users and its social network

However, we believe that the constraints on the number of participants and test queries did effect and may have caused some level of biasness in the evaluation results on accuracy and reliability of the ranking algorithms. In order to avoid this limitation, we have used click-through data that is recorded in search engine logs to simulate user experiences in Web search, and analyze it, as described in [19]. In general, when a user issues a query, the user usually checks search results in top to bottom manner. The user may click one or more results that look relevant and skips those documents that the user is not interested in. If our personalization mechanism ranks relevant results for the users higher in the search results list, the user might be more satisfied and browse through the re-ordered search results more than that of original search results. Therefore, we may utilize the user click history as a way to judge the level of satisfaction of the user to evaluate the ranking search accuracy. In this way, it has become easier for us to perform a large-scale evaluation. Furthermore, click-through data reflects the real world distribution of queries, users, and search scenarios. Thus, in our evaluation, usage of click-through data has brought results closer to the practical use cases in the evaluation of personalized search than that of using user surveys.

Click-through data in search engines can be seen as a set of triples (q, r, c) consisting of the query q, the ranking r presented to the user, and the set c of links the user clicked on. Listing 5 shows an example, the user asked a query, and received the ranking shown as order of results, and then clicked on the links. Since every query corresponds to one triple, the amount of data that is potentially available is virtually unlimited. Users, normally, do not click on links at random, but make a (somewhat) informed choice. While click-through data is typically noisy and clicks

Table 26.5 Average DGC for search results

Result set	DGC	Standard deviation
Original search results	0.518	0.119
Re-ordered search results	0.892	0.147

are not perfect relevance judgments, the clicks are likely to convey at least some information. Click-through data can be recorded with little overhead and without compromising the functionality and usefulness of the search engine. In particular, compared to explicit user feedback, it does not add any overhead for the user. The query q and the returned ranking r can easily be recorded whenever the resulting ranking is displayed to the user. For recording the clicks, a log file can be kept by a simple proxy system.

In order to collect the data and use it for experiments and testing, a simple Web search engine was built, that uses well-known Web search engines (like Google, Yahoo and Altavista) to collect the Web search results, and performs the re-ordering of the Web search results (as per user preferences) on client side. Our search engine works as follows: the users type query into the basic interface. This query is forwarded to the search engine. The results are returned by one of these basic search engines and the top 100 suggested links are extracted. Re-ordering of the search results is then performed and top 10 results are shown to the user. For each of the presented link, the system displays the title of the page along with its URL. The clicks of the user are recorded using the proxy system.

To be able to compare the quality of different retrieval functions, methods prescribed in [14] have been used. The idea is to present two rankings as A and B at the same time and then compare them after combining them as C. This particular form of presentation leads to a blind statistical test so that the clicks of the user demonstrate unbiased preferences. If the user scans the links of C from top to bottom, at any point he has seen almost equally many links from the top of A as from the top of B. To measure the ranking quality, we use the Discounted Cumulative gain (DCG) [12], which is a measure that takes into consideration the rank of relevant documents and allows the incorporation of different relevance levels. DCG is defined as follows:

$$DCG(i) = \left\{ \begin{array}{ll} G(1) & if\ i = 1 \\ DCG(i-1) + G(i)/\log(i) & otherwise \end{array} \right\}$$

where i is the rank of the result within the result set, and $G(i)$ is the relevance level of the result. We used $G(i) = 2$ for highly relevant documents, $G(i) = 1$ for relevant ones, and $G(i) = 0$ for non-relevant ones.

As shown in Table 26.5, automatic re-ordering of search results clearly improves search result quality. For example, the search results for query "football" with different users having different preferences have been reformulated by our system resulting in a better DCG.

The pure personalized results slightly overdue personalization, however, when combined with the original web ranks using the personalization, the original Google results are outperformed. The ranking quality obtained by re-ordering the search results based on the user preferences indicates the need for our approach of community-aware personalization strategies based on the information need. Click entropy, as introduced in [7], is defined as a measure of the variation in the information needs of users for a query as follows:

$$ClickEntropy(q) = \sum_{p \in P(q)} -P(p|q) \log P(p|q)$$

where, *ClickEntroy(q)* is the click entropy of query q. $P(q)$ is the collection of web pages clicked on query q. $P(p|q)$ is the percentage of clicks on web page p among all clicks on q, i.e., $P(p|q) = \frac{|Clicks(q,p,\bullet)|}{|Clicks(q,\bullet,\bullet)|}$

Click entropy is a direct indication of query click variation. If all users click only one identical page on query q, we have $ClickEntroy(q) = 0$. Smaller click entropy means that the majority of users agree with each other on a small number of web pages. In such cases, there is no need to do any personalization. Large click entropy indicates that many web pages were clicked for the query. This may mean that either a user has to select several pages to satisfy his/her information need, which means that the query is most likely an informational query. Therefore, personalization-based reordering of search results can help to in bringing more relevant results to the users or different users have different selections for a search query, which means that the query is an ambiguous query. In this case, personalization-based reordering of search results can be used to provide different web pages to different users, as per their needs.

We show the average search performance improvement of different personalization strategies on test queries with different click entropies in Fig. 26.2 that shows the improvement of personalized search performance increases with click entropy being larger, especially when click entropy is higher than 1.5. For click-based methods, individual-level personalization and group-based personalization, the improvement is limited for the queries with click entropy being lower, i.e. between 0 and 0.5. In the case of low click entropy, our approach brings only 0.37 % of improvement which is not statistically significant. It shows that the users have general consistent clicks for the queries with low click entropy, and thus, no personalization is necessary for the current search results. However, for the queries where click entropy is significantly higher, say greater than 3.0, the result is obviously different. Both individual-level personalization and group-based personalization gets a dramatic improvement by having more relevant search results. In terms of ranking and re-ordering of search results, both, the group-based personalization and the individual-level personalization improve by 25 %. This shows that the search queries with higher click entropy benefit more from personalization. Therefore, we perform personalization and re-ordering of search results, only when it is beneficial to do so (i.e. click entropy is significantly high).

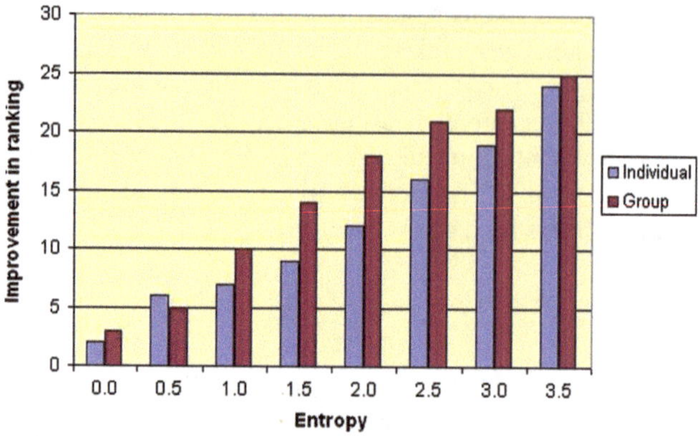

Fig. 26.2 Click entropy vs. improvement in ranking

26.4 Conclusions

In this book chapter, we presented our proposed solution to re-order Web search results based on the contextual information collected from a user's social network in a systematic manner. We have shown how the proposed system can help in bringing more relevant and interesting information for different users by re-ordering the search results from Web search engines, while avoiding irrelevant information. It enables the users to find out the information according to their interests in an easier and automated manner. We have developed various strategies, based on standard social network analysis techniques, for pulling out important publicly available information from the community of a user that is taken as important contextual information. It helps in extracting the required information of the community of a user from his/her social network and uses it to rank and re-order the search results of a Web search engine, based on the personal interests of the user and his/her community. Our design methodology in developing the community-aware personalized Web search kept our solution generic, to be able to customize it and apply it to any search scenario. We presented the overall architecture, described the ranking algorithms, and discussed the implementation and evaluation using well-known techniques and real-life datasets to show the viability of our proposed solution in real-life search scenarios.

References

1. Almeida, R.B., Almeida, V.A.F.: A community-aware search engine. In: Proceedings of International World Wide Web Conference (WWW 2004). New York
2. Anick, P.: Using terminological feedback for web search refinement: a log-based study. In Proceedings of WWW 2004, New York, pp. 89–95 (2004)

3. Berners-Lee, T., Hendler, J., Lassila, O.: The semantic web. Scientific American Magazine (2001). http://www.scientificamerican.com/article.cfm?id=the-semantic-web
4. Brin, S., Page, L.: The anatomy of a large-scale hypertextual web search engine. In: Proceedings of WWW, Santa Clara (1997)
5. Carminati, B., Ferrari, E., Perego, A.: Combining social networks and semantic web technologies for personalizing web access. In: Proceedings of the 4th International Conference on Collaborative Computing (CollaborateCom 2008), Orlando (2008)
6. Chen, H., Finin, T., Joshi, A.: An ontology for context-aware pervasive computing environments. Special Issue on Ontologies for Distributed Systems, Knowledge Engineering (2004)
7. Dou, Z., Song, R., Wen, J.R., Yuan, X.: Evaluating the effectiveness of personalized web search. IEEE Trans. Knowl. Data Eng. **21**(8), 1178–1190 (2009)
8. Freeman, L.: The development of social network analysis. Empirical Press, Vancouver (2006)
9. Google Personal (2009). http://labs.google.com/personalized
10. Granovetter, M.S.: The strength of weak ties. Am. J. Soc. **78**, 1360–1380 (1973)
11. Heath, T., Motta, E., Petre, M.: Computing word-of-mouth trust relationships in social networks from semantic Web and Web2.0 data sources. In: Proceedings of the Workshop on Bridging the Gap Between Semantic Web and Web 2.0, 4th European Semantic Web Conference (ESWC2007), Innsbruck (2007)
12. Jarvelin, K., Keklinen, J.: Ir evaluation methods for retrieving highly relevant documents. In: Proceedings of the 23rd Annual International ACM SIGIR Conference on Research and Development in Information Retrieval, July 2000, Athens (2000)
13. Jeh, G., Widom, J.: Scaling personalized web search. In: Proceedings of WWW 2003, pp. 271–279 (2003)
14. Joachims, T., Granka, L., Pan, B., Hembrooke, H., Gay, G.: Accurately interpreting clickthrough data as implicit feedback. In: Proceedings of the Conference on Research and Development in Information Retrieval (SIGIR), Salvador (2005)
15. McKeown, K.R., Elhadad, N., Hatzivassiloglou, V.: Leveraging a common representation for personalized search and summarization in a medical digital library. In: Proceedings of ICDL 2003, pp. 159–170. New Delhi, India (2003)
16. Morris, M.R., Teevan, J., Bush, S.: Enhancing collaborative Web search with personalization – Groupization, smart splitting, and group hit-highlighting. In: Proceedings of CSCW 2008. SIGCHI/Association for Computing Machinery, New York (2008)
17. Parr, B.: BREAKING News: Google announces social search. October 21st, 2009. http://mashable.com/2009/10/21/breaking-google-launches-social-search
18. Pattanasri, N., Jatowt, A., Tanaka, K.: Context-aware search inside e-learning materials using textbook ontologies. In: Advances in Data and Web Management. LNCS, vol. 4505/2009. Springer, Berlin (2009). doi:10.1007/978-3-540-72524-4, ISBN:978-3-540-72483-4
19. Shafiq, O., Alhajj, R., Rokne, J.G.: Community aware personalized web search. In: Proceedings of the 2010 International Conference on Advances in Social Networks Analysis and Mining (ASONAM 2010), Odense (2010)
20. Speretta, M., Gauch, S.: Personalizing search based on user search history. In: Proceedings of CIKM, Washington (2004)
21. Sugiyama, K., Hatano, K., Yoshikawa, M.: Adaptive web search based on user profile constructed without any effort from user. In: Proceedings of WWW, New York, pp. 675–684 (2004)
22. Tarjan, R.E.: A note on finding the bridges of a graph. Inf. Process. Lett. **2**, 160–161 (1974)
23. Teevan, J., Dumais, S.T., Horvitz, E.: Beyond the commons: investigating the value of personalizing Web search. In: Proceedings of the Workshop on New Technologies for Personalized Information Access (PIA), Edinburgh (2005)
24. Teevan, J., Dumais, S.T., Horvitz, E.: Characterizing the value of personalizing search. In: Proceedings of SIGIR 2007, Amsterdam, pp. 757–756 (2007)
25. Zeng, Y., Ren, X., Qin, Y., Zhong, N., Huang, Z., Wang, Y.: Social relation based scalable semantic search refinement. In: Workshop on Scalable Semantic Data Processing, Asian Semantic Web Conference (ASWC 2009), 7th December 2009, Shanghai (2009)

Chapter 27
Evolution of Online Forum Communities

Mikolaj Morzy

Abstract An Internet forum is a Web application for publishing user-generated content under the form of a discussion. The most important feature of Internet forums is their social aspect. Many forums are active for a long period of time and attract a group of dedicated users, who build a tight social community around a forum. With great abundance of forums devoted to every possible aspect of human activity, such as politics, religion, sports, technology, entertainment, economy, fashion, and many more, users are able to find a forum that perfectly suits their needs and interests. Communities of users forming around popular Internet forums undergo an evolution over time. Some Internet forums become more dense and saturated with users, some Internet forums dissolve in broader discussion topics. Forums can differ in ways they attract new users, maintain current users or decay in membership and posting intensity. In this paper we introduce a micro-community-based model for measuring the evolution of Internet forums. We show how simple concept of a micro-community can be used to quantitatively assess the openness and durability of an Internet forum. We also show that our model is capable of producing a taxonomy of Internet forums using unsupervised clustering method. We present the micro-community model, the set of basic statistics, and we apply the model to several real-world online forum communities to experimentally verify the correctness and robustness of the model.

M. Morzy (✉)
Institute of Computing Science, Poznan University of Technology, Poland, Piotrowo 2, 60-965, Poznan, Poland
e-mail: Mikolaj.Morzy@put.poznan.pl

T. Özyer et al. (eds.), *The Influence of Technology on Social Network Analysis and Mining*, Lecture Notes in Social Networks 6, DOI 10.1007/978-3-7091-1346-2_27,

27.1 Introduction

An Internet forum is a Web application for publishing user-generated content under the form of a discussion. Usually, the term *forum* refers to the entire community of users. Discussions considering particular subjects are called *topics* or *threads*. Internet forums (the Latin plural *fora* may also occasionally be used) are sometimes called Web forums, discussion boards, message boards, discussion groups, or bulletin boards. Internet forums are not new to the network community. They are successors of tools such as Usenet newsgroups and bulletin board systems (BBS) that were popular before the advent of the World Wide Web. Messages posted to a forum can be displayed either chronologically, or using threads of discussion. Most forums are limited to textual messages with some multimedia content embedded (such as images or Flash objects). Internet forum systems also provide sophisticated search tools that allow users to find messages fulfilling search criteria, to limit the search to particular threads or subforums, to search for messages posted by a particular user, to search within the subject or body of the post, etc.

Internet forums provide users with social environments. Usually, upon joining the forum a user pledges to adhere to the netiquette of a forum, i.e., the set of rules governing the accepted format and content of posts. Some forums are very strict about enforcing netiquette rules (e.g., a family forum may not tolerate any form of swearing or sexually explicit content), and some forums do not enforce netiquette rules at all. Two types of special users are present to protect the forum and enforce the netiquette. Administrators have a complete set of rights and permissions to edit and delete abusing posts, to manage threads of discussion, to change global forum settings, to conduct software upgrades, to manage users and their accounts, to ban users who do not comply with the netiquette, and to stick popular threads and create word filters for posts. Moderators enjoy a subset of rights and permissions granted to administrators. Moderators are commonly assigned the task to run a single forum or a single thread and moderate the discussion by issuing warnings to users who do not comply with the netiquette. Moderators can suspend users, edit and delete questionable posts, and temporarily ban users who breach the rules of the forum. Forums may require a registration and a login prior to posting a message, but there are also popular forums where anonymous users are allowed to post. Anonymity and pseudo-anonymity drastically lower the quality of data and information available on a forum. Besides, the registration requirement creates a strong liaison between a user and a forum, building durable social bindings. It is interesting to see how these ad hoc communities of users emerge, persist over longer periods of time, and eventually fade away.

Unfortunately, even the registration does not shield forum community from trolls, malevolent users whose sole intention is to spark heated discussion, ignite controversy, or post offensive and abusive contents. Trolls usually have no other merit or purpose than to irritate and offend other users, misusing pseudo-anonymity offered by the Internet. Trolling is just one example of the obtrusive social cost of cheap pseudonyms which can be created and used at no expense. Indeed, trolls fear no real retaliation for their vandalizing behavior other than a ban on a given identity. As the registration is almost always free of charge, there is no incentive for a troll to preserve her identity. Trolling, destructive as it may be, is an inevitable aspect of collaboration and interaction happening within a large community of diverse individuals. As the community matures, the profiles of collaboration and interaction change. We are interested in studying this slow process of gradual change.

This chapter focuses on means to quantitatively measure the evolution of Internet forum communities. We employ a simple model of micro-communities to observe how groups of users fluctuate, with new users joining micro-communities while other users leaving micro-communities. These small changes in content and structure of micro-communities allow us to infer various macro-measures of Internet forums. We identify key statistics that can be used to characterize various types of Internet forums and we verify our model by using an unsupervised data mining algorithm (hierarchical clustering algorithm) to recreate the taxonomy of a set of Internet forums based on the contents of our model.

The main contribution of the chapter consists in the following:

- The introduction of the micro-community model for measuring the evolution of Internet forum communities over time,
- The identification of key features that can be used to characterize an Internet forum community,
- The validation of the presented model using hierarchical clustering algorithm on a set of Internet forums.

27.1.1 Organization of the Chapter

The chapter is organized as follows. Section 27.2 contains an overview of the related work. In Sect. 27.3 we introduce the micro-community model for quantifying the evolution of social networks. We present the notion of a micro-community and we list basic properties of micro-communities measured under the model. Section 27.4 presents statistics gathered during Internet forum crawling that are used to measure and compare Internet forums. These statistics may be further used as input features for a clustering algorithm. We relate initial reports on the clustering of Internet forums in Sect. 27.5. The chapter concludes in Sect. 27.6 with a summary of findings and a future work agenda.

27.2 Related Work

Much research has been conducted on text mining and knowledge discovery from unstructured data. An interested reader may find a detailed summary of recent findings in this domain in [6] and [16]. In [6] the authors provide the examination of core text mining techniques, as well as discuss link detection methods, preprocessing techniques, and knowledge representation models for text mining and text analysis. The authors also provide examples of text mining algorithms applications in business intelligence, bioinformatics or social studies. In [16] the authors concentrate on the advanced aspects of text mining: automated text indexing, information retrieval and Web search, information extraction, automatic document summarization, etc. In addition, much work has been done on statistical natural language processing. Statistical methods for text mining are described and discussed in detail in [2, 10]. In [2] the authors present a very interesting method for automatic discovery of emotions from text. The emotional affinity of sentences is determined solely based on machine learning tools. The authors apply their algorithm to children's fairy tales and report on very encouraging results. Manning [10] focuses attention on statistical approaches to processing natural language text, presenting both the theory, mathematical and linguistic foundations, and examples of practical applications of statistical methods for text analysis.

Analysis of threaded conversations, which are the predominant pattern of communications in the contemporary Web, is an actively researched domain. In particular, many proposals have been submitted to derive social roles solely based on the structural patterns of conversations. Examples of earlier proposals include [7, 15]. In [7] the authors present a method of characterizing authors in Usenet newsgroups. In particular, the authors discover that using the second-degree egocentric networks they were able to clearly distinguish between different types of newsgroups authors. Viegas and Smith [15] perform a similar experiment, using AuthorLines visualization tool to display the activity of newsgroup authors throughout a year. The examination of the patterns revealed on the visualization allows them to develop a model of social roles played by different users. A thorough overview of structural patterns associated with particular social roles, that can be used as structural signatures, can be found in [5]. The authors examine a wide variety of networks from four different types of species (humans, apes, birds, non-primate mammals) representing very different relationships. Surprisingly, the similarities between networks are related to the type of the relationship and not to the species.

Most of the recent work has been performed on the basis of social network analysis methods [3, 4, 9], but the investigation of role typology has been an important challenge in sociology [12, 13]. Recently, more attention has been given to the identification of social roles that are not general, but specific to online communities. The existence of local experts, trolls, answer people, fans, conversationalists, etc. has been verified [8, 11, 14]. For instance, in [11] the authors show how the specific settings of online newsgroups influence the structure of communication between users. They also show how the effects of having a computer as the medium for communication (such as very short conversational sentences, misplaced messages, and specific language being utilized) leads to confusion and misunderstanding. The authors use their findings to propose a taxonomy of roles in newsgroups, which includes simple readers (or eavesdroppers), casual senders, and hosts. Moreover, the benefits of being able to deduce the social role of an individual without having to analyze the contents generated by that individual are becoming apparent [17–20].

Wenger and Snyder introduce the concept of a Community of Practice and show, in subsequent works, how these communities appear, how they maintain their online presence, and how these communitites can be used to manage knowledge resources.

27.3 Micro-community Model

In this section we introduce the micro-community model for the analysis of social network evolution over time. Each Internet forum induces a community of authors who contribute to the forum. The authors are attracted by the main subject of the forum and we can reasonably expect that the authors share interest in topics discussed on the forum. The entire community of users of a particular forum is difficult to analyze because even for narrowly defined subjects these communities tend to be large and diverse. Trends and regularities discovered at the level of the entire community may be too general to apply to individual authors. Hence, we have decided to discover smaller building blocks of communities, namely, micro-communities of Internet forum authors. The rationale behind the division of the community into micro-communities is that smaller micro-communities are more consistent and cohesive, thus leading to easier knowledge extraction.

The authors contributing to a forum create particular bonds when they write in the same topics. Co-authorship of a topic indicates shared interests, friendship or enmity, all of which express a sense of a micro-community. When two authors consistently co-author topics, we treat this fact as a strong confirmation that these authors belong to a common micro-community. The process of micro-community discovery consists of three stages. In the first stage we discover micro-groups of authors who co-author common topics within a particular period of analysis. A micro-community should be durable, i.e., it should span over many periods of analysis. In the second stage for each micro-group we are trying to identify predecessor micro-groups discovered in previous periods of analysis. Finally, in the third stage, related micro-groups from subsequent periods of analysis are aggregated to form a micro-community.

A *micro-group* is a group of authors who participated in at least *minsup* common threads, where the threshold *minsup* is defined as $minsup = \lfloor log_{10}(t_{cnt}) \rfloor$ and t_{cnt} denotes the thread count, i.e., the count of currently active threads on the forum. We have chosen to scale the *minsup* threshold logarithmically with respect to the number of posts, because human capability of participation in different topics of discussion is almost constant and it does not scale with the size of the forum. On the other hand, we observe that the authors are slightly more active on large forums, this is why instead of choosing a global constant, we modify the threshold marginally to improve its filtering power while not compromising its main goal.

The micro-groups are discovered using the Apriori algorithm [1]. Each topic is transformed into a set of authors participating in the topic. These sets form the transaction database for the Apriori algorithm. The result of the Apriori algorithm is the set of micro-groups discovered in the forum.

Let $U = \{u_1, \ldots, u_m\}$ denote the set of all contribution authors (or, more generally, users). Let $M_i^{(k)}$ denote an i-th micro-group of the size k. If the size of a micro-group is not relevant, we will refer to such i-th micro-group as M_i. Let T_F denote the set of all topics on the forum F, and let *support*(M_i) denote the number of topics in which the members of the micro-group M_i jointly participated (where the fact that a user u_j participates in topic t is denoted by $u_j \rightharpoonup t$):

$$support(M_i) = \frac{\left|\{t \in T_F : \exists u_j \in M_i : u_j \rightharpoonup t\}\right|}{|T_F|}$$

The Apriori algorithm iteratively computes frequent micro-groups based on smaller frequent micro-groups discovered in previous iterations. The algorithm works as follows. The smallest possible micro-group consists of a single author. In the first step, the algorithm generates the candidate set $C_1 = \{M_{u_1}^{(k)}, \ldots, M_{u_m}^{(k)}\}$, where $M_{u_j}^{(k)} = \{u_j\}$. Next, the support of all candidate micro-groups is computed in the database and the frequent micro-groups are retained as the set L_1. From then on, the algorithm generates the set C_k of candidate micro-groups of the size k by joining all frequent micro-groups belonging to the set L_{k-1} discovered in the previous step. In addition, the algorithm prunes all newly generated candidate micro-groups which contain any infrequent subset, i.e., which contain a subset that does not belong to L_{k-1}. The algorithm terminates at step q when there are no more candidate micro-groups to be generated from L_{q-1}.

Each micro-group represents a set of cooperating authors during a single period of analysis. In other words, a micro-group is a static snapshot of inter-author cooperation at a given point in time. In order to extend this notion to a sequence of periods, we must identify predecessors and successors of each micro-group. To enhance the continuity of micro-groups we do not constrain ourselves to only previous period, but for each micro-group we are looking for continuity in two predeceasing periods (i.e., a micro-group M_i discovered at period p_k might have been inactive during period p_{k-1}, but had been active during period p_{k-2}). We define the micro-group precedence relation $\prec$ in the following way:

$$M_i' \prec M_i \Leftrightarrow \frac{\left|M_i' \cap M_i\right|}{\left|M_i'\right|} \geq \alpha \wedge \frac{\left|M_i' - M_i\right|}{\left|M_i'\right|} \leq \beta \wedge M_i' \in p_{k-1} \cup p_{k-2}$$

In other words, for a micro-group M_i to be identified as the successor of the micro-group M_i', the following must be true:

- M_i must contain at least α members of the preceding micro-group M_i'
- M_i must not contain more than β new members,
- M_i' must have been discovered in one of the two preceding periods of analysis.

Let $\prec^*$ denote the transitive closure of the precedence relation $\prec$. The set of all predecessors of a micro-group M_i until period p_k is defined as

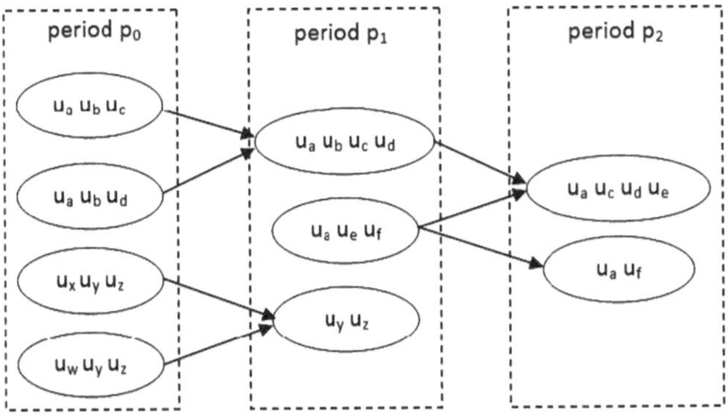

Fig. 27.1 Micro-groups and micro-communities

$$predecessors(M_i, p_k) = \{M_i' \in \bigcup_{j=1}^{k-1} p_j : M_i' \prec^* M_i\}$$

Micro-groups form a forest with respect to the precedence relation $\prec$. Edges in the forest represent the direction of the precedence relation and each level represents a single period of analysis. An example of such forest is depicted in Fig. 27.1. This forest can be searched for individual trees. Following the example, there are three levels in the forest representing three consecutive periods of analysis. All authors who belong to micro-groups constituting a single tree are aggregated to a single micro-community.

Let F denote the forest resulting from the precedence relation $\prec$, and let T denote a single tree present in the forest F. A *micro-community* MC_i is defined as

$$MC_i = \{u_j : u_j \in \bigcup_{M_i \in T} M_i\}$$

Again, using the example forest depicted in Fig. 27.1 we can observe two micro-communities, $MC_1 = \{u_w, u_x, u_y, u_z\}$ and $MC_2 = \{u_a, u_b, u_c, u_d, u_e, u_f\}$.

Micro-communities discovered using the above described procedure serve as the community model for the entire forum. They group authors who share common interests, discuss similar subjects and (probably) know each other, at least virtually. Due to the transitivity of the precedence relation $\prec$ a situation may occur when two authors u_q and u_r are aggregated to a micro-community despite never having participated in a common topic. This may happen if a micro-community is very durable and persists during several subsequent periods, undergoing a gradual exchange of members at the same time. Nevertheless, we still believe that it is legitimate to put such users into a single micro-community, because the transitivity of the precedence relation $\prec$ implies the similarity of interests of such users. In the next section we show how micro-communities discovered in Internet forum data can be used to extract statistics that are further used to quantitatively describe the evolution of online communities.

27.4 Statistics

In this section we present the quantitative characteristics of the datasets used in our experiments. We have focused on real-world datasets and vivid online communities. We have also targeted long-lasting communities with a record of past activities to make sure that the selected communities were undergoing a continuous evolution.

The data used in our experiments have been collected by a specialized crawler created on top of the popular WebSphinx library. We have chosen 34 different Internet forums as targets for the analysis. The emphasis was to create the set as diverse as possible. The following Internet forum aggregators were selected, and from each one a few particular forums were harvested and analyzed:

- acapella.harmony-central.com: forums devoted to classical music,
- www.christianforums.com: forums devoted to Christianity and religious conservatism,
- www.fanforum.com: forums on celebrities, gossips, movies and TV series,
- www.honda-tech.com: forums devoted to motorization, in particular, to the cars produced by Honda,
- www.inthemix.com: forums on current musical events worldwide (concerts, festivals, etc.),
- forums.macrumors.com: forums on Apple company rumors and products,
- photography-on-the.net: forums on photography,
- www.shroomery.org: forums for mushroom pickers,
- www.thestudentroom.co.uk: general discussion forums for students of British universities,
- www.vbulletin.com: technical forums on vBulletin system software.

As can be easily noticed, the set of selected forums is very diverse, ranging from general purpose discussion boards (student news, celebrity gossips), through more focused subjects (conservative Christians, photography), to highly specialized and narrowly defined forums (mushrooms pickers). The type of the Internet forum under consideration influences the characteristics of the forum. The participation in an Internet forum is tantamount to the participation in an established social community defined by the Internet forum subject. The degree of coherence of the community may vary from very strict (a closed group of experts who know each other), through moderate (a semi-opened group consisting of a core of experts and a cloud of visitors), to loose (fully opened group of casual contributors who participate sporadically in selected topics). The degree of coherence is closely related to the information value of the forum. Opened forums are least likely to contain interesting and valuable knowledge content. These forums are dominated by random visitors, and sometimes attract a small group of habitual guests who tend to come back to the forum on a regular basis. Discussions on opened forums are often shallow, emotional, inconsistent, lacking discipline and manners. Opened forums rarely contain useful practical knowledge or specialized information. On the other hand, opened forums are the best place to analyze controversy, emotionality, and social interactions between participants of the discussion. Their spontaneous and impulsive character encourages authors to form their opinions overtly, so opened forums may be perceived as the main source of information about attitudes and beliefs of John Q Public. On the opposite side one finds closed specialized forums. These forums provide high quality knowledge on selected subjects, they are characterized by discipline, consistency, and credibility. Authors are almost always well known to the community, random guests are very rare, and authors pay attention to maintain their status within the community by providing reliable answers to submitted questions. Closed forums account for a small fraction of the available Internet forums. The majority of forums are semi-opened forums that allow both registered and anonymous submissions. Such forums may be devoted to a narrow subject, but may also consider a broad range of topics. Usually, such forum attracts a group of dedicated authors, who form the core of the community, but casual authors are also welcomed. These forums are a compromise between the strictly closed specialized forums and the totally opened forums. One may dig such forum in search of practical information, or browse through the forum with no particular search criterion.

In order to measure the dynamics of Internet forum evolution over time we have selected a set of statistics. The values for statistics describing chosen Internet forums are presented in Table 27.1. Some statistics utilize the concept of a period, which is the time interval between subsequent forum snapshots, i.e., between subsequent sampling of the forum. The length of the interval depends on the popularity of the forum. Very large and dynamic forums should be sampled frequently, whereas small community-driven forums may be sampled less frequently. We have decided to compute the length of the period independently for each forum, using the following assumptions: a period cannot be shorter than 3 days and nights and each period must contain at least 20 posts (as computed from the average daily activity of the forum). Each period is rounded to the multiple of 24 h. However, periods must not be disjoint, because it would not permit the continuity of events at both ends of the period (e.g., the continuity of a micro-community existence). Therefore, after computing the initial length of the period, this length is extended by 40 % at each end of the period to form the final period that overlaps with its predecessor and successor. In this way, each event during the lifetime of a forum takes place within at most two periods, each period is at least 6 days and nights long, and each pair of consecutive periods shares 40 % of common events.

The statistics displayed in individual columns are as follows:

- **A**: total number of posts submitted to the forum,
- **B**: total number of threads of discussion on the forum,
- **C**: average number of posts per thread of discussion,
- **D**: age of the forum in days since forum creation,

Table 27.1 Internet forum statistics

Nazwa forum	A	B	C	D	E	F	G	H	I	J	K	L	M
iPhone	255,111	17,910	14.24	933	273.43	11.99	0.36	0	0	0.98	0.9	0.27	0.21
Heroes	238,441	1,078	221.19	1,074	222.01	4.57	5.15	0.01	0.01	0.99	0.97	0.13	0.1
General discussion and...	212,936	317	616.65	1,874	104.31	16.76	1.31	0.01	0.02	0.97	0.46	0.76	0.67
Nature & Landscapes	195,478	25,557	8.33	2,099	101.45	12.2	2.01	0	0.01	0.84	0.96	0.22	0.14
Conservative Christians	137,060	1,373	43.03	742	79.61	12.99	4.56	0.01	0.09	0.98	0.92	0.3	0.19
Societies	119,968	86	1,394.98	1,789	67.06	6.1	1.54	0.01	0	0.94	0.38	0.18	0.1
Chat	95,238	1,407	67.69	1,490	63.92	12.06	1.52	0.01	0	0.84	0.51	0.36	0.31
Gilmore girls	86,176	677	202.45	2,321	59.05	5.52	2.06	0.01	0	0.88	0.74	0.13	0.11
Amps	68,108	1,338	64.41	1,654	52.1	12.4	0.44	0	0	0.98	0.36	0.26	0.19
Kelly Clarkson	64,917	282	234.01	1,609	41.01	4.67	10.47	0.01	0.09	0.89	0.93	0.22	0.1
Sports	59,074	15	4,327.8	1,788	36.31	5.76	4.07	0.03	0	1	0.21	0.23	0.15
Bass forum	55,640	497	91.58	2,119	21.48	9.63	2.2	0.01	0.01	0.74	0.34	0.3	0.2
Photography	45,515	38	622.13	1,215	19.46	12.83	3.1	0.01	0.02	1	0.45	0.31	0.21
Applications and UCAS	28,751	1,946	11.9	1,289	17.97		0	0.01	0	0.46	0.53	0.14	0.07
Server configuration	27,357	9,223	6.03	3,379	16.47	2.13	1.81	0.01	0	1	0.35	0.02	0.03
vBulletin 3.8 questions...	23,764	4,994	4.22	1,324	15.92	0	3.13	0.03	0	0.24	0.58	0	0
Recording forum	23,641	3,650	7.5	2,384	11.48	3.6	1.46	0.01	0	0.91	0.17	0.07	0.06
Effects	23,164	1,090	6.79	651	11.37	0	0	0.13	0	0.62	0.07	0	0

MacOS	21,928	4,171	6.89	3,009	9.56	5.35	1.59	0.01	0	0.92	0.53	0.06	0.06
Sydney	21,076	114	119.9	1,454	9.4	19	1.42	0.02	0.02	0.46	0.19	0.47	0.37
Classifieds: buy	14,714	11,691	2.03	2,619	9.07	0	0	0.06	0	0.66	0.03	0	0
vBulletin suggestions and...	14,330	2,485	8.82	2,897	7.57	0	0.24	0.01	0	0.88	0.36	0.19	0.14
Brisbane and Gold Coast	13,669	108	132.69	2,062	6.95	13.14	0.7	0.02	0	0.62	0.29	0.33	0.22
Honda Civic/Del Sol (1992...)	9,487	763	19.28	2,413	6.1	0	0	0.04	0	0.84	0.03	0.08	0
iPhone programming	7,399	441	5.84	504	5.11	0	2.13	0.05	0	0.68	0.07	0	0.04
Craig Anderton's sound, studi...	6,889	219	31.46	1,460	4.72	6	0.73	0.03	0	0.75	0.04	0.08	0.1
Mac applications	6,214	1,350	7.03	2,300	4.12	0	0	0.04	0	0.56	0.03	0.06	0
Health and fitness	4,682	26	180.08	1,276	3.67	0	0	0.12	0	0.96	0.04	0	0
Missions & Evangelism	3,863	1,037	5.99	2,752	2.26	3	1.27	0.01	0	0.94	0.35	0.06	0.03
Computing and technology	2,574	33	49.12	927	1.75	0	0	0.19	0	0.63	0.14	0.13	0
Songwriting	1,874	138	27.99	2,608	1.48	0	0	0.08	0	0.96	0.03	0.21	0.13
Tunes & Tracks	1,621	55	34.07	1,858	1.01	0	0	0.11	0	0.99	0.08	0.08	0
MacBytes.com news discussion	1,146	134	8.55	1,515	0.76	0	0	0.5	0	0.31	0.05	0	0
Mushroom cultivation	861	40	21.53	2,305	0.37	0	0	0	0	0.2	0	0	0

- **E**: average number of posts per day,
- **F**: average openness of the forum, where openness is defined as the number of new authors joining a micro-community and staying within the micro-community for more than three periods,
- **G**: average durability of the forum, where durability is defined as the number of micro-communities that last more than three periods,
- **H**: average number of micro-groups per author,
- **I**: average density of the forum, where density is defined as the percentage of popular micro-communities to which more than 1,000 authors belong,
- **J**: activity of the forum, defined as the percentage of periods during which at least a single post has been submitted to the forum,
- **K**: percentage of active periods, defined as the ratio of the number of periods during which at least one micro-community has been started to the number of periods during which at least a single post has been submitted to the forum,
- **L**: average percentage of new authors in a micro-community,
- **M**: average percentage of authors who quit a micro-community.

In the next section we show how these statistics can be used to quantitatively measure the characteristics of various online forums.

27.5 Clustering of Internet Forums

Statistics presented in Sect. 27.4 has been fed to the hierarchical clustering algorithm in order to find subsets of similar forums. The analysis has been twofold. First, we have verified how basic static features related to forum activity can be used to group similar forums. Next, we have enhanced the model with parameters drawn from the discovered micro-communities. We have experimented with various clustering algorithms (K-Means, Hierarchical Clustering) and distance measures (euclidean, Manhattan distance, power distance). Below we report on the results obtained from the most promising experiment configurations.

Parameters used in the first experiment were: daily number of posts, forum age, active percentage of the forum, active percentage of time periods. The best combination of parameters for clustering algorithm proved to be Manhattan distance with Ward's cutoff criterion. The cutoff appeared at around 0.1, producing 6 distinct clusters (see Fig. 27.2).

The first cluster, which contains, among others, forums *Honda Civic/Del Sol*, *Health and Fitness*, *Computing and Technology*, *Tunes & Tracks*, has the following characteristics. The age of the forum lies between 2 and 7 years, the number of daily posts is kept very low (usually between 1 and 6) and, as a consequence, the active percentage of these forums is very low. Due to low posting frequency these forums experience prolongated periods of inactivity. We describe the forums falling into this category as *mature inactive expert forums*.

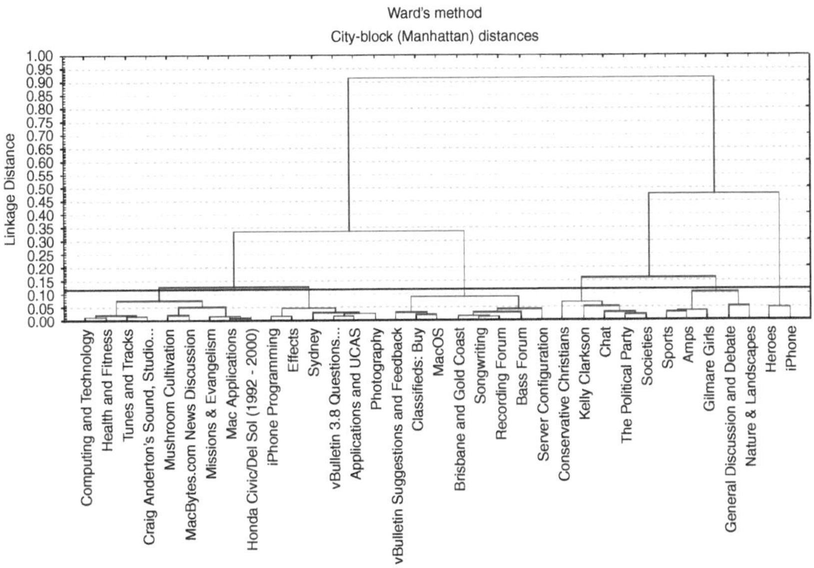

Fig. 27.2 Hierarchical tree of Internet forums – without micro-communities

The second cluster contains forums such as *Photography*, *Applications and UCAS*, *iPhone Programming*, etc. Their characteristics are as follows. These forums are relatively young, being active on average for 3 years. Similarly to the previous cluster, these forums have a relatively low volume of daily posts, ranging between 5 and 20 posts per day. However, first micro-communities begin to appear on these forums and initial social interaction can be detected. Although not so often as mature inactive expert forums, these forums may have possible long periods of inactivity. We refer to Internet forums such as these as *mature active expert forums*.

Let us now consider the fourth cluster containing forums *Conservative Christians*, *Societies*, *Gilmore Girls*, *The Political Party*, etc. All these forums display the following properties. These are usually quite stable forums, with long-established presence on the Web. Their average age is 4 years and they attract tens of posts per day. Micro-communities are common on these forums, but have a distinctive feature: almost all micro-communities appear frequently and are short-lived. These forums almost never experience any periods of inactivity. These forums can be generally characterized as *active community forums*.

Finally, consider the sixth cluster, consisting of two forums: *Heroes* and *iPhone*. These forums share the following distinct characteristics. Most of them are slightly younger than active community forums, counting on avereage 3 years. The most distinctive feature of these forums is the fact that they produce hundreds of daily posts. Similarly to active community forums, these forums frequently generate micro-communities of contributors, but these micro-communities are short-lived.

These forums never go silent and have absolutely no periods of inactivity. We refer to these forums as *novelty community forums*.

The above analysis employed static features of Internet forums, considering only the presence of micro-communities, but disregarding dynamic properties of micro-communities. In the second analysis we enhance the model by adding dynamic features of micro-communities. Our clustering algorithm is presented with the following features: average openness of the forum, average durability of the forum, average number of micro-communities per user, average density of the forum, and the percentage of active periods. For this set of features the Manhattan distance measure with Ward's cutoff criterion produced too many isolated clusters. Therefore, we used the power distance measure $d(\bar{x}, \bar{y}) = \sqrt[3]{\sum_i (x_i - y_i)^2}$ which resulted in 7 clusters with the cutoff at 0.3 (see Fig. 27.3). Let us now scrutinize selected clusters.

The first cluster, containing forums such as *Tunes & Tracks*, *Health and Fitness*, or *Computing and Technology*, has the following characteristics. These forums are extremely closed (or, conversely, characterized by very low openness). If micro-communities appear on these forums, they are volatile and do not last, as is indicated by very low durability measure. Users of these forums do not form large interwoven communities, leading to very low density measure for these forums. However, low density does not indicate the lack of micro-communities. Just the opposite is true, most users belong to several small micro-communities within these forums. These are the very large micro-communities that do not form within these forums, and even if they do, they exist for a very short period of time. The forums are active, but do not induce community bonds. We may characterize these forums as either *expert forums*, or *classified forums*. Interestingly, the same set of forums has been identified as a single cluster by the first clustering method.

Let us now examine the second cluster containing forums such as *Sydney, Brisbane and Gold Coast*, *Honda Civic*, or *Photography*. All these forums share the following characteristics. The forums are opened and friendly toward new users, who easily accommodate into the social structure of the forum. Micro-communities are not durable and tend to dissolve. Usually, users join a relatively small number of micro-communities (small average number of micro-communities per user), but they have no obstacles to join a group (large number of new users joining existing micro-communities). These forums do not exhibit any regular patterns with respect to activity and have very diverse activity periods. These are vibrant and active forums, with many micro-communities forming ad hoc, but only few surviving for a longer period of time. Users join these forums eagerly, but do not contribute or attach to them (except for a small core set of animators). We refer to these forums as *socially coherent forums* consisting of members of a large, heterogeneous community (students, music lovers, photographers).

The analysis of static and dynamic properties of the micro-community model allows for automatic forum classification. The model can be successfully applied both in static environment (where a single snapshot of the forum data is available, with no time perspective) and in the presence of additional time-related data. The model produces high quality clustering that is consistent with human intuition.

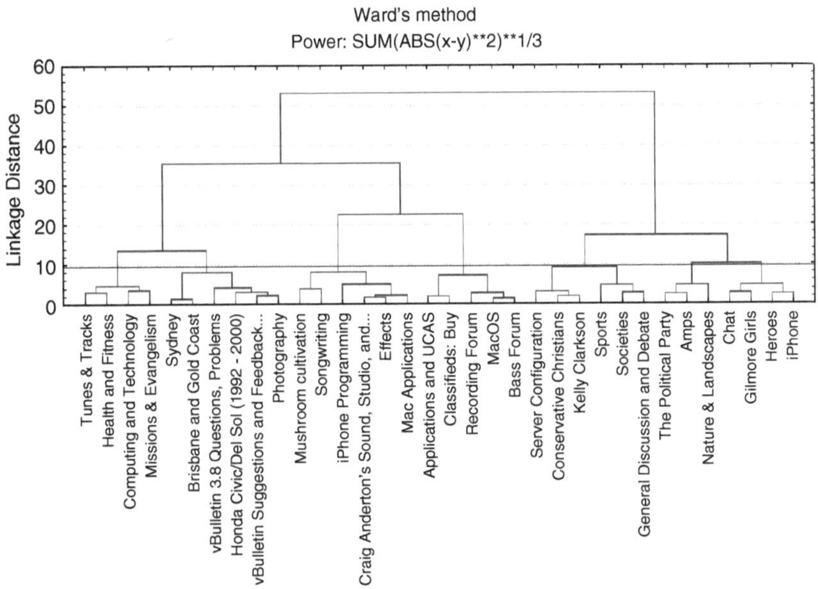

Fig. 27.3 Hierarchical tree of Internet forums – with micro-communities

27.6 Conclusions

In this chapter we have presented our initial findings in the domain of Internet forum evolution over time. We have introduced a new micro-community model for quantitatively measuring Internet forum characteristics and we have verified our model by the means of an unsupervised data mining algorithm, namely, hierarchical clustering, by producing a division of a set of Internet forums into clusters based solely on statistics found in our model and manually verifying the consistency and cohesion of the resulting clusters. We believe that our model correctly captures important features of Internet forum community evolution and allows for automatic tagging of Internet forums based on the observed characteristics of the communities.

The abundance of Internet forums, ranging from specialized to popular, makes the subject of mining Internet forums both interesting and very desirable. Internet forums hide enormous amounts of high quality knowledge generated by immense communities of users. Unfortunately, the lack of structure and standards makes the acquisition of this knowledge very difficult. Research presented in this chapter is a step towards automatic knowledge extraction from these opened repositories of knowledge. The statistics are fairly simple, but work surprisingly well in the real world. Rather than being a conclusive report, this chapter serves as the starting ground for further research into the evolution of online forum communities. In particular, we intend to focus our attention on the evolution of individual authors and to discover how the micro-evolution on the level of individual authors informs the macro-evolution of the entire community.

Acknowledgements Research supported by the Polish Ministry of Science grant N N516 371236.

References

1. Agrawal, R., Srikant, R.: Fast algorithms for mining association rules. In: Bocca, J.B., Jarke, M., Zaniolo, C. (eds.) Proceedings of the 20th International Conference on Very Large Data Bases, VLDB, pp. 487–499. Morgan Kaufmann, Hove (1994)
2. Alm, C.O., Roth, D., Sproat, R.: Emotions from text: machine learning for text-based emotion prediction. In: Proceedings of Human Language Technology Conference and Conference on Empirical Methods in Natural Language Processing, Vancouver, pp. 579–586. Association for Computational Linguistics, East Stroudsburg, (2005)
3. Brandes, U., Erlebach, T.: Network Analysis. Methodological Foundations. Lecture Notes in Computer Science, vol. 3418. Springer, Berlin/New York (2005)
4. Carrington, P.J., Scott, J., Wasserman, S.: Models and Methods in Social Network Analysis. Cambridge University Press, Cambridge (2005)
5. Faust, K., Skvoretz, J.: Comparing networks across space and time, size and species. Sociol. Methodol. **32**, 267–299 (2002)
6. Feldman, R., Sanger, J.: The Text Mining Handbook: Advanced Approaches in Analyzing Unstructured Data. Cambridge University Press, Leiden (2006)
7. Fisher, D., Smith, M., Welser, H.T.: You are who you talk to: detecting roles in usenet newsgroups. In: HICSS '06: Proceedings of the 39th Annual Hawaii International Conference on System Sciences, vol. 3, p. 59b. IEEE Computer Society, Washington, DC (2006)
8. Golder, S.: A typology of social roles in usenet. Ph.D. thesis, Harvard University (2003)
9. Hanneman, R.A., Riddle, M.: Introduction to Social Network Methods. University of California, Riverside (2005)
10. Manning, C.D., Schuetze, H.: Foundations of Statistical Natural Language Processing, 1 edn. MIT, Cambridge (1999)
11. Marcoccia, M.: On-line polylogues: conversation structure and participation framework in internet newsgroups. J. Pragmat. **36**(1), 115–145 (2004)
12. Merton, R.K.: Social Theory and Social Structure. Free Press, New York (1968)
13. Parsons, T.: The Social System, 2nd edn. Routledge, London (1991)
14. Turner, T.C., Smith, M.A., Welser, H.T.: Picturing usenet: mapping computer-mediated collective action. J. Comput. Mediat. Commun. **10**(4), 1–24 (2005)
15. Viegas, F.B., Smith, M.: Newsgroup crowds and AuthorLines: visualizing the activity of individuals in conversational cyberspaces. In: Proceedings of the 37th Annual Hawaii International Conference on System Sciences, 2004, pp. 10. IEEE Computer Society, Los Alamitos (2004)
16. Weiss, S., Indurkhya, N., Zhang, T., Damerau, F.: Text Mining: Predictive Methods for Analyzing Unstructured Information. Springer, New York (2004)
17. Welser, H.T., Gleave, E., Fisher, D., Smith, M.: Visualizing the signatures of social roles in online discussion groups. J. Soc. Struct. **8**(2), 564–586 (2007)
18. Wenger, E.: Communities of Practice: Learning, Meaning, and Identity, 1 edn. Cambridge University Press, Cambridge/New York (1998)
19. Wenger, E., Snyder, W.M.: Communities of practice: the organizational frontier. Harvard Bus. Rev. **78**(1), 139–146 (2000)
20. Wenger, E., Mcdermott, R., Snyder, W.: Cultivating Communities of Practice: A Guide to Managing Knowledge. Harvard Business School, Boston (2002)

Chapter 28
Movie Rating Prediction with Matrix Factorization Algorithm

Ozan B. Fikir, İlker O. Yaz, and Tansel Özyer

Abstract Recommendation systems are one of the research areas studied intensively in the last decades and several solutions have been elicited for problems in different domains for recommending. Recommendation may differ as content, collaborative filtering or both. Other than known challenges in collaborative filtering techniques, accuracy and computational cost at a large scale data still at saliency. In this paper we proposed an approach by utilizing matrix value factorization for predicting rating i by user j with the sub matrix as k-most similar items specific to user i for all users who rated them all. In an attempt, previously predicted values are used for subsequent predictions and we have investigated the accuracy of neighborhood methods by applying our method on Netflix Prize (http://www.netflixprize.com/). We have considered both items and users relationships on Netflix dataset for predicting movie ratings. Here, we have followed different ordering strategies for predicting a sequence unknown movie ratings and conducted several experiments.

28.1 Introduction

Recommendation systems are originated from different areas such as approximation theory, cognitive systems, information retrieval, prediction methods, and management science. Resnick and Varian describe recommendation systems as the opinion of users of community in order to help individuals to obtain their interests among a set of choices [8]. In mid 1990s recommendation systems has

O.B. Fikir
Aydin Yazilim Elektronik Sanayi A.Ş., TOBB University, Ankara, Turkey

İ.O. Yaz · T. Özyer (✉)
TOBB University, Ankara, Turkey
e-mail: ozyer@etu.edu.tr

T. Özyer et al. (eds.), *The Influence of Technology on Social Network Analysis and Mining*, Lecture Notes in Social Networks 6, DOI 10.1007/978-3-7091-1346-2_28,

become an individual research area [2, 3]. The taxonomy of technical design, item and evaluation characteristics have been given in detail [9]. In parallel to internet technologies, recommendation systems have been used more especially in e-commerce for movie, music, book, videos, pictures and etc.

There are very well known e-commerce examples such as Amazon, MovieFinder, eBay, Reel.com, and CDNOW. A detailed taxonomy of these techniques can be found in [9]. Past and future recommendation systems have been summarized in [2, 8].

As the massive information accessible via Internet grows exponentially, users have more difficulties to reach the needed information. There are various attempts to cope with the inherent problems in information filtering techniques with data mining techniques to come up with a solution [2, 5, 7].

Recommendation systems can be summarized in three approaches. Namely, the content based filtering, collaborative filtering and hybrid methods. Content based filtering, recommends something to user according to past preferences (s)he made. Content of the past preferences are significant for recommendation. Collaborative filtering relies on the past preference\rating correlation with other users. Based on this correlation, people with similar likes are taken into account for recommendation. Hybrid methods are the combination of both [2, 8].

Content based filtering is one of the oldest methods for percolating data. Systems using this method analysis the content of a set of items together with the ratings provided by individual users to infer which non-rated items might be of interest for a specific user. Basically, content based filtering uses utility function U(c,s), is computed with the utility of item s to user c. s content is composed of s1,s2,...,sk. Overall utility is based on U(c,si), $i = 1 \ldots k$ [2, 8]. Content based filtering has severe problems. User is limited to content has already been rated. Unrated content is ignored. To be able to do a better recommendation, user must do as many ratings onto content. This action is mostly disliked by users. Also, some other criteria as presentation, loading time can play a role in content rating and this is disregarded (Limited content and overspecialization and new user problem) [2, 3].

As in our daily life, we rely on the idea our friends, peers who share the same likes\dislikes and if they recommend an item, we are likely to enjoy it or vice a versa.

Collaborative filtering methods have been explained in [3, 8]. Tapestry [6] is one of the fist recommendation systems using collaborative filtering technique. Mainly, for U(c,s) utility function U(ci,s) is computed for all user ci. Collaborative filtering methods can be dependent on memory based and model based techniques [2]. Memory based and model based techniques have been surveyed in [2]. Model based methods are costly for model building whereas memory based model is easy to construct.

Contrary to content based filtering, collaborative filtering methods do not suffer some problems content based filtering does. Regardless of content, irrelevant items not seen previously can be dealt easily with collaborative filtering methods. Still, collaborative filtering methods have some problems as new user, new item and data sparsity problems. New user problem also exists in content based filtering. A new user's preferences must be learnt first. New item must also be rated by enough number of users. A general approach to rating for a user is rating small amount of item, so rating matrix is sparse. Similarities among users must be found in a sparse matrix [2].

Both content and collaborative filtering methods are used together to surpass the limitations of both methods. There are different approaches in hybrid methods. They can be enlisted as (1) the construction of collaborative and content based recommendation systems separately and combine them. (2) Incorporating content based filtering into collaborative filtering (3) Incorporating collaborative filtering into content based filtering and (4) constructing a unified recommender system that incorporates both collaborative and content based filtering. A detailed definition of hybrid methods and related examples of each approach has been given and supported with a digest of different literature studies on classification of recommender systems in [2].

Although the cost of recommending an item has increased in more complex structure, hybrid methods have been proposed to overcome shortcomings of content based and collaborative filtering techniques.

Our method performs a novel collaborative filtering method on the entire missing values. Iteratively, predicts ratings. The amount of surrounding knowledge of a missing value of a user, determines the order. The more knowledge, earlier the prediction is. As missing values are predicted they are used for latter missing values. We have proposed an algorithm for predicting all missing values and used QR factorization method for predicting each entry.

In this paper, we proposed a method for collaborative filtering. Our contributions are:

1. Our method restricts knowledge to k-similar items rated by the user and considers ratings of those who rated them all.
2. It follows an iterative rating procedure. All previously predicted ratings are used for rating other missing values.
3. Completing entire missing values in user-item matrix has been considered.
4. Our method follows an iterative method. Matrices with differing ranks are solved in order. Three different strategies have been employed: Decreasing rank order, Increasing rank order, and random rank order. Sub matrices with the rank are considered as surrounding information that can help rating other missing values.
5. Completing entire missing values in user-item matrix has been considered.

Besides, our method is believed to prevent round off errors come across in prediction of rating. This enables more accuracy for the subsequent rating predictions throughout the process.

The outline of the paper is as follows: Sect. 28.1 contains introduction; Sect. 28.2 summarizes the proposed work; Sect. 28.3 has the experiments and discussion. Section 28.4 has the conclusions and future work.

28.2 Proposed Method

28.3 Preliminary Work

Rating data can be represented as item-user matrix A of size mxn. We assume columns of the matrix represent the users; rows of the matrix represent the items that are rated. Each entry of column i contains the rating given by the user for all items. In mathematical point of view, ?? represents a linear transformation from user space to item space. Of course the matrix ???? is also a linear transformation from item space to user space. Each user u_j $(j = 1 \ldots n)$ rates items t_i $(i = 1 \ldots m)$ and user's rating for each cell is denoted as r_{ij}. The subscripts of r_{ij} indicates that the entry at the ith row and jth column of the matrix. It can be easily seen that $t_i \in \Re^n$ and $u_j \in \Re^m$.

If all the entries of ?? are fulfilled, item-user associations might be evaluated directly and easily. However, in most cases the matrix ?? is a sparse matrix. Entries can be missing because of several reasons. Items may not have been rated or values can be literally missing. After all, if we had chance to serve all the items to a particular user, the user evaluates each these items according to its own preferences. Hence, our goal in prediction is to reveal out all the missing parts to discover the user-item associations.

As mentioned above, rating prediction can be performed by considering either similarity between items or users (item-oriented vs. user-oriented). While rating r_{ij}, In item oriented approach the neighborhood function $N_k(t_i, u_j)$, designates the k-most similar items to t_i rated by the user u_j; in user based approach, the neighborhood function $N_k(u_j, t_i)$, designates the k-most users similar user u_j among all users who have rated t_i.

The most popular similarity metrics are pearson correlation coefficient and cosine similarity. Let u_j and u_k be two different users and S_{jk} represents the items rated by both users. Pearson similarity is:

$$\mathrm{sim}(u_j, u_k) = \frac{\sum_{t_p \in S_{jk}} (r_{pj} - \bar{r}_j)(r_{pk} - \bar{r}_k)}{\sqrt{\sum_{t_p \in S_{jk}} (r_{pj} - \bar{r}_j)^2 \sum_{t_p \in S_{jk}} (r_{pk} - \bar{r}_k)^2}}$$

Likewise similarity between two items is calculated as:

$$\mathrm{sim}(t_i, t_k) = \frac{\sum_{u_p \in S_{ik}} (r_{ip} - \bar{r}_i)(r_{kp} - \bar{r}_k)}{\sqrt{\sum_{u_p \in S_{ik}} (r_{ip} - \bar{r}_i)^2 \sum_{u_p \in S_{ik}} (r_{kp} - \bar{r}_k)^2}}$$

Where S_{ik} represents users who rate both t_i and t_k. Cosine similarity between users and items are:

$$\mathrm{sim}(u_j, u_k) = \cos(u_j, u_k) = \frac{u_j . u_k}{\|u_j\| \, \|u_k\|} \text{ and } \mathrm{sim}(t_i, t_k) = \cos(t_i, t_k) = \frac{t_i . t_k}{\|t_i\| \, \|t_k\|}$$

Both item-oriented and user-oriented approaches are given above. k-most similar neighbor will de determined by using similarity metric. In the next section, we will describe how we employ our ideas.

28.4 Rating Prediction Algorithm

Our prediction algorithm undergoes three phases. In the first phase, pairwise similarities between items are estimated. K most similar item is put in use for entry prediction. K-most similar items are retrieved and users who rated all are considered. This implies a smaller subset of users ($\leq n$). Our assumption is that matrix is sparse and the subset is very small. This is expected to get smaller as k increases. Thus we obtain a smaller region for rating prediction. Next, a matrix factorization method is applied for rating prediction. An iterative approach is utilized while completing all nonexistent entry values, so sub regions while doing rating prediction, we consider sub region with maximum rank value.

Algorithm CompleteRatings(A,k)

```
  //It completes nonexistent cells A(ui,tj) with k-most
  //similar items. A is of size mxn.
  Itemset(ti,uj) ←null S←null Ranks←null
  //Phase 1- Similarity matrix is estimated (in symmetric //case lower triangle would be sufficient)
  for i=1..m
    for j=1..m
      S[i,j]←sim(ti,tj)
  //Phase 2- Find N_k(t_i, u_j) and ranks of subregion
  for i=1..m
    for j=1..n
      if A[i,j] is missing then
      //The first k-most similar items to ti and rated by uj are estimated
            Itemset(ti,uj)←{tr|S[i,r]≤ S[i,r'] ∧ S[i,r']∉ itemset(ti,uj) ∧ size(Itemset(ti,uj))≤ k ∧ rated(tr,ui) j,r,r' ≤m}
      //Retrieve users rated all items in Itemset(ti,uj)
        Subusers(ti,uj)←{ur|∀t_s ∈ itemset(t_i, u_j) rated(ts,ur) }
      //Estimate the matrix rank
        Ranks(ti,uj)←getRank(Subusers(ti,uj),itemset(ti,uj))
      endif
  //in decreasing order, ascending order or this step is omitted in case random order
  sort(Ranks)
  while (Ranks is not empty)
    //Ranks is in sorted order. The most complete element
    //is popped out with address (ti,uj) and removed
    //Randomly one of (i,j) is picked from Itemsetfor
```

```
    //prediction
    element←pick(Ranks) //related to sort function above
    //pick retrieves kth element
    item_no←element.getItem()
    user_no←element.getUser()
    //Form matrix with the given info to find A[ti,uj]
    M←Construct(itemset(item_no,user_no),Subusers(item_no,user_no))
    //Solve the equation
    A[ti,uj]←Solve(M)
    Update(S) Update(Itemset)
    Update(Subusers) Update(Ranks)
  endwhile
```

The algorithm above completes ratings in matrix. We find $N_k(t_i, u_j)$ and users rated them. This is the sub region that has been used for predicting the movie rating of (ti,uj). In order, we randomly pick these sub regions and predict values. Based on the information, we get the matrix rank of the sub region composed of k-similar items rated by uj and all users rated those items. We keep ranks and use three different strategies to solve the equations. First, the ranks of matrices are sorted in ascending order; second in descending order and third is in random order. Ranks in sorted are taken individually and we apply matrix factorization method to find the empty cell (ti,uj). We update the information kept at each iteration. All the data resides at a database server.

Matrix Factorization Process (Solve (M)): For this section we assume that the temporal effects on the dataset have been ignored and we are trying to predict the undetermined rating rij. We can use either item-oriented or user-oriented approach in here. For simplicity, we will use item-based approach as also described in [4]. For given a set of neighbors, $N_k(t_i, u_j)$ they define the *interpolation weights* as $\{w_p | t_p \in N_k(t_i, u_j)\}$ and the prediction rule such that

$$r_{ij} = \sum\nolimits_{t_p \in N_k(t_i, u_j)} w_{pi} r_{ij}$$

$$\begin{bmatrix} r_{11} & r_{12} & r_{13} & r_{14} & r_{15} & r_{16} & r_{17} & r_{18} & r_{19} \\ r_{21} & r_{22} & r_{23} & r_{24} & r_{25} & r_{26} & r_{27} & r_{28} & r_{29} \\ r_{31} & r_{32} & r_{33} & r_{34} & r_{35} & r_{36} & r_{37} & r_{38} & r_{39} \\ r_{41} & r_{42} & r_{43} & r_{44} & r_{45} & r_{46} & r_{47} & r_{48} & r_{49} \\ r_{51} & r_{52} & r_{53} & r_{54} & r_{55} & r_{56} & r_{57} & r_{58} & r_{59} \\ r_{61} & r_{62} & r_{63} & r_{64} & r_{65} & r_{66} & r_{67} & r_{68} & r_{69} \\ r_{71} & r_{72} & r_{73} & r_{74} & r_{75} & r_{76} & r_{77} & r_{78} & r_{79} \end{bmatrix}$$

Suppose that we have nine users and seven items with ratings given. And we predict the rating r35 (the rating of third item given by the fifth user) and fifth user rated the items {t2,t4, t5, t6, t7 } and among these items the most similar ones to t3 are {t2,t4, t6, t7}. So the neighbor set becomes $N_4(t_3, u_5) = \{t_2, t_4, t_6, t_7\}$

The prediction rule implies that we can evaluate r35 such that:

$$r_{35} = \sum_{t_p \in N_4(t_3, u5)} w_{p3} r_{p5} = w_{23} r_{25} + w_{43} r_{45} + w_{63} r_{65} + w_{73} r_{75}$$

To find the weights above they construct a least square problem such that, in hypothetical dense case where all user but uj rated both ti and all its neighbor in $N_k(t_i, u_j)$.

$$\min_w \left\{ \sum\nolimits_{u_k \neq u_j} (r_{ik} - \sum\nolimits_{t_p \in N_k(t_i, u_j)} w_{pi} r_{pj})^2 \right\}$$

The optimal solution of the equation above will give us the weights $\{w_p | t_p \in N_k(t_i, u_j)\}$ Now get back to our example:

Suppose that users rated t3 and all its neighbors in $N_4(t_3, u_5) = \{t_2, t_4, t_6, t_7\}$ and users who rated them all are $\{u_1, u_3, u_4, u_7, u_9\}$

Here, we solve a system of linear equations as below. This matrix has been constructed with *Construct(itemset(item_no,user_no),Subusers(item_no,user_no))* in the algorithm *CompleteRatings* that returns matrix *B*.

The entries of the matrix above just obtained by the intersection of the entries of {t2,t4, t6, t7} and {ul, u3, u4, u7, u9}. If we write the equation above as: $B\omega = c$ then it becomes:

$$\underset{B}{\underbrace{\begin{bmatrix} r_{21} & r_{41} & r_{61} & r_{71} \\ r_{23} & r_{43} & r_{63} & r_{73} \\ r_{24} & r_{44} & r_{64} & r_{74} \\ r_{27} & r_{47} & r_{67} & r_{77} \\ r_{29} & r_{49} & r_{69} & r_{79} \end{bmatrix}}} \underset{w}{\underbrace{\begin{bmatrix} w_{23} \\ w_{43} \\ w_{63} \\ w_{73} \end{bmatrix}}} = \underset{c}{\underbrace{\begin{bmatrix} r_{13} \\ r_{33} \\ r_{43} \\ r_{73} \\ r_{93} \end{bmatrix}}}$$

Then the least square solution of this equation becomes $B^T B w = B^T c$and it's identical to the solution$Aw = b$. The solution of the equation is:

$$Bw = c \Rightarrow \tilde{w} = B^+ c$$

where B+ is the pseudo inverse of B. Suppose that the singular value factorization of B is $B = Q_1 \Sigma Q_2^T$. Then the pseudo-inverse of B is:

$$B^+ = Q_2 \Sigma Q_1^T$$

The r singular values of on the diagonal of $\sigma_1, \sigma_2, \ldots, \sigma_r$ on the diagonal of Σ(m by n) are the non-zero square roots of the non-zero eigenvalues of both BBT and BTB and the reciprocals ${}^1/_{\sigma_1}, {}^1/_{\sigma_2}, \ldots, {}^1/_{\sigma_r}$ are on the diagonal of Σ^+(n by m). The columns of Q1 are eigenvectors of BBT and The columns of Q2 are eigenvectors of BTB.

However, for least square solutions the singular value decomposition sometimes can go unstable because of machine round offs. To guarantee the numerical stability one can use the QR decomposition as a solution. A QR decomposition of real valued square matrix B is a decomposition of B as:

$$B = QR$$

Where Q is an orthogonal; R is an upper triangular matrix. The QR decomposition can also be applied to a mxn rectangular matrix with m>n as:

$$B = Q\begin{bmatrix} R \\ 0 \end{bmatrix}$$

Where Q is an m×m orthogonal matrix; R is an nxn upper triangular matrix. The bottom (m-n) rows of the right-hand side of the equation consist entirely of zeroes. If the matrix B is full-rank, which means the n column vectors of B are linearly independent, the QR decomposition guarantees the numerical stability caused by the machine round offs. If the column vectors of B are not linearly independent then we call the matrix B as *rank deficient*. The term *rank deficiency* is significantly important for the algorithm we applied. Using the QR decomposition the solution of the corresponding equation becomes:

$$Bw = c \Rightarrow \tilde{w} = R^{-1}Q^T c$$

In our algorithm we have already used both the QR and the singular value decomposition according to the dimension of the matrix we obtained. Especially if the matrix is rank deficient we use QR decomposition for the solution, otherwise we use the singular value decomposition.

To sum up, we have already covered the solution to the problem for a given user-item association. However, the problem can be easily extended filling the whole user-association matrix. As we already mentioned above the knowledge of a user has a direct impact on the determination of undetermined rating. For this reason we decide to extend the problem to the whole user-item associations instead of determining to only one undetermined rating.

Now consider the whole user-item association matrix contains undetermined ratings. The problem is filling the gaps or evaluating the undetermined ratings. To achieve the problem one must travel the whole the gaps and must determine the neighborhood of the related gap and then construct the least square problem. Now we know the dimension of least square problem matrix for each gap. Then we evaluate the undetermined rating where the matrix dimension is the largest. One of the gaps in the whole user-item association matrix has been filling. And then we must repeat the whole process for actual matrix. Filling a gap in the user-item association matrix does not affect every least square problem we have constructed. However those who are affected this procedure must be regenerated. After the regeneration the process keeps going until all the gaps in the user-item association matrix fulfilled.

28.5 Experiments and Discussion

We implemented in Java and all the information resides on MySQL server 5.0.75 database. Experiments are conducted on Intel Core 2 Duo CPU T7500 2.2 GHz, 3 GB Ubuntu machine. Experiments are taken on Netflix dataset [1]. In netflix We have 17,770 movies and 480,189 users. Ratings scale from 1 to 5.

We have several experiments with different k values for the k-most similar items.

Initially, we have taken initial dataset to test our algorithm we select 66 applicant ratings from probe dataset. Then for each applicant rating we evaluate prediction as described in [4]. Then we remove the applicant ratings from our item-association matrix and then we run our algorithm. The graph below illustrates results for the algorithm (Fig. 28.1).

We have extracted two different datasets (Dataset 1 and Dataset 2). Each dataset performed 6,000 movie predictions. Figures 28.2–28.7 are the results of cumulative root mean square errors as the ith movie is predicted (1...6,000) for both datasets. Results show that root mean square error fluctuates at the beginning and becomes tends to be show trend after the first movies. Prediction of RMSE becomes smooth and ends up with value between 1 and 1.2 in figures.

In both datasets we analyzed the rank information and given a set of sub matrices having sub user and sub itemset information unknown rating value has been predicted with different strategies. Sub matrices are solved in order. The order has been decided according to rank. Ranks of submatrices are sorted in descending order, ascending order, and random order. Random order has been calculated ten times and the average has been taken. In the first dataset, there is a sharp fall in RMSE and it increases slightly in Fig. 28.2.

In Fig. 28.3, RMSE increases upto 1.7 and then it falls above.

Random order falls down to 1 and stabilizes. RMSE takes a value slightly below 1.

In the second dataset, we have performed the same experiments and obtained results in Figs. 28.5–28.7. In the second experiment set, there is a steady increase up to 1.1 in RMSE in descending order case (Fig. 28.5).

In ascending order, RMSE increases up to 1.5 and end in 1.1 (Fig. 28.6).

Random order case has the same behavior as in previous two figures and becomes stable and ends at the same RMSE value finally (Fig. 28.7).

Abovementioned results consider the predicted values above 5 as 5; and below 0 as 0.

Fig. 28.1 Comparison of probe dataset ratings with [4] and actual ratings

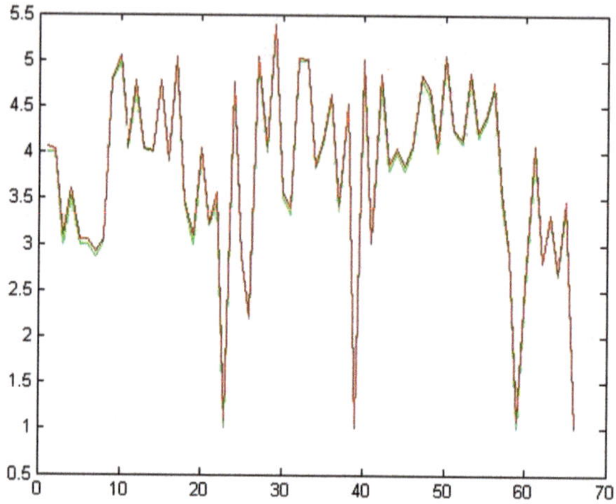

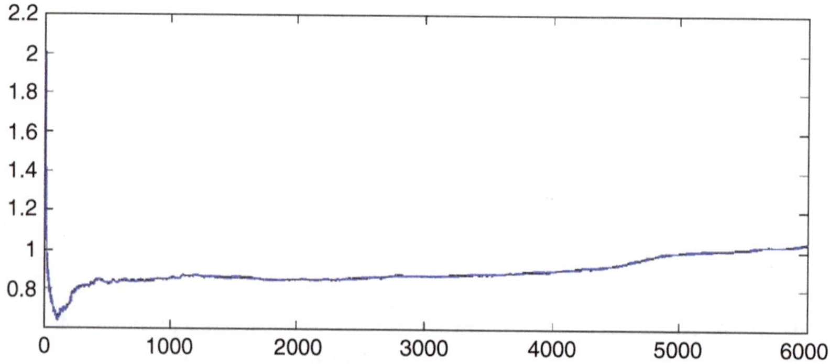

Fig. 28.2 Cumulative RMSE for movies data set 1[1. . . 6,000] in descending order

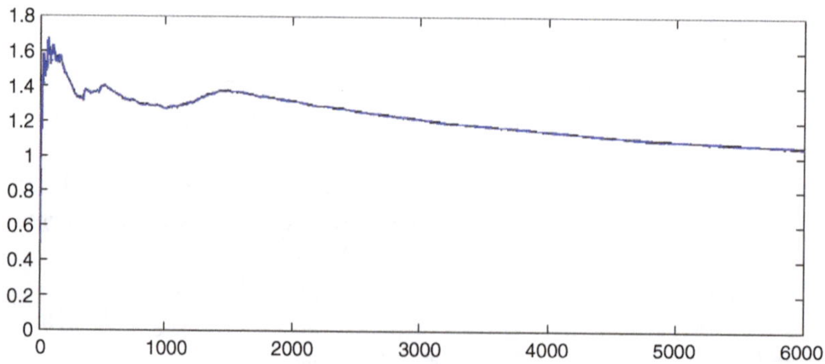

Fig. 28.3 Cumulative RMSE for movies data set 1[1. . . 6,000] in ascending order

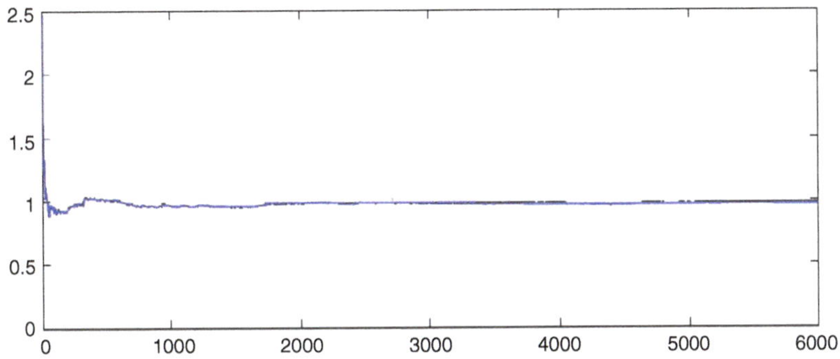

Fig. 28.4 Cumulative RMSE for movies data set 1[1...6,000] in random order

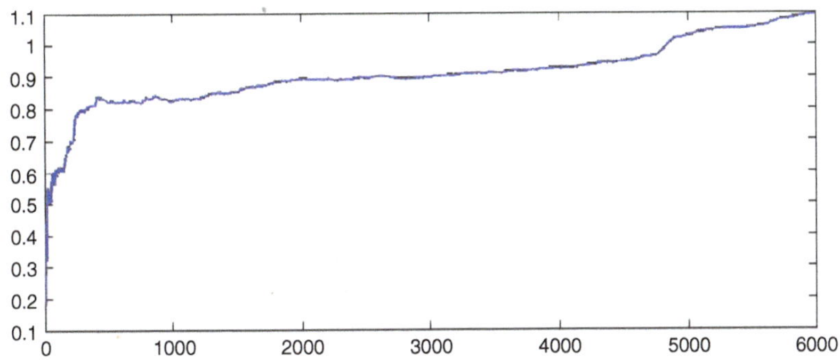

Fig. 28.5 Cumulative RMSE for movies data set 2[1...6,000] in descending order

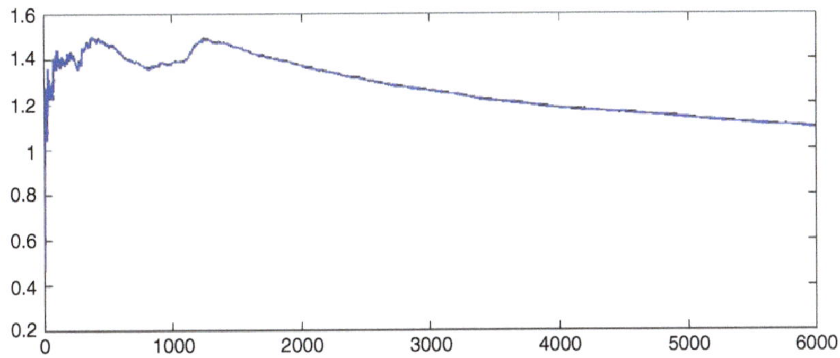

Fig. 28.6 Cumulative RMSE for movies data set 2[1...6,000] in ascending order

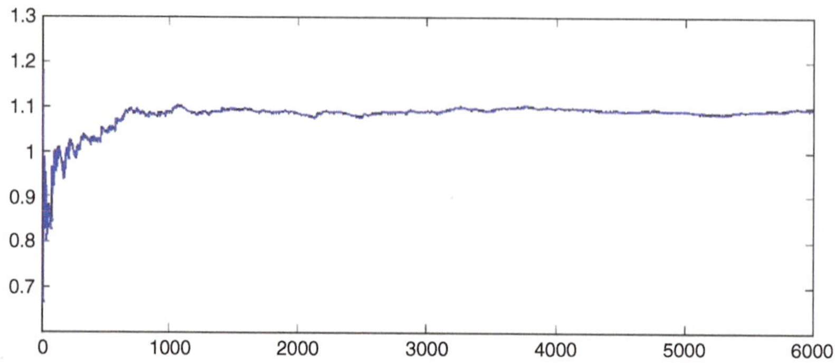

Fig. 28.7 Cumulative RMSE for movies data set 2[1...6,000] in ransom order

28.6 Conclusions

Even if the neighbors have been found logically to predict undetermined rating, there are major problems have been missed. The accuracy of the prediction does not depend on neither the neighborhood collection nor the methods be used. The concurrency of the data cannot be guaranteed just because of unavoidable reasons. One of them and may be the crucial one is *temporal effect*, e.g. items served in different times might be evaluated changeably by the users had similar taste. Another considerable reason is effect of *previous predictions*. We have suggested an algorithm that detects sub regions to be used in prediction and performed random accesses as well as starting from the problem with highest rank and lowest rank approaches for solving equation.

References

1. http://www.netflixprize.com/
2. Adomavicius, G., Tuzhilin, A.: Towards the next generation of recommender systems: a survey of the state-of-the-art and possible extensions. IEEE Trans. Knowl. Data Eng. **17**, 634–749 (2005)
3. Balabanovic, M., Shoham, Y.: Fab: content-based, collaborative recommendation. Commun. ACM **40**(3), 66–72 (1997)
4. Bell, R., Koren, Y.: Improved neighborhood-based collaborative filtering. In: KDDCup'07, San Jose (2007)
5. Faloutsos, C., Oard, D.W.: A survey of information retrieval and filtering methods. UM Computer Science Department, CS-TR-3514 (1995). http://hdl.handle.net/1903/436
6. Goldberg, D., Nichols, D., Oki, B.M., Terry, D.: Using collaborative filtering to weave an information tapestry. Commun. ACM **35**(12), 61–70 (1992)
7. Prabhakar, R.: Information retrieval algorithms: a survey. In: Proceedings of the Eighth Annual ACM-SIAM Symposium on Discrete Algorithms (SODA '97), pp. 11–18. Society for Industrial and Applied Mathematics, Philadelphia (1997)

8. Resnick, P., Varian, H.: Recommender systems. Commun. ACM **40**, 56–58 (1997)
9. Schafer, J.B., Konstan, J., Riedi, J.: Recommender systems in e-commerce. In: EC '99: Proceedings of the 1st ACM Conference on Electronic Commerce, pp. 158–166. ACM, New York

FSC
www.fsc.org
MIX
Papier | Fördert gute Waldnutzung
FSC® C083411

Kolibri 360 GmbH
Ferdinand-Jühlke-Straße 7
99095 Erfurt, Deutschland
produktsicherheit@kolibri360.de